Engaging the Doctrine of Jesus (and Mary)

Engaging the Doctrine of Jesus (and Mary)

A Traditional, Historical-Critical, and Mariological Christology

by
MATTHEW LEVERING

CASCADE *Books* • Eugene, Oregon

ENGAGING THE DOCTRINE OF JESUS (AND MARY)
A Traditional, Historical-Critical, and Mariological Christology

Copyright © 2025 Matthew Levering. All rights reserved. Except for brief quotations in critical publications or reviews, no part of this book may be reproduced in any manner without prior written permission from the publisher. Write: Permissions, Wipf and Stock Publishers, 199 W. 8th Ave., Suite 3, Eugene, OR 97401.

Cascade Books
An Imprint of Wipf and Stock Publishers
199 W. 8th Ave., Suite 3
Eugene, OR 97401

www.wipfandstock.com

PAPERBACK ISBN: 978-1-6667-0508-9
HARDCOVER ISBN: 978-1-6667-0509-6
EBOOK ISBN: 978-1-6667-0510-2

Cataloguing-in-Publication data:

Names: Levering, Matthew, author.

Title: Engaging the doctrine of Jesus (and Mary) : a traditional, historical critical, and Mariological Christology / Matthew Levering.

Description: Eugene, OR: Cascade Books, 2025 | Engaging the Doctrine of . . . series | Includes bibliographical references and index.

Identifiers: ISBN 978-1-6667-0508-9 (paperback) | ISBN 978-1-6667-0509-6 (hardcover) | ISBN 978-1-6667-0510-2 (ebook)

Subjects: LCSH: Jesus Christ—Historicity. | Jesus Christ—History of doctrines. | Mariology. | Bible. Gospels—Theology.

Classification: BT301.3 L50 2025 (paperback) | BT301.3 (ebook)

VERSION NUMBER 03/05/25

Contents

Acknowledgments | vii

Introduction | 1

Chapter 1
Conception and Birth | 55

Chapter 2
Teaching | 99

Chapter 3
Miracles | 176

Chapter 4
Cross | 235

Chapter 5
Resurrection | 304

Chapter 6
Ascension | 360

General Conclusion | 411

Bibliography | 421

Index | 479

Acknowledgments

This book has been in preparation since late 2020, and many debts have piled up. Let me first thank the Mariological Society of America for inviting me to give a keynote address on "Aquinas, Mary, and the Bible" to their May 2021 annual meeting, which took place over Zoom. Portions of the essay are included in chapter 2. Many thanks to the generous scholars who helped me to revise it, including Robert Fastiggi, Danielle Peters, and Joshua Revelle. In July 2022, I gave a keynote lecture—again via Zoom—to a conference sponsored by the University of Notre Dame Australia. My paper "Aquinas, His Interpreters, and Spirit Christology" recently appeared in the edited volume that arose from the conference: *Pneumatology at the Beginning of the Third Millennium*, edited by Kevin Wagner, Peter McGregor, and M. Isabell Naumann, (Eugene, OR: Pickwick, 2023), 163–85. The University of Notre Dame Australia is an inspiring place with a stellar faculty, including Kevin and Peter along with such luminaries as Tracey Rowland and Renée Köhler-Ryan. Although this paper is not in the present book, it provided an important stimulus for my research. In December 2022, at the invitation of Benjamin Mayes, I delivered "Glorified Bodiliness: Christ's Resurrection and Ours" at Concordia Theological Seminary in Fort Wayne, Indiana. I am greatly indebted the graciousness and valuable questions provided by Ben and the seminary community.

I also owe thanks to those who read and criticized the manuscript that became this book, especially David Moser, my colleague at the *International Journal of Systematic Theology* (where he serves as managing editor). David, a recent Catholic convert who now teaches at Franciscan Missionaries of Our Lady University in Baton Rouge, is not only a friend but also a former student of mine. David gave me valuable feedback in reading what was then an especially unwieldy manuscript. A current doctoral student at Marquette, Daniel Edwards, provided some especially timely criticisms that led me to undertake more rounds of revisions. I am very much in Daniel's debt.

ACKNOWLEDGMENTS

Another doctoral student, Derek Bruns, currently completing his degree at Australian Catholic University, performed the yeoman's task of adapting my footnotes to Cascade's style and also compiling the bibliography, which he did with meticulous skill. Derek has been a real pleasure to work with. Simon Gaine, OP, Robert Fastiggi, Michael Barber, Bill Wright, and Daniel Keating read the penultimate draft either in whole or in part, and they all made significant corrections and improvements, without being responsible for the final outcome. I am deeply grateful for their help and friendship.

My work has been made possible by the generosity of Jim and Molly Perry, who donated the funding for my chair at Mundelein Seminary, where I have taught for eleven years. These years at Mundelein have been a real blessing for me. In addition to the Perrys—who have also supported my Center for Scriptural Exegesis, Philosophy, and Doctrine—I owe thanks to Bishop Robert Barron, whose idea the chair was, and to the collegial encouragement of the administration and faculty of Mundelein Seminary. This is the third book in the Engaging the Doctrine series to appear from Cascade. As with other volumes in this series (which began with Baker Academic), I have focused my reading on scholarly literature available in English, due to the vast amount of literature published on each of the topics treated.

My brother, Brooks Levering, deserves a special word of deep appreciation for his encouragement over the past several years. He has read a large number of my books, going far beyond the call of fraternal duty. It has been a great consolation to me. His love of Jesus is inspiring.

I dedicate this book to my extraordinary wife, Joy Levering. Paul exhorts, "Let all that you do be done in love" (1 Cor 16:14). That is Joy's way of living. May Jesus bless you unto eternal life, giving you his Spirit to strengthen you at all times, and may Mary powerfully intercede for you, beloved Joy!

Introduction

The task of writing about Jesus Christ is overwhelming for all sorts of reasons, not least the fact that the depths of the incarnate Lord are endless, in addition to the fact that historical-critical scholarship about Jesus reveals immense complexities rooted in the New Testament texts and in the religious imagination of late Second Temple Judaism. Nevertheless, to write about Jesus is a joy. In the present book, I explore and confess the incarnate Lord who is filled with the Spirit, who was born of the Virgin Mary, who taught authoritatively and performed miracles, who sacrificed his life with supreme love to establish the new covenant and to redeem and divinize God's people Israel reconfigured around himself and open to the whole world, who rose from the dead in his glorified flesh, and who ascended to the Father and royally reigns even now by configuring his people to his cruciform love through the power of his Spirit.[1]

The book is the sixth volume of my Engaging the Doctrine series, a quasi-dogmatics—"quasi" because it is not comprehensive or speculatively unified. I have already written about Jesus elsewhere in the series while treating other major doctrines, and the present book itself has some significant gaps. In the series, I aim to offer a broadly Thomistic perspective on the central realities of Catholic faith while responding to contemporary concerns and controversies. My method is to allow the voices of numerous theologians and biblical scholars (past and present, with a fully ecumenical

---

1. For an alternative approach to these mysteries, engaging (as I do) with historical-critical scholarship, see Söding, *Verkündigung Jesu*. Söding emphasizes that the Gospels are portraits of Jesus that provide us with the truth of him, even while not being the kind of historical writing that we might want. For Söding, the reality of Jesus' cruciform love and embodiment of the kingdom is what stands out. Jesus is "God's love in person" (607). Söding suggests that historical-critical scholarship runs the risk of missing what the Gospels actually convey, due to historical critics' efforts to get behind the text in order to defend or criticize the veracity of this or that claim about Jesus. Where possible, my chapters in this book attempt to "think with" historical-critical scholars as part of sifting and evaluating the existing scholarship.

range) to be heard in their own integrity, both in the body of the text and in footnotes. It is by means of such painstaking exposition that I build gradually in each chapter toward my constructive conclusions, which in this book defend the truth of the Gospel portraits of, and the Church's dogmatic witness to, Jesus (and Mary). This book has been shaped by my desire to complement and supplement, not duplicate, my friend the Catholic theologian Thomas Joseph White's Thomistic masterwork *The Incarnate Lord*.[2]

In much recent scholarship, Jesus appears as a Second Temple-Jewish fanatic, a disciple of John the Baptist who increasingly identified himself as a more-than-human redeemer figure able to usher in the kingdom of God which did not appear. Partly in response to such scholarship (which is not entirely wrong) and partly out of desire to retrieve the Holy Spirit's centrality in forming Jesus' identity and public ministry, contemporary theologians have developed a "Spirit Christology" that begins with Jesus' baptism by John in the Jordan River and his public ministry as a Spirit-filled prophet, or else which prioritizes Pentecost over the incarnation as the basis for Christology.[3] In my view, however, understanding Jesus' fiery presence

---

2. See White, *Incarnate Lord*; and see also Mansini's insightful review essay, "Christology in Context."

3. See for example Habets, *Anointed Son*; and the particularly excellent work of Macchia, *Jesus the Spirit Baptizer*. See also D. Lyle Dabney's seminal essay "Starting with the Spirit." Habets's proposal is modest: "A Third Article Theology does not claim that starting with the First Article, the Father, or with the Second Article, the Son, is incorrect, or that starting with the Spirit is the only legitimate way to do theology today. That would be a gross reactionary move. Rather, the claim is that a Third Article Theology has not yet been attempted in any systematic or sustained way and that it is high time attempts were made in this direction. The goal is not to overturn the Great Tradition but rather . . . to enrich the received tradition with additional insights" (Habets, *Anointed Son*, 233). Habets goes on to offer some valuable criticisms of Amos Yong's *Beyond the Impasse*. For discussion of Spirit-baptism in Mark and Luke-Acts, see Buckwalter, *Character and Purpose of Luke's Christology*, 120–37, with reference to Menzies, *Development of Early Christian Pneumatology*. Buckwalter argues that Luke-Acts presents Jesus as ontologically equal to the Father (even while dependent on the Father as the Servant). By contrast, in view of Acts 2 and Peter's Pentecostal quotation of the prophet Joel's prophecy about the eschatological outpouring of the Spirit, J. R. Daniel Kirk argues against readings that entail Jesus' divinity as the incarnate Lord: "the Christology by which Peter interprets Joel's prophecy is not a Christology of divine ontology, or a Christology of divine incarnation, but a Christology of divine empowerment and divine supervision. The uniqueness of Jesus is found in God's working through him in life, death, and resurrection, attesting to God's approval of this uniquely empowered human agent, Jesus of Nazareth. In terms of ontology, Jesus is a man. In terms of deeds of empowerment, God is at work in him" (Kirk, *Man Attested by God*, 540–41). For another problematic perspective, see McCormack, *Humility of the Eternal Son*, 224: "So the most pressing question for our inquiry is this: is there any evidence for the conviction that the extraordinary things said or done by Jesus of Nazareth were the result of the Word acting through and upon him? Or were they, alternatively, the result of his

INTRODUCTION

requires going deeper—all the way to his conception, since from the outset he is radically unique. The Gospels testify to his unique presence from the outset: "Joseph, son of David, do not fear to take Mary your wife, for that which is conceived in her is of the Holy Spirit; she will bear a son, and you shall call his name Jesus, for he will save his people from their sins" (Matt 1:20–21); "The Holy Spirit will come upon you, and the power of the Most High will overshadow you; therefore the child to be born will be called holy, the Son of God" (Luke 1:35); "the Word became flesh and dwelt among us, full of grace and truth" (John 1:14).[4] Other than Mark, the Gospels all turn to Jesus' origins to account for the fact that he came among his people as the "Christ" and "the Son of God" (Mark 1:1). As the Catholic biblical scholar Harold Attridge remarks with the Gospel of John in view, "something quite spectacular happens to flesh when the Word hits it."[5]

---

endowment with the Holy Spirit? Certainly, the answer we give makes a significant difference. The first answer could incline us in the direction of an instrumentalization of the human (depending on the construct in question); the second presses unavoidably in the direction of the fully engaged humanness of Jesus in all of his extraordinary acts" (224). In my view, Jesus' unique endowment with the Spirit in fact is the result of the hypostatic union, insofar as the Word breathes forth Love. Drawing upon Kavin Rowe's exegesis of Luke 1, but taking it in a direction that Rowe does not, McCormack holds that "pneumatology does here [Luke 1] all the heavy lifting that would later be done in the church's dogma by the concept of a 'hypostatic union'—with one major difference. The unity of 'persons' that the Spirit constitutes is a unity of Jesus and his Father and not . . . a unity of Jesus with an eternal Son somehow to be distinguished from him. Jesus simply *is* the Son in Luke, and in the other three Gospels for that matter. Again, this does not preclude 'preexistence' but it is the 'preexistence' of the Spirit-filled Jesus we would have to be thinking about in that case, not of a 'Son' whose reality has been posited with the help of a cosmologically grounded metaphysics" (225). I consider McCormack to be confused on a number of fronts, but the core of the matter is his rejection of reflection upon divine transcendence—which is far more biblically grounded than he supposes. On the latter subject, see my *Scripture and Metaphysics*.

4. Raymond Brown points out that the Johannine terminology is quite theologically precise: "it is not said that the Word became *a* man, but . . . that the Word became man" (Brown, *Gospel According to John (i–xii)*, 13). As he goes on to say, "Verse 14a describes the Incarnation in strongly realistic language by stressing that the Word became *flesh*" (31). For background to the incarnation and John 1 in the Old Testament's tabernacle narrative, see especially Gary A. Anderson, *That I May Dwell Among Them*; and see also Evans, *Words and Glory*; Kerr, *Temple of Jesus' Body*; and Koester, *Dwelling of God*. Nicholas Perrin observes that the Gospels of Matthew and Luke (and not only John) "presuppose an extended and evolving traditioning process . . . on Jesus as Wisdom incarnate" (Perrin, *Jesus the Priest*, 234). Regarding the Spirit, J. R. Daniel Kirk is correct to notice that Jesus' "empowerment by the spirit is qualitatively continuous with that of other characters" (Kirk, *Man Attested by God*, 554). For Kirk, however, this supports the claim that Jesus is not ontologically God.

5. Attridge, "Genre Bending in the Fourth Gospel," 77. Attridge does not have in mind the theology of the incarnation as such, but he does have in mind the relationship between flesh and spirit/Spirit.

ENGAGING THE DOCTRINE OF JESUS (AND MARY)

I begin my reflections with Jesus at his conception, the conception of the Spirit-filled Messiah and Lord in Mary's womb.[6] The reality of Jesus Christ requires contemplating his incarnation and therefore contemplating the Spirit's presence and action not only in Christ but also in his conception and birth from his virginal mother Mary. It also requires insisting with Thomas Aquinas upon the Word's intrinsic relation to the Spirit: the Word who becomes incarnate is always the Word who, with the Father, breathes forth Love (i.e. the Spirit).[7]

---

6. The assumed foundation of this book is the work on the incarnation found in White, *Incarnate Lord*, especially chapter 1; White, *Trinity*; Riches, *Ecce Homo*; Weinandy, *Does God Change?*; Weinandy, "Aquinas: God *IS* Man"; Gorman, *Metaphysics of the Hypostatic Union*; Barnes, *Christ's Two Wills*; Daley, *God Visible*. See also Pope Pius XII, *Mystici Corporis*, §31: "at the first moment of the Incarnation the Son of the Eternal Father adorned with the fullness of the Holy Spirit the human nature which was substantially united to Him, that it might be a fitting instrument of the Divinity in the sanguinary work of the Redemption." White makes the same point: "The Spirit, who comes forth from the Word, reposes upon the human nature of Christ, fills him with grace, inspires his human actions of knowledge and love, and moves him from within to embrace the mystery of the Cross" (White, *Trinity*, 622). On Christ and the Spirit according to Aquinas, see also my *Engaging the Doctrine of the Holy Spirit*, chapter 4. In "Incarnate *De Spiritu Sancto*," 175, Dominic Legge shows that Aquinas offers "a rich Spirit-Christology"; and see Legge, *Trinitarian Christology of St Thomas Aquinas*. Ralph Del Colle defines Spirit Christology in a manner that accords with Legge's approach and that I find helpful: "By Spirit-Christology I mean envisioning the constitution and mission of the person of Christ in terms that establish an inter-relationship between the filiological and the pneumatological dimensions of Christology. In other words, reference to Jesus Christ is true to the gospel only when the christological event is understood to be a thoroughly trinitarian event, an event in which God effects salvation through the Son and in the Spirit" (Del Colle, "Spirit-Christology," 93). See also the discussion of the grace of union and Christ's habitual grace in White, *Incarnate Lord*, 87–91. As White maintains in a somewhat different context (discussing the human knowledge of Christ), "In a rightly ordered Christology . . . we should not be obliged to choose between an ontology of the hypostatic union and an anthropological theology that focuses upon the human actions of Christ" (White, *Incarnate Lord*, 67).

7. Perhaps the most urgent controversy about the incarnation today—in terms of impact among Christian laity—has to do with what it means to call Jesus the incarnate Word. The urge to separate "Jesus" and "the Word" appears in recent popular theological writings, building upon but going beyond Pierre Teilhard de Chardin (in the direction of process theology), by Richard Rohr, Diarmuid O'Murchu, Ilia Delio, OSF, and others. See Rohr, *Universal Christ*; O'Murchu, *Incarnation*; Delio, *Emergent Christ*. For a valuable response, see Dauphinais, "Creation Is Not Incarnation." Dauphinais sums up the controversy, using Rohr's thought to exemplify it: "Rohr criticizes the tradition's emphasis on the unique mode of divine presence in the incarnation and instead presents the message of the universal Christ as a recovery of the ubiquity of the divine presence. . . . According to Rohr, to focus on Jesus as the unique and personal Incarnation—as affirmed in the Catholic creeds—separates God from creation and Jesus from us" (275–76). Dauphinais puts forward aspects of Aquinas's theology that constructively address Rohr's anti-Chalcedonianism (276–78). For recent scholarly dalliance

INTRODUCTION

According to the Gospels, Jesus' birth from a virgin inaugurated the messianic age, one of tribulation and glory along the path of his love.[8] How this can be so—given the fact that it seems as though life goes on as before—is a central theme of the New Testament. Matthew and Luke proclaim Mary's virginity in her conception of Jesus. In her flesh, Mary makes manifest the eschatological power of what Christ is accomplishing. Mary's miraculous virginity and her virginal integrity in childbirth are signs of the inbreaking kingdom that has Christ the healer at its head. Recognizing Mary as Theotokos ("God-bearer"), believers avoid Nestorian conceptions that relinquish the unity of Christ's Person—the unity on which the eschatological power of his saving acts depends.[9]

(consciously or unconsciously) with the perspective that characterizes Rohr's Christology, see Hart, *You Are Gods* and Wood, *Whole Mystery of Christ*. Although he makes the necessary metaphysical and historical distinctions, Hart also presses on to say that "creation *is* the incarnation in the fullness of all its necessary historical and natural dimensions" (*You Are Gods*, 113). For his part, Wood claims, "The only way we fall into either idolatrous pantheism or world-denying theopanism in affirming the literal truth of 'God is the world' is if we assume a priori that creation is not Incarnation. . . . For if creation is Incarnation—if creation's logic is the whole Christ—then what is naturally improper to predicate of the world determines the world's whole truth no more than the fact that corpses do not rise from the dead determines the truth of Christ's resurrected flesh—which is to say not at all" (*Whole Mystery of Christ*, 202).

8. For an extended (but in my view exaggerated) critique of "inaugurated" eschatology as not giving sufficient place to the theology of the cross, see Harrigan, *Gospel of Christ Crucified*—although certain forms of inaugurated eschatology merit his critique. I agree with his contention that the Church "must have a theology of the cross that dictates its self-sacrificial mission in this age. Our practice of taking up the cross must be driven by a theology that tells us that this is what God is doing. Jesus is presently enthroned at the right hand of God extending the cross—that is, preaching repentance and forgiveness of sins in light of the coming day of God (Luke 24:47; Acts 2:38; 3:19; etc.). In other words, the theology and practice of the church needs to be both cruciform and apocalyptic" (*Gospel of Christ Crucified*, 263). Harrigan fears, "When the mission of God in this age (and thereby the mission of the church) becomes the inauguration of the kingdom and the age to come, the cross ceases to be the standard of this age" (263). In my view, Christ has inaugurated the kingdom and we can now share in it (including, to a degree, in his risen life), but only in and through the cross.

9. Informed by Sergius Bulgakov, Louis Bouyer proposes that "Mary is, not the final or complete realisation of Wisdom, but its supreme realisation on the plane of history. Mary is truly the Seat of Wisdom, of the uncreated Wisdom shown forth as a creature in her Son" (Bouyer, *Seat of Wisdom*, 196–97). For Bulgakov's Mariology, see Louth, "Mary in Modern Orthodox Theology," 234–38. On Mary as the "icon of the Spirit," see Pontifical International Marian Academy, *Mother of the Lord*, 5. As in the earlier cases of the tabernacle and the temple (see Exodus 40 and 1 Kings 8), the glory cloud or Holy Spirit descends upon Mary; see Pitre, *Jesus and the Jewish Roots of Mary*, 59–60. This traditional reading of Luke is dismissed, in my view mistakenly, in Brown et al., *Mary in the New Testament*, 122, 136. The authors state, "in interpreting the virginal conception of Jesus as the begetting of God's Son, we recognized that Luke is not talking about

When Jesus commenced his public ministry, he did so as an apocalyptic prophet and wisdom teacher. The evangelist Mark states, "Jesus came into Galilee, preaching the gospel of God, and saying, 'The time is fulfilled, and the kingdom of God is at hand; repent, and believe in the gospel'" (Mark 1:14–15). But for many scholars and theologians today, listening to what Jesus says in the Gospels is a near-useless enterprise, because Jesus' voice is irretrievably blurred with the evangelists'. When scholars do find traces of Jesus' voice, its authority is often absent.[10] Thus, it has become difficult for educated people to know or care what Jesus taught and believed. By contrast, I contend that the Gospels reveal extraordinary truth about God, Jesus, and us. This revelation is constitutive of the deposit of faith. Mary, then, exemplifies the faithful believer who ponders Jesus' words and deeds in her heart.

Jesus' miracles showed to his contemporaries that the divine eschatological battle against sin and death had become present in and through his person. For us today, however, the question is whether to understand miracles literally or to find naturalistic or solely symbolic ways of appreciating them.[11] The exorcism of the Gerasene demoniac, during which Jesus sends the demons into a herd of pigs, provides a test case. With that miraculous exorcism in view, I argue that Jesus' working of real supernatural miracles can be affirmed without supposing that the evangelists never invented details or changed their source material. The miracle at Cana—Jesus' first miracle according to the Gospel of John, and one that reveals much about his ministry—teaches us, through Mary, how to prepare for and understand Jesus' miracles.[12]

---

the incarnation of a pre-existent divine being. The idea of pre-existence is found in other NT works . . . , but it represents a different christology from that implied in the virginal conception" (122).

10. As David B. Capes says, Paul and other New Testament authors "associate Jesus with God (YHWH) in remarkable and even unprecedented ways. The linkage of Jesus with God is so strong that we must conclude that, very early, at the beginning of the Christian movement, influential voices such as Paul considered Jesus constitutive of God's unique identity" (Capes, "Jesus' Unique Relationship with YHWH," 88).

11. See Harvey, *Faithful History*, for an example of the latter, focusing on "sacred myth" and avoiding "the netherworld of metaphysics and doctrine" (92, 94).

12. Persuasively in my view, White argues that the incarnation is the heart of the matter: "Seeking to understand the New Testament claims about Christ non-ontologically is in the end a non-biblical enterprise. What must we maintain minimally, then, in order to take seriously the historicity of God in Jesus Christ? Here the theology of the hypostatic union is not too abstract but is in fact the correct indication of the concrete grounding for the historicity of the Logos in human flesh. It is precisely because it is the *person* of God the Son who *exists* as a human being that the actions carried out by this person and all that he undergoes in and through history are attributed truly and

INTRODUCTION

So impressed by Christ's cross was Paul that he told the Corinthians, "When I came to you, brethren, I did not come proclaiming to you the testimony of God in lofty words or wisdom. For I decided to know nothing among you except Jesus Christ and him crucified" (1 Cor 2:2). Imitating Paul, I seek to explore "the redemption which is in Christ Jesus, whom God put forward as an expiation by his blood, to be received by faith" (Rom 3:24–25). This task leads me to retrieve the theological perspective of Matthias Joseph Scheeben on sacrifice and to develop an interpretation of John 19 as depicting the new covenant sacrifice—parallel to the covenant sealing depicted in Exodus 24—with Mary (alongside the beloved disciple) in the role of faithful Israel, sharing in the salvific blood of Christ. The purpose of Jesus' sacrificial death is the establishment of the new covenant, the bond of love grounded in Jesus' perfect offering of praise in his sorrowful death, an offering of praise that constitutes the worship God desires from his beloved people.

I believe that Jesus rose from the dead and that this belief is reasonable. Since elsewhere I have treated his resurrection from various angles, I inquire in the present book into a topic that I have not previously treated but that is fundamental for the intelligibility of belief that he rose from the dead in a salvific way.[13] This topic is whether a *glorified* body can really be

---

realistically to God the Son. It is the second person of the Trinity who exists as a human being, from conception to natural death, so as to undergo all the stages of human development (biological, sensible, spiritual) that are proper to the human condition.... All of this happens to God in his human nature, as man. But it happens to *One who* exists as human. Thus it happens *to* the existent Son and Word, as the hypostatic subject of this history" (White, *Incarnate Lord*, 117). White goes on to say, "If the human nature of Jesus is created (which of course it is) it is created in such a way as to exist in the Word without damage or violence occurring to this human nature, with its inherent limitations but also with its proportional integrity and developmental history. The human nature of Christ is more humane and perfect because it is the human nature of God, but it is also that of a genuinely historical human being. Likewise, the existence of the Son made man does not serve to enslave or limit the gradual development of his humanity through time, but causes it to flourish in an appropriate and essentially normal human way" (*Incarnate Lord*, 118). White defends the trans-historical reality of "human nature" in his *Incarnate Lord*, 144–68, in response to M.-D. Chenu and others. Chenu's position is that (in White's words) "God himself took on historical flesh to bring to fulfillment the dynamic, ever-developing history of man, and so likewise, doctrine must be rearticulated according to the inner living historical spirit of a given age and in keeping with the adaptive evangelical life of the church in history" (White, *Incarnate Lord*, 145, summarizing Chenu, "Une Constitution Pastorale de l'Église"). White here critiques Chenu on human nature; and for an equally important critique of Chenu on dogma, see White, "Precarity of Wisdom," 93–102. See also Donneaud, "Constitution dialectique de la théologie et de son histoire selon M.-D. Chenu."

13. See especially my *Did Jesus Rise from the Dead?* Of course, there is more recent scholarly literature on the topic of Jesus' resurrection that deserves a response, including Chidgzey, "Subjugating Subjectivity"; Smith, "Parapsychology, Hallucinations,

called "flesh" or a "body," and whether resurrection at the end of time can really be the raising of the body that died. I delve into patristic, medieval, post-Reformation scholastic, and contemporary approaches to the glorified body. My goal is to defend the intelligibility of glorified bodiliness, with attention not only to Jesus but also to Mary, who has been assumed body and soul to her Son's right hand.

Jesus' ascension is no mere afterthought for me but rather is the culmination of his saving work and is constitutive of Christian life today. Elsewhere I have examined the ascended Jesus as high priest. Here I wish to reflect upon Jesus' ascension to *royal* rule—given that the world and even the Church may seem hardly to reflect Christ's reign.[14] As Matthew Thiessen says in his *A Jewish Paul*, for Paul—well aware of the world's ongoing

---

Collective Delusions"; and Elledge, *Resurrection of the Dead in Early Judaism*. Smith, like Dale Allison (and others) before him, maintains that "once we circumnavigate the red herring of veridical visions of the paranormal kind and apply what psychology can disclose about bereavement hallucinations and collective delusions . . . some form of hypothesis along these [hallucination-theory] lines is equally as valid as the traditional belief in bodily resurrection" ("Parapsychology," 253). Smith assumes that all Marian apparitions are false, and this provides an important plank in his argument. I argue in *Did Jesus Rise from the Dead?* that hallucination theories are less likely historically than the alternative that Jesus rose bodily from the dead, especially once one removes the normal default historical presumption against the existence of God (the God of Israel). Chidgzey argues that N. T. Wright practices not a critical realism but a soft objectivism or an empiricist realism, according to which it is possible for the historian to identify "a single, 'necessary', conclusion" ("Subjugating Subjectivity," 222). While Wright may at times open himself to this critique, I read him as holding that the conclusion that Jesus rose bodily from the dead is the most historically probable position and therefore in that limited sense a "necessary" conclusion for historians who seek the most probable reconstruction of what happened. A book that could have enriched my chapter in the present book, but was published too late for me to integrate it, is Rae, *Resurrection and Renewal*.

14. See Moltmann, *Resurrected to Eternal Life*, 20–21: "Jesus's resurrection from the dead also represents his appointment as *Lord* over the kingdom of God, over the world, over heaven and earth and all that exists. Christ's dominion is universal. . . . Believers do not live *under* Christ's dominion like slaves but rather *in* Christ's dominion as sisters and brothers of their 'first-born' brother, Jesus (Rom 8:29). . . . Even on our deathbeds, there is comfort in the fellowship of Christ, for the Resurrected is present even in death. Christ goes with the dying through the night of death into the eternal light. He is standing, so to speak, on the opposite shore to receive us. . . . There is something that connects life and death: the dominion of Christ—that is, believers' fellowship in Christ." Moltmann explains later in his book, "The history of humankind is the backstory of the real history of true life in the peace of the world's new creation. This new creation is the counterpart to the destruction rampant in this world of death and slaughter" (64). Moltmann, having lived through the Nazi regime and the Holocaust, knows well the evils of this world. He argues, "God's day is breaking. This beginning gives direction to our life journeys. The beginning was forged with Christ's entrance into this dark world" (69).

INTRODUCTION

disorder—"Jesus was a Jewish king . . . enthroned in his resurrection and ascension."[15] It is necessary, then, to reflect upon how the ascended Messiah reigns. I conclude by contemplating Mary's queenship: the new Adam reigns with the new Eve, and so the new creation (grounded not in worldly power but in self-sacrificial love) has begun.[16]

I. Two Emphases

Throughout the book—although more so in some chapters than in others—I draw upon an array of sources to develop a Christology that has two emphases. The first is mariological: I maintain that Jesus is not fully discernible without his mother Mary and what the Church believes about her. This follows not least from the fact that, in the words of Louis Bouyer, "Christ does not find his reason for being—nor his completion, for that matter—in himself."[17] The second involves bringing together traditional Christology with contemporary historical-critical biblical scholarship.[18]

---

15. Thiessen, *Jewish Paul*, 15. Thiessen adds, "Paul depicts himself as one authorized—chosen and called—to serve as a spokesperson on behalf of a king: Jesus the Messiah" (16).

16. For the significance of emphasizing the new creation, see Daniel J. Treier's "New Covenant and New Creation," arguing that "new creation" serves to ward off individualistic accounts of salvation that pay little attention to the suffering world.

17. Bouyer, *Church of God*, 275. See also Bouyer, *Seat of Wisdom*, 112–13. As he says, the history of the Spirit's work in Israel (and in the nations prior to Christ's coming) needs to be taken into consideration when reflecting upon the Spirit's role in preparing for and accomplishing the incarnation of the Word in Mary's womb. For discussions of Bouyer's Mariology, see Weill, *L'Humanisme eschatologique de Louis Bouyer*; Nepil, *Bride Adorned*, 153–95; and Heintz, "Mariology as Theological Anthropology." Bouyer wishes to emphasize how profoundly prepared the Jewish people were, so that the incarnation does not seem a meteor or an alien invasion into human history. Balthasar's cautionary remark would be accepted by Bouyer: "There is no question of a collective, not even the 'faithful people', producing the Redeemer-Messiah out of itself, in virtue of its own faith" (Balthasar, *Theo-Drama* 3:291); and for the same point regarding Mary's own holiness, see Ward, *Ordered by Love*, 143. See also Dalton, *Fulfilled Israel*, 307, on the centrality of Christ for everything: "Risen from the dead and enthroned in glory, he is fulfilled Israel par excellence. Just as the king cannot be understood as an isolated monad, so too the kingdom cannot be understood apart from the king. He is God-with-us. . . . Thus, even now, prior to the Parousia, in the regeneration/rebirth inaugurated by Christ (19:28), the people of the new creation are also being filled with his fullness as they live in, and live out, his greater righteousness and perfect love (5:20, 48). In this sense, *plērōsis* is *Christōsis*. In and through and with him, what has been consummated in the king has been inaugurated in his kingdom."

18. For a quite different approach to the same task, see Behr, *John the Theologian*. Behr argues that "in and through the Passion, the one Lord Jesus Christ becomes, as human, that which he, as God, always is. . . . Although it might sound rather aodptionistic

Historical-critical scholarship varies widely in quality and perspective, but it is too often neglected by theologians today. Let me briefly explain these two emphases of my book.

A Mariological Christology

Regarding the place of Mary in Christology, the Orthodox theologian John Zizioulas points out along lines with which I agree, "Christ without his body is not Christ."[19] Thomas Joseph White underlines that Mary "has the

---

(a man becomes God), it is not. The Passion is a transformative event, both *pathos* (as Melito) and *passage* (as Origen), as a result of which we no longer know Jesus through the properties by which we might have identified him before the Passion (height, shape of body, etc.), but now only know him as the Word of God. . . . [A]scending into heaven and to God through the Passion, while remaining that which he is, he nevertheless, *as human*, becomes that which he (the same one), *as God*, always is, the eternal Word of God: he, while remaining all that he is as human, is only known, as the iron in the fire is, by the properties of God, and God, in turn, while remaining unchanged, as does the fire when it receives the iron, is now, nevertheless, embodied, though the body is no longer measured by the space and time of our world to be seen in the world" (326). If I understand Behr correctly, he is saying that the man Jesus, through his passion, becomes "as human" God, even while "as God" the man Jesus had always been God. The problems here pertain first of all to what it is that makes Christ, "as human," God. The answer, in my view, is that due to the hypostatic union, Christ is the divine Person. This differs from what is meant by the distinction between "as human" and "as God" in Christ—a distinction that has to do with his two natures. The change that occurs through Christ's Pasch certainly involves the complete deification or glorification of Christ's humanity, which until the Pasch had not been fully deified, but this differs from the point made by the literal sense of Behr's words. For Behr, moreover, the "Passion" includes the other christological mysteries, including the resurrection and the birth of Jesus, but I do not see how this can be so, even if the birth of Jesus (or, for that matter, his incarnation) was never "independent" from—in the sense of autonomous or unrelated—the death, resurrection, and ascension of Jesus. Here I am in agreement with Alexis Torrance, *Human Perfection in Byzantine Theology*, 213: "By frequently enforcing a sharp dichotomy between the 'modern' view of history as 'what really happened' and the possibilities of a 'postmodern' retrieval of a premodern approach, something important may well be gained through creative rereadings of the text. However, something is also inevitably lost, for the simple reason that 'premoderns', including early Christians, did in fact believe in more than one historical 'event' in the life of Jesus as well as the ultimate significance of these events, even if their understanding of 'historicity' may well have been somewhat different from a straightforwardly modern view." For Behr, Christ "defines for us what it is to be God and what it is to be human, in one, at the same time," through "the *way* in which he dies as a human being" (*John the Theologian*, 327). While I agree that the way in which Jesus dies is revelatory, no act of human dying, no matter how great, could define from scratch "what it is to be God," unless one is operating within a framework of univocity—and even then one would likely read suffering into this finite "God."

19. Zizioulas, *Being as Communion*, 182. Zizioulas italicizes this statement.

greatest proximity to the mystery of Christ, in his incarnation, apostolic life, death, and resurrection."[20] I propose in this book that apprehending Christ in light of Mary, and Mary in light of Christ (with the light coming solely from Christ), is a necessary part of ascertaining the truth of Christ and his inauguration of the eschatological Israel. Drawing upon the seventeenth-century Catholic theologian Pierre de Bérulle, John Saward argues that "the guarantee of an authentic Christ-centeredness is Blessed Mary Ever-Virgin, above all the expectant Mary."[21] I agree with this claim. As the Vatican's Congregation for Catholic Education put it in 1980, "Christology is also Mariology"—a statement that I will elucidate in this book.[22]

Yet, Protestants generally remain unconvinced that Catholics have grasped the truth about Mary, and therefore my inclusion of Mary in this book on Jesus may provoke noteworthy concerns.[23] Many Protestants are concerned that the Church's Marian doctrines, even when they have clear biblical warrant, exalt a mere member of the Church (and thus, in a sense, the Church itself) to the level of Christ. Karl Barth puts the matter strongly: "where Mary is 'venerated,' where this whole doctrine with its corresponding devotions is current, there the Church of Christ is not."[24] Barth thinks that in Catholic theology, Mary's privileges and her participation in the mysteries of her Son generate "a relative rivalry with Christ."[25] Responding to Barth, the Catholic theologian Henri de Lubac observes that the "criticisms [from] the Reformation direction against the Catholic conception of the Church correspond with those it directed against the Catholic cult of our Lady."[26] De Lubac insists that the relationship of Mary to her Son in fact illuminates the relationship of the Church to Christ. He contends that Catholic Mariology is "the indispensable guarantee of the importance of

---

20. White, "Mariology and the Sense of Mystery," 219. See also the Pontifical International Marian Academy, *Mother of the Lord*, 3: "The person and the mission of Jesus the Savior casts light on the figure of the mother, that is, Christology enlightens Mariology. And, to a degree, Mariology makes a contribution to Christology."

21. Saward, *Redeemer in the Womb*, 74.

22. Congregation for Catholic Education, *Circular Letter Concerning Some of the More Urgent Aspects of Spiritual Formation in Seminaries*, 619.

23. Of course, some Protestant theologians and biblical scholars, such as Beverly Roberts Gaventa and Amy Peeler, have contributed significantly to reflection on Mary in relation to Jesus, as has Barth himself with respect to the virgin birth. See Gaventa, *Mary: Glimpses of the Mother of Jesus*; Peeler, *Women and the Gender of God*.

24. Barth, *CD* 1/2:143.

25. Barth, *CD* 1/2:145.

26. De Lubac, *Splendor of the Church*, 314. For discussion, quoting the same passage from de Lubac, see Nepil, *Bride Adorned*, 18.

the Incarnation and ... bears witness to the divine plan of associating God's creatures with the work of their own salvation."[27]

In my view, Catholic Mariology helps us to perceive the participation of Israel and the Church in the eschatological victory of Jesus Christ—and thus to perceive the full reality of Christ in his words and deeds. The Episcopal biblical scholar Amy Peeler states, "In the age of the Messiah, she [Mary] is the first slave [or 'handmaid'] upon whom God pours out the Spirit. As a maidservant of this κύριος (*kyrios*), she is the first in line to reap the eschatological benefits."[28] In my chapters, I will examine how Mary participates in her Son's "new era,"[29] although for reasons of space I generally can only present (rather than defend) the Church's Marian doctrines. When viewed in relation to Jesus, Mary "provides a template for all Christians whose primary identity resides in their relationship with Christ."[30] She exemplifies the eschatological power of grace, obedience, love, contemplation, intercession, and suffering. She is the Mother of God, Daughter Zion, the new Eve, the temple or ark in whom God dwelt, the mother of all believers, and the model of the Church. The inaugurated kingdom of Christ the King is not the realm of Christ alone in his glorified flesh, but also of Mary as "the ark of his covenant" and as the Queen, "on her head a crown of twelve stars" (Rev 11:19; 12:1), in accordance with the arrival of the wondrous marriage of Christ and his Bride the Church.

My perspective accords with *Lumen Gentium*'s appreciation for the "union of the mother with the Son in the work of salvation," properly

---

27. De Lubac, *Splendor of the Church*, 315. De Lubac refers for the same viewpoint to Journet's *L'Église du Verbe incarné*, 2:392.

28. Peeler, *Women and the Gender of God*, 80. Peeler emphasizes that all Jesus' followers, and Jesus himself (Phil 2 and elsewhere), are presented as "slaves" or servants. The language of slavery is thereby upended, without denying the oppressiveness of human systems of oppression built upon forced servitude. In this regard, Peeler directs attention to Lettsome, "Mary's Slave Songs," and Boss, *Empress and Handmaid*, 218. See also Schmemann, "Archetype of Mankind," 52: "Mary, the 'doule kyrion'—the 'slave of the Lord' (Lk 1:38)—stands in the very center of the Church's vision of the world, of man and life as the ultimate fruit and therefore the highest expression of that 'enslavement,' humility and obedience, without which there is no entrance into the mystery of man's true communion with God."

29. Peeler, *Women and the Gender of God*, 80. I do not mean to imply that Peeler accepts the Marian doctrines that Protestants traditionally reject. For Catholic theologians, she is most helpful with respect to the virgin birth. She argues, "The virginal conception reveals that the Messiah, whose body was crucified and resurrected, embraces male and female, and therefore can in a powerfully and beautifully inclusive way save all humans. In short, a male-embodied Savior with female-provided flesh saves all" (136–37, with reference to the similar point made by Behr-Sigel, *Ministry of Women in the Church*, 40, 59).

30. Peeler, *Women and the Gender of God*, 152.

understood.[31] As the Catholic theologian Theresa Marie Chau Nguyen has shown, de Lubac's work was influential upon *Lumen Gentium*'s chapter on Mary. Citing a wide array of patristic and medieval saints and theologians, de Lubac makes clear in *The Splendor of the Church* that Catholic Mariology "sums up symbolically, in its special case, the doctrine of human cooperation in the Redemption."[32] Far from competing with her Son, who is the sole Mediator and Redeemer, Mary displays the eschatological fruitfulness of Christ's work.[33] De Lubac's friend Joseph Ratzinger comments in a similar vein, with a focus on Christology rather than ecclesiology: "When one recognizes the place assigned to Mary by dogma and tradition, one is solidly rooted in authentic christology."[34] Ratzinger observes that the Church has taught each of the Marian dogmas—from Mary's status as Mother of God and perpetually virgin, to Mary's assumption and queenship—"in direct service to faith in Christ" and thus to Christology properly understood.[35] This is my viewpoint as well.

31. Vatican Council II, *Lumen Gentium* §57, 416. Chris Maunder comments, "Roman Catholic tradition historically has carried out a balancing act between its exaltation of Mary as the mother and helper of Jesus, while also asserting her humanity and speaking of her participation in the work of redemption as 'subordinate' or 'inferior' to that of Christ. In modern times, the compromise that this represents has been characterized in the language of 'Christotypical' and 'ecclesiotypical' Mariology. In the former, Mary is Christ-like in all respects other than divinity: her role is pre-ordained in the divine plan from eternity; she is sinless; she participates in Christ's redemptive mission; she mediates grace; she suffers with him at the cross; she is assumed body and soul into heaven. In ecclesiotypical Mariology, the emphasis is on Mary being on the side of humanity in the relationship with Christ: she is the Church in prototype; the first and ideal believer; the exemplary recipient of Christ's saving grace. Famously, at Vatican II in the 1960s, the Roman Catholic hierarchy, by a narrow majority, opted for the ecclesiotypical approach" (Maunder, "Introduction," 7). The distinction between "Christotypical" and "ecclesiotypical" has been exaggerated, since of course Mary is both—and is both in *Lumen Gentium*. She is "like" Christ only inasmuch as she receives a uniquely close participation in her Son's mission, and her unique participation makes her both mother of the Church and model of the Church (model disciple). See also the extensive reflection on Mary in Journet, *L'Église du Verbe incarné*, 2:651–757, treated at length (along with the perspectives of Matthias Joseph Scheeben, Hans Urs von Balthasar, Louis Bouyer, and Leo Scheffczyk) in Nepil, *Bride Adorned*. Nepil sums up, "When Mary and the Church are viewed in dogmatic relation, their Christological foundations are fortified. As mysteries of grace, the two find their sole foundation in the redemptive Incarnation of the God-man" (*Bride Adorned*, 250).

32. De Lubac, *Splendor of the Church*, 316. See Nguyen, *Splendor of the Church in Mary*.

33. See Vatican Council II, *Lumen Gentium* §60, 418. For further background, see Calkins, "Mariology at and after the Second Vatican Council."

34. Ratzinger with Messori, *Ratzinger Report*, 106.

35. Ratzinger with Messori, *Ratzinger Report*, 106. Of course, Ratzinger and de Lubac are in accord here. De Lubac observes, "*Soli Deo gloria*—everything in Mary

ENGAGING THE DOCTRINE OF JESUS (AND MARY)

Traditional Christology and Historical-Critical Biblical Scholarship

The Catholic theologian Simon Gaine, an eminent Thomist, has recently commented that "for Aquinas' followers, metaphysics and history ought not to be strangers to one another, but should be mutually enriching in the practice of Christology."[36] Gaine calls upon his fellow Thomists to integrate historical-critical biblical exegesis fully into contemporary Thomistic Christology. As he observes, most of the main challenges to Christology today come not from philosophy but from historical-critical biblical scholarship.[37] Since this is so, Thomistic theologians must "take account of the

---

proclaims that; her sanctity is wholly theological, for it is the perfection of faith, hope, and charity. Our Lady is the consummation of 'the religion of the humble'; the handmaid of the Lord effaces herself before him who has regarded her lowliness, marvels at his power, praises his mercy and faithfulness, and rejoices in him alone; she is his glory. The whole of her maternal role as far as we are concerned consists in her leading us to him" (de Lubac, *Splendor of the Church*, 376-77).

36. Gaine, "Jesus Christ," 675.

37. See for example the historical-critical doubts in Collins and Collins, *King and Messiah as Son of God*, 210-11 (a section written by Adela Yarbro Collins): "John differs from the Synoptic Gospels in its elaboration of the divine sonship of Jesus by identifying him with the 'word' (λόγος) in the sense of the Middle Platonic 'logos.' This 'logos' is akin to preexistent, personified wisdom. Wisdom was portrayed both as the first creature of God (Prov 8:22-23; Sir 24:9) and as begotten by God (Wis 8:3; Philo, *On Flight and Finding* 9 §§48-50). She is also portrayed as an eternal emanation of effulgence of God and as God's image (Wis 7:26). It is not clear whether Jesus as logos is portrayed as God's first creature or as eternal. The existence of the logos 'in the beginning' in John 1:1 could mean at the beginning of creation; the notion of the logos as the first creature is compatible with such an interpretation of the statement. The same is said of wisdom in the Greek version of Prov 8:22." I disagree with Collins here, as does Loke, *Origin of Divine Christology*, 155-59, and Hurtado, *Lord Jesus Christ*, 366-67. For an exhaustive analysis of the Johannine meaning of the λόγος, see Keener, *Gospel of John*, vol. 1; and see also Bauckham, *Testimony of the Beloved Disciple*, 239-52; and Myers, "Jesus the Son of God in John's Gospel." For Philo in *De fuga*, as Harold Attridge notes, "The Logos has God as his Father and Wisdom as his mother," is connected with light, constitutes the bond of all existing things (in accord with the Stoic doctrine to which Philo is indebted), reveals God, and is the Torah ("Philo and John," 54-55). Attridge describes Philo's "'rational mysticism' of the Logos" (55). Attridge comments, "Whether or not the Fourth Gospel read Philo, it knows something very much like this [Philonic] scheme and plays on many of the motifs at work in it throughout the gospel (light, name, Man/son of Man, divine begetting, shepherd). Finally it is true to the positive Philonic impulse: God is knowable through the Word. At two particular points the Gospel resembles crucial moves that the philosopher makes. (1) Both insist on the 'particular' pole of the universal-particular dichotomy, but John in a more radical way. Philo's angelic Logos comes to the soul as a surprise, as an invader from without. The Gospel's word comes to the believer in the person of Jesus who challenges acceptance. (2) Like Philo, the Fourth Gospel finds that knowledge is intimately connected to action: one knows who God is by obeying. For Philo, obedience is to Torah; for John it

challenge made to any Christology committed to traditional, metaphysical claims about Christ by the varied nature of the results of the historical-critical method."[38] Historical-critical scholarship cannot merely be given lip service. Gaine demands that Thomistic theologians enter fully "into the arena of historical debate in pursuing the construction of their own Christologies."[39]

---

is to the command to love displayed on the cross" (58). The mysticism of the Word that impacts the doctrine of the incarnation reveals a deep regard for the Johannine teaching about the Logos, including areas where John and Philo agree (though also including the many areas where John goes well beyond Philo). See also Siegert, "Logos, 'älterer Sohn' des Schöpfers und 'zweiter Gott'." For a firm separation of Philo from Paul's Wisdom Christology, see Lee, *From Messiah to Preexistent Son*, 288–89; but for a firm (and persuasive) tearing down of such a separation—pointing out the evident similarity between Philo's understanding of the Logos as the one "through whom" God creates and 1 Corinthians 8:6—see Giambrone, "Primitive Christology as Ancient Philosophy," 50–55.

38. Gaine, "Jesus Christ," 675. For a similar insistence upon bridging the gap between dogmatic theology and historical-critical exegesis, see Congar, "Theology's Tasks after Vatican II," 54–55. See also Le Guillou, *Christ and Church*, 338: "As a contemplation of the Mystery of Christ, Thomistic theology is oriented in two directions which may at first sight appear contradictory, but which are in fact absolutely complementary and necessarily joined to one another: a continually increasing concern for fidelity to the biblical structures, and a desire for an always greater technical refinement in the conceptual apparatus. We might even say that fidelity to the Scriptures must remain all the more constant as the technical refinement increases. It is nonetheless extremely difficult to preserve this balance, sustained by the Word of God, unless a living and permanent contact is maintained with Sacred Scripture and with the Fathers of the Church."

39. Gaine, "Jesus Christ," 676. See also, for Aquinas's own exegetical practice insofar as it informed his Christology—and for a helpful proposal for how best to develop a biblically grounded contemporary Christology—Daniel A. Keating's "Exegesis and Christology in Thomas Aquinas." Keating, a rare scholar who has published substantive works in the fields of patristics, systematic theology, and New Testament studies, offers a rich and balanced conclusion: "Thomas provides an impressive and canonically rich use of scripture both to anchor and illuminate teaching about Christ. In contrast to some systematic christologies today, Aquinas is rarely far from the biblical text and has constant recourse to it in such a way that the discussion always has biblical revelation in view. And he ranges over the whole Bible in all of its parts in a way that few today have competence to equal. And for Aquinas, the scripture is not just the 'data' that we work from, but provides revealed truth to which we must adhere. It is not just a 'source' for his theology but a bedrock authority we can stand upon. . . . Aquinas's manner of referring to the biblical text, however, is not sufficient for our context today. He could rely upon a generally understood and agreed upon view of scripture in the medieval university, and his method of citation builds upon this general consensus. Today, much more groundwork in, and explanation of, the biblical text itself is required. In short, systematic studies of Christology today require a deeper and fuller explication of the scriptural revelation than Aquinas needed to furnish in his day. . . . We face new challenges because of the array of critical approaches to the Bible that have surfaced

As Gaine recognizes, his project is in many ways nothing new. Along various lines, the task of integrating historical learning and scholastic dogmatic theology has characterized the past five centuries of Catholic theology. In the sixteenth century, marked by conflict between Renaissance humanism (and its historical discoveries, which fueled the Reformation) and various scholasticisms, Thomas de Vio Cardinal Cajetan risked his reputation in order to try to integrate Thomism with the insights of Renaissance humanism. Stimulated by his debate with Martin Luther, he followed up his commentary on the *Summa theologiae* with an equally ambitious commentary on the Bible, drawing heavily on humanist learning.[40] Other post-Tridentine theologians likewise combined Thomistic or more broadly scholastic insights with historical erudition. For example, Scheeben's heavily scholastic *Handbook of Catholic Dogmatics* contains a rich *ressourcement* of the church fathers and includes a deep dive into the Old and New Testaments in the original languages.[41] In my view, the early twentieth-century conflict between the *Ressourcement* theologians promoting biblical-patristic theology, on the one hand, and Thomists or neo-scholastics promoting scientific or scholastic theology, on the other hand, unnecessarily weakened and depleted both sides, opening the door widely for the religious liberalism that is now dominant in many Catholic theological circles.[42]

---

since the Enlightenment, requiring of us a keen awareness of the historical method and the critical questions that have been posed to the Bible in the modern era. We have a more complicated task than Aquinas did and so need to work more diligently to master a historically aware canonical reading of Scripture that nonetheless maintains the conviction of its divine inspiration and authority for Christian teaching. In this effort, Aquinas remains a model and inspiration. Though we cannot simply repeat his approach in every respect, we can gain lasting instruction on how to use scripture in teaching about the Incarnation, and at the same time learn about the content of Christology from this master of the sacred page" ("Exegesis and Christology in Thomas Aquinas," 529–30).

40. See O'Connor, *Cajetan's Biblical Commentaries*; Cuddy, "Sixteenth-Century Reception of Aquinas by Cajetan." See also Giambrone, "Aquinas between Abelard and Erasmus," where he challenges Thomistic theologians to grapple more seriously with the Renaissance humanist insistence that the Bible is best read in the original languages.

41. For background to Scheeben's method, see Carola, *Engaging the Church Fathers in Nineteenth-Century Catholicism*.

42. For a recent introduction to Christology and soteriology that seeks to combine the best of the *Ressourcement* and scholastic modes, see Begasse de Dhaem, *Mysterium Christi*. Begasse de Dhaem's volume draws heavily upon Bonaventure, the church fathers, Louis Bouyer, Joseph Ratzinger, and Gerhard Lohfink. While biblically informed, however, it is not up-to-date in biblical scholarship, although its chapter on modern Christologies attends briefly to Albert Schweitzer and Rudolf Bultmann. There are also chapters on Christology and soteriology from 1951 to the present, which engage succinctly with John P. Meier, N. T. Wright, Ratzinger, Lohfink, Bouyer, Karl Barth,

INTRODUCTION

The difficulty of implementing Gaine's program in today's academic context, however, can hardly be overestimated. As is well known, especially over the past two centuries, historical-critical biblical scholars have undertaken research that mounts notable challenges to the traditional Christian understanding of Jesus. The scope of these challenges can be seen in a recent best-selling book by Reza Aslan, titled *Zealot: The Life and Times of Jesus of Nazareth*. This book, though not in itself worth scholarly attention, can serve my purposes here insofar as Aslan sums up the perspective of an influential strand of (non-Christian) academic New Testament scholarship.

Aslan's main claims are the following. He portrays Jesus as an apocalyptic prophet who had illusory expectations about the imminent end of the world. He blames Paul and the evangelist John for deifying Jesus and inventing the "incarnation."[43] He thinks that the notion that Mary conceived

---

and Hans Urs von Balthasar. Another such work, cited by Begasse de Dhaem in the Italian, is Ladaria's *Gesù Cristo, salvezza di tutti*. Too often, *Ressourcement* theologians, especially those of my generation, have failed to engage in a serious way with biblical scholarship.

43. There is an ongoing debate regarding what it means for the Synoptic Gospels and Paul to have a "divine" Christology. In part, the debate centers around what to make of Second Temple Judaism's figures that have an quasi-divine or "divine" role, as can be found in Wisdom of Solomon, Daniel, 1 Enoch, the Dead Sea Scrolls, various apocalyptic texts, and so on. These figures include personified Wisdom, angels, Moses, Adam, and diverse messianic figures. Crispin Fletcher-Louis has made the case that in Second Temple Judaism, as demonstrated by a wide variety of texts (including some New Testament texts), God can and does "'share his own nature' with another entity (to use Philo's language) in a way that means a second entity is, so to speak, 'divine' but not *fully* included within the divine identity," so that the second identity can be said to "'manifest' or 'participate in' or 'share' the divine identity without being fully 'included' within it" (Fletcher-Louis, *Christological Origins*, 306). Here one can distinguish between "ontological" divinity (which is strictly one) and "functional" divinity (where God shares his throne with exalted agents who manifest God's presence but who are not ontologically or strictly God)—although Richard Bauckham challenges this distinction, arguing that it is preferable to speak of "divine identity" (Bauckham, *Jesus and the God of Israel*, 31). For works that follow Fletcher-Louis's lines—often with the work of Bauckham and Larry W. Hurtado as the main targets—see, among others, Kirk, *Man Attested by God*; Fletcher-Louis, *Luke-Acts*; Fletcher-Louis, *All the Glory of Adam*; Fletcher-Louis, "Worship of Divine Humanity and the Worship of Jesus"; Horbury, *Jewish Messianism and the Cult of Christ*; Litwa, *We Are Being Transformed*. For the contrasting case, though not always in disagreement with Fletcher-Louis himself, see such works as McGrath, *Only True God*; Hurtado, *Lord Jesus Christ*; Hurtado, *How on Earth Did Jesus Become a God?*; Bauckham, *Jesus and the God of Israel*; Hays, *Echoes of Scripture in the Gospels*; Rowe, *Early Narrative Christology*; Tilling, *Paul's Divine Christology*; Hill, *Paul and the Trinity*; Bates, *Birth of the Trinity*. For Old Testament background that can be used to favor a "functional" reading, see McClellan, *YHWH's Divine Images*, especially his Appendix, which is aimed against Bauckham along lines that (in my view) far too sharply distinguish between the philosophical and patristic ontological Creator-creature distinction and the ways of expressing the Creator's

virginally is an invention of Matthew and Luke, and perhaps simply a way of covering up Jesus' illegitimacy. He holds that Jesus' teaching was merely an opportunistic continuation of John the Baptist's, although Jesus inflated his own importance much more than did the Baptist. He concludes that Jesus never did anything truly miraculous. He asserts that the evangelists largely invented the details of the crucifixion narratives in service to their theological agendas, with the exception of the fact that Jesus was executed because he claimed to be king. He argues that Jesus' followers experienced ecstatic but deluded encounters with the "risen" Jesus after his death. He considers that the evangelists invented their resurrection narratives with the purpose of confounding skeptics, but, even so, "the notion of a man dying a gruesome death and returning to life three days later defies all logic, reason, and sense."[44] He deems that the biblical portrait of Jesus' ascension fits with Paul's spiritualized and Romanized Judaism that "required nothing for salvation save belief in Christ."[45]

Although Aslan's book is a popularization rather than a work of scholarship, it represents the basic perspective of a number of biblical scholars today.[46] His perspective has its roots in eighteenth-century thinkers, among

---

sovereignty and distinctiveness in the Old Testament and Second Temple Judaism. See also, in favor of the perspective of Bauckham et al., Staples, "'Lord, LORD,'" and the summary and extension of Staples's argument in Barber, *Historical Jesus and the Temple*, 60–64. Staples shows that the Old Testament never uses the formula "Lord, Lord" (which is frequently used in the Gospels with reference to Jesus) for a figure other than YHWH. In a recent unpublished lecture, Barber has instructively pointed out that in the Gospels it is John the Baptist who functions as the messenger of the Lord, and so it would hardly make sense to suppose that the divine terms in which the Gospels describe Jesus are equally intended to portray Jesus as a functional bearer of the Lord's name or messenger of Lord.

44. Aslan, *Zealot*, 174.

45. Aslan, *Zealot*, 215. For a sharp critique of oft-repeated ideas about the Zealots and about "the figure of Jesus as a Zealot" (*pace* Aslan's book title), registering the point that "a more critical reading of Josephus has brought about the collapse of the Zealot-hypothesis and the notion of a Galilee seething with revolutionary fervour," see Freyne, *Jesus, a Jewish Galilean*, 135–36. I note that Freyne, like Aslan, suggests that interest in Jesus' ascension ("as the risen Lord and Saviour") has from the outset been in tension with interest in Jesus' earthly life, although Freyne recognizes that "[l]iving a life as Jesus had lived his became an essential component of the early Christian *kerygma*" (*Jesus, a Jewish Galilean*, 172–73).

46. See also the recent work of Litwa, *How the Gospels Became History*; and *Iesus Deus*. For Litwa, the evangelists probably did not know they were writing fiction: "The gospel writers—insofar as their social and educational situation allowed—wrote their stories so that they took on the appearance of *historia*. Whether or not the evangelists *did* report actual events is a separate question and is not my concern. Evidently they *thought* they did" (*How the Gospels Became History*, 3). In Litwa's view, the New Testament authors drew widely upon Mediterranean ideas of divinity to portray Jesus. For

INTRODUCTION

them Edward Gibbon. Almost all Aslan's claims were already widely available by the 1840s, having been spread by David Friedrich Strauss and others. His emphasis on Jesus as a false apocalyptic prophet echoes the late-nineteenth-century work of Albert Schweitzer.

Among recent works of Catholic historical-critical biblical scholarship, John Meier's multivolume project *A Marginal Jew: Rethinking the Historical Jesus* sums up in a definitive fashion the challenge that historical-critical biblical scholarship poses to dogmatic Christology. Meier's work places Jesus firmly within the late-Second Temple context, marked by an intense eschatological fervor. His Jesus comes across as a zealous man and an effective preacher, but certainly not as Wisdom incarnate or the Savior of the world. At the outset of his first volume, Meier asks his readers to imagine the following scenario: "Suppose that a Catholic, a Protestant, a Jew, and an agnostic—all honest historians cognizant of 1st-century religious movements—were locked up in the bowels of the Harvard Divinity School library, put on a spartan diet, and not allowed to emerge until they had hammered out a consensus document on who Jesus of Nazareth was and what he intended."[47] Meier grants that the outcome would not be perfect; there

---

the case that the evangelists knew that (for instance) Jesus' resurrection did not happen, see MacDonald, *Mythologizing Jesus*; and Miller, *Resurrection and Reception in Early Christianity*. Arguing that Jesus in the New Testament is an ancient version of modern superheroes, MacDonald remarks, "A Jewish teacher named Jesus actually existed, but within a short period of time, his followers wrote fictions about him, claiming that his father was none other than the god of the Jews, that he possessed incredible powers to heal and raise the dead, that he was more powerful than 'bad guys' like the devil and his demons, and that after he was killed, he ascended, alive, into the sky. . . . Mark and Luke reshaped memories of Jesus by emulating the *Iliad* and the *Odyssey* to portray him with supernatural powers" (*Mythologizing Jesus*, 1–2).

47. Meier, *Marginal Jew*, 1:1. Meier suggests that the religious diversity would strengthen the objectivity of the results. Influenced by Bernard Lonergan and the biblical scholar Ben F. Meyer, Jonathan Bernier raises a helpful objection regarding how Meier understands "subjectivity as it relates to objectivity. It seems that Meier understands the religious commitments of these scholars as barriers to objectivity, subjectivities to be set aside as these persons seek to know historical truth"—whereas from the perspective of Lonerganian critical realism, "such setting aside does not so much advance as hinder the work of historical understanding," which proceeds not by renouncing subjectivity but by "allowing that subjectivity to come to full maturation" through moving "from a pre-objective subjectivity to an objective subjectivity" (Bernier, *Quest for the Historical Jesus*, 159–60). For the significance of *ecclesial* reading of Scripture—missing from Meier's project, but ultimately inescapable (and fundamental to my own engagement with historical-critical biblical scholarship)—see Paddison, *Scripture*, influenced by Karl Barth and Stanley Hauerwas, among others. See also Kereszty, "Reflections on the Method of J. P. Meier"; Barron, *Priority of Christ*, which includes a trenchant response to Meier. Kereszty draws upon Paul Ricoeur, "Objectivity and Subjectivity in History."

would be unresolved issues and none of the historians would be fully satisfied with the consensus document. Nevertheless, says Meier, "something would be gained. We would have a rough draft of what that will-o'-the-wisp, 'all reasonable people,' could say about the historical Jesus."[48] In his view, such a reconstruction can well serve Jewish-Christian dialogue, ecumenical dialogue, and the interchange between Christians and nonbelievers.

Meier knows that his "historical Jesus" is a reconstruction rather than being the "real Jesus," but inevitably his readers (and sometimes Meier himself) conflate the two. *Pace* Meier, no historical reconstruction of Jesus could form the basis for Christian faith-based dialogues, given the assumptions built into the modern academic notion of "history."[49] Modern historiography has no place for divine providence and divine action. As a result, historical reconstruction of Meier's kind typically results in a portrait of Jesus that turns him into merely another "John the Baptist . . . or one of the prophets" (Matt 16:14), that is, into a man of his day who might have caused his fellow Jews to marvel (see Matt 22:22) but who cannot speak

---

48. Meier, *Marginal Jew*, 1:2. In a later volume, Meier sums up his own view of Jesus on the basis of his historical reconstruction: Jesus was "the Elijah-like prophet of the end time who seeks to regather all Israel and prepare it for God's kingdom (imminent and yet somehow present)" (Meier, *Marginal Jew*, 4:415). At least, the historical Jesus thought of himself in this way (and, for Meier, also deemed himself to be the Davidic Messiah). For a response to Meier's view that Jesus saw himself as the eschatological Elijah, see Allison, *Constructing Jesus*, 267-70, concluding that the evidence is insufficient.

49. Again, this is not to say that historical-critical work should have no role in such dialogues, granted, of course, that there will be sharp differences among historical-critical scholars, with the result that some scholars will have more to contribute to faith-based dialogues. For his part, discussing Jesus' divinity in Matthew's Gospel, Hays argues that "it is far too simple to say that the relation between the Father and the Son is 'hierarchical' and subordinationist; Matthew's narrative offers . . . far too many clues of a richer unity in identity. And to speak of a 'christological window' that relates Jesus to YHWH merely in terms of 'agency' or 'perceptual equivalence' is at once to superimpose foreign categories upon Matthew's text and to subvert the explosive theological logic of the story. Indeed, if we may press the point, it is to suggest that the disciples who worship Jesus in Matthew 14:33, 28:9, and 28:17 are actually guilty not only of a category mistake but of idolatry. *Matthew highlights the worship of Jesus for one reason: he believes and proclaims that Jesus is the embodied presence of God and that to worship Jesus is to worship YHWH*—not merely an agent or a facsimile or an intermediary" (Hays, *Echoes of Scripture in the Gospels*, 174-75). By contrast, J. R. Daniel Kirk, indebted to W. D. Davies and Dale C. Allison Jr., contends that this worship is offered simply to the Davidic Christ who is (or is to be) enthroned at the right hand of God: see Kirk, *Man Attested by God*, 375; and see 246-53 for the argument that Matthew 14:33 simply means that Jesus, as the Davidic Christ, shares in Godlike qualities without ontologically being God: here Kirk cites Heil, *Jesus Walking on the Sea*, 171.

authoritatively to later times, since his mentality was trapped in his own religiously eccentric and fanatical culture.[50]

As Thomas Joseph White points out, it is a mistake when Catholic theologians, embracing such reconstructions, proceed as though "[h]istorical study of Jesus in what is presupposed to be a post-metaphysical age permits us to recover anew the truth of Christianity that lies behind the artifices of ontological doctrine."[51] White and Meier agree that historical-critical scholarship is important and that "knowledge of the empirical, historical-cultural conditions of Christ can invite us to a deeper reflection about the mystery of the incarnate Word."[52] But historical-critical reconstruction can-

---

50. On the understanding of history, see my *Participatory Biblical Exegesis*. See also Van Wart, "Aquinas's Eschatological Historiography"; and the chapter on providence in Boersma, *Five Things Theologians Wish Biblical Scholars Knew*, 64–86; as well as Boersma, "Sacramental Interpretation," where Boersma demonstrates (no doubt to Wright's surprise) the heavy presence of typology within Wright's exegesis. Darren Sarisky comments that "the direction [biblical] reading takes is a consequence of the reader's beliefs about God (or denial of God's existence): one's stance here carries implications for the aim of interpretation as well as for the interpretive strategies that seek to fulfill that goal. Theological exegesis is an interpretive response to the Bible that is the product of construing the reading subject and the object to be read in connection with God" (Sarisky, *Reading the Bible Theologically*, xi). See also Johnson, *Real Jesus*, 81–133, including a detailed and helpful critical evaluation of Meier's first two volumes on 127–33. While Johnson values Meier's emphasis on the eschatological dimension of Jesus' ministry and Meier's sense that Jesus was understood to be a miracle-worker, Johnson insists that the historical skepticism intrinsic to Meier's method must be applied consistently, and he suggests that Meier fails by this measure in his use of the criteria for judging an incident's historicity. Strictly speaking, Johnson is correct to be skeptical of Meier's method, but I think biblical scholars should continue—as Brant Pitre, for example, does—to argue for historical probability and attempt to discern Jesus' intentions. Such efforts at historical reconstructions can generate insights, so long as they are not taken as gospel. For a critique of some aspects of Johnson's *Real Jesus*—especially Johnson's appeal to religious experience—see Hays, "Reading Scripture in Light of the Resurrection," 49–50. See also Gerd Theissen's helpful proposal regarding what he calls "the criterion of plausible historical context," in Theissen and Merz, *Historical Jesus*, 117.

51. White, *Incarnate Lord*, 37. See also the extended discussion of this point, building upon White and Sarisky, in Stevenson, *Consciousness of the Historical Jesus*, Part 1.

52. White, *Incarnate Lord*, 58. Here may be the place to point out that in John's Gospel, the Christology of the divine Word runs throughout Jesus' history. Ruben Bühner states, "While the absolute term ὁ λόγος does not come up again after the prologue, its underlying concept and implications can indeed be found throughout the Gospel of John. Jesus proclaims the word of God: 'He whom God has sent speaks the words of God' (John 3:34). Moreover, like God's word, Jesus' speech is a redemptive power, and his saying effects purification: 'You have already been cleansed by the word that I have spoken to you' (John 15:3). Like God's Word in the context of creation, Jesus' words in the narrative of the Fourth Gospel have creational power when Lazarus is raised from the dead at Jesus' command (John 10:43). In all of these aspects, the Fourth Gospel takes up the tradition also found in Isa 55:11 and transfers it to Jesus' words:

not provide the *foundation* for Christology. After all, Christians maintain that properly to know Jesus means to know him as the divine Son of the Father. Such knowledge requires faith, which exceeds what human historical reason can know.[53] Jesus explains in the Gospel of John: "I am the way, and the truth, and the life; no one comes to the Father, but by me ... Believe me that I am in the Father and the Father is in me; or else believe me for the sake of the works themselves" (John 14:6, 11).[54] Since we can know the works, faith in Jesus is not unreasonable; but knowing Jesus *as the incarnate Son*—the mystery of the incarnation, his eternal existence with the Father—involves personal, Trinitarian depths that exceed what reason as such can know without the grace of faith.

In this light, White observes aptly, "Ultimately ... none of the conditions of Christ's life can be fully understood except by recourse to supernatural faith, for only at this level of reflection do we attain to the deepest ontological core of his person."[55] Biblical exegesis that brackets faith—and

---

'So shall my word be that goes out from my mouth; it shall not return to me empty, but it shall accomplish that which I purpose, and succeed in the thing for which I sent it.' Finally, just as the Logos belongs to the divine identity without fully comprising the one God within the Jewish wisdom tradition, so also Jesus and his father are said to be 'one'. ... (John 10:30). Therefore, although Jesus is never again depicted explicitly with title ὁ λόγος after the prologue, the essential aspects and implications linked to this Logos Christology are continued throughout the Fourth Gospel" (Bühner, *Messianic High Christology*, 163).

53. Regarding faith in the incarnation, Brian E. Daley, SJ, comments, "Many modern theologians ... question whether it is intellectually responsible for Christian believers, in an age characterized by an empirically grounded view of truth ... and a suspicion of the mythic character of religious narrative, to continue to assert that Jesus *is* genuinely the eternal Son of God who lived, died, and rose again in history as a complete human being" (Daley, *God Visible*, 26). For Daley, it is not unreasonable to believe in the incarnation—and he thinks the church fathers help—but reason needs the aid of faith.

54. Bühner observes, "John's concepts of the incarnation of a truly divine being, as well as his presentation of Jesus as an uncreated being, cannot be deduced from earlier messianic motifs" (Bühner, *Messianic High Christology*, 170). In my view, however, the Johannine developments are not foreign to the realities described in earlier New Testament texts. Indeed, Bühner does see significant continuity: "With regard to earlier messianic motifs, John adopts, develops, deduces, and sometimes creatively invents motifs in order to present his distinctive high Christology. Thus, some of his motifs are more or less directly adopted from earlier discourses, such as the use of the God predicate. Other motifs are taken up by John and are further developed, such as the idea of the special power of the messiah's words. Furthermore, the inclusion of the Jewish wisdom tradition is an innovation of the early Jesus movement that reaches its peak in the Johannine prologue but could nevertheless have been easily deduced from earlier messianic hopes, which sometimes reveal close functional similarities between the messiah and Wisdom" (170).

55. White, *Incarnate Lord*, 58. For an exposition of faith, drawing upon Aquinas,

thereby also inevitably brackets the faith-filled interpretations given by the Gospel writers—has missed the very personhood of Jesus of Nazareth, which cannot later be added as icing on the cake. We cannot first know the incarnate Son strictly "historically" (in the modern sense of history, bracketing divine presence and action) and then, theologically, add the fact that he is the divine Son, without this second step altering almost everything that had been presumed to be known about the "historical" Jesus.[56]

Nevertheless, once the limitations of historical reconstruction have been recognized, Meier's efforts are not in vain. Historical-critical Jesus research is highly instructive for Christology.[57] This research uncovers a great deal about the religious categories, worldviews, leading figures and movements, and modes of discourse prevalent in Jesus' day. The "historical" Jesus is a Jesus firmly embedded within his Second Temple Jewish and Galilean context. Since Jesus was a Galilean Second Temple Jew, such research

---

Bonaventure, and Joseph Ratzinger, see Ramage, "Unless You Believe, You Will Not Understand." See also, for a broadly similar point from a Kierkegaardian direction—arguing that the Old Testament prophecies themselves are not enough, without the gift of faith, to ground all the connections revealed by Jesus and the Gospels—Crump, *Encountering Jesus, Encountering Scripture*. Crump is rightly critiquing an apologetics that argues that Jesus' fulfillment of the Old Testament prophecies is easily evident and that the New Testament's use of the Old is always demonstrably accurate. Although occasionally he overstates his case, his central (and accurate) argument is that historical reasoning *alone*, highly valuable though it is, cannot ground faith in Christ: "Clinging to reason's supremacy will make it impossible ever to believe in Christ. . . . Once a person becomes a believer and stands inside the circle of faith, the perception of faith standing *against* the understanding is seen in retrospect as faith *transcending* the understanding" (112). Crump's book would have benefited from making use of the full range of Second Temple Jewish literature.

56. For further insights in this vein, see East, *Church's Book*; Wright and Martin, *Encountering the Living God in Scripture*; and Stevenson, *Consciousness of the Historical Jesus*. See also the vision of the influential nineteenth-century scholar Ferdinand Christian Baur, who (in Johannes Zachhuber's words) "emphatically affirms 'objective,' impartial, historical research as a first, separate step to which is then subsequently added a philosophical or theological interpretation. The latter, it is assumed, will furnish all that has consciously been left out at first, meaning, values, teleology: all those concerns that ultimately motivate our interest in history, whether religious or otherwise" (Zachhuber, "Absoluteness of Christianity," 303).

57. Stevenson, in his *Consciousness of the Historical Jesus*, at times seems to suggest—although I think his viewpoint is in fact more positive—that historical-critical scholarship will need to be entirely reformed (rebuilt upon a better metaphysics and epistemology) before it can be of value in Christology. This is the position of Seth Heringer, who criticizes historical criticism especially in light of postmodern challenges to historical positivism: see Heringer, *Uniting History and Theology*; and see also Rowlands, *Metaphysics of Historical Jesus Research*. In my view, the fact that historical-critical scholarship generally needs a better philosophical foundation should not blind theologians to the fact that it still has much to contribute in its current form.

greatly assists our knowledge of Jesus. Theologians can and should integrate this research in ways that enrich Christology. As White comments, "historical study ... can help us to clarify what is and is not reasonable to believe concerning the *historical mode* in which a given mystery was unveiled historically."[58] There are many important things present in this "historical mode." As should be clear, it is no minor dimension!

Thus, the Catholic biblical scholar Anthony Giambrone highlights Jesus' "inauguration of a new eschatological cult and a new temple" as "the eschatological high priest, rightful heir to supreme headship of the chosen people's cult."[59] When Giambrone contextualizes and unpacks this historical reconstruction—aided by theological and canonical commitments that he and I share—I find his defense of Jesus' institution of the cultic priesthood (and of the Petrine office) to be extraordinarily helpful. Another Catholic biblical scholar, Michael Patrick Barber, has demonstrated that the Gospel of Matthew's Davidic Christology presents Jesus as the eschatological temple-builder and as the one who establishes the Church's leaders (preeminently, but not exclusively, Peter) as priests.[60] For his part, the Catholic biblical scholar Brant Pitre has published historical-critical studies arguing that Jesus understood his death on the cross as an atoning sacrifice (setting in motion "an eschatological Passover"); that Jesus at the Last

---

58. White, *Incarnate Lord*, 58. Regarding the historical mode of early christological reflection, Hurtado points out that "earliest Christian reverence for Jesus seems to have drawn upon pre-Christian Jewish tradition, especially ancient Jewish ideas about God having what we term a 'principal agent.' That is, typically in earliest Christian sources, Jesus is linked with God and is given a unique status in relation to God—for instance, as God's 'Son' or 'Messiah' (Christ) or 'Word' or 'Servant.' In ancient Jewish sources, this sort of 'principal agent' role is played sometimes by a great angel (such as Michael), sometimes by a great human figure of the past (such as Moses or Enoch), and sometimes by one of God's own attributes (such as divine Wisdom or God's Word, pictured in personified forms)" (*How on Earth Did Jesus Become a God?*, 21). But Hurtado insists that there are "very real differences between ancient Jewish reverence for martyrs, messiahs, or other figures, and the distinctive pattern of devotion to Jesus in early Christian sources.... The fact is that we simply have no evidence that any figure, whether human or angelic, ever featured in the corporate and public devotional practice of Jewish circles in any way really comparable to the programmatic role of Jesus in early Christian circles" (21–22). See also Bühner, *Messianic High Christology*, 130, where Bühner, while otherwise accentuating parallels between the New Testament and other Second Temple Jewish texts, grants at least that "there are only rare parallels in which a figure besides the one God was the recipient of 'cultic' worship in early Judaism." Almost all New Testament scholars agree that the ontological divinity of Jesus is attested by some New Testament texts.

59. Giambrone, *Bible and the Priesthood*, 12, 187. This emphasis on Jesus' eschatological mission (his kingdom-inauguration) does not entail the conclusion that Jesus was a failed prophet of the imminent kingdom of God, along Albert Schweitzer's lines.

60. See Barber, *Historical Jesus and the Temple*.

Supper understood himself to be instituting "an eschatological Passover meal" with himself as the "eschatological Passover lamb, whose blood would be poured out and whose body would be eaten by the eschatological priests of a new cult"; and that Jesus understood himself to be both human and much more than human (namely, divine).[61] Pitre's books are informed by Catholic theological commitments but equally reflect profound historical-critical erudition.

Overall, however, much Catholic biblical scholarship since Vatican II has focused on making the case that core Catholic doctrines are *not* found in Scripture or that Jesus knew nothing about them.[62] Giambrone therefore judges that, in general, the historical-critical "domain of the knowledge of Jesus has become a sterile field, void of ecclesial harvest."[63] Furthermore, efforts to reunite the theological and exegetical domains have had little success. Giambrone remarks, "The longed-for grail of a reintegrated theological culture, where systematic and biblical studies stand reconciled in a shared love of *sacra doctrina*, is an intellectual hunt that not infrequently wanders off in unlikely alchemical directions."[64] The goal or "grail" is a shared language through which biblical scholars and dogmatic theologians pursue the same questions and truly communicate with each other. Giambrone calls for "a disciplined discourse, pitched at a level fully fit for academic discussion, in which both sides can exercise their proper dialogical part."[65]

If a shared language is unattainable—and I do not have any illusions that I have achieved it here—then Giambrone proposes that theologians and biblical scholars should at least read one another's books assiduously. I have tried to do exactly this in preparing the present volume. Catholic theologians often blame biblical scholars for the current divide, but significant blame should go to theologians who have often only dipped into biblical scholarship and do not bother to keep current in the field. Again, the point is not that historical research provides a *neutral* substratum of facts or can "establish the biblical-theological content [of Scripture] apart from

---

61. Pitre, *Jesus, the Tribulation, and the End of the Exile*, 515; Pitre, *Jesus and the Last Supper*, 517; Pitre, *Jesus and Divine Christology*.

62. On the reception of *Dei Verbum* and post-Vatican II biblical scholarship, see Giambrone, *Bible and the Priesthood*, 23–35; Wright, "*Dei Verbum*"; Vall, "Two Trajectories in the Reception of *Dei Verbum*"; Reasoner, "Twentieth-Century Drama of Scripture's Literal Sense"; Johnson and Kurz, *Future of Catholic Biblical Scholarship*. See also Giambrone, "*Vera et Sincera de Iesu*," focusing on *Dei Verbum* §19 and the historical truth of the Gospels, in light of (among other things) Joseph Ratzinger's exegetical project.

63. Giambrone, "Introduction," 3.

64. Giambrone, "Introduction," 7.

65. Giambrone, "Introduction," 8.

philosophical and doctrinal presuppositions."[66] In fact, sacred Scripture itself is one of the divine realities that historical-critical methodologies must exclude, since there is no purely immanent historical ground that justifies either reading the books of "Scripture" as a canon or reading the New Testament as a unity (with the Gospel of John illuminating the Gospel of Mark, for instance[67]). Theologians rightly insist upon reading the New Testament primarily in light of the canonical Old Testament rather than primarily in conversation with Second Temple Judaism.[68]

At the same time, theologians must not neglect Second Temple Judaism's complex and fascinating reception of Israel's Scriptures, since it was within the matrix of this reception that Jesus lived and preached. Indeed it would be absurd to proceed without the vast erudition of historical-critical biblical scholarship. Biblical scholars are expert in an array of ancient Near Eastern and Hellenistic texts, practices, genres, and patterns of thought within which the New Testament texts fit. Due to their expertise, biblical scholars can identify theologically significant differences between the various New Testament texts, whereas theologians (myself included) tend to neglect or obscure these differences for the purposes of constructive canonical

---

66. Boersma, *Five Things Theologians Wish Biblical Scholars Knew*, 5. Boersma, of course, disagrees with such a claim. For Scot McKnight, "theology is a conversation about Scripture" (McKnight, *Five Things Biblical Scholars Wish Theologians Knew*, 37, referencing Jones, *Practicing Christian Doctrine*, 2). Catholic theologians can agree with this definition of theology, but only when Tradition is fully appreciated. See Congar, *Tradition and Traditions*.

67. While this is standard for theological exegesis of Mark as inspired Scripture, it can also be done from a historical-critical perspective, arguing that John corrects and augments Mark: see Anderson, "John and Mark."

68. For further (christological) engagement with the canonical Old Testament, see my *Engaging the Doctrine of Israel*; and see also my two co-authored books with Michael Dauphinais, *Wisdom of the Word* and *Holy People, Holy Land*. See also Meyer, *Jesus the Jew in Christian Memory*. Although a number of earlier historical-critical scholars strove to interpret Jesus in his Jewish context, Meyer is still basically correct to point out that in the past four decades, "Historical Jesus research underwent nothing short of a complete reversal, from interpreting Jesus in contrast to Second Temple Judaism to understanding him as deeply rooted in that context" (*Jesus the Jew in Christian Memory*, 181). In her view, the result has been to reveal the radical distance of Jesus from contemporary Christians—with the exception of marginalized Christians whose experience mirrors the suffering of the Jewish people under Roman rule—and his corresponding (relative) closeness to contemporary Jews. Theologically, Meyer argues that the next step for Christian theology should be "making space to express what has not been achieved in Christ instead of simply asserting reconciliation with God as something that has mainly already occurred" (187). Although I think Christian dogmatic theology has always been able to express what has not yet been achieved in Christ, Meyer is right that Christian dogmatic theology needs to show how the Jewish Jesus is not distant from contemporary Christians.

interpretation.[69] Biblical scholars know the Second Temple Jewish and ancient Near Eastern background and context of the New Testament texts, whereas theologians may fall into naive interpretations by misunderstanding the "plain sense" due to a failure to recognize the texts' background and context.[70] Biblical scholars are often profoundly attuned to the theology being articulated by the biblical texts in which they are expert. Even though theologians should confidently affirm that the Church's dogmatic teachings about Christ and salvation are true—and truly "biblical"—it would be beyond foolish for theologians to allow the divide to continue to grow between scriptural reading that locates Jesus in his Second Temple context and scriptural reading that confesses Jesus as the incarnate divine Son and the crucified and risen Lord of history.[71]

---

69. For a helpful balance, see Matera, *New Testament Theology*; and Matera, *New Testament Christology*. See also McKnight, *Five Things Biblical Scholars Wish Theologians Knew*, 21, warning that "a single-minded approach to systematics often blunts the diversity of the Bible, and this silences alternative voices in the Bible itself. Very few theologians I read do well at combining or even articulating the kingdom vision of Jesus with the soteriological and ecclesiological vision of the apostle Paul, and that must butt up against the nearly complete absence of anything like a theology of Hebrews at work in systematic theologies." In my view, systematic theologians should operate with the presumption that the diverse scriptural voices strongly cohere—much in the same way that, analogously, systematic theologians can and should presume that the diverse (orthodox) patristic voices generally cohere. The presumption of Spirit-guided ultimate coherence and the seeking out of such coherence—counter-cultural in the contemporary world that privileges difference—do not mean that differences are not theologically significant, but nevertheless a theology that underplays these differences is not thereby invalid. McKnight offers his own guiding biblical "frame" or narrative expressing Jesus' worldview of "theocracy, monarchy, and christocracy" (108), but he adds: "this is a narrative that (for me at least) best explains the narrative Jesus was using, but it does not explain the narrative framework at work for the apostles John, Paul, Peter, or James, and it does not get us into the narrative at work behind the book of Hebrews. There is some overlap in my narrative . . . with the book of Revelation, but Revelation has its own narrative, and it, too, needs to be seen for what it is" (110).

70. McKnight goes so far as to say, "The fruition of contextual studies in the twentieth and twenty-first centuries may well be the most important contribution made by those in biblical studies" (*Five Things Biblical Scholars Wish Theologians Knew*, 23; and see chapter 3 of his book for a full exposition of why systematic theology must learn from such work). Note that McKnight is aware that all Christians today inevitably "are reading a mediated Bible" in the sense that seminal thinkers and creedal developments of the past impact our understanding of the biblical texts (30); and he also appreciates the inexhaustibility of scriptural meaning: "Scripture is living and breathing and pulsating with throbbing possibilities" (33).

71. Here I differ from—while still valuing—Reno's *End of Interpretation*. I agree with the critique lodged by Markus Bockmuehl in his review of Reno's book: see Bockmuehl, "Reno Contra Mundum."

Beyond reading books by biblical scholars, what approaches might theologians take in order to help overcome the divide? In my recent *Reconfiguring Thomistic Christology*, I propose a partial solution: more attention to the New Testament's typological-eschatological portrayal of Jesus Christ, in accordance with the groundbreaking work of biblical scholars such as Richard Hays, Richard Ounsworth, and Leroy Huizenga—and also in accordance with the exegesis and theology of the church fathers.[72] In the New Testament, among the main typological figures of Jesus are Adam, Isaac, Moses, Joshua, and David. That Jesus understood himself as the eschatological Son of David (the New David) seems highly likely. I think Jesus also understood himself to be recapitulating, in an eschatological mode, other central figures of Israel's Scriptures.[73] Certainly the inspired authors of the New Testament understood him in these ways. The typologies' central purpose is to show how, in God's providence, Jesus brings Israel's history and cosmic history to fulfillment by conquering Israel's enemies, forgiving sin through his new covenant sacrifice as the eschatological temple, revealing himself to be the new Passover Lamb of the new Exodus, teaching and embodying Torah, and so on.[74]

Thus, in writing about Jesus' transfiguration in light of "scribal expectations of an eschatological high priest," Giambrone pays close attention to Second Temple traditions about a new David, new Moses, new Aaron, new Phineas, new Elijah, and new Adam.[75] Indeed, Giambrone maintains that

---

72. See my *Reconfiguring Thomistic Christology*; and see Hays, *Reading Backwards*; Hays, *Echoes of Scripture in the Gospels*; Perrin, *Jesus the Priest*, 144–65; Ounsworth, *Joshua Typology in the New Testament*; and Huizenga, *New Isaac*. For a further explanation and defense of Hays's approach, in response to criticisms raised by N. T. Wright, Ben Witherington III, and others, see Hays's "Figural Interpretation of Israel's Story." Hays observes, "The testimony of the Gospel writers makes sense and has validity if and only if the God to whom the Gospels bear witness is *real*, and if he is the same God as the God of Abraham, Isaac, and Jacob. Further, their testimony makes sense only if that God has providentially scripted history. . . . The Gospels claim not only that God is the author of the story of Israel but also that Jesus is the climactic consummation of that story" (84).

73. See also Le Donne, *Historiographical Jesus*.

74. Without reference to typology, see Markus Bockmuehl's helpful emphasis on Jesus' "Israel-centered mission and message," focused upon "the deliverance and renewal of Israel" (Bockmuehl, "God's Life as a Jew," 75)—although I would add an equal sense of the messianic reconfiguration of Israel around Jesus.

75. See Giambrone, "'Why Do the Scribes Say?'" The quotation comes from the title of the essay on 301. Giambrone comments, "Fluid Second Temple exegesis, which was inclined to multiply its mediators, resulting in a pluriform eschatology with scripturally based chief agents aplenty, was also marked by an unmistakable scribal trajectory prone to fuse these agents and generate a conglomerate messianic colossus, precisely such as we triumphantly confront in Jesus in the Gospels" (333–34). For a persuasive

Jesus himself experienced these typologies with extraordinary depth: Jesus "found himself in Scripture" because, as God's Servant, he "heard God's Word addressed to him with perfect directness, an almost unimaginable immediacy."[76]

In the present book, however, I have not taken this typological path. Instead, I offer a variation on a traditionally Thomistic project, namely, meditating on the mysteries of the life of Christ—as Aquinas does in the *Summa theologiae*. But, again, the context in which I write has been shaped by biblical scholarship. The Anglican biblical scholar Scot McKnight remarks, "Sometimes I read theologians and Jesus seems absent. More often he has become an abstraction."[77] I take this statement to be a challenge to present Jesus of Nazareth within his first-century Jewish context and also as the incarnate Son and (risen and ascended) universal Savior.

In his *Messianic High Christology*, the biblical scholar Ruben Bühner points out that other Second Temple Jewish texts already contained a number of elements found in New Testament Christologies, including "the messiah's preexistence, the notion of his presence at the act of creation, his

---

critique of Giambrone's overall argument in "'Why Do the Scribes Say?,'" see Gregory Vall's review of *The Quest for the Historical Christ*, 133–34—but Giambrone's speculative claim about Jesus' typological self-understanding still strikes me as correct.

76. Giambrone, "*Scientia Christi*," 276. Giambrone argues further, "So quickened was the Lord's knowledge of Scripture that this personal script of his unique destiny spoke to him with the living voices of the historical subjects and the divine *auctor* of the Word. Jesus' experiential understanding of his identity and mission came through a spectrum of historical encounters with the Scriptures. Each had an *event* quality, extending from humble hearing (or reading) of the Word in its liturgical proclamation to, at the far end, extraordinary infusions of supernatural grace and light—actual graces always configured to the normative shape of the Scriptures. For the Son who lived perfectly by every word that falls from the mouth of God, however, the immediacy of his hearing was *unbroken*" (285).

77. McKnight, *Five Things Biblical Scholars Wished Theologians Knew*, 151. McKnight adds, "If biblical scholars want to operate as doctors of the church, they will need to respect the historic theological foundations found in the creed, but respect requires engagement and even challenging some points. If systematic theologians want to operate as doctors of the church, they will need to engage paradigm-shifting contributions of biblical scholars" (150). For a similar concern, but much more pointed in its criticism, see the Evangelical biblical scholar Ben Witherington III's *Problem with Evangelical Theology*. The solution that Witherington proposes is simple: "All of these Protestant systems are to one degree or another products of Western and Enlightenment ways of reading the New Testament. But the authors of the New Testament were not late Western Christians. They did not live in an almost exclusively Gentile world, nor did they labor in the shadow of Augustine, Aquinas, Luther, Calvin, or even Wesley. They were Jews, and they thought like first-century Jews. The way forward is in part the way backward—to earlier exegetes, more Jewish contexts, a better understanding of the biblical world into which NT words were spoken" (*Problem with Evangelical Theology*, 227–28).

sitting on the Divine throne, his heavenly descent to earth, his appearance with typical signs of theophanies, and his superhuman power, as well as the description of him using 'monotheistic language,' the application of the God predicate to him, and . . . the idea of him being worshipped."[78] Arguably, one reason for this is that the core elements in Bühner's list have antecedents in canonical prophetic texts that, in accordance with providence of the God of Israel, were interpreted in the late Second Temple period along lines that prepared Israel for the coming of Jesus. Indeed, Christology requires firmly acknowledging God's providential preparation of the matrix of the Second Temple Judaism(s) in which Jesus lived and moved.[79] Just as the Old Tes-

---

78. Bühner, *Messianic High Christology*, 184–85. In my view, Bühner exaggerates these parallels, but enough of them are present nonetheless. Bühner adds, "Granted, for most of the 'parallel' texts . . . we do not know whether they were directly known by Paul or any other New Testament writer. However, they give us evidence for the wider contemporary discourses within the very same linguistic community to which the earliest members of the Jesus movement also belonged" (185). He is willing to grant that "the concepts of Jesus' divinity also took on views that cannot be found in earlier messianic concepts. But—and this is the crucial point—even those Christological developments that do not have a one-to-one parallel in earlier messianic concepts are still deeply connected to the given messianic language, which is why we should still view them as part of the wider messianic discourse" (186). Bühner goes on to describe the distinctiveness of early Christian messianism in terms of three elements: the sheer quantity of "superhuman" elements attributed to Jesus, as well as new "superhuman" motifs such as incarnation; the fact that these elements are attributed to a particular man, Jesus of Nazareth; and the fact of Jesus' weakness and crucifixion. The newness of the concept of a suffering Messiah is defended by Bühner against Boyarin, *Jewish Gospels*, 129–56.

79. For a statement of the problem—but in my view an exaggerated statement—see Paul J. DeHart, *Unspeakable Cults*, 225: "The cultural terms which conveyed Jesus' peculiar excellence for his era, the 'divine' marks that effected his deity in his contemporary world, are largely inscrutable to all save specialist historians. The symbolic systems which were the inevitable substance of his humanity and within which his deity was realized are for the most part foreign to the values that modern people might cherish. Thus, when historical investigation attempts to make contact with Jesus yet simply sets aside the categories which framed the cult of his deity, the purely human remainder that is exhibited will all too likely show up as at once blandly familiar in his own context, bizarre in ours." I can see what DeHart means regarding some (or even many) historical investigations, but I think that most of the categories and symbolic systems of Jesus' day are not so foreign today as DeHart supposes, granted that some important elements (such as the ones listed by Bühner) will require instruction—generally provided by the New Testament itself, especially when read in light of the Old Testament. Historically speaking, I do not think the Gospels accurately be summed up, along lines conceded by DeHart (while he argues that the Spirit can overcome the seeming deficiency and enable a living faith), as "a farrago of borrowed Syrian cultic legends and dubiously applied Jewish messianic oracles layered over the barely visible lineaments of an obscure enthusiast" (236). Where DeHart and I agree, however, is with regard to the needful "integration of Jesus and his cult as an organic (semantic)

tament texts presage and point toward Jesus in various ways but without anticipating the radical newness of the mode in which he brings various elements together, so also the Second Temple texts (building upon Old Testament texts) presage and point toward Jesus in various ways without containing anyone like the man who bursts off the pages of the New Testament.

II. Twentieth-Century Catholic Christologies: A Brief Sampling

In response to historical-critical challenges, a number of prominent twentieth-century Catholic theologians attempted to rethink Christology from the ground up.[80] They sought to do justice to Jesus' eschatological words

---

complex" (63). As DeHart says, "The more the mental world of early Christians is assumed to be confined within the conceptual horizon of the Old Testament writings and priestly or proto-rabbinic ideologies, the harder it is to see by what religious logic the notoriously strict centralization of worship on YHWH came to be suspended to such an outrageous degree in the case of Jesus of Nazareth. Even the wisdom speculations of preexistent Sophia and the apocalyptic visions of the Son of Man really do not get us very far toward an actual cult of Jesus" (61). Quite rightly (but inseparably from Jesus' radical distinctiveness), DeHart concludes that "divinization can be seen as a cultural dynamic that Jesus himself might well have actively participated in, providing terms for his own self-understanding as well as for the acceptance and deeper exploration of that self-understanding in his cult" (91).

80. See the blunt historical remarks offered by Bingemer et al., "Editorial," 7–8: "Christology is going through a sort of 'second modernity'. The first came into being when biblical criticism forced the interpretation of the mystery of Christ through concepts inherited from the Fathers and the Scholastics to be revised, imposing abandonment of the—till then normal—literalist reading of the texts. The beginnings of the second can—for Catholicism, not without the fraternal influence of Protestant theology—be assigned to Vatican II, when not only was the need to continue what had been started recognized, but its cultivation received an official boost. . . . Centuries of christology marked by the lofty reflection of the fourth Gospel and by the dogmatic pronouncement of Chalcedon changed the divinity of Christ into such a dominant starting point that it is appropriate to speak of a sort of a-historical 'Monophytism' in theological speculation and of a certain 'mythologism' in popular imagery. Today it is no longer possible to continue with a vision that, as has so often been said, tends to regard Jesus as a divine being who descended from on high and passed through our world only to return to heaven. There is a real hunger for rescuing the reality of his human life, of his fellowship in the flesh with our sorrows and joys, with our quests and our hopes—in a word, of being able to see him and feel him as a model for our lives who, secure in the love of God, gave himself up to effective love of his brothers and sisters and opened himself out to the great hope of the final Kingdom." There is a real irony here, in that clothed in historically minded language, the authors of this editorial end up with a paean not to the Jesus of Second Temple Judaism but to early-twentieth-century religious liberalism of the kind associated with Adolf von Harnack and Alfred Loisy. This is especially ironic given that this issue of *Concilium* aims, according to the

and deeds and to New Testament data such as Jesus' solidarity with the poor. They also sought to distance themselves from patristic and medieval portraits of Jesus (and Mary) that now seemed ahistorical and untenable.

In my view, these theologians were partly on the right track. As noted above, it is imperative to incorporate biblical scholarship within christological reflection on the incarnate Lord. The alternative would be to cease to offer credible testimony to Jesus of Nazareth, and to sit by while the Christian faith withers. Nevertheless, many of these theologians conceded too much, or set out on eccentric paths, despite their real insights.

For instance, under the influence of mid-twentieth-century German exegetes, Karl Rahner maintained that Jesus was a prophet of the kingdom, but he left it an open question whether Jesus thought of himself as the Messiah or understood his death as redemptive. Rahner also thought it possible to leave open the question of the empty tomb, although he affirmed the resurrection.[81] For Rahner, it is the exalted Christ—and our experience of

---

authors of this editorial, to respond critically to Joseph Ratzinger/Pope Benedict XVI's *Jesus of Nazareth*.

81. See Rahner, *Foundations of Christian Faith*, 248–49, 267, 283. For Rahner on Christ's resurrection, see also his "Position of Christology," 210–13, which takes a firmer line than his later *Foundations of Christian Faith*. For full (and critical) accounts of Rahner's Christology, see Marshall, *Christologies in Conflict*, 15–114; Schrader, *Thomistic Christocentrism*, 159–205 (in dialogue with the Salmanticenses—see Salmanticenses, *On the Motive of the Incarnation*); and White, *Incarnate Lord*, 91–101, 442–47. Marshall sums up the problem, "For Thomas [Aquinas], Jesus Christ 'is God', explicitly in virtue of that which distinguishes him from us as a human being, rather than that which we hold in common with him. For Rahner, it seems, Jesus 'is the absolute saviour' in so far as he is the first instance of a general pattern which we can realize in common with him. And . . . because for Rahner the saving character of this pattern logically depends upon its being at least potentially common to us and him, that which distinguishes him from us as human beings need never have a place in 'the idea of an absolute saviour'" (*Christologies in Conflict*, 188). See also the exposition of the Christologies of Rahner, Sobrino, and Balthasar—in light of religious pluralism—in Oakes, *Infinity Dwindled to Infancy*, 350–72. For instructive critiques of Rahner's Christology vis-à-vis the hypostatic union, Christ's knowledge, nature and grace, and Christ's resurrection, see White, *Incarnate Lord*. White's critique of Barth and Schleiermacher is apropos here: "[B]oth think *univocally* about the being-in-act of operations (Jesus's consciousness of religious dependence, Christ's human obedience) as in some way equivalent with or susceptible to signifying formally the being in act of substantial being (the subsistent person of Christ in his unity of being with the Father). This is what leads each of them, in two very different ways, to seek to locate the divine-human union in Christ in the human actions of Jesus. In addition, then, Barth does not identify accurately what distinguishes the operations of the divine and human natures of Christ. Human operations become direct windows into the operation of the deity itself, as if the two were somehow equated" (65). For a defense of Schleiermacher against White's critique, arguing in part that Thomistic and Greek metaphysics are no longer helpful in light of contemporary philosophy, see Ralston, "Schleiermachian Rejoinder"; and see

him—that assures us of the everlasting meaningfulness of the universal human experience of self-transcendence and that thereby makes sense of the symbolism found in biblical eschatology.[82] Rahner states in a representative passage, "We are . . . able to grasp, in Jesus and our love for him, that neither he nor we in him, with our individuality and our history, perish when we approach the burning and unconditional immediacy of God, but that we will continue to exist and be definitively saved."[83]

In Rahner's view, Jesus did not intend to found a Church. Jesus had a "temporally imminent expectation" regarding the end of all things and "this expectation was not fulfilled in the way in which he presented it to himself and formulated it in words."[84] Yet, Rahner also maintains that Jesus' imminent eschatological expectation has an "absolute significance" today, even though as a temporal claim, Jesus was mistaken.[85] The reason for its "absolute significance" is that Jesus fully opened himself to his transcendentality. Rahner states that Jesus' experience of the "holy mystery" is of "a hidden closeness, a forgiving intimacy" and "a love which shares itself."[86] Jesus is what humans, at the height of their transcendental experience, are supposed to be.[87] This claim, however, makes transcendental experience

---

White's response (largely engaging Barth, and joining with Barth in a critique of Erich Przywara's view of analogy), "On the Ecumenical Work of Reforming Christology." See also Hans Boersma's defense of core elements of Platonic (and, though Boersma does not say so, in this case also Aristotelian-Thomistic) metaphysics as crucial "theoretical building blocks without which Christian doctrines are difficult or impossible to uphold": Boersma, *Five Things Theologians Wish Biblical Scholars Knew*, 43.

82. Rahner explains, "If anyone understands the Resurrection *aright*, if at the centre of his own existence, he yearns for his own resurrection since on any true anthropology, he can only understand himself as a man who hopes for that which is described in terms of resurrection, then, in my belief, he has also achieved an *a priori* perspective such that, while it certainly does not excuse him from the *free decision* of faith in the Resurrection of Jesus, still at the same time it does justify him in believing in such a thing as the Resurrection of Jesus, i.e. in accepting the Easter experience of the disciples as a matter of his own intellectual honesty" ("Position of Christology," 213).

83. Rahner, "Jesus Christ and Christology," 15.

84. Rahner, "Jesus Christ and Christology," 23.

85. Rahner, "Jesus Christ and Christology," 23.

86. Rahner, *Foundations of Christian Faith*, 131.

87. Regarding the broader issue of the intelligibility of "human nature" and its distinction from divine grace (aside from Rahner's claims about transcendental experience), White notes that Vatican II's *Gaudium et Spes* "proposes a very developed interpretation of what constitutes human nature, as intellectually distinguishable from the life of Christian grace, and yet simultaneously underscores that the healing, strengthening, and fulfillment of the former are only made possible by recourse to the latter. If nature is not *historically and existentially* separable from the mystery of God's gracious action in history, it is nevertheless distinguishable and can even be appealed

the ultimate measure, before which Jesus in his human specificity risks fading away or (as has happened in postconciliar Germany) simply being cast aside as a misguided late-Second Temple Jewish prophet.[88] Although Rahner affirms Chalcedon, as Thomas Joseph White observes, "Rahner locates the ontological union of God and man in Christ in the same place where Nestorianism typically locates it: uniquely in the spiritual operations of the man Jesus.... Just in this way, then, he makes the basis for the hypostatic union a union of 'mere' moral cooperation between the man Jesus Christ and God."[89]

---

to *precisely as a way toward understanding* the goodness of the mystery of life in Christ" (White, *Incarnate Lord*, 130). White persuasively argues that some concept of "human nature" as such—i.e., in its own integrity, as distinct from its graced or fallen states (and White recognizes that this "pure nature" never existed historically, important though it is to conceive of human nature as such)—is necessary for Christology. White sums up his view: "without a properly understood concept of pure nature, it is impossible to claim (1) that moral evil (which is prevalent in human nature in its actual state) is in truth unnatural; (2) that we can only become perfectly human (with a restored nature) by the grace of Christ; (3) and that what is true for human nature in general is the case in a unique way concerning Christ" (*Incarnate Lord*, 131; cf. 142–43). If we do not have some concept of what it means to be human, we will not be able to make a case for Christ as manifesting perfect humanity. Indeed, White's examination of Rahner's revision of "pure nature" along lines that, in fact, resonate with Dominican criticisms of Francisco Suárez's account of "pure nature" is particularly instructive in this context. Instead of "pure nature" one can say "integral nature." See also Torrell, "Nature and Grace in Thomas Aquinas."

88. In "Position of Christology," Rahner allows the following regarding Jesus' Second Temple-Jewish identity: "If Jesus understood himself to be the eschatological event of salvation in the absolute, and the Mediator of salvation in the absolute, and if this self-understanding on the part of the pre-Easter Jesus can, with sufficient certainty be recognized as present in him even by modern historical and critical exegesis, then we have found an adequate point of departure for the christology of the Church. At the same time this is not to deny, but on the contrary to imply, that in the dimension of Jesus' own conscious reflection upon himself, this self-understanding of his can in its turn have a history of its own. And this history in itself only attained its definitive fulness in his Resurrection" (206; cf. 187–89, 195–96 on Jesus' explicit self-understanding in contrast to later Christology). Rahner also takes care to clarify that his position "does not imply that this absolute assent of faith in Jesus Christ has nothing whatever to do with the data of history with which exegetical speculation is concerned. If someone came to us and proved to us positively and unambiguously that for instance Jesus himself either never existed at all or *certainly* understood himself merely as having some kind of religious mission to arouse his fellow men with a message which had nothing whatever to do with himself, his own person, and what he himself did, then our faith would no longer have that reality of saving history as its content, then our faith would be vain" (191).

89. White, *Incarnate Lord*, 76. He adds, "On Rahner's model, the 'grace of union' has been in effect reduced solely to a union of 'habitual grace'" (77). White comments that the hypostatic union is not only utterly unique, but also "is a mystery without pure analogy in the order of sanctifying grace. For Christ cannot be understood adequately even by comparison with saints or holy persons who possess by grace a most perfect

INTRODUCTION

For his part, Edward Schillebeeckx argued that Jesus did indeed rise but that no one ever saw him after his death. He asks rhetorically, along lines that render Jesus' resurrection implausible: "May it not be that Simon Peter—and indeed the Twelve—arrived via their concrete experience of forgiveness after Jesus' death, encountered as grace and discussed among themselves (as they remembered Jesus' sayings about, among other things, the gracious God) as the 'evidence for belief': the Lord is alive?"[90] For Schillebeeckx, Jesus' ministry was notable for his ability to reestablish wholeness in people's lives. On this view, salvation, as a lived reality, consists in ethical conduct that mends a broken world. The mark of the kingdom here and

---

degree of human union with God. Such union is real: sanctifying grace does permit moral cooperation with God and the indwelling presence of God in the soul of the human person. It does not, however, constitute a substantial or hypostatic union, as if by grace a human being might 'become' a subsistent divine person. Consequently, there is no perfect analogy either in the order of nature or in the order of grace for the hypostatic union" (White, *Incarnate Lord*, 84). White sums up: for Rahner "Jesus's relational consciousness to the Father is that which gives him his identity as the Son of God. [Jon] Sobrino prolongs this idea by historicizing the developmental consciousness of Jesus, who relates more and more to the Father, becoming *progressively*, in some real sense, the Son of God" (122). The solution, as White makes clear, is to hold that "the human conscious activity of Jesus (while not *constitutive*) is in fact *indicative* or *expressive* of his hypostatic identity as the Son" (122).

90. Schillebeeckx, *Jesus*, 391. Schillebeeckx is integrating and (in certain ways critically) responding to such scholars as Marxsen, *Auferstehung Jesu als historisches und theologisches Problem*; Seidensticker, *Auferstehung Jesu in der Botschaft der Evangelisten*; and Pesch, "Zur Entstehung des Glaubens und die Auferstehung Jesu." Rahner differentiates himself sharply from this view: "If anyone says they [the apostles] were precisely people who were religiously inclined, who could not bear to be parted from their Master, and so precisely ended by conjuring up the idea that he had risen from the dead—if anything of this kind is intended to be taken as a serious explanation of the apostles' experience, then this again belongs to the realm of uncritical rationalism" ("Position of Christology," 213). I critique Schillebeeckx's perspective at some length in *Did Jesus Rise from the Dead?*; and see also Wright, *Jesus and the Victory of God*, 21–27. For Schillebeeckx's further thoughts, originally published in 1978 in Dutch, see his *Interim Report*. For a similar trajectory, though applied to Jesus' whole life and to the goal and impact of the historical-critical quest, see Queiruga, "Jesus," 36: "[Jesus'] contemporaries had direct experience of Jesus; he comes to us through interpreters. The deep meaning of inquiry into the 'historical Jesus' consists precisely in moving beyond this interpretation in order to attain, through it, the *same experience* and to interpret it in *our* culture." For instance, Queiruga contends, "Jesus' actions and sayings call us to be a participatory Church, servant and committed to tolerance, freedom, and justice. The new quests for the historical Jesus, even if they do not expressly recognize this, have their underlying justification here and are obeying a sure instinct of faith" (37). It is no surprise when Queiruga goes on to recall "the favourable impression Schillebeeckx made on me by recognizing the problems he had left open and unfinished at the end of his *Jesus*" (40), problems that for Schillebeeckx (and Queiruga) do not undermine the path taken by Schillebeeckx.

now is radically open table fellowship and a refusal to exclude anyone from the circle of care.

Indebted to some (now outdated) exegetes of his era, Schillebeeckx denies that Jesus was an apocalyptic preacher. Jesus instead preached a "good news" that differs in notable ways from what apocalyptic texts proclaim. As in traditional liberal Protestantism, Schillebeeckx holds that at the core of Jesus' message is the following insistence: "Soon God will be king, and right relations among men will prevail."[91] According to this perspective, Jesus focused entirely upon his hearers' present relationship with God. Schillebeeckx states, "All that matters to Jesus is people in their relationship to God, and God in his care and concern for people."[92] For Jesus, says Schillebeeckx, the kingdom is present wherever people are acting to assist others in achieving "wholeness of being"—where people are surrendering themselves to the will of God through "orthopraxis."[93] Again, this does not sound like the Jesus of the New Testament, and in fact, as Thomas Joseph White observes, "the 'conclusions' of his massive exegetical effort" turned out to "be practically irrelevant within ten years of their publication."[94]

For his part, Jon Sobrino strove to fit the words and deeds of Jesus into the categories of economic and political liberation as understood in the 1970s. Like some biblical scholarship of his era, Sobrino claims that "the decisive thing for Jesus was not himself or the church, but the Kingdom of God."[95] He criticizes conciliar Christology in the name of a supposedly more historically grounded exegesis focused upon the kingdom. He too, however, ends up interpreting the Gospels along the lines of nineteenth-century religious liberalism. For example, he states, "What Christian faith says is that God becomes present in humanity, that God certainly became

---

91. Schillebeeckx, *Jesus*, 173. For the same message in Adolf von Harnack, see the discussion in Ratzinger, *Introduction to Christianity*, 198–200.

92. Schillebeeckx, *Jesus*, 150.

93. Schillebeeckx, *Jesus*, 153.

94. White, *Incarnate Lord*, 476. For criticisms of Schillebeeckx's hermeneutics, see 470–86.

95. Sobrino, *Jesus the Liberator*, 106; see also Sobrino, "Coming Kingdom or God's Present Reign"; and—much earlier—Sobrino's *Christology at the Crossroads*. Sobrino defines the kingdom of God as "the just life of the poor" (*Jesus the Liberator*, 131), with "the poor" being the economically and politically marginalized. For a similar approach, with similar problems, see Gustavo Gutiérrez's seminal *Theology of Liberation*. For concerns about the main lines of liberation theology, see Boersma's succinct remarks in *Five Things Theologians Wish Biblical Scholars Knew*, 115–18; and see Schall, *Liberation Theology in Latin America*. Schall's book contains 125 pages by Schall, followed by essays by Hans Urs von Balthasar and others, along with various Church documents, including the International Theological Commission's "Human Development and Christian Salvation."

present in Jesus, and that God is not going to become more present in anyone other than in Jesus."[96] This is not a description of the incarnation at all, but rather of the divine indwelling in a man.

In Sobrino's view, Christology is only now incorporating the centrality of the kingdom of God for Jesus, which prior to the late nineteenth century had not been adequately understood. Sobrino thinks the parables have a historical basis in Jesus' own preaching, and he argues that their central message is that the poor and the outcast will receive a preferential place in the kingdom that is about to arrive. In light of Jesus' urgent proclamation that people must repent and live in accordance with the coming kingdom, Sobrino deems that the kingdom consists simply in justice, peace, reconciliation, and happiness—the absence of anything contrary to God's will for human flourishing. Sobrino sums up, "the Kingdom of God is the just life of the poor."[97] Ultimately, this kingdom will involve "the radical overcoming of death" and the "fullness of life" in Christ, rejoicing in the goodness of God who gives life to the poor.[98] In my view, while the kingdom of God is not less than this, it is much more.

For Hans Urs von Balthasar, the solid historical ground on which Christology can be rebuilt is Jesus' unique mission-consciousness, attested by the Gospels. Balthasar states, "The words of the Gospels point concentrically to his peerless sense of mission. . . . Whether explicitly or implicitly, Jesus must have acted as if he were the Archimedean point of the religious history of the world."[99] I think this is both an important insight into Jesus

---

96. Sobrino, *Christ the Liberator*, 199. For discussion of Sobrino's Christology, see Oakes, *Infinity Dwindled to Infancy*, 356–62; White, *Incarnate Lord*, 107–11.

97. Sobrino, *Jesus the Liberator*, 131.

98. Sobrino, *Jesus the Liberator*, 133. Sobrino adds, "As utopic principle, this God goes on instigating good things for the poor, in history and against history: hope, the struggle for justice, peace, community. . . . And this God goes on enabling us to combine in history such apparently irreconcilable things as the struggle for justice and work for peace, efficacy and gratuitousness, action and contemplation, activity and spirit. . . . As long as all this remains a reality, God is being seen to be present in the Kingdom, and the Kingdom is being seen to be 'of God.' In this way, in the historical dimension, building the Kingdom is walking toward God, till all the principalities—the anti-Kingdom—are overthrown and God is all in all" (134).

99. Balthasar, *Theo-Drama* 3:26–27. As Balthasar is aware, his emphasis on Christ's consciousness both fits with and, in some very significant ways (especially with respect to Balthasar's argument that Christ's mission is to bear our punishment, that is, to bear God's wrath against sin), differs from the tradition stemming from Friedrich Schleiermacher's emphasis on Christ's God-consciousness. Some context regarding this tradition is provided by Vidu, *Atonement, Law, and Justice*, 133–76. Vidu notes that for Schleiermacher's liberal Protestant successor Albrecht Ritschl—whose work remains influential today, often in subterranean ways—we must affirm "the methodological and epistemological priority of Christian consciousness. We have no access to God, no

(and the Father and the Spirit), and an insufficient basis for understanding the incarnation.[100] Furthermore, Balthasar contends that the differentiation of Father and Son depicted in the Gospels properly "involves the positing of an absolute, infinite 'distance' that can contain and embrace all the other distances that are possible within the world of finitude, including the distance of sin"; and he argues that "God unloaded his wrath" upon Jesus on the cross.[101] These elements and others like them seem mistaken on a number of grounds.

Balthasar correctly sides with those who highlight Jesus' status as an eschatological prophet. As Balthasar makes clear, Jesus claims to do what

---

knowledge of sin, except through the influence of Christ, present in the church. Unlike Schleiermacher, however, Ritschl understands this influence not as mystical, acting on the preethical level of our desires, but in terms of the kingdom, which is a moral principle. In other words, the influence of Jesus extends through history not by what is, after all, despite Schleiermacher's claim to the contrary, a magical method of transmission. Rather, Jesus affects the course of human history through the foundation of an ethical and historical body, his kingdom" (*Atonement, Law, and Justice*, 163).

100. I agree here with White, *Incarnate Lord*; and Stevenson, *Consciousness of the Historical Jesus*.

101. Balthasar, *Theo-Drama* 4:345; 4:323. For background in Hegel's writings, and for Balthasar's ultimately anti-Hegelian purposes, see my *Achievement of Hans Urs von Balthasar*, chapter 2. A strongly appreciative view of Balthasar's Christology is found in Turek, *Atonement*. For critical reflections, see Brotherton, *One of the Trinity Has Suffered*; Schrader, *Thomistic Christocentrism*, 206-37 (in dialogue with the Salmanticenses). For further critical discussion, with which I agree, see White, *Incarnate Lord*, chapters 6-9; and White, *Trinity*, 402-6, 579-83. White points out that "kenotic Christology," as found in various forms in Gottfried Thomasius, Karl Barth, Sergius Bulgakov, Wolfhart Pannenberg, Hans Urs von Balthasar, Walter Kasper and others, is in part a result of an attempt to embrace historical-critical perspectives without excluding creedal Christian claims about Jesus. As White affirms, "the Paschal mystery does manifest for us, in and through the human agony, death, and resurrection of Christ, the relations of the persons and the processions of the Son and Holy Spirit from the Father. The human obedience of the Son in his passion is proper to his created nature alone, but it is also expressive of his personal intentions and willing. Therefore even Jesus's human acts of obedience do reveal to us something of his personal relation to the Father, a relation that is constitutive of his divine identity. . . . The transposition from the Paschal mystery to the consideration of the immanent life of the triune God is legitimate and necessary. It has to be done in a twofold respect. One must avoid the extreme of reducing the immanent life of the Trinity to that of a historical life among us (based upon an anthropomorphism derived from the human character of the cross event), and one must avoid severing all connection between the cross and the revelation of the inner life of the triune God, so as to fall into a kind of practical Sabellianism" (White, *Incarnate Lord*, 378). I make a similar point in my *Scripture and Metaphysics*, chapter 4. From a Balthasarian perspective that envisions more continuity between Balthasar and Aquinas than I think there is on these matters, see Franks, "Thomistic-Balthasarian Comments." See also White's response to Franks and others: White, "On the Ecumenical Work of Reforming Christology."

only God can do. Jesus requires that people follow him and surrender their lives for his sake, and he promises salvation as the reward. He promises the rest that only God can give. He claims to be the one who will judge the world, and he teaches that building our lives upon his words is the only solid foundation. With regard to the above, Balthasar develops a "theo-dramatic" portrait of Jesus that comports in crucial ways with the Jesus of the Gospels. Even here, however, Balthasar does not give sufficient place to Jesus' two wills, divine and human. Instead he tends to conflate the former into the latter.[102]

Bernard Lonergan's christological work, published in English as *The Incarnate Word* and *The Redemption*, belongs to the height of mid-twentieth century neo-scholastic theology. In its English edition, Lonergan's *The Incarnate Word* (originally published in Latin in 1960 as a textbook) contains four parts, which move from the more concrete to the more speculative. He begins with a first part on "The Teaching of the New Testament on the Hypostatic Union." He proceeds scholastically by offering a thesis, identifying its theological "note" or dogmatic weight, and identifying the most important opponents of the thesis (e.g., the Arians and Immanuel Kant, among others).

---

102. For discussion, see White, *Trinity*, 554; and see White, "Two Natures of Christ in the Crucifixion," 132, where he points out that in Balthasar's trilogy "there is little or no real recourse made to the classical teaching of dyothelitism and the Third Council of Constantinople (680–681), that posits that there are two wills in Christ, human and divine. Obviously Balthasar does not deny the truth of this doctrinal teaching and its patristic roots. He famously wrote a major study of Maximus the Confessor, arguably the most important of the twentieth century. However, in his mature work, Balthasar simply rarely alludes to the mystery of the two wills of Christ and it plays no thematic role in his thinking. Or perhaps we could say that it is an idea subject to radical reinterpretation in light of a kenotic notion of the mission of Christ. Consequently, in the *Theo-Drama*, for example, the human willing of Christ in his temporal mission and obediential freedom is alone indicative in a quasi-univocal way, of the inner life of the Trinitarian persons' relations. When the Son obeys the Father as man in time, we see into the self-surrendering love of the eternal Son as God and even see by a mirroring reciprocity the kind of kenotic love that the Father has for the Son from eternity. The human will of Christ is thus not depicted as distinct from and subordinate to his divine will in an instrumental fashion (as with Damascene for example), nor is his divine will depicted as identical with that of the Father and the Spirit, as that of God (the three persons having one will that is identical with the divine nature). Instead we are presented with something like an inverted monophysiticism, where the kenotic life of the Son in his identity with man manifests precisely only in his human nature as such what it is for him to be Son in his very person, eternally, as self-surrendering love." For further discussion of the point that "the human nature of Jesus (his body and soul) is an instrument of his person, in an analogical and unique sense of the term," see White, *Incarnate Lord*, 113–16.

Lonergan distinguishes between "narrative history" and "critical history."[103] The New Testament texts, he recognizes, are narrative history, written with apologetic, artistic, and prophetic purposes in view. His description of the task and resources of the critical historian is helpful. Insofar as critical history leaves out the mind or perspective that the historian brings to the task, however, critical history is insufficiently critical of its own pre-understanding or prejudices. Along Newmanian lines, Lonergan proposes, "*Methodical* history arises, therefore, when historians realize that there is no human inquiry without presuppositions. They are careful to distinguish two things: one is the intelligible pattern that shines forth in data as though they were interconnected of themselves; the other is the intelligible pattern that proceeds from the historian's own preunderstanding."[104] Although Lonergan's knowledge of historical-critical New Testament scholarship does not appear to have been extensive, he insists upon the necessity of the labor of understanding "the teaching of the New Testament . . . according to its own conceptualities."[105]

Beginning with the New Testament understanding of "God," Lonergan explores the progressive development of the distinction between "Father" and "Son" and how Jesus began to teach this distinction via his use of titles such as "Son of man." Titles such as "Son of God" or "Lord," he argues, exhibit a "retrospective pattern," that is, they become intelligible by looking back to the Jesus of history after his resurrection.[106] He attributes to John 1:1–4 an "*inverse retrospective pattern*, which begins from pre-existence and moves to the man, either living on earth or reigning in heaven."[107] Lonergan's approach allows for historical-critical suppositions about the development of early Christology, while also providing a foundation in the New Testament (and in the words of Jesus himself) for Christian dogmatic faith.[108] He also treats the Ecumenical Councils and their teaching on the

103. Lonergan, *Incarnate Word*, 19.
104. Lonergan, *Incarnate Word*, 21.
105. Lonergan, *Incarnate Word*, 35.
106. Lonergan, *Incarnate Word*, 45.
107. Lonergan, *Incarnate Word*, 47.
108. In this regard, C. Kavin Rowe has recently suggested that Luke's own starting point—not only the Gospel of John's—is the incarnation of the Lord, although of course this is inseparable from Jesus' activity in the world. Rowe comments on Luke 1:43 (in light of Luke 1:25), "In this crucial moment of Jesus' introduction, Elizabeth's confession effects a duality in the referent of the word κύριος between the as yet unborn and human κύριος of Mary's womb and the κύριος of heaven, who has taken away Elizabeth's shame (1:25 κύριος; the only other time Elizabeth speaks in the Gospel). . . . In light of the fact that κύριος was, if not written in the LXX MSS around the time of the NT, at least the *qere* for the tetragrammaton among Greek speaking Jews and

incarnation, and he does so with some sophistication. In the final part of the work, he engages speculative issues such as the metaphysical status of Christ's body and soul (whose "act of existence" pertains to the subsisting divine person), the metaphysical unity of the incarnate Word, and the consciousness of Christ.

Lonergan's *The Redemption*, as it appears in English translation, comes from the 1964 Latin edition of *The Incarnate Word*, in which it constituted Part Five. It contains insights that he worked on in the late 1950s, and it displays his exegesis of the Greek text of key passages of the New Testament regarding Christ's cross. He is indebted to Catholic biblical scholars of the 1940s and 1950s, such as Stanislas Lyonnet, Luigi Moraldi, and Bruce Vawter. His speculative creativity appears throughout, as for instance when he asks "why God became human, why so many ages had to wait for the Savior, why he came to the Jewish people, why the spread of the faith is so slow, why there have been so many heresies," and so on—to which he replies that the answer is that "it is the way of God's justice to act through secondary causes and in accordance with their natures. This is why God himself became human, that he might be a secondary and proportionate

---

Christians, and in light of the fact that Luke reflects this and even makes explicit use of it for his 'christological' exegesis of the Old Testament, it is all the more startling that he interjects κύριος for Jesus in the middle of numerous uses of κύριος that refer clearly to YHWH. . . . [T]he dramatic moment of 1:43 in the narrative bespeaks a kind of unity of identity between YHWH and the human Jesus within Mary's womb by means of the resonance of κύριος" (Rowe, *Early Narrative Christology*, 40). For a critique of Rowe's perspective, arguing that for Luke Jesus becomes "Lord and Christ" through the divine enthronement produced by his resurrection, see Kirk, *Man Attested by God*, 541–45 and 567, where—in addition to critiquing Buckwalter's argument regarding Jesus and the Spirit—Kirk concludes: "Luke's scriptural Christology is most often a functional Christology and, importantly, it never leaves the reader to conclude that Jesus is, in some mysterious way, playing the role of Israel's God in anything other than a mediated fashion." Much depends here upon what it means for the Son to play "the role of Israel's God." For arguments for ontological preexistence of the Son in Luke, see—in addition to Rowe—Gathercole, *Preexistent Son*, 161–64, 168–69, 181–89, 231–42; Buckwalter, *Character and Purpose of Luke's Christology*; and Hays, *Echoes of Scripture in the Gospels*, 243–64. See also the critique of Gathercole's approach to the Synoptic Gospels in Collins and Collins, *King and Messiah as Son of God*, 123–48. Adela Yarbro Collins (who wrote this section) recognizes that "[i]n the *Similitudes of Enoch*, the preexistent Son of Man is presented as the messiah. He is also . . . described in terms of divine wisdom. . . . So, like the author of the *Similitudes of Enoch*, Paul may also have conceived of Jesus, as the preexistent messiah, in terms of preexistent and personified divine wisdom. Although there is less evidence that Mark presented Jesus as preexistent, if the hypothesis about Paul just discussed is correct, it would be analogous to Mark's presentation of Jesus as the hidden Son of Man" (148). For a sharp contrast to Yarbro Collins's link between the *Similitudes of Enoch* and Paul, see Tilling, *Paul's Divine Christology*, 232–33.

cause in restoring all things (Ephesians 1.10) and making all things new (2 Corinthians 5.17)."[109] He offers a theology of the cross grounded in Christ's satisfaction fueled by supernatural charity, ensuring, as Ligita Ryliškytė notes, that "the justice of the cross is not a retributive (transactional) justice but redemptive (agapic) justice, that is, reconciling, restoring, and transformative justice."[110] Lonergan describes his overall position—which he developed both philosophically and theologically, and which centrally involves friendship and forgiveness—as the "Law of the Cross," unfolding historically and eschatologically.

Lonergan's *Method in Theology* (1971), his essay "The Transition from a Classical Worldview to Historical Mindedness" (1967), and other similar writings such as "Revolution in Catholic Theology" (1972)—all of which build upon his early work *Insight* (1957)—call for the transposition of the writings of all theologians who wrote prior to the full emergence of modern historical consciousness. He especially has in view the neo-scholastics. Thus, in "Revolution in Catholic Theology," Lonergan compares the "old-style dogmatic theologian" (who proceeds much like Lonergan did in *The Incarnate Word* and *The Redemption*) with the postconciliar recognition of the need for a much greater specialization and for a better "grasp of what is meant by a person's historicity."[111] Highlighting cognitional theory and religious experience, he argues that in future Catholic theology "one's basic terms will refer to conscious operations and one's basic relations will refer to conscious relations between operations.... From cognitional theory and

---

109. Lonergan, *Redemption*, 363.

110. Ryliškytė, *Why the Cross?*, 440. This perspective fits well with other neo-scholastic theologies of the cross, although Lonergan has his own way of tracing the dialectical progression from Augustine through Anselm and Aquinas, focusing on justice and power, humility and pride, satisfaction and punishment, and charity and satisfaction. In his "Law of the Cross," Lonergan recognizes, as Ryliškytė says, that "true love in a fallen world is cruciform" (441). Ryliškytė draws out the eschatological implications: "Christ's triumph on the cross introduces a new finality in history, thereby providing means for the recovery of human progress.... By the Father's good pleasure, in and through the whole Christ [inclusive of the Church], comes the transformation of the human good as ordered to the glory of God. Though the new order is fully realized only eschatologically, the renewed finality already takes hold in history through the recurrence of forgiveness and the diffusion of friendship. Both of them are constitutive of the emergent *agape* network—the higher integration of the human good of order that is realized in and through the dialectical unification of all things in Christ" (443). See also Ryliškytė's excellent further discussion of the Law of the Cross in *Why the Cross?*, 444–56.

111. Lonergan, "Revolution in Catholic Theology," 197.

epistemology one can go on to setting up a metaphysics, that is, to state in general what one knows when one does come to know."[112]

Lonergan's appreciation for specializations is helpful, since without such specialization the kind of erudition that biblical scholarship requires would not be possible. But his emphasis on cognitional theory and transposition is, contrary to his expectations, rather dated. His christological writings remain important for his dogmatic insights, but these writings are hampered by the fact that he was himself neither particularly conversant with historical-critical exegesis nor correct in his later view that classical metaphysical language must now be transposed.[113]

Jean-Hervé Nicolas's work is less widely known than that of the above thinkers, but he makes a significant contribution.[114] His Christology is generally well-versed in Jesus' Second Temple context, although in his view it is clear enough that Jesus founded the Church, established the Petrine office, and prepared the Church to function for as long as needed. He argues for the truth of Jesus' preaching of the *imminent* kingdom, because the kingdom of God is present wherever Jesus is present, and Jesus is present in the Church. The kingdom will come in its fullness only when Jesus comes in glory, at the final judgment. Even now, however, the Church participates in "the permanent present of the resurrected Christ."[115]

Nicolas considers that the central categories that prepared for Christ are those of the royal mediator of salvation (grounded in the figure of David), the priestly mediator of salvation (grounded in the figure of Aaron), and the prophetic mediator of salvation (grounded in the figure of Moses).

---

112. Lonergan, "Revolution in Catholic Theology," 199.

113. For christological (and soteriological) work drawing upon Lonergan, see also Ormerod, "Sacred Heart, Beatific Mind"; Wilkins, "Love and Knowledge of God in the Human Life of Christ"; Doran, "Nonviolent Cross." See also, more broadly, Wilkins, *Before Truth*.

114. Of course, many other important twentieth-century theologians could also be mentioned, especially Réginald Garrigou-Lagrange, OP and various Protestant theologians. See Garrigou-Lagrange, *Christ the Savior* and *Our Saviour and His Love for Us*; and see also Garrigou-Lagrange, *Mother of the Saviour*. Among Protestant theologians, see, for example, Thomas F. Torrance's often instructive *Atonement*. Along lines that anticipate some important elements of what I say in chapter 4, Torrance emphasizes that "Jesus thinks of himself at the last supper, as the [Isaianic] servant who inaugurates the new covenant in his body and blood. . . . The Son offers his life and death in a covenant sacrifice for the remission of sins and the establishment of covenant communion between God and humanity" (21–22; cf. 39–41 on covenant and atonement in the Old Testament). Torrance goes on to distinguish between redemption conceived in terms of *"padah"* (by a mighty hand), *"kippur"* (by expiatory sacrifice), and *"goel"* (by a kinsman-advocate): see *Atonement*, 53.

115. Nicolas, *On the Incarnation and Redemption*, §544.

Other important categories, he notes, were the Angel of the Lord, the hypostasized divine Wisdom, and the Danielic Son of Man.[116] Nicolas points out that Pauline texts such as Colossians 2:9, Ephesians 1:3–10, and Titus 2:13 maintain Christ's divinity. Philippians 2:6–11 affirms Christ's preexistence, as does Colossians 1:15–20.[117] Paul also regularly speaks of Jesus as "Lord," κύριος, using the title by which the Septuagint translates YHWH.

In this light, Nicolas discusses the title "Son of Man" used frequently by Jesus in the Gospels. In the book of Daniel, this title has to do with the exaltation of the Messiah but not with suffering. In the Gospels, by contrast, the title is linked with the suffering servant of Isaiah 52–53.[118] This unique connection, Nicolas argues (along now outdated lines), must have been made by Jesus himself. Similarly, in Nicolas's view, the prayer of Jesus in which he proclaims "no one knows who the Son is except the Father, or who the Father is except the Son and any one to whom the Son chooses to reveal him" (Luke 10:22) must have come from Jesus rather than from the evangelists.[119] On a variety of grounds, Nicolas concludes that Jesus taught

---

116. On the Danielic Son of Man, see Perrin, *Jesus the Temple*, 107–8.

117. Patrick Henry Reardon adds such passages as Romans 8:3 and Galatians 4:4 (which portray God as sending his Son into the world), along with 2 Corinthians 8:9 and possibly Romans 1:3, as further Pauline testimony to Christ's preexistence. See Reardon, *Reclaiming the Atonement*, 100–101, 106. For various recent scholarly perspectives, see Gathercole, *Preexistent Son*; McCready, *He Came Down from Heaven*; Dunn, *Christology in the Making*, 113–25; Yai-Chow Wong, "Problem of Preexistence in Philippians 2:6–11"; Byrne, "Christ's Preexistence in Pauline Soteriology." A number of these authors are responding to Karl-Josef Kuschel's *Geboren vor aller Zeit?*. Among English-language studies on this topic, Lee's *From Messiah to Preexistent Son*, 182–99, also deserves attention. Lee argues that "the sending formula ["God sent his Son" (found in Galatians 4, Romans 8, John 3, and 1 John 4)] is in fact rooted in the pre-existent Son Christology developed from the early Christian exegesis of messianic psalms (Ps 110:1 and Ps 2:7) in the light of Jesus' self-consciousness of divine sonship and divine mission" (*From Messiah to Preexistent Son*, 284). For a valuable study by a Catholic theologian engaging most of the above authors, see Durand, "Christ's Mission Implies His Preexistence."

118. Nicolas draws this point from Feuillet, "Trois grandes prophéties de la Passion et de la Résurrection," 69, and from Bouyer, *Fils éternel*, 206.

119. For support for this view, see Pitre, "Historical Jesus and the Apocalyptic 'Thunderbolt.'" Pitre begins by noting that Matthew 11:25–27 // Luke 10:21–22 has been "widely ignored or deemed unhistorical in many major studies of the historical Jesus" (170). A few scholars have asserted at least its partial authenticity, including Wilhelm Bousset, Rudolf Bultmann, and W. D. Davies and Dale C. Allison Jr. Some scholars affirm its full authenticity, including Craig Keener, Joseph Fitzmyer, SJ, and Marinus de Jonge. Albert Schweitzer uses the passage to suggest that "it is possible, though not probable, that Jesus believed in his own pre-existence" (Schweitzer, *Quest of the Historical Jesus*, 254–55).

his own divinity, although his disciples did not understand him until after the resurrection and the outpouring of the Spirit.

Indebted especially to Aquinas, Nicolas devotes much attention to the hypostatic union. It is not a "substantial" union, since that would meld the two natures; nor is it an "accidental" union, since if it were, then the two natures would not really be united. It is comparable to the union of soul and body (as Augustine and many others teach), in the sense that a human person subsists in the spiritual and material aspects of his or her nature. Delving into the issue of how the human nature of Jesus Christ, which is individuated, does not constitute a human person, Nicolas argues that "individuation, by which a substance is complete, does not yet confer subsistence *in se*."[120] Nicolas probes at some length into what is meant by "subsisting in the Word." He rejects the notion (held by Charles Billot and Maurice de la Taille) that this subsisting can mean that God is the "actuating act" of the human nature.[121] He also denies that this subsisting can be explained in terms of graced consciousness, as Anton Günther proposed and as Karl Rahner likewise suggested.[122] The ontological union cannot be the consciousness of that union, since being and consciousness are one in God but not in humans. He holds instead that the subsisting occurs by the mode of a "real relation" of union.

Nicolas grants that Jesus experienced some kinds of ignorance. As he states, "In the Gospels, Jesus does not seem to know all things in advance. He poses questions, and most importantly, in all the expressions of his knowledge, He appears to be very dependent on his cultural milieu."[123] Nicolas contests Augustine's dictum that ignorance is the result of sin. It suffices to say that Jesus did not reason erroneously, even though Jesus did partake "in the common and naturally inevitable errors of the men of His cultural milieu."[124] Nicolas largely adopts Jacques Maritain's way of understanding Jesus' vision of God as located in his "supra-consciousness" and as refracted (by illumination) in his natural knowledge. While Jesus' self-consciousness gradually awakened, at all times "it was a self-consciousness of being the Word and at the same time of being a man."[125] Although Jesus

---

120. Nicolas, *On the Incarnation and Redemption*, §277.
121. Nicolas, *On the Incarnation and Redemption*, §286.
122. Nicolas, *On the Incarnation and Redemption*, §288. See, among other places, Rahner, "Dogmatic Considerations on Knowledge and Consciousness in Christ"; Rahner, "Current Problems in Christology"; Rahner, "On the Theology of the Incarnation."
123. Nicolas, *On the Incarnation and Redemption*, §344.
124. Nicolas, *On the Incarnation and Redemption*, §348.
125. Nicolas, *On the Incarnation and Redemption*, §364.

knew from the start that his mission was to die for our sins, some details only gradually became clear to him.

Nicolas emphasizes against liberation theology that salvation has an eschatological character and is primarily redemption from sin and death.[126] The gospel impels us to try to liberate others from economic and political oppression, but such liberation is not the eschatological salvation won by Christ. For salvation to be offered to all human beings, Christ's expiatory death was needed, in accordance with Isaiah 53 and various New Testament texts. Nicolas rejects some ways of understanding Christ's death, including the notion that Christ was punished for us. Christ did indeed bear our punishment (death), but he did so freely and God the Father was not punishing him. As priest, Christ offered perfect worship, inclusive of his perfect sacrifice, to the Father.[127] Christ's self-offering on the cross was a cultic, sacrificial act.[128]

In my view, Nicolas's exposition could be enriched by further integration of the concrete realities of Jesus' historical context as found in biblical scholarship.[129] Consider for instance Giambrone's way of arguing that Jesus "accepted an eschatological scenario something broadly like that of the Essenes: two chief agents, twinned priestly and royal messiahs of Aaron and Judah."[130] Giambrone proposes that after the death of John the Baptist, Jesus perceived that these two identities came together in himself as the royal and priestly Messiah.[131] Nicolas is aware that Jesus is both priest and (Davidic)

---

126. With respect to the latter (and in view of Orthodox theology rather than of debates about the motive of the incarnation), Reardon aptly cautions, "Some Christians have pursued a logic according to which our redemption requires nothing more than the Incarnation. According to this logic, the event of the Incarnation was sufficient—all by itself—for man's redemption, inasmuch as the enfleshing of God's eternal Word conferred immortality and theosis on human nature in the person of Christ," as though "by the very fact of the Incarnation, God and man are *already* 'at one'" (Reardon, *Reclaiming the Atonement*, 118). When it comes to the issue of the motive of the incarnation, all parties can agree with Reardon's observation: "Why, then, did God become man? To join us to Himself. Union with God—theosis—is the full fruit of redemption. God's Son assumed our complete humanity in order to save and sanctify our complete humanity" (134).

127. See Nicolas, *On the Incarnation and Redemption*, §517.

128. See Nicolas, *On the Incarnation and Redemption*, §520.

129. See the extensive engagement with biblical scholarship in Part One of Le Guillou's *Christ and Church*. Part Three of this book offers a rich account of Aquinas's theology, with extensive attention to his biblical commentaries.

130. Giambrone, *Bible and the Priesthood*, 270. For a link to John 1:19–23, see Fitzmyer, "Qumran Literature and the Johannine Writings," 126.

131. See also Perrin, *Jesus the Priest*, 7: "while scholars will regularly sling around terms like 'messiah' or 'messianic', and then unselfconsciously shift over to seemingly

INTRODUCTION

king, as the New Testament makes clear. But in Giambrone's hands, there is much more contextual depth to the notions of "priest" and "king," and it becomes clearer how the royal Messiah Jesus was able to institute the priesthood by transforming the Passover rite into the sacramental sacrifice of the Eucharist. Giambrone shows how Jesus' cross involved a "high priestly action" in which, at the Last Supper, he enabled his disciples to share.[132] In the process, Giambrone shows that Jesus' expectation of the imminent arrival of the kingdom does not contradict his founding of a Church with priestly hierarchy and liturgical rites. As Giambrone puts it, "The Church, sanctified and governed by the purified priesthood of our high priest and great shepherd of the sheep,

interchangeable terms like 'king' or 'royal', we still have hardly begun to elucidate how the Jewish messianic concept, variegated as it was, *brought together the royal aspects and priestly aspects.*" Perrin makes a strong case that "in many a first-century mind the ultimate significance of the promise of Davidic restoration lay not in its implications of political autonomy (as important as autonomy might be) but in its cultic entailments, for as pressing as the problem of Roman occupation might have been, even more acute was the festering defilement of the temple" (7). See also Perrin's *Jesus the Temple*, where he argues that "countless first-century Jews were desperately looking for the full return from exile, the restoration of the tribes, and—the point of it all—the establishment of proper worship. From Israel's perspective, the *telos* of human history, the anticipated climax of the scriptural narrative, was to be set on the stage of the final temple. This was the only appropriate venue in which Israel could lay hold of its destiny: the worship of the Creator God. Against this backdrop, Jesus of Galilee entered the stage of history. Against this backdrop, too, Jesus was dramatizing his unprecedented claim that the kingdom temple was *now* materializing through him and his followers" (*Jesus the Temple*, 184). In *Jesus the Temple*, as in *Jesus the Priest*, Perrin combines royal and priestly aspects of Jesus' self-understanding. Citing Qumran (11Q13), he proposes that Jesus played "not only the role ascribed to the Zecharian shepherd-king, but also the role ascribed to the Melchizedekian high priest.... The land needed to be not only re-deeded, but also re-purified, for only on a purified land would it be possible to enjoy pure worship. For Jesus no less than the Qumran covenanteers, both tasks—crucial for the future salvation of Israel—would fall to the eschatological high priest, Melchizedek" (*Jesus the Temple*, 168). Perrin draws these aspects together in his account of Jesus as the eschatological temple. In Perrin's view, "Jesus of Nazareth's most distinctive activities, healings/exorcisms, and meals were public signs that he had reconstituted time, space, and a people around himself, the new convergence of heaven and earth, the new temple" (*Jesus the Temple*, 179). The new temple is the kingdom of God, because "what else is the temple of God but the palace of Yahweh, the location from which he, as one enthroned between the cherubim, rules and dwells" (*Jesus the Temple*, 181). For the convergence of royal and priestly dimensions of Jesus' mission, see also Barber, "New Temple, the New Priesthood, and the New Cult," 101–24, drawing upon Jeremiah 30 among other texts.

132. Giambrone, *Bible and the Priesthood*, 271. Jesus "creates a rite that represents and makes present his own personal passion" (271). By contrast, Jens Schröter is only willing to say (of Paul's account of the Last Supper) that it is "a tradition that cannot be traced back—at least in this form—to the earthly Jesus, but represents an early Christian reminiscence of the meaning of the Last Supper" (Schröter, *From Jesus to the New Testament*, 81).

served by a ministry binding together heaven and earth, is this prophesied newness" of the kingdom—even if not yet in its consummated form.[133]

III. The Plan of the Work

At the risk of some repetition—indeed not so much the risk but the reality—let me describe in detail the planned structure of this book, which will help the reader better understand my choice of sources as well as the diversity of approaches among the chapters. Overall, my structure is similar to the one adopted by the Romanian Orthodox theologian Dumitru Staniloae. His Christology begins with the Incarnate Word according to Scripture and tradition, and then addresses in distinct chapters "The Saving Power of the Incarnate Word," "Jesus as Prophet and Teacher," "Jesus as High Priest and Supreme Sacrifice," and "Jesus as Risen Lord and King."[134]

Recall that my first chapter treats the birth of Jesus and the question of whether the doctrine of the virgin birth adds anything important to Christology, given the difficulties involved in defending the biblical testimony to this miracle. Briefly, I explore the case against affirming the historicity of the virgin birth, as set forth by Andrew Lincoln, among others. I then examine christological reasons for the fittingness of the virgin birth, drawing upon Karl Barth and Hans Urs von Balthasar. Indebted to Aquinas, and along lines found in Balthasar as well, I also distinguish the "virginal conception" from the "virgin birth." The latter undergirds the Catholic doctrine that Mary remained virginal in giving birth, without suffering any damage to her bodily integrity—a miraculous sign of the eschatological new creation. I explore how Aquinas develops his theology of the incarnation in view of Mary's childbearing, inasmuch as his theology of the incarnation is guided by his anti-Nestorianism. My chapter emphasizes that Christ's virginal conception and virgin birth are signs of the eschatological inbreaking of the kingdom of God.

Chapter 2 turns to the teaching of Jesus, asking whether he reveals anything much—or else was merely another late-Second Temple Jewish apocalyptic (eschatological) prophet and wisdom teacher.[135] I set forth the

---

133. Giambrone, *Bible and the Priesthood*, 273.

134. See Staniloae, *Person of Jesus Christ as God and Savior*.

135. For discussion of Second Temple Jewish eschatology, distinguishing between "restoration eschatology" and "apocalyptic eschatology" (a distinction that should not be exaggerated, since apocalyptic eschatology includes the restoration of Israel in some form), see Wright, *Lord's Prayer*, 30–33; cf. 80–82, 94–95, 99; and see also the distinction between "eschatological" and "apocalyptic"—with the former signaling the imminent arrival of the eschaton (the final end time), and the latter signaling apocalyptic

position of Albert Schweitzer and others that Jesus was a misguided prophet of the imminent arrival of the kingdom of God. In response to such claims, I argue that Jesus' teaching reveals a great deal, including that he is the Son of God, possessed of divine authority. The work of Sigurd Grindheim and Brant Pitre demonstrates, in my view, Jesus' own "high Christology." Claiming immense (indeed divine) authority, Jesus reveals truths about God, himself, and us. To exemplify this point, I turn to some of Jesus' best-known teachings: his parables (such as that of the good Samaritan) and his Sermon on the Mount. In this context, I interact with the work of the biblical scholars Amy-Jill Levine, Frank Matera, and Gerhard Lohfink, whose differences are instructive. Levine focuses on Jesus as a great wisdom teacher, which he was; while Matera and Lohfink add the eschatological dimension and the claim of Jesus to radical authority. As a final step, I explore Mary's "pondering" of the mysteries of her Son "in her heart" (Luke 2:19) and her command "Do whatever he tells you" (John 2:5). Mary's response to Jesus' teaching embodies what the Catholic theologian Aidan Nichols calls the "*theologia prima*" that is "doxological contemplation . . . leading to the glorifying of God's grace by hearers of the Word."[136]

My third chapter takes up the miracles of Jesus and the question of whether they were invented by the evangelists, who lived in a culture that was credulous about miracles and that assumed a prophet would necessarily perform miracles. After providing some initial background, I compare Bonaventure's understanding of the function of Jesus' miracles—focusing upon his *Commentary on Luke*—with that of N. T. Wright. As a test case, I give special attention to the story of Jesus' exorcism of the Gerasene demoniac and the resulting drowning of the herd of pigs, a story with notable

---

events such as the temple's destruction—in Stevenson, *Consciousness of the Historical Jesus*, chapter 8. Wright remarks, "Jesus teaches about the kingdom of God (Luke 4:43; cf. Matt. 4:17), and the Lord's Prayer features the petition 'Your kingdom come' (Matt. 6:10; Luke 11:2). This teaching about God's end-time action as king and the related petition that God bring his kingdom to the world make sense within the eschatological teachings about God acting as the king in the end-time (e.g., Isa. 52:7-10; Dan 2, 7; Zech. 14). . . . Jesus teaches that this eschatological action of God is in some respects present in him and his ministry and in other respects is something to be realized fully and plainly at a future time" (32-33). For his part, E. P. Sanders argues that Jesus adopted John the Baptist's "restoration eschatology" but reordered it around himself: "he called 'twelve' with himself as their head; he dramatically pointed to the coming of a new or renewed temple; and perhaps he rode into Jerusalem on an ass. Finally, he symbolized the coming kingdom in a banquet shared with the 'twelve'" (Sanders, *Jesus and Judaism*, 340). For a critique of Sanders for underestimating the importance of ritual purity for Jesus—and for linking the term "sinners" with the wicked rather than with the ritually impure—see Chilton, "E. P. Sanders and the Question of Jesus and Purity."

136. Nichols, *Theologian's Enterprise*, 51-52.

historical difficulties. Here I examine the interpretive proposals of various biblical scholars, among them Wright, Nicholas Perrin, and Matthew Thiessen. I also explore Luke Timothy Johnson's recent book on miracles, which is a response to the skepticism of the influential nineteenth-century Protestant scholar David Friedrich Strauss, whose brilliant work (including his treatment of the Gerasene demoniac) I survey. Johnson does not defend the historicity of every miracle story or of every element of the stories, but he affirms that Jesus performed miracles as part of his ministry.[137] I conclude the chapter with the Protestant biblical scholar Craig Keener's examination of post-biblical miracles, in the context of Christian intercessory prayer and the unique mediation of Mary—focusing once more on Mary's actions at the wedding at Cana in John 2.

Chapter 4 addresses the cross of Jesus as the new covenant sacrifice that redeems us from sin and death and draws us into the divine life.[138] After briefly addressing concerns about sacrifice that have been articulated by such thinkers as Eleonore Stump and Denny Weaver, I provide biblical background to Jesus' death as a new covenant sacrifice, focusing upon

---

137. See Wright, *Lord's Prayer*, 97: "Matthew and Luke both show the association of the kingdom of God with Jesus's exorcisms. Both evangelists record a saying of Jesus in which he interprets the significance of his exorcism ministry: 'If it is by the Spirit of God that I cast out demons, then the kingdom of God has come upon you' (Matt. 12:28; cf. Luke 11:20). . . . Jesus acts here as the divine warrior-king who defeats his enemies (i.e., the demons) and rescues his people from their power." For the exorcisms as "prophetic dramas" that demonstrate that "the Kingdom of God is bursting into this world" through "the hidden reality of Satan's defeat," see Hooker, *Signs of a Prophet*, 36–37. See also the historical point made by Rodriguez, *Structuring Early Christian Memory*, 210: "Jesus' exorcisms were at the heart of Jesus in early Christian memory" (210; cf. 199–201 on Matt 12:28//Luke 1:20, arguing that here "Jesus enacts—literally rather than symbolically—the liberation of the children of Israel from the oppressive, foreign powers and at the same time enacts God's judgement against those powers" [201]).

138. For a critical reflection on early Christian claims to "newness," focusing especially upon the phrase "new covenant" but ranging across the New Testament (along with some post-biblical writings such as the *Didache*), see Klawans, *Heresy, Forgery, Novelty*, 117–58, in light both of non-Christian "ancient Jewish anxieties toward innovation" (117) and later Christian accusations of heresy on the ground of innovation. Klawans aims to show "the Jewish background of Christian heresiology" and also to demonstrate the newness of "the open embrace of newness that took hold among Jesus's followers and the writers of many New Testament texts" (159, 161). Although he recognizes the acceptance of newness in prophetic discourse in the pre-Second Temple period (and the existence of a good deal of camouflaged newness in the Second Temple period), he does not sufficiently allow, so far as I can see, for the real possibility of newness that is indeed divinely willed fulfillment of or development of what has come before. Instead, his book hammers home "early Christianity's Janus face: the supersessionist critique of Judaism on the one side, the heresiological condemnation of perceived new Gods and newer prophets on the other"—"the irony that heresy and supersessionism are the structural inverses of each other" (162).

the Last Supper and its connections to Exodus 24, with the help of Joseph Fitzmyer, Brant Pitre, Scot McKnight, and others. Drawing upon recent biblical scholarship by Francis Moloney, Rekha Chennattu, Alexander Tsutserov, and especially Sherri Brown, I then argue that in fact not only the Synoptics but also John 19:25–27 portrays Jesus' cross as the new covenant sacrifice, recapitulating and transcending Moses' and the people's covenant-sealing actions in Exodus 24. In John 19, Jesus has the role of offerer, altar, and victim, while faithful Israel is represented by Mary and by the beloved disciple at the foot of the cross. In light of these biblical foundations, I examine Matthias Joseph Scheeben's rich account of sacrifice as uniting the elements of love and satisfaction. Scheeben places the Old Testament image of the altar fire at the center of his understanding of Jesus' sacrifice, on the grounds that the glorification of God (and not simply the removal of sin) is the central purpose of sacrifice not only in the Old Testament but also in the New. Dumitru Staniloae does something similar when he praises "the Son's initiative to offer Himself as sacrifice for the people."[139] My theology of the cross as the new covenant sacrifice understands "sacrifice" along Scheeben's lines, while adding the element of covenantal fulfillment. I conclude by exploring what Scheeben has to say about Mary's motherhood and her participation in his redemptive cross, in light of my reading of John 19.

Chapter 5 examines Jesus' resurrection and the question of whether the notion of an immortal, glorified body is intelligible rather than being a contradiction in terms. In the New Testament, Jesus' resurrection is depicted in relation to our future resurrection. A key part of defending the intelligibility of Jesus' resurrection, therefore, consists in defending the reasonableness of believing in the possibility of risen and glorified *bodiliness*. With appreciation for the mystery, the Catholic biblical scholar William

---

139. Staniloae, *Person of Jesus Christ as God and Savior*, 111. Staniloae mistakenly thinks he is opposing the standard Roman Catholic perspective when he adds, "The sanctification of Him who wants to sacrifice Himself and of His sacrifice once offered do not have a meaning worthy of God except when understood as manifestation of the will for communion on behalf of the Father and as acceptance on behalf of Christ as man, or as beginning of the realization of communion and as its realization indeed ... Understood in this, the only possible manner, Christ's death no longer appears as the offering of a substantive satisfaction to the offended honor of God on behalf of men, or as the expiation of a substantive punishment in their stead, for the same reason. Western theology, both Catholic and Protestant, has not known another modality of man's liberation from sin except that of suffering death for him or the amnesty on the basis of a satisfaction offered to God. The Holy Scripture and the Holy Fathers see the solution beyond this external alternative, namely in God's movement toward communion, which is also imprinted within the human being. In both other cases God remains external, punishing, or He places the human being from without into a movement of satisfaction" (113).

Wright remarks, "In the resurrection, Jesus is raised to an eschatological mode of life, and his humanity is totally transformed by divine glory."[140] Some theologians, including most recently Steven Harris, argue that it is best to avoid all speculation, insofar as possible, about the mystery of risen and glorified bodiliness. In my view, however, there are a number of important things that need to be said, since believers will otherwise lose a concrete sense of what to hope for. Put simply, our eschatological imagination needs to be strengthened. Both for Jesus and for us, the glorified body must be in some fundamental sense be the same body as the one that died; if it were not the same, it would be not a resurrected body but a mere replica of the body that died. But this seems to entail that the glorified body must be composed of the same matter as the body that died, a claim that causes significant problems. A glorified body must also be a body that can no longer suffer or die, but this mode of existence seems incommensurable with real material bodiliness. In response to such difficulties, my chapter explores the arguments and insights of numerous figures from the patristic period onward, including Origen, Johann Gerhard, Sergius Bulgakov, Kathryn Tanner, Gregory of Nyssa, Augustine, Albert the Great, Ted Peters, John Polkinghorne, and Jeffrey Schloss. I seek a middle position between over-spiritualization of the glorified body and exaggeration of the glorified body's identity in every respect with our present body. Since my theme is Christ's glorified body in relation to ours, I bring the chapter to a close with reflection upon Mary's bodily assumption.

My sixth and final chapter investigates the ascension of Jesus. The world and the Church continue to suffer from sin and death in a manner that seems to cut against belief in the present reign of the Messiah. In this context, I explore the significance of Jesus' ascension. I begin with texts from the Qumran and other Second Temple literature that have in view a messianic priest-king. Informed especially by the monographs of Timo Eskola and Félix Cortez on the Letter to the Hebrews, I suggest that Jesus' priestly work can primarily be associated with his cross, whereas his ascension can primarily be viewed as an ascent to royal enthronement at the right hand of the Father. The ascended Christ presently reigns through self-surrendering love rather than through the customary modes of worldly power, and therefore the signs of his reign, and the salvation he brings, are markedly different from the signs of the reign of a king who rules by worldly power.[141] As Thomas Aquinas observes, commenting on Hebrews 1:8, "The

---

140. Wright, *Lord's Prayer*, 99.

141. Along these lines, for discussion of Henri de Lubac's trenchant critique of Marxist philosophy of history, Joachimite theology of history, and liberation theology (including Edward Schillebeeckx's appropriation of critical theory and his conflation of

'throne' belongs to him according to his divine nature, inasmuch as he is God: *The king of the whole earth is God* (Ps 46:8). But as man it belongs to him as a result of his passion, victory, and resurrection."[142] In light of Christ's enthronement as king, I conclude by discussing Mary's unique queenship in representing the Bride (the Church).

Each of the six chapters draws a link to Mary as participating in the mysteries of her Son's life and as modeling our participation. In chapter 1, the link is Mary's role in Christ's coming into the world; by miraculously conceiving and giving birth to Christ, she shows the power of the eschatological new creation. In chapter 2, the link is Mary's pondering upon all things related to her Son in a spirit of obedience. In chapter 3, the link is Mary's active participation in the miracle at Cana—the miracle by which Jesus symbolizes the inauguration of the new-covenant marriage of God and humanity. In chapter 4, the link is Mary's participation in Christ's redemptive work through her standing at the foot of the cross. She represents God's faithful people sharing in the sacrificial blood that seals the new covenant. In chapter 5, the link is Mary's bodily assumption, by which the new Adam brings to himself the new Eve in the glory of the new creation or inaugurated kingdom. In chapter 6, the link is Mary's queenship, by which she shares in her Son's reign, as ultimately the whole Church is called to do. These discussions of Mary—in light of the noncompetitive, kenotic primacy of Jesus[143]—exhibit the truth that (in Romano Guardini's words) "every step

---

the kingdom of God with the world's progressive perfecting in justice), see Hillebert, *Henri de Lubac and the Drama of Human Existence*, 131–68, 210–13.

142. Aquinas, *Commentary on the Letter of Saint Paul to the Hebrews*, §60, p. 29. See Bühner, *Messianic High Christology*, 153, observing that beyond the Gospel of John, "the epithet 'God' is used of Jesus solely in 1 John 5:20 and Heb 1:8. In Hebrews, however, it is only taken from a biblical quotation from Ps 45:7LXX." I will discuss the historical-critical issues much more thoroughly below, including in footnotes to quotations from Aquinas and others whose thought is unacquainted with historical-critical insights.

143. I interpret Jesus' *kenosis* as his humility and his self-emptying or self-surrendering love, and so I agree with the approaches taken by John M. G. Barclay, Beverly Roberts Gaventa, Grant Macaskill, John McGuckin, Han-luen Kantzer Komline, Thomas Joseph White, OP, and David Fergusson (among others) in Nimmo and Johnson, *Kenosis: The Self-Emptying of Christ*—a volume prepared in honor of Bruce Lindley McCormack on the occasion of his retirement from teaching. I do not follow in the path of kenotic theologians such as Gottfried Thomasius, and I also differ from the position formulated by McCormack in his *Humility of the Eternal Son*. For McCormack—attempting (impossibly in my view) to adhere strictly to the principle "Nothing will be said of the immanent life of God that does not find a firm and clear root in the economy"—"*Kenosis* . . . refers to that *ontological receptivity* in relation to the human Jesus by which the identity of the Son is established in eternity (as the personal property of the second 'person' of the Trinity, we might say) and the unity of the

the Lord took towards fulfillment of his godly destiny Mary followed."[144] For insights into Mary, I will draw upon biblical texts and also upon the Greek and Latin church fathers, Bernard of Clairvaux, Aquinas, Gregory Palamas, Scheeben, neo-scholastic theologians, Balthasar, Bouyer, and others.

***

Despite the glory of Christ that has been revealed, there is far more to come: Christ will come in glory and bring all things to consummation. Thus, the seventh and final chapter of this book is yet to be written, and Christ alone can write it—infinitely better than my meager writing—in his own time. Until Christ comes in (unimaginable) glory, his mysteries will be somewhat veiled. "For now we see in a mirror dimly, but then face to face" (1 Cor 13:12). "Come, Lord Jesus!" (Rev 22:20).

Christological subject is secured in time. Insofar as ontological receptivity makes the Son to be an experiencing participant in the suffering and death of the human Jesus, the gap opened up traditionally between the natures of Christ by a prior commitment to simplicity and impassibility (so that suffering and death are confined to the human nature alone) is overcome. *Kenosis*, then, is just this: that ontological receptivity on the part of the eternal Son that makes the humility and obedience of Jesus to be his 'own'—not merely in a figurative possessive sense but in a sense that makes it clear that the subject of that human attitude and activity is *also* the eternal Son" (McCormack, *Humility of the Eternal Son*, 19). In my view, McCormack confuses or mixes the divine and human natures in such a way as to exclude divinity in any transcendent sense of the term, but this is a price that McCormack is willing to pay, as he makes clear in his critiques of Cyril of Alexandria and of Chalcedon, and in his further discussion of what divinity entails. McCormack notes that "any repair of Chalcedon would have to begin with the surrender of simplicity and impassibility" (58), but this would turn God into a finite being among finite beings. As Thomas Joseph White maintains, "The one who suffers in kenosis is the very one who alone can truly save us effectively, in virtue of his hidden eternal power. He who suffered, died, and descended into hell as one of us is the one who can redeem all of us and, indeed, remake creation. . . . [E]ven as we say rightly that the human self-emptying unto death of Christ can and does truly reveal intratrinitarian personal communion and the uncreated love of God as the fundamental ground of the world, we must preserve the analogical interval between the divine freedom of Christ as God and the freedom of Christ as human, between the uncreated deity in its perfect power to remake all things, and the fragile created nature in which God lives kenotically in solidarity with us, in his perfect humanity, subject to suffering and death" (White, "Divine Perfection and the Kenosis of the Son," 154–55). See also the similar defense of Chalcedonianism in Legge, "Remedy for Confused Kenoticism"; and for background regarding Thomasius and others, see McCormack's "Kenoticism in Modern Christology."

144. Guardini, *Lord*, 14.

Chapter 1

Conception and Birth

I. Introduction

My main point in this chapter is that the Spirit-filled Son comes into the world in a manner reflective of his identity as the inaugurator of the new creation. As the angel tells the shepherds in Luke 2:10-11, "I bring you good news of a great joy which will come to all the people; for to you is born this day in the city of David a Savior, who is Christ the Lord." That the Messiah is born of a virgin is a glorious eschatological sign.

In recent centuries, the virgin birth has become a controversial doctrine, doubted even by some Christians. Jean Daniélou observes, "The question of the historicity of the gospels is a fundamental one for our faith: if Christ was not really conceived by the Holy Spirit, did not really rise from the dead, then our faith is in vain."[1] It is easy enough to agree with this re-

---

1. Daniélou, *Infancy Narratives*, 1. Daniélou is indebted to the Jewish scholar Robert Aron's defense of much of the contents of the infancy narratives: see Aron, *Jesus of Nazareth*. Daniélou goes on to say about Luke 1:26-38 and Matthew 1:18-25, "these two passages give evidence that 'that which is conceived in her is of the Holy Spirit' (Matthew 1:21). This affirmation is repeated in the Apostles' Creed, which sums up the whole Christian faith. For many people it is a real stumbling-block—and it certainly is from the point of view of reason. Yet it is upon this very stumbling-block of truth that the twentieth-century Christian pledges his faith and his word, for he knows that the love of God is supremely free and that 'with God nothing will be impossible' (Luke 1:37)" (*Infancy Narratives*, 13). At the same time, Daniélou freely grants, against biblical literalism, that "Luke's presentation of the episode [the Annunciation] contains certain elaboration, certain features borrowed from earlier biblical stories" (17). See also Allison, *Constructing Jesus*, 451: "If Luke thought of his stories about the conception, birth, and youth of John and Jesus as being more haggadic than historical, is it not odd that he sandwiched them between a preface that makes him sound like a would-be historian and a sentence full of bona fide chronological data?" Allison grants that texts

mark inasmuch as it touches upon Christ's resurrection. But how important really is the claim that Jesus of Nazareth was conceived by the power of the Holy Spirit and born of a virgin?[2] Given that it is a difficult doctrine to defend, Christians can be tempted to relinquish it. At least, one might be excused for devoting little attention to it.

One problem is that Mary's virginity appears to add very little to the theological import of the coming of the Messiah into the world. Indeed, most of the New Testament, including the letters of Paul, exhibits no knowledge of the virgin birth.[3] If Jesus had not been born of a virgin, Christian faith arguably would be little affected. Jesus' incarnation, passion, and resurrection do not depend logically or in any other way upon his having been born of a virgin. Jesus could still be the divine Son of the Father even if Joseph was Jesus' biological father. While it is evident that the events of Jesus' conception and birth are significant for Christian faith, it is not immediately evident that adding the miraculous element of Mary's virginity makes these events any more significant.

In this chapter, I affirm in faith that Mary virginally conceived and gave birth to Jesus, and I argue for the plausibility of the biblical testimony to this reality and for its extensive theological import. If Jesus is the incarnate Lord, then a miraculous conception—in which certain elements of Near Eastern and Greco-Roman myth are historically realized, now mediated through God's covenantal relationship to his people Israel[4]—makes

---

such as 3 Maccabees, however, do present fiction in a historical format. See Johnson, "Third Maccabees."

2. Litwa, for example, rejects the historicity of the virginal conception of Jesus in his *How the Gospels Became History*, chapter 5. He argues, "It is not that the evangelists *borrowed* from the stories of Perseus, Heracles, or Minos to present the idea of divine conception. Stories of divine conception were culturally common coin in the ancient Mediterranean world and could be independently imagined and updated in distinct ways" (Litwa, *How the Gospels Became History*, 87). Litwa's examples—he focuses on Plutarch's account of Plato's divine conception—have long been well known, and Christians have never imagined that God was not providently preparing for Jesus both in Israel and in the world. For further reflection on the examples that Litwa brings forward, see Talbert, "Miraculous Conceptions and Births in Mediterranean Antiquity"; Peeler, *Women and the Gender of God*, 27–28; and Myers, *Blessed among Women?*.

3. Some scholars have gone so far as to suggest that even the Gospels of Luke and Matthew may not teach a virgin birth. See Roberts, *Complicated Pregnancy*; Parrinder, *Son of Joseph*; Freed, *Stories of Jesus's Birth*. Andrew T. Lincoln raises this possibility in his *Born of a Virgin?*, but he rightly rejects it (see 104–5).

4. For mythic accounts of impregnation by a deity, see Peeler, *Women and the Gender of God*, 21–30. Peeler notes that the infancy narratives "assiduously avoid any hint of sexual encounter" (22). See also the section on "Myth and Prophecy" in Balthasar, *Seeing the Form*, 628–43. Balthasar comments, "Israel's distinctive character is to be found in the mediating movement between, on the one hand, the myth which lies

eminent sense as a divine action. This is so because Jesus' coming into the world inaugurates the new creation. Mary's virginal motherhood, therefore, is a preeminent eschatological sign. Daniélou cites Irenaeus in this regard: Jesus is "the new Adam who is to inaugurate the new creation. With this, the virginal motherhood of Mary . . . is given its proper significance. As Irenaeus put it so marvelously, just as the first Adam was formed from the virgin earth, so the second Adam must be formed from a virgin."[5]

My chapter has four main sections. The first section canvasses recent scholarly debate about the historicity of the biblical testimony to the virgin birth. I suggest that there are sufficient reasons for upholding the historicity of this event, even though affirming the virgin birth ultimately requires faith. Second, I set forth the insights into Mary's virginal motherhood found in the work of the Protestant theologian Karl Barth and the Catholic theologian Hans Urs von Balthasar. Their reflections on the virgin birth concur in insisting upon its christological importance, although they differ sharply regarding the truth of Catholic Marian doctrine more broadly.[6] Third, I

---

behind it and which it must time and again repel and deny (particularly in the form of Canaan's fertility cults) in order to remain faithful to its own idea, and, on the other hand, that second point of convergence in the future towards which Israel is striving ever more clearly without, nevertheless, being able to anticipate it or construct it in actual imaged form. Israel's history is the upward movement from the level of myth as type to the level of Christ as antitype, and this movement is the historical transposition of mythical existence into Christian existence. This transposition, however, can be achieved in no other way than by breaking up and, in fact, shattering the mythical image of totality conceived by this understanding of reality and of the world, on behalf of a new totality which lies in the point of convergence in the future" (634). Balthasar draws here upon von Rad, *Theologie des Alten Testaments*, 2:112-25. There is no doubt that Scripture is rich in mythic and figural imagery, but this is what should be expected given that, in God's plan, "the Old and New Testaments form the indispensable relational system, the geometric field of co-ordinates, the supernatural table of categories, the necessary historical canvas upon which alone the intended figure [Jesus Christ] could be drawn" (*Seeing the Form*, 647).

5. Daniélou, *Infancy Narratives*, 29, citing Irenaeus, *Demonstration of the Apostolic Preaching*, 32.

6. Manfred Hauke comments (along lines I mentioned briefly in my Introduction), "In theology we find two diverse schools of thought, visible above all during the 1950s and at the beginning of Vatican II: a somewhat Christocentric tendency and another that is ecclesiocentric. The Christocentric (or 'Christotypical') tendency insists above all on the divine maternity of Mary and derives from this principle all the other privileges of our Lady. Here Mary appears intimately associated with Jesus Christ and faces us along with him. The ecclesiocentric (or 'ecclesiotypical') tendency, in contrast, describes Mary most of all as a 'type of the Church': in the Blessed Virgin, in her openness to Christ, we find the essential traits of the reality of the church" (Hauke, *Introduction to Mariology*, 7-8). For Hauke, the fact that Vatican II placed the treatise on Mary within the Dogmatic Constitution on the Church (*Lumen Gentium*), when combined with the fact that Paul VI during the Council solemnly bestowed upon Mary the title

treat Cyril of Alexandria's and Thomas Aquinas's anti-Nestorian presentations of Mary as Theotokos, with attention as well to some contemporary scholarship on this theme. My purpose in this section is to defend Aquinas's understanding of Mary's virginal motherhood, including her *virginitas in partu*. I do so on eschatological and anti-Nestorian grounds. Fourth and finally, I examine Aquinas's theology of the fittingness of the hypostatic union, which bears upon the evaluation of the virgin birth. Throughout the chapter, I seek to clarify and defend the theological necessity of affirming Jesus Christ's birth from a virgin.

II. Recent Debates about the Historicity of Mary's Virginal Conception of Jesus

In a recent book arguing against the historicity of the claim that Mary virginally conceived Jesus, the Protestant biblical scholar Andrew Lincoln explains that he fully affirms the salvific significance of Jesus' coming into the world. He observes that Jesus' birth is "related to his identity as the second 'person' of the triune God. It is the point in history at which the Son of God assumed human form. Exploring *this* birth has momentous significance."[7] He denies that everything miraculous in the Gospels is mere invention, and he believes that Jesus is the incarnate Lord. Yet, he thinks that the modern biological understanding of procreation (in which the male Y chromosome must come from a male), the genre of the infancy narratives, the existence of other traditions in the New Testament regarding Jesus' conception, and the ancient world's practice of linking the births of notable figures with miraculous events should lead Christians to interpret the narratives about the virginal conception in a metaphorical rather than a literal historical manner.[8]

"Mother of the Church," offers some support to both sides. For his part, Hauke is committed to providing a distinctive treatise on Mary rather than treating Mary within either Christology or ecclesiology. He points out that Mariology is connected intrinsically with "Christology, ecclesiology, pneumatology, supernatural anthropology, and eschatology" (Hauke, *Introduction to Mariology*, 10).

7. Lincoln, *Born of a Virgin?*, 6. See also, in a similar vein, Pederson et al., "Fully Human and Fully Divine." For a response to Lincoln's rejection of the historicity of the virgin birth, see Crisp, *Analyzing Doctrine*, 162–78. Lincoln responds to Crisp in "Bible, Theology, and the Virgin Birth." See also Crisp's earlier chapters on the virgin birth in his *God Incarnate*. For broader exegetical background, see Fornberg, "Annunciation."

8. Lincoln insists, "Given what we now know about reproduction, a literal virginal conception means that Jesus would not have 'become like his brothers and sisters in every respect' (Heb. 2.17)"—because God would have had to supply the Y chromosome, thereby (in Lincoln's view) separating Jesus' humanity from the Adamic evolutionary

Lincoln goes just a step further than the Catholic biblical scholar Raymond Brown. Like Lincoln, Brown underscores the "enormous difference" between Matthew 1–2 and Luke 1–2 and points out that the wondrous events at Jesus' birth hardly seem to square with the later presentation of Jesus as basically unknown at the time of his baptism. Brown seems to imply that skepticism about the virgin birth is in order. He says on the one hand that Christians should "avoid both a naive fundamentalism that would take every word of these accounts as literal history and a destructive skepticism that would reduce them to sheer mythology."[9] But on the other hand, in his view it is possible that the evangelist Matthew, aware of the fact that Jesus was born very early in Mary and Joseph's marriage, invented the detail of a virginal conception and explained it as the transcendent fulfillment of the motif of Old Testament the motif of the barren woman rendered fruitful by

---

stream (*Born of a Virgin?*, 261). Against this viewpoint, I do not think that God's miraculous transformation of part of the genetic material provided by Mary would make Jesus' human nature no longer Adamic or would entail that Jesus no longer receives his human nature from Mary. My position thus accords broadly with that of Kerr, "Questioning the Virgin Birth," which Lincoln critiques. Lincoln draws upon such works as Brown, *Birth of the Messiah*, 517–31; and Miller, *Born Divine*. Raymond Brown does not take Lincoln's position, even while recognizing that historical research can only arrive at tentative findings in this matter.

9. Brown, *Coming Christ in Advent*, 9–10. For skepticism, see also Schaberg, *Illegitimacy of Jesus*; Welburn, *Myth of the Nativity*; Räisänen, "Begotten by the Holy Spirit"; and Lüdemann, *Virgin Birth?*. In *The Birth of the Messiah*, Brown argues, "The fact that Matthew can speak of Jesus as 'begotten' (passive of *gennan*) in 1:16,20, suggests that for him the conception through the agency of the Holy Spirit is the *becoming* of God's Son. In tracing the 'backwards' application of christological language ... one observes that, besides 'beget,' the verbs 'make' (Acts 2:26), 'elevate' (5:31), 'designate' (Rom 1:4), and 'give [a name] to' (Philip 2:9) are used to describe the way in which the christological titles came to Jesus from God after the resurrection (or exaltation). This vocabulary, at least sometimes, reflects a stage of thought wherein Jesus *became* God's Son (or Messiah or Lord) only at the resurrection—a thought pattern corrected by the movement of the christological moment to the baptism. Yet, even after this correction, the divine baptismal declaration of Jesus as Son without any prehistory (as in Mark 1:11), left open the possibility of understanding the baptism as an adoption, so that Jesus would not have been God's Son before the baptism. This impression has been corrected by the further movement of the christological moment to conception, as witnessed in Matthew's and Luke's infancy narratives. However, there was another direction in the backwards movement of the christological moment in early Christian thought, a movement toward pre-existence, exemplified best in the hymns of the NT (Philip 2:6; Col 1:15; John 1:1). Conception christology and pre-existence christology were two different answers to adoptionism ... Christian theology soon harmonized the two ideas" (*Birth of the Messiah*, 141). See also Lincoln's argument that in the context of the Hellenistic and ancient Near Eastern world, it can be seen that "[t]he virginal conception was a conventional way of elaborating Jesus' status as Son of God" (Lincoln, *Born of a Virgin?*, 126).

God.[10] Rather than speculating further, Brown argues that the evangelists Matthew and Luke are primarily making a christological point—namely, that Jesus is the Son of God from the outset. The stories reveal Jesus' "role as the dramatic embodiment of the whole of Israel's history."[11]

Even so, Brown knows that the question of the historical truth of the virginal conception will not go away.[12] He is aware that the biological and

---

10. See Brown, *Birth of the Messiah*, 143; see also his "Appendix IV: Virginal Conception," 517–33, and "Appendix V: The Charge of Illegitimacy," 534–42.

11. Brown, *Coming Christ in Advent*, 10; see also the connections between Luke 1–2 and the "Isaianic new exodus" and Isaianic Servant shown by Beers, *Followers of Jesus as the 'Servant'*, 91–97, with reference more broadly to Fuller, *Restoration of Israel*. At the same time, as Brown notes, "we have no evidence that a virginal conception of the Messiah was expected in Judaism" (30). Amy Peeler makes the same point: "Matthew and Luke certainly did not get this idea [virginal conception] from the Judaism of their day. The stories of Israel provide many points of connection with Jesus's birth narratives, especially the early days of Moses and Samuel, but these or any other accounts do not suggest virginal conception. Matthew's use of *parthenos* in Isa 7:14 proves the point. If Matthew gives this text a miraculous interpretation, it is because he is reading backward. Isaiah 7:14 did not give him the idea of a virginal conception. Such a thing was not known in Israel" (Peeler, *Women and the Gender of God*, 128). Peeler directs attention to Moyise, *Was the Birth of Jesus according to Scripture?* However, see Bühner, *Messianic High Christology*, 113 (cf. 120): "the probable early Jewish interpretation of Isa 7:14–16 and Luke 1 share a similar background. On this basis, the messianic rereading of Isa 7 and other early Jewish messianic texts can aid our understanding of Luke 1:26–28 regardless of a direct literary dependency. If scholars such as Rösel are right and the reference of παρθένος [in the Septuagint] to a virgin is the most natural way of understanding the text, at least for Jews acquainted with Egyptian traditions, then the concept of Jesus' virginal conception has an almost perfect parallel within Second Temple messianism . . . [E]ven if there was no such direct parallel and the members of the early Jesus movement were the first to understand Isa 7:14 as referring to a virgin, there were at least already similar concepts within the messianic discourse of Second Temple messianism (see Ps 109:3LXX; 1QSa II 11f.)." See Rösel, "Jungfrauengeburt des endzeitlichen Immanuel"; and see Holtz, *Jungfrauengeburt und Greisinnengeburt*. I should note that Brown's and Peeler's positions seem more plausible to me than Bühner's: although the latter offers interesting observations (especially regarding the conception of Isaac according to Philo and Jubilees), I find his examples ultimately rather weak.

12. Brown reiterates, "a Christian who wishes to give proper respect to the evangelists' teaching is still faced with the delicate decision as to whether a questioning of the biological supposition brings into question the main christological affirmation" (Brown, *Birth of the Messiah*, 529). Brown says the same with regard to the creed: "Consistent church teaching has been invoked to support the historicity of the virginal conception, and certainly one can cite a virtual unanimity from A.D. 200 to 1800. For many of us this is an extremely important, even deciding factor. But the point made in discussing the previous factor needs to be repeated here. The virginal conception under its creedal title of 'virgin birth' is not primarily a biological statement, and therefore one must make a judgment about the extent to which the creedal affirmation is inextricably attached to the biological presupposition. Moreover, in the period of unanimity, opponents of the virginal conception were, for the most part, denying the divinity of Jesus. That is not necessarily true today" (529).

christological affirmations are closely bound together in the minds of most Christians. He therefore determines that questioning the virginal conception as a biological reality should be avoided by Christian biblical scholars because it will shake the faith of simple believers.[13] From this cautious but not particularly reassuring perspective, he affirms solely that "the *scientifically controllable* biblical evidence leaves the question of the historicity of the virginal conception unresolved."[14]

For Brown, the stories of the virginal conception aim primarily to demonstrate that Jesus "is so much God's Son that God is his only Father, not through sexual intervention but through the same power of the Spirit that brought life into the world at the creation."[15] This same emphasis on the Spirit's power appears in the work of the Protestant biblical scholar James D. G. Dunn, who casts doubt both upon the virgin birth (without explicitly denying its historicity) and upon the infancy narratives as a whole, while suggesting that we should retain the "core tradition" that "Jesus was born of God's Spirit in a special way."[16] After raising the possibility that Matthew and Luke were attempting to cover up Jesus' illegitimacy, Dunn suggests that this viewpoint at least—held by Jane Schaberg and Gerd Lüdemann, among others—is unwarranted by historical reconstruction. Arguing that there is "heavy typologizing" in the birth narratives, Dunn comments, "Are there, then, no historical facts concerning Jesus' birth to be gleaned from the birth narratives? The prospects are not good."[17]

---

13. See Brown, *Birth of the Messiah*, 529: "Two points should be remembered. First, in orthodox Christian belief, Jesus would be God's Son no matter how he was conceived, since his is an eternal sonship not dependent upon the incarnation. Second, for ordinary Christians the virginal conception has proved an effective interpretive sign of that eternal divine sonship; and we should not underestimate the adverse pedagogical impact on the understanding of divine sonship if the virginal conception is denied." He adds in the same vein that, over the centuries, "the historical alternative to the virginal conception has not been a conception in wedlock: it has been illegitimacy through adultery by Mary... But illegitimacy would destroy the images of sanctity and purity with which Matthew and Luke surround Jesus' origins and would negate the theology that Jesus came from the pious Anawim of Israel... For many less sophisticated believers, illegitimacy would be an offense that would challenge the plausibility of the Christian mystery" (530).

14. Brown, *Birth of the Messiah*, 527, directing attention to his *Virginal Conception and Bodily Resurrection of Jesus*.

15. Brown, *Coming Christ in Advent*, 36. In the Gospel of Luke, the fact that John the Baptist's conception (while miraculous) required sexual intercourse whereas Jesus' did not, indicates for Brown Luke's emphasis on "the uniqueness of Jesus who, even in conception and birth, is greater than the Baptist" (63).

16. Dunn, *Jesus Remembered*, 347–48.

17. Dunn, *Jesus Remembered*, 343–44.

For his part, Anthony Giambrone deems Luke's infancy narrative to be cast "in a distinctly Judean historiographical mold," by which he means two things. First, Luke displays an "evident proximity to local birth traditions about Jesus known to have been circulating in Judea at an early date" (but with the caveat that such local traditions were viewed skeptically by the more critical historians of Luke's day); and, second, Luke writes with Israel's Scriptures in view and should be understood "as a kind of *continuator* of Israel's national literature" whose writing involves a heavy "scriptural patterning."[18] For Giambrone, judgments about the historicity of the virgin birth are inevitably judgments not only about the text, but also about the ethical stance of the evangelist Luke as a whole. Giambrone judges the latter positively. Although one does not come away from Giambrone's essay with a strong sense of the virgin birth's historicity, he shows that it makes sense as part of Luke's overall testimony.[19]

Amy Peeler offers what seems to me to be a much stronger reason for affirming the Gospels' testimony. Namely, had the evangelists invented Mary's virginal conception, they would have been undermining the very understanding of Jesus for which they wished to advocate. While there are plenty of virginal conception stories in polytheistic Hellenistic and ancient Near Eastern cultures, Israel did not have such stories. Citing Tacitus's observations about Jewish monotheism and rejection of the pagan deification of kings, Peeler remarks, "Luke and Matthew present a theological system . . . which claims the supremacy of the Most High God. Virginal conception stories, on the basis of their contextual roots, introduce the specter of a

---

18. Giambrone, "'Lying Historians' and Luke 1–2," 84–85, 90. Giambrone draws upon a wide array of materials, but noteworthy here are Jung, *Original Language of the Lukan Infancy Narrative*—which Giambrone deems interesting if ultimately unsuccessful—and especially Sterling, *Historiography and Self-Definition*.

19. Giambrone accepts the miracle in faith. As he points out in another essay with respect to historical-critical biblical scholarship, "historical reason by its own contingent formal object deals always and only in probabilities . . . Much of history simply lies forever beyond our science's grasp . . . Historical criticism, to begin, cannot insist on ever playing the judge, haughtily eschewing the servant's role of illumining the background. In this sense, the reach of faith is in no way limited in its positive assent to the modest 'proofs' of science. The ample use of the *non liquet* card is an open invitation to faith. At the same time, the serene confidence essential to faith never tempts it to act as a superhuman surrogate for plodding, mental labor, which retains its proper scope of judgment entirely unimpaired. Human *ratio* deepens (rather than 'purifies') faith's delicate conviction, gives it new dimension, by drawing it ever more into the light of understanding from the dark seat of *memoria* where God touches the mind" (Giambrone, "*Vera et Sincera de Iesu*," 37–38). See also LaVerdiere and Bernier, *Firstborn of God*, 5: "The infancy gospels, as well as the prologues of Mark and John, are the gospels in miniature, introducing the principal themes of their Gospel accounts, including the mission, ministry, Passion, and Resurrection of Jesus."

pantheon of gods."²⁰ As Peeler goes on to say, the Hellenistic and ancient Near Eastern parallels would have been deeply concerning to the evangelists when writing about Jesus' conception: "The parallels open wide the suggestion that Jesus was a demigod like many others."²¹ In addition, Matthew and Luke's narratives of virginal conception only intensify the suspicion—brought against the Gospels by the second-century Roman author Celsus, to whom Origen responded—that Jesus was an illegitimate child.²²

On these grounds, Peeler considers that the evidence tilts in favor of historicity—or at least in favor of the view that the evangelists "heard that it happened this way and wanted to be faithful communicators of testimony."²³ Peeler cites an early work by Brown in which he offers a similar conclusion: "No search for parallels has given us a truly satisfactory explanation of how early Christians happened upon the idea of a virginal conception—unless, of course, that is what really took place."²⁴

In the final volume of his *Jesus of Nazareth* trilogy, Joseph Ratzinger likewise takes a positive view of the historicity of these stories. Ratzinger reflects first upon the narrative of Luke 1. After the angel Gabriel foretells that Mary will bear a son who will be the everlasting Davidic king and Son of God, the following exchange occurs between Mary and the angel Gabriel: "Mary said to the angel, 'How will this be, since I do not know man?' And the angel said to her, 'The Holy Spirit will come upon you, and the power of the Most High will overshadow you; therefore the child to be born will

---

20. Peeler, *Women and the Gender of God*, 129–30. Peeler draws attention to Tacitus, *Histories* 5.5 (LCL 249), 185. Lest the fact of Greco-Roman philosophical "monotheism" be forgotten, see the comparison of Second Temple Jewish monotheism with pagan monotheism in Giambrone, "*Interpretatio iudaica*"; and Giambrone, "Primitive Christology as Ancient Philosophy."

21. Peeler, *Women and the Gender of God*, 130.

22. Peeler observes in this regard that Jane Schaberg's "work is criticized for developing arguments from silence, but these gaps become noticeable because of the things Matthew and Luke *do* say. Schaberg argues that the evangelists were writing these stories apologetically, to dispel the even more scandalous stories of rape that were circulating" (Peeler, *Women and the Gender of God*, 131). Peeler responds to Schaberg's position: "Her argument rests on locating rumors documented much later in the time before the writing of Matthew and Luke. The cause and effect could have worked in the other direction: if the evangelists had not brought the issue of Jesus's unusual origin to the fore with the virginal conception stories, far fewer would have wondered (and gossiped) about it" (131).

23. Peeler, *Women and the Gender of God*, 132. Daniélou offers a further argument for historicity, namely, the details about Joseph in Matthew 1:18–25, which otherwise would have been completely unnecessary and indeed impediments to acknowledging Jesus' Davidic ancestry. See Daniélou, *Infancy Narratives*, 31–38.

24. Brown, *Virginal Conception and Bodily Resurrection of Jesus*, 65.

be called holy, the Son of God'" (Luke 1:34-35).²⁵ As Ratzinger says, one may reasonably ask why Mary does not assume that her childbearing would come about through sexual intercourse with her husband Joseph.²⁶ But Ratzinger focuses his attention instead upon the angel's reply. In making clear that Mary's conception will be virginal and will be by the power of the Holy Spirit, the angel presents Mary in the role of the temple covered with the *shekinah* or sacred cloud that marks out God's presence.²⁷ The virginal conception is momentous for understanding Mary's role.

25. For connections to the scenes of Jesus' baptism and transfiguration, see Brown et al., *Mary in the New Testament*, 118, 121. See also the eschatological emphasis of De Long, "Angels and Visions in Luke-Acts," 83-84: "Gabriel tells Mary her future pregnancy will happen through the Holy Spirit, which he describes as a power of the Most High that will overshadow her ... His explanation combines the eschatological expectation of a renewing Spirit (Isa 32:15; 44:3-4) with the apocalyptic image of God's glory (δόξα) overshadowing ... and filling the tabernacle in the form of a cloud (Exod 40:35). This linguistic correspondence suggests that just as the divine presence overshadowed the tabernacle in Israel's past, so it will now overshadow Mary in the eschatological present of a miraculous conception." Regarding the term "holy" (and the Holy Spirit's presence), Loren T. Stuckenbruck and Gabriele Boccaccini make the following connection, which is intriguing but insufficient to account for all the things that the verse is revealing: "If Matthew and Luke's Gospels knew of the charge that Jesus has an unclean spirit (as it appears in Mark, for example), they did not draw on it directly, but rather drew on a much older tradition to represent Jesus another way: as one born of the *holy* Spirit (Matt 1:18, 20; cf. Luke 1:35) ... A plausibility structure for the notion that the adjective *holy* was intended at some stage as a contrast to *unclean* is supplied by the stories of Noah's birth found in 1 En. 106-7 and the Genesis Apocryphon (at 1Q20 II-V)" (Stuckenbruck and Boccaccini, "1 Enoch and the Synoptic Gospels," 9).

26. Ratzinger observes, "Mary sees no way, for reasons that are beyond our grasp, that she could become mother of the Messiah through marital relations" (Ratzinger, *Jesus of Nazareth* 3:35). Similarly, Peeler comments, "Gabriel has told her of events that will happen in the future: you *will* conceive, you *will* bear, you *will* name. The natural thing would be for Mary to assume that this will happen when she consummates her marriage. But she makes no such assumption. Something about what Gabriel has said makes her ask about the mechanics of this good news" (*Women and the Gender of God*, 71). In Peeler's view, Mary's "question reveals that she has already perceived that he [the angel Gabriel] is not speaking about a typical pregnancy because he is not speaking about a typical son" (72).

27. For further discussion, see Anderson, *That I May Dwell Among Them*, 204, describing how "the theology of John 1:14 was amplified in a Marian direction: she who was to bear the Word of God was also the one who fashioned the fabrics of the temple in which the Word had formerly dwelt. In this way Mary was imagined as a living, breathing temple into which the Creator of the universe had taken up residence." Anderson specifies, "When Ezekiel, for example, spoke of Israel's eager hope for the rebuilding of the temple (Ezek. 40-43) and the return of God's presence to dwell within it (43:1-4), Christian homilists almost uniformly assumed that the ultimate referent was the person of Mary. Indeed, in the icons used during the Marian feasts in the Eastern Church, Ezekiel is almost always shown holding his temple, a figure for the person of Mary" (205).

Most concerning to Ratzinger is why the virgin birth was not mentioned by Paul and thus is absent in the earliest Christian texts. In response, he proposes that the virginal conception of Jesus makes sense once Jesus has been understood in a deeper way that takes time. It is first necessary for "the evolving complex of Christological doctrine" and "the confession of Jesus as the Christ, the Son of God" to take firm shape, as it begins to do in Paul.[28] Ratzinger adds that the virgin birth makes it more difficult to affirm that Jesus is descended from David, and so the infancy narratives are not simply inventing details to support Jesus' status.

Ratzinger assumes that "the conception and birth of Jesus from the Virgin Mary is a fundamental element of our faith."[29] As noted above, this is the

28. Ratzinger, *Jesus of Nazareth*, 3:53. For Ratzinger's theology of biblical inspiration and biblical truth—which includes the aspect of development, but without losing touch with the deposit of faith as given once and for all by Christ and his apostles—see Pidel, *Inspiration and Truth of Scripture*. For a sharp critique of Ratzinger's project, see Borgman, "Opening up New History." Borgman comments, "Much of what has been discovered and developed in theology in recent times is attacked [by Ratzinger] because it differs from the traditional way of seeing and presenting the Christian tradition" (64). For Borgman, however, Ratzinger shares something fundamental with Rahner, Sobrino, and Schillebeeckx—something that Borgman rejects. For these giants of postconciliar theology, "The question was not—although at times it was hard to avoid thinking it was—what we, as modern people, can still reasonably believe about Jesus, given the level of historical knowledge. The question was how to think God's saving presence in Jesus among us, and therefore, for instance, what Jesus' proclamation of the Kingdom of God really meant. And how—not the least important question— we can still consider this Jesus as our redeemer and liberator, although he lived 2000 years ago" (69). Borgman goes (he thinks) a step further, although in my view Rahner, Sobrino, and Schillebeeckx join him. He identifies "a major change in understanding religious faith. Faith can no longer be seen as holding on to an unchanging, stable and in this sense certain foundation. It should be seen as an ongoing exploration of the space God's liberating faithfulness opens up for us, individually and collectively . . . [T]hinking about Jesus' identity as something present in our understanding of him in our lives as his disciples implies that Jesus' identity is not stable. He cannot just seem, but he really can be different things to different people and different communities" (70–71). Jesus is what we experience him to be, and this experience changes and differs radically across time and space.

29. Ratzinger, *Jesus of Nazareth*, 3:57. In a review of Ratzinger's book, the Catholic biblical scholar Nathan Eubank observes, "Matthew and Luke's birth narratives contain some of the most notorious difficulties in the New Testament as well as some of its richest theology. One would expect the gulf between history and theology to appear wider here than ever, but in fact Ratzinger comes closer to a synthesis of history and canonical-theological exegesis . . . Following Joachim Gnilka, he proposes that the birth narratives draw on family traditions, with Mary herself singled out as one of Luke's sources. He defends the historicity of the virgin birth and the census under Quirinius (Lk 2:1–5), as well as the birth in Bethlehem. Many scholars will be frustrated by the near-absence of arguments in favor of this high view of the historicity of the infancy narratives, but . . . Ratzinger plays to his strengths by keeping his historical arguments

claim about the virgin birth that is most contested today among theologians. The Protestant theologian Millard Erickson underscores that Jesus' "being both divine and human did not depend on the virgin birth," just as "Jesus' sinlessness was not dependent on the virginal conception."[30] Erickson does not think the virgin birth is fundamental to Christian faith, though he holds that it really happened.[31] Jürgen Moltmann states simply that the virgin birth "is not one of the pillars that sustains the New Testament faith in Christ," and he does not believe the virgin birth took place.[32] Many more theologians holding some variation of this position could be named.

III. Barth and Balthasar

In my view, however, Mary's virginal motherhood is one of the pillars of Christian faith. The Son inaugurates the new creation from the moment of his conception in Mary's womb. In her virginal womb, we see the fulfillment of Daughter Zion (bridal Israel), of God's temple filled with the divine presence, and of the ark of the covenant that bears the word of God.

In support of this valuation of Mary's virginal motherhood, let me turn to two twentieth-century theological treatments, by Karl Barth and Hans Urs von Balthasar, respectively. Barth and Balthasar are notable for their robust defense of the truth of Mary's virginal motherhood, whose

---

brief. Though Ratzinger takes a high view of the historicity of the infancy narratives, his understanding of historicity is capacious, leaving room for Matthew and Luke's creative theological work" (618). Eubank is less optimistic than Ratzinger about the overall historicity of the infancy narratives, but Eubank does not challenge or deny the virgin birth.

30. Erickson, *Christian Theology*, 689.

31. See Erickson, *Christian Theology*, 690. Erickson points out that the virgin birth is a sign of Jesus' uniqueness, of our dependence upon God, and of God's sovereign power over nature and history. See also the similar view of van der Kooi and van den Brink, *Christian Dogmatics*, 295; and cf. 575: "Vatican II placed Mariology within ecclesiology, ending the tendency that began in the tenth century to make it a part of Christology instead, which granted Mary a structural role in the work of redemption. The promulgations of 1854 (immaculate conception) and 1950 (Mary's ascension) are the fruit of that older model, which was based on an analogy between Christ and Mary. In the more recent approach the person of Mary represents our receptivity and the response of the church to Christ. She does not have a place next to Christ but bears an important function for the church that is en route."

32. Moltmann, *Way of Jesus Christ*, 79. For the same view, see also, among many others, Macquarrie, *Christology Revisited*. The Catholic theologian Uta Ranke-Heinemann lost her chair at the University of Essen due to stating this belief in 1987. See Ranke-Heinemann, *Eunuchs for the Kingdom of Heaven*, 346–48.

importance they insist upon. They do this, however, in different ways in accordance with the Protestant-Catholic divide regarding Marian doctrine.[33]

Karl Barth

Barth begins his discussion of the virgin birth by referencing the fundamental christological dogma: "God's revelation in its objective reality is the incarnation of His Word, in that He, the one true eternal God, is at the same time true Man like us."[34] For Barth, the reality of the incarnation is revealed to us in the most intimate and extraordinary way: the miracle of "the conception of Jesus Christ by the Holy Ghost or His birth of the Virgin Mary."[35] In other words, the path to the christological dogmas (Nicea, Ephesus, Chalcedon, and so on) runs through faith's assent to the virginal conception of Jesus in Mary's womb. Barth argues that the concreteness and historical particularity of the incarnation—the fact that "everything ascribable to man . . . can now be predicated of God's eternal Son"—are present to us through the virgin birth.[36]

In Barth's view, the detail regarding Mary's virginity came into the Gospels of Matthew and Luke simply because it was a clear entailment of what was otherwise known about Jesus. As he puts it, "A certain inward, essential rightness and importance in their connexion with the person of Jesus Christ first admitted them [the stories of the virginal conception and birth] to a share in the Gospel witness."[37] He then proceeds to probe into what characterizes this "essential rightness and importance": why does it matter so decisively for Christology that Jesus was born of a virgin? Here Barth seeks a "dogmatic *a posteriori* understanding" of why this detail is present in Scripture and why the Church lifted it up and gave it a relatively central position, as for instance in the Apostles' Creed.[38]

According to Barth, what the detail of the virgin birth does first is to accentuate the place of mystery. The virgin birth primarily shows that there is no human way to understand the coming of Jesus. God's free action

---

33. For an influential Protestant response to Barth, arguing against the historicity of the virgin birth, see Pannenberg, *Jesus*. Regarding the problems with Pannenberg's theology of the incarnation, see Olson, "Self-Realization of God."

34. Barth, *CD* 1/2:172.

35. Barth, *CD* 1/2:173. For further discussion of Barth's Mariology and his understanding of the virgin birth, see Resch, *Barth's Interpretation of the Virgin Birth*.

36. Barth, *CD* 1/2:146–47.

37. Barth, *CD* 1/2:176.

38. Barth, *CD* 1/2:177.

is the sole explanation of everything related to Jesus Christ's coming into the world. Of our own resources, humans could neither bring about this coming nor even understand this coming. That Jesus was born of a woman shows that the coming of true God and true man, the coming of the incarnate Lord, was "a real event accomplished in space and time as history within history."[39] But that Jesus was born of a *virgin* shows that only God accomplishes this; it is the work of God, not a human work. Barth sums up his argument: "The dogma of the Virgin birth is thus the confession of the boundless amazement of awe and thankfulness called forth in us by this *vere Deus vere homo*. It eliminates the last surviving possibility of understanding the *vere Deus vere homo* intellectually," that is, as something human intellectual resources as such could grasp.[40]

Barth goes on to explain further why the virgin birth undermines the pretensions of human reason vis-à-vis the incarnation. It might seem that the detail of the virgin birth fits with pagan notions and therefore actually inflates or echoes human reasoning or mythmaking. As Barth points out, however, there was no preparation in Judaism for a Messiah who would be born of a virgin. Even if one reads Isaiah 7:14 as describing a "virgin," it is not a messianic text.[41] The infancy narratives cut against the pagan myths, which in fact do not describe a real incarnation, since they deal in gods rather than the living God. The infancy narratives do not portray a mythic symbol of divine-human communion; instead they emphasize—Barth

---

39. Barth, *CD* 1/2:177.
40. Barth, *CD* 1/2:177.
41. For the suggestion that not only Matthew's Gospel, but also Luke 1:27–32 makes a connection to Isaiah 7:10–17, see Sri, *Rethinking Mary in the New Testament*, 35–36, drawing upon numerous scholars (and allowing for the tentative character of their conclusions). On Matthew 1:1:23, see also the position of Collins and Collins, *King and Messiah as Son of God*, 137–38 (a section written by Adela Yarbro Collins): "What then was the catalyst that evoked a miraculous reading of Isa 7:14? The best explanation is that the author of Matthew and his predecessors were aware of Greek and Roman stories about great men being fathered by deities with human women. The Isaian prophecy enabled followers of Jesus to interpret the origin of Jesus as equally or even more miraculous, since his Father is not just one among many so-called gods, but the Creator of all things." J. R. Daniel Kirk and John Nolland add that (in Kirk's words) "the transition from the name Jesus to the name Immanuel and then back again to Jesus works because Immanuel carries connotations of God's saving presence through a human person, not through God's own incarnation. The paradigm of idealized human Christology suffices to contain the Immanuel identification, in the absence of other compelling evidence that a divine human is intimated" (Kirk, *Man Attested by God*, 369, with reference to Nolland, "No Son-of-God Christology in Matthew 1.18–25," 3–12). In my view, a better approach to Matthew 1:23 in the context of the whole Gospel—even if the debate will never be decisively settled on historical-critical grounds—is found in Hays, *Echoes of Scripture in the Gospels*, 162–75, in critical dialogue with Kupp's *Matthew's Emmanuel*.

reiterates—that Jesus' origins involve a profound mystery, utterly grounded in divine action and divine revelation. Assenting to the virgin birth entails assenting to "God was in Christ," an assent made by faith.[42] Thus, the virgin birth is the divinely chosen sign of the incarnation.

According to Barth, Schleiermacher rejects the virgin birth as a necessary part of Christian dogma because Schleiermacher thinks he can understand the virgin birth from within the parameters of the "old creation." In fact, however, the virgin birth is the sign of the mystery of the new creation, God doing a radically new thing, incomprehensible in terms of the "old creation."[43] In the virgin birth, God gives us a sign of the coming of the kingdom of God through the incarnate Lord. In conjunction with the sign that is the empty tomb, the sign that is the virgin birth serves to "mark out the existence of Jesus Christ, amid the many other existences in human history, as that human historical existence in which God is Himself, God is alone, God is directly the Subject, the temporal reality of which is not only called forth, created, conditioned and supported by the eternal reality of God, but is identical with it."[44]

As Barth says, the origins of other human beings are haphazard, in the sense that the sexual intercourse of the parents is not directed specifically toward the specific child who comes forth. By contrast, Jesus is radically intended by God. Barth interprets this in terms of its implications for Jesus as the fullness of divine revelation. He argues that the virgin birth "denotes the fact that God stands at the start where real revelation takes place—God

---

42. Barth, *CD* 1/2:179.

43. See Barth, *CD* 1/2:180. For a sympathetic portrait of Schleiermacher's concerns, see Lincoln, *Born of a Virgin?*, 214–39. Lincoln does not aim to defend all aspects of Schleiermacher's Christology. But he does think that "Schleiermacher's specific critique of the virgin birth tradition is a telling one and he makes a strong case for seeing it as both superfluous and possibly harmful to adhering to the confession that Christ is God incarnate . . . In particular, the questions that Schleiermacher raises and that will not go away include the following: (i) If Scripture is the primary source for theology, what difference does it make to the doctrine of the virgin birth once its human and historical conditionedness is properly recognized and literary and historical criticism is applied to the birth narratives? How is the diversity of views on the incarnation in the New Testament among the witnesses of Paul, the Synoptics and John to be handled and what impact does this have on the virgin birth tradition? (ii) What difference, if any, does a questioning of the historicity of a virginal conception make to an orthodox Christological confession of the full humanity, full divinity and sinlessness of Christ? (iii) How is a rethinking of the virgin birth in relation to incarnation to be treated in relation to the Church's tradition as expressed in the creeds and formulations of the early councils? (iv) What role in the rethinking of the tradition is played by the relation of the doctrine of the virgin birth to contemporary knowledge and thought forms?" (*Born of a Virgin?*, 238–39).

44. Barth, *CD* 1/2:182.

and not the arbitrary cleverness, capability, or piety of man."[45] As I would put it somewhat differently, the virginal motherhood of Mary reveals the unique Fatherhood of God vis-à-vis Mary's Son who comes into the world as Redeemer, inaugurating a new creation.

Barth is arguing not only with Schleiermacher but also with the Protestant theologian Emil Brunner.[46] According to Brunner as described by Barth, the virgin birth involves not mystery but mere biology. Brunner casts doubt upon the virgin birth on the grounds that it threatens to turn the incarnation into a biological conundrum. In response, Barth observes that the Christian tradition never probed into the "how" of the incarnation. In fact, "the sign did not in the least explain the thing signified. Rather it brought to light essentially and purposefully its very inexplicability."[47]

On these foundations, Barth discusses the creed's confession that Christ was conceived by the Holy Spirit and born of the Virgin Mary. He again highlights the divine sovereignty and the dimension of mystery, and he underscores that "Jesus Christ is the real son of a real mother."[48] Christ is genuinely and fully a man—just not in precisely the same way as other humans, since he has no human father. This fact supports the sheer mystery of the Son of the Father becoming flesh. God is completely sovereign over and active in this event. Man participates in the event, but in creaturely receptivity, not in co-sovereignty. Repeatedly, Barth emphasizes that the virgin birth demonstrates that human resources as such are not able to bring about the incarnation of the Son; there is "no such entrance gate of revelation into our world."[49] Thus, Christ opens up a radical new humanity precisely in the mode by which he takes up Adamic humanity. Barth responds to the traditional view that the virgin birth was appropriate because the act of sexual intercourse entails concupiscence and transmits original sin. He argues that the heart of the matter is not human sinfulness—which he deems to be a given, whether or not sexual intercourse is involved—but rather is God's sovereignty in acting upon us so as to become man. In the Virgin Mary's absolute receptivity, God's work of revelation and incarnation exhibits "non-willing, non-achieving, non-creative, non-sovereign man," or "man who can merely receive, merely be ready, merely let something be done to and with himself."[50] God, not man, is sovereign in the virginal conception of Jesus Christ.

---

45. Barth, *CD* 1/2:182.
46. See Brunner, *Mediator*.
47. Barth, *CD* 1/2:184.
48. Barth, *CD* 1/2:185.
49. Barth, *CD* 1/2:188.
50. Barth, *CD* 1/2:191. Barth considers it significant here that the male (the human

Barth also attends to the work of the Spirit. The Spirit's role connects the incarnation with our adoptive sonship in the Son, which is effected by the Spirit's power. Barth clarifies that of course the Spirit is not the father of the incarnate Son. God sovereignly accomplishes the incarnation of the Word in the womb of Mary, but not as though merely "substituting" in the natural order for the contribution of the human father.

In sum, Barth shines light on three main elements of the virgin birth that are important for Christology: the revelation of the only Son's Father and thus the revelation of the full divinity of the fully human Son; the revelation of the intrinsic relationship of Christ and the Church (through the Spirit's power); and the revelation of Christ as the divinely willed new Adam.

Hans Urs von Balthasar

The contemplation of Mary's virginal motherhood is taken further by Hans Urs von Balthasar, along Catholic lines. One such line that Balthasar pursues is Mary's relationship to covenantal Israel. Like Bouyer, he observes that Mary "is the perfect embodiment of the 'Daughter of Sion', the Virgin destined for her Covenant Spouse."[51] The long-promised and prophesied marriage between God and Israel takes place in a certain sense in Mary, who in this respect is not only the perfect type of faith-filled, waiting Israel, but is also the perfect type of the Church of Christ the Bridegroom.

Much like Barth, Balthasar underscores that Jesus' mission comes from his divine Father. In everything, Christ is obedient to his Father; even as a child, he is faithfully doing the work of his Father (see Luke 2:49). Although Jesus' adoptive father Joseph plays a significant role in protecting the holy family from the wiles of Herod, Jesus' mission is not in intrinsic relation to Joseph. Instead, Jesus embodies the mission of the Son coming into the world as the manifestation of the divine Father's love. Balthasar argues, "Jesus knows that he is one with his mission, and this means that he owes his entire being to the heavenly Father who has sent him. This would be impossible if he also owed his existence to an earthly father, for he would be indebted to the latter for part of his 'I', while owing nothing to him with regard to his mission."[52]

---

father) is absent, given the tendency in human history for men to exemplify striving and the grasping of sovereignty. I should add that while Mary is open to God's work, however, Mary is certainly under sin for Barth.

51. Balthasar, *Theo-Drama* 3:177. For further discussion of Balthasar's Mariology, see Gardner, "Balthasar and the Figure of Mary."

52. Balthasar, *Theo-Drama* 3:177.

In Mary, Israel contributes to the incarnation of the Word; the incarnation is not a sheer inbreaking of the sovereign God as though there was no significant preparation or as though Israel had no cooperating role (*pace* Barth). Balthasar deems that "in Mary, the (Abrahamic) faith that characterized this Covenant becomes a contributory element in the Incarnation."[53] Mary, then, is more than—but not less than—purely receptive. At the same time, moved by the Spirit, Jesus' mission is to obey and make manifest his Father. Mary's role is to serve Jesus' mission, a role that has spiritual and bodily dimensions. She experiences "virginal conception and birth" and so she knows that Jesus is no ordinary Son.[54] She embodies Israel's bridal faith and hope. Balthasar comments, "Without this spiritual handing on [of the Scriptures and hope of Israel], which takes place simultaneously with the bodily gift of mother's milk and motherly care, God's Word would not have really become flesh. For being-in-the-flesh always means receiving from others."[55] These are elements not found in Barth, though surely he could agree with them in part. For Balthasar, Jesus' mission is both radically new and the fulfillment of God's entire history with his people Israel—and Israel's role is summed up by Mary. The newness of Jesus' mission has its ground in his status as the Son, who "receives *himself* from the Father—both once for all and in an eternal *and* temporally ever-new 'now.'"[56]

Mary's motherhood extends from her Son to all those who are members of Christ's Body. In this regard, Balthasar identifies a passage from Book IV of Irenaeus's *Against Heresies* according to which there is no longer "any distance and difference between the pure womb that bears the Head [Christ] and that which bears the Church's members."[57] At other points in patristic writings, Mary appears as the most exalted member of the Church. Balthasar also observes that early Mariology, against the Gnostics, had to emphasize her real human motherhood of Jesus. Her virginal motherhood is grounded in her interior receptive obedience to God's word. She never could have been

---

53. Balthasar, *Theo-Drama* 3:177.

54. Balthasar, *Theo-Drama* 3:176. Thomas G. Weinandy, OFM, remarks, "Mary's virginity is significant only in relation to her motherhood. The preserving of Mary's virginity within the act of her son's conception clearly manifests that the nature of the act by which Jesus is conceived is none other than an act of the Holy Spirit . . . To highlight that Mary remained a virgin in the act of conception highlights the singular nature of the act of conception, that of the Holy Spirit, and thus the singular nature of her motherhood. The singular nature of her motherhood highlights the singular identity of her son—'thus the child to be born of you will be called holy, the Son of God' (Lk 1:35)" (Weinandy, *Jesus Becoming Jesus* 1:11–12).

55. Balthasar, *Theo-Drama* 3:177.

56. Balthasar, *Theo-Drama* 3:180.

57. Balthasar, *Theo-Drama* 3:303.

physically the virginal mother of Christ had she not interiorly possessed faith in its "virginal" integrity. Mary's holiness links her to her Son (as the new Eve) and to the Church (as the type and mother of the Church). In opposition to the tendency to force a choice between Christotypical and ecclesiotypical views of Mary, Balthasar remarks, "the more personal and unique Mary's relationship with Christ is understood to be, the more she represents the concrete epitome of what we mean by 'Church.'"[58]

As Balthasar says, the Fathers, in their contemplation of Mary's virginal motherhood, elevated "the fact of the Virgin Birth into something essential to salvation history."[59] In his reflection on Mary's virginal motherhood, Balthasar examines how Mary's motherhood ensures her Son's full continuity with Adamic humanity and with the people of Israel, while also (as *virginal* motherhood) serving as a sign of the newness of the inbreaking of God and his kingdom. She is Israel as the holy and virginal Bride of YHWH; she is the ark of the covenant that bears God's word; she is the God-bearing temple with its closed gate; she is the closed garden of the Song of Songs.[60] Balthasar discusses the prophecy of Isaiah 7:14 about the "virgin," as cited in Matthew 1:23. Balthasar is well aware, as were the Fathers, that "in classical Old Covenant terms, virginity implies unfruitfulness and brings disgrace."[61] But matters are different in the inaugurated eschatology of the new covenant. As both virgin and mother, Mary exemplifies the new covenant reality while standing also within the old covenant. Again, she is most blessed because she believed, not because of family ties; and her physical motherhood of Jesus is joined intrinsically to her purity of faith.[62]

---

58. Balthasar, *Theo-Drama* 3:304–5.

59. Balthasar, *Theo-Drama* 3:327. In this context, Balthasar is speaking explicitly of the relatively common (in the Greek East) patristic view that separated sexuality from the original state of humanity, a view that I think deeply mistaken but that, as Balthasar shows, can still help us to appreciate virginity as an eschatologically proleptic state.

60. As Weinandy says, "[T]he Holy Spirit, through his act of overshadowing Mary, builds a living temple—a new Holy of Holies within which the living most holy God now newly dwells among his people, a dwelling that is most unprecedented and unanticipated. Mary, as the new living temple in whom the Son of God dwells bodily, then becomes the living prophetic image of the future church . . . This Spirit-filled communion between Jesus and Mary, this living communion between Jesus' flesh and Mary's flesh, establishes her as the first member of the church as so fashions her as its living icon, for through her act of faith she conjoins herself to the very act of the Holy Spirit, by which her son is conceived within her womb" (*Jesus Becoming Jesus*, 12). See also, more broadly, Bonino, *Reading the Song of Songs with St. Thomas Aquinas*.

61. Balthasar, *Theo-Drama* 3:329.

62. See Wright, *Lord's Prayer*, 62: "In the family scene, when Jesus speaks of his mother and brothers, he does so in terms that recall the 'good soil' ([Luke] 8:8) in the parable: 'My mother and my brothers are those who hear the word of God and do it'

Balthasar addresses Mary's *virginitas in partu*—the fact that her bodily integrity was not corrupted or harmed by the coming forth of her Son from her womb. The church fathers strongly affirmed this doctrine, as did the Catholic Church's tradition up to the twentieth century.[63] In Balthasar's view, meditation on Mary's virginal motherhood requires the doctrine of her *virginitas in partu*. It does so because of the nature of the incarnation itself. Not only is Mary the type of the Church (which preserves her full integrity of faith and sacraments in giving birth to adoptive sons and daughters in the Son), but most importantly Balthasar highlights "the sign quality of the human body as such and of virginal integrity in particular."[64]

Balthasar explains that the virginal integrity of Mary is intended to exhibit the power and mission of Christ. His mission accomplishes healing, restoration, and salvation. Mary's virginal motherhood serves as a sacramental sign of his work, manifesting the inbreaking of the new creation. Thus, Mary's body as such is not a site of damage or corruption, but rather is a sign of the power of the new creation that Christ brings. The spiritual integrity of the Church is reflected by Mary, in her virginal motherhood, both physically and spiritually. Thus, for christological and ecclesiological reasons, "the Virgin retained her virginity,"[65] inclusive of her bodily virginal integrity—miraculous indeed, but far less miraculous than the incarnation of her Son.

In sum, Balthasar carries forward some of the elements that we found in Barth while reconfiguring others and adding new ones. Balthasar agrees with Barth that the virgin birth helps to reveal the fact that Christ is the Son of the divine Father. Balthasar puts this in terms of Christ's mission not having a temporal origin: Christ carries forward in time his eternal procession, now manifesting his Sonship (and the love of the Father) in a temporal mode. Balthasar also agrees with, while revising and expanding upon, Barth's connection between Mary's virginal conception and the fact that she is the type of the Church. For Barth, the Church is shaped by the

---

(8:21). Jesus's kin are those who receive the word he teaches and then put it into practice... Jesus and his disciples form a family, a kinship group, and this family has Jesus' Father for their Father." Sharing the same divine Father is given a twist by Nicholas Perrin, who argues with respect to the Lord's Prayer that "by calling on God as 'Father', Jesus and his disciples were asking Yahweh to do in their own time what God had done in the exodus, namely, repurpose the machinations of the wicked for atoning ends. So, then, by praying just this prayer, Jesus and his disciples were going on record before God that they were prepared to accept this appointed suffering, thereby exercising their newly acquired priestly role" (Perrin, *Jesus the Priest*, 43).

63. See for example Bonaventure, *Commentary on the Gospel of Luke*, 73, ch. 1, §62.
64. Balthasar, *Theo-Drama* 3:333.
65. Balthasar, *Theo-Drama* 3:334.

sovereign Lord and is passive and receptive in relation to the Lord, since the Church stands under judgment (as does Mary). The virginal conception, in Barth's view, underscores God's absolute sovereignty over the event of the incarnation and over the Church. Balthasar, by contrast, explores Mary's cooperation and holiness, and Balthasar also expands upon the connection between the virginal conception and the Church in order to draw in other elements, such as Mary's virginal integrity *in partu*. Third, Balthasar concurs with Barth's view that the virginal conception and virgin birth are a sign of the inbreaking of the kingdom or new creation. Balthasar, however (much like Bouyer and other Catholic thinkers), makes more connections to the old covenant, and especially to the figure of "Daughter Zion," God's Bride. Balthasar also notes that virginity itself has eschatological implications.

I should add that in Balthasar's view, Mary remained a virgin after Jesus' birth and did not have other children. This is of course hardly a well-accepted view among biblical scholars, or even among many Catholic theologians today. Biblical scholars generally assume not only that Jesus had brothers and sisters but also that Jesus experienced (in Stephen Barton's words) serious "conflict in [his] relations with his natural kin," as Mark 3:22–32 can be read to imply.[66] But the Gospels' references to Jesus' "brothers and sisters"

---

66. Barton, *Discipleship and Family Ties in Mark and Matthew*, 78. Barton remarks, "If, then, [Mark] 3.22–30 is 'damnation history' so far as the scribes are concerned, is it so for Jesus' family as well, given the setting of vv. 22–30 in vv. 20–35? The most appropriate answer is probably a qualified affirmative. The odium of blasphemy which the evangelist attaches to the scribes does extend, to some degree at least, to the story of Jesus and his family in the bracketing verses" (77). But Barton does not demonstrate why this is so. Mark 3:31–35 makes the point that Jesus' new covenant family is based upon faith. We read, "And his mother and his brethren came, and standing outside they sent to him and called him. And a crowd was sitting about him; and they said to him, 'Your mother and your brethren are outside, asking for you.' And he replied, 'Who are my mother and my brethren?' And looking around on those who sat about him, he said, 'Here are my mother and my brethren! Whoever does the will of God is my brother, and sister, and mother.'" This point need not, however, be taken as excluding his kin from the new covenant family of Jesus. Nor does it require conflict between Jesus and his "brethren," let alone between Jesus and his mother—although it may imply a lack of understanding of some kind (not, however, blasphemy against the Spirit working through Jesus). Barton hastens to point out that Mark does not anywhere attribute to Jesus' family the unbelief he attributes to the scribes and to Judas. Barton holds that Matthew and Luke sharply disagree with Mark's presentation (including by omitting Mark 3:20–21): "Whereas Mark has Jesus' kin issue a summons at a distance, Matthew has them reverently seeking to speak to him (12.46), and Luke has them wanting to see him but being prevented from so doing by the crowd (8.19–20)" (*Discipleship and Family Ties in Mark and Matthew*, 79). Again, however, the notion that Matthew and Luke are concealing Jesus' conflict with his mother Mary (and with his "brothers and sisters") is one that Barton and others create by means of their interpretation of Jesus' words about his new covenant family. For the same perspective as Barton's, see Brown

need not indicate that Mary had additional children. The Catholic biblical scholar James Prothro has recently argued on biblical grounds that the evidence leans toward the conclusion that Mary had no further children.[67] Prothro explores the range of meaning of the Greek "ἀδελφοί/αί," as well as the fact that "the Aramaic way to unambiguously designate 'cousins' is somewhat cumbersome or often specific to one's paternal side."[68] In addition, he considers it significant that Hegesippus, in his lost second-century history of the Church (quoted by Eusebius of Caesarea), identifies Symeon/Simon—and therefore also James—as Jesus' cousin (ἀνεψιός).[69] Hegesippus, who claimed knowledge of Jesus' extended family, elsewhere calls James the "brother" (ἀδελφος) of Jesus.

Furthermore, when Mark 6:3 and Mark 15:40-41 are compared with each other in light of Luke 24:10, it appears that there was a Mary who was close to Jesus and who was the mother of James and Joseph (listed in Mark 6:3 as among Jesus' "ἀδελφοί") but who was not the mother of Jesus. Prothro comments, "One can hardly imagine the Synoptic evangelists—particularly Luke—listing Jesus' mother second after Mary Magdalene (contrast John), or distinguishing her among other Marys by the names of James and/or

---

et al., *Mary in the New Testament*, 54-59, 63. But the authors of this volume go on to draw, with regard to the Gospel of Luke, the link between Mary's place in Christ's blood-relation family and Mary's place in the new covenant family that, in my view, Mark may also be expressing: "One may also compare [Luke] 1:42, 45 to 11:27-28, the scene where a woman in the crowd raises her voice to say to Jesus: 'Happy [*makaria*] the womb that bore you, and the breasts you sucked'; but Jesus responds, 'Happy rather those who hear the word of God and keep it.' In both instances there is a blessing or beatitude in reference to physical motherhood; and then a greater emphasis on the one who believes the things spoken to her or the one who hears the word of God and keeps it. Mary, the handmaid of the Lord (1:38), meets the criterion and gains the beatitude of the Christian believers whom Acts 2:18 calls the servants and *handmaids* of the Lord" (*Mary in the New Testament*, 137). Of course, Mary is more than this, but she is not less than this—and I see no reason to hold that she is less than this in Mark's eyes.

67. See Prothro, "Semper Virgo?" For further discussion, see Blinzler, *Brüder und Schwestern Jesu*, as well as—in much less detail—Braine, "Virgin Mary in the Christian Faith," 898-904; Hauke, *Introduction to Mariology*, 194-97. For the view that the New Testament evidence is not conclusive, but can be read either in support of Jesus' having full brothers (and sisters) or in support of Jesus' brothers (and sisters) being the children of Joseph by an earlier wife, see Bauckham, "Family of Jesus." See also Bauckham's defense of the view that Jesus' brothers and sisters were children of Joseph but not of Mary in Bauckham, *Jude and the Relatives of Jesus*; and Bauckham, *Gospel Women*.

68. Prothro, "Semper Virgo?," 88.

69. Prothro notes that this reading depends upon interpreting δεύτερον as modifying ἀνεψιός, which Prothro shows is the most likely meaning. See also Pitre, *Jesus and the Jewish Roots of Mary*, 125, for the view that Hegesippus clearly meant "cousin."

Joses/ph rather than Jesus. It is simply implausible."[70] He reasons that Mary the mother of James and Joseph may be the "Mary of Clopas" mentioned in John 19:25. According to Eusebius, Clopas was Joseph's brother, and was the father of Symeon/Simon. If so, then Mark 6:3's statement that Jesus is the "ἀδελφός" of "James and Joses and Judas [cf. Jude 1] and Simon" means that they were Jesus' cousins.[71]

IV. Theotokos: Cyril of Alexandria and Thomas Aquinas

At the Council of Chalcedon, the Church confessed Jesus Christ to be "begotten before the ages from the Father as regards his divinity, and . . . the same for us and for our salvation from Mary, the virgin God-bearer, as regards his humanity."[72] Two decades prior to Chalcedon, during the controversies that were dogmatically decided at the Council of Ephesus, Cyril of Alexandria had much to say about the "God-bearer." His opponents the Nestorians held that Mary is mother of Christ, but not mother of God, the reason being that Mary gave birth only to Christ's humanity.[73]

---

70. Prothro, "Semper Virgo?," 92. Pitre adds the following arguments from his reading of John 19: "First, notice that John identifies the second woman at the cross as 'his mother's *sister*, Mary' (John 19:25). Although it's easy to miss the point, this verse provides important support for the word 'sister' (Greek *adelphē*) being used to refer to someone other than a blood sister. It seems extremely unlikely that Mary's parents would have given both her and her sister the name Mary. However, the text makes perfect sense if John is using the word 'sister' to refer to a close relative of Jesus' mother. Second, and even more important, when John refers to this woman as 'Mary the wife of Clopas' (John 19:25), he gives us an important clue to the identity of 'the other Mary' referred to by Matthew and Mark. If John is referring to the same Mary that Matthew and Mark say was present at the crucifixion and burial of Jesus—Mary the mother of James and Joses—then we have further evidence that James and Joses are *not* the sons of Jesus' mother. Nor are they the sons of Joseph by a previous marriage. Instead, they would be the sons of another man—a man named Clopas" (*Jesus and the Jewish Roots of Mary*, 122–23). For the opposite view, tentatively suggesting that Mary the mother of Jesus is the mother of four other sons (James, Joses, Judas, and Simon), see Levine, *Witness at the Cross*, 89–90.

71. Prothro concludes, "Any answer to whether Mary had natural children after Jesus involves speculation and weighing probabilities and possibilities. I hope that the above has shown that the non-Helvidian positions [i.e., the positions that hold that Mary had no other children] are warranted if not preferable, and that on exegetical grounds. However, the above has only addressed the apparent falsifying criterion for the dogma of Mary's perpetual virginity. The positive claim that she remained *semper virgo* cannot be verified by exegetical or historical inquiry" (Prothro, "Semper Virgo?," 95).

72. Council of Chalcedon, "Definition of the Faith," 86.

73. See Cyril of Alexandria, *On the Unity of Christ*, 64. For a succinct discussion

This section of my chapter will examine the birth of Jesus from Mary in relation to the Nestorian controversy. As both Cyril and Chalcedon recognize, Mary did not give birth to the human nature as such; rather, Mary gave birth to the person Jesus. This person is the divine Son. Christ's human nature has a temporal origin whereas his divine nature does not, but his human nature cannot subsist on its own. Instead, it subsists only, and always, as the human nature of the Son. Therefore, when Mary gave birth to Jesus Christ according to his humanity, she gave birth to the incarnate Son.

In this vein Cyril of Alexandria emphasizes, "For he who is and exists from all eternity, as he is God, underwent birth from a woman according to the flesh."[74] The child virginally conceived by Mary is the divine Son. Although the divine Son as such did not originate in Mary's womb, it is *not* the case that the human nature alone originated in Mary's womb. What originated in Mary's womb is the fruit of the hypostatic union: Jesus Christ, the incarnate Son. For Cyril, then, contemplating the birth of Jesus provides an opportunity to fathom an extraordinary mystery. Jesus simply is the Son, because the Son is the person in whom the human nature subsists. Thus—to put the matter in terms of the birth of Jesus—"the Word of God the Father born of God before all ages and times . . . in these last times of the present age, has been born of a woman according to the flesh."[75]

Cyril of Alexandria is cited in Aquinas's *Catena Aurea* on the Gospel of Luke, and Aquinas also knows Cyril's theology through the documents of the Council of Ephesus and through John of Damascus.[76] Let me now turn

---

of Cyril's Christology in its context, see Daley, *God Visible*, 190–95; and for further analysis, see Loon, *Dyophysite Christology of Cyril of Alexandria*; Keating, "Christology in Cyril and Leo"; Keating, "Baptism of Jesus in Cyril of Alexandria"; McKinion, *Words, Imagery, and the Mystery of Christ*. Describing Cyril's Christology, McKinion makes two especially important points: "First, the Incarnation is not a puzzle whereby two pieces are joined together; it is the becoming human of the Word. Second, the manner in which the Word united human nature to himself, thereby becoming a human being, is ineffable. It is not a technical process of combination. Cyril's christology had a different starting point from either of those two. It is therefore misguided to speak of him as being midway between Nestorius and Apollinarius. Cyril was actually on a different spectrum than either of them. Instead of beginning with two objects—the Word and a human being—Cyril began with the Word's act of condescension on behalf of humankind" (McKinion, *Words, Imagery, and the Mystery of Christ*, 225). See also on related matters O'Keefe, "Impassible Suffering?"; Keating, *Appropriation of Divine Life in Cyril of Alexandria*; Keating, "Twofold Manner of Divine Indwelling in Cyril of Alexandria"; and Congar, *Parole et le Souffle*.

74. Cyril of Alexandria, *On the Unity of Christ*, 69.

75. Cyril of Alexandria, *On the Unity of Christ*, 75. For Christ and the Spirit, see for example Cyril of Alexandria, *Commentary on John*, 2:197, 260.

76. On the latter, see Elders, *Thomas Aquinas and His Predecessors*, chapter 13. See also Barnes, *Christ's Two Wills in Scholastic Thought*.

to the Virgin Mary in Aquinas's anti-Nestorian Christology. Jean-Pierre Torrell remarks that in the *tertia pars* of the *Summa theologiae*, "Aquinas puts in relief the two great essential truths of the motherhood of Mary and her virginity."[77] But Torrell also notes with reference to Mary's *virginitas in partu* that Aquinas's "insistence on the physical sign of her virginity can be surprising for a modern reader."[78]

In the *tertia pars*, question 28 treats the virginity of Mary.[79] In article one, on the virginal conception, the fourth objection is particularly important because it contends that to be a member of the human race one needs to be generated according to the human mode, namely, sexual intercourse between a man and a woman. The fifth objection makes a similar case: since a human body is comprised of semen from a male, it seems that a body not composed in such a way would not be human.[80]

These objections have to do with whether Jesus has a true human nature, something that the Nestorians considered to be put at risk by Cyril's Christology. In response, Aquinas argues that human nature, as such, does not need to come forth from a man and a woman.[81] Adam was directly created by God, but he still had human nature. In the womb of Mary, God's power can act upon the ovum in a manner sufficient to bring forth a human child (including by ensuring that the needed chromosomes are present, not least the Y chromosome, something that Aquinas is unaware must be done).[82]

77. Torrell, "S. Thomas et la Vierge Marie," 1096.

78. Torrell, *Jésus le Christ chez Thomas d'Aquin*, 493.

79. For background see Torrell, *Jésus le Christ chez Thomas d'Aquin*, 492–500.

80. Myers notes, "For Aristotle, the *pneuma* is part of the unique contribution from male semen that initiates life in the matter provided by the woman . . . Galen mixes Aristotelian ideas with his two-seed theory that allows for *pneuma* to be provided by both the male and female, though the male's provision is of greater heat and, therefore, potency, thus supplying the necessary 'motion' for life" (*Blessed among Women?*, 61). Drawing from the work of Gwynn Kessler, Myers adds that "later Second Temple Jewish sources *do* convey familiarity with Aristotelian ideas by describing the male's 'virile' and causative seed, which shapes the nourishing female blood" (*Blessed among Women?*, 61). See Kessler, *Conceiving Israel*; and see also Thiessen, "Legislation of Leviticus 12 in Light of Ancient Embryology."

81. In making his point, Aquinas draws upon Aristotle's faulty biology. For discussion, contrasting Aquinas's use of Aristotle with his use of Genesis in the same reply to the fifth objection (and arguing that "difficulties or solutions that claim to stay on the biological level alone can only constitute a distorted path" for resolving issues pertaining to Mary's virginal conception), see Torrell, *Jésus le Christ chez Thomas d'Aquin*, 495.

82. Recall Andrew Lincoln's point that if Jesus' flesh came solely from his mother, then he could not have had a male Y chromosome and so he could not be fully human (in continuity with Adam), since his conception would have required a special divine creation (of a Y chromosome). In response, Daniel J. Treier grants that God miraculously enables the presence of the Y chromosome. Without functioning as a father, God

Aquinas's central point in the body of the article is that it is fitting that a miracle should be involved in Jesus' conception in Mary's womb. Although Mary truly conceives Jesus in her womb, the incarnation is not a normal event, and so it is appropriate that God highlight its uniqueness by enabling Mary to conceive in her womb in a unique way. Aquinas—much like Balthasar and Barth—states that the incarnation is the entrance into the world of "the true and natural Son of God," and so it makes sense that he has no other "father than God."[83]

Aquinas reflects further upon the fittingness of the incarnate Son having no human father. As he says, the purpose of the incarnation is for human beings to become adopted children of God, sharing in the inheritance of the Son. This filial adoption occurs when we are "born again as sons of God" through the power of divine grace.[84] Just as our adopted sonship occurs by the grace of the Holy Spirit rather than by a natural process, so also it is fitting that the incarnation occur not *solely* by a natural process. The Spirit is responsible for the conception of Christ (see Matt 1:20 and Luke

---

miraculously (in a manner beyond our understanding) augments the genetic material given by Mary, so as to produce the full forty-six chromosomes normally given by sperm and egg. Rightly, Treier does not think this is a problem for the traditional viewpoint. The chromosomal miracle does not entail that Jesus was not fully human, since it does not change the fact that he possesses a human nature in full. See Treier, "Virgin Territory?," 375. See also Peeler's response to Lincoln's concern that (in Peeler's words) "Jesus's difference from all other humans *by virtue of his singular maternity* could destroy the aim of the incarnation itself, the recapitulation of the human race" (Peeler, *Women and the Gender of God*, 133). Peeler counters, "Possessing a Y chromosome that was supplied by God rather than a human male could still afford Jesus this flesh-and-blood humanity that can experience the full human condition. The unique nature of his body by virtue of the virginal conception does not destroy his salvific solidarity" (135). A similar response to Lincoln on this point appears in Crisp, *Analyzing Doctrine*, 171 (cf. his full discussion on 170–73, 176): "The missing genes are a product of divine action just as the generation of the human race is ultimately the product of divine action. If God decides to provide the requisite Y chromosome to generate a human male by means of a miracle..., why think that this new genetic material coupled with the genes supplied by the Virgin do not add up to a new human individual after the moment of syngamy? There is no 'abstract speculative category' of humanity at work here, just a particular condition that (I suppose) needs to be met in order for the divine agent who brought about the human race to bring about a new human individual by means of a miracle." In this discussion, a salutary warning comes from Juan Eduardo Carreño in "Theology, Philosophy, and Biology," 77, emphasizing that God does not do an "*assisted fertilization*" (as though divine causality were ontologically on the same level as creaturely causality) and ruling out parthenogenesis. See also the problematic brief proposal—undermining Mary's real motherhood—by Thomas, "If Not Parthenogenesis."

83. Aquinas, *Summa theologiae* III, q. 28, a. 1.

84. Aquinas, *Summa theologiae* III, q. 28, a. 1. See also Spezzano, *Glory of God's Grace*, 179–207, especially 192–207.

1:19-20), and likewise the Spirit is responsible for our becoming adopted sons in the Son.⁸⁵ Indeed, the Catholic philosopher David Braine argues that the virginal conception is more than fitting, since if Jesus were the natural son of Joseph and Mary, then Jesus' "divinity would then be not key to his natural identity and existence but, as it were, an extra gift, one of his properties, or, in Aristotelian terms, 'accidents.'"⁸⁶ In such a case, says Braine, Jesus would have been interiorly divided. His human nature or human existence would have been natural—willed by God within the natural order—whereas his divinity would be accidental.

To my mind, Braine's argument most likely does not hold; I think God could have willed that the incarnate Son have a human father. But Braine's argument supports the fittingness that Aquinas and others perceive. Without compromising his full humanity, the origin of Jesus is entirely from God the Father through the power of the Holy Spirit. As Barth puts it, God is utterly sovereign in his conception; and as Balthasar puts it, Jesus' "mission" is utterly from the Father. Aquinas recognizes that for all other humans, the coming-to-be of a human nature entails the coming to be of a human person. Since Jesus' human nature subsists in the person of the Son rather than subsisting as a human person, the presence of the divine Father and the Holy Spirit at the origins of Mary's Godbearing befits the radical uniqueness of Jesus' humanity.

The second article of *Summa theologiae* III, question 28 asks whether Mary preserved her virginal integrity during Christ's birth.⁸⁷ Aquinas re-

85. See Emery, "Holy Spirit in Aquinas's Commentary on Romans," 144-49; and see also Emery, *Trinity*. See also the extensive background in Somme, *Fils adoptifs de Dieu par Jésus Christ*.

86. Braine, "Virgin Mary in the Christian Faith," 878-79.

87. Torrell comments, "For Thomas, there is no doubt about Mary's *virginitas in partu*, but it is necessary to recognize that this affirmation about Mary is a matter less anciently attested than the virginal conception" (Torrell, *Jésus le Christ chez Thomas d'Aquin*, 496). The first text that clearly teaches Mary's *virginitas in partu* is Leo's Tome, and it was also taught by Pope Martin I and, in solemn fashion, by Pope Paul IV. Graebe points out that rejection of Mary's *virginitas in partu* undermines the traditional doctrine of the virgin birth not least by "reducing it to the natural consequence of the virginal conception," thereby separating out the birth itself as not part of the miracle (*Vessel of Honor*, 300). Graebe also comments that the doctrine helps to highlight Mary's status as the intact vessel of the Word and Mary's status as "the Virgin Bride" or Daughter Zion (*Vessel of Honor*, 302). See also the defense of the doctrine in Laurentin, *Short Treatise on the Virgin Mary*, 324-34; and, for a constructive advancement of Aquinas's position, Ku's "Fittingness of Mary's Virginity in Birth." Citing *Summa theologiae* III, q. 45, a. 2, ad 1 and ad 3, Ku remarks, "The miraculous subtlety effecting the virgin birth was 'of glory' but not 'of a glorious body.' This was a proleptic manifestation: Christ's subtlety in the virgin birth 'represented' the future subtlety of his body" ("Fittingness of Mary's Virginity in Birth," 461).

marks in the second objection of this article that an affirmative answer would seem to undermine the human concreteness of the incarnation. Aquinas states in this objection, "nothing should have taken place in the mystery of Christ, which would make His body to seem unreal. Now it seems to pertain not to a true but to an unreal body, to be able to go through a closed passage; since two bodies cannot be in one place at the same time."[88]

In reply, Aquinas first observes that Isaiah 7:14—as quoted in Matthew 1:23—states that "a virgin shall conceive and bear a son." Aquinas therefore feels biblically justified in holding that Mary was virginal not only in conceiving Jesus but also in bearing or giving birth to him, and in Aquinas's view this entails physical integrity.[89] As a matter of fittingness, he underscores the principle that Christ, in order to show the truth of his incarnation, "mingled wondrous with lowly things. Wherefore, to show that His body was real, He was born of a woman. But in order to manifest His Godhead, He was born of a virgin."[90] In Aquinas's view, for Mary to be a virgin in conceiving her Son is a miracle that is fittingly paired with the miracle of her continuing to bear the marks of virginity in giving birth.

For Aquinas as for Balthasar, Christ comes as the healer, the one who inaugurates the eschatological new creation.[91] Fleshly damage involves bodily "corruption" and tends in the direction of death. As Aquinas observes, Christ's incarnation has among its primary purposes "that He might take away our corruption."[92] Since the incarnation has this purpose,

88. Aquinas, *Summa theologiae* III, q. 28, a. 1, obj. 2.

89. See also Aquinas, *Commentary on Isaiah*, no. 250, p. 119: "Likewise they [Jewish scholars] object that in Hebrew it does not say *virgin*, but *alma*, which, according to them, signifies a marriageable young girl, as found in Genesis 24:16 concerning Rebecca; where we [in the Vulgate] have *an exceedingly comely maid*, they also have *alma*. And even if it said *bethula*, which, according to them, signifies a virgin, this does not necessarily mean that she conceives while remaining a virgin, because it may be that she who was a virgin at the time of the prophecy, should conceive afterwards, having been corrupted by the seed of a man. To which is to be said that it would be no sign at all if a young woman should conceive, and even a corrupted virgin. The Lord, however, wished to signify something great." In *Commentary on Isaiah*, no. 253, p. 120, Aquinas cites Matthew 1:23 and explains that the meaning is that "'a virgin,' remaining a virgin, 'shall conceive,' in giving birth, 'bear a son.'" See also *Commentary on Isaiah*, no. 1140, p. 543, where Aquinas discusses Isaiah 66:7, "before she was in labor, she gave birth." Like Irenaeus, Gregory of Nyssa, Jerome, Augustine, and other church fathers, Aquinas interprets this mystically as a reference to Mary. In III, q. 28, a. 3, *sed contra*, Aquinas discusses Mary's perpetual virginity in light of the Fathers' interpretation of Ezekiel 44:2, "This gate shall remain shut; it shall not be opened, and no one shall enter by it; for the Lord, the God of Israel, has entered by it; therefore it shall remain shut."

90. Aquinas, *Summa theologiae* III, q. 28, a. 2, ad 2.

91. See Novakovic, *Messiah, the Healer of the Sick*.

92. Aquinas, *Summa theologiae* III, q. 28, a. 2.

Aquinas concludes with Augustine that "it is unfitting that in His birth He should corrupt His mother's virginity. Thus Augustine says in a sermon on the Nativity of Our Lord: 'It was not right that He who came to heal corruption, should by His advent violate integrity.'"[93]

In the *sed contra* of this article, Aquinas highlights a sermon he believes to have been preached at the Council of Ephesus, a sermon that suggests that the virgin birth did not corrupt Mary's virginal integrity. Aquinas draws his central insights from this anti-Nestorian sermon. The sermon states, "Whosoever brings forth mere flesh, ceases to be a virgin. But since she gave birth to the Word made flesh, God safeguarded her virginity so as to manifest His Word, by which Word He thus manifested Himself: for neither does our word, when brought forth, corrupt the mind; nor does God, the substantial Word, deigning to be born, destroy virginity."[94] The integrity or uncorruptedness (or wholeness) of Mary has significance for revealing that it is the *incarnate Word* who comes forth.

Aquinas deems it fitting that, just as the virginal conception of Christ is both ordinary in certain respects and extraordinary in others, so the same is true of the virgin birth. The conception of Christ, which is both a real human conception in Mary's womb and a miraculous virginal conception caused by the Holy Spirit, reflects the Son's humanity and divinity. Similarly, the virgin birth reflects both Christ's humanity and divinity, in that Christ truly passes through the birth canal while miraculously not causing Mary any bodily damage.[95]

In defending the doctrine of the virgin birth, the Protestant theologian Daniel Treier asks rhetorically "whether. . . God would have allowed the entirety of Christendom to get fundamentally off track on a vital doctrine for almost two thousand years."[96] Treier argues that the answer is no, and he suggests that for Christians who believes in the doctrine of the incarnation this point should weigh heavily in support of the truth that the infancy

---

93. Aquinas, *Summa theologiae* III, q. 28, a. 2; translation slightly altered. Graebe examines some mid-twentieth-century misunderstandings of Aquinas's position on Mary's *virginitas in partu*: see Graebe, *Vessel of Honor*, 58–60, 67.

94. Aquinas, *Summa theologiae* III, q. 28, a. 2.

95. As Prothro puts it, "many events in the economy of salvation are simply odd and singular, effected by God as peculiar 'signs' that break from natural patterns—which the virgin's motherhood was prophesied to be (Isa 7:14). If one holds this regarding Christ's conception, what offense is it to apply this also to a miraculous parturition? If one is thinking purely in terms of implications (again, not a sufficient method for determining veracity), one could easily say that parturition without travail is not a lessening of the incarnation but a 'sign' that this birth heralds the Son who will break the adamic curse (cf. Gen 3:16)" (Prothro, "Semper Virgo?," 96).

96. Treier, "Virgin Territory?," 379.

narratives convey. Treier notes that Protestants, Catholics, and Orthodox will agree about this "tradition-historical factor."[97]

In his conclusions regarding Mary's *virginitas in partu* as constitutive of the mystery of the virgin *birth*—the full entrance of the incarnate Son into the world—Aquinas is operating along just such weighty tradition-historical lines, grounded in the church fathers' reading of Matthew 1:23, Isaiah 66:7, and Ezekiel 44:2.[98] According to the Catholic theologian Brian Graebe, the doctrine that Mary's bodily integrity was not damaged by childbirth was explicitly defended by numerous church fathers, appeared in

---

97. Treier, "Virgin Territory?," 379. For appeal to creedal tradition from a Reformed perspective, see also Crisp, *Analyzing Doctrine*, 174; but Crisp adds an important caveat (one which Treier would likely agree, at least when it pertains to Catholic and Orthodox Marian doctrines not shared by Protestants): "The point of the creeds and confessions of the church is to ensure that believers do not have a mistaken view of the doctrine in question, and hold to the right form of doctrine. That is why the issue of the *filioque* is such a running sore in the life of the church; it is a clause added unilaterally by one branch of the church to an ecumenically agreed upon instrument of catechesis—namely, the Nicene Creed" (175). Crisp assumes a "branch" theory of the Church's structure, although, of course, neither "branches" in existence (if the Church really can be thought of in terms of "branches," which I do not grant) at the time of the addition of the *filioque* would recognize Protestant Christianity as a "branch." For further reflection on tradition-historical thinking, see Kuhner, "Ignatius of Antioch's *Letter to the Ephesians* 19.1 and the Hidden Mysteries."

98. Treier is well aware that Catholics will be quick to point out this implication of Treier's proposal. Thus, he notes that some Catholic scholars gladly "concede . . . that the explicitly scriptural case for the virgin conception is, like those for Mary's immaculate conception and bodily assumption, tenuous—but traditional dogmas these remain" (Treier, "Virgin Territory?," 378). While firmly disagreeing with the dogmas of the immaculate conception and assumption of Mary, Treier accepts that Christians should not suppose that only doctrines demonstrable by historical-critical methods are truly biblical doctrines. As Treier notes, without rejecting historical-critical scholarship and its insights, we can recognize that some "assumptions implicit in modern historical argumentation can gradually lead even scripturally committed Trinitarian Christians to deny or fundamentally reinterpret articles of ecumenically orthodox faith" (Treier, "Virgin Territory?," 378). Representing a standard Eastern Orthodox position, Sergius Bulgakov argues that although the dogma of the Immaculate Conception fails on various grounds, Mary never committed a sin, never felt a desire to do so, and was graced in the womb by the Holy Spirit. He states, "She remained sinless all along this path which terminates in her unwavering station at the cross. The Mother's station on Golgotha at the cross of her Son reveals the purity and the sinless sacrificial quality of her entire life which prepared her for Golgotha" (Bulgakov, *Burning Bush*, 9). He adds, "In its countless divine services dedicated to the Mother of God, the Holy Orthodox Church firmly and clearly teaches the absolute sinlessness of Mary in her birth, her holy childhood and adolescence, in the Annunciation, in the birth of her Son and throughout her entire life" (Bulgakov, *Burning Bush*, 9). Bulgakov criticizes the dogma of the Immaculate Conception in part because of the Catholic doctrines of original sin and of the divine creation of each human soul, doctrines that he contests.

Pope Leo's Tome at the Council of Ephesus in relation to the Theotokos, and was taught consistently by the medieval doctors.[99] For instance, recalling that the curse associated with Eve's fall has to do with pain in childbearing (Gen 3:16), Bernard of Clairvaux proclaims: "Eve's curse was transformed in our Virgin, for she bore a child without pain . . . A virgin gave birth and remained inviolate after the birth; she possessed the fecundity of offspring with the integrity of her flesh."[100]

For Aquinas, then, the doctrine of the virgin birth communicates the truth about what God accomplished in the childbearing of the new Eve: a woman has given birth without damage to her bodily integrity, because her Son is the incarnate Lord, the new Adam, who inaugurates the new creation, freed from all suffering and corruption. This emphasis on the eschatological new creation is found also in Barth and Balthasar, though in different ways (with Barth rejecting the Catholic doctrine). As professed by the Second Vatican Council's Dogmatic Constitution on the Church, *Lumen Gentium*, "the birth of Our Lord . . . did not diminish his mother's virginal integrity but sanctified it."[101]

---

99. See Graebe, *Vessel of Honor*, 33–42. See also Nichols, *Deep Mysteries*, 57, referencing "the teaching of the Lateran Synod, which preceded the Sixth Ecumenical Council."

100. Bernard of Clairvaux, "Sermon for the Sunday within the Octave of the Assumption," 206–7. For discussion of the scope of Bernard's Mariology, see Gambero, *Mary in the Middle Ages*, 131–41; Graef, *History of Doctrine and Devotion*, 184–89.

101. Vatican Council II, *Lumen Gentium* §57, 416. The *Catechism of the Catholic Church* makes the same point, quoting *Lumen Gentium* (and citing numerous earlier magisterial teachings): "The deepening of faith in the virginal motherhood led the Church to confess Mary's real and perpetual virginity even in the act of giving birth to the Son of God made man. In fact, Christ's birth 'did not diminish his mother's virginal integrity but sanctified it'" (*Catechism of the Catholic Church*, §499). Weinandy argues that it would be more fitting for the new Eve to suffer physical pain in childbirth. The reversal of Adam and Eve's sin and its curses is accomplished by Christ through entering into suffering and death and reversing the curse from within. Likewise, it seems appropriate that Mary should have entered into pain in childbirth so as to reverse the curse (given to Eve) from within. Weinandy explains, "As Christ, in becoming human, assumed the penalty of Adam's sin and so, on the cross, transformed it into an act of loving salvation, so Mary assumed the curse of Eve, giving birth in pain, and so transformed it into a loving act of giving birth to the one who would free humankind from all pain and suffering" (Weinandy, "Annunciation and Nativity," 229). For Weinandy, Mary could have experienced this pain in childbirth even while miraculously preserving her bodily integrity, although he does not rule out the possibility that Jesus' birth damaged her bodily integrity (depending upon what is required by the Church's magisterial tradition, which Weinandy does not here resolve). Although it was fitting that Mary enter into the suffering and death endured by Christ on the cross, I think the virgin birth was a sign of the inauguration of the new creation and therefore did not involve pain; here I agree with see Nichols, *There Is No Rose*, 19, and especially

Aquinas is well aware of the objections raised against Mary's perpetual virginity, objections first expressed by Helvidius in the fourth century.[102] Aquinas's discussion of these issues relies upon Augustine's reading of Scripture, specifically Ezekiel 44:2 where the prophet receives the following command in his vision of the eschatological temple: "This gate shall remain shut; it shall not be opened, and no one shall enter by it; for the Lord, the God of Israel, has entered by it; therefore it shall remain shut." In Aquinas's view, Augustine's mariological interpretation of this verse deserves to be accepted, given the verse's reference to the eschatological age that Christ inaugurates. But Aquinas also gives reasons of fittingness for Mary's perpetual virginity, including Joseph's knowledge that the conception of Jesus had been accomplished by the Holy Spirit—which would have made Mary's womb a sacred temple in Joseph's eyes—and also the fact that Mary, having given birth to the perfect Son, would have devoted all her attention to that Son rather than striving for more children.[103]

Pitre, *Jesus and the Jewish Roots of Mary*, 134–58, whose analysis of Isaiah 66:7–8 in relation to Revelation 12:1–6 is instructive (and consistent with the church fathers and Aquinas). Among recent notable Catholic theologians who suggest that the birth of Jesus damaged Mary's bodily integrity, Weinandy names Karl Rahner, Otto Semmelroth, and Jean Galot—and to this list can be added Walter Kasper and Gerhard Müller (in his *Was heißt*, 100–104). On the issue of whether Mary's perpetual virginity has been solemnly taught by the Catholic Church and thus is "de fide," see also Fastiggi, "Fr. Peter Damian Fehlner on Divine Maternity," 83–84, where Fastiggi revises the position he took in his "Francisco Suárez, S.J. (1548–1617) on Mary's *Virginitas in Partu* and Subsequent Doctrinal Development." For the main lines of the twentieth-century debate, see Bastero, *"Virginitas in Partu* en la Reflexión Teológica del Siglo XX"; Graebe, *Vessel of Honor*, 55–111; Hauke, *Introduction to Mariology*, 190–92. For Karl Rahner's influential article, see his *"Virginitas in Partu."*

102. For discussion, see Torrell, *Jésus le Christ chez Thomas d'Aquin*, 497–98.

103. These reasons of fittingness have been reiterated and insightfully developed in a recent essay by John C. Cavadini, drawing upon Origen and Augustine. See Cavadini, "Sex Life of Mary and Joseph." See also John Behr's chapter on the Church as Virgin Mother and on Mary as a "symbol" of the Church in his *Mystery of Christ*. For Behr, to ask questions about the historicity of the infancy narratives is beside the point, because "the Mary that we are presented with in the infancy narratives ... and at the Feast of Annunciation is already described in terms of the gospel of the crucified and risen Lord: the infancy narratives of Matthew and Luke are already told as a proclamation of the gospel (in the full sense), and Mary is presented here in the fullness of the theological vision made possible by the Passion ... As Mary is known to have given birth to the Word of God only from the perspective of the Passion and exaltation of Christ, when seen and understood through the matrix of scripture, her conception and birth of Christ is already presented in these terms—to the tomb corresponds the womb" (*Mystery of Christ*, 136). To my mind, while Behr is correct in part, the question of historicity cannot be avoided. For the extension of Behr's perspective to the figure of Jesus, see Behr, *John the Theologian*, 326: "it is not through the historical reconstruction of the life of Jesus, on the basis of New Testament texts, that we encounter the Word of

In the first article of question 30, Aquinas highlights the spiritual or personal dignity of Mary at the Annunciation. She is no mere channel for the incarnate Lord; God does not simply make use of her womb. It is fitting that "she should be informed in mind concerning Him, before conceiving Him in the flesh."[104] Aquinas quotes Augustine, who points out (in accord with Jesus' teaching in Mark 3:35) that it is more blessed to conceive Christ in one's heart—to have faith—than to conceive Christ in one's womb. If Mary were simply a conduit in conceiving and gestating Jesus, then her role in this extraordinary event would be a merely physical one, less than fully personal.[105]

Aquinas therefore insists that Mary's virginal conception of Jesus involved the fullness of her graced intellect and will. She receives the angel's communication about the plan of salvation; she enquires into this plan, asking how it could be since she is a virgin; and she consents with great faith and complete freedom of will. She thereby becomes a real "witness of this mystery," offering to God the full obedience of faith in welcoming, by the power of the Spirit, the incarnate Son of the Father.[106] Indeed, Mary's consent is the greatest act that a mere human being (as distinct from the God-man) ever accomplished. She is so personally, intelligently, and spiritually engaged in her act of faithful obedience that we can rightly say of the Annunciation: "the Virgin's consent was besought in lieu of that of the entire human nature."[107] Her "yes" is a profound profession of faith: "I

God, but through the unveiled Scriptures (the Old Testament), and their distillation in the scripturally mediated writings of the Gospels." I disagree simply with the either/or.

104. Aquinas, *Summa theologiae* III, q. 30, a. 1.

105. Peeler comments, "Mark's scant reference to her, which holds a particular weight as the earliest gospel tradition, positions motherhood, even her motherhood, in relation to Jesus as an act of faith over and above an act of biology (Mark 3:31–35, where Jesus concludes, 'Whoever does the will of God is my brother and sister and mother') . . . Hence, this exchange, which some have read as evidence of her limited faith in her son, is instead included so that she might not be limited to the act of bearing her son" (Peeler, *Women and the Gender of God*, 150).

106. Aquinas, *Summa theologiae* III, q. 30, a. 1.

107. Aquinas, *Summa theologiae* III, q. 30, a. 1. See also Pope Leo XIII, *Octobre Mense*, §4: "The Eternal Son of God, about to take upon Him our nature for the saving and ennobling of man, and about to consummate thus a mystical union between Himself and all mankind, did not accomplish His design without adding there the free consent of the elect Mother, who represented in some sort all human kind, according to the illustrious and just opinion of St. Thomas, who says that the Annunciation was effected with the consent of the Virgin standing in the place of humanity"; as well as Leo XIII's *Fidentem Piumque*, §3. The Anglican theologian Edward Bouverie Pusey registers a concern with the way in which some devotional Catholic books "have delighted to dwell on the Incarnation, as though our redemption depended upon the 'fiat' of Mary. For, although God,—in conformity with that His wondrous condescension, whereby He reverences (if I may so speak) the free will with which He has endowed

am the handmaid of the Lord; let it be to me according to your word" (Luke 1:28, 38). In light of Luke 1:38, Aquinas concludes that the marriage of God and humanity takes place in the incarnation—a marriage not lacking the free consent of humanity. Mary's active spiritual role ensures that in the incarnation, "there is a certain spiritual wedlock between the Son of God and human nature."[108]

This emphasis on Mary's spiritual role in the incarnation—her faith and love—is echoed by more recent theologians, including Balthasar and Bouyer. Pope John Paul II teaches in his encyclical *Redemptoris Mater*: "Mary's faith can also be *compared to that of Abraham* . . . In the salvific economy of God's revelation, Abraham's faith constitutes the beginning of the Old Covenant; Mary's faith at the Annunciation inaugurates the New Covenant."[109] In *Daughter Zion*, Joseph Ratzinger goes further in this direction. He states that "the image of Mary in the New Testament is woven entirely of Old Testament threads."[110] In his view, Mary's participation in

---

us, and will not force our will—would not accomplish the Incarnation without the free will of His creature, yet, of course, there was nothing really in suspense. Had He indeed, amid the manifold failures which He has allowed in His work of grace, willed to allow this scope also to free-will, that it should reject the privilege of being Theotokos, and so have offered it to one who would not accept it, the Incarnation might have been delayed for a while; it could not have failed. But He did not so will" (Pusey, *First Letter to the Very Rev. J. H. Newman*, 23). Aquinas affirms that Mary was predestined in the order of grace, but in Aquinas's view this fact should not hinder in any way our praise for Mary's fiat, just as the fact that Jesus was predestined does not hinder our praise for Jesus' willingness to endure the cross. For testimony from Orthodox, Catholic, and Protestant theologians and biblical scholars to the praiseworthiness of Mary's free consent, see Peeler, *Women and the Gender of God*, 84–86.

108. Aquinas, *Summa theologiae* III, q. 30, a. 1. See also Torrell, *Jésus le Christ chez Thomas d'Aquin*, 505–6. Torrell observes that for Aquinas's medieval predecessors, notably Albert the Great and Bonaventure, "Mary is little more than the place where this union is accomplished ('the nuptial chamber'); this is perhaps the reason why the scholastics could envisage, at least in the abstract, that the incarnation could have been accomplished without the knowledge of Mary" (Torrell, *Jésus le Christ chez Thomas d'Aquin*, 506).

109. John Paul II, *Redemptoris Mater* §14, 69. For Mary's faith in relation to Abraham's, see also the excellent discussion in Reardon, *Reclaiming the Atonement*, 171–73. Louis Bouyer comments further, "It is to her [Mary] that the supreme announcement of the Word is to be made; in her is to take effect the divine initiative that will bring into being the new creation. Her faith will utter that 'fiat' necessary to a creation which is not a creation from nothing, but from human freedom under sentence of death and in need of new life. The Church has always, in reflecting on St Luke's narrative, been convinced that Mary's faith was the supreme fulfilment of all the Old Testament holiness, a holiness of preparation, aspiration, acceptance and consent to the divine plan in a growing detachment from self" (Bouyer, *Seat of Wisdom*, 119).

110. Ratzinger, *Daughter Zion*, 12.

the event of the incarnation is the participation of representative Israel. Ratzinger's perspective is particularly significant for my purposes because, like Aquinas, he suggests that by attending to Mary we ensure that Christology does not fall into Nestorianism, which "surgically removes God so far from man that nativity and maternity—all of corporeality—remain in a different sphere."[111]

Similarly, the Catholic theologian Aaron Riches has explored the anti-Nestorian significance of Marian doctrine. He examines how Aquinas pushed back against some Nestorian elements widely present in medieval Christology.[112] Aquinas is indebted to the Third Council of Constantinople, which focused on the divine and human wills of Christ. He takes up John of Damascus's understanding of Christ's human nature and human will as a rational "instrument" through which the person of the Son works.[113] In Riches's words, "the Son is the subject of this human nature, the one who directly constitutes the reality of this nature and its action insofar as it is 'one' with him, apart from whom it neither acts nor exists."[114] Thus, Aquinas carries forward what can be termed the Cyrillian and anti-Nestorian perspective. Aquinas advanced a "Cyrillian doctrine of Christ's single divine *esse*" and "a rich theology of theandric synergy."[115]

I will close this section by describing the way that Riches integrates Mary into his account of Aquinas's Cyrillian Christology. Riches proposes that the doctrine of Mary as Theotokos in her virginal motherhood is "the

---

111. Ratzinger, *Daughter Zion*, 35.

112. Nestorian tendencies affect the Christologies of Peter Lombard, Hugh of St. Victor, and Anselm of Laon as well as other significant figures such as Gilbert de la Porrée, Peter Abelard, and William of Champeaux.

113. See John of Damascus, *On the Orthodox Faith*.

114. Riches, *Ecce Homo*, 183. See also Reichmann, "Aquinas, Scotus and the Christological Mystery."

115. Riches, *Ecce Homo*, 16. By contrast, see McCormack, *Humility of the Eternal Son*, 64: "The truth is that the Chalcedonian Definition *as it stands* can never succeed in producing the single-subject Christology for which it strove with might and main. It can never succeed because a *real* relation of Jesus to the 'person of the union' can never be allowed so long as one remains committed to the idea of impassibility. But in the absence of this real relation, the unity of the 'person' would always remain in doubt and the tendency to regard Jesus on occasion as an independent subject (and, indeed, a hypostasis) in his own right would prove inescapable. One might rightly say: there lurks in the heart of every Cyrilline theologian a 'Nestorius' (or, at least, a 'Theodoret'!) just waiting for an opportunity to emerge." McCormack references, but criticizes, Brian E. Daley, SJ's claim that Cyril was a theologian primarily driven by Scripture who succeeded in defending the unity of Christ: see Daley, "'One Thing and Another'"; and see also Daley, *God Visible*. For a Thomistic defense of the Son's impassibility, see Steven J. Duby, *Jesus and the God of Classical Theism*.

essential constituent of a properly non-dualist Christology," with the result that "the Jesus-Mary relation is so integral to the incarnational fact, and therefore to a coherent Christocentrism, that a Christology without a full Marian account fails to be incarnational in any meaningful way and is reduced to mere abstraction."[116] Contemplating the mystery of the virgin birth is intrinsic to Christology, because the virginal conception of Jesus is not merely something strange that happened to him. The fact that he is a single subject (the divine Son of the Father) is at the center of God's eschatological inbreaking, and it is also the very center of Mary's Godbearing.

Jesus' humanity, Riches emphasizes, is that of a member of the people of Israel. Therefore, it matters that his virgin mother is the fulfillment of Daughter Zion. Contemplation of Mary—her obedience and faith, her place in the eschatological fulfillment that God is placing in motion—is important for understanding who Jesus is as the incarnate Son. Riches states, "Only *ex Maria* can we develop an account of the significance of the particularity of *this* Jewish flesh, *this* birth in time and place, *this* Davidic ancestry out of which *this* 'one' is born the Messiah of Israel."[117] Scholars who barely mention Mary can still say a great deal about Jesus the Messiah

---

116. Riches, Ecce Homo, 17.

117. Riches, Ecce Homo, 226. For discussion of Mary's ancestry—including whether Jesus was of Davidic descent through Mary and not only through his adoptive father Joseph—see Cover, "Historically, Was Jesus's Mother from a Priestly Family?." From what can be surmised via historical reconstruction, Cover argues that Mary did not descend from David. For one thing, in Luke 1:26, Mary is called the kinswoman of Elizabeth, who is of Levitical descent (see Luke 1:5). For another thing, Mary is never identified as a daughter of David. Cover also notes that Matthew 1's genealogy fails "to prove the very thing it set out to demonstrate: that Jesus was the son of David by patrilineal descent"—although Matthew 1 makes clear that "Jesus was legally Joseph's (and therefore David's) son" ("Historically, Was Jesus's Mother from a Priestly Family?," 135). As to whether Mary was in fact of Levitical (priestly) descent, Cover concludes that historically the answer must remain unclear, with some evidence in favor and some against. See also the remark of H. Daniel Zacharias that Matthew's "genealogy is dynastic rather than biological" (Zacharias, *Matthew's Presentation of the Son of David*, 38). Without rejecting the genealogy's historicity, Zacharias holds that "Matthew did not intend to relate an exhaustive family tree in his genealogy, but rather to trace both Jesus' descent from the father of the Israelite nation, and more importantly his royal descent from David" (38). Lastly, see the valuable insight of Meyer, *Jesus the Jew in Christian Memory*, 127: "Two-Natures Christology was historically meant to reinforce and ensure Jesus' humanity. His humanity refers back to geography, culture, and the history of his life, today called 'context.' The Jewishness of his context shines through New Testament texts and is manifest in latent memories of the Church . . . But it is also this most human Jewishness that maintains the reference to the God of Jesus, the God of the Bible. In this sense, the historical Jewishness of Jesus, primarily informing Christological discourse, is highly relevant for the core of theology, the question of God par excellence. 'Truly divine' means union with the God of the Jews."

and Davidic king who fulfills the covenants of God with Israel; but understanding Jesus in full requires reflection upon Mary. As Riches says, Mary plays "an integral role . . . both in the incarnational event of her Son and the event of mystical union of those being joined to him in his mystical body."[118]

V. The Fittingness of the Incarnation in Mary's Womb

The first two articles of question 1 of the *tertia pars* treat the fittingness of the incarnation and whether the incarnation was necessary for the restoration of the human race. Thus far in this chapter, I have tried to provide biblical, contemporary (Protestant and Catholic), patristic, and medieval reasons for giving the virgin birth (and thus the virginal conception) a central place in Christology. In this final section, I will briefly expand upon the first two articles of question 1 of the *tertia pars* in order to further display how the Christian understanding of the incarnation benefits from placing Mary's virginal motherhood in the foreground.

Article 1 asks whether it was fitting that God become incarnate. At the core of Aquinas's answer is the principle, drawn from Romans 1:20, that it is highly fitting that "by visible things the invisible things of God should be made known" and that, indeed, the whole universe was created precisely in order for this revelation to take place.[119] The invisible things of God include such realities as the goodness, wisdom, justice, and power of God. All these things, Aquinas notes (indebted to John of Damascus), are sublimely made known by the incarnation.

I would add that these things are *also* made known by the miracle of Mary's virginal motherhood. In his goodness, God bestows upon Mary a blessing that no human resources could have bestowed; and this blessing—to be mother of the Messiah and mother of God—goes beyond any gift ever given to any other mere human being. In his wisdom, God establishes Mary as the eschatological fulfillment of Daughter Zion, the virginal bride who responds to God with supreme faith and who thereby bears the fruit of restoration and redemption. In his justice, God rewards the graced humility of Mary by enabling her to bear the Messiah.[120] In his power, God works a

---

118. Riches, *Ecce Homo*, 230.

119. Aquinas, *Summa theologiae* III, q. 1, a. 1, *sed contra*. For further discussion, see my "Variations on a Theme by Paul."

120. See the clarification offered by Nichols, *There Is No Rose*, 39: "Thomas asks [in his *Commentary on the Sentences*] . . . whether Mary might be said to have merited the incarnation—to have been, so to say, its moral cause. Is this perhaps an implication of

miracle in Mary's womb and reveals that the son of Mary is none other than the divine Son. The conception of this Son in Mary's womb by the Holy Spirit is mirrored by the conception of many sons and daughters in the womb of the Church.

Aquinas does not draw these links here, and so I am extending his thought. In article 1, Aquinas argues that because God is infinite goodness, it is fitting (though not necessary in a strict sense) for God to share his goodness by becoming incarnate.[121] Drawing upon Pseudo-Dionysius's *The Divine Names*, Aquinas observes, "It belongs to the essence of goodness to communicate itself to others... Hence it belongs to the essence of the highest good to communicate itself in the highest manner to the creature."[122] There can be no higher self-communication of God to the creature than becoming incarnate. The incarnation not only stands as the supreme sharing of the divine life with creation, but also the incarnation is the path by which God redeems and deifies fallen creatures. Given God's goodness, the miracle of the union of the divine and human natures in the person of the Son is supremely fitting.

This chain of reasoning should include the woman in whose womb the incarnation took place. Other than the incarnation itself—the union of the divine and human natures in the person of the Son—there is no greater gift in the orders of creation and grace than to be the mother of God. Mary's motherhood is not solely physical, but rather is a body-soul reality grounded in the fact that Mary is "full of grace" (Luke 1:28) and is therefore able to proclaim with all her heart and mind, "Behold, I am the handmaid of the Lord; let it be to me according to your word" (Luke 1:38).[123] Aidan Nichols

---

the Lukan angel's description of her as 'full of grace'? Thomas's answer to his own question is negative, and yet he adds an important qualification to that negation. Once the incarnation was divinely decreed, Mary merited that it should take place specifically in her and in no other woman—deserving as much by the merit or accolade of fittingness, of *convenientia*." Of course, this meriting was entirely the fruit of grace. For a similar point, arguing that the doctrine of Mary's Immaculate Conception serves to protect the Reformers' principle *sola gratia*, see Oakes, *Theology of Grace in Six Controversies*, 225–46.

121. For background, especially in the theology of Robert Grosseteste, see Hunter, *If Adam Had Not Sinned*.

122. Aquinas, *Summa theologiae* III, q. 1, a. 1.

123. For feminist concerns, see Peeler, *Women and the Gender of God*, 77–78: "She [Mary] refers to herself as the δούλη (*doulē*), a female slave, of the Lord. Such self-naming might only be evidence of a woefully commonplace example of female acquiescence to oppression. Several dynamics of the relationship between Mary and the Lord complicate and eventually rule out that conclusion, however... [T]o be a slave of the Most High God is to claim a position of unparalleled importance. Such a statement is congruent with the system of reversal about which Mary will soon sing: in the economy

describes Mary's role in terms that many Catholic theologians, including Aquinas, have adopted before him: "For . . . Thomas, although the hypostasis of the Son has no inherent relation to the Virgin according to the Son's eternal generation from the Father, that hypostasis *does* have an inherent relation to her person through the assumption of the human nature that originates from her."[124] Mary herself, through grace, is uniquely caught up in the self-diffusive goodness manifested in the hypostatic union.

With regard to the second article, on the restoration of the human race, a similar argument can be unfolded. The cornerstone of Aquinas's *respondeo* in this article is John 3:16, "For God so loved the world that he gave his only-begotten Son, that whoever believes in him should not perish but have eternal life."[125] Aquinas recognizes that God could have accomplished the restoration of the human race in many other ways, but God chose this way—the (redemptive) incarnation—because it was supremely fitting. Aquinas provides two sets of reasons of fittingness with respect to the incarnation. The first set has to do with "furtherance in good," the

---

of this Lord, to be low is to be raised high (Luke 1:48). To be a servant of this Lord, then, is to grant one access to the sovereign of all creation . . . She has gained access to the court, and an unrivalled proximate access at that." In fact, the entire New Testament describes Christ's followers as God's servants or slaves, as Peeler shows through an extensive review on p. 79; and Christ himself became a "servant" (Phil 2:7; cf. Mark 10:45; Luke 22:27; John 13). See also, for the way in which medieval women committed to serving God found strength in Mary, Newman's *From Virile Women to Woman Christ*.

124. Nichols, *There Is No Rose*, 41. Nichols shows that in his *Commentary on the Sentences*, Aquinas adopts a less helpful presentation of Mary's role. In this early writing, Aquinas is a bit less fully "Cyrillian" and more inclined (unconsciously) toward Nestorius. Nichols explains, "The *Writing on the Sentences*, coming as it does from Thomas's first period as master in Paris, antedates . . . his full exposure to the Greek Fathers, and above all to Cyril and the Acts of Ephesus and Chalcedon. As a consequence, the Marian content he gives his theology of the incarnation in the *Scriptum* does not start with an account of the hypostatic union between the divine Son and humanity in Mary's womb, which is where in the *Summa theologiae*, after discussing the fittingness of the incarnation, he will begin. In the *Writing on the Sentences*, Thomas will end with the hypostatic union, but he will not begin from there. Where he starts is with Mary herself and what she furnished for the incarnation . . . [T]he scheme he presents in the *Writing* has been criticized. It sits somewhat uneasily, it has been said, with the key dogmatic assertion [i.e. the hypostatic union] to which it is juxtaposed. Its logic runs: Mary's generation of the humanity of Jesus leads to the divine assumption of that humanity which in turn leads to union with the person of the Word. In the mystery of the divine motherhood, the Word thus assumes from Mary the humanity of Jesus according to what might be called a 'genetic order' where parts come, at any rate logically, if not chronologically, before the whole. Consequently, Mary, a biological provider, seems in her own person extrinsic to the order of the hypostatic union properly so-called" (37–38, 40).

125. Quoted in Aquinas, *Summa theologiae* III, q. 1, a. 2, *sed contra*.

second set with "withdrawal from evil." In the first set, the first reason is that the incarnation founded true faith by revealing Truth in person; the second reason is that the incarnation strengthened hope by giving us the divine Son as our partner in the flesh; the third reason is that the incarnation inflamed charity by demonstrating God's love for us; the fourth reason is that the incarnate Lord reveals the path of a virtuous life that leads to eternal life; and the fifth reason is that the incarnation makes possible our sharing in Christ's humanity so as to share in his divinity.

Meditation on Mary's virginal motherhood concretizes these aspects of the incarnation still further. The incarnation grounds faith; Mary exemplifies the perfection of faith in Luke 1:38 and elsewhere. The incarnation strengthens hope; Mary's Magnificat (Luke 1:46-55) is an extraordinary profession of hope.[126] The incarnation fuels charity; Mary's charity-filled heart "magnifies the Lord" and "rejoices in God my Savior" (Luke 1:46-47). The incarnation sets an example of the path of a truly virtuous life; Mary follows that path, in accordance with what Simeon tells her at the temple: "Behold, this child is set for the fall and rising of many in Israel, and for a sign that is spoken against (and a sword will pierce through your own soul also)" (Luke 2:34-35). Lastly, the incarnation reveals that our vocation is to participate in the divine life through Jesus Christ. Mary's participation in Christ's life, from the moment of the incarnation through his cross, is intense and unique in its character.

It may seem that in all five of these ways, I am speaking simply of Mary's motherhood, with the virginal dimension being peripheral and unnecessary. But in fact, the faith, hope, charity configuration to Christ's manner of life, and openness to the gift of divine life that comes through Christ are all, in Mary, enhanced by the fact that everything comes to her utterly as God's gift, and that as a virgin mother Mary is fully free to devote herself entirely to this gift. As not merely a mother through intercourse with

---

126. For background, drawing the connection to Hannah's song of praise in 1 Samuel 2:1-10, see Hays, *Echoes of Scripture in the Gospels*, 197-98: "the reader who knows 1 Samuel will hear Mary singing a harmonious descant to Hannah's song of praise. Both of these hymns expand their praises beyond the immediate occasion of childbirth to celebrate God's vindication of the people as a whole, symbolized in 1 Samuel 2:10 by images of the shattering of God's adversaries and the exaltation of God's anointed king . . . It is not merely coincidental that the language of Hannah's song reappears in Psalm 113, the first of the cycle of Hallel psalms sung before the Passover meal in Jewish tradition; the Passover celebrates God's powerful intervention to 'raise the poor from the dust and lift the needy from the ash heap' (1 Sam 2:8; Ps 113:7) by bringing Israel out of Egypt. If the hearers of Luke's Gospel understood this link between Hannah's hymn of deliverance and the Passover, they might well have understood that Mary's song, too, should be heard in this same tradition, as a song celebrating the impending deliverance of Israel, this time through Mary's own offspring."

Joseph but rather a mother because of the power of the Holy Spirit, Mary can *literally* attribute everything to God: "For behold, henceforth all generations will call me blessed; for he who is mighty has done great things for me, and holy is his name" (Luke 1:48–49). Mary's virginal fruitfulness—at the conception and birth of her son, and throughout her life—stands as a type of the Church's faith, hope, love configuration to Christ's manner of life, and preparation for the blessedness of life in God.

With respect to the incarnation's supreme fittingness for our "withdrawal from evil," Aquinas provides the following five reasons. First, the incarnation shows that God does not prefer the angels over man, which is important given the fallen human propensity to honor Satan and to wish to be bodiless spirits. Second, the incarnation shows the great dignity that humanity has in God's eyes. Third, it destroys human pride because the gift of the incarnation is entirely unmerited. Fourth, it exhibits the wondrous humility of God, and thereby undermines pride. Fifth, the incarnate Lord establishes justice by bearing the penalty of all sin.

Again, I think these points can be extended by reflection on the incarnation in light of Mary's virginal motherhood. Given that the incarnation shows that God does not prefer angels over man, the concreteness of the incarnation in Mary's womb amplifies this point. The incarnation shows the great dignity of humans, and Mary echoes this when she proclaims "henceforth all generations will call me blessed" (Luke 1:48; cf. 1:54). The incarnation destroys human pride because it is unmerited, and the corresponding gift that the Virgin Mary receives is entirely grace, entirely God's work. The incarnation shows God's amazing humility, and this humility is only amplified by the realization that the incarnate Son is conceived and born in and through Mary. The incarnation leads to the establishment of justice and righteousness, and Mary's response to the annunciation—her faith and obedience—signals just such an eschatological new ordering, as does her proclamation in her Magnificat (anticipating the restoration of Israel) that God "has scattered the proud in the imagination of their hearts, he has put down the mighty from their thrones, and exalted those of low degree; he has filled the hungry with good things, and the rich he has sent empty away. He has helped his servant Israel, in remembrance of his mercy, as he spoke to our fathers, to Abraham and to his posterity for ever" (Luke 1:51–55).

Recall that in discussing the conception of Jesus, Aquinas states, "That the Son of God took to Himself flesh from the Virgin's womb was due to the exceeding love of God: where it is said (John iii. 16): *God so loved the world as to give His only-begotten Son.*"[127] This verse from John's Gospel connects

---

127. Aquinas, *Summa theologiae* III, q. 32, a. 1.

Aquinas's reflections on the virginal conception with his reflections on the fittingness of the incarnation. Aquinas holds that the virginal conception is proclaimed to be the work of the Holy Spirit because the Spirit is properly Love and Gift, and the virginal conception of the Son is the sheer gift of God. Moreover, Aquinas adds, "the term of the Incarnation was that that man, who was being conceived, should be the Holy One and the Son of God. Now both of these are attributed to the Holy Ghost.... Just as other men are sanctified spiritually by the Holy Ghost, so as to be the adopted sons of God, so was Christ conceived in sanctity by the Holy Ghost, so as to be the natural Son of God."[128] The fact that the conception was virginal, therefore, has christological significance and, correspondingly, ecclesiological significance as well. The Virgin Mary's role illuminates the truth about her Son.

VI. Conclusion

As we saw, it is possible to argue that the virgin birth does *not* have significance for Christology and therefore can today be discarded, given the possibility that the evangelists invented it as part of their theological portraiture of Jesus. In response, I have argued in this chapter first that historical-critical exegesis does not in fact require us to renounce the virgin birth, as Amy Peeler shows (with some aid from Ratzinger and others). Second, I emphasized that Mary's virginal motherhood has a crucial place in manifesting the new creation begun by the incarnation.

Drawing upon Barth and Balthasar, I noted that Mary's virginal motherhood accentuates the following aspects of the incarnation: God's sovereignty; Jesus' status as the unique Son of the Father; Jesus' inauguration of the new creation or the eschatological age through the power of the Holy Spirit; the fulfillment of the covenantal figure of Daughter Zion; Jesus' status as "the first-born among many brethren" (Rom 8:29); and Mary as the type of the Church, joined to Jesus in faith and holy obedience by the grace of the Spirit. As the Protestant theologian Zoltán Dörnyei says—appreciating the eschatological new creation without explicitly recognizing Mary as the type of the Church—"the infusion of the Spirit [e.g., Rom 8:9–11; 1 Cor 2:4; 1 Thess 1:5] suggests a powerful reality in the believers' lives, and it is highly noteworthy that this infusion of the divine into the corporeal parallels the process underlying the Incarnation whereby the corporeal pregnancy of Mary was the work of the Holy Spirit."[129]

---

128. Aquinas, *Summa theologiae* III, q. 32, a. 1.
129. Dörnyei, *Progressive Creation and the Struggles of Humanity in the Bible*, 135.

The second half of this chapter explored these themes through the anti-Nestorian Christology of Cyril and Aquinas. I briefly treated Aquinas's Mariology, as found within his Christology in the *tertia pars*. I also directed attention to his Cyrillian theology of the incarnation, drawing upon Aaron Riches's insistence that Christology should be deeply attentive to the Theotokos. The links between the theology of the incarnation and the Theotokos stand out in reflecting upon Aquinas's reasons for the fittingness of the incarnation.

Let me add here one final note, drawn from question 35 of the *tertia pars*. Discussing Christ's nativity, Aquinas applies what he has said earlier about the incarnation: because the union of the two natures takes place in the person of the Son, "whatever belongs to the divine and to the human nature can be attributed to that Person."[130] The mother of Christ is therefore the mother of God. Aquinas also examines whether Christ should have been born in Bethlehem and whether Christ's birth took place at a fitting time.[131] It was appropriate, he argues, that the Messiah or Davidic King be born in Bethlehem, and it was fitting that the truly glorious Davidic King be born into the world of seemingly glorious Caesar Augustus. All these things remind us that through Mary's miraculous conception and birth of her Son, the world was radically changed: an entire new reality—eschatological in scope and power—came to be.

Thus, it makes sense that in this context Aquinas makes much of the eschatological prophecy found in Micah 5:2, "But you, O Bethlehem

---

Dörnyei continues aptly, "the release of the Spirit to believers 'in Jesus' name' (John 14:26) can be seen as the expansion of the new creation process that was set into motion by the Incarnation" (135).

130. Aquinas, *Summa theologiae* III, q. 35, a. 4.

131. For historical-critical arguments that Jesus was indeed born at Bethlehem, but that Matthew and Luke were both embarrassed by this fact and had to invent explanations for it (since the Messiah was not expected to be born in Bethlehem), see Croy, *Escaping Shame*. In Croy's view, "Luke, like Matthew, was wrestling with a stubborn historical tradition of a birth in Bethlehem. Luke knew that the career of Jesus was rooted in Galilee, so he had to explain how the child of a Galilean couple could be born in Bethlehem of Judea. Luke knew that at some point in the past Augustus had initiated an aggressive plan to organize the empire through a series of provincial censuses, one of which was carried out in Judea. But the chronology of this census, the connection with Quirinius, and the mandate to return to one's ancestral home are impossible obstacles [to historicity] . . . Luke erred in his report of the census, and therefore some other reason must account for Mary and Joseph's presence in Bethlehem when Jesus was born" (162). Croy argues that the real reason Mary and Joseph were in Bethlehem was "the potential for social opprobrium connected with an *apparently* illegitimate birth" (162). Croy believes that Jesus was, in fact, virginally conceived—and that Mary did indeed receive some social opprobrium. With regard to the theological significance of this opprobrium, he directs attention to Stauffer, "Jeschu ben Mirjam."

Ephrathah, who are little to be among the clans of Judah, from you shall come forth for me one who is to be ruler in Israel, whose origin is from of old, from ancient days."[132] This chapter has argued that the virginal conception and birth of the Spirit-filled incarnate Son opens up this new mode of rule, through a Davidic King who is the son of Mary of Nazareth and who is the Son of God. In part natural, in part miraculous, we find in Mary's childbearing the wondrous sign of the God of Israel's new creation.

---

132. Croy argues that, historically speaking, "the 8th century BCE prophet was probably not speaking of the Messiah, certainly not a Messiah akin to the eschatological figure that developed in subsequent centuries . . . Mic 5:2 was not necessarily speaking about the literal birth of a ruler at all. 'Coming forth from Bethlehem' was a figurative way of speaking about a Davidic lineage, whether it involved that village as a birthplace or not" (Croy, *Escaping Shame*, 34). These arguments are not persuasive regarding the ultimate prophetic meaning of Micah 5:2.

Chapter 2

TEACHING

I. INTRODUCTION

My argument in this chapter is that the Spirit-filled Son, inaugurating the new creation or kingdom of God, is "the true light that enlightens every man" and the source of truth for all people (John 1:9, 17). In Matthew's account of the transfiguration, the Father's voice in the Spirit-cloud proclaims, "This is my beloved Son, with whom I am well pleased; listen to him" (Matt 17:5). Jesus delivers powerful teachings to which we should adhere.

Readers of the Gospels will recognize that, as the Jewish New Testament scholar Amy-Jill Levine says in commenting upon Jesus' teaching in the temple, "Jesus is a master teacher."[1] The Protestant biblical scholar Nicholas Perrin puts the matter even more fulsomely but no doubt accurately, focusing on Jesus' rhetorical abilities. He states, "By all accounts, Jesus was a rhetorical genius. Whether teaching the crowds out in the open countryside or instructing his disciples in private, he displayed a rare combination of creativity, flair and profundity that made him an unrivalled communicator."[2]

---

1. Levine, *Entering the Passion of Jesus*, 67. On Jesus as a master teacher whose central message flowed from his "apocalyptic eschatology" proclaiming the imminent arrival of the kingdom of God (marked by the restoration of Israel and all manner of earthly blessings), see Allison, *Constructing Jesus*, 24–25, 32–43; and indeed, see the entirety of 31–220, where Allison provides his account of Jesus' eschatology as an "apocalyptic prophet" (85). In light of Levine's important work, this may be the place also to mention Homolka, *Jewish Jesus Research*.

2. Perrin, *Jesus the Priest*, 91; cf. 288. Perrin devotes focused attention to the parable of the Sower, found in all three Synoptic Gospels. He reads this parable in light of the parables of the mustard seed and of salt, also found in all three Synoptic Gospels.

Not surprisingly, therefore, Jesus' words or message—the content of his teaching—mattered greatly to his hearers and to Jesus himself. As James Dunn remarks, Jesus "placed a tremendous weight of significance on his teaching and expected his disciples to do so too."[3] The first Christians understood Jesus to have delivered an authoritative, indeed divine teaching.[4]

All four Gospels portray Jesus as constantly teaching, whether in front of crowds, in the presence of his disciples privately, or with individuals such as Nicodemus. He teaches in discourses, in parables, and in disputations. He teaches about a wide range of matters, including the character of God, his own Sonship and mission, human destiny, the kingdom of God, judgment and repentance, divine and human mercy and love, human and demonic sin, Israel and its restoration, the temple, the Torah, his cross and resurrection, marriage, wealth, politics, discipleship and mission, the reward his disciples will receive, the meaning of the Last Supper, and so on. The Gospels present him as the eschatological or apocalyptic wisdom teacher focused on teaching about the kingdom of God. By all accounts, he was a man who taught with divine authority, preparing his disciples "to become teachers themselves, teaching others what the Teacher commanded them."[5]

He argues that Jesus' worldview is shaped by Ezekiel 36 and various texts from Isaiah, including Isaiah 27 and 55. For Perrin, Jesus had in mind the coming of the kingdom understood as the eschatological temple and "an eschatologically radiant Zion" (116)—a kingdom of priests, whose mission including suffering to atone for the sins of the people and thereby to assist in ushering in the fullness of the kingdom.

3. Dunn, *Jesus Remembered*, 702.

4. See Loke, *Origin of Divine Christology*, 166.

5. Burridge, *Four Gospels, One Jesus?*, 98. Burridge has the Gospel of Matthew specially in view here. Bruce Chilton remarks along lines that are pertinent here, "there has been a tendency to interpret Jesus' teaching as a set of abstract assertions without precise context. Considered in the abstract, Jesus' sayings can be reduced to a few banalities, the supposed religious truth that remains the same through the ages" (Chilton, *Pure Kingdom*, 102). Chilton holds that Jesus was an apocalyptic sage who sought to bring about the kingdom, constituted by a renewed temple and by the renewed fellowship of all Israel: "His initial intention was that the Temple would conform to his vision of the purity of the kingdom, that all Israel would be invited there, forgiven and forgiving, to offer of their own in divine fellowship in the confidence that what they produced was pure" (126). When this did not work—when his renewal of the temple was rejected—Jesus then taught that his disciples' meal practice would be the center of the kingdom (which is the divine presence), radiating outward in table fellowship rooted in the power of God's presence to demand and create righteousness and purity. See also Chilton's *Feast of Meanings*, where he argues that Jesus ultimately came into fatal conflict with the temple authorities by representing "his communal meals as fitter occasions of God's presence than sacrifice in the Temple" (79). To my mind (if I have understood him correctly), Chilton underestimates Jesus' program, although the elements he highlights have a place.

In the Synoptic Gospels, on which my chapter will focus, Jesus teaches preeminently in his parables and his Sermon on the Mount, the latter of which is found in the Gospel of Matthew but whose elements also appear in the Gospel of Luke (and, to a certain extent, the Gospel of Mark). Introducing the Sermon on the Mount, with its portrait of Jesus as the eschatological new Moses,[6] the evangelist Matthew tells us: "Seeing the crowds, he [Jesus] went up on the mountain, and when he sat down his disciples came to him. And he opened his mouth and taught them" (Matt 5:1–2). As the Protestant biblical scholar Martin Hengel comments, "Here Jesus teaches the disciples and the people from the Mount, as God himself gave the law from Mount Sinai, the new 'Torah of the Messiah', which begins with the beatitudes."[7] Matthew's Gospel presents Jesus as a divine lawgiver who teaches and embodies "eschatological existence in the Spirit."[8] The Catholic theologian Jacques Philippe explains Jesus' teaching in the Sermon on the Mount by interpreting the whole Sermon in light of the beatitudes, with their call to the fullness of blessedness. He concludes, "This New Covenant Jesus promulgates on the mount of the Beatitudes is not just a moral law . . . Even more deeply than a code of conduct, no matter how exalted, it is a path toward the happiness of the Kingdom."[9]

In this chapter, I seek to reclaim Jesus' teaching, set forth scripturally under the Spirit's inspiration, as authoritative divine revelation. I do so in accord with the lesson of the Sermon on the Mount (and specifically Matthew 7:24–27), as succinctly articulated by the Protestant biblical scholar Jonathan Pennington: "the one who listens to Jesus and practices what he teaches is . . . wise."[10] Jesus taught with divine authority as the one who was inaugurating the kingdom of God. Indeed, Jesus is presented as the kingdom of God

---

6. See Allison, *New Moses*.

7. Hengel, *Four Gospels*, 161.

8. Mohrlang, *Matthew and Paul*, 126; see also my *Aquinas's Eschatological Ethics*. The phrase I have quoted from Mohrlang, however, comes in his description of Paul. Mohrlang presents Matthew and Paul in terms of a dialectic between law (Matthew) and grace (Paul), but I find this inadequate.

9. Philippe, *Eight Doors of the Kingdom*, 6. Philippe goes on to say, "On Calvary, Jesus was absolutely poor, afflicted, meek, hungry, and thirsty for justice, merciful, pure of heart, a maker of peace, persecuted for justice. Practicing each of the Beatitudes to perfection, he received in fullness, through his resurrection and glorification, the promised reward, the joy of the Kingdom of Heaven. Greater yet, he received power to admit into his Kingdom any man or woman, even the greatest of sinners" (8). Numerous other commentators—both classical and contemporary—have likewise read the sermon in light of the Beatitudes.

10. Pennington, *Jesus the Great Philosopher*, 67.

in person, and his authority "is the authority of charity."[11] His oral teaching, therefore, demands our closest attention, especially given that for biblical Israel "knowledge of God was the key to life" and that for the New Testament "Jesus explains the Father to us."[12] The Catholic theologian Michael Dauphinais puts the matter simply, along lines that describe Aquinas's perspective and my own: "As presented by Aquinas, Christ is the teacher who willingly communicates his divine learning (*scientia*) to others."[13]

---

11. Mansini, "Authority and Charity of Christ," 139; cf. 143 on how Jesus' authority is verified not ultimately by an external measure but by its "self-authentication" which "leads us to recognize who he is." For a helpfully succinct discussion of the kingdom, see Strauss, *Jesus Behaving Badly*, chapter 11. Strauss notes, "In Jesus' teaching and throughout the New Testament, the arrival of God's kingdom is connected to various events: (1) Jesus' public ministry of teaching and miracles, (2) his sacrificial death on the cross, (3) his resurrection as the beginning of the end-time resurrection, (4) his exaltation to the right hand of God and pouring out of the Spirit, (5) the worldwide proclamation of the gospel, (6) the destruction of the temple and the end of the Old Testament sacrificial system, and (7) the return of the Son of Man to consummate the kingdom. In short, the kingdom arrives through the entire 'Jesus event'—his life, death, resurrection, ascension, and glorious coming to judge and to save" (*Jesus Behaving Badly*, 166–67). Strauss interprets Matthew 10:23, where Jesus tells his disciples that they "will not finish going through the towns of Israel before the Son of Man comes," as a reference to the "destruction of Jerusalem in A.D. 70" (179). Richard B. Hays comments, "hasn't the passage of time disconfirmed the literal apocalyptic hopes of the NT writers? The answer is, simply, no. The NT itself already makes clear that the duration of the present age is uncertain and the date of Christ's return unknowable to mortal kind" (Hays, "Eschatology," 389); and Witherington makes a similar point in *Jesus the Seer*, 289: "However near Jesus may have thought some preliminary eschatological events may have been, and however much he may have believed God's Dominion was already breaking into human history during his ministry, he did not offer up a timetable for the conclusion of the eschatological events, nor did he make specific predictions about the timing of some of the individual things he believed would happen at the end of human history." For further discussion, see my chapter on the Holy Spirit and the kingdom of God in *Engaging the Doctrine of the Holy Spirit*; and see Hays et al., *When the Son of Man Didn't Come*. They note that Jesus is even now already with his followers; and, as for the delay in the consummation of all things, "The conditional and hortatory nature of prophecy explains a great deal of the non-fulfillment of the prophesied kingdom of God," especially with regard to God's forbearance in bringing judgment upon his wayward people (259). Simon Gaine, OP has responded critically and constructively to *When the Son of Man Didn't Come* in his "Veracity of Prophecy and Christ's Knowledge." Gaine argues that one may suppose that Jesus knew of particular conditions or causes that, had they taken place, would have quickly brought about his Parousia, whereas in fact these conditions or causes (e.g., the embrace of Jesus' teaching and preaching by his contemporaries) did not hold.

12. Pennington, *Jesus the Great Philosopher*, 72.

13. Dauphinais, "Divine *Communicatio* as the Formal and Material Principle of Aquinas's *Summa Theologiae*," 187. See also, for an emphasis on Christ's charity (inseparable from his wisdom), John Emery, OP's "Aquinas's Christology of Communication."

My chapter will start with two sections that introduce some contemporary debates about whether Jesus taught anything truly noteworthy. In these sections, I will contrast the perspective of Vatican II's *Dei Verbum* with that of skeptical interpreters of the Gospels, especially Albert Schweitzer, and I will contend that Jesus taught his own divinity, among other things. Since it is not possible to survey all of Jesus' teachings, I will then devote the bulk of the chapter to three of his parables and to short portions of his Sermon on the Mount, focusing upon the relationship between Jesus' eschatological proclamation and his wisdom teaching. In this vein, Perrin has recently remarked that "perhaps *the* central problem of historical Jesus studies" is "the tension between Jesus as sage (speaker of universal truths) and Jesus as apocalyptic prophet (predictor of future cataclysmic events)."[14] Although I believe that Jesus prophesied the destruction of the temple and spoke about the coming tribulation which would be followed by the consummation of the kingdom of God, Jesus' eschatological proclamation also involved wisdom teaching, since he had in view the time of the Church—the time (however long or short) of the inaugurated but not yet consummated kingdom. Understanding his parables and Sermon requires finding a way to integrate his eschatological and sapiential themes.

The three parables that I will explore are the parable of the good Samaritan, the parable of the laborers in the vineyard, and the parable of the prodigal son. Rather than expositing these parables directly, I have chosen to read them through the eyes of Amy-Jill Levine and Gerhard Lohfink, who offer complementary perspectives that will help us to appreciate both

---

14. Perrin, *Jesus the Priest*, 5. In Perrin's view, Jesus' moral teaching, "though eventually lending itself well to being principalized in different directions, was in the first instance intended to apply to the specific conditions occasioned by the tribulation. Issued as a guide for negotiating the current trials in the current eschatological crisis, Jesus' teachings were fundamentally eschatological in nature" (5–6; cf. 222, arguing that Albert Schweitzer's understanding of Jesus' moral teaching as an "interim" ethics for a very short period "was far closer to the truth than most scholars today are willing to admit"). I agree with Perrin that Jesus' hour was the "eschatological crisis" and that the prophesied eschatological tribulation was endured by Jesus in constituting the new temple; but I think Jesus never intended his teaching solely for the specific conditions of his day, except in the sense that his teachings apply wherever the Church is sharing in his sufferings. I note that Perrin offers a welcome emphasis on the Church: "the historical Jesus' conception of absolute surrender had a vertical *and* a horizontal aspect, demanding that self-surrender unto God be expressed through self-surrender unto the community—and vice versa" (6), grounded in what Perrin deems to be Jesus' self-understanding as the new temple: "Poised between two ages, Jesus commended an ethic that was both particular to the hour of tribulation and universally reflective of the unchanging character of God. The 'already' and the 'not yet', Jesus the prophet and Jesus the sage, converge within and easily subsume themselves under the category of Jesus the new temple" (Perrin, *Jesus the Temple*, 189).

the richness and the coherence of Jesus' wisdom teaching and his eschatological proclamation. Second, I will examine the Catholic biblical scholar Frank Matera's interpretation of the beatitudes and of two other portions of the Sermon on the Mount. The final section of the chapter will suggest that Mary, as presented by Luke and John, exemplifies the way in which Christian believers should receive Jesus' teaching.

II. Setting the Stage

At the outset of his Gospel, the evangelist Mark reports that after arriving in Capernaum, "immediately on the sabbath he [Jesus] entered the synagogue and taught. And they were astonished at his teaching, for he taught them as one who had authority, and not as the scribes" (Matt 1:21-22). The Protestant biblical scholar Runar Thorsteinsson observes, "Mark presents Jesus as the wise man par excellence, a master of argumentation and debate."[15] It will

---

15. Thorsteinsson, *Jesus as Philosopher*, 55. Thorsteinsson argues that the evangelists drew upon the example of Greco-Roman philosophers in their portraits of Jesus, but I do not think he makes a strong case, although there is inevitably some overlap between Jesus' words and deeds and those of some philosophers. That overlap, and its importance, is the subject of Jonathan T. Pennington's helpful *Jesus the Great Philosopher*. Pennington argues that Scripture offers an ethics that is "imitative" and "agentic," and therefore is properly understood as a form of virtue ethics, which he defines as focusing "not just on the external issues of right and wrong but on our interior person and our development to be a certain kind of people" (*Jesus the Great Philosopher*, 75). He makes the case that "at the core of the sermon [on the mount] is a virtue-focused ethics. Jesus's critique of the Pharisees is that they lack wholeness or integration (Matt. 5:48), because although they perform good deeds and obey God's laws, they lack something more important—a heart of love that is attuned to God and to others" (75-76). By contrast, Michael C. Legaspi holds, "The Gospels generally steer clear of virtue language found in some Hellenistic Jewish writings. What belongs to the ethical realm, then, is framed not in terms of rational continence or particular states of soul but rather in terms of life lived under divine authority, in the context of the kingdom. In the Sermon on the Mount (Matt 5-7) and the parallel Sermon on the Plain (Luke 6:17-49), Jesus orients the conduct and motivation of the disciples toward the reality of the kingdom" (Legaspi, *Wisdom in Classical and Biblical Tradition*, 220). I agree with Legaspi (as does Pennington) that the Sermon on the Mount orients disciples toward the Kingdom (and obedience to the divine King, Christ), but Pennington is correct that such obedience is not opposed to virtue ethics, which in fact cannot ultimately be sustained without an account of law. See also Wright, *After You Believe*, which—while sometimes disdaining Plato and Aristotle—has chapters not only on the kingdom of God, but also on "Three Virtues, Nine Varieties of Fruit, and One Body" and "Virtue in Action: The Royal Priesthood." I concur fully with Wright's way of putting the matter: "Royal priests [i.e. Christians] are, in short, to work at revealing the glory of God to the world. That is the task of the renewed temple. But if, as in John's gospel, the glory of God is revealed when Jesus of Nazareth goes to the cross as the supreme act of love (John 13.1; 17.1-5), then we should expect that God's glory will be reflected out into

already be clear that Mark's emphasis on the uniquely authoritative mode and content of Jesus' teaching resonates with the other Gospels. Although many of the greatest of Jesus' parables are found only in the Gospel of Luke, in the Gospel of Mark we read, "With many such parables he spoke the word to them, as they were able to hear it; he did not speak to them without a parable, but privately to his own disciples he explained everything" (Mark 4:33–34).[16]

Despite the fact that Jesus devoted much of his ministry to teaching, it seems to some scholars that Jesus taught relatively little that is new. On this view, Jesus was simply an eschatological prophet whose ideas differed only marginally from those of his religiously zealous peers. Michael White remarks in this vein that "Jesus did not come as the founder of a new religion."[17] In White's view, the teachings that eventually caused a breach with Judaism likely came not from Jesus but from his later followers. Even when biblical scholars maintain that Jesus' teaching was distinctive because he considered himself to be the Messiah of Israel who was inaugurating "the apocalyptic end times" and who would soon usher in the kingdom, they often deem this central teaching of the imminent kingdom to be false.[18]

By contrast, the Second Vatican Council's Dogmatic Constitution on Divine Revelation, *Dei Verbum*, considers Christianity to be grounded firmly in the teaching of Jesus. *Dei Verbum* presents Jesus Christ as proclaiming and embodying the fullness of revelation. It affirms that God "sent his Son, the eternal Word who enlightens all men, to dwell among men and to tell them about the inner life of God."[19] *Dei Verbum* closely connects Jesus' words with his deeds. Jesus brought divine revelation to its fullness "by the total fact of his presence and self-manifestation—by words and works, signs and miracles, but above all by his death and glorious resurrection from the dead, and finally by sending the Spirit of truth."[20] I note that Athanasius said something similar in the fourth century. He remarks that Jesus,

---

the world when Jesus's followers learn the habits of mind, heart, and life that imitate the generous love of Jesus and thus bring new order, beauty, and freedom to the world. It is hugely important that we see these habits precisely as *virtues*, not simply as 'principles' to be 'applied' or 'values' to be 'embraced'" (*After You Believe*, 234).

16. Pennington comments, "It has been estimated that at least 35 percent of Jesus's teaching in the Gospels is parabolic in form. We can count over sixty different parables that Jesus used" (*Jesus the Great Philosopher*, 62). Pennington points out that Greco-Roman philosophers also used parables.

17. White, *From Jesus to Christianity*, 95.

18. White, *From Jesus to Christianity*, 158.

19. Vatican Council II, *Dei Verbum* §4, 751.

20. Vatican Council II, *Dei Verbum* §4, 752.

through his actions, "teaches those who would not learn by other means to know Himself, the Word of God, and through Him the Father."[21] In all this, Jesus' oral teaching is never merely secondary or unnecessary, since, as *Dei Verbum* says, he "promulgated [the Gospel] with his own lips."[22]

What exactly did Jesus communicate in his oral teaching?[23] On the one hand, *Dei Verbum* allows for a certain degree of complexity when faced with this question. We have no writings by Jesus. Jesus's oral teaching comes to us mediated by the apostles, who, however inspired, are merely human teachers. Regarding the various human authors of the scriptural texts, *Dei Verbum* states, "Rightly to understand what the sacred author wanted to affirm in his work, due attention must be paid both to the customary and characteristic patterns of perception, speech and narrative which prevailed at the age of the sacred writer, and to the conventions which the people of his time followed in their dealings with each other."[24] On the other hand, *Dei Verbum* makes clear that the New Testament faithfully communicates the truth that Jesus himself taught. *Dei Verbum* comments in this regard that the four Gospels "faithfully hand on what Jesus, the Son of God, while he lived among men, really did and taught for their eternal salvation, until the day when he was taken up (cf. Acts 1:1–2)."[25]

The problem of ascertaining what Jesus taught arises forcefully (though certainly not only, given the fierce debates that have shaped the history of Christian division) in the domain of historical-critical biblical scholarship. Already in the late eighteenth and early nineteenth centuries, thinkers such as Edward Gibbon and Thomas Jefferson articulated widespread intellectual doubts about the Gospels' accuracy.[26] The relevant historical-critical

21. Athanasius, *On the Incarnation* §14, 43.

22. Vatican Council II, *Dei Verbum* §7, 753.

23. Ross McCullough aptly remarks that Jesus is "a kind of microcosmos, 'in whom are hid all the treasures of wisdom and knowledge' (Col. 2:3): in whose history all history can be read"; and, furthermore, "when Christ's wisdom is communicated to us, it is not just some abstract property representing ideal human wisdom: it is the wisdom formed by the concrete growth in stature of Jesus of Nazareth" (McCollough, *Freedom and Sin*, 198, 194). Jesus' wisdom and teaching cannot be separated from his life, death, and resurrection, or for that matter from the life of his Mystical Body.

24. Vatican Council II, *Dei Verbum*, §12, 57–58.

25. Vatican Council II, *Dei Verbum*, §19, 761.

26. Jefferson nicely expresses the viewpoint of more than two centuries of liberal Christianity (now fading away as a concretely Christian phenomenon, leaving in its wake post-Christian societies along with culturally assimilated denominational leaders) when he observes: "The truth is that the greatest enemies to the doctrines of Jesus are those calling themselves the expositors of them, who have perverted them for the structure of a system of fantasy absolutely incomprehensible, and without any foundation in his genuine words. And the day will come when the mystical generation of Jesus, by the

problems were well known in 1850 when John Henry Newman's brother Francis published his spiritual autobiography, *Phases of Faith*, describing his loss of confidence not only in dogma but in Scripture.[27] By the time that the Cambridge scholar F. C. Burkitt wrote a preface to the 1910 English edition of Albert Schweitzer's *The Quest of the Historical Jesus: A Critical Study of Its Progress from Reimarus to Wrede*,[28] intellectual doubts about the Gospels had spread to the general public, as had the view that Jesus was simply a fanatical Jewish apocalyptic "prophet" who did not really reveal anything but who instead wrongly announced the imminent end of the world as we know it. Burkitt deems that Christians must "reckon with the Son of Man who was [falsely] expected to come before the apostles had gone over the cities of Israel, the Son of Man who would come in His Kingdom before some that heard our Lord speak should taste death, the Son of Man who came to give His life a ransom for many, whom they would see hereafter coming with the clouds of heaven."[29] From this perspective, Jesus' eschatology falsified the core of his proclamation, but Burkitt considers that Jesus' spirit of hope and trust in God lives triumphantly on.

In Schweitzer's view, like that of David Friedrich Strauss, Adolf von Harnack, and Alfred Loisy, the Hellenizing Gospel of John and the equally Hellenizing church fathers hid the real Jesus from view, despite the fact that the Synoptics preserved a record of the fanatical apocalyptic prophet. Schweitzer argues that the work of the German historical-Jesus scholars of the eighteenth and nineteenth centuries was flawed but nevertheless served a good purpose in helping to throw off the "supernatural nimbus" that had obscured the Jewish Jesus.[30] He thinks that it is unclear whether Jesus

---

supreme being his father in the womb of a virgin, will be classed with the fable of the generation of Minerva in the brain of Jupiter. But we may hope that the dawn of reason and freedom of thought in these United States will do away with all this artificial scaffolding, and restore to us the primitive and genuine doctrines of this the most venerated reformer of human errors" (quoted by Mitchell in his *Gospel According to Jesus*, Appendix One, 280). Mitchell praises and aims to promote Jefferson's view of Jesus' teaching. See also Sanders, *Historical Figure of Jesus*, in which Sanders observes, after surveying Jefferson's view and other similar positions, "Matthew and Luke (to whom we owe the Sermon on the Mount and the Good Samaritan) would not have appreciated having Jesus' teaching separated from their own theological conviction that God sent him to save the world" (8). Sanders adds, however, that "the way in which they [Matthew and Luke] composed their books allows the reader to pick and choose" (8).

27. See Newman, *Phases of Faith*. I treat this work at length in chapter 3 of my *Newman on Doctrinal Corruption*.

28. See Burkitt, "Preface," v–vii.

29. Burkitt, "Preface," vi.

30. Schweitzer, *Quest of the Historical Jesus*, 4. For study of Schweitzer's work, offering a helpful critique, see Thate, *Remembrance of Things Past?*, Part One. Unfortunately,

thought of himself as the Messiah. According to Schweitzer, Jesus was in the grip of a fanatical eschatology.

In the penultimate chapter of his *The Quest of the Historical Jesus*, Schweitzer compares his own earlier book *Das Messianitäts- und Leidensgeheimnis. Eine Skizze des Lebens Jesu* to William Wrede's 1901 book *Das Messiasgeheimnis in den Evangelien. Zugleich ein Beitrag zum Verständnis des Markusevangeliums*.[31] Whereas Schweitzer advocates a "thoroughgoing eschatology," Wrede contends that "Jesus came forward as a teacher, first and principally in Galilee. He was surrounded by a company of disciples, went about with them, and gave them instruction. . . . He is fond of discoursing in parables."[32] In Wrede's view, Jesus' teachings brought him into trouble because of his free attitude toward Torah observance, eventually resulting in his crucifixion. Wrede suggests that the evangelist Mark has overlaid the real Jesus with a supernatural coloring. By introducing the theme of the messianic secret, Mark (and those who influenced him) sought "to give a Messianic form to the earthly life of Jesus"—but this impulse was restrained, Wrede posits, by people still alive who remembered that Jesus did not ascribe messianic import to himself.[33]

In Schweitzer's view, by contrast, eschatological fervor colors every aspect of Jesus' words and deeds. Jesus' eschatology is deeply "dogmatic" or theological. These elements are not a later overlay but go back to Jesus himself. Simply put, Jesus "looked forward to His Messianic 'Parousia' in the near future," and Jesus acted accordingly.[34] Jesus' teaching was ordered to his mission to bring about the imminent arrival of the kingdom. His fundamental message was simple: since the kingdom is now at hand, people must repent. The purpose of the parables was to enable the elect of God, those who have ears to hear, to prepare for the coming kingdom. Similarly, the beatitudes simply describe the attributes of those who are "predestined to the Kingdom."[35]

That ends up in postmodern perspectivalism, grounded in Jesus as the great model of transgressing and subverting tradition. For a sharp contrast between Schweitzer (and his reception in recent decades) and the broader outlook of Marie-Joseph Lagrange, OP, see Giambrone, "German Roots of Historical Jesus Research." For Lagrange's alternative, see his *Messianisme chez les Juifs*; and see also his *Sens du christianisme d'après l'exégèse allemande*.

31. See Schweitzer, *Messianitäts- und Leidensgeheimnis*; Wrede, *Messiasgeheimnis in den Evangelien*.

32. Schweitzer, *Quest of the Historical Jesus*, 331, 338.

33. Schweitzer, *Quest of the Historical Jesus*, 339.

34. Schweitzer, *Quest of the Historical Jesus*, 351.

35. Schweitzer, *Quest of the Historical Jesus*, 355.

For Schweitzer, then, the only "revelation" or significant teaching that Jesus offered was that the kingdom (the end of history as we know it) was about to appear, just as the harvest follows the time of sowing—but in fact the kingdom did not appear.[36] Schweitzer holds that Jesus intended to bear in his own body the final eschatological tribulation on behalf of all God's elect people, from which would supposedly arise immediately the kingdom of God.[37] As a result, says Schweitzer, modern people cannot credibly build a theology upon Jesus. In fact, modern people can only find Jesus deeply troubling, "a stranger and an enigma" rather than "a Teacher and Saviour," even though the figure of Jesus as portrayed by Paul can still be inspiring.[38]

36. Schweitzer argues that John the "Baptist and Jesus are not . . . borne upon the current of a general eschatological movement. The period offers no events calculated to give an impulse to eschatological enthusiasm. They themselves set it in motion by acting, by creating eschatological facts" (Schweitzer, *Quest of the Historical Jesus*, 370). More eloquently, Schweitzer puts it this way: "There is silence all around. The Baptist appears, and cries: 'Repent, for the Kingdom of Heaven is at hand.' Soon after that comes Jesus, and in the knowledge that He is the coming Son of Man lays hold of the wheel of the world to set it moving on that last revolution which is to bring all ordinary history to a close. It refuses to turn, and He throws Himself upon it. Then it does turn; and crushes Him. Instead of bringing in the eschatological conditions, He has destroyed them. The wheel rolls onward, and the mangled body of the one immeasurably great Man, who was strong enough to think of Himself as the spiritual ruler of mankind and to bend history to His purpose, is hanging upon it still. That is His victory and His reign" (Schweitzer, *Quest of the Historical Jesus*, 370–71).

37. See Schweitzer, *Quest of the Historical Jesus*, 389; and, for agreement with Schweitzer on Jesus' intention to bear the eschatological tribulation, see Wright, *Jesus and the Victory of God*, 577–91; Dunn, *Jesus Remembered*, 808–9; Pitre, *Jesus, the Tribulation, and the End of the Exile*. Schweitzer adds the claim that even in Jesus' last days, no one except his disciples knew that he was the Messiah. Speaking for many contemporary biblical scholars, Craig A. Evans remarks, "I think that Jesus did anticipate setting up a messianic administration that would displace the religious establishment of Jerusalem. We see this in Jesus' reply to James and John (Mark 10:35–40), which clearly anticipates the disciples sitting with Jesus. We see this in Jesus' promise to the twelve that they would someday sit on thrones judging the twelve tribes of Israel (Matt 19:28 = Luke 22:28–30) . . . [T]he reference to building a new Temple 'without hands' may have originally referred . . . to this new community, the nucleus of the small but growing kingdom" (Evans, "From Anointed Prophet to Anointed King," 454; and see also Evans, "Twelve Thrones of Israel," arguing that "Jesus envisioned the full restoration of Israel in every sense, political, economical, and cultic. His proclamation of the kingdom of God, which conceived of the very presence of God at work in the human sphere, presupposed this vision" [479]).

38. Schweitzer, *Quest of the Historical Jesus*, 399. Famously, Schweitzer adds that historical-critical scholarship "loosed the bands by which He had been riveted for centuries to the stony rocks of ecclesiastical doctrine, and rejoiced to see life and movement coming into the figure once more, and the historical Jesus advancing, as it seemed, to meet it [i.e., modernity]. But He does not stay, He passes by our time and returns to His own. What surprised and dismayed the theology of the last forty years

Schweitzer's position is widespread today, and—as should go without saying—this makes it difficult for Jesus' teachings, as found in the Gospels, to be received as authoritative truth. The Protestant biblical scholar E. P. Sanders sums up his *The Historical Figure of Jesus* by remarking, "Jesus thought the kingdom of God was at hand, and his disciples had accepted his message . . . [H]e may have died disappointed . . . The coming kingdom had sounded so marvellous! The last would be first, the meek would inherit the earth. These expectations were not fulfilled, at least not in any obvious way."[39] Sanders thinks that the disciples truly believed they saw Jesus risen from the dead. Whether they actually did so, or simply hallucinated in one way or another, is impossible (Sanders holds) for historians to say. Similarly, Bart Ehrman argues that Jesus thought that the apocalyptic day of the Lord had now arrived, that the temple would be destroyed, and that he himself would very soon be made king over the glorious kingdom of God.[40]

---

was that, despite all forced and arbitrary interpretations, it could not keep Him in our time, but had to let Him go. He returned to His own time, not owing to the application of any historical ingenuity, but by the same inevitable necessity by which the liberated pendulum returns to its original position" (Schweitzer, *Quest of the Historical Jesus*, 399). Schweitzer thinks that spiritual and ethical significance flows across the centuries from the figure of Jesus and remains of value. Schweitzer sees Paul as a key inventor of this Jesus, known spiritually rather than historically. He concludes, "it is not Jesus as historically known, but Jesus as spiritually arisen within men, who is significant for our time and can help it. Not the historical Jesus, but the spirit which goes forth from Him and in the spirits of men strives for new influence and rule, is that which overcomes the world . . . The abiding and eternal in Jesus is absolutely independent of historical knowledge and can only be understood by contact with His spirit which is still at work in the world" (401). Jesus' "spirit" consists in his radical negation of this world, that is, his ability to reject the goods of this world in order to selflessly serve higher goods. Wright responds, "Schweitzer was right to say that 'apocalyptic' was central for Jesus, but wrong to think it meant the end of the world, and wrong to suppose that an eternally valid core of meaning could emerge from the failure of the world to end on time. No. Jesus went to Jerusalem to enact and embody the coming kingdom, in which YHWH would be king of all the world. He died the way all failed Messiahs die. If the story ended there, its only real message would be the one Juvenal learned as a schoolboy, writing exercises in rhetoric. Retire from public life altogether; you'll sleep better . . . The category of failed but still revered Messiah . . . did not exist. A Messiah who died at the hands of the pagans, instead of winning YHWH's battle against them, was a deceiver, as the later rabbis (and Christians) said of Bar-Kochba. Why then did people go on talking about Jesus of Nazareth, except as a remarkable but tragic memory? The obvious answer is the one given by all early Christians actually known to us . . . : Jesus was raised from the dead" and has thereby conquered sin and death, inaugurating the kingdom and pouring out the Spirit to spread the inaugurated kingdom (Wright, *Jesus and the Victory of God*, 658–59). For the impact of Christ's kingdom-inauguration in the world, against all complacency, see Spence, *Promise of Peace*, 89–90.

39. Sanders, *Historical Figure of Jesus*, 276.

40. I agree that Jesus thought these things, but Ehrman also assumes, mistakenly

Ehrman supposes that the transition from the Synoptics to Paul reveals the shift "from seeing Jesus as his own disciples did during his ministry, as a Jewish man with an apocalyptic message of coming destruction, to seeing him as something far greater, a preexistent divine being who became human only temporarily before being made Lord of the universe."[41]

Another notable biblical scholar, Dale Allison, accepts Schweitzer's general outlook but holds that Jesus need not have been consistent. In Allison's view, Jesus could have been a wisdom teacher at times, while also inconsistently (since humans are not consistent) at other times proclaiming the imminent arrival of the kingdom.[42] Like Schweitzer, Harnack, and Loisy, the Protestant biblical scholar Marcus Borg proposes that Jesus' teaching, while wrongheaded, should still inspire us.[43] Despite the fact that the kingdom of God failed to come, Borg argues that the notion remains beneficial: "the Kingdom of God is what life would be like on earth if God were king. It is God's dream as dreamed by the great figures of the Jewish tradition: Moses, the prophets, and for those of us who are Christians, Jesus. It is a dream for the earth."[44]

---

in my view, that Jesus believed that all suffering and death were about to come to an end and that the final judgment was imminent. For Ehrman, it is axiomatic that Jesus did not foresee the Church (the persecuted community of Jesus' followers, obeying his commandments, proclaiming the gospel, and practicing the sacraments) lasting more than a generation. For historical-critical background to Jesus' "belief that even constitutional features of the eschaton—the shape of eschatological Israel, the purity of God's people, and even the temple of the eschaton—were already coming into existence," see Bryan, *Jesus and Israel's Traditions*, 243. I do not accept all of Bryan's judgments, but his work is a good starting point.

41. Ehrman, *How Jesus Became God*, 371.

42. See Allison, *Constructing Jesus*, 91–94. See also Freyne, *Jesus, a Jewish Galilean*, 140: "there is nothing incompatible between a worldview that expects God's imminent judgement and a concern for right living in the present. Recent discussion of the Wisdom writings from Qumran Cave 4, especially 4Q416–418, shows how naturally and freely Jewish thinking in the circles within which both John and Jesus moved could combine a sapiential and an apocalyptic understanding of life."

43. See von Harnack, *What Is Christianity?*; Loisy, *Gospel and the Church*. For background to von Harnack, see Teubner, "Jesus and the Ascent of *Wissenschaft*"; Beiser, *German Historicist Tradition*; Hector, *Theological Project of Modernism*. For background to Loisy, see Hill, *Politics of Modernism*. See also Rosa, "Essence of Christianity."

44. Borg, *Heart of Christianity*, 135. For criticism of Borg's viewpoint, see various works of N. T. Wright and see also Chilton, "Jesus within Judaism," 187–88: "Borg makes Jesus into a hero of religious experience; any consideration of the setting of his teaching within Judaism is made subsidiary to the claim that his mystical insight was profound and that it was mature at a relatively early stage in his life."

III. Jesus' Self-Understanding

To say the least, Jesus did not share the modern skepticism about the authority of his teaching. In my view, he taught his own divine status, as part of his enabling human beings to know the true God and God's wisdom for human salvation, and in accordance with his acting with divine power (forgiving sins, performing miracles, and so on).[45] Scholars often hold that Trinitarian doctrine arose in the Church because of scriptural pressure pointing toward the divinity of Christ (and the Spirit). As the biblical scholar Carey Newman observes, this answer "serves to drive the Trinitarian debate further back in time, to the first days of the Christian movement and, potentially, even to Jesus himself."[46] Indeed, I maintain that just as Newman suggests, "Jesus himself" is the source of divine Christology.

45. For further reflection, see White, "Trinitarian Consciousness of Christ." White gladly grants that "Jesus of Nazareth expressed himself in a typically human way, as one who is conscious of himself within the given culture and linguistic tropes of his age" (121). But White adds that Jesus "did so nonetheless as one who was also humanly aware that he is the transcendent Son of God and who was aware, however numinously, that he can and does act in unity with the Father and with the Holy Spirit . . . As depicted in the Gospels, the historical Jesus is aware, however clearly or vaguely, of his divine origin and capacity to work with the Father and the Spirit. Consequently, his actions of miraculous healing, like his words and parables, as well as his suffering and death, *reveal a set of personal relationships* that he is aware of as man. They reveal his personal intimacy with the Father and the Spirit, and therefore implicitly manifest to us the true inner identity of God as Trinity" (121). White argues against the positions of Wolfhart Pannenberg, Karl Rahner, and N. T. Wright in this regard. He observes that what they miss—without thereby being heretical—"is the acknowledgment that Jesus's knowledge of his own identity is a key dimension of the mystery of the Incarnation and likewise has important soteriological consequences [cf. Matthew 11:27; John 14:6] . . . Salvation is not only about his atoning death (as Pannenberg risks to make it), or even about union with the divine (as Rahner risks to make it), but also about initial and eventually perfected human knowledge of the Trinity. Salvation is effectuated ultimately, in other words, by our union with God through knowledge of love of God by faith in this life and by vision in the next. Jesus of Nazareth can only illuminate us—as distinct from being illuminated himself by the Father in his resurrection—if he is able during his earthly life to manifest the truth about God in his teaching, actions, miracles, and suffering unto death. He manifests to us in his historical earthly life that he is one with the Father, and is truly God with us, giving us to know God in himself" (110–11). I note that Hans Urs von Balthasar accounts for this via his notion of Jesus' absolute mission-consciousness, which arguably requires some knowledge on Jesus' part of who he himself is.

46. Newman, "From (Wright's) Jesus to (the Church's) Christ?," 282. Newman argues further, "Wright makes Jesus a credible, crucifiable, apocalyptically minded, first-century Jewish prophet and messiah . . . [But] it is not at all clear how Jesus, the prophet to Israel, and Jesus, the Messiah of Israel, become Jesus, the Lord of the church. The shoulders of Wright's Jesus do not appear to be sturdy enough to bear the christological weight the church willingly placed upon them. Wright appears to have dissolved all

In all the Gospels, Jesus claims divine prerogatives.[47] Historical-critical biblical scholars have not neglected to notice this. For instance, the Protestant biblical scholar Aquila Lee has devoted a well-respected monograph to arguing in favor of "Jesus' self-consciousness of his divine sonship."[48] Another Protestant biblical scholar, Sigurd Grindheim, contends that Jesus "invested his own words with the same authority as God's words" because he "thought himself to be God's equal."[49] According to Grindheim, Jesus regularly claimed divine titles such as "bridegroom" and "king" in order to indicate that "he takes God's place in interacting with the world."[50]

Even James Dunn, who maintains that it is likely that Jesus claimed no explicit titles at all, supposes that Jesus understood himself to be uniquely God's eschatological spokesman and agent.[51] The Jewish biblical scholar Israel Knohl has suggested that Jesus, influenced by Qumran, was crucified by a court comprised of Sadducees for the blasphemy of claiming to be the "son of God" with at least "a quasi-divine status."[52] Nicholas Perrin holds that

the potential ontological elements of Christology into narrative. That is, for Wright, Christology is simply this: Jesus is the chief protagonist in the stories he tells and enacts" (287). Presumably Wright's answer is the resurrection of Jesus, which he does not explore in *Jesus and the Victory of God*.

47. See for example Johnson, *Living Jesus*, 136–37: "Mark's Jesus reveals a depth of being and of power that points to an origin in God. His first words—'The time has come to completion, and the rule of God has come; turn about and believe the good news' (1:15)—are at the very least those of a human person who claims to know the course of history and God's plan and has the prophetic authority to call people to change their lives . . . Similarly, Jesus declares, self-referentially, that 'the Son of man has power on earth to forgive sins' (2:10) and that 'the Son of man is Lord of the Sabbath' (2:28) . . . Although Jesus eschews knowledge of the end-time, in so doing he refers to God as his Father and to himself as Son (13:32), and does so immediately after declaring that 'heaven and earth will pass away but my words will not pass away' (13:31). It is not simply that Jesus' speech and the declaration of God reveal his special status, however. Mark shows Jesus working wonders—feeding the multitudes (6:30–44; 8:1–10), stilling the storm (4:35–40), walking on the water (6:45–52)—that demonstrate a power over creation itself and demand an answer to the question 'Who therefore is this person that even the wind and the sea obey him?'"

48. Lee, *From Messiah to Preexistent Son*, 30. Lee is indebted to his teacher I. Howard Marshall's *Origins of New Testament Christology*.

49. Grindheim, *God's Equal*, 124.

50. Grindheim, *God's Equal*, 133.

51. Dunn, *Jesus Remembered*, 762; cf. 707.

52. Knohl, *Messiah Confrontation*, 158. Focusing on the Gospel of Mark, Bernardo Cho argues that "it is only after Jesus openly declares his identity as Israel's royal messiah that he is seen as deserving death (Mark 14:63–64) . . . Raymond Brown is absolutely correct that nowhere in the pre-Markan sources does the claim to messiahship alone suffice to accuse someone of blasphemy . . . Simply *to claim* to be the messiah—let alone truly *to be* the messiah—is not to commit blasphemy. And yet, the high priest

Jesus "was confident that the divine power rested not only in his movement but also, in some inscrutable way, within himself in particular."[53] Likewise, in his *Jesus and Divine Christology*, Brant Pitre finds that it is historically probable that Jesus repeatedly presented himself as divine. Pitre shows that such a self-understanding would not have been entirely out of line for a man of Jesus' place and time—assuming that Jesus also understood himself to be Israel's Messiah, able to work miracles by divine power.[54] As Pitre re-

accuses Jesus of that. In this way, the lack of clarity in Mark on what kind of offence Jesus perpetrates is not incidental, as it highlights the illegitimacy of the Sanhedrin's verdict" (Cho, *Royal Messianism*, 188-89). Cho goes on to say that the issue in Mark seems to be Jesus' claim about his coming enthronement in heaven: "By deploying OG Ps 109:1 and OG Dan 7:13, Mark 14:62 emphasizes that the one about to be crucified is the messianic son, whom God will soon enthrone in heaven before the eyes of his enemies. It is one thing to envisage a messiah who will be seated on an exalted throne, as in the *Similitudes of Enoch*; it is a whole other thing to find a living person, bound as a criminal, predicting his own ascension in such a manner over against the temple rulers" (189). See also the similar perspectives of Wright, *Jesus and the Victory of God*, 643-44; and Evans, "In What Sense 'Blasphemy'?"; and see the exchange on the trial and the charge of blasphemy in Zaas and Craig, "Interactive Discussion," 30-32. In Zaas's view, the charge of blasphemy is unlikely to have historical grounds; whereas for Craig, it is likely that "Jesus' notion of the kingdom of God's coming in himself was . . . perceived as blasphemous precisely because it attempted to replace the Temple as the focus of Judaism with himself . . . [The] perceived attack on the Temple itself was thought to be blasphemous in Jewish sight because Jesus arrogated to himself a type of authority that no person could have arrogated to himself" (31). For further reflection, focused not on the blasphemy charge but on Mark's theme of Jesus as the hidden Son of Man (who will fulfill Daniel 7:13-14 in two stages, first through enduring tribulation and second in his future glorious coming), see Collins and Collins, *King and Messiah as Son of God*, 150-52—a section written by Adela Yarbro Collins.

53. Perrin, *Jesus the Temple*, 169; see also 288: "Jesus was convinced that the godhead was already fully and uniquely present in his person and this not least on account of his election, confirmed through baptism."

54. See Pitre, *Jesus and Divine Christology*. Pitre observes on the concluding page of his book, "the best explanation for why the early church took several centuries to debate and discuss how Jesus could be both the divine messiah and yet somehow distinct from 'the one God, the Father almighty,' is because Jesus himself had spoken and acted as if he were divine without abandoning early Jewish monotheism" (351). For the opposite position, see Bart D. Ehrman's popular book *How Jesus Became God*, to which Pitre responds. Ehrman sums up his viewpoint: "we have numerous earlier sources [than the Gospel of John] for the historical Jesus: a few comments in Paul (including several quotations from Jesus's teachings), Mark, Q, M, and L, not to mention the finished Gospels of Matthew and Luke. In none of them do we find exalted claims of this sort. If Jesus went around Galilee proclaiming himself to be a divine being sent from God—one who existed before the creation of the world, who was in fact equal with God—could anything *else* that he might say be so breathtaking and thunderously important? And yet none of these earlier sources says any such thing about him. Did they (all of them!) just decide not to mention the one thing that was most significant about Jesus? Almost certainly the divine self-claims in John are not historical. But is it

marks, "in contrast to the age-old assumption that at the time of Jesus, most Jewish people were waiting for a merely human messiah, recent scholarship suggests that *'the divinity of the messiah'* was a significant part of the early Jewish messianic landscape."[55]

Along these same lines, if somewhat cautiously with respect to Jesus' own self-understanding, Ruben Bühner argues that the context of Second Temple messianism makes it quite possible that "a Jew in the first century CE was already believed during his lifetime to have some divine authority or to be an otherwise superhuman figure," capable of making "divine claims" and of being crucified for what some other first-century Jews deemed to be blasphemy.[56] Dale Allison sums up the matter eloquently: "No follower of Jesus,

---

possible that Jesus considered himself divine in some other sense? I have already argued that he did not consider himself to be the Son of Man, and so he did not consider himself to be the heavenly angelic being who would be the judge of the earth. But he did think of himself as the future king of the kingdom, the messiah" (*How Jesus Became God*, 125–26). Ehrman rejects the view that Jesus supposed that he would become divine when he became king. Also worth noting—in response to Ehrman and others, especially Peppard's *Son of God in the Roman World* and Dunn's *Did the First Christians Worship Jesus?*—is Loke, *Origin of Divine Christology*. Loke demonstrates that the "highest Christology was present among the earliest Christians" (47). Against scholars who deny that Second Temple Jews were monotheistic and worshiped only "the one God of Israel," Loke points out, "the premise that Jesus was regarded as truly divine in earliest Christianity is based on what the earliest Christian Jewish leaders thought about worship and divinity"—and they certainly "held to a strict view according to which worship implied recognition of divinity in the sense of being on the Creator side of the divide" (57). For further discussion, see also Loke's disagreements with—and agreements with—Hurtado, *Lord Jesus Christ*, in Loke, *Origin of Divine Christology*, 119–33; and see the essays in Bird, *How God Became Jesus*.

55. Pitre, *Jesus and Divine Christology*, 14.

56. Bühner, *Messianic High Christology*, 190–91. Bühner contends that the worldview of many Jews in Jesus' time included "various divine beings with a basic boundary that separates the one God of Israel among all those divine beings," giving supremacy to the one God but understanding the implications of this supremacy in various ways (189; cf. the fuller account provided on pages 10–20, critiquing aspects of the positions of Larry Hurtado and Richard Bauckham). In Bühner's view, scholarly efforts to differentiate between "higher" and "lower" conceptions of Jesus' divine status are mistaken. He argues, for example, that "[e]ven if John may have thought so, we have no basis for the assessment that the author of the Gospel of Mark would have agreed with him that being uncreated is the sign of a higher level of divinity than sitting at the right hand of God" (189). I think this is an exaggeration. It is only logical, not something unavailable to first-century Jews and Christians, to apprehend that being uncreated is indeed a "higher level of divinity"—assuming one has to use the term "level"—than being a man exalted to the divine throne. Here I agree with Gabriele Boccaccini's essay (critiqued by Bühner), "Jesus the Messiah." Boccaccini is not defending traditional Christian doctrine as such; see his "How Jesus Became Uncreated"; and his "From Jewish Prophet to Jewish God." Regarding Jesus' crucifixion for blasphemy, Bühner adds, "One might ask why there is evidence that the claims regarding the divinity of Jesus were objected to so heavily

to our knowledge, ever called Paul divine or reckoned him a god. Christians did, however, say astounding things about Jesus, and that from the very beginning. The differing evaluations, I submit, had something to do with who those two people actually were."[57] Allison does not mean that Jesus actually is divine but rather that he likely presented himself that way, as the (future) king of the kingdom of God.[58] Allison concludes, "We should hold a funeral for the view that Jesus entertained no exalted thoughts about himself."[59]

Let me briefly discuss Pitre's and Grindheim's arguments in more detail. As Pitre shows, in at least three of Jesus' reported miracles—Jesus' calming of the storm, Jesus' walking on water, and Jesus' transfiguration—Jesus is depicted as acting in ways that Israel's Scriptures attributed to God alone. Likewise, Jesus' teaching includes "riddles" in which Jesus is presented as on par with God. His apocalyptic ministry includes claims to be the heavenly Son of Man and to be the only one able to make known the Father. John the Baptist, too, seems to have anticipated a divine or quasi-divine Messiah. Lastly, Jesus is more than once accused of blasphemy, and this accusation stems from Jesus proclaiming himself to be divine or quasi-divine. Pitre

---

by contemporary Jews as early as the first century CE if analogous ideas were already present in earlier messianic models. The reason for this objection is to be found within the diversity of Second Temple Judaism in general and of Second Temple messianism in particular. That is, expectations of a superhuman messiah did not represent the whole messianic discourse of their time" (*Messianic High Christology*, 191; cf. 195–97 for Bühner's argument that the claim that Jesus was divine became a real sticking point between Jews and early Christians only in the second century, since prior to that time, the notion of complementary "powers in heaven" was possible within Jewish discourse).

57. Allison, *Constructing Jesus*, 304.

58. For Allison—debating here with John Meier, in whose view Jesus understood himself to be the Davidic Messiah—it is most likely that Jesus understood himself "as *messias designatus*: he saw kingship as a hope or a destiny, not an accomplishment" (*Constructing Jesus*, 290). In this regard, Allison agrees with Lindars, "Re-enter the Apocalyptic Son of Man," 61–62. In *Historical Jesus and the Temple*, 117–36, Michael Patrick Barber builds upon and significantly strengthens Allison's argument for Jesus' messianic self-understanding,

59. Allison, *Constructing Jesus*, 305. Here Allison is responding directly to Borg, "Was Jesus God?," 147: "I don't think people like Jesus have an exalted perception of themselves." See also Borg's *Meeting Jesus Again for the First Time*, where Borg, while leaving open the question of whether Jesus thought of himself as the "son" of the Father or as the child of divine Wisdom, nevertheless grants: "But when 'Son of God' is seen instead as one metaphor among several, it opens up the possibility of a much richer understanding of the significance of Jesus as experienced and expressed in the early Christian movement. The issue is no longer believing that Jesus was literally the Son of God, but appreciating the richness of meaning suggested by the multiplicity of Christological images" (110–11). In fact, here Allison and Borg may not be all that far apart, since Allison, while fascinated by Jesus, does not as a historian profess Jesus' ontological divine Sonship in *Constructing Jesus*.

examines the above actions and teachings as reported in the Gospels, and he argues in favor of their historicity. Whether or not he is correct in every instance, he builds a strong case that not only the evangelists but also Jesus himself considered Jesus to be the divine Son.[60]

For his part, Grindheim first examines the Qumran documents and other Second Temple Jewish texts. He points especially to 1 Enoch (generally thought to be roughly contemporaneous with Jesus and to be pre-Christian), which I will describe somewhat more fully in chapter 6. The Enochic "Son of Man" sits upon the divine throne as the eschatological judge, and he "has functions that are known to belong exclusively to God."[61] Yet the Enochic Son of Man, despite possessing some divine characteristics

---

60. I thank Brant Pitre for allowing me to read his book, *Jesus and Divine Christology*, in manuscript. See also Collins and Collins, *King and Messiah as Son of God*, 173-74 (a section written by Adela Yarbro Collins): "It is plausible . . . that Jesus spoke about the one like a son of man in Daniel as a heavenly messiah who was coming soon or who would be revealed soon. The text of Daniel already presents this figure as God's agent in exercising eternal kingship. The *Similitudes of Enoch* present the same figure as God's agent in the final judgment. *4 Ezra* presents him as God's agent in defeating the nations, gathering the people of Israel, and defending them. After his crucifixion, some of his followers had visions of Jesus as raised from the dead and exalted to heaven. These visions were interpreted in terms of Dan 7:13-14 and Psalm 110, both read messianically . . . If his followers had hoped that Jesus would take the role of messiah of Israel during his earthly lifetime, this hope was transformed by his death and resurrection into an expectation of his coming or being revealed as a heavenly messiah, the Son of Man. At that time he would act as God's agent in ruling, judging, and defending God's people . . . [T]he idea of a heavenly messiah opens the door to speculation and rhetoric about preexistence. The notion of preexistence intensifies the divine status of the heavenly messiah . . . The understanding of Jesus that emerged after his resurrection involved his kingship over Israel and over the entire world. Given the practice of the imperial cults, it is not surprising that Jesus was viewed as a god and that worship of him became an alternative to the worship of the emperor." Thus, Collins does not say that Jesus understood himself as divine or quasi-divine, but she comes close to doing so—albeit with a heavy dose of skeptical suggestion that Jesus and his followers were deluded. In the Conclusion to their book, the Collinses state, "The Synoptic Gospels do not present Jesus as preexistent" (209).

61. Grindheim, *God's Equal*, 161. See the cautionary note provided by Bühner: "the text of the Parables is available only in Ethiopian manuscripts from the late Middle Ages. Not one fragment containing the original Semitic language of the Parables has survived, and comparison with the Ethiopian text from other parts of 1 Enoch, where at least a few Greek or Semitic fragments are available, suggests that the Ethiopian text of the Parables should be treated with caution" (*Messianic High Christology*, 131-32). For further background to the Enochic Son of Man, see—from a vast array of literature—Hannah, "Elect Son of Man of the Parables of Enoch"; Walck, *Son of Man in the Parables of Enoch and in Matthew*; Fletcher-Louis, *Christological Origins*, chapter 5; Grabbe, "'Son of Man,'" 182-88; Alexander, "From Son of Adam to a Second God"; Davila, "Of Methodology, Monotheism and Metatron"; and Rowland and Morray-Jones, *Mystery of God*, especially 33-61.

and functions, "is also distinguished from God, and he is seen to be inferior to him."⁶² Grindheim argues that Jesus, in his words and deeds, exalted himself beyond the status of the Enochic Son of Man in claiming divine authority and power. In the Gospels, Jesus teaches that he is in some way subordinate to the Father while also being equal to the Father. By contrast, the Enochic Son of Man is not equal to the Father.⁶³ Here Delbert Burkett's observation is of value, although Burkett does not deny that the Enochic Son of Man in certain ways influenced the Gospel portraits: "The significant differences between the Enochic figure and the Gospel Son of Man indicate that the latter developed independently of the former."⁶⁴

One final note before moving on. I affirm *Dei Verbum*'s teaching that the Gospels "faithfully hand on what Jesus, the Son of God, while he lived among men, really did and taught for their eternal salvation, until the day when he was taken up (cf. Acts 1:1–2)."⁶⁵ But although I am persuaded that the Gospels are rooted in eyewitness testimony (cf. Luke 1:2) and that the Gospels contain what Jesus really taught, this does not commit me to the view that the evangelists simply wrote down exactly what Jesus said or exactly what eyewitnesses recalled him saying, as distinct from the evangelists making their own creative contributions in accordance with the ancient genre of biography.⁶⁶ As Hans Urs von Balthasar remarks, moreover, this

---

62. Grindheim, *God's Equal*, 163.

63. See Grindheim, *God's Equal*, 167, 188. Regarding Jesus' use of the title "Son of Man," see Grindheim, *God's Equal*, 189–204, as well as Mogens Müller's history of the interpretation of this title as used by Jesus: see Müller, *Expression 'Son of Man' and the Development of Christology*.

64. Burkett, *Son of Man Debate*, 121. Burkett, however, holds that historical-critical scholarship should remain agnostic about whether the title Son of Man goes back to Jesus himself.

65. Vatican Council II, *Dei Verbum* §19, 761. Pitre argues in *Jesus and Divine Christology* that historians can seek, not the exact words of Jesus, but the "substance" of his words—that is, words that plausibly originated (in their core content) with Jesus.

66. See Keener, *Christobiography*. Keener notes, "While biography was firmly rooted in historical information, it also potentially allowed significant flexibility in details. In general, human memory preserves primarily the gist, rather than all the details" (325). Ancient biographers, while certainly not creative in an unrestricted manner (and while committed to historical truth), were expected to be able to adapt the chronology, to conflate some events, to omit marginal characters, to write speeches (under certain conditions), to shape the telling of the story in accord with a moral and theological perspective, and to invent some details for the sake of the story's flow. For Keener on memory and eyewitness testimony, see *Christobiography*, 365–496, including Keener's emphasis that "Jesus was a teacher with disciples" and these disciples would have transmitted reliable memories of Jesus (401). For the claim that "the gospels seemed true because they were written in historiographical discourse with historiographical tropes that gave the impression of historicity"—despite in fact being "mythic"—see

issue has a further dimension for those who recognize in faith, as I do, that the ascended Jesus guided and governed (through the Spirit) the words that are attributed to him by the inspired authors of Scripture.[67]

For the purposes of this chapter, it suffices that Jesus' parables and Sermon on the Mount exhibit a profound fit with what we know about Jesus otherwise. Receiving them as a true expression of what he taught is reasonable. Of course, the portions of Jesus' teaching that I treat in this chapter do not come close to exhausting the content of his teaching, but they can serve as a good start for understanding the vision of reality that he taught, including his own self-understanding.

Litwa, *How the Gospels Became History*, 62; and see also the argument that "seeing" and "remembering" in the Gospel of John show that an "eyewitness" can be someone who was not present but who has rightly understood the event in the power of the Spirit, in Dewey, "Eyewitness of History." I discuss eyewitness testimony in more detail in my *Did Jesus Rise from the Dead?*, chapter 2. See also the works referenced therein, especially Bauckham, *Jesus and the Eyewitnesses*; Dunn, *Jesus Remembered*, 192–254; Gerhardsson, "Secret of the Transmission"; Mournet, *Oral Tradition and Literary Dependency*; Kelber and Byrskog, *Jesus in Memory*; Rodriguez, *Structuring Early Christian Memory*; Byrskog, *Story as History*; Kirk and Thatcher, "Jesus Tradition as Social Memory"; and McIver, *Memory, Jesus, and the Synoptic Gospels*. For other recent engagements with memory studies in the context of Jesus research, see Schröter, *From Jesus to the New Testament*, 49–70 (for German developments and the influence of Paul Ricoeur); Havukainen, *Quest for the Memory of Jesus*; Thate, *Remembrance of Things Past?*, Part Two.

67. See Balthasar, *Seeing the Form*, 538–44. Quite different is Paul J. DeHart's claim, "The scandal for belief in Jesus Christ is precisely Jesus of Nazareth, the 'larval' form of the total event of Christ . . . Jesus, once recognized in the Gospels and in worship, must still continually be reidentified in new forms, much as a target must be 'reacquired'; belief oscillates between his initial larval form and the local phases of its current metamorphosis, an identity under unending construction (as long as history lasts). The biblical figure in its particularity somehow contains *in nuce* this entire later development, but repels any direct attempt to perceive its unity with his elusive presence now, much less with his completed future 'imago'" (DeHart, *Unspeakable Cults*, 223). Some degree of elusiveness and even "larval" articulation (allowing for later unfolding) is true and unavoidable, but DeHart has exaggerated the degree and thereby underestimated the power of Scripture (in the Tradition) to present the true "form" (to use Balthasar's terminology) of Jesus. DeHart similarly contends against the identification of Jesus as the (doctrinal) source of the apostolic and post-apostolic Church: see 228, indebted to Walter Bauer's influential *Orthodoxy and Heresy in Earliest Christianity*—though I agree with DeHart's later point that the Church's complicity in sin, for instance sins of injustice and hatred against the Jewish people, obscures the truth about Jesus to a degree, just as Paul in Acts 20 (without doubting the efficacy of the communication of the Gospel) warns will be the case. Certainly, "[a]ll recognitions of Jesus are embedded within the larger, unfinished process of faith living in history," but DeHart's rhetoric of "the unfolding ecclesial event of Jesus' pneumatic future" flies too close to the historicist wind (*Unspeakable Cults*, 232), despite his appeal to the Spirit and (albeit in an overly limited way) to the value of "biblical remembrance of his past" (233).

ENGAGING THE DOCTRINE OF JESUS (AND MARY)

III. The Parables of Jesus: Levine and Lohfink

Amy-Jill Levine

As Amy-Jill Levine shows, the parable of the prodigal son is often interpreted in an anti-Jewish way, as if Jesus were introducing a merciful Father set against the Pharisaic Jews' view of an unforgiving and stern divine Judge, or as if the elder son represents the Pharisaic Jews' arrogant works-righteousness and Jesus reveals that salvation comes by grace.[68] Another anti-Jewish reading holds that the younger son (due to the story about his involvement in pig-farming) represents the gentiles while the elder son represents the Jews and their anger at "God the Father's outreach beyond the so-called chosen people."[69]

---

68. Levine, *Short Stories by Jesus*. For a perspective on Jesus similar to Levine's, see Zaas, "Who Was Jesus?," 15–20. Zaas states, "I continue to be struck, as a Jew, by many aspects of Jesus' life and teachings, even if the claims that his followers made about his person are irrelevant to my religious life. I am struck by the Jewishness of Jesus, and by the pointedness of the critique of Jewish hypocrisy which pervades his teachings in the Gospels. Jesus stood against the sin of religiosity, the notion that what God desires is religiousness rather than justice, the notion that persons whose religiousness is a mask for their viciousness are the worst of sinners. This idea, born among the Hebrew prophets but expressed with Jesus' characteristic simplicity and vigor in the Gospels, links this teacher with what is best in Jewish ethical thinking. If Christian readers of the Gospels persisted, most of the time, in thinking of Jesus as standing in opposition to *Jewish* hypocrisy and not to religious hypocrisy in general, that does not detract from the force of what Jesus himself stood for, and stood against. The Jesus of the Gospels is a Jewish teacher of righteousness, no matter how unrecognizable to Jews the church has made him" ("Who Was Jesus?," 19). I hold that Jesus' teaching, in the Gospels, is more (though not less) than such ethical teaching, and so I agree with William Lane Craig who, in his companion-piece to Zaas's, observes: "In recent years, New Testament scholarship has reached something of a consensus that the historical Jesus of Nazareth came on the scene with an unprecedented sense of divine authority—the authority to stand and speak in God's place" (Craig, "Who Was Jesus?," 21). Let me also mention Zaas's powerful testimony to the radical scandal caused by Christian persecution of Jews, beginning with the early Christian (intra-biblical) denunciation of those Jews who did not accept Jesus as the Messiah and gathering force across the centuries. Zaas remarks, "My generation is the generation of the children of Holocaust survivors, and, however much Christians may disavow this horror, these survivors remember that their tormentors all claimed to be Christians, all understood that the Messiah was the Jesus of Nazareth" ("Who Was Jesus?," 18; Zaas's point is damning even though, as Donald A. Hagner responds in the same volume in his "Jesus," 46, the Nazi perpetrators of the Holocaust were not believing Christians).

69. Levine, *Short Stories by Jesus*, 30. For the parables of the rabbis and comparison with Jesus' parables—including many close parallels—see McArthur and Johnston, *They Also Taught in Parables*; Stern, *Parables in Midrash*; Evans, "Jesus and Rabbinic Parables, Proverbs, and Prayers"; Evans, "Parables in Early Judaism."

Levine argues that none of the above interpretations accurately assesses the parable—and I agree. In her view, somewhat less persuasively but still instructively, the parable makes clear that the lost son is actually the elder one.[70] The father is seeking desperately to make his family whole. Levine denies that the father here is God the Father. It makes more sense, she argues, to interpret the parable as really being about a human father and sons. After all, the father makes a number of mistakes that abet the mistakes of the younger son. By acquiescing to the younger son's request, the father goes against the wise advice of Sirach 33:23–24 and commits a foolish act by giving away half of his property while he is still alive. Humanly speaking, the father does not raise and discipline his younger son in a good way.

When the father rejoices to see his younger son, Levine points out, this is what we should expect. It is not true that in the ancient Near East a father would lose his paternal honor by running toward his son; nor, in the parable, has the father disowned the son. We should not be surprised to see that the father loves his son and has compassion on him, since this is what many fathers do in every culture, including the Jewish culture of Jesus' day. The notion that Jesus is "inventing a new theology that rejects the supposed Jewish or Old Testament God of wrath in favor of the Christian or New Testament God of love" is mistaken.[71] After all, the God of the Old Testament consistently has compassion and love for his wayward people. Levine also pushes back against christological readings for which Jesus stands in the place of the younger son, in solidarity with sinners. Levine points out, "the prodigal squandered his inheritance; Jesus did not. The prodigal sinned; Jesus did not."[72]

Instead, Levine interprets the elder brother's anger in light of the biblical tradition of rivalry and conflict between two sons. She notes that the story of the younger brother describes his returning to his father, whereas the story of the elder brother describes his returning to the house. The tension consists in whether the Father will be able to unify his family. It is the elder son who is interiorly "lost" vis-à-vis the father.[73]

---

70. For a much different interpretation, arguing that the parable has resurrection and eschatology in view (although adding an argument about resurrection to angelomorphic life that seems perhaps a stretch), see Fletcher-Louis, *Luke-Acts*, 90–96. See also Kirk, *Man Attested by God*, 558–59, which adopts some of the readings of the parable rightly warned against by Levine.

71. Levine, *Short Stories by Jesus*, 62.

72. Levine, *Short Stories by Jesus*, 66.

73. For a different interpretation, see Stern, *Rabbi Looks at Jesus' Parables*, 185–95. Stern sums up Jesus' aim: "The disadvantaged and needy identified with the first son [the prodigal one] and reveled in the father's immediate and unconditional acceptance of his returning child. Jesus reminded them that God would welcome them completely

Having reached this stage in the interpretation of the parable, Levine turns her focus to Luke's framing of the parable. She suggests that this framework likely was not Jesus' own, and she argues that it is the Lukan framework that has produced anti-Jewish readings of the parable. Luke 15 begins with a strong critique of the Pharisees and scribes. Levine proposes that in this way, "Luke leads readers to see the elder son as representing Pharisees and scribes who object to Jesus's table fellowship with sinners."[74]

---

and unconditionally once they repented. Even the most depraved sinner would be accepted in love. In the World to Come, a great celebration awaited every sinner who repented. But time was short. The banquet was already prepared and would begin soon. Those who didn't atone now would be left outside and destroyed. It didn't matter how much property, wealth, or status a person possessed. They were irrelevant in the kingdom of heaven . . . Regardless of their good works and their diligence in maintaining the law, those who were proud or jealous or judgmental of others were sinners. By not accepting God's willingness to welcome in love even the most debased penitent, they were thwarting God's will . . . The 'scribes and Pharisees' who murmured against Jesus' dining with sinners were like the older son, who complained about his father's decisions to welcome back his wayward son unconditionally, to exalt him to a position of respect and authority, and to organize a feast in his honor. Jesus reminded these detractors of their own doctrine that God rejoiced when any sinner repented" (194).

74. Levine, *Short Stories by Jesus*, 70. For Levine, Luke (a gentile) was anti-Pharisee while Jesus was not, or at least was much less so. I think, however, that Jesus was calling out real problems among the Pharisees of his day, with whom, of course, he had much in common. For background, see the essays in Chilton and Neusner, *In Quest of the Historical Pharisees*; and see Meier, *Marginal Jew*, 3:311–40, taking a moderate position: "The dirty little secret of NT studies is that no one really knows who the Pharisees were—though many thought they did before a wave of more critical studies hit the academic beach in the 1970s . . . A summary of what we can say with fair probability about Jesus' relation with the Pharisees might run like this: All Gospel sources testify to Jesus' interaction with Pharisees during the public ministry. The tone of the interaction is often adversarial. This is not surprising, since both Jesus and the Pharisees were competing to influence the main body of Palestinian Jews and win them over to their respective visions of what God was calling Israel to be and do at a critical juncture in history. Debates between Jesus and the Pharisees tended to be of a halakic (legal, behavioral) rather than of a doctrinal nature. Such debate probably involved questions like divorce, fasting, tithing, purity rules, observance of the sabbath, and in general the relative importance of various external observances. As part of the prophet-like polemic of Jesus against his debating partners, he may at times have proclaimed woes against Pharisees and attacked them in open or veiled ways in some of his parables" (311, 339). See also Le Donne, "Jewish Leaders," 204: "The disputes between the [Pharisaic] schools of Hillel and Shammai were diverse and profound . . . In one episode of this ongoing rivalry, Dosa ben Harkinas called a fellow Jew 'the first born of Satan' for associating himself with the school of Shammai (*y. Yebam.* 5e). Harkinas's harsh words were spoken in the first century CE and directed at his own brother, Jonathan. We may even have evidence that the followers of Shammai rose up to commit an act of mob violence against Hillel in the Jerusalem temple (*t. Ḥag.* 2.11). According to this Tosefta account, Hillel averted their violent intentions by distracting them with a discussion concerning sacrificial practice. There can be no doubt that the rabbis have colored this

Later commentators, then, intensify this outlook by identifying the angry and sullen elder brother with "restrictive Judaism," and by suggesting that the younger brother represents the inclusion of the gentiles into the family of God.[75] Levine emphasizes that the younger brother, however, is a Jew and does not appear to have eaten pork. Moreover, Levine observes that the Judaism of Jesus' day was not terribly restrictive. She comments, "Why Jews would find gentiles worshipping the God of Israel 'painful' is unclear. Given that gentiles were welcome to worship with Jews in the synagogue and in the Jerusalem Temple, where the outer court was called the Court of the Gentiles, the pain is not self-evident."[76]

For Levine, the parable's point is that the elder son is in need of the father's love. The father, therefore, calls the elder son his "son" or "child" (Luke 15:33) and pledges his permanent love. As Levine describes the father's perspective, "Were either brother to be missing, the family would not be whole."[77] On this view, the parable shows the difficulty of holding

---

story in favor of Hillel. Nonetheless, it shows the severity of the internal hostilities between Pharisaic schools." Le Donne's conclusion is apt: "it will be helpful to remember that Jesus's arguments with these Jewish leaders [scribe, Pharisees, Sadducees] reflect an ongoing power struggle of partisan politics and religious division" (204).

75. Levine, *Short Stories by Jesus*, 70.

76. Levine, *Short Stories by Jesus*, 71. Sean Freyne casts some doubt on the existence of a "Court of the Gentiles." He provides helpful background: "Jubilees reflects the immediate aftermath of the reform of Antiochus and the desecration of the Jerusalem temple, so that its conservative attitude on the issue of the gentiles is, perhaps understandable. A century later, the Psalms of Solomon, especially Ps. 17, is a response to Pompey's takeover of Jerusalem and his entry into the holy place in 67 BCE. It envisages the holy city being purged from all gentiles and the nations subjected to Israel's rule (Pss. of Sol. 17.20, 28, 30). It is among the Qumran sect that these xenophobic attitudes find their most extreme expression. Thus, 4Q Florilegium (4Q 174) declares that into the house which Yahweh will establish (Exod. 15.17f.) 'never will enter the Ammonite, the Moabite or the Bastard, or the foreigner or the proselyte, never, because there he will reveal his ones'. So absolute is the position adopted here that it could easily be read as a direct counter to the openness of Isa. 56.7 and the claims of those who were inspired by it. 11Q Temple Scroll is no more yielding on the subject of gentiles offering sacrifice in the temple. In the detailed plan of the temple put forward by this work the outer court is solely for women, unlike the Herodian temple, where the outer court was divided by a low wall that carried warning inscriptions, threatening the penalty of death for any gentile who might pass beyond that point (JW 5.193; JA 15.17). This has given rise to the notion that there was 'a courtyard of the gentiles' in that temple, even though no ancient source mentions one. The wall and the inscription at least indicate that gentiles had been given some limited access to the temple area, but there is no question of their being able to approach the altar of sacrifice as Isaiah had foreseen" (Freyne, *Jesus, a Jewish Galilean*, 156–57).

77. Levine, *Short Stories by Jesus*, 73. In his *Sacramental Charity*, Anthony Giambrone gets closer to the heart of the matter when he argues that in fact we should pair the parable of the prodigal son with the parables of the dishonest steward (Luke

a family together. The father overindulged the younger son and underindulged the elder son. Thus the parable is primarily about how to identify the "lost" member of one's family and how to ensure that this lost member does not become permanently alienated. The parable can be extended to apply to the whole world. It is important, for instance, that Ishmael (the elder son) and Isaac (the younger one) be reconciled, and that Jacob and Esau be reconciled. The contemporary application speaks to the need for the reconciliation of Christians, Jews, and Muslims. As will become clear below, I disagree with her interpretation, even while I think she is correct to perceive that Jesus in his wisdom teaching cares about family reconciliation.

Let me next turn to Levine's interpretation of the parable of the good Samaritan. She first observes that interpreters often understand the parable to be about the need to set aside religious, national, or political differences in order to care for each and every person, especially the oppressed or vulnerable, as a beloved neighbor. In this standard reading of the parable, the observant Jews (a priest and a Levite) failed to do the act of love that their enemy, the Samaritan, did. Too often in interpretations of this parable, "the Samaritan comes to represent the Christian who has learned to care for others or to break free of prejudice, whereas the priest and the Levite represent Judaism, understood to be xenophobic, promoting ritual purity over

---

16:1–13) and the rich man and Lazarus (Luke 16:19–31). Connecting the prodigal son with the dishonest steward—along lines suggested by Michael Austin—Giambrone observes, "Both characters, the Prodigal Son and the Prodigal Servant, ultimately face a crisis due to their grave misuse of money; then they realize a (self-interested) plan to procure hospitality for themselves (15:17–19; 16:4). Though neither story ever uses the word μετάνοια, the theme fills the whole context (e.g. 15:7; 16:30), and the note is struck in 16:3, when the steward significantly asks the Lukan 'repentance question': τί ποιήσω (3:10, 12, 14; 10:25; 18:18; Acts 2:37; 22:10). It was exactly this query that John the Baptist answered, in counseling penitent sinners to produce fruit in works of charity" (*Sacramental Charity*, 238). The connection between the parable of the prodigal son and the parable of the rich man and Lazarus is even tighter, as Giambrone shows in detail, drawing upon Hanna Roose (although Giambrone differs from Roose in notable ways). Giambrone's application of all this to Jesus' critical engagement with the Pharisees draws upon the work of Kilgallen, "Luke 15 and 16." With Jesus' eschatological proclamation and the Pharisees' general rejection of it in view, Giambrone notes, "Luke thus offers a trio of interrelated stories, and one can make out the narrative arc. The Pharisees, like the Elder Brother, grumble, but are urged to rejoice in the repentance of sinners. Jesus' subsequent praise of the wisdom of escaping judgment through almsgiving only earns the Pharisees' mocking laughter, however. Jesus thus counters with a dire warning, indicating that the greedy Pharisees stand in grave need of self-rescue by repentance, shown in charity to the poor. Significantly, resurrection imagery punctuates this three-pointed narrative arc at every step" (*Sacramental Charity*, 240–41; cf. 243). See also Austin, "Hypocritical Son"; Roose, "Umkehr und Ausgleich bei Lukas."

compassion, proclaiming self-interest over love of neighbor, and otherwise being something that needs to be rejected."[78]

How then should we better interpret the parable of the good Samaritan? Again, Levine begins by suggesting that it is likely that Luke has repackaged material derived from Jesus in order to promote Luke's own emphasis on repentance and forgiveness as well as his negative view of the Jewish religious leaders (Pharisees, scribes, and lawyers). For Jesus' audience, says Levine, "lawyers would likely have been positive figures and their connection to Torah a good thing."[79] Luke, however, frames the parable of the good Samaritan as Jesus' response to a treacherous question put to him by a lawyer, who calls Jesus "Teacher" but does not mean it.

Moreover, the question asked by the lawyer—"Teacher, what shall I do to inherit eternal life?" (Luke 10:25)—is not a real question, according to Levine, because Jews who believed in eternal life did not see it as "a commodity to be inherited or purchased."[80] Jesus himself teaches in Luke 10:28 and 18:20–22 that to receive eternal life we should follow the Decalogue and lead self-sacrificial lives, but he does not thereby think we *earn* the covenantal gift of eternal life. In Levine's view, Jesus attempts to draw the lawyer away from focusing on eternal life and back toward the present life. Jesus' response "do this, and you will live" (Luke 10:28) echoes Leviticus 18:5 and Deuteronomy 30, both of which are focused on what a person must do in order truly to live here and now.

According to the Torah, a "neighbor" is someone inside the community. There is another term for outsiders who reside within Israel and whom God commands his people to treat with love and care. Israelites must love both the outsider and the neighbor, but in the framing of the parable, the lawyer's question "who is my neighbor?" means, in essence, "who is *not* my neighbor?" and can therefore be treated less well. At stake, Levine suggests, is Jesus' commandment to love one's enemy, including enemies who are not Israelites and who do not live in the land. The Torah requires that Israelites treat foreign enemies with respect, but it does not require the Israelites to love them. Jesus likely draws upon Proverbs 25:21–22 for his teaching on love of enemy, and he may also be drawing upon the fact that in Hebrew the words "evil" and "neighbor" are written in the exact same way (they differ only in vowels, which are not present in Hebrew writing). While the

---

78. Levine, *Short Stories by Jesus*, 80.

79. Levine, *Short Stories by Jesus*, 82.

80. Levine, *Short Stories by Jesus*, 85. I think Levine here underestimates the place of merit (and eschatology) in Second Temple Judaism; on this point, see Anderson, *Sin*, and many recent works by other scholars. Merit does not exclude grace. For Second Temple Jewish understandings of grace, see Barclay, *Paul and the Gift*.

framework is Luke's, then, Levine thinks the core of the parable quite possibly comes from Jesus.[81]

Surveying the history of interpretation of the parable, Levine notes that the church fathers depicted Jesus as the good Samaritan, and the heartless priest and Levite as the Law and Prophets. Almost equally problematically, contemporary scholars often argue that observant Jews of Jesus' day would have kept their distance from tradesmen such as the man in the ditch, since such tradesmen could not strictly observe Torah. In response, Levine observes that Pharisees such as Paul *were* tradesmen (in Paul's case, a leather worker), and, besides, Pharisees were not so petty as to worry about the possibility that a person had broken a commandment when faced with a victim of violence.

Other contemporary interpreters cast aspersions on priests and Levites as members of a supposedly hated "elite," even though in Jesus' day the priests and Levites inherited their position and often had neither power nor wealth. Some priests and Levites were elite, but many were not. Still other contemporary interpreters blame Jewish law regarding ritual contamination by touching corpses[82]—ignoring the fact that the priest and Levite are depicted as traveling *away from* the temple, and also ignoring the fact that for Jewish Law touching a half-dead person for restorative purposes is a good deed, as is burying the dead. Levine observes that for Josephus, burying an unattended corpse is a strict religious duty.[83] In addition, the ritual

---

81. By contrast, Craig A. Evans comments that "it is probable that the context into which the Lukan evangelist placed the parable is true to its original intent. The point of the parable in its present context is to provide an answer to the Pharisees who criticized Jesus for associating with 'sinners' (Luke 15:1–2). The point is that the Torah-observant Jew should rejoice when the sinner sees the error of his ways and seek reconciliation" (Evans, "Reconstructing Jesus' Teaching," 163). Evans thinks that the parable is likely part of Jesus' original oral teaching.

82. See for example Zimmermann, *Puzzling the Parables of Jesus*, 306.

83. This point is made also by Stern, *Rabbi Looks at Jesus' Parables*, 213. Matthew Thiessen likewise warns against reading this parable as though it "demonstrates that Jews, perhaps especially the priestly and religious elite, have interpreted the law in such a way that it discourages them from pursuing actions of compassion and mercy" or as though Jesus is attacking "some sort of Jewish legalism" (Thiessen, *Jesus and the Forces of Death*, 114, 118). On the contrary, in Thiessen's view, "Luke's Jesus believes himself to be adhering to the Jewish law," with the caveat however that "the Jewish law, like any legal code, contains potential interpretive issues" (114). The issues here consist in how to understand the relationship between Leviticus 21:1–3 and Deuteronomy 21:23. Thiessen astutely remarks (partly in response to Levine), "In exceptionally rare circumstances these two divine commandments might come into conflict, a situation that Luke's Jesus constructs in his answer to the lawyer. Given the commandment to bury the dead, what was a priest to do if he discovered a neglected corpse in need of burial? Should he contract corpse impurity in order to bury the dead body in obedience both

purity required of a priest differed sharply from that required of a Levite. The Torah required all Jews to treat with care both neighbors and strangers, and so the priest and Levite would have had no excuse for their negligence. Levine states, "Saving a life is so important that Jewish Law mandates that it override every other concern, including keeping the Sabbath."[84]

For Levine, one point that Jesus wished to convey is a simple one: do not worry about eternal life but instead worry about caring for people here and now. But another point has to do with the role of the Samaritan. For Jesus' audience, a Samaritan would have been the last person they expected to hear praised. Jesus' audience would have expected a story about a priest and a Levite, but certainly not a Samaritan—let alone as the hero of the story. In the parable, the Samaritan shows the same "compassion" that the father shows in the parable of the prodigal son (Luke 10:33; Luke 15:20).

Jesus' audience thought of Samaritans as oppressors. Shechem, the original Samaria, was a place of rape and murder in the books of Genesis and Judges. In the period of the kings, the Samaritans were idolaters and opponents of the Davidic kingship, until the Assyrian empire conquered the Northern Kingdom (Samaria).[85] During the return of the Judahites from their Babylonian captivity, the Samaritans who had remained in the land opposed the returning exiles. The Samaritans went on to build their own temple (on Mount Gerizim) in the early fourth century BC. They did not assist the Maccabean revolt, in part because Samaria had been rebuilt

---

to this reading of Deuteronomy 21:32 and to the priestly command to love one's neighbor (Lev 19:18)? Or should he avoid the corpse and corpse contamination in obedience to the legislation of Leviticus 21:1–3? For that matter, what was a priest to do if he discovered a body that, as in Jesus's story, might or might not be a corpse?" (115–16). Arguing that Jews in Jesus' day debated such matters rather than having a unanimous viewpoint, Thiessen maintains that Jesus (without rejecting the laws regarding ritual purity) "argues that the laws of Leviticus 19:18 and Deuteronomy 21:23 take legal precedence over the law of Leviticus 21:1–3" (118). Thiessen emphasizes that Jesus does not thereby, in the name of compassion, do away with concern for ritual purity: "In Jesus's story, a priest or Levite who contracts corpse contamination in order to see whether the man is still alive does so with the result that he either (a) preserves the life of the beaten man and therefore saves the world from one more corpse and its concomitant, never-ending ability to pollute or (b) buries the man's remains, thereby honoring and loving the dead man, and marks the burial site so that other people do not unwittingly contract corpse impurity . . . Exercising compassion does not undermine the ritual purity system; it ultimately confirms it" (119). See also Bauckham, "Scrupulous Priest and the Good Samaritan," cited appreciatively by Thiessen.

84. Levine, *Short Stories by Jesus*, 102.

85. For background, see Judge, *Other Gods and Idols*. A thesis of Judge's book is that "the sequence of events associated with the fall of the Northern Kingdom marks the end of the Old Testament's battle on the domestic front against the worship of YHWH via divine images" (xv).

in 333 as a Greek city. In 128, the Jewish ruler John Hyrcanus burned down the temple on Mount Gerizim, but Herod rebuilt this temple for the Samaritans.[86] The point is that the Samaritans had been in intense conflict with the people of Judah for many centuries.

Furthermore, the Samaritans claimed to possess the true interpretation of the Torah that had been misunderstood, they believed, by the people of Judah. They rejected the work of Ezra, along with the prophetic books and indeed everything other than the Pentateuch. Levine adds a capstone: "The Jewish king Herod the Great took a Samaritan woman named Malthace as one of his wives"—the very woman whose son was Herod Antipas, the dissolute ruler who ordered John the Baptist's death.[87]

Shortly before the parable of the good Samaritan, Luke reports that despite Jesus' overtures, the people of a Samaritan village refused to "receive him, because his face was set toward Jerusalem" (Luke 9:53). His disciples were thunderstruck at this rude rejection. James and John even asked Jesus whether they should call down fire from heaven to destroy the villagers—a request that Jesus rebuked. Thus, the Samaritan was not a mere religious

---

86. For further detail, see Stern, *Rabbi Looks at Jesus' Parables*, 215. Stern adds, "Some twenty years before Jesus' ministry, a group of Samaritans defiled the Jerusalem Temple by strewing it with human bones. The enmity and mistrust Jews felt were expressed in a series of laws. Jews normally said 'Amen' after an Israelite recited a blessing, but Jews were commanded not to say 'Amen' after a Samaritan said a blessing. Two witnesses normally certified a document. However, if one of the two witnesses was a Samaritan, the document was invalid . . . A man who had intercourse with a Samaritan woman (even though he could marry her) paid a fifty-shekel fine. Samaritan women were unclean, and Samaritan men defiled whatever they touched. The half-shekel tax to support the Temple was not accepted from a Samaritan even when he offered it voluntarily" (215).

87. Levine, *Short Stories by Jesus*, 107. For background, see Chilton, *Herods*; and see also Freyne, *Jesus, a Jewish Galilean*, 164–65: "Herod's lavish project with regard to the temple is often seen as his way of placating Jewish religious sensibilities. This judgement is not an adequate explanation, however, since he had introduced into Jerusalem other aspects of the gentile way of life, such as the amphitheatre, without any compunction . . . His intentions are better understood as self-glorification in the best Hellenistic style by endowing Jerusalem with a temple that could match those of other great temple-cities of the east such as Palmyra, Jerash and Petra. He thus hoped to win good-will and admiration from the far-flung Jewish Diaspora, as well as recognition from his Roman patrons . . . This change in the symbolic status of the Jerusalem under Herodian patronage within the larger Roman world throws the magnitude of Jesus' symbolic action/word into bolder relief. Jeremiah's words [against the temple: see Jeremiah 7 and 26] were a reminder to his co-religionists that religious worship, devoid of ethical sincerity were valueless in the sight of Yahweh. Jesus' action, while affirming that aspect of prophetic insight, also represented a throwing down of the gauntlet to the imperial power that basked in the reflected glory of this extraordinary architectural statement."

outsider; rather, Samaritans were strong opponents or enemies both of Jews and of Jesus himself.

In Levine's reading, the parable goes much deeper than a mere lesson about tolerance, let alone a lesson showing how intolerant Jewish Law is. Rather, Jesus offers a lesson about ending a cycle of violence. Second Chronicles 28:8–15 describes a battle between the kingdoms of Judah and Israel (Samaria) in which the victorious Samaritan army, after being sharply chastened by a prophet, actually clothes, feeds, anoints, and restores its Judean captives. In this case, the Samaritans acted like the good Samaritan, and the Jews were in the place of the victim on the side of the road. The Samaritans in this case did what God wills: they showed compassion or mercy.

Jesus urges that his audience needs to take seriously the possibility of Samaritan goodness. Thus, for Levine "[t]he parable, in its original setting, is not about the type of prejudice that creates people on the margins; it is about hatred between groups who have similar resources."[88] To overcome such hatred requires acknowledging the good actions of one's enemy. This is not easy, given the ingrained enmity and the historical and contemporary reasons for it. Levine compares Jesus' parable to Israelites today telling a story of a "good Hamas member" or to Palestinians in Ramallah today telling a story of a "good Jew." She concludes that the point of the parable is that we must tell such stories and imitate the good Samaritan in the story, because "[t]he divine is manifested only through our actions."[89] When religious people focus on differences and on long-standing enmities, they impede the expression of the divine on behalf of true reconciliation.[90]

I will discuss one more parable treated by Levine, the parable of the laborers in the vineyard (Matt 20:1–16).[91] As suggested by Isaiah 5, the

88. Levine, *Short Stories by Jesus*, 112.

89. Levine, *Short Stories by Jesus*, 114.

90. Similarly, Stern concludes that "Jesus addressed the parable to Jewish listeners—to convey ideas Jesus wanted Jews to consider, in order to overcome their antipathy to Samaritans and others traditionally despised in Jewish society, and to broaden their understandings of the biblical commandment 'Love your neighbor'" (Stern, *Rabbi Looks at Jesus' Parables*, 218–19).

91. Ruben Zimmermann observes that in the Gospel of Matthew, "The parables consider and reflect upon ethical questions with a view toward both individual and social ethics. And parables are used to consider eschatological questions, sometimes working with a strong apocalyptic dualism as well as with imperatives (Matt. 24:52; 25:13: 'Keep awake!') and harsh concluding sentences (e.g. 'there will be weeping and gnashing of teeth,' see Matt. 13:42, 50; 22:13; 24:51)" (Zimmermann, *Puzzling the Parables of Jesus*, 263). While cautioning against reducing Jesus' teaching solely to teaching about the kingdom in parables, he suggests that Matthew supports such a portrait: "that Jesus announced the 'kingdom of God in parables' was, to a significant extent, actually developed by Matthew . . . There is a large number of parables in both

vineyard in Israel's Scriptures is a symbol of Israel—with God as the owner of the vineyard.[92] Arguing once more that "Jesus was more interested in how we love our neighbor than how we get into heaven,"[93] Levine maintains that the parable is about how economic life should be oriented in God's community.

Levine notes that traditional Christian interpretations of the parable see it as anti-Jewish. For the church fathers, the first-hired worker is Adam, the later-hired workers are Abraham and Moses, and finally the last-hired are Jesus and the gentiles. For more recent readers, the workers who complain are the ever-grumbling Jews, who are about to lose the vineyard to the gentiles. Other contemporary interpreters see the last-hired workers as people of a different race, with the first-hired workers as Pharisaical opponents of multiculturalism. Levine argues that all these readings trade in anti-Jewish stereotypes, and all of them enable readers to avoid the economic challenge intended by the parable.

Aware that there are some economic interpretations of the parables today, Levine summarizes a few of these. Not uncommon is the notion that the landowner is exploitative. In this interpretation, Jesus' purpose is to help all parties to see that the landowner has been exploiting them, so that all parties can unite with each other in labor negotiations. In response, Levine notes that there is no real evidence of severe economic distress or

---

Mark and Q, and both writings also frequently refer to the kingdom of God. It was only Matthew, however, who prominently introduced the parables of Jesus as 'parables of the kingdom' and used the formula 'the kingdom of heaven is like . . .' ten times" (*Puzzling the Parables of Jesus*, 264). Luke's scope is broader: "In the introductions to so-called figurative sayings (e.g., 'the physician who is to heal himself,' Luke 4:23), similitudes (e.g., 'humility and hospitality,' Luke 14:7), parables (e.g., 'the widow and the judge,' Luke 18:1), and example stories ('the Pharisee and the tax collector,' Luke 18:9), Luke simply refers to all of these as παραβολή" (295).

92. For an analysis of Jesus' eschatological use of the image of the vineyard, including in his parable of the laborers in the vineyard, see Bryan, *Jesus and Israel's Traditions*, 47–72; and on this parable see also Barber, *Historical Jesus and the Temple*, 171–79, 207–12, including a critique of the anti-Jewish interpretations of the parable. The eschatological dimension of the parable is neglected by Levine. For Bryan, the parable of the laborers in the vineyard emphasizes "the absolute freedom of God in the giving of the eschatological blessings of the kingdom even to those within Israel who by all accounts do not deserve it and who by the accounts of some at least had already cut themselves off from elect Israel" (68). To my mind, the likelihood of the parable having an eschatological import is high, whether or not Bryan is correct (and here Levine would rightly be most opposed) that "[t]he workers who complain about the generosity of the vineyard owner to those who came late in the day most naturally correspond to the Pharisees and teachers of the law in the Jesus traditions" (68). Bryan directs attention to Beasley-Murray, *Jesus and the Kingdom of God*, 117–19.

93. Levine, *Short Stories by Jesus*, 215.

exploitation in the Galilee of Jesus' time. Levine concurs, however, that the parable is about labor relations. She probes into the meaning of the Greek term for "householder," arguing that the term does not suggest reference to God—although she grants that the householder *may* represent God in the parable. The rate paid by the householder was a denarius, the customary wage at the time. The strange part of the parable, she observes, is that the householder keeps going out to find more workers; he never seems to have hired enough.

In Matthew 20:8, the phrase "owner of the vineyard" is better translated "Lord of the vineyard," since the term is *kyrios*. Levine therefore suggests that the point of the parable may be to instruct us in good economic practice by calling us to imitate the Lord/householder. What then is the significance of the fact that the householder decides to pay each worker the same (fair) wage, no matter when during the course of the day the worker was hired? In her view, the last line of the parable—"So the last will be first, and the first last" (Matt 20:16)—is here placed on Jesus' lips as a framing device by the evangelist, and cannot "serve as the 'moral' of the parable," given that the parable makes all the workers equal in pay rather than establishing an upside-down hierarchy in which the first switch places with the last.[94]

Instead, her interpretation of the parable boils down to Jesus' concern that everyone should receive enough to live on.[95] She quotes ancient Jewish texts that express a similar concern, arguing that in God's eyes all persons are equally beloved. The payment of equal (and never unfair) wages for unequal work indicates that the person in charge of the funds is acting as God acts. Each worker should receive what is needed to live. Indeed, business

---

94. Levine, *Short Stories by Jesus*, 233.

95. For another economic interpretation of the parable of the laborers in the vineyard, see Sirico, *Economics of the Parables*, 29–37. Davies and Allison comment, "Perhaps 20.1–5 served Jesus as an apology for his ministry, which belonged to the last hour: God's grace goes to the undeserving ('tax collectors and sinners') and gives them the same reward (the kingdom) others receive—and where is the justice in that? Opponents could have posed the question, or perhaps the twelve raised it when promises given to them were offered to others. But the story may also have functioned in a more general fashion to set forth a lesson not about 'realized eschatology' but about divine goodness and future rewards: God's generosity transcends human expectations, and grace disallows calculation of recompense. While Christians in the past have unfairly characterized Judaism as dominated by mechanical notions of reward, any religion that makes God a judge will have adherents who imagine the last judgement as a weighing of merits. And it is quite possible that, with his parable about equal payment for unequal work, Jesus was countering such thinking. He did not attack the idea of reward . . . But, as in 25.31ff., so here too: reward is surprise because God's ways are not our ways" (Davies and Allison, *Critical and Exegetical Commentary on the Gospel According to Saint Matthew*, 3:70).

owners should hire as many people as economically possible, thereby ensuring that as many people as possible receive the dignity of a living wage. Levine argues that for Jesus, as for the Torah, "the rich who fail to open their hand will receive eschatological punishment."[96] But the point of the parable is not only aimed at the rich. It is aimed at all of us, since we all need to recognize that rather than living by greed or private benefit, we need to live and act so that as many people as economically possible receive what is needed to live. When we act in this way, "we learn what it means to act as God acts, with generosity to all."[97]

Levine's Jesus is wise, but his teaching—at least as represented by his parables—cannot be said to *reveal* much. His parables provide instructive and challenging teaching about the need for reconciliation in families (the prodigal son) and among nations (the good Samaritan), as well as about the need for people to seek the common economic good rather than mere private wealth (the laborers in the vineyard). But in her reading, the parables

---

96. Levine, *Short Stories by Jesus*, 236. See Räisänen, "Resurrection for Punishment?." Interestingly, Räisänen thinks New Testament texts favor hell as annihilation: "Paul is rather reticent concerning the fate of the wicked. He does assume that sinners and unbelievers will have a fate different from that of the believers and speaks of their 'destruction' (Rom 2,12; 9:22; 1 Cor 1,18; 2 Cor 2,15; 4,3; 1 Thess 5,3; Phil 1,28; 3,19), probably thinking of their annihilation. He seems to assume the resurrection of the *righteous only*: the dead *in Christ* (1 Thess 4,16) or 'those of Christ' (1 Cor 15, 23) will rise when Jesus returns... In a Q section, Jesus encourages his followers to confess him before humans: 'Do not fear those who kill the body but cannot kill the soul; rather fear him who can *destroy* both soul and body in hell' (Q 12,45). It would seem that those punished will be totally annihilated, body and soul. The Gospel of John seems to lack the notion of eternal torment. Those who do not believe are 'condemned already' (John 3,18); without faith in Jesus one can only 'perish' (3,16). The evil-doers will rise to the 'resurrection of condemnation' (5,25–29), but as God's wrath is expressed as a denial of life, they are annihilated" ("Resurrection for Punishment?," 366-67; and see also, for background to "Q"—and for the argument that it was not a single document and contained some Aramaic sources—Casey's *Aramaic Approach to Q*. Räisänen grants that in Mark 9:43–48; Matthew 13:42, 22:13, 24:51, 25:30, and 25:41; and Luke 16:24—along with Revelation 14:9–11, Jude 13, and 2 Peter 2:17—there are strong images of everlasting torment).

97. Levine, *Short Stories by Jesus*, 237. Stern's interpretation is similar to Levine's but goes a step further. He writes, "For Jesus, it was not the amount of money involved but the principle, since each laborer received a subsistence wage, barely enough to sustain the worker and his family. The laborer's wife and children would go hungry. The vineyard owner understood this. Out of his compassion for the plight of the poor and the unemployed, he paid a full day's wage. In that sense, he was generous. According to Jesus, God was generous with humans the same way. Such was the measure of his compassion that He provided a place in His kingdom to the most egregious sinners. Jesus reminded those who saw themselves as better and who criticized Jesus' association with outcasts that, in the process, they were condemning God and disassociating themselves from His endeavors" (Stern, *Rabbi Looks at Jesus' Parables*, 103–4).

TEACHING

do not teach anything that Jews did not already know about God, and the parables teach next to nothing about Jesus himself. She emphasizes that Jesus' teaching is about human life and good human action. In sum, for Levine the authority of Jesus' teaching is that of a good rabbi and nothing more; and his message is not that of the (divine) eschatological Messiah inaugurating the kingdom of God in his person, but rather that of a wise man offering good counsel for how families, communities, and nations might flourish in the present life along paths sanctioned by what the Jewish people already knew about God.[98]

---

98. For background to Levine's perspective, see her *Misunderstood Jew*. She emphasizes, "When Jesus is located within the world of Judaism, the ethical implications of his teachings take on renewed and heightened meaning; their power is restored and their challenge sharpened. Jews as well as Christians should be able to agree on a number of these teachings today" (21; cf. 34–41 on the parables). She later says in a similar vein, "To understand Jesus, he must be seen as provocative enough both to prompt some to leave their homes and families and to follow him and to prompt others to regard him as insane or demon possessed. This means, at the very least, that his message is not an easy one to follow. Jesus demanded of his followers an economic overhaul and a nonviolent response to injustice. The former is at best impractical; the latter is psychologically difficult. Neither is beyond the competencies of most individuals, but Jesus asked for even more" (217). In Levine's view, Jesus' message also required such things as selling all one's property and giving the proceeds to the poor, abandoning one's family, and absolute celibacy (218). At the same time, Levine does not devote explicit or sustained attention to the eschatological character of Jesus' words and deeds, and instead she attributes the New Testament's "eschatological enthusiasm" to his early Jewish followers who believed that he had risen from the dead (60). Levine reconstructs the disappointment of some of these followers: "As the delay of justice, the finality of death, and the rapacity of Rome continued, some of Jesus's early followers may well have returned to their homes and families. The social experiment of living by forgiving debts and trespasses, treating all in the group as members of one's own family, and recognizing that they were part of the inbreaking of the kingdom of heaven remained only a beautiful memory and an unfulfilled hope. They would need to wait for someone else" (62; after these Jews left, Levine suggests, Peter and Paul took the message to the Gentiles, who embraced it and radically transformed it). See also Levine's *Sermon on the Mount*. Levine reads the sermon as being about "living into the kingdom of heaven by helping to create it on earth . . . When the community does the divine will, then the community is in the image of the divine" (*Sermon on the Mount*, 109, 114). She concludes, "For Jesus, life meant being part of a community. His comment in Luke 17:21, 'The kingdom of God is among you,' demonstrates that communal presence. When people take seriously the Sermon on the Mount—when they conquer their anger, when they love not only their neighbors but also their enemies—the kingdom is present . . . Neither Judaism nor Christianity is a finished project; both traditions are looking forward to that messianic age where there is real peace on earth and real peace in the human heart" (125).

ENGAGING THE DOCTRINE OF JESUS (AND MARY)

Gerhard Lohfink

Let me now turn to the quite different perspective of the Catholic biblical scholar and theologian Gerhard Lohfink. In Jesus' parables, says Lohfink, the framing theme is "the urgent advent of the reign of God and . . . the 'here and now' of the rule of God in Israel."[99] Jesus' parables are not simply wisdom regarding morality and human life. They have to do instead with Jesus' announcement of the kingdom of God. After all, the one who speaks the parables is no ordinary wisdom teacher, but rather understands himself as having a mission to inaugurate the kingdom of God as Israel's Messiah.

On the basis of his study of some Old Testament parables, Lohfink notes that we should expect Jesus' parables to make an argumentative case for something and to have a striking climax. Parables may sometimes possess a double meaning, as in the case of the parable that the prophet Nathan told to King David—in response to which David unwittingly pronounced a death sentence upon himself. The climax of a parable may often be one of condemnation, just as we find in Isaiah 5, which tells the story of the planting of a beautiful vineyard (symbolic of God's bride Israel) and God's lament over its unfruitfulness, which will result in its destruction by God.

Ezekiel 16 is a parable along these lines. God condemns faithless Israel as an adulterous wife. Lohfink notes that in Ezekiel 16, "The faithlessness of the city of Jerusalem toward its God is depicted with extreme intensity and severity. The city has become a whore. She has given herself over to all the sins of the Canaanites."[100] Ezekiel 16, Lohfink observes, offers a parable in the form of an allegory. It was an allegory that described real sufferings that the city of Jerusalem and the kingdom of Judah were then undergoing, due to the Babylonians. The allegory is filled with images that aim to lead the

---

99. Lohfink, *Forty Parables of Jesus*, 6. For a recent study of the parables—much indebted to Lohfink although in more direct conversation with the philosopher William Desmond—see Duns, "Reconfigured Through the Word."

100. Lohfink, *Forty Parables of Jesus*, 19. Lohfink comments, "For us listeners today the parable of the faithless wife is harder to understand than Jotham's fable or Isaiah's song of the vineyard. For example, one needs to know that in the ancient world of paganism the exposure of children in marshes and barren wastes was common practice. Girls especially were simply thrown away soon after birth. One needs to know that a newborn child was rubbed with finely-ground salt and then tightly swaddled, not merely for reasons of hygiene but above all in order to protect it from demons. One must know that even earrings and nose rings had apotropaic significance: they were supposed to barricade the body's orifices so demons could not enter. One must know that Hosea and Jeremiah had previously described God's covenant with Israel in terms of marriage and named participation in the fertility cults of the Canaanites as whoredom and adultery" (21). For further discussion of such prophetic texts, see the first chapter of my *Engaging the Doctrine of Marriage*.

people to recall what God did for his people in electing them, making covenant with them, establishing the Davidic kingdom, and so on. God appears in the parable as a lover who has been rejected despite all that he has done. The parable ends by confirming that God still greatly loves his people. The people will undergo a profound judgment (i.e. the exile), but this will not be the end of the story of God's love for them. God promises to establish with Israel an everlasting covenant: "Yes, thus says the Lord God: I will deal with you as you have done, who have despised the oath in breaking the covenant, yet I will remember my covenant with you in the days of your youth, and I will establish with you an everlasting covenant" (Ezek 16:59–60).

Lohfink argues that Jesus' parables about the kingdom of God should be interpreted in light of such prophetic parables about eschatological judgment and restoration.[101] He points to John 15:1–8 (the vine and the branches) as an example of a "parable" that builds upon a metaphor, contains a firm admonition, and ends with a promise of everlasting union. Lohfink's key point in this context is that "behind the authentic Jesus parables stands . . . a claim beyond all grasping."[102] That claim is the inauguration of the kingdom of God.

Whether directly or implicitly, Jesus' parables consistently alert his hearers to the coming kingdom, and often to his own role in it. Lohfink argues that in his parables Jesus teaches about God's accomplishing his rule in Israel and in the world, over against the forces (human and demonic) that oppose his rule. In the Gospels, "the reign of God is, in principle, already present in Jesus, but it still has to establish itself throughout the world, against the powers opposed to God. Thus it has both a present and a future aspect."[103] With regard to the future aspect, Lohfink notes that various New Testament writings speak of a coming "day of the Lord"—the *parousia* or Second Coming of Jesus.[104] In the Gospels, however, Jesus is already overthrowing the powers of darkness and inaugurating the kingdom by his presence.

---

101. For background to restoration eschatology, see Eskola, *Narrative Theology of the New Testament*; Bryan, *Jesus and Israel's Traditions of Judgement and Restoration*.

102. Lohfink, *Forty Parables of Jesus*, 24.

103. Lohfink, *Forty Parables of Jesus*, 42.

104. Discussing a parable found in Luke, N. T. Wright argues that the notion of Jesus' second coming "looks much more like a post-Easter innovation than a feature of Jesus' own teaching. Even granted that Jesus' hearers did not always grasp what he said, it strains probability a long way to think of him attempting to explain, to people who had not grasped the fact of his imminent death, that there would follow an indeterminate period after which he would 'return' in some spectacular fashion, for which nothing in their tradition had prepared them" (*Jesus and the Victory of God*, 635). This may be so, but "post-Easter innovation" is not the right way of putting it, since the risen Jesus himself could have been the teacher of this "innovation." Moreover, some of Jesus'

Let me now turn to Lohfink's reading of the three parables whose interpretation by Levine I have surveyed above. The first is the parable of the prodigal son. Reading the parable in the context of Jesus' first two parables in Luke 15 (the parable of the lost sheep and the parable of the lost coin), Lohfink gives the parable the title "The Lost Son," as Levine also did. Lohfink begins his interpretation by praising Luke's narrative artistry. In his view, Luke is the one who has linked these three parables together; in each case something treasured is found. Lohfink ascribes to Luke the last line of the parable of the prodigal son, where the father says, "It is fitting to make merry and be glad, for this your brother was dead, and is alive; he was lost, and is found" (Luke 15:32). Overall, however, Lohfink considers that the parable of the prodigal son derives from Jesus.

Along lines that Levine discounts, Lohfink argues that no ancient Near Eastern patriarch would have run to greet someone; instead, the patriarch would wait with dignity at the doorstep. In his view, ancient readers would have been impressed by the father's running to greet the returning prodigal son. Whether or not Lohfink is correct here, the father's greeting is certainly accentuated by the fact that not only does the father run toward the son, but the father embraces and kisses his son before the son has even spoken. Lohfink points this out and adds that the father goes still further: the father "interrupts the son's confession of guilt and orders that a festal garment, a ring, and shoes be brought for him"; and the father orders the slaughter of the fatted calf so as to hold a feast.[105]

No doubt, the father pulls out all stops in order to welcome the son back to the family. Recall that for Levine, the meaning of the parable is family reconciliation—and so the most difficult and important task is the father's reconciliation of the embittered elder son to himself. By contrast, Lohfink considers that Jesus' audience would have seen the reference to the prodigal son's working on a pig farm as a symbolic indication of the son's having lost his faith. Lohfink observes that not only has the bankrupt son gone to work for a gentile, but also "no Jew in the employ of a Gentile could live his faith. Among the Gentiles there was no kosher food, no Sabbath, no way of keeping the law."[106] Surely the fact that he ended up as a hired man on a pig farm signifies his distance from his Judaism and not only his material deprivation.

---

words and deeds indicate an expectation of an indeterminate period prior to the full arrival of the kingdom, as for instance his institution of the Eucharist at the Last Supper.

105. Lohfink, *Forty Parables of Jesus*, 82.
106. Lohfink, *Forty Parables of Jesus*, 82.

Unlike Levine, Lohfink sees a dynamic of guilt, repentance, and profound mercy being played out between the prodigal son and the father. In Lohfink's view, the son returns with the sincere intention of confessing guilt for his waywardness. (Here inevitably the prophetic charge that Israel had been guilty comes to mind.) The son is truly repentant. The father runs toward the son with absolute mercy. The father is so merciful that the son's speech is never the focus of the father's attention. The father is already utterly merciful prior to the son's speech, and so the son's speech changes nothing. Lohfink suggests that Jesus is giving his audience a portrait of the power of the divine Father's grace. The father takes the initiative in reconciling his son. Indeed, the father's seeing his son "while he was yet at a distance" (Luke 15:20) indicates symbolically, Lohfink argues, that "this father was expecting his son; he yearned for him; his very yearning had drawn the son back."[107] The point here is that the father stands for the divine Father who loves and yearns for his people Israel, while the son stands for wayward Israel, on the path back to God (freed from captivity to the gentile idolatry symbolized by the pig farm).

Lohfink does not spell all this out, but instead moves on to attend to the father's relation to the elder son. Much like Levine, Lohfink considers this relationship to be crucial to the story. Just as the father goes out to the younger son, so the father goes out to the elder son when he discovers that the elder son, too, has been "lost" in the sense of being estranged from the father. The father does not demand that the elder son come to him inside the house, but instead goes out personally to invite the elder son to come in. The father's initiative (or grace) again strikes Lohfink as significant.

Unlike Levine, Lohfink considers that the elder brother really does stand for the Pharisees, who are often Jesus' opponents in the Gospel of Luke. Lohfink does not consider it historically unlikely that the Pharisees would have thought that others were prodigal and had not been living in accord with God's will for redemption. The Pharisees arguably would not have accepted the notion of God offering full mercy and grace without conditions to the younger son. When the father comes out to talk to the elder brother, the father says that "this your brother was dead" (Luke 15:32). It seems reasonable to suppose that the Pharisees would indeed have concurred in this estimation of the spiritual state of the younger brother. But the father's unrestricted joy at the son's return, and the father's drawing the prodigal son directly into the feast without any further conditions, are the sticking points. The father's response to the prodigal's return seems like

---

107. Lohfink, *Forty Parables of Jesus*, 83.

foolishness to the elder son, who wonders why the father has never acted in this joyfully foolish way toward him.

It is notable that Lohfink does not discuss a passage that Levine emphasizes: "Son, you are always with me, and all that is mine is yours" (Luke 15:31). Lohfink may take it for granted that for Jesus it is a matter of course that the Pharisees, as members of God's Jewish people, are beloved inheritors of all that God has. They are members of the covenantal people of Israel. There is no doubt that God loves them. The question, however, is whether they will respond to the mercy that God is now offering to all in and through Jesus.

As in the parable, the father (representing the heavenly Father) reaches out to reconcile his children and to invite them to the eschatological feast. Jesus himself, in his ministry, "went after the lost and the sinners (Luke 19:1–10). He ate with sinners and the despised (Mark 2:15). He defended them against their accusers and those who looked down on them."[108] The message of Jesus was one of unconditional mercy for sinners. Lohfink emphasizes that in revealing the divine mercy, Jesus reveals the meaning of his own actions. Jesus' actions and those of God (and the father in the parable) go together. Thus, Jesus' teaching in the parable of the prodigal son is revelatory of the truth about God, Jesus, and Israel/humankind.

If, as Lohfink supposes, the elder son in this parable symbolizes the Pharisees who in Luke's Gospel oppose Jesus, then why does Jesus focus on reconciling sinners but not, seemingly, concern himself with reconciling the Pharisees? Without doubt, Jesus ate and freely interacted with people who were "public sinners," something the Pharisees avoided in accordance with the warning found in Psalm 1:1–2.[109] Jesus did this in order to make clear God's love for the most broken people, not to signify God's approval of their sins. The prodigal son in the parable stands in the position of these sinners (and of the gentiles as well). Lohfink specifies why the Pharisees took serious offense at what Jesus was doing and teaching: "What they saw as scandal was not that God can forgive even serious sin. People in Israel had always believed that. What embitters the Pharisees and scribes here is that salvation is being promised to people who have not changed their ways at all."[110] Does Lohfink mean that, in the parable and in Jesus' teaching and actions as a whole, no repentance or conversion is expected or needed on the part of those who would follow Jesus and share in his eternal life? Clearly the Gospels (and Paul) repeatedly indicate the opposite: for example, consider

---

108. Lohfink, *Forty Parables of Jesus*, 85.
109. Lohfink, *Forty Parables of Jesus*, 86.
110. Lohfink, *Forty Parables of Jesus*, 86.

Jesus' statement just prior to the parable of the prodigal son: "whoever of you does not renounce all that he has cannot be my disciple" (Luke 14:33). What then does Lohfink mean?

He explains that Jesus' opponents differ from Jesus with regard to what conversion entails and with regard to how it is that God's mercy is given to sinners. For the Pharisees, says Lohfink, repentance and conversion will necessarily entail "unconditional return to Torah and complete restitution," and the reception of God's mercy follows upon the person's return to Torah.[111] Lohfink finds this stance in the parable's characterization of the elder son. According to Lohfink, the elder brother (representing Jesus' opponents) holds, "The one who has caused damage must make restitution. Someone who has lived a life like that of his brother must not have it too easy. Such a person must first demonstrate that he or she has really changed."[112] The elder brother is shocked that the father immediately arranges for a feast and treats the prodigal brother as though all were more than well. If some Pharisees did indeed hold to a similar viewpoint as did the elder brother, I can hardly blame them, but it is clear that Jesus' position is different. Lohfink points out that Jesus' position is reflected in Psalm 103:10–12, "He does not deal with us according to our sins, nor repay us according to our iniquities. For as the heavens are high above the earth, so great is his mercy toward those who fear him; as far as the east is from the west, so far does he remove our transgressions from us." The father (representing the divine Father) takes the initiative, draws us back to himself, and calls us to his eschatological feast. As for the elder brother, at the end of the parable it is still an open question whether he will join the feast with a joyful heart, as the father is urging him to do.

In this light, Levine's question is an urgent one: does anti-Judaism (given the connections between Pharisaic Judaism and Rabbinic Judaism) inevitably result from reading the parable as Lohfink does, namely, as a parable about repentance, grace, and forgiveness, with the father symbolizing God, the prodigal son symbolizing public sinners (and gentiles), and the elder brother symbolizing Jesus' opponents the Pharisees? Lohfink does not address this issue directly, although he makes clear that it is understandable that some persons opposed Jesus on the ground that he minimized the place of Torah observance in redemption. For Lohfink, Jesus' position is plausible only if Jesus truly is the Messiah inaugurating the kingdom of God. The father in the parable acts along eschatological lines. Lohfink observes that "the father's attitude positively turns this world upside down,"

---

111. Lohfink, *Forty Parables of Jesus*, 86.
112. Lohfink, *Forty Parables of Jesus*, 86.

insofar as "in the person of the father, the new world of the reign of God breaks through."[113] Grace, mercy, and feasting are the marks of the reign of God; and there is real repentance present as well.

Lohfink thinks that the prodigal son repents, takes "the road back to his father," and makes a sincere "confession of guilt" in which he truly—and not merely for the sake of self-interest—asks forgiveness from God and from his father: "Father, I have sinned against heaven and before you; I am no longer worthy to be called your son" (Luke 15:21).[114] But the main initiative in this story of eschatological grace, mercy, and feasting belongs to the father, who in this regard represents both God and Jesus. Jesus is thereby teaching in a revelatory fashion about his identity as the supreme image of the Father and about his eschatological mission.

Lohfink does not deny that merciful paternal love already existed in the world of Jesus' day. Just as Levine says, such paternal love surely was not unheard of in Israel. Indeed, "self-surrendering and self-forgetting love" is present in our world today, and not only as a shocking eschatological inbreaking.[115] The Messiah does something radically new, but also fulfills Israel's relationship with its God in accordance with the highest impulses of human nature.

In the Gospel's own context, the claim that the arrival of the Messiah, joined to the inauguration of his kingdom, serves to reconfigure Torah does not seem anti-Jewish. In my view, it becomes anti-Jewish only when Jesus' Pharisaic opponents are equated with the Jewish people of later generations.[116] Jesus is revealing God's invitation to sinners to repent and enter into the eschatological feast that is the kingdom of God. Jesus is thereby revealing, indirectly, his own identity and role. His eschatological proclamation encounters opposition from all sides, including from his own followers. The parable makes clear that God will never abandon or stop loving the elder son—just as God will never stop loving any of his children.

The second parable that I discussed above is the parable of the laborers in the vineyard. As we saw, for Levine the parable offers Jesus' instructions regarding greed and the common good: the purpose of wealth is to ensure that everyone has enough to live. In Lohfink's view, the first phrase of the parable, "For the kingdom of heaven is like" (Matt 20:1), probably derives from the evangelist rather than from Jesus. If so, then does Lohfink consider the parable to have eschatological import?

---

113. Lohfink, *Forty Parables of Jesus*, 88.
114. Lohfink, *Forty Parables of Jesus*, 84.
115. Lohfink, *Forty Parables of Jesus*, 88.
116. For further discussion, see my *Engaging the Doctrine of Israel*.

He begins with some background. During the grape harvest, every hour is important and so a landowner could return repeatedly to the marketplace to find more workers. But in the economic context of Roman-controlled Galilee, farms tended to be owned by the very wealthy and worked by day-laborers. The day-laborers made enough money in a full day's work to feed their family for that day, but if they missed a day's work, their family would go hungry. This context helps to explain why the laborers who worked the *whole* day wanted their efforts to be rewarded proportionately, even though the wage they received—a denarius—was a fair wage.

For Lohfink, the heart of the parable consists in Jesus' putting his finger upon the presence of rivalry and envy within the economic order. We often compare ourselves with each other and strive to have more than our neighbor. In the kingdom of God, by contrast, such rivalry has no place. Thus, the landowner in the parable represents the inbreaking of the eschatological kingdom. He symbolizes both God and Jesus. In the parable we see how the standards of this-worldly justice are subverted, and instead God's rivalry-free economy bursts forth. I note that the point is not that persons who reject rivalry were absent among the Jewish people, whether in Jesus' time or in any time. The point is that the rejection of rivalry is indeed a sign of the eschatological kingdom breaking into the world. The landowner is not acting irrationally by the standards of the kingdom.

Lohfink argues that in Jesus' community of disciples, he sought to inscribe the kingdom-standards of solidarity and mercy. In Lohfink's view, this mode of living out the reign of God posed a threat to some of the social norms on which the Jewish leaders relied. In his eschatological community, Jesus insists upon a higher standard. The sharp critique of rivalry appears frequently in Jesus' instructions to his (often rivalrous!) disciples.

Thus, Lohfink maintains that the parable is ultimately about the eschatological harvest that Jesus is accomplishing. Inaugurating God's kingdom, Jesus works in his authoritative, revelatory words and deeds to bring about "what Israel's Torah had always sought: sisterhood and brotherhood, equality and freedom."[117] The messianic community, as the inaugurated kingdom, must be a realm in which all receive a sufficiency. This is an economic message (as Levine likewise holds) that is fundamentally an eschatological message revelatory of the truth about God, Jesus, and human life.

The third and final parable is that of the good Samaritan. Setting the stage, Lohfink suggests that the original audience might have understood the priest and Levite to be heading home from serving in the temple in Jerusalem,

---

117. Lohfink, *Forty Parables of Jesus*, 95. This way of putting it sounds noticeably modern, and its terms would need to be better defined.

since a number of priests lived in Jericho in Jesus' day. Like Levine, Lohfink notes the bitter enmity between Jews and Samaritans. Indeed Lohfink adds a further detail: "During Jesus' lifetime a group of Samaritans succeeded in scattering human bones throughout the columned halls and other parts of the temple during a Passover feast in order to make the holy place 'unclean.'"[118] No doubt, therefore, the comparison that Jesus makes, with the Samaritan being given the hero's role, would have been shocking to his audience.

Lohfink, like Levine, rejects the notion that the priest and Levite passed by the victim because they feared becoming ritually unclean. Both Levine and Lohfink think that the parable has to do with the reconciliation of nations or communities that are at enmity with each other. But Lohfink goes further, in an explicitly eschatological direction. He argues that for Jesus, the eschatological restoration of the twelve tribes requires the healing of the breach between the Judeans and the Samaritans. Jesus therefore tells a parable in praise of the mercy shown by a Samaritan, in order to make clear that in his eschatological community, the fullness of Israel will be gathered together. Like Levine, Lohfink knows that the compassion to victims and strangers shown by the Samaritan is commanded by the Torah and exemplified in 2 Chronicles 28:15, among other places. The parable should not be read as a critique of a supposed Jewish narrowness or particularity by contrast to Jesus' love of neighbor. What Lohfink adds, however, is that the compassion commanded by the Torah often did not manifest itself in practice: biblical Israel, like all human societies, fell short of the divine command. Jesus' point is that such compassion must manifest itself in the eschatological community that he is inaugurating. As I would put it, the great mark of Spirit-filled human life is actually to love one's neighbor as oneself. To love in this way is to love as Jesus loves and to love other people in the selfless and generous and merciful way that God does.

In sum, Lohfink's attention to Jesus' eschatological inauguration of the kingdom shows that Jesus' parables reveal truths about God, Jesus, and us that entail that Jesus is more than simply another teacher of Israel. In his life and work he embodies the stance of the merciful father in the parable of the prodigal son. He reveals the absolute grace and mercy of God the Father as well as our need for repentance and conversion so as to enter into the eschatological feast as reconciled sinners. He reveals that the inauguration of the kingdom means that Israel will be restored and rivalries will come to an end.

I should add that I am aware that many historical-critical scholars are less sanguine about our ability to trace these parables to Jesus. For instance,

---

118. Lohfink, *Forty Parables of Jesus*, 119.

regarding the parable of the good Samaritan, John Meier argues that its "intricate structure and verbal patterns are Luke's redactional creation [building upon Mark 12:28–34], and it is this redactional creation that is paralleled perfectly in the parable that follows."[119] In Meier's view, since every aspect of the parable can be plausibly shown to be Lukan, there is no core that can be shown to be grounded in Jesus' own words. Meier thinks that scholars who hold the contrary are engaging, historically speaking, in wishful thinking. In his view, a few Lukan parables *may* go back, in part, to traditions originating with Jesus, but not the two Lukan parables treated above—and not the parable of the laborers in the vineyard either.[120]

I see no need to limit what can plausibly be said to go back to Jesus only to what can be shown (in the Gospel of Luke) *not* to bear the marks of Lukan artistry. The question is whether Jesus taught things of the above kind and taught them through parables. There are strong grounds to suppose that he did. As the Gospel of Mark reports in describing Jesus' teaching ministry, he taught large crowds and "he taught them many things in parables" (Mark 4:2)—and indeed "he did not speak to them without a parable" (Mark 4:34). Mark only includes a few parables by comparison with the profusion of parables found in Luke, but Mark makes clear that his presentation is not exhaustive (Mark 4:33).

With Birger Gerhardsson, I think that "the origins of the gospel tradition" are in fact "to be found in the torah of Jesus himself," and that we should remember that to his earliest followers "Jesus was indeed much more than an earthly teacher."[121] On this basis, I would accentuate the eschatological element even more than does Lohfink. Although the Gospels testify to the confusion experienced by the disciples, the Gospels also make clear that Jesus is the Messiah who now reigns as king: the kingdom has been inaugurated. Approvingly summarizing Scot McKnight's work, the Protestant biblical scholar Joshua Jipp has argued that "the gospel is the proclamation that Jesus's entire life brings Israel's story to its climax and centers upon Jesus's messianic lordship."[122] For Jesus to understand himself as inaugurating the kingdom means that he both spoke and acted with extraordinary authority. He understood himself, in N. T. Wright's words, as the one who was doing what only God could do: "he acted upon a vocation

---

119. Meier, *Marginal Jew*, 5:203.

120. See Meier, *Marginal Jew*, 5:210. For a response to Meier's reading of the Parable of the Wicked Tenants—a response that challenges Meier's skeptical viewpoint on a number of grounds—see Barber, *Historical Jesus and the Temple*, 210–12.

121. Byrskog, "Introduction," 9 (discussing Gerhardsson).

122. Jipp, *Messianic Theology of the New Testament*, 13.

to do and be for Israel and the world what, according to scripture, only Israel's god can do and be."[123]

Part of hearing Jesus' teaching properly, therefore, is to recall that it made him powerful enemies and led him to crucifixion. In claiming to be the (divine) Messiah, he incurred the charge of blasphemy and died for it. This is the charge that the Gospel of Matthew depicts with Daniel 7 in view: "And the high priest said to him, 'I adjure you by the living God, tell us if you are the Christ, the Son of God.' Jesus said to him, 'You have said so. But I tell you, hereafter you will see the Son of man seated at the right hand of Power, and coming on the clouds of heaven.' Then the high priest tore his robes, and said, 'He has uttered blasphemy'" (Matt 26:63–65). In the Gospel of Mark, when confronted with the same question, Jesus answers "I am" (Mark 14:62), and he depicts himself as sharing in the divine power and glory along the same Danielic lines.[124] In the Gospel of John, the charge of blasphemy is a regular occurrence, with Jesus identifying himself as "I am" in John 8:58 (in response to which his hearers try to stone him) and claiming "I and the Father are one" in John 10:30 (again eliciting the threat of stoning).[125] Jesus associates himself with the divine name repeatedly in the Gospel of John, as for instance John 17:11, where he prays, "Holy Father, keep them in your name, which you have given me."[126] His hearers make the problem clear: "you, being a man, make yourself God" (John 10:33).[127]

---

123. Wright, *Jesus and the Victory of God*, 649.

124. For background, see Perrin, *Jesus the Priest*, 269–80; Bühner, *Messianic High Christology*, 65–95; and Boyarin, "Jewish Reader of Jesus," 10–12. Boyarin argues that the development of a suffering (and exalted) divine-human Messiah could easily have been spearheaded by an apocalyptic Jewish interpreter such as Mark: "Jesus Jews might very well have innovated but ... even when they did so, they did so 'Jewishly'" ("Jewish Reader of Jesus," 12). In dialogue with Boyarin, Bühner makes a similar case, granting that Mark 14 contains some distinctive christological notions while demonstrating that "Mark 14 develops its distinctive high Christology in dialogue with texts [such as Psalm 110] and high messianic ideas that were already believed by at least some Jews in the Second Temple period" (*Messianic High Christology*, 93). As Bühner says, "the high priest's question and charge of blasphemy as well as Jesus' answer all refer to divine messianic expectations" (95).

125. On John 10:30, see Bauckham, "Biblical Theology and the Problems of Monotheism," 104–6, with reference to Appold, *Oneness Motif in the Fourth Gospel*.

126. See Gieschen, "Divine Name as a Characteristic of Divine Identity," 76–77.

127. For discussion, see Ashton, *Understanding the Fourth Gospel*, 91–94, whose main argument is well summed up in Behr, *John the Theologian*, 170–71: "It cannot be, as Ashton rightly observes, that Jesus appeals to Psalm 81:6 simply to reassure his audience that the term 'god' can be used loosely, for it would never then have provoked the reaction that it did. The background for the reaction is found, rather, in the various ways in which this Psalm was being read. Some took the word 'gods' as 'angels', as it is rendered in the Peshitta version, as J. A. Emerton pointed out ('God stood in the

TEACHING

To say that Jesus sharply challenged his Jewish contemporaries, including his own disciples, and accused them of blindness and spiritual arrogance is simply to report the evident testimony of the Gospels. According to the Gospels, he was unsparing in his criticisms of the Jewish leaders, even if he also could show respect for them and for their authority.[128] Many people

congregation of God, he judges amongst the angels . . . "You are angels, . . ."'), and as is also done elsewhere in the Peshitta and targumim, as well as texts from Qumran. On the other hand, in some of the texts from Qumran, such as the songs for the Sabbath sacrifice, there appear, alongside other heavenly beings, such as princes and angels, other beings called *elim* and *elohim*: Carol Newsom translates the second by 'godlike beings', while Geza Vermes, though properly translating both by 'god', puts scare quotes around the second, when it is used for beings other than God. Moreover, in the Melchizedek text (11Q13), the 'God' who has taken his place in the divine council (Ps. 81:1) is taken as referring to Melchizedek himself, who had appeared on earth as a human being (Gen. 14:18-20). With this background of the ways in which Psalm 81 was being read, its use by Jesus becomes more striking. As Ashton concludes, however, 'the big difference is that in the Fourth Gospel the whole heavenly court is encapsulated in the person of Jesus; apart from the Father he alone is given the title'. He alone is not simply one of the sons of the Most High, but 'the Son of God' and himself 'God' (cf. 1:1; 1:18. . .; 20:28)." See also Frey, "Between Jewish Monotheism and Proto-Trinitarian Relations." Frey recognizes that John's Logos goes beyond earlier "binitarian" models: "As θεός, the Johannine Logos is even more than what is expressed by the predication δεύτερος θεός in Philo. His divinity is not merely a share in the divine nature; it is divinity in the sense that the Logos clearly belongs to the realm of the creator, uncreated. He is *divine* in the sense that he is uncreated" (209). Frey also comments, "The unity with the Father stated in 10:30, deliberately with the neuter and the plural verb . . . , is not understood as a simple fusion of two figures into one, but as an inseparably close relationship, described by the metaphor of love (3:35; 17:24), and as being rooted in the premundane realm of the creator" (219). For a somewhat contrasting viewpoint, arguing that John's goal was to defend the Christian claim that Jesus was the Messiah or final agent of God's purposes—and that, motivated by this goal, John proclaimed that Jesus was "the person whom the Name/Word became" and the person "as whom the Word/Name returned to heaven"—see McGrath, *John's Apologetic Christology*, 231. For further viewpoints, see Novenson, "Jesus the Messiah"; Bühner, *Messianic High Christology*, 143-72, including his remark on 161 that "the prologue of John certainly depicts the Logos much closer to the one God" than can be said of Melchizedek in 11QMelch; Hayward, "'Lord is One'"; North, "Monotheism and the Gospel of John." Hayward places John's discourse within the context of Qumran, and he argues that "Johannine statements about the Divine Unity and the role of Jesus as shepherd represent, *inter alia*, one particular stance towards matters which were particularly sensitive and controversial in first century Judaism," namely, matters pertaining to "the identity of the legitimate Temple, and the proper manner of affirming God's Unity as required by the *Shema*'" ("'Lord is One,'" 154). On John and Qumran, and on Jesus' divinity in the Gospel of John, see also Bauckham, *Testimony of the Beloved Disciple*, 125-36, 239-52.

128. For discussion of Jesus' unsparing criticisms, see Keith, *Jesus Against the Scribal Elite*, 4-5, 57-59, although at one point Keith paints Jesus as a fanatic: "There is a wild look in his eyes, sweat pouring down his forehead, and spit flying off his lips when he yells, 'Woe to you, scribes and Pharisees, hypocrites!' (Matt. 23:13, 15, 23, 25, 27, 29; cf. 23:16)" (5). Keith points out that E. P. Sanders deems the conflict between

found his teachings off-putting and rejected him, although many others followed him devoutly.¹²⁹ The Protestant biblical scholar Chris Keith observes, "Jesus's very status as a teacher was controversial. The scribal authorities likely disagreed with what he taught and how he taught it, but a central part of the problem was that, from their perspectives, Jesus did not have the right to be teaching in the first place."¹³⁰ This situation surely exacerbated his conflict with the educated Jewish leaders.

Jesus and the scribes/Pharisees to have been largely invented by the evangelists and the later Church: see Keith, *Jesus Against the Scribal Elite*, 143–48, citing Sanders, *Jesus and Judaism*, 246–75, and Sanders, *Historical Figure of Jesus*. For Sanders, "there was no substantial conflict between Jesus and the Pharisees with regard to Sabbath, food, and purity laws" (*Jesus and Judaism*, 265). Sanders concludes, "Jesus himself looked to a new age, and therefore he viewed the institutions of this age as not final, and in that sense not adequate. He was not, however, a reformer" (*Jesus and Judaism*, 269). Michael Patrick Barber accepts that Jesus really did engage in substantial conflict with the Pharisees, including with regard to the food laws (although Barber argues that Jesus did not annul these), but Barber shows that this does not mean that Jesus was anti-Jewish: see Barber, *Historical Jesus and the Temple*, 12, 19; and see also Barber's interpretation of Matthew 27:24-25 on 109. As Barber points out, in Matthew 23 we find "Jesus's endorsement of the Pharisees' teaching authority" (77), despite Jesus' excoriations of the Pharisees in that chapter. On Jesus' conflict with the Pharisees, see also Banks, *Jesus and the Law in the Synoptic Tradition*, 173–81.

129. For the latter, see Mansini, "Authority and Charity of Christ," 170: "Great crowds went out to listen to him (Mk 1:45, 3:7), and they followed him from place to place (Mt 14:13–14, 15:39). It is an understatement to say that people liked to be around him; they came near to crushing him (Mk 3:9). The crowds so pestered him and the disciples that they could not even eat (Mk 3:20) . . . What did they go out to see when they went out to see Jesus? They went out to see authority joined to charity." Mansini describes this "authority joined to charity" by employing Aquinas's rich theology of charity in relation to the Spirit's gifts of wisdom and understanding, charity's interior effects, and the relationship of knowledge and charity.

130. Keith, *Jesus Against the Scribal Elite*, 6. Keith argues that "factors such as social class and literate education stood at the cradle of the controversy over Jesus of Nazareth . . . Jesus was not a member of the authoritative scribal elite class, but acted in some ways as though he were, and managed to convince some of his audience that he was" (6). In my view, Jesus really was greater than the scribes in his knowledge and teaching. Keith's book provides a detailed argument for the thesis that "controversy over Jesus's status as a teacher in fact provides the foundation for why his miraculous activity, exorcistic activity, and even the content of his teachings proved worthy of the authorities' attention" (12). I am not persuaded by this viewpoint. Nevertheless, Keith rightly points out, "The Gospels of Mark and Matthew portray Jesus as a teacher outside scribal circles [cf. Mark 6:3], while Luke portrays him as a member of the scribal elite; meanwhile John's Gospel [cf. 7:15] reports simply that Jesus's literate education and scribal status were matters of debate among his audience" (14). For Keith, it is possible that Jesus knew how to "sign a contract and read directional signs," but Jesus lacked the literate education in Torah that would have justified his claim to be able teach about God and Torah (31). Michael L. Satlow goes further, emphasizing Jesus' loose relationship to Israel's Scriptures: "The Gospel texts themselves are unclear about

Regarding Jesus' true identity, Paul remarks, "None of the rulers of this age understood... for if they had, they would not have crucified the Lord of glory" (1 Cor 2:8).[131] In the Gospels, his disciples too—and not only the Jewish and Roman leaders—are generally portrayed as not understanding, and they abandon Jesus when he is arrested. Jesus' teaching made people deeply uncomfortable, as the Gospel of John shows in Jesus' bread of life discourse (where Jesus states, "unless you eat the flesh of the Son of man and drink his blood, you have no life in you" [John 6:53]).[132] The evangelist sums up, "After this many of his disciples drew back and no longer walked with him" (John 6:66). Hans Urs von Balthasar puts it this way: "Jesus is the man who burns with God's fire," and such fire will be comfortable for no one.[133] To say this is not to descend into anti-Semitic tropes against the ongoing Jewish people, but rather is to notice that Jesus is deeply challenging for all people.

IV. The Sermon on the Mount and the Beatitudes

In his *Jesus of Nazareth: From the Baptism in the Jordan to the Transfiguration*, Joseph Ratzinger explores Jesus' teaching in his Sermon on the Mount. In the sermon, Ratzinger observes, "Jesus' 'I' is accorded a status that no teacher of the Law can legitimately allow himself."[134] The evangelist Matthew makes clear that Jesus' claim to divine authority was recognized by his audience, which was shocked by it. We read in Matthew 7:28, "And when Jesus finished these sayings, the crowds were astonished at his teaching, for he taught them as one who had authority, and not as their scribes." Jesus' teaching provokes a reckoning with his identity.

---

how much scripture Jesus knew, and whence he knew it. The Gospels do show Jesus 'teaching,' which seems to mean citing a few verses of scripture and explaining them. Yet when Jesus communicates with his disciples, he much prefers to use actions and parables rather than scripture and its interpretation; scripture per se appeared to have played a marginal role in his religious life. The authors of the Gospels, following Paul, would reframe Jesus's life around his fulfillment of scriptural prophecies, but it is likely that Jesus—even if he saw himself as God's anointed (a much debated point in New Testament scholarship)—never quite framed his own life in that way" (Satlow, *How the Bible Became Holy*, 208). Satlow here ignores the scriptural imagination that fuels the parables and, even more, the actions of Jesus.

131. See Allison, *Constructing Jesus*, 396–98.

132. For discussion of John 6, see especially Behr, *John the Theologian*, 148–60, drawing upon an array of biblical scholars; and see also Moloney, *Signs and Shadows*.

133. See Balthasar, *Theo-Drama* 4:60.

134. Ratzinger/Benedict XVI, *Jesus of Nazareth*, 1:102.

For Chris Keith, this reckoning is heightened by Matthew in service of Matthew's contention that Jesus was "the scribes' serious pedagogical rival," despite being an uneducated laborer.[135] But Matthew does more than show Jesus as a "rival": Matthew portrays "Jesus as a teacher superior to Moses" and equal to "God the lawgiver."[136] Ratzinger sums up the result: "Either [Jesus] is misappropriating God's majesty ... or else ... he really does stand on the same exalted level as God."[137] Jesus' claim to have divine authority stands behind his eschatologically charged wisdom teaching in the Sermon on the Mount.

Frank Matera's perspective concurs with that of Ratzinger. Briefly comparing the Sermon on the Mount with the Gospel of Luke's (much shorter) Sermon on the Plain, Matera notes that the core teachings are the same in both versions. Much of the material that Luke does not include in the Sermon on the Plain, he includes later in his Gospel. Perhaps somewhat controversially, Matera argues that "[m]ost contemporary scholars ... would acknowledge that the content of the two sermons has its origin in

---

135. Keith, *Jesus Against the Scribal Elite*, 57. Satlow remarks, "By the time Jesus died, around 30 CE, scripture was emerging as a powerful presence in Jewish life in Judea and Galilee. Citing a text carried authority, even among the Pharisees. Most people would have had access to these texts only through their oral recitation and explanation by a 'teacher,' who himself (or herself) may have been reciting from memory. Scribes were the one class that would have had access to written versions of texts" (Satlow, *How the Bible Became Holy*, 208). Satlow dismisses Jesus as a garden-variety itinerant who nevertheless "was an independent thinker" and quarreled with the Pharisees about "relatively small and technical points of practice," while probably conceiving of himself "as a wonder-worker, healer, and prophet in addition to teacher"—in "a religious landscape that was dotted with healers, wonder-workers, and prophets" (*How the Bible Became Holy*, 203). As Satlow explains Jesus' background, "He was unlikely to have received much of a formal education, and his knowledge of scripture would have been acquired through occasional attendance at the synagogue and perhaps the teachings of local Pharisees. It would thus have been ad hoc, aural, and disjointed. Nevertheless, scripture and the lessons associated with it clearly intrigued him" (*How the Bible Became Holy*, 201). For further discussion of Galilee in Jesus' day, see Freyne, *Galilee and Gospel*, a collection that builds upon Freyne's earlier monographs and also engages critically (and insightfully) with Horsley, *Galilee: History, Politics, People*.

136. Keith, *Jesus Against the Scribal Elite*, 57.

137. Ratzinger/Benedict, *Jesus of Nazareth*, 1:103. Ratzinger observes that this insight is the heart of Jacob Neusner's objection to Jesus' Sermon on the Mount in Neusner's *Rabbi Talks with Jesus*. Neusner perceives that Jesus claims "to be Temple and Torah in person" and therefore Jesus claims to stand in the place of God (Ratzinger/Benedict XVI, *Jesus of Nazareth*, 1:111). Neusner asks the disciple of Jesus two questions: "So I say to the disciple, is it really so that your master, the son of man is lord of the Sabbath? Then ... is your master God? And that forms the crux of the matter" (Neusner, *Rabbi Talks with Jesus*, 71, 74).

the teaching of Jesus," despite the significant redactional activity of Matthew and Luke.[138]

In the Gospel of Matthew, the Sermon on the Mount is the first of five major discourses delivered by Jesus to his disciples, and it is the most important one. Prior to the Sermon, Matthew has introduced Jesus' identity and made clear that he is the Messiah and the obedient Son of God who makes manifest the divine presence and redemptive power. Jesus' teachings in the Sermon directly precede his miraculous deeds in Matthew 8–9.[139]

Matera argues that the Sermon on the Mount offers not simply a philosophical or rabbinic teaching but rather the authoritative teaching of the divine Messiah who reveals God's will. The sermon challenges us to live in accordance with Jesus' eschatological model—to live as citizens of God's inaugurated kingdom and to imitate Jesus' own imaging of the Father. Matera considers the Sermon to be fully eschatological, though in the sense of inaugurated, not consummated, eschatology.[140] Now that Jesus has inaugurated the kingdom and reigns at the right hand of the Father, sending

---

138. Matera, *Sermon on the Mount*, 8. For Satlow, "One of the best examples of what 'teaching' meant at this time, both for Jesus and other contemporary Jews, might be the Sermon on the Mount. After a short set of blessings, Jesus launches into a series of teachings on enigmatic laws found in the Pentateuch . . . The Sermon on the Mount might constitute our best evidence for what exactly happened in a synagogue in first-century CE Galilee (even though this sermon, of course, was taught outside). In this sermon, Jesus never introduces the verse that he explains with, 'You read in the Torah.' Instead, he uses the phrase, 'You have heard it said' or 'You have heard that it was said to those of ancient times.' This points to the ad hoc way in which his audience would have known scripture" (*How the Bible Became Holy*, 201).

139. On Matthew 8's identifications of Jesus as "Lord," see O'Donnell, "Insisting on Easter," arguing that "the suppliants' κύριος is a Christologically charged designation that demonstrates their acknowledgement of Jesus' divine authority" (200). See also Staples, "'Lord, LORD'"; and Barber, *Historical Jesus and the Temple*, 60–64.

140. See also, along the same lines, Pennington, *Sermon on the Mount and Human Flourishing*. Pennington comments, "Jesus provides in the Sermon a *Christocentric, flourishing-oriented, kingdom-awaiting, eschatological wisdom exhortation*" (15). When Pennington treats the beatitudes, he argues that the background is especially the prophecy of Isaiah, especially Isaiah 61. Recall that Isaiah 61—to which Jesus refers in Matthew 11:5 and Luke 4—begins with the Servant announcing the eschatological victory: "The Spirit of the Lord God is upon me, because the Lord has anointed me to bring good tidings to the afflicted" (Isa 61:1). The prophecy continues with the Servant announcing healing for the brokenhearted, freedom for captives, and comfort and gladness for those who mourn. He foresees the day of the Lord on which God will triumph and Israel will be restored in righteousness and well-being, so that the holy people of Israel will all be priests of God and will receive the riches of the nations, the blessings of salvation and righteousness, and "everlasting joy" (Isa 61:7). Pennington argues that the beatitudes do two things at once: they call believers into the virtues of true flourishing (righteousness and peace-making mercy), and they inscribe these virtues within an eschatological vision of the day of the Lord's triumph (kingdom).

his Spirit upon his disciples, "[t]he sermon is the norm for discipleship because it teaches disciples to live in the sphere of God's kingdom."[141] If the kingdom of God had not been inaugurated, Matera suggests, the sermon would be unlivable. But the kingdom has been inaugurated and is present in the person of Jesus by the power of the Spirit. Matera states simply, "The sermon is an ethic for the kingdom of God. Apart from the kingdom, it makes little sense."[142]

In the sermon, Jesus authoritatively reveals God and God's will for Jesus' followers, who "live in the sphere of God's rule," assuming that they truly follow Jesus.[143] The main point of the sermon is the holiness of God that must be emulated by human beings, empowered by the grace of the Spirit that fuels the kingdom.[144] Jesus must be obeyed, because he is the Messiah, the Son of God, and the one who "proclaims and inaugurates the kingdom of heaven."[145] The gift of faith in the Messiah enables Jesus' followers to hear, obey, and live Jesus' teachings.

---

141. Matera, *Sermon on the Mount*, 5.

142. Matera, *Sermon on the Mount*, 12.

143. Matera, *Sermon on the Mount*, 12.

144. Matera explains, "The Christian moral life is not a matter of observing rules and regulations, although it often appears that way. It is a life lived in response to God's grace; it is a life made possible by the new life believers have received from God in Christ through the power of the Holy Spirit. Thus the nature of Christian obedience—what Paul calls the obedience of faith—is rooted in the gift of salvation. Believers strive to live in a particular way because of the gift of salvation that God has given them in Christ. Whereas the Pauline letters express this gift in terms of the Spirit, the Synoptic Gospels focus on the salvation the kingdom of God has inaugurated. The kingdom that Jesus proclaimed, and into which he entered by his saving death and life-giving resurrection, opens a new sphere where believers can live in a new way. No longer under the power and rule of Satan, those who embrace the kingdom have entered the realm of God's rule where all things are possible. Having turned from the rule of the one who brings them to sin and death, they have embraced a new way of life made possible by the gift of the kingdom, which is nothing less than God's rule over their lives. This is why Jesus' Sermon on the Mount begins with a series of blessings that assure his disciples of the final beatitude that will be theirs when the kingdom is revealed in all of its power" (Matera, *Sermon on the Mount*, 27).

145. Matera, *Sermon on the Mount*, 29. Pennington observes, "Jesus is not simply repeating the words of God and calling people to repentance/renewal. Rather, he is making a bolder claim than this—he is now the arbiter of the truth of God (cf. 7:24, 29; 21:27; 24:35; 28:18–20)" (Pennington, *Sermon on the Mount and Human Flourishing*, 181). On the basis of Pennington's observation here, one can see how Jesus' teaching in the Gospel of Matthew stands in fundamental agreement with Jesus' teaching in the Gospel of John. According to his own teaching, his identity is inscribed into that of God; and our destiny involves becoming configured to him and sharing in the divine life. In John's Gospel, of course, Jesus' divine identity is front and center. He teaches with authority because he is the Word made flesh, the divine Word who "was in the

TEACHING

Let me focus here on two controversial passages: Jesus' teaching about nonresistance (Matt 5:38–41) and Jesus' teaching about love of enemy (Matt 5:43–48). This section of the sermon reflects, in Dale Allison's view, his followers' "recollection of a series of sentences that Jesus uttered on more than one occasion, or even uttered regularly, perhaps something like a stock sermon."[146] Jesus' teaching of nonresistance begins as follows: "You have heard that it was said, 'An eye for an eye and a tooth for a tooth.' But I say to you, Do not resist one who is evil" (Matt 5:38–39). The interior quotation is from Exodus 21:24 and Leviticus 24:20, whose intention was to limit the scale of retribution or vengeance. As Matera points out, Jesus was not the first to try to limit retribution even further. On the contrary, Proverbs 20:22 teaches, "Do not say, 'I will repay evil'; wait for the Lord, and he will help you"; and Proverbs 24:29 similarly instructs, "Do not say, 'I will do to him as he has done to me; I will pay the man back for what he has done.'" Thus, the people of Israel already knew that vengeance, in which individuals take justice into their own hands, is not a godly path.

At the heart of the Torah, Jesus suggests, is a commitment to letting go of such violence. One must not respond to violence against oneself with further violence, however justified the latter might be. Matera articulates Jesus' logic as follows: "It begins with the premise that resisting evil does not overcome evil. To the contrary, resistance gives evil its power and force."[147] What then can overcome evil? The answer is love. Ultimately, stopping the evil that plagues human life requires bringing into the world a goodness that is the very opposite of the *modus operandi* of evildoers.[148]

In his letters, Paul echoes this teaching of Jesus.[149] Paul exhorts in Romans 12:19–21, "Beloved, never avenge yourselves, but leave it to the wrath

---

beginning with God" and "was God" (John 1:1–2). In the Sermon on the Mount, Jesus' claim to divinity is equally clear for those who perceive what is implied by his words about imitating him and about his authority over Torah.

146. Allison, *Constructing Jesus*, 381. Allison devotes pages 305–81 to reflection on the overlapping portions of Matthew 5 and Luke 6, which Allison, following scholarly convention, terms Q 6:27–42.

147. Matera, *Sermon on the Mount*, 61.

148. Levine comments, "Jesus offers what the biblical scholar Walter Wink called the 'third way': rather than escalate the violence, and rather than lose personal dignity, face the perpetrator by making the violence and so the wrongness of the situation clear. What looks like humiliation to an outsider—being slapped, stripping naked, carrying gear—becomes an opportunity of expressing agency. By offering the left cheek, the victim resists humiliation by displaying agency and courage" (*Sermon on the Mount*, 40).

149. For various perspectives on the relationship between Paul and the Gospels, see the essays in Bird and Willitts, *Paul and the Gospels*. Notably, see Stanley E. Porter's demonstration that "the position of Luke and Paul toward the Parousia may have more in common than has often been thought. Whereas Paul is typically depicted as

of God; for it is written, 'Vengeance is mine, I will repay, says the Lord.' No, 'if your enemy is hungry, feed him; if he is thirsty, give him drink; for by so doing you will heap burning coals upon his head.' Do not be overcome by evil, but overcome evil with good." Paul here is quoting passages from Deuteronomy 32:35 and Proverbs 25:21–22. Paul similarly teaches in 1 Thessalonians 5:15, "See that none of you repays evil for evil, but always seek to do good to one another and to all." Matera directs attention to these passages, and he argues that Jesus' refusal to employ the instruments used by evildoers is authoritative. Those who dominate and oppress must be engaged from within a new logic of love.

Matera knows that this counsel of Jesus' (and Paul's) seems impracticable. It is clear, for example, that if evildoers such as the Nazis are not forcefully opposed, they will wreak unspeakable harm, as they did until they were crushed by the Allied troops. In response to such concerns, Matera argues that Jesus is not here offering a set of casuistic rules. Instead, Jesus is revealing to us what God knows: evil in the human heart is only overcome (or transformed) by the manifestation of goodness. Jesus gives us his own example on the cross: he dies out of love for sinners, and thereby manifests love, the one thing that can transform sinful hearts. As his followers, we are commanded authoritatively to follow his example.[150] In the world, the

---

expecting an unqualified imminent return, he himself indicates his belief in an in-between stage, an already and not yet perspective on the parousia. Whereas Luke is typically depicted as having abandoned and even attempted to minimize an imminent return, he himself also indicates an in-between stage, an expectation of future events still present even during this Church age" (Porter, "Luke?," 166).

150. Interestingly, Legaspi holds that the command to carry our cross and follow Jesus (Luke 14:27; Matthew 10:38) is a profoundly anti-social command. Legaspi argues, "This statement about carrying the cross is not a general platitude about the inevitability of suffering, a recognition that 'everyone has a cross to bear,' or, in the softer language of Longfellow: 'into each life some rain must fall.' It is rather a statement about the shape and direction of one's life" (*Wisdom in Classical and Biblical Tradition*, 221). So far, so good. But Legaspi proceeds to take it much further than I think accurate: "Jesus's listeners would have understood that one who 'carries the cross' has already been sentenced to die by the authorities. What remains of his life is only a short path to certain death. The cares of ordinary life—the fortunes of one's children, responsibilities to one's parents, the struggle to stay ahead in the world—no longer have a claim on the prisoner. He thus 'hates' his relatives 'and even life itself' (Luke 14:26; see Matt 10:37) because his condemned state prevents him from giving attention to the obligations that once structured his life. He is functionally indifferent to them. His many obligations have dwindled to one. The idea is not merely to follow Jesus unto death (though this too is required) but to follow Jesus single-mindedly because, ultimately, it is only life in the coming kingdom that matters" (221–22). In my view, Legaspi exaggerates here. Believers must "follow Jesus single-mindedly" and follow him above following anything else (no matter how dear), but believers must do this in Christlike love. Jesus does not annul the Decalogue, including the commandment to honor one's parents; on the contrary, he

community that in faith obeys Jesus' command will suffer. But Christians must fight evil by displaying the goodness and love that Jesus embodied on the cross—which is the only hope for transforming the fallen creation.[151]

Such a stance, Matera knows, is an eschatological ethics, accessible to those who have received Jesus in faith as the Lord and have entered through the Holy Spirit into the life and love of the inaugurated kingdom. Jesus knows that his commands are not easy. He states, "You . . . must be perfect, as your heavenly father is perfect" (Matt 5:48). The translation here can be misleading, since the meaning of the Greek word *teleios* in this context is "to be whole, entire, undivided in allegiance and devotion to God"—just as God is "whole, entire, and undivided."[152] But this nuanced meaning of "perfect" does not lessen the challenge, which is an invitation to share in the kingdom of God.

Matera takes a similar approach to Jesus' command to love one's enemies.[153] As Jesus says, in general we love those who love us. We reciprocate

---

affirms it. Believers will give attention to their obligations, because love requires this. For a better approach to these issues, see Dicken, "Luke and the Cross."

151. In Pennington's view, Jesus' teaching of nonresistance should not be understood literalistically but rather should be seen as an invitation to "look inward and become a different kind of people" (Pennington, *Sermon on the Mount and Human Flourishing*, 197). When we are wronged, we should commit ourselves to "nonretaliatory righteousness" (197). We need to become like Jesus, who was willing to go to the Cross without inflicting a retaliatory cross upon others. Agreeing with Pennington's view, I discuss and defend just war doctrine (and legitimate self-defense) in my *Betrayal of Charity*, chapter 7.

152. Matera, *Sermon on the Mount*, 64. The deeper understanding of the Torah that Jesus proposes is one that is grounded firmly in perfection or wholeness of the God of Israel. Pennington states, "God the Father is known to be *teleios* with respect to the topic in each paraenesis—God does not murder, but is forgiving; God is faithful to his marriage covenant (with Israel; cf. the extensive allegory in Hosea); God is honest and keeps his covenant oath; God forgives and gives even to those who dishonor him; and God loves even his enemies" (Pennington, *Sermon on the Mount and Human Flourishing*, 206).

153. Ernst Käsemann argues that the command to love one's enemies has no parallel in the Gospel of John, where Jesus commands his disciples to love one another but does not command them to love outsiders. For Käsemann's influential perspective, see Käsemann, *Testament of Jesus*, 59–60; and see also the extension of Käsemann's arguments in Campbell, *Kinship Relations in the Gospel of John* and in Sanders, *Ethics and the New Testament*, 91–100. For a persuasive response to Käsemann, Campbell, Sanders, and others on this point, see Moloney, *Love in the Gospel of John*. Moloney explains, "Jesus challenges all disciples to continue his mission of making love known by becoming beloved disciples, believing without seeing ([John] 20:2–10, 29), and he founds a community on a pastor who must profess his love in words and action (21:15–19) . . . [A]ll the love commands directed to the disciples in the Gospel are missionary. Within the context of the dramatic presentation of Jesus' love for his disciples in the footwashing and the gift of the piece of bread (13:1–38), during which he tells the disciples that his actions are to reveal the living presence of the divine among them (v. 19: *I am he*), he issues his first command to love. They are to love one another as he has loved as a

love, but we do not show love toward those who threaten to hurt and even kill us. (Recall that the Samaritan is an example of just such an existential enemy vis-à-vis the Jewish people of Jesus' day.) Matera remarks upon the connection between Jesus' command regarding love and the previous command regarding nonresistance. In both cases, Jesus is requiring his disciples "to treat those who mistreat them in a wholly new way."[154] Rather than giving what we get, we must break out of the circle of worldly reciprocity

---

sign to everyone, not just to the community itself, that they are disciples of Jesus ... They have been chosen and appointed by Jesus as his friends, people who love one another so that they may go out and bear much fruit, a fruit that will abide ([15:]14-16). The 'bearing of fruit' is not an inner-community process but a mission that flows from the love that they have for one another, matching the love of Jesus" (*Love in the Gospel of John*, 35, 206-7). Admittedly, in Moloney's view 1 John's love commandment, in the context of deep religious hostilities, makes for a tension: "reading 1 John's statement on love in a setting of the rejection of 'the other' within contexts that reflect conflict indicates that *living* the perfect law of love in the community that produced and then inherited the Gospel of John was more difficult than *proclaiming* it" (198). See also Popkes, *Theologie der Liebe Gottes in den johanneischen Schriften*; Skinner, "Virtue in the New Testament"; and Meier, *Marginal Jew*, 4:478-646. Meier argues, "The inextricable bond between loving God and loving one's brother that 1 John 4:20-21 affirms could possibly be a 're-reception' (or simply a distant echo?) of Jesus' double command of love by the Johannine community. This is an intriguing conjecture, but only a conjecture. In the end, unlike Mark's double command of love and Q's command to love one's enemies—both of which we have judged authentic—the love command in the Fourth Gospel should probably be honored simply as a great contribution of the evangelist (and/or the final redactor), reflecting creatively on the core Christian message in the light of both the OT and his community's tradition" (Meier, *Marginal Jew*, 4:571-72).

154. Matera, *Sermon on the Mount*, 62. See also Perrin's comment on Luke 11:4, "forgive us our sins, for we ourselves forgive every one who is indebted to us": "For Luke, 'to forgive those who have sinned against us' finds its supreme expression when believers respond to their enemies by interceding for their forgiveness before God. For Luke's readers in the early Christian community, then, to obey Luke/Q 11.4 was to take up a priestly role. That the historical Jesus also shared and indeed promulgated this interpretation of his own prayer is not difficult to prove. In Matthew 5.44 ('But I say to you, Love your enemies and pray for those who persecute you'), the authenticity of which is undisputed, Jesus makes clear that one of the distinctive markers of his followers would be a shared commitment to pray for those who bore tangible malice towards the community. Such prayer was to be not a begrudging act, but rather born out of an attitude of love and compassion. This is not to say that Jesus' followers obeyed this injunction with unflinching consistency: on the contrary, the reports that have come down to us record just the opposite [see Luke 9:52-56; Matt 26:50-52//Luke 22:49-51//John 18:10-11]. Nevertheless, the prayer embodies an ideal that was central to the movement's *modus operandi*" (Perrin, *Jesus the Priest*, 49). For the point that "prayer and politics go hand in hand for those endowed with the apocalyptic imagination" and so "students of the historical Jesus have given too little attention to the importance of prayer in the unfolding of his ministry, especially in view of the emphasis on contemplation and reflection for the seer/wise person within both the wisdom and apocalyptic traditions" (including John the Baptist), see Freyne, *Jesus, a Jewish Galilean*, 141.

and embody a radical love—a love that flows from the fact that Jesus has truly inaugurated the kingdom and truly reigns. Adding a further element to this discussion, Nicholas Perrin comments, "Jesus' ethical vision marks a significant departure from other sectarian conceptions of the day, especially those which envisaged the latter-day priests as instruments of divine retribution. Here the typical expectation was that Yahweh's priests would mete out justice, sometimes violent justice, to the enemies of God."[155]

At the same time, the distinctiveness of Jesus' teaching, while real, should not be exaggerated. Proverbs 25:21–22 offers the clearest precedent and, as noted above, is quoted by Paul in Romans 12. There are other precedents, such as Proverbs 24:17, "Do not rejoice when your enemy falls, and let not your heart be glad when he stumbles"; and Exodus 23:4–5, "If you meet your enemy's ox or his donkey going astray, you shall bring it back to him. If you see the donkey of one who hates you lying under its burden, you shall refrain from leaving him with it, you shall help him to lift it up."[156] These passages confirm what Jesus himself says, "Do not think that I have come to abolish the law and the prophets; I have come not to abolish them but to fulfill them" (Matt 5:17). His authoritative teachings draw out the central divine intentions of Torah.[157]

---

155. Perrin, *Jesus the Priest*, 50. Perrin later points out with regard to Jesus' teaching in Mark 12:29–31 on the love of God and love of neighbor, "While the calls to love God and love humanity are sometimes paired in both pre-Christian and post-Temple Jewish texts, and similar attempts to summarize Torah could have quite possibly been current in Jesus' day, neither the former fact nor the latter possibility should detract from the innovativeness of this exegetical move. That the double love commandment was already 'in the air' at the time is rendered unlikely by, among other factors, the fact that the early Christian movement was the first to assert Leviticus 19.18 as *the* summarizing commandment. Nor do we have any traditions prior to Jesus coordinating these two verses, much less elevating either one to the status of a leading principle" (*Jesus the Priest*, 218–19).

156. See Levine, *Sermon on the Mount*, 41–42.

157. In *Jesus and Judaism*, E. P. Sanders suggests that we should not place much weight on Matthew 5:17. In Sanders's view, "Jesus may have said something like Matt. 5.17," but "[i]n its present setting 5.17 points to a strict legalism which no one will attribute to Jesus. Can the saying be preserved by creating for it a new setting or combining it with other sayings? It is my judgment that we cannot be confident of reconstructed settings which provide new meanings" (262). Sanders goes on to argue that it is likely that Matthew 5:17—6:18 was entirely invented by the evangelist, or at least does not go back to Jesus, with the exception of 6:9–13. For a different perspective, probing into what Jesus likely meant by fulfillment of the law, see Hays, *Echoes of Scripture in the Gospels*, 122–23, where Hays comments: "for all his affirmation of the Torah, Matthew's account of what obedience to Torah actually entails has some distinctive features over against other contemporary forms of *halakhah*. Surprisingly, Matthew is silent about circumcision, and his position on purity laws is emphatically nonpharisaic, as shown by his account of Jesus' rejection of oral Torah—'Why do you break the commandment

Jesus appears to misquote Torah when he states, "You have heard that it was said, 'You shall love your neighbor and hate your enemy'" (Matt 5:43). The commandment in Leviticus 19:18 to "love your neighbor as yourself" contains no instruction regarding hating one's enemy, and God never commanded the people of Israel to hate their enemies. As Levine pointed out, the commandment to "love your neighbor as yourself" was generally understood to cover both fellow Israelites and foreigners who lived in the land. The Torah also made clear that the people of Israel were to be respectful rather than oppressive toward foreign nations and toward people who lived in other lands. But some biblical texts speak of hatred of enemy, as for instance various psalms, including Psalm 139:21-22, "Do I not hate them that hate you, O Lord? And do I not loathe them that rise up against you? I hate them with perfect hatred; I count them my enemies."[158]

Is it possible to love one's real enemy? I note that Augustine and Thomas Aquinas provide detailed and nuanced accounts of an ordering of love, in which certain neighbors to whom one has debts of gratitude or duty, such as

---

of God for the sake of your tradition?' (Matt 15:3)—and his casual stance on food and purity laws: 'It is not what goes into the mouth that defiles a person, but it is what comes out of the mouth that defiles' (15:11). Again, here, we see the concern with purity of heart as the key issue for Matthew: '... what comes out of the mouth proceeds from the *heart*, and this is what defiles' (15:18). Matthew's concern is not to advocate a program of rejecting Jewish food laws but rather to shift the emphasis to purity of heart as the Torah's chief concern. How are such teachings to be squared with the claim that Jesus has come not to abolish the Torah but to fulfill it? Clearly, Matthew is operating with a flexible theological notion of 'fulfillment' that is not rigidly identified with literal performance of all the law's commandments. Jesus' fulfillment of the law is partly related to his own embodied enactment of its meaning ... but it is also connected to a particular *hermeneutical construal* of Torah. This becomes especially clear in Matthew's handling of the lawyer's question about the greatest commandment (Matt 22:34-40) . . . The climax of the pronouncement in Matthew is this: 'On these two commandments hang all the law and the prophets.' These two commandments, in other words, are not merely the greatest or the most important, the ones at the top of the list; rather, they have a systemic, structural, and hermeneutical role. All the other commandments in Torah are *suspended from* these two pillars. It is a matter not just of priority but of *weight-bearing*. This claim is fully consistent with Matthew's insistence that in Jesus' teaching the law remains in force. Yet, at the same time, the passage inescapably proposes a particular *hermeneutical reconfiguration of Torah*, one in which *love* becomes the most determinative requirement." See also Banks, *Jesus and the Law in the Synoptic Tradition*, 251-52: "it is not so much his [Jesus'] relationship to the Law that he [Matthew] is concerned to depict ... as how the Law now stands in relationship to Jesus as the one whose teaching and practice transcend it and fulfill it and to whom all attention must now be directed."

158. Here it is also worth noticing Matthew 5:21-26 and 6:12-15, where Jesus commands his followers to renounce anger and practice forgiveness—along lines that are closely paralleled by Sirach 27:30—28:7. See Hays, *Echoes of Scripture in the Gospels*, 123-25.

one's children and one's parents, take priority.[159] In addition, Augustine and Aquinas clarify what pertains to love of enemy: such love does not involve the emotion of love, for example. But the point is that Jesus commands us to live in a sharply different way from how people (including most professed Christians!) actually live. Followers of Jesus must truly love—pray for, seek the good of, care for—those who threaten and oppose them existentially. Instead of rising up in hatred against enemies, believers must rise up in love, commending them to God's bountiful love and even being willing to die out of love for them.[160] Believers must act as an eschatological people who know God's love and who are fearless in sharing it, since God has conquered death in Christ.

Matera quotes 1 Peter 3:9 in this regard: "Do not return evil for evil or reviling for reviling; but on the contrary bless, for to this you have been called, that you may obtain a blessing." When our hearts are wholly devoted in Christ to the God of love, we can truly love all those whom God loves without fearing for our lives and our possessions.[161] I note that such love does not entail allowing enemies or injustice a free hand. Love of enemies can and often does involve action to stop people from committing injustices. The point is simply that "just as God does not discriminate in his love for humanity, neither should disciples discriminate in their love for others."[162] Arguably—and with-

---

159. For discussion, see my *Betrayal of Charity*.

160. In her commentary, Levine focuses on praying for enemies, which is difficult enough (even if not as difficult as laying down our lives for enemies, something that Levine certainly does not rule out). She states, "To love our enemies as ourselves—which first requires that we, in fact, love ourselves (a point that cannot be taken for granted)—is not easy. It means praying not only for the rival team or the obnoxious boss but also for the neo-Nazi and the KKK member. They, too, are in God's image and likeness, no matter how deformed that image has become. God forbid that we would descend into that same deformity by rejoicing in the sufferings of others, even those whom we would call the enemy" (Levine, *Sermon on the Mount*, 42–43).

161. See Barron, *And Now I See*, 6. This is a constant theme of Barron's, drawing upon Dorothy Day and Thomas Merton.

162. Matera, *Sermon on the Mount*, 65. Pennington observes that "kingdom-entering righteousness is seen as that heart-fueled way of being in the world that accords with God's nature" (Pennington, *Sermon on the Mount and Human Flourishing*, 201). He links the command to love enemies to the seventh beatitude, "Blessed are the peacemakers, for they shall be called sons [or children] of God" (Matt 5:9). To be a true peacemaker is to love one's enemies; for just such love configures us to the Son of God, Jesus, who died out of love for sinners. As Pennington notes, the connection here between God (as supremely merciful love), Jesus as the Son of God, and ourselves as imitators of God and Jesus is found throughout the New Testament. He points to such passages as Ephesians 5:1–2; 1 John 4:7–12; and 1 Peter 1:13–25—to which many others could be added. See also Davies and Allison, *Critical and Exegetical Commentary on the Gospel according to Saint Matthew*, 1:554; and, without direct reference to

out triumphalism (given Christian history!)—this is possible only within the inaugurated kingdom, through the power of the Holy Spirit.

Let me underscore that although Jesus teaches a "greater righteousness,"[163] including in certain instances (such as divorce and remarriage) foregoing what the Torah itself permits, Jesus does not claim that the visible community of his followers will automatically excel in holiness. Jesus warns that "the salt of the earth" (here symbolizing his followers) can lose its savor (Matt 5:13).[164] The Sermon on the Mount is filled with warnings against various vices. To draw from the Sermon on the Mount the notion that Jesus' visible followers will necessarily be better than other people is to turn the message of the sermon on its head.[165] Far from justifying an attitude of self-congratulation, Jesus warns that some professed believers will be found outside the kingdom, while those whom they have condemned as outsiders ("the tax collectors and the harlots") enter into the kingdom (Matt 21:32).[166] In the sermon, Jesus makes clear that some of his followers will be "false prophets, who come to you in sheep's clothing but inwardly are ravenous wolves"; the standard for discernment in this respect will be whether people bear "good fruit" (Matt 7:15, 17). Even more explicitly, Jesus teaches: "Not every one who says to me, 'Lord, Lord,' shall enter the kingdom of heaven, but he who does the will of my Father who is in heaven" (Matt 7:21). He foretells that among the persons who seem to be his greatest followers, there will be some who have separated themselves from the life of the kingdom.

That said, the Beatitudes of the Sermon on the Mount describe the blessings that Jesus' followers now receive in part and will receive fully "when the kingdom is revealed in all of its power," that is, at the presently unknown time when Jesus will come in glory to consummate the kingdom.[167] Matera

---

the Sermon on the Mount, Jensen, *Affirming the Resurrection of the Incarnate Christ*, 175–76.

163. Matera, *Sermon on the Mount*, 65.

164. On this "salt," arguing that it has a priestly import, see Perrin, *Jesus the Priest*, 112–28.

165. See Durand, *Jésus contemporain*, 85–88. Durand underlines that "faith in the victory of Christ does not justify any institutional triumphalism" (85).

166. See Martens, "'Produce Fruit Worthy of Repentance.'" As Martens notes, "the central issue in the anti-Judaism polemic of these parables of judgment—just as it is throughout all of the New Testament, whatever the specific topic being treated—is christological in nature. Christians today need to be extremely sensitive to issues regarding anti-Semitism and careful not to repeat the sins of their forbears, many of whom were anti-Semites in blaming the death of Jesus on the Jewish race" (173).

167. Matera, *Sermon on the Mount*, 27. In various parables in the Gospels, Jesus indicates that the time of his coming cannot be predicted or known. In his eschatological

argues that the list of beatitudes in Matthew 5 sets forth "the new life Jesus' disciples have begun to enjoy, and will enjoy in its fullness at the end of the ages."[168] When people are poor in spirit, mourn, are meek, hunger and thirst for righteousness, are merciful, are pure in heart, are peacemakers, and are persecuted for righteousness's sake, they already are experiencing the eschatological blessings of kingdom life in Christ.[169]

Even if persons who possess the attributes named in the Beatitudes have not yet received "the final or eschatological blessing" or the "gift of final salvation," such persons are on the way, which is Jesus himself.[170] They have "embraced the kingdom" and have abandoned earthly attachments.[171] Their state of present blessing consists in the relationship that they have with God in Jesus Christ. Insofar as they "have surrendered everything and now depend solely upon God," they belong to the kingdom and will inherit the fullness of the Kingdom.[172] Jesus can teach this with assurance and authority because of

---

sayings, he seems to indicate that it will be soon, and indeed Paul (for example) expected it to be soon. In the Gospel of Matthew, Jesus gives various hints about the final tribulation that will precede his coming, but he adds obscurely, "[b]ut of that day and hour no one knows, not even the angels of heaven, nor the Son, but the Father only" (Matt 24:36). According to Paul, we can marry or not marry—we can go on living along normal lines, or we can live solely for the kingdom (Paul favors the latter)—but the one thing we must do if we wish to live within the inaugurated kingdom is to cleave to nothing earthly but to cleave to God above all in an "undivided devotion" (1 Cor 7:35). Paul describes this spiritual attitude as follows: "from now on, let those who have wives live as though they had none, and those who mourn as though they were not mourning, and those who rejoice as though they were not rejoicing, and those who buy as though they had no goods, and those who deal with the world as though they had no dealings with it. For the form of this world is passing away" (1 Cor 7:29–31).

168. Matera, *Sermon on the Mount*, 28. For parallels between the Beatitudes and later rabbinic texts, see Dalman, *Jesus-Jeshua*, cited in Evans, "Jesus and Rabbinic Parables, Proverbs, and Prayers," 269–70. See also Perrin's point that "Luke's first three beatitudes (viz. 'Blessed are the poor'; 'Blessed are those who mourn'; 'Blessed are those who hunger and thirst for righteousness') have as strong a claim as any material in preserving the dominical voice . . . While there may be some difference of opinion as to *why* Jesus spoke these sayings, most of us can at least agree *that* he spoke them. That fact alone puts the Beatitudes into an elite category of authenticity" (Perrin, *Jesus the Priest*, 128). Like Pennington, Perrin notes the influence of Isaiah 61 upon the beatitudes.

169. In dialogue with contemporary biblical scholarship, patristic interpretations, and Thomas Aquinas's theology, William C. Mattison III proposes that the list of beatitudes correlates well with a list of virtues: faith=poor in spirit; temperance=mourn; fortitude=meek; hope=hunger/thirst for righteousness; justice=merciful; prudence=clean of heart; and charity=peacemakers. See Mattison, *Sermon on the Mount and Moral Theology*, 47.

170. Matera, *Sermon on the Mount*, 31.

171. Matera, *Sermon on the Mount*, 32.

172. Matera, *Sermon on the Mount*, 33.

who he is, the Messiah and divine Son. In him, the kingdom or rule of God has broken into the world. A "new creation" has appeared.[173]

Can people who mourn and are persecuted really be experiencing blessing at the same time? Matera argues that the mourning in view here is preeminently mourning for the sins (including one's own sins) that "have prevented the church from being a light to the nations," just as the people of Israel mourned over the exile and mourned over the sins of the people.[174] Part of the blessing of holiness is mourning over sin, one's own and the world's. Likewise, with the blessing of holiness comes persecution in this world. Jesus himself was persecuted and so too will be his followers. Matera comments in this regard, "Jesus the Messiah . . . exemplifies what he proclaims in his life."[175] In his teaching, Jesus reveals the eschatological life of blessing that he himself embodies as the incarnate Lord.[176] This can

---

173. Matera, *Sermon on the Mount*, 34.

174. Matera, *Sermon on the Mount*, 35. See my *Engaging the Doctrine of Israel*, especially the final chapter.

175. Matera, *Sermon on the Mount*, 43. Pennington emphasizes that the Beatitudes illuminate "Jesus' own way of being in the world" (Pennington, *Sermon on the Mount and Human Flourishing*, 148). Jesus teaches his followers to act as he himself acts. In the antitheses that follow upon the Beatitudes—"You have heard that it was said . . . But I say to you" (Matt 5:21–22; 5:27–28; 5:31–32; 5:33–34; 5:38–39; 5:43–44)—Jesus hammers home the point. He teaches us to become godlike by imitating him because he is "God with us" (Matt 1:23), bearing divine authority. With respect to Jesus' exemplification of his teaching, Legaspi raises an intriguing, but in my view mistaken, claim about Paul's worldview: "When Paul describes this divine wisdom, he does so in a way that is akin to the Gospel writers' presentation of wisdom as something finally embodied or incarnated in Jesus. Yet Paul steers sharply away from the idea that Jesus is a sage or purveyor of wisdom. For Paul, Christ is wisdom. But to grasp this, one must understand that it is Christ *crucified* who is 'the wisdom of God' (1:24)" (Legaspi, *Wisdom in Classical and Biblical Tradition*, 229). Certainly Paul emphasizes Christ crucified as the ultimate revelation of wisdom, but Paul also understands Jesus to be an authoritative teacher or sage, as for instance regarding divorce and remarriage.

176. Perrin takes the Beatitudes in a somewhat different direction from that of Matera and Pennington, although he would agree with them (and they with him) in many respects. Perrin states, "Given that blessings were typically associated with the priestly role in the daily life of ancient Israel, there is no reason to exclude Jesus' beatitudes, even as they invoked the eschatological high priest of Isaiah 61, as blessings in this technical sense. On this likely scenario, the Beatitudes were originally neither a general description of future blessedness nor a series of detached reflections on life, but rather an efficacious speech-act in which Jesus, functioning as a priest, imparted real blessedness in real time on his hearers. By offering blessings at will and well outside Jerusalem, Jesus had entered into direct competition with the temple. . . . [T]hese observations raise the possibility that Matthew's nine-fold arrangement of the Beatitudes was part of his design to portray Jesus as the eschatological high priest and his beatitudes as his issuing *ex officio sacerdotis* a new Aaronic blessing for an extraordinarily special *yom kippur.* . . . Matthew's nine beatitudes may well be giving expression to his conviction

be specified further—more speculatively—as Nicholas Perrin does when he argues in light of Jesus' royal-priestly role, "Matthew's carefully arranged beatitudes seek to preserve the memory of a recurring, ritualized speech-act, taking place between, on the one side, Jesus as the eschatological high priest, and, on the other side, 'the poor' as recipients of his blessings."[177] On this view, Jesus' parables are prophetic teachings that reflect his priestly and messianic office, formalized in his beatitudes.

V. Hearing and Obeying God's Word: Mary

Thus far in this chapter, I have sought to present an exegetical case for the unique authority and eschatological resonance of Jesus' teaching, as well as for his self-understanding as the divine Messiah empowered to teach his people divine wisdom. Let me conclude the chapter with some reflection upon Mary as a model of how believers should receive and live his teaching.

According to the Gospel of Luke, the angel Gabriel proclaims the gospel to Mary at the annunciation. She is told that she will virginally conceive and bear a son who "will be called the Son of the Most High" and who will receive "the throne of his father David" and "reign over the house of Jacob for ever" (Luke 1:32–33). In response, Mary questions the angel, and then she proclaims, "Behold, I am the handmaid of the Lord; let it be to me according to your word" (Luke 1:38). At the birth of Jesus, similarly, the shepherds proclaim the gospel to Mary. Immediately after Jesus' birth in Bethlehem, an angel tells the shepherds who are watching their flocks in the fields around the town: "Be not afraid; for behold, I bring you good news of a great joy which will come to all the people; for to you is born this day in the city of David a Savior, who is Christ the Lord" (Luke 2:10–11).[178] The shepherds rush to find Mary and the baby, and when they do so, they tell her what they have learned. In response, "Mary kept all these things, pondering them in her heart" (Luke 2:19). Mary does the same thing when Jesus, now twelve years old, tells her: "Did you not know that I must be in my Father's house?" (Luke 2:49; cf. 2:51).[179]

---

that Jesus has surpassed Aaron (much as Jesus surpasses Moses; cf. 5:21–42) by offering not three blessings but three sets of three blessings" (Perrin, *Jesus the Priest*, 133).

177. Perrin, *Jesus the Priest*, 134. Perrin draws a connection to the ritualized blessings of the Qumran community, as reconstructed by Nitzan, "Benedictions from Qumran." For Perrin, "Jesus as priest explains both Jesus as messiah and Jesus as prophet" (*Jesus the Priest*, 137).

178. On the shepherds in the context of other details, see Lewis, "Inn."

179. For background, see Hays, *Echoes of Scripture in the Gospels*, 200–201. Hays states, "In these passages, there is no scriptural quotation, or even anything that could

Thus, Mary's response to the word of God is twofold. First, she embraces it and expresses firm obedience to it. Second, she ponders it. In response to the authority of the gospel, she shows obedience and humility, not in a passive mode but in the mode of active contemplation.

The Gospel of John communicates something similar about Mary. The narrative of the wedding at Cana is filled with symbolism, beginning with that of a marriage (symbolizing the covenantal marriage of God and his people, which Jesus is inaugurating). Mary first tells Jesus that the hosts have run out of wine. She brings the need for the wine of salvation to the attention of Jesus. Recall the imagery of Isaiah 25:6, which describes the day of the Lord's victory in terms of "a feast of fat things, a feast of choice wines." Amos 9:13 also employs such eschatological imagery: "the mountains shall drip sweet wine, and all the hills shall flow with it. I will restore the fortunes of my people Israel."[180] Responding to Mary, Jesus tells her that his "hour" has not yet arrived—a response that refers to his cross. Mary then tells the servants: "Do whatever he tells you" (John 2:5). Jesus gives the servants some commands, through which he works a miracle. He changes the water of purification into the wine of the eschatological marriage.[181]

The servants at the wedding represent the members of the inaugurated kingdom, who "listen to her Son as the people Israel listened to the Lord at Sinai."[182] As "an intermediary between her Son and the members of the

---

be considered a clear allusion. But the reader steeped in Scripture might well hear an echo of Genesis 37:11, in which Jacob ponders the words of his similarly precocious son Joseph, who had reported prophetic dreams signifying his own future lordship over his parents and eleven brothers. Jacob scolds him for talking presumptuously; however, the narrator then remarks, 'So his brothers were jealous of him, but his father *kept the word* . . .' (Gen 37:11 LXX)" (201). Hays also directs attention to Daniel 7:28 LXX, where Daniel "fixed the word in [his] heart." As Hays says, "in both Daniel 7 and Luke 2, the word 'kept in the heart' offers a prophetic foreshadowing of the deliverance and vindication of Israel through the person of an exalted messianic figure whose kingdom will have no end (cf. Luke 1:33; Dan 7:14)" (201).

180. The mountain symbolism here is fulfilled not in John 2 at Cana, but (among other places) in the feeding miracles of Matthew 15:29-39 and John 6:3-14. For discussion, see Perrin, *Jesus the Temple*, 174-76, in light of Isaiah 24-25, Ezekiel 34, and Exodus 24.

181. For discussion, see McWhirter, *Bridegroom Messiah*. For a study of the image of the eschatological wedding banquet in the Synoptic Gospels, with attention to the image's roots in the Old Testament and in the Second Temple context, see Long, *Jesus the Bridegroom*. Long focuses on the end of exile (through a new exodus) and the restoration of Israel. See also the discussion of the miracle at Cana—with attention also to patristic interpretations—in Hengel, "Dionysiac Messiah," although Hengel's reading of the status of Mary in this miracle story is woefully inadequate.

182. Martin and Wright, *Gospel of John*, 58. Earlier Martin and Wright point out, "Scripture often personifies the people of God as a feminine figure, such as the Lord's

household," Mary tells the servants to obey Jesus' words.[183] What Jesus commands, the servants should obediently believe and do. This is an indication of Jesus' divine authority, as is the ensuing miracle. It is also a clear expression of how we should hear and respond to Jesus' teaching. When Jesus reveals something about God, himself, and us, we should embrace it. His teachings are challenging because he requires us to imitate his path and to embody his own love. It is no wonder that Mary, in the Gospel of John, makes manifest her obedience to the word of God precisely by her presence at the foot of the cross, the center of divine love.

Commenting on John 2:5—Mary's command to the servants, "Do whatever he tells you"—Thomas Aquinas remarks that even though Jesus had seemed to refuse her, Mary did not lose hope in Jesus' mercy. Moreover, Mary's command "Do whatever he tells you" is the epitome of justice, since "perfect justice consists in obeying Christ in all things."[184] Mary's words describe how we should respond to Jesus' teaching: namely, by understanding the nature of his divine authority and by obeying him. We thereby show ourselves to be under the rule or kingdom of God.[185]

---

covenantal bride. In the Old Testament, Israel is personified as 'daughter Zion' (Ps 9:15; Isa 62:11; Zeph 3:14) or as the children of Mother Zion (Isa 66:7-9; see also 60:1-7), and in the New Testament, the Church is personified as the bride of Christ (2 Cor 11:2; Eph 5:29-32; Rev 19:6-8; 21:2, 9). At Cana, the mother of Jesus appears as the embodiment, in a single person, of the faithful, obedient people of God. Just as the people Israel expressed perfect faithfulness to God at the covenantal wedding at Mount Sinai—'We will do everything that the Lord has told us' (Exod 24:3; see 19:8; 24:7)—so too the mother of Jesus instructs those present at the wedding to 'Do whatever he tells you' (2:5; compare Luke 1:38). The mother of Jesus is the model of those obedient to God: she both displays and encourages perfect covenant faithfulness and love for God" (Martin and Wright, *Gospel of John*, 57).

183. Martin and Wright, *Gospel of John*, 58.

184. Aquinas, *Commentary on the Gospel of John: Chapters 1–5*, §354, 138.

185. I emphasize that Mary's obedience is not passive but active, rooted in her pondering of her Son. Without reference to Mary, Michael Legaspi argues that faith in Christ puts an end to human (i.e. non-Christian) wisdom: "Though the Gospel writers do not speak explicitly of a binary opposition between divine and human wisdom in the way Paul does, they share with Paul a sense that human wisdom has come to an end with the advent of Jesus and the formation of the new Christian collective. Inasmuch as the evangelists portray Jesus as the incarnation of the divine *logos* (John 1:14) and as wisdom personified (e.g., Matt 23:34 but see Luke 11:49; Matt 11:28), they exclude the possibility that others—scribes, Pharisees, or sages of any sort—possess knowledge or authority superior to that of Jesus" (Legaspi, *Wisdom in Classical and Biblical Tradition*, 241–42). I agree that Jesus possesses superior knowledge or authority, but I do not see why that means that "human wisdom has come to an end"—after all, Mary's active pondering includes learning from the shepherds (Luke 2) and, if Matthew 2 can instruct us, from the Magi as well. In Acts 17:28, Paul makes appeal to Greek poets. Non-Christian wisdom is relativized but not negated by the coming of Christ. For Legaspi,

Indebted to Bernard of Clairvaux, Bonaventure offers a commentary on Mary's words, "Behold, I am the handmaid of the Lord; let it be to me according to your word" (Luke 1:38). Mary's consent to the word of God, Bonaventure observes, exhibits three elements: humility, love, and faith. Together, these elements constitute the stance from which we should respond to Jesus' teaching. Mary's faith is present already when she opens her mouth to reply to the angel Gabriel. She immediately "believed that what the angel had said was true."[186] Interiorly, she conceived faith before she spoke her exterior words of consent. Here Bonaventure finds a parallel with Psalm 116:10, which in his Latin psalter reads "I believed, and therefore I spoke." Bonaventure cites Elizabeth's praise of Mary's faith: "blessed is she who believed that there would be a fulfilment of what was spoken to her from the Lord" (Luke 1:45).

The second element according to Bonaventure is humility, which Mary expresses in the phrase, "I am the handmaid of the Lord." As a parallel, Bonaventure recalls the humility shown by Abigail, when David asked her to become his wife: "Behold, your handmaid is a servant to wash the feet of the servants of my lord" (1 Sam 25:41). Bonaventure suggests that the greatness of Mary's grace corresponded to the greatness of her humility. The latter can be measured by the fact that the angel announced that Mary was going to receive the immeasurable dignity of being the virgin mother of the Messiah, and Mary responded with pure humility rather that with pride.

The third element is love, and Bonaventure finds this in Mary's words, "Be it done to me according to your word." Mary consents with love, with desire that God's will for her and for the salvation of the world take place. Bonaventure finds a resonance here in Psalm 119:173, which in his psalter reads, "Be it done by your right hand to save me."

Mary's response to God's word is marked by the elements that should characterize our response to Jesus' teaching: faith, humility, and love. Bonaventure remarks that these three elements should also characterize our prayer, and so Mary's response, "let it be to me according to your word," is an expression of prayer. When we hear Jesus' teaching, we should humbly embrace its truth in faith and love, and we should also pray that his words will come about in our lives, in the Church, and in the whole world.

What does Bonaventure say about Mary's "pondering" of the shepherds' words (Luke 2:19)? He connects it with the practice of the wise person

---

the New Testament proclaims "a way of life marked less by knowledge than by piety and integrity," but I think that the New Testament's constant proclamation of truth about Christ and of the importance of knowledge is consistent with the later church fathers who also insist upon the value of knowledge.

186. Bonaventure, *Commentary on the Gospel of Luke: Chapters 1–8*, 78, ch. 1, §67.

who meditates continually upon truth. He compares Mary's pondering to the response to instruction urged by Sirach 50:28: "Blessed is he who concerns himself with these things, and he who lays them to heart will become wise." Mary takes the wisdom of the gospel into her heart and contemplates it. In so doing, Mary is the opposite of the fool, whose mind "is like a broken jar," able to hold nothing (Sir 21:14). Discussing Mary's pondering of the truth about her Son, Bonaventure remarks that Mary fulfills the symbolism of the ark of the covenant in which the Ten Commandments were stored. Mary truly "contains the mysteries of God's words," and, even more, Mary understands them.[187] Bonaventure applies to Mary the testimony of the psalmist, "I have laid up your word in my heart" (Ps 119:11).

Bonaventure also briefly reflects upon Mary's response to her Son's words after she and Joseph found him in the Temple in conversation with the teachers. After Jesus says to her, "How is it that you sought me? Did you not know that I must be in my Father's house?" (Luke 2:49), Mary does not immediately understand his meaning. But the evangelist presents Mary as continuing to reflect upon his words. She "kept all these things in her heart" (Luke 2:51). Bonaventure suggests that this passage has in view the entirety of Jesus' words and actions toward his parents. Mary kept in her heart the entire mystery of Jesus' childhood. She did so, says Bonaventure (echoing Bede), "so that she might produce testimony with regard to time and place."[188] He compares Mary's role here to the role of the disciples who witnessed Jesus' transfiguration. Acting upon Jesus' instruction, the disciples "kept the matter to themselves, questioning what the rising from the dead meant" (Mark 9:10). During Jesus' life there were mysteries witnessed by both Mary and the disciples that did not yet possess their full meaning, since their meaning would be unfolded by later events. In faith, we ponder mysteries whose meaning will fully be revealed when we enjoy the beatific vision in the consummated kingdom of God.

For Aquinas and Bonaventure, therefore, Mary is a model of how to receive Jesus' teaching. We are to recognize its authority and obey it. We can only do so if we receive it in faith, humility, and love. We must keep it close to our heart and ponder it, both because wisdom should regularly be meditated upon and put into practice, and because the teaching of Jesus contains eschatological dimensions that we cannot yet fully understand.

Let me add that Bonaventure quotes from Bernard's *Homilies in Praise of the Blessed Virgin Mary*. When Bernard arrives at Mary's response— "Behold, I am the handmaid of the Lord; let it be to me according to your

---

187. Bonaventure, *Commentary on the Gospel of Luke: Chapters 1–8*, 170, ch. 2, §40.

188. Bonaventure, *Commentary on the Gospel of Luke: Chapters 1–8*, 220, ch. 2, §109.

word"—Bernard identifies it as exhibiting wondrous humility, a mark of divine grace. Bernard observes that the angel Gabriel has just praised Mary in an extraordinary way and has announced that God wants to give Mary the highest possible vocation among mere humans. Bernard admits that if the Church came to Bernard and bestowed upon him some honor, then he, being a sinner, would puff up with pride. But Mary did the very opposite. Her response offers a lesson for monks, who, Bernard observes, all too often crave honors and become angry when they are slighted, or else pursue other worldly commendations. Mary's "let it be to me" indicates her great desire that God's word be accomplished—a desire due to her love. Mary prays that the word of the angel will become, in her womb, the living incarnate Word. This is a total response to God's Word.

Amy Peeler discerns in Mary's pondering of and obedience to God's Word not only a receptive embrace of divine truth, but also proclamation.[189] Wisdom means being taught by the Lord and then teaching others about the Lord. Mary teaches others by her Magnificat, by her words to the servants at Cana, and by participating with the disciples in prayer and praise at the "upper room" after Jesus' ascension (Acts 1:13–14). As Peeler says, Mary is among the "testifying group" at Pentecost, where, in accordance with Joel's prophecy as quoted by Peter in Acts 2:18, Mary likely "testified vocally and publicly to the fulfillment of God's promises in her son Jesus."[190]

VI. Conclusion

Employing well-known teachings of Jesus, this chapter sought to make a twofold case, in accordance with Jesus' own self-understanding and in support of the divine authority and power of Jesus' teachings for our salvation. First, Jesus' teachings are consistent with the overall portrait of Jesus that the Gospels provide. His words are borne out by his own revelatory deeds. Second (and related to the first), Jesus' teachings are simultaneously wisdom-teachings and thoroughly eschatological. The Protestant biblical scholar Suzanne Watts Henderson remarks, "In Mark's gospel, Jesus' teaching ministry figures as a constituent part of his apocalyptic proclamation."[191] The same thing is true in

---

189. See Peeler, *Women and the Gender of God*, 153. For Peeler, this entails women's inclusion in the Episcopalian priesthood, but I do not think it does from a Catholic perspective, in which proclamation involves many other vocations as well.

190. Peeler, *Women and the Gender of God*, 183–84.

191. Henderson, *Christology and Discipleship in the Gospel of Mark*, 55. Henderson differentiates Jesus' teaching from the Greco-Roman model of a teacher who gathers disciples in order to impart (in Vernon K. Robbins's words) "the system of thought and action that he himself embodies" (Robbins, *Jesus the Teacher*, 55, quoted in Henderson,

TEACHING

the Gospels of Matthew and Luke, as we have seen. Levine shows that there is great wisdom for everyday life in Jesus' parables, and her perspective is complemented by Lohfink's, which underlines that these parables are strongly eschatological in their import. In Matera's work, we saw that the Sermon on the Mount contains much wisdom-teaching and constitutes an eschatological ethics for the (non-triumphalist) inaugurated kingdom.

Jesus' teaching reflects his unique prophetic authority, grounded in his divine identity as the Son of God. The proper response to Jesus' teaching is enunciated by Mary: "Do whatever he tells you" (John 2:5) and "I am the handmaid of the Lord; let it be to me according to your word" (Luke 1:38). Those who desire to remain in fellowship with Jesus must, as Perrin puts it, manifest "an ongoing commitment to receive the teachings of Jesus."[192]

Both the parables and the sermon contain much doctrinal content about God, Jesus, and Israel/Church. The God of mercy who meets us in Jesus Christ commands the works of mercy—in the case of the parable of the Good Samaritan, specifically "charity towards the poor," including "monetary almsgiving," as Anthony Giambrone has shown.[193] Given the cultic role of almsgiving in Second Temple Judaism, Giambrone demonstrates that Jesus' moral teaching in the parable of the good Samaritan is tied to a proper understanding of the cross and of the eschatological temple, as well as of the requirements for sharing in the priestly work of Jesus.[194]

Christology and Discipleship in the Gospel of Mark, 55). While Jesus does gather disciples for this purpose, Henderson notes the following difference: "Though Greco-Roman literature features philosophers-teachers who actively recruit followers, they do so on the basis of remarkable words or deeds that inspire their pupils' loyalty; only after much convincing proof do the leaders earn the right to be surrounded by those who would learn from an espouse their teachings" (*Christology and Discipleship in the Gospel of Mark*, 55-56). For Henderson, Jesus calls disciples—and they immediately obey and follow him, well before he has said or done anything noteworthy—because he understands himself (as do his followers) as the one through whom the Kingdom is about to spring forth. Henderson goes on to argue insightfully that in the Gospel of Mark, "the Twelve become more than just ardent spokesmen for the coming reign of God; they will wield its very power, in both word and deed" (242; cf. Mark 6).

192. Perrin, *Jesus the Priest*, 141.

193. Giambrone, *Sacramental Charity*, 175, indebted to Heiligenthal, "Werke der Barmherzigkeit oder Almosen?." Giambrone argues persuasively, "In evaluating the extended understanding of 'neighbor' presented in Luke 10:25-37, it is important not to mistake the actions of the Good Samaritan. They belong in every way to the world of almsgiving, though the word ἐλεημοσύνη does not appear" (Giambrone, *Sacramental Charity*, 171). See also such studies as Hays, "By Almsgiving and Faith Sins Are Purged?," focusing on the church fathers.

194. See Giambrone, *Sacramental Charity*, 311-13. In email correspondence, Michael Patrick Barber pointed out to me the fact that, for Giambrone, the christological reading of the parable in the fathers coincides with Luke's imagery of the good

A similar connection between Jesus' moral teaching and the underlying doctrine of God and Christ appears in the work of the Catholic biblical scholar Nathan Eubank. Eubank observes that the parable of the laborers in the vineyard should be read in the context of Matthew 19's portrait of Jesus' encounter with the rich young man, whom Jesus commands to sell all that he has and to follow Jesus.[195] Jesus tells the rich young man that if he does what Jesus commands, he "will have treasure in heaven" (Matt 19:21). When the rich young man goes away sad, Jesus warns his disciples that it is easier for a camel to go through the eye of a needle than for a rich man to enter God's kingdom. The disciples are alarmed, but Jesus reassures them that "with God all things are possible" (Matt 19:26). Jesus promises them a great reward for the sacrifices they have made in following him. It seems that the parable of the laborers in the vineyard undermines the lesson of Matthew 19, because in the parable those who work longer hours fail to receive a greater reward. In response, Eubank notes that each worker receives the reward he was promised, so the promise of "treasure in heaven" is not reneged upon. But the parable addresses a further question: "what is the fate of those who have not earned treasure in heaven?"[196] The answer given by the parable is that even such persons will be rewarded far beyond their deserts.[197]

The parable of the laborers in the vineyard has evident moral implications, identified by both Levine and Lohfink. All should receive a sufficiency

---

samaritan who promises to repay whatever is necessary on his return (Luke 10:35)—a statement that mirrors Jesus's parable about his future eschatological return in Luke 19.

195. See Eubank, *Wages of Cross-Bearing and Debt of Sin*, 95. For interpretation of Matthew 19, see the opening of Pope John Paul II's encyclical *Veritatis Splendor*, available at www.vatican.va; and see also chapter 1 of Levine, *Difficult Words of Jesus*, although some of Levine's comments strike me as mistaken, such as her suggestion that Jesus aimed to direct the rich young man's attention away from eternal life and her corresponding claim about the rich young man, "I think this man is single . . . Had he a family, he might be less worried about inheriting eternal life. He could live on through his children and his grandchildren" (*Difficult Words of Jesus*, 4). It is worth noting that "eternal life," as in John's Gospel and in some synoptic texts, may simply mean the "kingdom of God": see Allison, *Constructing Jesus*, 188.

196. Eubank, *Wages of Cross-Bearing and Debt of Sin*, 96.

197. Eubank finds something quite similar in 2 Baruch 24:1–2 and 4 Ezra 8:31–36, which emphasize both that God will do justice, and that God's mercy to sinners will be extraordinary. As Eubank sums up, "God will indeed repay those who have stored up heavenly treasure and will be merciful to those who have not"—although Eubank adds that the parable "does not discuss the fate of those who fail to do any work for the kingdom," who may end up like the "goats" who, having done no works of mercy, find themselves damned in Jesus' account of the final judgment in Matthew 25:31–46 (Eubank, *Wages of Cross-Bearing and Debt of Sin*, 98). For a reading similar to Eubank's, though without Eubank's interest in merit, see Hultgren, *Parables of Jesus*, 41.

from their labor, and the community must not fall into rivalry. Here as elsewhere, it is apparent that Jesus teaches an eschatological vision, possible not within normal human life but instead rooted in his cross and resurrection and his outpouring of the Holy Spirit. As Eubank makes clear, Jesus' teaching has to do with more than morality. It is about the final judgment and about the justice and mercy of God, and it also involves the doctrine of merit in relation to Jesus' salvific sufficiency.

Given that Jesus' teaching possesses divine authority—even when he is simply instructing us in wise living, without necessarily going beyond other Jewish wisdom teachers of his era—let me conclude this chapter by asking more directly what it means for him to teach *as the incarnate Lord*. For the Gospels, as the Protestant biblical scholar Benjamin Wold points out, "Jesus is the quintessential expression of wisdom," or "embodied and personified wisdom dwelling with humanity."[198] The Gospels generally attribute extraordinary knowledge to Jesus. We find many statements such as Luke 6:8, "he [Jesus] knew their thoughts," and John 2:25, "he knew all men and needed no one to bear witness of man; for he himself knew what was in man." The Protestant biblical scholar Collin Bullard notes that, in John's Gospel, "Jesus' omniscience results in his complete awareness of not only his own divine being and the future course of the story, but also the minds of characters."[199] Bullard shows that the something similar holds in the Gospel of Luke as well. For Luke, Jesus' ability to know the thoughts of others is a divine ability that Jesus "possesses by virtue of his identity as Lord."[200]

---

198. Wold, "Jesus among Wisdom's Representatives," 317–18. See also Witherington, *Jesus the Sage*. For focus on Jesus' (apocalyptic) prophetic ministry, see Witherington, *Jesus the Seer*, chapter 8, with critical reference to Allison, *Jesus of Nazareth* and to Wright, *Jesus and the Victory of God*.

199. Bullard, *Jesus and the Thoughts of Many Hearts*, 175.

200. Bullard, *Jesus and the Thoughts of Many Hearts*, 178. Bullard adds, "Our conclusion, when set in the context of broader discussions of NT Christology, contributes one more to the list of features which comprise Yahweh's character or identity in the OT and which scholars have observed being attributed to Jesus in the NT. There are numerous attributes shared between Jesus and the God of Israel which have been the subject of critical inquiry: God and Jesus share the κύριος title; Jesus is included in the divine identity as ruler and creator; Jesus receives worship alongside God. These represent some of the major points of discussion in recent research, but the list may also include other features of God's character which Jesus possesses, such as the ability to forgive sins, to bestow the spirit, or, as we have argued, to plumb the depths of the human heart" (181–82). Bullard hypothesizes that behind such claims is the Christian experience of the risen Jesus, as does Hurtado in his *Ancient Jewish Monotheism and Early Christian Jesus-Devotion*. Although there is no doubt about the significance of Jesus' Resurrection for his followers' confession of his divine status, I agree with Grindheim, Pitre, and others that Jesus himself—not simply Jesus according to the Gospels—taught his own divinity. For further reflection, advancing a number of helpful arguments (both

In response, many scholars assume that such passages are invented or vastly exaggerated: Jesus "was a scribal-illiterate Galilean who . . . managed to dupe a few unlearned audiences."²⁰¹ By contrast, I hold that Jesus really did have the profound knowledge attributed to him by the Gospels. Yet, it is clear that Jesus spoke and thought in Second Temple language and cultural modes, and that he was a relatively uneducated man even by the standards of his day.²⁰² In my view, however, there is good reason to suppose that his human knowledge accorded with his dignity as the Spirit-filled divine Son whose task it was to inaugurate the kingdom of God. Thomas Joseph White has pointed out that if Jesus in his human mind did not know the Father intimately, then Jesus could not have always known and obeyed the will of the Father. For Jesus to be able to obey the divine will at all points, and to reveal the Father perfectly, he must in his human knowledge have known the divine will.²⁰³

Although N. T. Wright has argued that Jesus was aware of his vocation to do what only YHWH could do and to bring to fulfillment all YHWH's covenantal promises, Wright deems it docetic to suppose that Jesus had some "sort of 'supernatural' awareness of himself, of Israel's god, and of the relation between the two of them."²⁰⁴ In fact, for Wright, Jesus "must have

theological and exegetical) in favor of Jesus' uniquely broad knowledge, see Stevenson, *Consciousness of the Historical Jesus*.

201. Keith, *Jesus' Literacy*, 184—describing a viewpoint that is not his own. Keith defines "scribal-illiterate" as one not trained in the interpretation of Torah (as distinct from simply illiterate). He grants that "some members of Jesus' audience(s) could have concluded that he was a scribal-literate teacher if he cited Scripture during his pedagogical sessions or his interpretive battles" (185). This line of reasoning is, as such, clearly quite far from the profound knowledge attributed to Jesus by the Gospels. For another perspective, see John Meier's contention that "[t]he historical Jesus is both deeply steeped in the Jewish Scriptures—as well as the legal debates about them—and at the same time open to the cultural influences of the larger Greco-Roman world" (Meier, *Marginal Jew*, 4:573).

202. As Keith says, "Whether one considers Jesus a scribal-literate or scribal-illiterate person impacts one's conception of Jesus as a Jewish teacher and, ultimately, how one sees Jesus functioning in the culture of his day" (*Jesus' Literacy*, 190). Of course, it is possible that Jesus' wisdom was infused by God or acquired through his own unique intelligence, so that he did not need to be taught by scribes. Keith does not address this possibility directly.

203. See White, *Incarnate Lord*, 247.

204. Wright, *Jesus and the Victory of God*, 653; see also Wright's statement at 649 (repeated at 653) that Jesus "acted upon a vocation to do and be for Israel and the world what, according to scripture, only Israel's god can do and be." For an appreciative and, at the same time, helpfully critical assessment of Wright's project (especially as articulated for example in *Jesus and the Victory of God*, 661–62), see Hays, "Story, History, and the Quest for Jesus." Hays argues that all too often for Wright, "'The church' . . . seems to offer chiefly an oppressive and misleading hermeneutical framework that

had to wrestle with the serious possibility that he might be totally deluded," and Wright supposes that Jesus, in daring to do what only God could do, was making "a great Pascalian wager."[205] But if that is all it was—if without real knowledge he dared to try to "personify" YHWH's return to Zion[206]—then he was deluded and fanatical. Other biblical scholars, however, have pushed

---

obscures the real Jesus. To discover that real Jesus we must bracket out the church's received traditions about him and reread the NT with a fresh (modernist?) historical consciousness. Only then will we truly know Jesus in two ways: through our own experience (prayer, etc.) and in our historical reconstruction. Experience and critical history rescue us from the misreading of Jesus in these terms, but it is one important strand of his working methodology" (113). Note that Hays goes on to offer five major gains achieved by Wright's work. In Hays's view, the major weaknesses of Wright's work consist in Wright's over-systematization (so that the distinctive voices and narratives of the NT tend to be lost—as an example Hays points to Wright's argument that "the parable of the prodigal son [is] a story about Israel's exile and restoration" [117]) and Wright's relativizing of the Church and the canon as providing the faithful context in which Scripture is read and understood.

205. Wright, *Jesus and the Victory of God*, 606, 609.

206. Wright, *Jesus and the Victory of God*, 615. See also Tan, *Zion Traditions and the Aims of Jesus*. For background from Jesus' Galilean context pertaining not so much to YHWH's return to Zion as to the symbolism of Zion itself, see Freyne, *Jesus, a Jewish Galilean*, 116, where Freyne observes, "Ever since the profanation of the temple by Antiochus Epiphanes in the mid-second century BCE, Mount Zion had been turned into a fortress as well as a holy place. In Jesus' day, Herod the Great had built the Arx Antonia, a fortress that housed a Roman garrison . . . Resistance to such foreign exploitation of the religious centre hardened into militant nationalism. In the first revolt against Rome the rebel forces had made the temple mount the location of their final stand, leading eventually to its destruction by Titus and his army . . . Similar feelings were current in Galilee also. Just 30 years after Jesus' death, the Jewish citizens of Gamla had a coin struck locally whose legend runs: 'For the freedom of Zion, Jerusalem the holy'. Such ideas were surely current in Jesus' day also. Galilean Jewish villagers sought to retrieve their Maccabean/Hasmonean past as a way of resisting the Romanization of their world by the Herodian rulers, typified by such centres as Sepphoris and Tiberias, and resented the encroachment on their traditional way of life. Jesus had rejected both the Herodian cities and the Hasmonean-style militarism based on the holy war ideology. His was a more open perspective on Jewish ethnic identity. If Zion was to be a meaningful symbol for him and his movement it would have to strike a different note to either fortress Zion or triumphant Zion" (cf. 144-49 for more on Jesus' view of "the Herodian dynasty as doomed to apocalyptic annihilation" [147] and Jesus' avoidance of Sepphoris and Tiberias). Notably, Freyne reconstructs an earlier Isaian "servants of Yahweh" community that sought "a humbled Zion, like the humbled servant" (116-17), and he proposes that this earlier community "provides a highly important analogue for Jesus and his group, and may well have functioned as an inspiration for his project" (117). For more on Jesus and Jerusalem, arguing that for Jesus "the servant-Zion tradition in Isaiah offered possibilities for challenging the hegemony of the temple aristocracy in Jerusalem," see Freyne, *Jesus, a Jewish Galilean*, 152. Freyne's perspective, which accords with N. T. Wright's on Jesus' politics, is indebted to Theissen, "Political Dimension of Jesus' Activities."

in a better direction. I discussed above the work of Sigurd Grindheim and Brant Pitre, who, as we saw, make the case that Jesus claimed to be divine without ceasing to recognize himself to be a man.[207] Trying to apprehend such a claim, Giambrone has suggested that Jesus' self-knowledge may have involved more than one stage. In Giambrone's view, the Gospels' testimony to a theophany at Jesus' baptism has historical plausibility.[208] If saints such as Ignatius of Loyola have received mystical experiences of the Trinity, then surely Jesus could have received something similar but far more intense. Specifically, Jesus at his baptism may have recognized himself to be "implicated in the words, 'You are my Son.' The Spirit's unction thus radiates through all Jesus' senses and his soul and somehow involves Christ within the Trinitarian processions in a way entirely unique."[209] Even if one holds, as I do, that Jesus maintained an intimate knowledge of his Father throughout his life, Giambrone's emphasis on this intimate knowledge rising to explicit consciousness through scriptural and "sacramental" means is intriguing.

Further insights are found in Simon Gaine's *Did the Saviour See the Father?* Gaine argues that the New Testament broadly affirms that "Jesus enjoyed the extraordinary identity of the divine Son of God" and that "a claim to an extraordinary knowledge appropriate to this Son is surely implied."[210]

207. It seems to me that Wright might accept this. He comments, for example, that among Second Temple Jews speculations about a "second god" (as in the work of Philo) were quite possible, and he also notes that Rabbi Akiba appears to have held that the Messiah (whom Akiba deemed to be Simeon Bar-Kochba) would sit on a throne at the right hand of God: see *Jesus and the Victory of God*, 627–28. Wright also notes in light of Matthew 11:25–27//Luke 10:21–22 that "the possibility of Jesus' having a particular intimacy with the one he called 'father' is not . . . a new and strange idea added on to the outside of the rest of the portrait. It appears quite naturally as the inside of the picture, making sense of, and giving depth to, all the rest" (650; see also Lee, *From Messiah to Preexistent Son*, 137–43). If an event like the transfiguration occurred, Wright adds, this would have only confirmed Jesus' sense of his radical uniqueness and intimacy with the Father.

208. For the same viewpoint, see also Perrin, *Jesus the Priest*, 61–70. Perrin concludes, "*Something* happened that day, something large. From that day forward, Jesus dedicated himself to a new calling, complete with a unique register of narratives and vocabulary, all revolving around his identity as the self-proclaimed 'Son' and his association with the Spirit" (66).

209. Giambrone, "*Scientia Christi*," 281–82. For a partial criticism, see Gregory Vall's review of Giambrone's *Quest for the Historical Christ*, 133.

210. Gaine, *Did the Saviour See the Father?*, 20. See also John Saward's argument that "St. Thomas' doctrine of the human knowledge of the incarnate Son is in complete conformity to the data of Sacred Scripture. A threefold pattern emerges from a reading of the Gospels: an experimental knowledge in which our Lord grows and develops (Luke 2:52); an extraordinary prophetic knowledge of the future and of men's hearts (Matt. 9:4; 12:25; etc.); and an intimate knowledge of the Father that is higher and more direct than faith (Matt. 11:27): St. John's Gospel describes it as 'seeing' (John 3:11;

Among Gaine's most significant observations is the point that "a Christ who is the herald of the kingdom of heaven sits easily with a Christ who possesses extraordinary knowledge of God: such an extraordinary teacher must doubtless know something extraordinary to teach."[211] White augments this point by observing that Jesus' unique knowledge enabled him to sorrow intensely for our sins and to cry out on the cross as our redeemer. In White's words, "Through his cry of agony and desire, Jesus intends (through his consciousness of himself as the eschatological Son of Man) to inaugurate the kingdom of God."[212]

At the same time, ignorance also is present in Jesus. White distinguishes various modes of Jesus' human knowledge, including (beatific) knowledge that exceeds the domain of concepts and that therefore allows for ignorance in the conceptual domain of acquired knowledge.[213] This distinction can account for Jesus' profession of ignorance of the "day" or the "hour" of the consummation of the eschaton, in accordance with Matthew 24:36: "But of that day and hour no one knows, not even the angels in heaven, nor the Son, but the Father only."[214] The biblical scholar Daniel

---

31–32; 6:45–46; 8:38). Nowhere does the New Testament suggest that Jesus came to know that he was God the Father's eternal Son by deduction or by information from a human person. At no point does it describe him as a believer" (Saward, *Redeemer in the Womb*, 69). For the historical-critical argument that John knew and (in part) rewrote Mark's Gospel, see the essays in Becker et al., *John's Transformation of Mark*.

211. Gaine, *Did the Saviour See the Father?*, 20.

212. White, *Incarnate Lord*, 338. White concludes, "Christ's words on the cross are eschatological in nature. His cry tends toward the final possession of a gift of redemption for humanity that is not yet fully possessed. Furthermore, the theological affirmation of such a mixed state of expectation and suffering in the soul of Christ is entirely compatible with (and in fact complementary to) the teaching of St. Thomas concerning Christ's knowledge of both the Father and sinful humanity in and through his crucifixion. The knowledge of the Father's will afforded by the beatific vision is not the cause of suffering in itself, but of confidence and consolation. Yet because this same vision is accompanied necessarily by intense knowledge of human evil in the world, it is also the source of both profound redemptive desire and intense agony. Jesus experiences in his ordinary consciousness as man a deeper suffering on our behalf because of this grace" (338–39). In this section, White is responding to various interlocutors, including Karl Barth and Hans Urs von Balthasar, who interpret the cry of dereliction as indicative of despair (as Christ undergoes the punishment of all who are alienated from God) or, analogously, of an intra-Trinitarian separation or suffering. See also—building upon White's work—Nolan, "Christ's Human Nature and the Cry from the Cross"; and, for further background, Rossé, *Cry of Jesus on the Cross*.

213. For further discussion, defending the value of going beyond (as White does) strict adherence to Aquinas's own position on these matters, see Gaine, "Some Recent Arguments."

214. Aquinas, like his fellow medieval theologians and like many of the church fathers, does not grant that Jesus' acquired knowledge is less than perfectly full, but

Assefa has rightly contrasted 1 Enoch's eschatological timetable with that of the Gospel of Matthew, given that Matthew "underlines ignorance" and emphasizes "the motif of surprise" with regard to the timing of the consummation of the kingdom.[215]

Returning to the Gospel of Matthew, we find that Matthew gives Jesus "a status and a relation to the Father that are superior to those of 'the angels of heaven.'"[216] William Wright comments about Jesus' words in Matthew 11:27—"All things have been delivered to me by my Father; and . . . no one knows the Father except the Son and any one to whom the Son chooses to reveal him"—that Jesus (or the evangelist) is using technical language that pertains to radically unique teaching authority.[217] Martin Hengel, indebted to Joachim Jeremias, arrives at a similar conclusion regarding this verse: Jesus "speaks both at the behest and in the authority of the Wisdom of God."[218]

White feels free to differ from Aquinas in this regard, as I do. For further background see Madigan, *Passions of Christ in High-Medieval Thought*, chapter 4, titled *"Christus Nesciens? Was Christ Ignorant of the Day of Judgment?"*

215. Assefa, "Matthew's Day of Judgment in the Light of 1 Enoch," 213.

216. Wright, *Lord's Prayer*, 54.

217. See Wright, *Lord's Prayer*, 52; and see also, in favor of the historical authenticity of this text, Pitre, "Historical Jesus and the Apocalyptic 'Thunderbolt.'" Wright goes on to say, "Jesus's words about himself as the Son echo things said in ancient Jewish literature about the Wisdom or Word of God as a heavenly figure. For instance, Jesus says that 'no one knows the Father except the Son' (Matt. 11:27). Similarly, Wisdom 9 says that God's personified Wisdom, who exists in heaven with God, knows him. 'She . . . knows your works . . . understands what is pleasing in your sight . . . [and] knows and understands all things' (vv. 9, 11). Jesus, given his unique, intimate knowledge of the Father as the Son, is alone able to reveal the Father (Matt. 11:27). Similarly, in Wisdom 9, Solomon prays that God would send his Wisdom into the world to make God's ways known to people: 'Send her forth from the holy heavens, and from the throne of your glory send her, . . . that I may learn what is pleasing to you' (v. 10; cf. 8:4; 9:17–18). In light of such allusions to God's Wisdom, Jesus seems to be implicitly identifying himself here as the Word or Wisdom of God in the flesh. As such, Jesus knows the Father in a way that no one else does, and on the basis of his unique relationship with the Father, Jesus alone can make the Father known in a unique, unparalleled way" (52).

218. Hengel, "Jesus as Messianic Teacher of Wisdom," 88. Hengel adds that "we must view the three essential elements God's Wisdom, God's kingdom and the Son of Man as closely bound together. Basically they are already related to each other in the apocalyptic of Daniel and the Similitudes of Enoch" (93). See also Hays, *Echoes of Scripture in the Gospels*, 157, where Hays shows that Matthew 11:29 alludes both to Sirach 51:26–27 and, even more literally, to Jeremiah 6:16. On this basis, Hays suggests that "Jesus' gracious word about 'rest for your souls' in Matthew 11:29 evokes the same ominous overtones found in Jeremiah 6: this is an offer of divine grace, but refusal of the offer leads to disaster" (*Echoes of Scripture in the Gospels*, 157).

In sum, more than a mere human teacher—since he is the Spirit-filled incarnate Son—Jesus is the definitive source of wisdom. Jesus knows that the temple will be destroyed, and he knows that at the eschatological consummation, all peoples "will see the Son of man coming on the clouds of heaven with power and great glory" (Matt 24:30). He knows that the kingdom is present in himself and that his words and deeds offer God's salvation. Knowing all this about God, himself, and us, he proclaims to us with divine authority, "The time is fulfilled, and the Kingdom of God is at hand; repent, and believe in the gospel" (Mark 1:15).

Chapter 3

Miracles

I. Introduction

The main argument of this chapter is that when the Spirit-filled incarnate Son began teaching and preaching, announcing the inauguration of the kingdom of God, he also performed supernatural miracles. Mark reports that at the outset of Jesus' public ministry, the people of Capernaum witness a miraculous exorcism performed by Jesus, and "they questioned among themselves, saying, 'What is this? A new teaching! With authority he commands even the unclean spirits, and they obey him'" (Mark 1:27). Jesus' divine authority includes the power to work miracles.[1]

---

1. I note that there is no first-century equivalent term to "miracles." Some scholars hold that the category of "miracle" is anachronistic. For background in this regard, see Eric Eve, *Jewish Context of Jesus' Miracles* and *Healer from Nazareth*. As various scholars have shown, the distinction between a "supernatural miracle" and (for example) a sudden natural cure of a major illness is foreign to the first century, in part because Second Temple Jews believed that physicians can only cure others by the help of God, even when employing natural remedies (see Sirach 38). In my view (and also, to an extent, in Eve's view), more must be said about Jesus' "miraculous" deeds. Although some or even many of them may have been "natural"—I see no reason to deny this—Jesus performed some deeds that fit under the category of "supernatural" miracle, in which he exercised the divine power directly. Eve states, "For the biblical authors a miracle was not primarily a breach in the natural order; it was primarily a significant act of God. It would, of course, have to be a suitably surprising, unusual act of God, or there would be no reason to regard it as a miracle; a miracle is an event that excites wonder through being strikingly unexpected. So perhaps the best definition of a miracle in the biblical sense is 'a strikingly surprising event, beyond normal human capacity, believed to be a significant act of God'. Such an act could be worked either directly on God's initiative or in response to prayer, or through some suitable intermediary such as a prophet or an angel" (Eve, *Healer from Nazareth*, xvii). He proposes that we should

MIRACLES

According to the Church's dogmatic tradition, Jesus Christ is one divine person whose actions make manifest his inseparably united two natures, divine and human. Unlike mere humans who must call upon the action of God in order to perform miracles, Christ in the Gospels has the (divine) power to do miracles directly. As Aquinas says, drawing upon Pope Leo the Great's Tome, "true miracles cannot be wrought save by divine power, because God alone can change the order of nature"; and therefore Christ performs miracles by his own divine power even while his "human nature is the instrument of the divine action, and the human action receives power from the divine."[2]

The Gospels are full of Christ's miraculous works, though his miracles do not extend to saving himself (or his people) from his cross. Thomas Joseph White describes the New Testament portrait: "Christ is able to cure the sick, raise the dead, and even forgive sins. Christ is also subject to human suffering, death, and resurrection from the dead. The subject who acts is one, but acts always both as God and as man, simultaneously able to do what only God can do, and able to suffer what only a human being can suffer."[3] White spells this out further in terms of the "communication of

---

distinguish between "miracles," which can have a natural explanation, and "anomalous miracles," which lack any possible natural explanation and that he therefore deems to be "essentially unhistorical"—post-Resurrection exaggerations and inventions (160). My argument, by contrast, is that Jesus performed "acts of God" (miracles) that were not and could not have been accomplished by natural causes, but rather flowed from Jesus' own exercise of divine power. Eve affirms, as I do, that "Jesus' healings and exorcisms served both to authenticate Jesus' standing as an eschatological prophet (to others and to himself) and as a symbolic enactment of the eschatological kingdom of God he proclaimed" (144); but Eve thinks these healings and exorcisms were performed through Jesus' exceptional God-given natural capabilities as a healer, and Eve also thinks that Jesus' proclamation of the imminent kingdom turned out to be false (162, 165–66, 168). For Eve, the miracles reported by John—including Jesus' turning of water into wine and his raising of Lazarus—are unhistorical, serving "the interests of John's heightened Christology" (158). I note that very similar miracles are present in the Synoptic Gospels, and so the appeal to "John's heightened Christology" is beside the point. Given his definition of miracles, Eve rejects efforts to ground belief in the incarnation in Jesus' miracle-working. See also Eve, "Meier, Miracle and Multiple Attestation."

2. Aquinas, *Summa theologiae* III, q. 43, a. 2. Some charismatic Protestants and Catholics have argued that Jesus at his baptism received power from the Holy Spirit to perform miracles *primarily through his human nature*, but I disagree with this perspective.

3. White, *Incarnate Lord*, 21; and see also White, *Trinity*, 574: "When, for example, the Lord Jesus heals a blind person, it is only the Son as man who wills humanly to stretch out his hand, touch the blind man, and say, 'I will it.' It is the Son as true God, however, with the Father and the Holy Spirit, who acts divinely to heal in and through his concrete act of human touch, and he does so in virtue of the divine power residing in him as Lord. Furthermore, the human action of the Son made man is the human

idioms," in which the one person of Christ, the Word or Son, is able to act as God and as man. Instructed by Maximus the Confessor, the Church affirmed Christ's two wills and two operations—divine and human—at the Third Council of Constantinople in 680-81.[4]

Whereas White's approach to the miracles of Jesus begins both with the biblical data and the post-Chalcedonian understanding of the communication of idioms, contemporary understanding of Jesus' miracles typically has a quite different starting point. Specifically, contemporary thinkers often interpret Jesus' miracles as either natural events (exaggerated by his audience or the evangelists) or as symbolic expressions of aspects of universal human spiritual experience. Rather than maintaining that the Gospels

---

action of God the Son, and so it reflects as *personal* action the relation of origin of the Son from the Father and of the Spirit from the Father as the Son. The Son works as one from the Father, and in the Spirit of his Father. The concrete action of Christ's healing within history, as a human being with divine power, thus manifests that he is the Lord, one who truly comes from the Father, not only in his temporal mission, but also in his procession as Son, from all eternity."

4. White also notes the "inverted monophysitism" that one finds in modern Christologies inspired by Hegel, whose thought (influenced by the seventeenth-century Lutheran Tübingen school) transformed the "communication of idioms" into an account of the divine Son's freedom—as God, not simply in his humanity—to act not as God but as man, in radical self-surrender: see White, *Trinity*, 553-57. White comments that for Hegel (for whom theology provides symbols that can be rightly interpreted by philosophy in terms of unfolding Spirit) and from a Hegelian theological perspective, "In virtue of the Incarnation, God is able to take attributes of human finitude, such as temporality, suffering, and death, into his own divine essence. The foundation for this capacity of the deity is located in God's freedom, his capacity to self-identify even with his ontological contrary by way of self-exploratory diremption" (554). White sums up: "modern Trinitarian theologians tend to retain from Hegel . . . the notion of a process of alienation and reconciliation that takes place between the eternal persons of God, one that is in some way constitutive of their divine nature. The history of God with us, including in his human finitude, suffering, and death, becomes either constitutive of or at least expressive of the eternal mystery of God the Trinity in itself" (555-56). White is drawing here from Hegel, *Lectures on the Philosophy of Religion*, 3:452-69. He is indebted for his analysis especially to Bruce D. Marshall, "Absolute and the Trinity"; and Powell, *Trinity in German Thought*. The modern Christologies he has in view include those of Sergius Bulgakov, Hans Urs von Balthasar, Karl Barth, Karl Rahner, and many others. The result, he notes, is that "modern Trinitarian theology has all too often drifted toward an obsession with the analogy or likeness between the immanent Trinity and the supposed economic Trinity (which I have argued is an ontological fiction), and in doing so has either projected human attributes onto the divinity of Christ, or has used distinctly human traits to distinguish the Trinitarian persons (such as command and obedience, or mutual and free self-surrender, suffering, and detachment)" (*Trinity*, 687). He concludes quite rightly, "A Trinitarian theology that takes the economy seriously might more profitably consider the analogy or likeness between the human nature of Jesus and the divine nature of Jesus. How does the human nature of God reveal his divine nature (without any confusion of the two)?"

describe real miracles performed by Jesus, many educated people today assume that these stories are the fruit of the late-Second Temple cultural expectations and credulity. Indeed it is true that Jesus' contemporaries would have assumed that Jesus, an eschatological prophet, *must* have performed miracles—even if he never actually performed any real ones. It is also evident that we now can explain scientifically some cures (and some diseases) that seemed mysterious in the first century.

In this chapter, I argue that Christians should embrace the claim that Jesus performed supernatural miracles by his divine power. As a first step, I will explore the perspectives of some nineteenth-century religiously liberal Protestants, who when faced with the difficulty (philosophical and historical) of defending miracles, interpreted them in a strictly symbolic way. Second, I will survey the ways in which Bonaventure and N. T. Wright treat Jesus' miracles, arguing that much can be learned from both the medieval saint and the modern biblical scholar about Jesus' purposes and about how to interpret the Gospels' miracle stories in a theologically nuanced and historically plausible fashion. Third, as a key to my own constructive approach to the miracle stories, I delve into the narrative of Jesus' exorcism of the Gerasene demoniac, a story told in the Synoptic Gospels in somewhat contradictory versions and that includes the strange detail of the death of the pigs. My focus is on the various ways that this story has been interpreted by contemporary New Testament scholars, including Wright, Nicholas Perrin, and Matthew Thiessen. Fourth, I set forth the insights of the Catholic biblical scholar Luke Timothy Johnson, who defends miracles within a larger "remythologized" context.

The above building blocks serve as the foundation for my contention that we should accept the biblical testimony that Jesus did real miracles and we should do so without falling into biblical literalism. As a fifth step, then, I turn to the greatest critic of the miracle stories: the nineteenth-century religiously liberal Protestant David Friedrich Strauss. I focus especially upon his interpretation of the miracle of the Gerasene demoniac, which he argues is absurd. He tries to compel an either-or: either we must read the miracle stories as containing no error, in which case one's energy is consumed by efforts to defend every detail; or we must read the miracle stories as exhibiting the mistaken worldview of late-Second Temple Jews. In response, drawing upon the above resources, I seek to discern the limitations of literalism from within a broader affirmation (against Strauss and others) that Jesus performed supernatural miracles.[5]

---

5. For historical-critical criteria by which to differentiate miracle stories that are probably authentic from miracle stories that are probably invented, see Evans, "Jesus and Jewish Miracle Stories," 213–27. Evans deems the story of the healing of the

Sixth and finally, I take up Craig Keener's recent study of postbiblical miracles. I do so in light of the role of the Virgin Mary as intercessor, grounded in her miraculous intercession with her Son at the wedding feast at Cana according to the Gospel of John.

II. Nineteenth-Century Approaches: Herrmann and Schleiermacher

Faced with a societal loss of faith brought about by philosophical idealism and historical-critical biblical scholarship, nineteenth-century German Protestant theologians spearheaded a complete reinterpretation of Christianity, including Scripture. Their re-envisioning provides a useful initial point of entrance into the controversies about Jesus' miracles.

Let me begin briefly with Wilhelm Herrmann, the teacher of Karl Barth. In lectures and publications from the early twentieth century, Herrmann—like many of his nineteenth-century predecessors—tries to salvage the truth of Christianity by arguing that it is reducible to our personal experience of God and Jesus. As he puts it, "We can be saved only by a reality presented to us as a fact of our own experience, a reality indubitable as our need."[6] According to Hermann, Jesus is incontestably a fact of our own experience, because it is "the impression of his moral purity and vitality" that sparks faith in us.[7] We experience his inspiring moral consciousness as the answer to our need for redemption from sin and union with God.

Hermann points to Luke 7:36–50 as a paradigmatic example of how Jesus manifested himself. In this story, Jesus has gone into a Pharisee's house in order to eat. A notoriously sinful woman arrives, weeps in his presence, kisses his feet, and anoints his feet with ointment. The Pharisee concludes from this event that Jesus cannot be a true prophet, since Jesus has allowed himself to be touched by a sinner. Jesus tells a parable in order to correct the Pharisee. Turning to the sinful woman, he then informs her that her display of repentance and faith means that her sins are forgiven (Luke 7:48).

Gadarene demoniac to be probably authentic, in part due to its place in "Q." He defends "the essential historicity of the miracle tradition" in the Gospels (214). I agree with Evans that Jesus did miracles, although I am less confident about the criteria. For a better approach to "criteria" for assessing historicity, see chapter 2 of Barber, *Historical Jesus and the Temple*, responding in part to John P. Meier's defense (in the volumes of his *Marginal Jew*) of the traditional criteria, and in part to the criticisms of the criteria by such scholars as Dale C. Allison Jr., Morna D. Hooker, and Chris Keith. Barber's approach is especially indebted to Allison, *Constructing Jesus*.

6. Herrmann, *Systematic Theology (Dogmatik)*, 116. This book is comprised of course notes taken down by students.

7. Herrmann, *Systematic Theology (Dogmatik)*, 117.

Herrmann argues that here we have an example of Jesus' saving work, operating by love and by "the quiet power of his Person."[8] It is not that Jesus miraculously forgave the sins of the woman. There is no such miracle here. Rather, the woman became experientially aware in his presence that she was *already* forgiven. As Herrmann describes the experience of redemption, "we become aware in a fact of our experience that the same God who judges us for our sins still seeks us to unite us with himself."[9] For Herrmann, this is miracle enough.

8. Herrmann, *Systematic Theology (Dogmatik)*, 117. Such a Jesus does not need to do miracles. Something like this Jesus appears in the otherwise stimulating book by Feldmeier and Spieckermann, *God Becoming Human*, insofar as the authors privilege "Q." Surveying Jesus' public ministry, Feldmeier and Spieckermann comment: "After successfully resisting these temptations, Jesus appears publicly and proclaims the rule of God. This includes his mighty deeds, his miracles, and his exorcisms, which are the fulfillment of the prophetic promises and thus show that God's rule is dawning (cf. Luke 11:20 par. Matt 12:28). But Jesus' mighty deeds occupy only a relatively small space in Q, in comparison to Jesus' words. The Son of God is portrayed in this branch of the tradition first and foremost as a teacher. In sovereign autonomy, he understands the biblical God as Father and interprets him as Father through his love and mercy, both recapitulating the Old Testament witness to God and at the same time intensifying it. This is linked with the demand that the Father God who is defined by his kindness and mercy must be made the point of reference, in the sense of an *imitatio Dei* that gives orientation to the existence and the conduct that Jesus requires of those who follow him" (268). One fears that Feldmeier and Spieckermann have here produced a twenty-first-century version of the liberal Protestant fatherhood of God and brotherhood of man. This fear is intensified when Feldmeier and Spieckermann go on to say, in a Schleiermachian mode: "Jesus knows the God of heaven and of earth as the ground of his existence that sustains him and determines him, as his Father—and therein, he knows himself as Son. This reciprocity of love (for nothing else than this is involved here) was already the basis of Jesus' answers in his dialogue with the devil at the beginning of Q, where he acknowledges the Father as his one and all" (271).

9. Herrmann, *Systematic Theology (Dogmatik)*, 118; cf. 136–39. Herrmann does not leave the cross out of this equation. The cross has an important effect in revealing God's love for sinners (as distinct from changing the human race from an unjust condition). Herrmann states in his typical experiential mode, "It was his cross that first brought home to his community the assurance that he was ready to do and suffer anything for those who had begun to feel in his Person the heart-constraining power of God. But in the cross such men always see the complete manifestation of the fact of God's desire to say to them that their guilt, however grievous it be, shall not separate them from him. This is the forgiveness of God which we experience" (124). Hermann goes on to downplay the actual resurrection appearances, along lines similar to the postconciliar Edward Schillebeeckx: "these disciples were bound to say to themselves subsequently that even without any such appearances what they had previously learnt ought to have assured them that for Jesus his death was the completion, not the negation, of his obedience, and was so far a victory (Luke xxiv. 25–26; John xx. 29; Phil. ii. 8) . . . The same is true of ourselves. Our assurance that Jesus is alive and is not separated from us is not primarily based upon a report of events such as these [i.e. the resurrection appearances]; for it is already implicit in the faith created and maintained in us by the

Likewise, Herrmann's predecessor Friedrich Schleiermacher argues that the centrality of experience—understood by Schleiermacher in terms of the "feeling of absolute dependence"—means that Christianity does not need to affirm miracles.[10] Miracles pale in comparison to the only true "miracle," namely the immutable interdependence of nature, to which science bears witness and which Christ helps us to appreciate through the power of his own feeling of absolute dependence. For Schleiermacher, "supernatural" miracles are an offense to the divine orderer: why would the one to whom our feeling of absolute dependence testifies wish to break his ordering of nature? A true account of "omnipotence" will insist that God gets things right the first time, without need for the disruption caused by miracles. In fact, says Schleiermacher, the more that people understand and appreciate nature as such, the less they believe in miracles; and such people exhibit more "of that reverence for God which is the expression of our fundamental feeling."[11]

What then to make of the biblical miracles? Schleiermacher suggests that they should not be interpreted as anything supernatural—and, indeed, neither is "the revelation of God in Christ" anything supernatural.[12] Christ exhibits the greatest possible God-consciousness or feeling of absolute dependence, thereby manifesting "God" as perfectly as God can be manifested. But Christ does this fully as a man, without need for the supernatural. Schleiermacher concludes, "On the whole, therefore, as regards the miraculous, the general interests of science . . . and the interests of religion seem to meet at the same point, *i.e.* that we should abandon the idea of the absolutely supernatural because no single instance of it can be known by us, and we are nowhere required to recognize it."[13] This does not mean that the supposed miracles performed by Christ did not happen; it simply means that if something like them did happen, then they have a naturalistic explanation, even if they remain religiously significant.

---

power of Jesus, under whose influence we stand. For a firm faith it would, of course, be self-evident that Jesus cannot have perished in death and departed from us . . . If we accept such fact as God's gift to us, this real obedience of faith will help us then to have unqualified joy even in the narratives of the appearances of the Risen Lord (contradictory and obscure though they are to the historian), and of his communion with the disciples. It will then be enough for us that this at any rate was the way in which the picture of these events established itself in the minds of those men who, as the first generation of a new humanity, lived in the power of the Person of Jesus. The fact that what happened at that time remains by God's will veiled from us will then cease to trouble us" (Herrmann, *Systematic Theology (Dogmatik)*, 126–27).

10. Schleiermacher, *Christian Faith*, 178–79.
11. Schleiermacher, *Christian Faith*, 179.
12. Schleiermacher, *Christian Faith*, 180.
13. Schleiermacher, *Christian Faith*, 183.

Schleiermacher is aware that people of Jesus' day assumed that prophets would be wonderworkers. In Schleiermacher's view, Jesus turned this expectation upon its head. He lays stress upon the point—later developed (as we will see) by David Friedrich Strauss—that "Christ, when signs and wonders were demanded of Him, refused to do them."[14] The prophets' wonderworking aimed to support their prophetic predictions, but Christ did not make such prophecies or need such support. Instead, Schleiermacher characteristically emphasizes that "faith in His [Christ's] relation to the Messianic idea was meant to proceed solely from the direct impression made by His Person."[15] It is the spiritual impression made by Jesus that is the key. Jesus certainly did good to others in a manner that was interpreted as miraculous, but such "miracles" were never the basis for people's recognition of Jesus. Although some of Jesus' contemporaries may have been impressed by witnessing one of his "miracles," none of his miracles are needed today in order for us to be impressed by "the character, as well as . . . the scope and duration, of Christ's spiritual achievements."[16]

14. Schleiermacher, *Christian Faith*, 448. For Strauss's critique of Schleiermacher's Christology as historically implausible and also as unsatisfying in its claims regarding divine presence, see DeHart, *Unspeakable Cults*, 119–36. DeHart is attracted, in ways that I am not, by Schleiermacher's understanding of "miracle" (even if DeHart does not accept Schleiermacher's view of divine presence) and by Schleiermacher's suggestion that Jesus exercises "a redemptive influence operating along the lines of formal rather than (though in combination with) efficient causality" (135). I agree with DeHart's conclusion that "Schleiermacher's Christological approach . . . fails to deliver a genuinely historical incarnation" (137). In an effort to fix Schleiermacher's understanding of the divine presence in Jesus and us, DeHart appeals to Aquinas's understanding of God's presence in all things, God's presence by grace in the saints, and God's presence in Christ through the divine being. Like DeHart, I find this understanding to be needed in Christology. DeHart also rightly notes that "Aquinas's notion of incarnation by assumption makes it possible to allow the entire psychic apparatus of Jesus, as such, to remain in the realm of immanent causality. The being of God in him is not a restricted zone within the structure of his subjectivity, but is the incorporation of the entirety of that structure in its historical actualization instrumentally within the personal self-relation of God" (148).

15. Schleiermacher, *Christian Faith*, 448.

16. Schleiermacher, *Christian Faith*, 449. This is the central point of Vander Schel, *Embedded Grace*. Vander Schel comments, "Within Schleiermacher's dogmatic theology, the historical appearance of Christ that inaugurates the Reign of God signals the one true miracle of the created world and indeed the miracle of miracles" (223–24). For Vander Schel, this is fitting, because, rather than "revealing an accidental invasion of transcendence into an otherwise immanent historical system," it reveals "the divine redemptive activity of Christ transforming the natural and historical world from within, bringing creation to its completed fulfillment and perfection . . . [Schleiermacher's] account both highlights the gratuitous character of redemption through Christ and emphasizes that this higher life is conditioned at every step by the existing structures and ongoing development of the natural world," through "the new form of human

In sum, the sole enduring and decisive "miracle" is the impressiveness of the person of Jesus, who is the highest manifestation of spiritual nature, bringing to fulfillment (and transcending) the example of all his predecessors. In this sense, Scripture reveals a true miracle, namely, the person of Jesus as the culmination, climax, and *sine qua non* of the "total spiritual miracle" of the Bible.[17] Jesus remains supremely relevant so long as he continues to inspire us through his God-consciousness and through the personal impression he leaves upon our souls.[18]

The problem, however, is that the Jesus of the Gospels—the Jewish Jesus of first-century Galilee and Judea—has little in common with the Jesus contrived by Schleiermacher and Herrmann. Furthermore, if Jesus was not God incarnate acting to conquer sin and death as the Messiah of Israel—if Jesus did not inaugurate the kingdom of God with divine authority and life-giving power—then Jesus and his exemplary consciousness are not of much interest today.[19]

---

historical living that proceeds from Christ . . . For Schleiermacher, the supernatural marks a further differentiation within the created world: the historically developing reality of the Reign of God that originates in the redemptive activity of Christ and is gradually expanding over the entirety of human living" (224–25). Granted the accuracy of Vander Schel's portrait of Schleiermacher's viewpoint, I am not persuaded that this is a plausible account either of the New Testament, or of post-biblical history, or of "grace" as a (salvific) natural dynamism enacted by Jesus.

17. Schleiermacher, *Christian Faith*, 449. See the interesting addendum provided by Dunn, *Jesus Remembered*, who notes about Schleiermacher's understanding of the New Testament: "Schleiermacher was able to use John's Gospel as not only a source but the primary source for his *Life of Jesus*. It was precisely the Fourth Gospel's portrayal of a Jesus deeply conscious of his relation as Son to God as Father which substantiated Schleiermacher's focus on Jesus' 'God-consciousness.' But ironically by the time Schleiermacher's lectures were [posthumously] published (1864) his major prop had been undermined" (40). See also Kelsey, *Schleiermacher's Preaching, Dogmatics, and Biblical Criticism*.

18. For further background, see Marshall, "God Almighty in the Flesh," pointing out that "Western Christianity, both Catholic and Protestant, is now beset by a crisis of faith, and has been for close to two centuries. At its most basic—or, we might say, its most blatant—the crisis consists in the unambiguous denial, precisely by Christians, that Jesus is true God, God almighty in our flesh . . . First in Germany and then more widely, Protestant theologians repeatedly sought a Christology that clearly maintained, in Friedrich Schleiermacher's phrase, that Jesus is 'redeemer alone and for all,' without having to maintain that Jesus is God almighty in the flesh. The solution was to see in Jesus the perfect *homo religiosus*, the human being who confronts us not with God in the flesh, but with a perfect human relationship with God . . . By way of the Christian community, we can have contact with this archetypal *homo religiosus* and thereby come into the relationship with God for which we secretly long, a relationship like his, though not fully equal to it" (347–48). Marshall directs attention not only to Schleiermacher, but also to Dorner, *Entwicklungsgeschichte der Lehre von der Person Christi*.

19. Despite the efforts of Troeltsch, *Absoluteness of Christianity and the History*

MIRACLES

In his discussion of Jesus' miracles in the *Summa theologiae*, Thomas Aquinas comments, "God enables man to work miracles for two reasons. First and principally, in confirmation of the doctrine that a man teaches. For since those things which are of faith surpass human reason, they cannot be proved by human arguments... Secondly, in order to make known God's presence in a man by the grace of the Holy Spirit."[20] In the previous chapter, we saw that Jesus taught the inauguration of the kingdom of God in and through himself—a kingdom marked by the forgiveness of sins, the conquest of death, and adoption into God's own life through the Holy Spirit. Aquinas holds that Jesus' miracles confirm the presence of this eschatological kingdom and display Jesus' unique authority as the incarnate Lord.[21]

---

of Religions, 158–62. Troeltsch concludes, "However much the figure of Jesus may be concealed under early Christian apologetics or dogmatic systems based on naïve traditions, it is plainly evident that what constantly radiates from him is the marvelous spontaneity with which he expressed so simply what is highest and most profound, connecting this in the most natural way with the belief that he had been sent by the Father. When the clouds of research have lifted, this final result will remain forever, and he who sympathetically involves himself with the diverse truths and values of mankind and seeks his way accordingly will discover in this completely free spontaneity, which is at the same time the expression of the purest and most concentrated religious power, an indication of the highest revelation of the divine life that holds sway over us" (161).

20. Aquinas, *Summa theologiae* III, q. 43, a. 1.

21. Pitre points out that "when it comes to the question of whether Jesus spoke or acted as if he was divine, many contemporary Jesus researchers are ... emphatic that the miracles attributed to Jesus did not lead anyone to believe in his divinity" (*Jesus and Divine Christology*, 43). Pitre argues that, on the contrary, Jesus according to the Gospels performed some of his miracles in order to make manifest his identity, and in at least three of these miracles—his calming of the storm, his walking on the sea, and his transfiguration—"a strong case can be made that ... Jesus is acting and speaking as if he is not just any kind of deity or heavenly being, but in some sense equal with the one God of Israel" (45). Pitre sums up his case: "In the stilling of the storm, Jesus demonstrates the divine power of the Creator when he commands the wind and the waves, something which Jewish Scripture says God alone possesses. When Jesus walks on the sea and identifies himself with the divine self-designation 'I am,' he is also doing something that Jewish Scripture says only God can do—walk on the sea. Finally, in the transfiguration on the mountain, not only do the disciples see Jesus's appearance changed into that of a heavenly being come down to earth, but the reason Moses and Elijah appear is because they were the two great figures who experienced theophanies on Mount Sinai but were not able to see the face of God. In the transfiguration of Jesus, however, the one God who appeared to Moses and Elijah on Mount Sinai now has a human face" (108). It is crucial to note that Jesus is not simply a "heavenly being" but quite literally divine in the sense of the God of Israel.

III. Bonaventure and N. T. Wright

Let me now turn to two figures to whom I wish to give special attention, on the grounds that they can help in different ways to move us beyond a skeptical approach to Jesus' miracles. Bonaventure's outlook is similar to Aquinas's, but his perspective is given further nuance by means of his sensitive employment of intertextuality and the spiritual sense. While fully affirming Jesus' miracles, he avoids a simple literalism by allowing for a complex set of meanings in the miracle stories. For his part, N. T. Wright places Jesus' miracles in their Second Temple eschatological context, and he argues that his miracles should not be ruled out by believers in the existence and covenantal work of Israel's God. Neither Bonaventure nor Wright makes the miracles into mere symbols of human experience of Jesus or God, but neither do they simply dismiss such experience.

Bonaventure on Luke 7

I will begin with Bonaventure, focusing my attention on his exegesis of Luke 7.[22] In Luke 6:17-49, Luke narrates Jesus' Sermon on the Plain. After this presentation of Jesus' teaching, Luke 7 is devoted to miraculous works of Jesus. Jesus heals a centurion's slave and he raises a widow's son who had died. He tells the disciples of John the Baptist, in response to their inquiry into whether he is the Messiah: "Go and tell John what you have seen and heard: the blind receive their sight, the lame walk, lepers are cleansed, and the deaf hear, the dead are raised up, the proof have good news preached to them" (Luke 7:22).[23] Claiming the divine power to forgive sins, he forgives the sins of a prostitute.

Commenting on the transition from the Sermon on the Plain to Luke 7's description of Jesus' miracles, Bonaventure remarks: "Now that the Evangelist has treated the truth of Christ's teaching, he here commends that teaching by showing *the sublimity of the Teacher*."[24] The miracles, in other words, are signs of the truth of what Christ has taught. The purpose of the miracles is to lead us to believe Jesus' teaching by manifesting the greatness of the Teacher.

---

22. For further background to Bonaventure's exegesis, see especially Dales, *Divine Remaking*; and see also Bougerol, "Bonaventure as Exegete"; Drago, "L'esegesi di S. Bonaventura nei suoi commentari"; and Karris, "St. Bonaventure as Biblical Interpreter."

23. For historical-critical background to Luke 7:18-23, see Rodriguez, *Structuring Early Christian Memory*, 120-28.

24. Bonaventure, *Commentary on the Gospel of Luke: Chapters 1-8*, 567, ch. 7, §1.

When speaking of the Teacher's "sublimity," Bonaventure argues that Luke 7 presents three things that should enable us to perceive how extraordinary the teacher Jesus is. The first is Jesus' power, the second is the acclaim that Jesus receives, and the third is Jesus' wondrous mercy. These three things confirm that the teaching of Jesus is "perfect and complete" and therefore is (as Bonaventure says) the fulfillment of Sirach 43:27, "Though we speak much we cannot reach the end, and the sum of our words is: 'He is the all.'"

With regard to Jesus' power, Bonaventure explores Jesus' healing of the centurion's slave who was at the point of death and Jesus' raising of the dead son of the widow at Nain. The two miracles go together, Bonaventure says, because in these miracles Jesus shows power not only to heal the body but also to restore the body-soul union.[25] At the end of his interpretation of the healing of the centurion's slave, Bonaventure adds: "*Spiritually* and according to *the allegorical sense* the miracle is to be understood as *the cure of the Gentile people*."[26] He arrives at this allegorical interpretation because the healing is the healing of a Roman centurion's slave, and the gentiles were in slavery to sin—specifically to idolatry. He appeals to Galatians 4:3, "when we were children, we were slaves to the elemental spirits of the universe." He interprets these elemental spirits as the demons or idols set up and worshiped by the gentiles. Thus, when Jesus heals the slave of the Roman centurion, this entails that the Roman (a gentile and, presumably, a worshiper of false gods) is healed of idolatry.

---

25. For an approach that supports Bonaventure's point here, see Bolt, *Jesus' Defeat of Death*. Citing evidence regarding disease and life expectancy in the ancient Near East, Bolt shows how severely "Mark's early flesh-and-blood readers . . . lived under the shadow of death" (1). Bolt demonstrates how the healing/exorcism stories in Mark's Gospel served, among other purposes, "to focus upon Jesus whose life, death and resurrection addressed their mortality and gave them the hope of their own future resurrection" (1). As Bolt says, "each condition depicted in the healing and exorcism scenes brought the sufferer close to death itself and/or under the sway of the dead. As such, each of the . . . stories relates to Jesus' defeat of death" (271). For a less helpful perspective, one that reflects both the prevalence of disease and early death in Jesus' day and our own attitudes toward trauma, see Kim, *Messiah in Weakness*, 97: "Wherever Jesus goes, he meets many sick people, whose bodies and souls are so severely ruined and broken that they can no longer live normally. They are deprived of human dignity and society as a whole does not pay much attention to them . . . In this dire situation, what Jesus could do is to offer solace and ask for God's mercy on their behalf. In doing so he was involved in curing them by relieving their anxieties and leading some to the process of healing. The nature of Jesus' healing is, as some scholars believe, close to a 'village psychiatrist' who helps the patients deal with their psychosomatic symptoms." Kim cites Capps, *Jesus the Village Psychiatrist*.

26. Bonaventure, *Commentary on the Gospel of Luke: Chapters 1–8*, 581, ch. 7, §17.

There is also the tropological or moral sense of the narrative of the healing of the centurion's slave. Jesus' miracle is a tropological sign of the healing of those sickened by sin. The centurion, in the role of penitent, begs Jesus for healing. Bonaventure recalls that Jeremiah 31:18–19 gives voice to true penitence: "bring me back that I may be restored, for you are the Lord my God. For after I had turned away I repented; and after I was instructed, I struck my thigh; I was ashamed, and I was confounded." Bonaventure also reflects upon the fact that, in healing the centurion's slave, Jesus does not actually go into the house. The "house" here signifies, in the tropological sense, a person's soul. At issue is *"the condescension of divine compassion* which draws near to the house of the sick person by the infusion of grace," just as God does according to Zechariah's song (Luke 1:77) when God works "to give knowledge of salvation to his people in the forgiveness of their sins."[27]

Bonaventure also applies the literal sense of the miracle story to the spiritual and sacramental life of believers. When begging Jesus to heal his slave, the centurion exhibits reverence and humility. The centurion urges, "Lord, do not trouble yourself, for I am not worthy to have you come under my roof; therefore I did not presume to come to you. But say the word, and let my servant be healed" (Luke 7:6–7). Bonaventure compares the centurion's humility to the humility of the tax collector Zacchaeus in Luke 19. In Bonaventure's hands, the miraculous healing of the centurion's slave serves to instruct believers about how we should act in relation to Jesus present in the Eucharist. With reverence and humility, we should welcome him to our "house" (our soul), either by reverently consuming the Eucharist or by reverently abstaining. The centurion symbolizes the latter: he exhibits faith-filled reverence toward Jesus, and his slave is healed without having Jesus enter into the centurion's "house." By contrast, Zacchaeus is healed when Jesus enters into his "house."

According to Bonaventure, we need to keep in mind that the miracles are teaching tools. In the early chapters of Luke, the people follow Jesus primarily to hear his teaching. He is above all a teacher, teaching about God, himself, and us. Recall Luke 4:14, after Jesus has completed his temptation in the wilderness: "And Jesus returned in the power of the Spirit into Galilee, and a report concerning him went out through all the surrounding country. And he taught in their synagogues, being glorified by all."[28] Luke

---

27. Bonaventure, *Commentary on the Gospel of Luke: Chapters 1–8*, 583, ch. 7, §18. For background to Zechariah's song, see Hengel, "Song about Christ in Earliest Worship," 234.

28. For background to the temptation narrative in the context of Luke's whole Gospel, see Hays, *Echoes of Scripture in the Gospels*, 208–9, emphasizing that Luke consistently underlines the value of Torah and that Torah plays an important role in

confirms this portrait of Jesus as above all a teacher by reporting (Luke 4:16–21) Jesus' actions at Nazareth. Attending synagogue on the Sabbath, Jesus reads aloud Isaiah 61:1–2, a messianic text regarding the coming of the kingdom. Jesus then proclaims, "Today this Scripture has been fulfilled in your hearing" (Luke 4:21).[29] The congregation, which knew him from the many years he lived in their midst, "spoke well of him, and wondered at the gracious words which proceeded out of his mouth" (Luke 4:22). When Jesus arrived at Capernaum, similarly, he taught "them on the sabbath; and they were astonished at his teaching, for his word was with authority" (Luke 4:31–32). When large crowds followed him and urged him to stay for a while, he replied, "I must preach the good news of the kingdom of God to the other cities also; for I was sent for this purpose" (Luke 4:43).

Bonaventure emphasizes this prophetic dimension of Jesus' ministry. The reason Jesus traveled to Nain, says Bonaventure, was to teach; and the reason that "his disciples and a great crowd went with him" (Luke 7:11) was to learn. Here Bonaventure makes reference to various Old Testament texts that speak of the communication of wisdom, among them Deuteronomy 33:3, which in Bonaventure's Vulgate version reads, "They that come to sit at his feet, will receive of his instruction" (the RSV reads "they followed in your steps, receiving direction from you"), and Proverbs 13:20, "He who walks with wise men becomes wise." The power and mercy of the kingdom of God preached by Jesus are manifested in the power and mercy of Jesus working a miracle. Jesus' mercy appears when he comforts the disconsolate widow at Nain, and his power appears "in the word commanding the dead man to rise."[30] Notice the response of the crowd when the dead man returns

---

Jesus' teaching. In addition, as Hays goes on to say, "the description of God offered in Jesus' teaching strongly affirms continuity with Israel's confessional tradition" (215). Hays also discusses Luke 4's presentation of Jesus as "the Spirit-anointed Servant figure whose mission is the liberation of Israel" (225; see also 226–30 with attention to Isaiah 61:2 LXX).

29. On Jesus' use of Isaiah 61, see Evans, "From Gospel to Gospel." For historical-critical background to Luke 4:16–30—which arguably "represents the Lukan programmatic vision," focused on the judgment and restoration of Israel and "the reestablishment of YHWH's reign in Zion (i.e., the kingdom of God)"—see Rodriguez, *Structuring Early Christian Memory*, 138–73 (quotations at 139 and 173).

30. Bonaventure, *Commentary on the Gospel of Luke: Chapters 1–8*, 587, ch. 7, §23. Craig Evans points out that, in comparison with roughly contemporaneous Jewish wonderworkers, "rarely does Jesus *pray* for healing or for other miracles . . . Jesus' style is very different. He speaks the words and the cure is effected. Moreover, he speaks and acts in his own name. He says, 'I will it' (Mark 1:41; 2:11), not 'God wills it'" (Evans, "Jesus and Jewish Miracle Stories," 215). In drawing this comparison, Evans criticizes the reductive readings of Geza Vermes and Morton Smith: Vermes, *Jesus the Jew*; Smith, *Jesus the Magician*. Evans appreciatively cites Howard C. Kee as sharing his reservations

to life: they praise Jesus as a "great prophet" (Luke 7:16) and therefore as a teacher, though also a wonderworker. In Jesus, they recognize that "God has visited his people" (Luke 7:16).

For Bonaventure, the miracle of the raising of the widow's son at Nain accomplishes two things. First, the dead man is raised and this makes the mother rejoice. There is a parallel here, as Bonaventure notes, with what Elijah did in 1 Kings 17, where Elijah raised a widow's son; although in Elijah's case, he had to beg God, "O Lord my God, let this child's soul come into him again" (1 Kgs 17:21)—whereas Jesus simply commanded, "Young man, I say to you, arise" (Luke 7:14).[31]

Even more important is the second thing accomplished by the miracle. Namely, the miracle spread faith. Bonaventure highlights Luke 17:16, "Fear seized them all; and they glorified God, saying, 'A great prophet has arisen among us!'" Bonaventure turns here to various Old Testament passages, such as Sirach 43:30, "When you praise the Lord, exalt him as much as you can; for he will surpass even that. When you exalt him, put forth all your strength, and do not grow weary, for you cannot praise him enough." Jesus' miracles, like his teaching, cause people to praise God. This in itself is an eschatological sign, a sign of the coming of God to Zion as Redeemer, as Bonaventure implicitly suggests by quoting Isaiah 59:19, "So they shall fear the name of the Lord from the west, and his glory from the rising of the sun."[32]

---

about Vermes's position: see Kee, *Medicine, Miracle and Magic in New Testament Times*. Anthony Giambrone, OP, adds the point that Jesus' miracles are generally associated with particular places, a fact that has significance in light of contemporary emphasis on memory in New Testament studies: see Giambrone, "Memorializing Miracles."

31. For these raisings as figures of Jesus' resurrection, see Harris, *Refiguring Resurrection*.

32. Bonaventure, of course, does not use the phrases "eschatological sign" or "sign of the coming of God to Zion as Redeemer." Steven Bryan notes, "All four Gospels indicate that a sign was requested from Jesus. On more than one occasion, the crowds or the Pharisees demand a sign, a demand that Jesus either flatly refuses or enigmatically evades (Mark 8.11–12; Matt. 12.38; 16:1; Luke 11.16; John 6.30; cf. 1 Cor. 1.22). The episodes suggest that in the first century the manifestation of a sign or signs was an expectation placed on prophetic claimants" (Bryan, *Jesus and Israel's Traditions*, 34). Bryan directs attention to Hooker, *Signs of a Prophet*. He summarizes Hooker's contribution: "Hooker helpfully distinguishes prophetic actions from oracles and isolates three particular types of actions by OT prophets: (1) actions which manifest the epiphanic power of God, bringing with them salvation or judgement; (2) actions which as 'dramatic presentations of truth' manifest the divine will to do something not presently observable; (3) actions which as authenticating miracles or proofs neither effect deliverance or judgement nor symbolize the intended will of God but rather authenticate the prophet and his message" (Bryan, *Jesus and Israel's Traditions of Judgement and Restoration*, 35–36). Bryan argues that the "sign" the people requested was of the first kind, whereas Hooker thinks it was of the third kind. But (I note) surely actions of the first kind would also "authenticate the prophet and his message."

Bonaventure points out that praising and glorifying God is not enough by itself; we must also understand who is the Mediator of salvation in order to have proper faith. The people's response to Jesus' raising of the son of the widow at Nain shows that they perceive that Jesus is the Redeemer and Mediator. As Bonaventure observes, when they say "A great prophet has arisen among us!," this is an allusion to the new Moses—the true Mediator—promised in Deuteronomy 18:15, where Moses foretells, 'The Lord your God will raise up for you a prophet like me from among you, from your brethren—him you shall heed.'"[33] Jesus is this foretold prophet, as his miracle of raising the dead man makes clear. Christ's power to work miracles, therefore, combines with his teaching to reveal his identity as the divine Redeemer, in whom "God has visited his people" (Luke 7:16).

N. T. Wright on Jesus' Miracles

A similar insight, from a historical-critical perspective, is found in N. T. Wright's *Jesus and the Victory of God*. Jesus' miracles are not random; instead, their purpose is to confirm Jesus' teaching—and at the center of Jesus' teaching is the inauguration of the kingdom of God. As Graham Twelftree says with respect to Jesus' miracles of exorcism, "the source of his power-authority for exorcism was in the wholly new eschatological Spirit of God."[34] Jesus' exorcisms were miracles that effected the eschatological deliverance he proclaimed in his teaching. In Twelftree's view, Jesus believed that the "exorcisms which *he* performed—by or through the eschatological Spirit of God—meant that the kingdom of God had come."[35]

---

33. For further exploration of Christ as the new Moses, see my *Reconfiguring Thomistic Christology*, chapter 3, with its references to biblical scholarship, the church fathers, and Aquinas; and see also Hengel, *Four Gospels*, 158–61; and DeJong, *Prophet Like Moses (Deut 18:15, 18)*.

34. Twelftree, *Jesus the Exorcist*, 217. Twelftree comments, "we can say that the awareness of the presence and empowering of the eschatological Holy Spirit had so given him a consciousness of his messianic identity that for Jesus the hoped-for kingdom had arrived, not only because of the activity of the Holy Spirit, but also because it was *he* who, in the Spirit, was casting out demons. Therefore, it is only half correct to say 'Where the *Spirit* is there is the kingdom.' Jesus' understanding is better reflected by saying that where the *Spirit* is operative in *Jesus* there is the kingdom" (*Jesus the Exorcist*, 218, citing Dunn, *Jesus and the Spirit*, 49). For further discussion of exorcism in Second Temple Judaism—for which the main (but not sole) evidence is the New Testament—see Eve, *Jewish Context of Jesus' Miracles*, especially chapter 12.

35. Twelftree, *Jesus the Exorcist*, 218. In Steven Bryan's view, however, the Jewish people asked Jesus for a greater sign to show that the kingdom was arriving, namely, one that "by close analogy with one of God's great redemptive acts in the time of the Exodus and Conquest unmistakably demonstrated the truth of Jesus' claim that the

Wright echoes Twelftree, but with an emphasis on the inauguration of the kingdom rather than on its full arrival, and with attention to "signs" of the kingdom. Thus, Wright observes that "from the perspective of a follower of Jesus at the time, his mighty works will have been interpreted within the context of his overall proclamation: they would be seen as signs that the kingdom of Israel's god was indeed coming to birth."[36] The miracles or "mighty works" were not, Wright argues, the central thing. Rather what was central was whether God had placed in motion the arrival of the eschatological kingdom, in which God would put all things to rights, beginning by renewing the temple, accomplishing the forgiveness of sins, and restoring God's people Israel. Jesus' contemporaries were focused on his teaching about the kingdom, which his miracles appeared to confirm. Wright explains that Jesus' fellow Jews, upon hearing of his miracles, would have sought to assess them "by seeing what else this strange prophet was up to, and what he was saying."[37] Since he taught largely in parables, his parables would have been particularly important.

Wright thinks that as a historical matter, the evidence points to the historicity of Jesus' doing miracles. Jesus' contemporaries and followers remembered him as a wonderworker. In Jesus' day, however, doing miracles would not have been proof of divine origin or even divine sanction. As Jesus' opponents pointed out, his miracles could be wrought by Satan. Luke describes this negative response: "Now he was casting out a demon that was mute; when the demon had gone out, the mute man spoke, and the

---

time of fulfilment had come" (Bryan, *Jesus and Israel's Traditions*, 39). In favor of his view, Bryan adds the point that "in John 6, a demand for a sign comes *after* the feeding miracle, though John portrays those who make the demand as precisely those who had witnessed the miracle" (39). Bryan notes that his view accords with that of Gibson, *Temptations of Jesus in Early Christianity*, 183–93. For my purposes, Bryan's position can be correct without negating the fact that the miracles of exorcism (for example) were eschatological signs. On the exorcisms as, in Jesus' view, "evidence of God's restoration of a fallen creation" and "evidence that God's end-time salvation is arriving through Jesus' words and actions," see Mark Strauss, *Jesus Behaving Badly*, 31; cf. 167. Strauss concludes, "Jesus' miracles confirm that he is not here to defeat the Roman legions or to establish Israel's glorious empire. He has a much greater goal. He is here to defeat humanity's ultimate foes: disease, death, sin and Satan" (32–33).

36. Wright, *Jesus and the Victory of God*, 191.

37. Wright, *Jesus and the Victory of God*, 191. As Craig Evans notes, "it seems highly unlikely that a *Wunder-Jesu* tradition grew up in order to fill out messianic beliefs about Jesus. Messianic beliefs simply did not require a prospective messiah to heal and exorcize demons. One should hardly expect, therefore, early Christians to find it necessary to create such a large number of miracle stories" ("Jesus and Jewish Miracle Stories," 222). Evans grants, however, that the Gospels contain some miracle stories that are "late and obvious fictions" and that "in the transmission of the texts of the Gospels themselves we are able to observe the infiltration of pious legend and embellishment" (227).

people marveled. But some of them said, 'He casts out demons by Beelzebul, the prince of demons'" (Luke 11:14–15).[38] In Luke 11, Jesus responds to these critics. He states that his miracles serve to overthrow slavery to sin and death, which are the marks of the demonic realm. If on behalf of *Satan* he is overthrowing the powers of sin and death, then, says Jesus, Satan has become divided against himself so as to seek his own ruin. Since this is absurd, then (as Jesus observes) it must really be the case that his miracles are inaugurating not the kingdom of Satan but the kingdom of God.

The biblical scholar Eric Eve remarks (in agreement with Gerd Theissen) that Jesus was unique "in seeing eschatological salvation realized in individual acts of healing and exorcism."[39] In his discussion of Jesus' miracles, Wright pays attention first to these healings and exorcisms. In addition to their physical effects, these miracles had the effect of restoring the person to the worshipping community: the person would no longer be judged ritually unclean. These miracles therefore correspond to Jesus' words and deeds about the welcoming of sinners. Wright highlights that the Gospel narratives about these miracles confirm that the miracles were aimed at supporting his preaching about the kingdom, what Wright calls "the great fulfilment, the great renewal, the time when Israel's god would at last become king."[40]

In the Gospels, Jesus often exorcises people with symptoms that today we would diagnose as a physical illness. The Gospels portray demons

---

38. For discussion of the Matthean version of this passage (Matt 12:23–29), see Gerhardsson, "Mighty Acts and Rule of Heaven," 40: "Jesus is to the Pharisees and scribes an imposter (πλάνος) and magician, receiving his might from Beelzebul, while he is to the Church *Immanuel*: he embodies the divine 'blessing', God's healing forgiveness to his people—in short, *the rule of Heaven* of which the prophets had spoken." Gerhardsson argues that Matthew 1:18–25, in which the child in the womb is named "Emmanuel" or "God with us," serves as the interpretive key to the Gospel's miracle stories (healings, exorcisms, forgiveness of sins, feeding the hungry, and so on). Similarly, Donald A. Hagner points out that Jesus in Matthew 12:28 "clearly asserts the presence of the kingdom" (as distinct from its future consummation): see Hagner, "Matthew's Eschatology," 52. See also, more broadly, Gerhardsson, *Mighty Acts of Jesus*, in which he sharply distinguishes Jesus' miracles of healing from his other miracles.

39. Eve, *Jewish Context of Jesus' Miracles*, 380; see Theissen, *Miracle Stories of the Early Christian Tradition*. See also Stanton, *Gospels and Jesus*, 197.

40. Wright, *Jesus and the Victory of God*, 194. As William C. Spohn puts it, "What did Jesus have to say about his own connection to the emerging reign of God? Typically, he invited the curious to pay attention to the works he was doing and to draw their own conclusions. They had to perceive what was going on in front of them. His encounters, healings, exorcisms, preaching, and association with outcasts were prophetic 'performances.' They indicated that Jesus thought himself to be intimately involved with the reign of God. When he was doing these things, the God of Israel was doing them. Jesus' opponents did not miss the point" (Spohn, *Go and Do Likewise*, 82).

as coming out of the exorcised persons, who then no longer suffer from the physical symptoms of illness. What does Wright make of such narratives? He argues that, from a Second Temple Jewish perspective, and from a contemporary Christian perspective in which the existence of angels and demons is affirmed, it is reasonable to suppose that the Messiah Jesus was at war with demonic powers.[41] The New Testament presents the world as under the control of Satan, insofar as the world is in the grip of sin and death. When Jesus performs exorcisms, these are not fulfillments of prophecies or even acts that Second Temple Jews would necessarily have expected from the Messiah, but their meaning is evident enough.[42] For Wright as for Twelftree, Jesus and his followers believed that "the defeat of Satan was taking place in the exorcistic ministry of Jesus," even if "Satan is to be finally defeated in the last judgement."[43]

I should add that Wright does not spend much time defending the historicity of Jesus' miracles, beyond affirming that Jesus did actual (supernatural) miracles. For instance, regarding Jesus' raising of the widow's son at

---

41. For background to biblical, Second Temple Jewish, and Christian perspectives over the centuries, see Bonino, *Angels and Demons*.

42. Likewise, Twelftree holds that "prior to the New Testament . . . there is no specific connection made between exorcism and eschatology. That the connection is found in authentic words of Jesus but not found before Jesus, it appears that *it was Jesus himself who made this connection between exorcism and eschatology*" (*Jesus the Exorcist*, 220). For a different (and to my mind persuasive) viewpoint, see Klutz, "Grammar of Exorcism." Comparing Jesus to Qumran's *Genesis Apocryphon*, in which Abraham is presented as an exorcist, Klutz contrasts "Abram as exorcistic intercessor and Jesus as exorcistic embodiment of divine power" (160). Klutz also argues that Jesus' exorcisms aimed to reestablish ritual purity, in a way that "both assumed the validity of the demonology-impurity semiotic system and simultaneously flouted it. For in tacitly relabeling as 'pure' those whom the guardians of the purity system had marginalized as impure and demonized, Jesus was critiquing the traditional Priestly health care system. And while such a critique need not have been seen as putting Jesus in a functional slot normally understood in his context to be reserved for God, it certainly is consonant with the sort of authority that . . . was implicit both in his direct exorcistic style and in the employment of his name by others, in his own lifetime, as a powerful source of exorcistic might" (163–64). For further discussion see Klutz's *Exorcism Stories in Luke-Acts*, chapter 2, including his demonstration that "Luke 8.26–39 derives much of its force from allusions to the LXX" (109), especially 1 Kings 17:18, Isaiah 58:6–7, and Psalm 105:7–12. Klutz concludes his chapter, "Jesus looks more like a god in this episode than like a mere charismatic healer or prophet. And the story is not void of clues regarding which god Jesus should be compared to; for the allusions to Scripture in this narrative encourage the reader to compare Jesus not only to the prophet Elijah but even to the Lord God himself, whose paradigmatic destruction of the Egyptian army in the Red Sea is re-enacted in the descent of Legion and the pigs into the lake" (*Exorcism Stories in Luke-Acts*, 150). See also Stanton, *Gospels and Jesus*, 238–39.

43. Twelftree, *Jesus the Exorcist*, 221.

Nain, Wright in a brief allusion to this story tones it down by describing it as "the healing of the widow's son at Nain."[44] Wright focuses not on the miracle but on the fact that Jesus was acclaimed by the witnesses as a prophet: "a great prophet has arisen among us!" (Luke 7:16). The model for a prophet was Elijah, known as much for his teaching—his warnings to the people of Israel about the coming judgment—as for his miracles. Wright argues, "Like Elijah or Jeremiah, Jesus was proclaiming a message from the covenant god, and living it out with symbolic actions."[45]

As Wright describes it, Jesus' proclamation of the kingdom was "a warning of imminent catastrophe, a summons to an immediate change of heart and direction of life, an invitation to a new way of being Israel."[46] In Wright's view, the catastrophe actually happened: the destruction of Israel's temple, due to misunderstanding Jesus and choosing instead the path of violent conflict against the Romans.[47] But Jesus' new way of being Israel happened as well: Israel's Torah and temple, and Israel's other symbols, were reconfigured around the Messiah, now with the Messiah at the center.[48]

---

44. Wright, *Jesus and the Victory of God*, 165.

45. Wright, *Jesus and the Victory of God*, 167. For reflection upon how the performance of miracles (including exorcisms) comports with Jesus' status as a prophet, see Eve, *Jewish Context of Jesus' Miracles*, 384–86.

46. Wright, *Jesus and the Victory of God*, 172.

47. For a recent notable study of Jesus' teachings about the destruction of the temple, see Barber, *Historical Jesus and the Temple*, chapter 4, citing (among many others) Holmén, *Jesus and Jewish Covenant Thinking*, 300; and Bryan, "Jesus and Israel's Eschatological Constitution," 3:2850. Barber shows that Jesus, in a prophetic sign pointing to coming judgment due to the Jewish leaders' rejection of him, likely did prophesy the temple's destruction. He observes that Jesus' denunciations of the temple leadership were hardly unparalleled: "Other Jews in the first century expressed concerns that the temple authorities had become unfaithful. For example, 1QPesher to Habakkuk (1 QpHab) describes the high priest as the 'wicked priest' . . . , speaking of how he had robbed the destitute . . . Josephus reports that the chief priests were known to commit violence against lower ranking priests (cf. *Ant.* 20.179–81, 207). The sinfulness of the priests is also recounted in 1 Enoch and other first-century Jewish texts" (Barber, *Historical Jesus and the Temple*, 92). See also the reflection on the destruction of the temple in Wright, *Lord's Prayer*, 162, where Wright argues that Matthew 24 (paralleled by Mark 13 and Luke 21) "presents Jesus interconnecting the end of the Jerusalem temple with the end of the cosmic age." Wright observes insightfully, "The former is a partial and anticipatory instantiation of the latter; that is, the eschatological reality of the end of the world is partially realized in history in the destruction of the Jerusalem temple. Just as the eschatological reality of the end can be partially instantiated in historical events (before its full realization at the actual end of days), so too can the eschatological trial be partially, but genuinely, realized in the lives of his disciples throughout history" (*Lord's Prayer*, 162).

48. For this approach to understanding Jesus' proclamation of the imminent kingdom, see, in addition to Wright, Andrew Perriman's *Coming Son of Man* (among many

The inaugurated kingdom began with the community gathered by Christ around the apostles.

Thus, in Wright's view as in Bonaventure's, Jesus' miracles are not intelligible outside the broader context of his teaching—including his mission to build up his Church. When Wright treats Jesus' parables, he reads them as deeply "apocalyptic and allegorical" and as reflective of "the main thrust of Jesus' work," which was "to bring to birth a new way of being the people of god."[49] The parables belong to Jesus' apocalyptic "prophetic praxis," inclusive of his miracles.[50]

Wright grants that many of Jesus' miracles may possess naturalistic explanations. This does not concern Wright, unless one is making an *a priori* claim that miracles cannot exist. Wright points out that the term "miracle" may also be misleading, inasmuch as it seems to imply something absolutely extrinsic to this world, whereas Jesus' miracles expressed the presence of a divine authority enabling creation to be *even more itself*. Repeatedly, Wright emphasizes that Jesus' miracles and his teaching co-implicate one another: "in first-century terms the main thing that would be 'seen' in the mighty works was not a supernatural display of power for its own sake but the coming of Israel's god in power to save and heal."[51]

Bonaventure's perspective is quite similar to Wright's in certain ways. As we saw, Bonaventure is attentive to the manner in which Luke 7, with its miracle stories, builds upon the Sermon on the Plain in Luke 6. Bonaventure argues that once Luke depicted "the truth of Christ's teaching" in Luke 6, Luke in chapter 7 "commends that teaching by showing the *sublimity*

---

other examples). See also my *Engaging the Doctrine of Israel*; and see, on the temple, such works as Hoskins, *Jesus as the Fulfillment of the Temple in the Gospel of John*; and Gray, *Temple in the Gospel of Mark*.

49. Wright, *Jesus and the Victory of God*, 181. Wright supposes that for "pre-critical" readers such as Bonaventure, the miracles were simply confirmations of Jesus' divinity. As we saw in Bonaventure, this was not in fact the case.

50. Wright, *Jesus and the Victory of God*, 182. For other instances of first-century Jews who were popularly embraced as prophets (all of whom, except for John the Baptist, were active after Jesus' death and Resurrection), see Evans, "From Anointed Prophet to Anointed King," 442–47, drawing largely upon Josephus as well as Horsley and Hanson, *Bandits, Prophets, and Messiahs*, and Aune, *Prophecy in Early Christianity and the Ancient Mediterranean World*. In each case, the Romans or Jewish leaders responded harshly, generally leading to the death or flight of the prophet. Evans comments, "The danger to the establishment that these popular prophets posed is obvious. Roman action in every case was calculated to pre-empt what was probably correctly perceived as the initiation of social and political upheaval" ("From Anointed Prophet to Anointed King," 443). See also Evans's "Messianic Claimants of the First and Second Centuries," 73–76.

51. Wright, *Jesus and the Victory of God*, 193.

of the Teacher"—not simply in terms of Jesus' divinity (although only God can raise the dead as Jesus does in Luke 7:14-15) but also in terms of the manifestation of the gospel of the kingdom to the disciples of John and to the crowds and in terms of Jesus' *"overflowing mercy."*[52] Bonaventure shows these things by continual reference to a wide span of Old Testament passages, the great majority of which I did not quote above and which serve to exhibit Jesus as the one who fulfills God's covenantal work and God's Torah. For Bonaventure, as we saw, Jesus comes primarily as a teacher who is the eschatological "great prophet" foretold by Moses, in accordance with the words of John the Baptist's father Zechariah (quoted by Bonaventure): "Blessed be the Lord God of Israel, for he has visited and redeemed his people" (Luke 1:68).[53]

I do not mean to exaggerate the similarities between Wright's interpretation and Bonaventure's. Wright grants that Jesus' miracles have symbolic meanings that pertain to Jesus' mission of kingdom inauguration, but Bonaventure finds spiritual senses that go beyond what Wright would affirm. For instance, in reflecting upon the dead young man of Luke 7:12, Bonaventure compares him symbolically to two other dead persons raised by Jesus, namely, Jairus's daughter (Mark 5) and Lazarus (John 11). Bonaventure suggests that the girl symbolizes persons who sin in the heart, the young man symbolizes persons who sin in actual deed, and Lazarus symbolizes persons who are habitual sinners. Bonaventure then compares these three (the girl, the young man, and Lazarus) to three persons raised by Elijah and Elisha. Bonaventure's purpose is to exhibit, by an allegorical meditation, what it means to be truly restored to life and thus what the inauguration of the kingdom involves spiritually.

I am not suggesting that Wright thinks it reasonable to go down such paths when interpreting Scripture (though I agree with Bonaventure on this point). Nevertheless, Bonaventure and Wright are united in appreciating the unity of Jesus' teaching and miracles within Jesus' mission to enact the eschatological "coming of Israel's god in power to save and heal."[54] The claim that Jesus did supernatural miracles makes sense within this context, assuming that one believes Jesus is the divine Messiah.

---

52. Bonaventure, *Commentary on the Gospel of Luke: Chapters 1-8*, 567, ch. 7, §1.

53. Quoted in Bonaventure, *Commentary on the Gospel of Luke: Chapters 1-8*, 591, ch. 7, §30.

54. Wright, *Jesus and the Victory of God*, 193. For further discussion of Jesus' healing miracles in Second Temple context, see Kahl, *New Testament Miracle Stories*.

IV. The Gerasene Demoniac and the Pigs

Wright does not commit himself to defending the historicity of every Gospel story about an exorcism undertaken by Jesus. But he does address a particular Gospel story that has long troubled readers, one which Twelftree deems "both the most astounding of the Synoptic exorcism stories and the one with the most textual and history of tradition problems."[55] This narrative describes the healing of the demoniac who lived in a graveyard on the other side of the Sea of Galilee (Mark 5, paralleled in somewhat different terms in Matt 8 and Luke 8). When Jesus heals this man, the demons who had dwelt within him receive Jesus' permission to enter into a herd of pigs. When the demons do so, the pigs immediately rush down a steep bank and drown in the sea. Even if we believe that Jesus performed supernatural miracles, how should we interpret strange miracle narratives such as this one? Eric Eve points out that this depiction of "pigs rushing into a lake and drowning themselves is unlikely to be historical. Pigs do not stampede, but they can swim. Moreover, Gerasa was over 30 miles from the lake."[56]

In his novel *The Rings of Saturn*, the German writer W. G. Sebald makes fun of this Gospel story and uses it to call into question the veracity and sanity of the Gospels as a whole. Traveling in southern England, the narrator of *The Rings of Saturn* stumbles upon a large herd of pigs with an intelligent, mournful, and submissive mien, dwelling on a bluff by the sea. Thinking back to the now long-lost Christian faith of his childhood, he remembers the story of the demoniac and the pigs. He recalls that in his catechetical classes as a boy, no teacher could explain "what the story of the mad Gadarene meant," and he wonders from whence this strange story came—especially since the story would seem to reflect "a serious error of judgment" on Jesus' part in allowing the demons to enter the pigs.[57] If the evangelist invented the pigs as characters because of their unclean status, then in Sebald's opinion this would be even worse than if the story were true, because it would mean that "human reasoning, diseased as it is, needs to seize on some other kind [of animal] that it can take to be inferior and

---

55. Twelftree, *Jesus the Exorcist*, 72. Twelftree directs attention to such works as Pesch, *Besessene von Gerasa*; and Detweiler and Doty, *Daemonic Imagination*. As Twelftree observes, "parallels to the pigs phenomenon are found in Jewish as well as Hellenistic literature. For example, it is found in Josephus *Antiquities* 8.48, Philostratus *Life* 4.20, and *Acts of Peter* 2.4.11" (*Jesus the Exorcist*, 74). Twelftree shows that a number of interpreters have tried to argue (in his view quite unsuccessfully) that the story of the exorcism goes back to Jesus whereas the details about the pigs were added later. For Twelftree, the story as a whole "most probably reflects tradition that rightly belongs to the original Jesus story" (*Jesus the Exorcist*, 87).

56. Eve, *Jewish Context of Jesus' Miracles*, 381n2.

57. Sebald, *Rings of Saturn*, 66-67.

thus deserving of annihilation."⁵⁸ For Sebald, the heroes of Mark 5 are the pigs, our fellow creatures.

Wright takes up Mark 5 and tries to make sense of it. In his view, the story requires sympathizing with the fact that from the Jewish perspective "Jesus is surrounded by places, people and influences that belong to the enemies of YHWH and his people."⁵⁹ For many Jewish people of Jesus' day, says Wright, there would have been the hope that the Messiah would drive the ritually unclean Romans out of the land of Israel. Arguably, then, Jesus is here battling against Israel's enemies, whose demon-driven idolatry is symbolized by the pigs.⁶⁰ From this perspective, the death of the pigs is a symbolic motif, in accordance with Wright's overall perspective: Jesus will overcome the demonic forces of idolatry by inaugurating his kingdom. Idolatry will be overcome without the Messiah needing to conquer the Romans, since the Messiah's real battle is with demonic powers.⁶¹

---

58. Sebald, *Rings of Saturn*, 67. For (unsuccessful in my view) psychological interpretations of this miracle story, focusing respectively on scapegoating and unresolvable trauma, see Girard, *Scapegoat*, 165–83; and Thate, *Godman and the Sea*, 132–56.

59. Wright, *Jesus and the Victory of God*, 195.

60. For the argument that the New Testament (like the Old Testament) is far too negative about gentile religion, see Johnson, *Among the Gentiles*. Johnson argues, "Early Christianity . . . reveals itself to be not only a religious movement that rapidly becomes Gentile culturally and demographically but one that increasingly reveals the same 'ways of being religious' as are evident in the Greco-Roman world," for instance "participation in divine benefits and moral transformation," along with "transcending the world" and "stabilizing the world" (276). Johnson's definition of religion in terms of experience, practices, and broad convictions, however, lacks the key element of the truth and adequacy of the object of worship.

61. See Shively, *Apocalyptic Imagination in the Gospel of Mark*, 39. For possible—though in my view, not probable—connections to 1 Enoch, see Elder, "Of Porcine and Polluted Spirits"; although for more persuasive, but still tentative, connections with the Book of Watchers in light of Jesus' cleansing of the temple (with links to Enoch's vision of the eschatological temple and to Enoch himself), see Freyne, *Jesus, a Jewish Galilean*, 157–63. Hans M. Moscicke observes, "For Mark, Jesus's scapegoat-like expulsion of Legion signals God's banishment of hostile cosmic powers from their positions of authority over the nations (i.e., binding the 'Strong Man,' Mark 3:27) and augurs God's kingdom reign, in which Gentiles are released from bondage to these powers (and their earthly counterparts) and welcomed into the family of God (Mark 3:13–19, 31–35)" (*Goat for Yahweh, Goat for Azazel*, 92). Moscicke takes this further along what seem to me to be much more speculative lines: "the Watchers tradition [1 Enoch] appears to have made a noticeable impact upon Mark's Gerasene narrative. But Mark's evocation of the Enochic myth is not unrelated to the elimination-ritual atmosphere of the exorcism. Rather, in light of the former, the Gerasene exorcism mimics the cosmic, scapegoat-like expulsion of Asael/Azazel, anticipating God's eschatological judgment of Satan and his associates. The demons' fear of being cast into the 'abyss' (Luke 8:31) or of being tormented 'before the time' (Matt. 8:29) confirms this apocalyptic and ritual component of the exorcism tradition" (*Goat for Yahweh, Goat for Azazel*, 92).

I note that there are connections here with the kind of allegorical reading present in Bonaventure.

Wright's former colleague Nicholas Perrin goes much further. Perrin strongly defends the historicity of Mark 5:1–20's account of the Gerasene demoniac. In his view (a controversial one given the manuscript tradition), the connection of the miracle story with Gerasa—thirty miles from any large body of water—is a scribal error. The town of Gergesa, named in some early manuscript versions of Mark 5:1–20 though not in the earliest extant manuscripts, had a steep cliff that adjoined the Sea of Galilee. But could pigs, which tend not to move in herds and which can swim, actually rush together into the sea and drown? Perrin argues that such a thing should be expected in a real miracle: pigs do exactly what they normally *would not* do. In the ancient world, says Perrin, it was expected that an exorcist would transfer the demons to some other bodily carrier. He concludes, "Objections to the basic integrity of this passage as a historical window on Jesus fall short. Their force typically derives from not only speculative source-critical hypotheses . . . but also a strange determination to distance Jesus, who was obviously regarded as remarkable in his own time, from remarkable actions."[62]

62. Perrin, *Jesus the Temple*, 159. John P. Meier takes the opposite view. He grants that it is historically possible "that an exorcism of Jesus did take place somewhere in the environs of the pagan city of Gerasa and that the unusual venue of the exorcism helped anchor it in the oral tradition" (Meier, *Marginal Jew*, 2:651). Meier notes that it was likely Origen's championing of Gergesa that led to its presence in some early manuscripts. As Meier says, "'Gerasenes' as the original reading in Mark easily explains the change to 'Gadarenes' or 'Gergesenes.' If one of the latter two had been the original reading, one would be hard pressed to explain how 'Gerasenes' would up in many early and excellent manuscripts" (651). Meier concludes on this basis: "Since the story most likely arose on Palestinian soil or adjoining territory, and since presumably the native storyteller would have known that Gerasa was nowhere near the Sea of Galilee, our decision that 'Gerasenes' belongs to the earliest form of the story confirms the view that the original story of the Gerasene demoniac did not include the incident of the pigs rushing into the Sea of Galilee . . . Even apart from the secondary swine, it is difficult to say how much of the story may be pressed for historical facts . . . Certainly, as the story stands in Mark, it serves the theological purpose of symbolizing the bringing of the healing, liberating message of the Christian gospel to the unclean Gentiles, a mission undertaken proleptically by Jesus himself. This overarching theological program must make us leery about accepting various details of the story as historical data" (652). Yet, Meier thinks that there may be a "historical residue," given that the Bible mentions "Gerasenes" only in this story, and given that "Decapolis" is mentioned nowhere else in ancient literature. Meier affirms Franz Annen's supposition that even if mission-minded early Christians invented much of the story, nevertheless any such invention (in the context of the early debate about mission to the gentiles) "would have been useful against the opponents only if both groups of first-generation Palestinian Christian Jews knew and accepted the fact that Jesus had indeed performed an exorcism in the region of Gerasa" (653). See Annen, *Heil für die Heiden*.

Perrin adds that Jesus' activity as an exorcist was rooted in his self-understanding as "the tribulation-bearing shepherd" (see Zech 13:7–9), given that God had promised that on the Day of the Lord, God would "remove from the land . . . the unclean spirit" (Zech 13:2).[63] On behalf of the "Most High God" (Mark 5:7), Jesus came to Gerasa/Gergesa in order to combat and drive out the demons brought by the gentiles, with their false gods and their imperial greed. The demons' name "Legion" (Mark 5:9) connects them to the Romans.[64] Perrin notes that the Roman soldiers stationed near Gergesa would have partly depended upon pigs for food, and so Jesus' action would have achieved both symbolic and practical ends. In addition to pigs being unclean for Jews, the wild boar served as the mascot of the Tenth Legion (to which the Gergesene soldiers belonged) and was well known as a symbol of Roman power. Jesus, in "driving two thousand living Roman mascots into the sea," acted with power to renew and restore the land of Israel.[65] Perrin concludes that this miracle story makes sense and Jesus himself likely set these events in motion.[66]

---

63. Perrin, *Jesus the Temple*, 162. Perrin comments, "While most contemporary readers of the Gospels are conditioned to think of the afflictions of an 'unclean spirit' as occurring strictly on an individualized level, we are probably on firmer ground in thinking of this ministry of exorcism as indicating something far deeper and broader—the eschatological removal of a spirit that bedevils the land as a whole. This insight in turn sharpens our understanding of Jesus' ministry as a whole and the temple cleansing in particular. On reconsideration, it seems that the final target of Jesus' temple action was not the idolatrous 'false prophets' who occupied the high-priestly office: the real enemy consisted of the invisible forces of darkness which inspired them . . . In situating Jesus' exorcistic activity within the context of Zechariah 13, that is, as a symbolic expression of Yahweh's imminent intention to purify the land of idolatry and dark spiritual forces, we recognize its inextricable political charge within the first-century context" (163).

64. Perrin notes that "the Romans maintained a detachment of the Tenth Legion (*Fretensis*) right next door in Hippos" (*Jesus the Temple*, 166). He goes on to say of the story, "I submit that Jesus stands behind it all. First of all, if, as I have argued, this encounter with the demoniac is a prophetic speech act, in effect declaring that the 'unclean spirit' of pagan Rome was due to be dislodged, then its orchestration makes much more sense as having been the brainchild of Jesus' creativity rather than the fancy of Mark or pre-Markan tradition" (167).

65. Perrin, *Jesus the Temple*, 167.

66. Perrin adds, "Jesus, though clearly violating the purity codes of his day and clearly, too, incurring in this event what for any other Jew would have been defiling contact in that gravesite, remains unscathed . . . Perhaps Jesus' remarkable lack of concern for his unclean environment in Mark 5.1–20, rather than being evidence of his flouting purity laws, speaks to his conviction that the laws have been redefined according to the eschatological moment. If Jesus was convinced that he himself was the temple, perhaps he reasoned—in a way that other counter-temple groups of his era did not—that he himself was not just the medium of divine power but its very locus on earth. What if, in other words, the location and methods of Jesus' exorcistic

For his part, the Protestant biblical scholar Matthew Thiessen reads the story in light of Jewish purity laws, whose value (within a Jewish understanding of God, the community, and temple worship) he defends, arguing that "compassion animates the Jewish purity system; it was a protective and benevolent system intended to preserve God's presence among his people," a presence that must be approached in a manner appropriate to the glory of God.[67] With respect to Jesus' exorcism of the Gerasene demoniac, Thiessen points out that "to anyone attuned to the purity systems of early Jewish thinking, impurity saturates the entire scene: impure *pneumata*, tombs that house impure corpses (cf. Num. 19), and impure pigs (cf. Lev. 11 and Deut. 14). The man's encounter with Jesus . . . results in the man's deliverance from all of these sources of impurity."[68]

---

practices could be attributed to a radical self-identity as the embodied eschatological temple?" (*Jesus the Temple*, 169–70). This "what if" describes Perrin's own position, of course—one that strikes me as reasonable.

67. Thiessen, *Jesus and the Forces of Death*, 11. Thiessen's perspective resonates with that of Chilton, "Jesus within Judaism," 200 (building upon and summarizing Chilton, *Temple of Jesus*): "Jesus, in other words, must be understood, not over and against Judaism, nor alongside it, but from within; necessarily, that implies he is to be apprehended as having a positive definition of purity. That definition is cognate with an aspect of Jesus' ministry which is usually overlooked: his programmatic concern with the issues of who is fit to sacrifice, how a person might be considered clean, when food might be taken with whom, and what should be sacrificed. Forgiveness for Jesus established an eschatological purity among people whose fellowship and sacrifice opened the way for the kingdom of God. That programmatic understanding explains his intentional insistence upon communal eating, and the 'last supper' in particular." For his part, Perrin points out that in Jesus' feeding miracles in the wilderness, Jesus does not worry about ritual purity: "first-century Judaism maintained strict prescriptions for the Jew *and* his or her table fellows. In the normal course of things, to eat with one who was ritually impure was to incur impurity. But unless the Gospel traditions have deliberately and independently distorted the record, purity concerns do not seem to have entered into the thinking of Jesus and his disciples as they administered these mass feedings" (*Jesus the Temple*, 171). In Mark 8, the second feeding miracle even appears to have taken place in gentile territory and to have included gentiles. On Jesus' eating with "sinners," see also Chilton, *Feast of Meanings*, 27 and elsewhere.

68. Thiessen, *Jesus and the Forces of Death*, 145. For background to the Levitical understanding of impurity (and related elements), see Sklar, *Sin, Impurity, Sacrifice, Atonement*. Peter J. Leithart conceives of the salvation brought by Jesus largely in terms of the breaking down of the barriers and boundaries of the Levitical purity laws, which Leithart views as divine pedagogy for a "fleshly" or fallen (Leithart uses the term "stoicheic") world whose true or ultimate purpose—radical inclusion in God's community—is revealed by Jesus. Leithart states, "The entire sacrificial system was designed to bring Israel near so that divine Husband and human Bride could feast together at the house of Yahweh. Yahweh accommodated himself to the post-Edenic, fleshly situation of Israel. Israelites themselves did not approach Yahweh but drew near through animal mediators, animals whose flesh was destroyed so that they could be transfigured and ascend, as the worshiper could not, into Yahweh's presence. Israelite priests ate in the

MIRACLES

Indebted to Peter Bolt, Thiessen reads this story in the context of Jesus' words in Mark 3, where Jesus is accused—by his own friends as well as his enemies—of being out of his mind or even demonically possessed. As his healing of the demoniac shows, Jesus is able to overcome the strength of Satan because Jesus, far from being under Satan's sway, is stronger than Satan and can defeat him. The demoniac had been too strong to be bound by his neighbors, and so he went around harming himself in the tombs. Thiessen observes, "No one is strong enough (*ischyō*) to subdue him, until Jesus arrives. Jesus plunders the house of these demons and steals their possession—the man—from their control."[69] For Thiessen, the pigs are a peripheral detail, symbolizing the ritual impurity that Jesus has come to heal.

---

holy place, but only under controlled conditions; Israelites could eat and drink and rejoice before the Lord, but only at a distance from his fiery presence.... When Yahweh came in the flesh, the need for that stoicheic apparatus began to end. In Jesus, Yahweh himself sat at human tables and ate food with them. This was what Torah aimed at from the outset. It was what Torah encouraged Israel to dream of. Jesus did what Torah always aimed to achieve, to make it possible for the Creator and his rebellious creatures to share space, to live and walk together in a common garden, to share a common table. Yahweh's entire program in Torah was designed to make human beings his 'companions' in the original sense of the word—God and humans as sharers of bread. The ministry of Jesus is what the sacrificial system looks like after Eden's curse is overcome. Jesus qualified people to draw near to his table. He touched lepers and dead bodies, and instead of contracting their contagious miasma, his cleansing life flowed to them. Lepers were cleansed; a woman's defiling flow of blood was stopped. The table fellowship of Jesus is the sacrificial system under poststoicheic conditions" (Leithart, *Delivered from the Elements of the World*, 137–38; see 228–30, 233–34 for further reflections).

69. Thiessen, *Jesus and the Forces of Death*, 145. Thiessen comments more broadly, "The purification mission of Jesus in the Synoptic Gospels extends beyond the three sources of ritual impurity (*lepra*, genital discharges, and corpses) mentioned in priestly literature to demonic sources of impurity as well. The demonic realm is no longer free to plague humanity unopposed. . . . The demons thought they had free rein on earth to do as they pleased, yet the Gospel writers portray Jesus's invasion of the world to take it back from the demonic and to establish God's kingdom. In this sense, Jesus's actions in the Synoptic Gospels parallel later rabbinic depictions of Israel's tabernacle, which also expelled demons from the earth" (Thiessen, *Jesus and the Forces of Death*, 147; see also Bolt, *Jesus' Defeat of Death*, 146–47). Thiessen concludes along lines I find particularly important, since they indicate Jesus' status as the eschatological Temple (thus implicitly reconfiguring Israel's ritual purity laws, although Thiessen goes on to deny that such reconfiguration belongs to Jesus' self-understanding): "Jesus's presence on earth introduces a power of holiness within the terrestrial realm that is both radically opposed to and stronger than the demonic. If some contemporaries of the Gospel writers were ascribing this same function to Israel's tabernacle (and by extension to the Jerusalem temple), since it housed the holy God of Israel, then the Gospel writers might have been implying that the holiness of Israel's God was housed in the person of Jesus in a way that actualized God's control over the demonic forces that plagued humanity" (Thiessen, *Jesus and the Forces of Death*, 148; and see also 161: "Matthew's Jesus argues that there is something now here that is even greater than the temple, so

Would Sebald accept such interpretations? He is firmly focused on the pigs, whose death he finds tragic and whose symbolic role (as "unclean" animals) he finds absurd and distressing. For Wright, Perrin, and Thiessen, however, it is appropriate that Jesus—and the evangelists—work within Jewish symbolic categories.[70] These categories have meaning, and (as Mary

---

it must take precedence over the Sabbath. He acknowledges that his disciples work on the Sabbath, yet they are, in his mind, compelled to do so in a way that compares to the priestly obligation to work on the Sabbath"). In contradistinction to Kazen's *Jesus and Purity Halakhah*, Thiessen holds that the evangelists retained Jewish understandings of ritual purity and saw Jesus as able to restore ritual purity. I think Jesus did what Thiessen describes, but at the same time Jesus also reconfigured and transformed ideas of ritual (and, in certain ways, moral) purity, without explicitly setting aside the laws of ritual purity. As noted above, Leithart offers an account of how Jesus did this (even if I have doubts about some details of Leithart's account); and see also Barber, *Historical Jesus and the Temple*, 65–66, 71–73; as well as (for the opposite viewpoint from Thiessen's) Witherington, *Many Faces of the Christ*, 30–34. In Perrin's words, "precisely in his status as the temple of God, Jesus believed that his presence and activity, through which the divine was mediated to the earthly, served to impart purity. A new temple meant a new way of configuring purity: from now on, those who sought to worship Jesus properly would have to align themselves with the cause and movement of Jesus" (*Jesus the Temple*, 182). In my view (for further discussion see my *Engaging the Doctrine of Israel*) in the apostolic age, the apostles held that Jews who believed in Jesus as the Messiah and Lord could (or, in some cases, should) continue practice the ritual laws, but they should do so out of piety, not out of a sense that obedience to such laws was necessary for salvation. See also John P. Meier's argument that "the authentic Jesus tradition [i.e. what can be reconstructed as historically deriving from Jesus himself] is completely silent on the topic of ritual purity" (Meier, *Marginal Jew*, 4:414). Meier holds that "it is a basic mistake to try to find one coherent line of thought or systematic approach to the Mosaic Law on the part of Jesus. Christian theologians in particular are often driven by a desire to find some 'principle' (love is the perennially favorite candidate) from which Jesus' various teachings on the Law can be derived or deduced. But there is no such principle . . . Jesus saw himself as an eschatological prophet and miracle worker along the lines of Elijah. He was not a systematic teacher, scribe, or rabbi; he was a religious charismatic . . . The religious charismatic, implicitly or explicitly, claims to know directly and intuitively what God's will is in a particular situation or on a particular question" (414–15).

70. Peter Bolt argues that the primary context for the evangelists may actually be the Greco-Roman one: "The pigs are often taken as a signal that this incident took place in non-Jewish territory. The Jews' avoidance of the pig was certainly known in the Graeco-Roman world, even if the reasons for it were little understood . . . However, instead of reading with Jewish eyes, the Graeco-Roman readers are more likely to understand the significance of the pigs according to their own cultural framework . . . In the cultural framework of the Graeco-Roman readers, the pigs are the usual chthonic sacrifices; they are involved in purificatory rites; and they act as a substitution for a person in order to rid them from the influence of the *daimones*. If so, these pigs moving from the man into the sea could be seen as a sacrifice to the underworld gods, which draws off the unclean spirits for the cleansing of the man" (Bolt, *Jesus' Defeat of Death*, 152–53). It is possible and even probable that the Graeco-Roman readers of the story interpreted it in this way, but in my view the primary context for the Gospels remains the Jewish one.

Douglas and Jonathan Klawans have shown[71]) their meaning is far more than mere scapegoating, let alone a priestly rejection of the created goodness of pigs. Wright deems it reasonable to affirm that Israel's God is the Creator and Redeemer, and Wright holds in faith that there exist demons that are a deeply troubling part of the struggle between good and evil that characterizes human lives.[72] Perrin and Thiessen further fill out a plausible context in which this miracle story makes sense, even if Perrin's argument for Gergesa (rather than Gerasa) may be a stretch.

Like Thiessen, Wright interprets the story of the miraculous healing of the demoniac as full of symbolism regarding Jesus' battle with "the satan and his hordes."[73] Wright contends that in this miracle narrative, "Jesus is going into what was thought of as an enemy territory, taking on (from the Jewish point of view) the demon of uncleanness and hostile paganism, and defeating the real enemy instead, demonstrating that victory in the acted symbolism of the death of the pigs."[74] The pigs have a symbolic role in Jesus' work of eschatological transformation, part of the larger cosmic battle (and battle against idolatry) to which both Bonaventure and Wright are attuned. Arguably, the symbolism of the pigs, within the context of transformation, provides an opening for the spiritual sense.

V. Luke Timothy Johnson on Biblical Miracles—in Light of Wright and Bonaventure

Even if one agrees with some or much of the above about the Gospels' miracle stories in their original (and later Christian) contexts, however, the skeptical questions have hardly yet received their full due. The skeptical questions pertain both to how we should engage worldviews that accept the miraculous and the demonic—worldviews that often exhibit credulity—and to how we should approach the New Testament witness (which is clearly not historical reportage of the kind historians undertake today) without jeopardizing our historical sense.

Let me give a concrete example of the debate over these matters. The Protestant biblical scholar Richard Bauckham argues for the "general reliability of the sources," both with respect to the evangelists' sources and with

---

71. See Klawans, *Impurity and Sin in Ancient Judaism*; and Douglas, *Leviticus as Literature*.

72. See Wright, *History and Eschatology*.

73. Wright, *Jesus and the Victory of God*, 196.

74. Wright, *Jesus and the Victory of God*, 196.

respect to the Gospels themselves.[75] In response, however, Dale Allison asks, "Should I trust, because Mark says so, that a number of demons once jumped from a man into a herd of pigs?"[76] For Bauckham, the exorcism stories, including the one involving the pigs, should be treated as likely to be true.[77] In his view, the fact that they are so detailed and striking suggests that they originated in reliable eyewitness memories. At least, they are *as likely* to be based upon reliable memories as is the claim—affirmed by Allison—that "Jesus was an exorcist."[78] Like Allison, Bauckham recognizes that the historian can only arrive at probability, not certainty. But if Jesus was actually an exorcist, says Bauckham, then there would have been eyewitnesses who had "good memories of specific exorcisms by Jesus," and their detailed stories would not have been easily manipulated by the evangelist.[79]

Allison's point is not to affirm pure skepticism, as though miracles could not happen (he thinks they can). As a historian, however, he argues that much modesty is needed about the power of reconstructions or plausible arguments to ground solid *historical* conclusions. He thinks that in most matters, the historian simply does not have enough evidence to make a judgment or even to assert a probability one way or the other. If a miracle story looks like a good symbolic story, it may just be a good symbolic story.

---

75. Bauckham, *Jesus and the Eyewitnesses*, 608. See also Bauckham's "General and the Particular in Memory," 28–51.

76. Allison, "Memory, Methodology, and the Historical Jesus," 15. See also Allison, *Constructing Jesus*, 18; and Allison, "Historians' Jesus and the Church," 81: "Despite all the ingenious efforts, has anyone really unveiled good public arguments for concluding that Jesus uttered or did not utter the golden rule (Matt 7:12 par. Luke 6:31), the parable of the rich man and Lazarus (Luke 16:19–31), the command not to let the left hand know what the right hand is doing (Matt 6:3), or the parable of the wicked tenants (Mark 12:1–12)? And who has established that a herd of pigs did or did not run over a cliff when Jesus was nearby? Is it not time to quit pretending that such things can be done?" Allison goes on to propose a way of continuing to evaluate the Gospels historically, even if not at the level of such details.

77. I think that Bauckham makes a typo when, referring to Allison's list of exorcism stories (or exorcism-related events), he cites number eight rather than number nine. The latter is the story of the healing of the demoniac and the death of the pigs. Number eight is simply Mark 3:15, where the evangelist states that Jesus gave the twelve disciples "authority to cast out demons." Bauckham writes—surely meaning to say "9" rather than "8"—that on Allison's list, "five stories (6, 8, 10, 11, 15) are each highly distinctive. They are the kind of exceptional events that are exceptionally well remembered precisely because of their distinctiveness. As we know, peripheral details may not be remembered well, but the narrative core, the 'gist' that makes each story the distinctive story it is, is what we should expect to have been well remembered" (Bauckham, "General and the Particular in Memory," 49).

78. Bauckham, "General and the Particular in Memory," 49.

79. Bauckham, "General and the Particular in Memory," 50.

After all, the evangelists had significant narrative leeway within certain parameters, just as did other ancient historians.[80]

In this debate, it seems to me that the recent work of Luke Timothy Johnson deserves attention, and so I will now turn to it. In his book *Miracles*, Johnson offers a detailed historical-critical analysis of the story of the Gerasene demoniac. He also provides a broader account—emphasizing the (reasonable but not reducible to reason) worldview of faith—of how to understand the Gospels' testimony to real miracles. I will begin with his analysis of the Gerasene demoniac and then explore what his broader account of miracles may contribute to this chapter's discussion.

Johnson's interpretation of the miracle of the healing of the demoniac accords with that of Wright in its emphasis on the eschatological current that undergirds the story. But Johnson adds significant further details. As he observes, Mark states that the demoniac "lived among the tombs" (Mark 5:3) and had become too strong for anyone to bind him. The latter detail echoes Mark 3:27, where Jesus remarks that "no one can enter a strong man's house and plunder his goods, unless he first binds the strong man." The "strong man" in Mark 3:27 is explicitly Satan. Thus, it is highly significant that the demoniac cannot be bound. The demoniac lives in the tombs and is no longer treatable as a human being. Johnson comments that the man "is utterly enslaved to the demonic power that drives him to isolation, misery, and self-destruction."[81]

Mark also states, "Night and day among the tombs and on the mountains he was always crying out, and bruising himself with stones" (Mark 5:5). Yet it is this same man, rather than the townspeople, who comes to meet Jesus when Jesus crosses the Sea of Galilee. This man seems to have known he needed greater help than any mere human could provide. At the same time as the demoniac runs toward Jesus and worships, the demons in the man complain bitterly. Mark depicts this interior division by noting that when the man worships Jesus, the man's voice at the same time cries out, "What have you to do with me, Jesus, Son of the Most High God? I adjure

---

80. See Bauckham, *Jesus and the Eyewitnesses*, 595 for discussion of this point. My perspective accords with Samuel Byrskog's summation of the genre of ancient historiography, which he extends to the work of the evangelists: "Since the historians always were involved in more or less complex narrativizing processes, their use of persuasive rhetorical techniques in preparing as well as composing their writings is not to be underestimated . . . [T]he historians employed a core of factual truth, enabling them to adhere to 'the laws of history' throughout an extensive narrativizing process." See Byrskog, *Story as History—History as Story*, 303. See also, on the possible presence in the Gospels of *consciously* fictionalized details or stories, in conjunction with details understood by the evangelists to be historical, Allison's *Constructing Jesus*, 435-61.

81. Johnson, *Miracles*, 199.

you by God, do not torment me" (Mark 5:6–7).[82] According to Mark, these words, so antithetical to the man's actions, arise because Jesus had already begun the exorcism. Upon seeing the man, Jesus had commanded, "Come out of the man, you unclean spirit!" (Mark 5:8).

According to Johnson, the term "legion" (Mark 5:9) is not primarily a reference to the structure of the Roman military, but rather is a way of saying that there are many demons possessing the man. The mingling of the singular and plural forms indicates the complexity of the man's demon possession. The term "legion" makes an imaginative link to Satan's army. Johnson comments, "The metaphor of Satan as ruler of a counterkingdom is metaphorically expanded with the demons and spirits imagined as soldiers."[83] These demonic soldiers have completely taken over the man's life. The lesson that Johnson draws is connected with the apocalyptic worldview of the day—shared by Jesus—according to which "exorcisms are acts of liberation from a rule opposed to God that holds humans captive."[84] This captivity cannot be undone by mere human power, since it is a matter of "a cosmic battle between God and powers inimical to God's rule over creation," so that a victory over demon possession can only be accomplished through "the overcoming of one spiritual domination by another powerful enough to overcome it."[85] Jesus, armed with the Spirit, has such power.

When Jesus liberates the man from the demonic "legion," he permits the demons to go from the man into the pigs, which then rush down the steep bank and drown. Mark next offers a counterpoint to the detailed description of the demoniac prior to his liberation. Alerted by the dead pigs' herdsmen, the townspeople arrive and see "the demoniac sitting there, clothed and in his right mind" (Mark 5:15). Previously he had been wandering among the tombs; now he is sitting peacefully. Previously he had been deranged; now he is reasonable. Previously he had been unpresentable; now he is clothed. Indeed, he is so fully liberated from Satan's power that he now wishes to follow Jesus and to serve him alone. Jesus, however, prevents the liberated man from entering the boat with him and instead asks the man to serve in another way: "Go home to your friends, and tell them how much the Lord has done for you, and how he has had mercy on you" (Mark 5:19).

---

82. I note here the argument of North, "Jesus and Worship, God and Sacrifice." In the New Testament, he argues, "our translation of προσκυν as 'worship' betrays us. It does not mean 'worship' if we are thinking of the exclusive 'worship' that God demands and God alone should receive . . . It means the profoundest respect and it implies no more" (189).

83. Johnson, *Miracles*, 199.

84. Johnson, *Miracles*, 197.

85. Johnson, *Miracles*, 197–98.

MIRACLES

The point is that freedom from slavery to Satan entails freedom for serving the Lord Jesus.

In this light, Johnson draws a connection between the liberated demoniac and the "young man" who appears before and after Jesus' resurrection. According to Mark, after the disciples have fled and while Jesus was being led away by the Roman soldiers, "a young man followed him, with nothing but a linen cloth about his body; and they seized him, but he left the linen cloth and ran away naked" (Mark 14:51–52). The actions and clothing of this young man express instability. But after the resurrection, a "young man" (Mark 16:5) appears again, this time sitting peacefully in the otherwise empty tomb, when Mary the mother of James, Mary Magdalene, and Salome find it open and enter it. The "young man"—whether or not he is the same young man is unclear—is dressed nicely and is well apprised about the risen Jesus' whereabouts.

Armed with these details, Johnson points back to Mark 3:27 (and Mark 1:7) in light of "Mark's fondness for triadic literary structures," with the liberation of the Gerasene demoniac in Matthew 5 at the middle of the Gospel and the "young man" of Matthew 14 and 16 at the end.[86] As noted above, Mark 3:27 presents Jesus as powerful enough to conquer the "strong man," that is, Satan. Johnson argues that Mark intended to compare the liberation of the demoniac to the restoration of the "young man," so as to underline the point that Jesus' resurrection has conquered the demonic powers that enslave people. Those whom Jesus has liberated "can no longer be 'with Jesus' [after the resurrection and ascension] but can tell all 'how much Jesus [has] done' for them."[87]

Thus, by his divine power, Jesus is overcoming the "legion" of God's opponents who have enslaved human beings to sin and death. This "legion," as Wright says, consists not in Roman soldiers but rather in the soldiers of Satan. Wright sees many elements of the story as symbolic, as does Johnson. Johnson downplays the symbolism of the pigs, while Wright thinks that this element adds to the overall reference to Israel's opponents. Neither Wright nor Johnson states that this particular miraculous event did not happen, but both suggest that the story is imbued with deep symbolism, reflecting the art of the evangelist and the broader theological point that the evangelist wishes to make about the liberation brought by Jesus.[88]

---

86. Johnson, *Miracles*, 200.

87. Johnson, *Miracles*, 202.

88. See also the spiritual reading of Mark 5:1–20 offered by the Old Testament scholar Lefebvre, *Comment tuer Jésus?*, 153–67.

Johnson insists that the Jesus "who works wonders and whose entire presence is a revelation of God's power in the world" is the real Jesus, not an embarrassment that historical criticism can put to the side for purposes of serious inquiry.[89] The rejection of the miraculous in human life brings with it the rejection of such things as the sacraments and the resurrection of the dead (both Jesus' resurrection and our future bodily resurrection). Johnson argues that in a miracle, what happens is that "God's implicit presence and power has, in this instance, been experienced in a more direct and explicit fashion."[90] Miracles, says Johnson, are always ambiguous in the sense that they need not be interpreted as miracles. Miracles are described in the symbolic imagery of the persons who experience them, and they require interpretation both during and after the miracle.

What "myth" does, according to Johnson, is to provide a symbolic framework and language for describing supernatural agency. "Myth" is therefore not something false, but rather it opens up a way of speaking about non-empirically-verifiable entities and agents. For Johnson, statements such as "participation in the Spirit" or "participation in Christ" count as "mythic," not in the normal sense of that term, but in the sense of involving a worldview that goes far beyond the empirical. Death is an empirical reality, but "new creation" is a "mythic" reality even though quite real. By committing ourselves in faith to this worldview, we can recover "the ability to imagine the world that Scripture imagines"—a way of putting the matter that Johnson draws from Richard Hays.[91]

In my view, Johnson is wise to focus on "the function and meaning of the miracles as they appear in the Gospels."[92] As he knows, since historians easily perceive the ways in which the evangelists shape the miracle narratives for literary and theological impact, it is difficult for historians (qua

---

89. Johnson, *Miracles*, 27. As Johnson says earlier, "The crisis of the present age is that the culturally most influential forms of Christianity have capitulated to a worldview that effectively eliminates the miraculous from serious consideration . . . Rationalistic skepticism characterizes the classic historical-critical approach to the Old and New Testaments: academic engagement with miracle stories tends to be dismissive when it appears at all. In so-called historical Jesus research, the miracles ascribed to Jesus are regularly 'bracketed' in favor of a portrayal of Jesus based on his sayings or on his prophetic (political) actions" (19). See also Johnson, *Real Jesus*.

90. Johnson, *Miracles*, 63.

91. Johnson, *Miracles*, 75. Johnson adds with great insight: "such reframing requires the most strenuous and consistent efforts of the community of faith to resist doublemindedness and recover the purity of heart that enables it to perceive and celebrate God's powerful presence not only in the words of Scripture from the past but also in the experiences of humans in the present" (75). For a similar "reframing," see the essays in Hays, *Conversion of the Imagination*.

92. Johnson, *Miracles*, 168.

historians) to be able to come to a firm conclusion that a specific miracle, as reported in the Gospels, took place. It is clear that many of Jesus' contemporaries thought of him as an exorcist and wonderworker, but, as Allison says, there is generally not sufficient evidence for or against the historicity of specific miracles. Historians cannot determine with certitude whether or not Jesus' signs and wonders have a naturalistic explanation.

While recognizing the limits of historical methods, Johnson counts himself firmly among those who believe that Jesus worked supernatural miracles. As the Gospel of Matthew explains, Jesus did his miracles of exorcism and healing precisely in order to demonstrate the eschatological inbreaking of the kingdom of God: Jesus is the one who "took our infirmities and bore our diseases" (Matt 8:17; cf. Isa 53:4). When Johnson examines the miracle narratives as a whole, he argues that acceptance of Jesus' miracles depends on a sense of God as the good Creator, sustaining all things and doing battle with the forces of sin and death. We need first to understand creation in such a way as "to see the world not as a fixed set of operations that we can grasp and control at will, but as a mysterious and ever-surprising coming-into-being whose workings we only partially and fitfully understand."[93]

I note that this approach to Jesus' miracles supports a retrieval of Bonaventure's spiritually rich mode of allowing Scripture's meaning to unfold in typological, moral, and anagogical directions, reflective of the depths of God's creative and redemptive work to which Scripture testifies and which we presently experience.[94] When Bonaventure comments upon Jesus' healing of the centurion's slave who was at the point of death, it is not for nothing that Bonaventure makes reference to the Word's creative power. Commenting upon the centurion's statement "But say the word, and let my servant be healed" (Luke 7:7), Bonaventure remarks that this statement is "[a]s if he were saying: 'Nothing is impossible with you' [cf. Luke 1:37]. For you are that Word through which 'all things were made,' as John 1:3 says. You are that 'word which heals all,' as Wisdom 16:12 has."[95] This deliberate joining of Christ as Creator with Christ's healing and redemptive power makes a crucial contribution to apprehending Christ's miracles.

A similar contribution is found in Bonaventure's commentary on Luke 7:14, where Jesus proclaims to the dead young man, "Young man, I

---

93. Johnson, *Miracles*, 281.

94. For Johnson's deep appreciation of patristic typology and allegory, see Johnson and Kurz, *Future of Catholic Biblical Scholarship*. See also the valuation of allegory in Boersma, *Five Things Theologians Wish Biblical Scholars Knew*; and Raith, "Aquinas, Allegory, and Paul's Use of the Old Testament."

95. Bonaventure, *Commentary on the Gospel of Luke: Chapters 1–8*, 577, ch. 7, §12.

say to you, arise." Bonaventure comments that Christ speaks in this way to the dead man in order to demonstrate that the one speaking is the creative Word: "So in Christ, because flesh has been joined with the eternal Word, *the exterior voice* is joined with him *to speak interiorly*, who is the beginning of every *creation*. And this is obvious in the works of the six days of creation in Genesis 1:1–31. And he is also the beginning of all *restoration*."[96] Here Bonaventure once again quotes Wisdom 16:12, which refers to God's healing word. Johnson's interpretation of the exorcism of the Gerasene demoniac makes room for this miracle-affirming worldview as well as for the apocalyptic imagination of Jesus' day, even while Johnson focuses on the theological and literary moves made by the evangelist rather than speculating on the historicity of the elements of a particular miracle story.

IV. David Friedrich Strauss

I hope that the above has provided a foundation for examining the nineteenth-century Protestant thinker David Friedrich Strauss's highly influential—and highly skeptical—stance toward Jesus' miracles. For good reasons, Strauss is often presented as a demythologizer who rejected the historicity of the Gospel narratives in his 1835 work *The Life of Jesus*.[97] Wright, for instance, describes Strauss's book as an attempt "to bring Christianity into line with rationalism, and with speculative Hegelian philosophy, ruling out the miraculous by means of an *a priori* (and having no difficulty in showing that many of the orthodox rationalizations of miracles were simply laughable)."[98] Certainly Strauss rejected the miraculous and exhibited a Hegelian bent, but his approach to Jesus' miracles builds upon much more than a mere *a priori* assumption about their impossibility.

Johnson gets it right when he describes Strauss as "sophisticated" and, in certain ways, "pioneering."[99] As Johnson points out, Strauss claims

96. Bonaventure, *Commentary on the Gospel of Luke: Chapters 1–8*, 588–89, ch. 7, §25.

97. For background to Strauss's work, see Howard, *Religion and the Rise of Historicism*, especially chapter 3. As Howard says, "the tools of criticism that Strauss employed, and that led him to question both orthodox and Hegelian formulations of Christian belief, had already been developed by de Wette. Indeed, on most important issues, de Wette directly influenced Strauss . . . Most important, Strauss's debt to de Wette can be seen in the parallels between their conceptions of myth. De Wette applied the mythic principle largely but not exclusively to the Old Testament and only indirectly to the person of Jesus Christ; Strauss applied it exclusively to the New Testament and directly to the person of Jesus Christ" (79–80).

98. Wright, *Jesus and the Victory of God*, 18.

99. Johnson, *Miracles*, 18; and see Dunn, *Jesus Remembered*, 31, 34: "Between

to be arguing against both rationalistic and supernaturalistic interpretations of Jesus' miracles. Rationalistic Christian interpreters of Strauss's day explained Jesus' miracles by providing a naturalistic interpretation, often wildly implausible (and anti-Semitic), for how the "miracle" truly occurred. On this view, for instance, the feeding of the five thousand depicts the amazing new generosity of previously greedy Jews who were inspired by Jesus' message. At the other extreme, as Strauss observes, supernaturalistic interpreters simply assume that the miracle narratives are literal reports of what happened.

Having ruled out these two approaches, Strauss observes that Jews in Jesus' day functioned within a worldview shaped by "mythic" categories such as the category of "Messiah." He argues that the Gospels are committed to these categories and therefore must be read as "mythic" rather than historical in any modern sense of that term. Recall that Johnson defends "mythic" symbolism and language as necessary for the description of divine agency and divine mysteries pertaining to the intersection of God and creatures. Strauss's category of the mythic, by contrast, collapses into rationalism, since for Strauss anything that might pertain to the divine cannot be historical. Strauss differs from earlier liberal Protestant rationalisms solely in that he does not attempt to squeeze a miracle narrative into a naturalistic explanation.[100]

[Hermann] Reimarus and Strauss the miracles of Jesus became the focus of interest, and there were various attempts on rationalist premises to save the historicity of the Gospel accounts. Contradictions could be explained, by postulating, for example, that there were three different healings of blind men at Jericho . . . Reimarus and Strauss should be compulsory texts for any course on Jesus of Nazareth, not simply as part of the story of the quest [for the historical Jesus] itself, but because the issues they pose remain issues to this day." For further background, see Beiser, *David Friedrich Strauß, Father of Unbelief*. Beiser observes, "Neither in its methods nor in its conclusions was Strauß's book anything new. Since the beginning of the eighteenth century, the idea that parts of the Bible are mythical had been steadily gaining ground. The theory of myth had been originally formed to explain pagan religion; but it was eventually applied to the Bible itself. At first it was applied to the Old Testament; but, later in the eighteenth century, it was extended to parts of the New Testament. Strauß was well aware of these historical precedents, acknowledged them, and deliberately built upon them. He never claimed that his theory of myth, or that his method of critique, were new. All that was original about his book was that, for the first time, the theory of myth was applied to all four gospels of the New Testament" (7). See also chapter 13 of Beiser's book for discussion of Strauss's 1864 *Das Leben Jesu für das deutsche Volk bearbeitet*. Beiser notes that in this 1864 volume, Strauss holds that "even though Jesus initially refused to be called messiah [due to its political implications in the popular mind], he later accepted this term and therefore understood himself to be the son of God, a semi-divine being . . . A person was has such a conception of himself suffers from self-delusion (*Überhebung*); he has a shaky hold on reality and lacks all judgment and common sense" (*David Friedrich Strauß, Father of Unbelief*, 230).

100. See Johnson, *Miracles*, 18.

Strauss's approach to Jesus' miracles is often even more subtle than Johnson perceives. Strauss argues *on New Testament grounds* that the New Testament authors or their sources invented Jesus' miracles.[101] He highlights the places in the Gospels where Jesus is presented as refusing to perform miracles. After citing various texts that demonstrate that the Messiah was expected to perform miracles, Strauss notes that the preeminent Old Testament figures set the terms for the kinds of miracles that the Messiah must perform. He shows that these are precisely the kinds of miracles that the Gospels attribute to Jesus. Moses miraculously delivers food and water to the people on the exodus; Jesus, as the new Moses and the Messiah, must also provide miraculous food and drink. Elisha miraculously restores sight to the blind; so too must Jesus. Elijah and Elisha raise the dead; so too must Jesus. In Isaiah 35:5–6, we learn that when God the Redeemer comes, "Then the eyes of the blind shall be opened, and the ears of the deaf unstopped; then shall the lame man leap like a deer, and the tongue of the mute sing for joy." All this must happen when the Messiah arrives.

In accordance with the mythic worldview in which a "Messiah" was thought possible, says Strauss, Jesus might have sought to do miracles in order to establish himself as the Messiah. But in Matthew 12:38–40, Jesus seems to say that the only miracle he will do will be his resurrection. We read, "Then some of the scribes and Pharisees said to him, 'Teacher, we wish to see a sign from you.' But he answered them, 'An evil and adulterous generation seeks for a sign; but no sign shall be given to it except the sign of the prophet Jonah. For as Jonah was three days and three nights in the belly of the whale, so will the Son of man be three days and three nights in the heart of the earth.'"[102] This saying is striking, not only because Jesus was not in the tomb for that long (according to the Gospel of Matthew itself), but also because the Gospel of Matthew seems to be undermining its own claim that Jesus performed miracles.[103]

This was not the only time that Jesus rejected the demand to perform miracles, at least if the Gospel of John is to be credited. In John 2, Jesus cleanses the temple, overthrowing the tables of the money-changers. He

---

101. See Strauss, *Life of Jesus*, vol. 2. This edition is based upon the fourth German edition, published in 1840.

102. Steven Bryan interprets the "sign of Jonah" as "an impending, irrevocable judgment" upon Israel (Bryan, *Jesus and Israel's Traditions*, 42). Bryan argues, "Jesus used language which deliberately evoked Israel's awaited restoration, but when asked to support such language with a manifestation of divine power modelled after the wondrous epiphanies of the Exodus and Conquest, he flatly refused, offering instead the sign of the Son of man—the sign of approaching and unavoidable judgement" (45).

103. For the contrary interpretation of this text, see Davies and Allison, *Critical and Exegetical Commentary on the Gospel According to Saint Matthew*, 2:354.

justifies himself by claiming to enjoy a special relationship to God: "you shall not make my Father's house a house of trade" (John 2:16). Not surprisingly, his fellow Jews are surprised and distressed, but they try to allow for the possibility that he had a good reason for this prophetic action. They ask Jesus, "What sign have you to show us for doing this?" (John 2:18). Jesus responds that he will give them the sign (or miracle) of his resurrection. He says with his death and resurrection in view, "Destroy this temple [i.e. his body], and in three days I will raise it up" (John 2:19). If this is Jesus' only sign, then it may appear that Jesus did no miracles prior to rising from the dead.

Strauss is well aware that both the Gospel of Matthew and the Gospel of John present Jesus doing plenty of signs or miracles. Why then, however, were his fellow Jews asking whether he would perform a sign? Perhaps, Strauss posits, they did not deem Jesus' miracles to be miraculous enough and were waiting for something greater. It may be the case that they were waiting for a specific sign, namely, "a sign from heaven" (Luke 11:16)—something greater than merely casting out demons. It may also be the case that when Jesus says that "no sign shall be given to this generation" (Mark 8:12), Jesus means by "this generation" solely the Pharisees or his opponents. But the Gospels report many miracles and surely the Pharisees or other opponents of Jesus witnessed at least one of them. If the resurrection of Jesus was the sign that Jesus' opponents were supposed to see, the problem arises that none (or few) of Jesus' enemies received resurrection appearances.

Taking these options into account, Strauss raises the possibility that at least in some texts, Jesus firmly "repudiated the working of miracles" and made clear that he would not work any, despite the expectations generally placed upon the Messiah.[104] In favor of such a view is the fact that in the book of Acts Jesus' miracles are almost never mentioned—the exceptions being Acts 2:22, where Peter says, "Men of Israel, hear these words: Jesus of Nazareth, a man attested to you by God with mighty works and wonders and signs which God did through him in your midst, as you yourselves know"; and Acts 10:38, where Peter recalls "how God anointed Jesus of Nazareth with the Holy Spirit and with power" and "how he went about doing good and healing all that were oppressed by the devil, for God was with him." Generally speaking, Strauss maintains, the early Christian preaching appears to be based not on any miracles done by Jesus but only on the miracle of his resurrection. Indeed, Strauss puts it more strongly (and in my view unpersuasively): it is generally the case that "the miracles of Jesus appear to be unknown, and everything is built on his resurrection."[105]

---

104. Strauss, *Life of Jesus*, 2:238.
105. Strauss, *Life of Jesus*, 2:239.

Strauss builds more support for the argument that Jesus actually did no miracles by pressing the question of why Jesus' resurrection looms so large in the apostolic preaching. After all, if the dead son of the widow at Nain, the dead Lazarus, and a dead girl were all raised by Jesus, why would Jesus' own emergence from the tomb be such a big deal? Strauss suggests that the answer is that none of these miracles happened, and so the resurrection of Jesus was the first miracle that the disciples of Jesus thought themselves to have witnessed. If Jesus had done all sorts of miracles, then the apostles would have trumpeted these miracles in their proclamation of the gospel; but the book of Acts and the letters of Paul seem to indicate otherwise.

In the end, Strauss actually presents himself as a defender of the New Testament, not as a skeptic. He makes the case that it is simply a question of which Gospel passages we choose to believe. As he puts it, "Ought we, on account of the evangelical narratives of miracles, to explain away that expression of Jesus [in Matthew 12:38-40 and John 2:18-19], or doubt its authenticity; or ought we not, rather, on the strength of that declaration, and the silence of the apostolic writings, to become distrustful of the numerous histories of miracles in the Gospels?"[106] In fidelity to the Gospels, he says, it is necessary to distrust the Gospels; one cannot accept on face value the mutually contradictory passages, and so one must choose which texts to accept. Strauss argues that it is better to accept Jesus' plain statement that he will not give any messianic signs. The messianic signs or miracles that we find in the Gospels are understandable given the Jewish worldview in which the Messiah was expected to perform certain miracles—an expectation that the evangelists or their sources ensured was not disappointed, since otherwise their audience might not have believed in Jesus' messianic identity.

This is an ingenious approach to Jesus' miracles, in two respects. First, Strauss insists that denying the historicity of the miracles is an act of fidelity to notable Gospel evidence. Second, Strauss attributes the presence of miracles in the Gospels to the pressure of the Old Testament and Second Temple expectations rather than to the exigencies of Jesus' own mission.

Strauss does not come to the above position without undertaking a review of the Gospels' narratives about Jesus' miracles. He points out that in the Synoptic Gospels, the exorcising and healing of demoniacs is front and center. Describing the Gerasene demoniac, he notes that the demons speak through the man, and the man is afflicted with a disturbed mind and undertakes "attacks of maniacal fury against himself and others."[107] He emphasizes that, according to the Synoptics, Jesus believed in Satan and in demon possession as an explanation for all kinds of maladies. Jesus thereby

---

106. Strauss, *Life of Jesus*, 2:239.
107. Strauss, *Life of Jesus*, 2:240.

manifests a first-century Jewish worldview that cannot be retrieved today. Strauss finds a similar outdated worldview among the ancient Greeks, who held that many diseases were caused by evil spirits; and he adds that the notion of demon possession derives from the Persians and is found not only in the Synoptics but in contemporaneous Jewish sources such as Josephus.[108]

Strauss goes on to pit the "old theology" (orthodox Protestantism) and the "new theology" (rationalism or liberal Protestantism) against each other. The "old theology" believed in demonic possession on the grounds of the "authority of the Jesus and the evangelists," thus failing to recognize the historical context and the Persian influence in the development of the first-century Jewish notion of demon possession.[109] The "new theology" is aware of the problem and no longer contends that physical and mental maladies are caused by demon possession. But the "new theology" insists that, nevertheless, in the time of Jesus some maladies *were* caused by demon possession, and Jesus knew which ones those were. In addition, the "new theology" argues that the "demonic" is not a realm of personal beings; instead the "demons are understood to be mere effluxes and operations, by which the evil principle manifests itself."[110]

Strauss's representative new theologian is the Protestant Hermann Olshausen, influenced by Friedrich Schleiermacher and best known for his New Testament exegesis. Olshausen, who died not long after the publication of Strauss's book, offers an interpretation of the healing of the Gerasene demoniac. According to Olshausen (as presented by Strauss), when Jesus says "Come out of the man, you unclean spirit" and receives the response "What have you to do with me, Jesus, Son of the Most High God? I adjure you by God, do not torment me" (Mark 5:7-8), Jesus' next question—"What is your name?" (Mark 5:9)—cannot be directed toward the demons.

---

108. Along lines outdated today, Strauss reports: "If it must be admitted that the Hebrews owed their doctrine of demons to Persia, we know that the Deves of the Zend mythology were originally and essentially wicked beings, existing prior to the human race; of these two characteristics, Hebraism as such might be induced to expunge the former, which pertained to Dualism, but could have no reason for rejecting the latter. Accordingly, in the Hebrew view, the demons were the fallen angels of Gen. vi, the souls of their offspring the giants, and of the great criminals before and after the deluge, whom the popular imagination gradually magnified into superhuman beings. But in the ideas of the Hebrews, there lay no motive for descending beyond the circle of these souls, who might be conceived to form the court of Satan. Such a motive was only engendered by the union of the Graeco-roman culture with the Hebraic: the former had no Satan, and consequently no retinue of spirits devoted to his service, but it had an abundance of Manes, Lemures, and the like,—all names for disembodied souls that disquieted the living" (Strauss, *Life of Jesus*, 2:246).

109. Strauss, *Life of Jesus*, 2:246.

110. Strauss, *Life of Jesus*, 2:249.

In Olshausen's view, it must instead be directed toward the man. The demons' answer, however, suggests that they are speaking through the man: "My name is Legion; for we are many" (Mark 5:9).

Strauss catches Olshausen here in an implausible effort to shore up predetermined rationalistic theological opinions. Since Olshausen deems that the demons are not personal beings, they cannot have a conversation with Jesus and they have no names or distinct identities. Olshausen's claim that Jesus asks the man (not the demons) "What is your name?" strikes Strauss as being "plainly in opposition to the whole context, for the answer, *Legion*, appears to be in no degree the result of a misunderstanding, but the right answer—the one expected by Jesus."[111] Trying to account for the demoniac's physical symptoms, Olshausen also claims (in Strauss's words) that "the preponderance of evil in the man must have weakened his corporeal organization, particularly the nervous system, before he can become susceptible of the demoniacal state."[112] In response, Strauss points out that many people have weakened or disordered nervous conditions without being morally wicked. As Strauss concludes, Olshausen is stretching to find a naturalistic explanation for the demoniac's symptoms, but if there were such a naturalistic explanation, then exorcism would not be necessary.

Strauss argues that the fundamental problem is that Olshausen has tried "to modernize the New Testament conception of the demoniacs" along lines that are not only implausible, but also should be offensive to anyone who respects the text of the New Testament.[113] The better approach is to respect the first-century Jewish worldview. For Strauss, we cannot today accept this worldview as our own, but we can do it the favor of trying to understand it. We can also recognize that a number of the maladies described in the Gospels were psychological ones. It should not surprise us that Jesus' commanding presence was able to calm psychological distress. We should expect that such events would be interpreted as miraculous within the worldview of the day.

The story of the Gerasene demoniac has parallel versions in Matthew, Mark, and Luke, and Strauss shows the absurdity of efforts to harmonize the versions. As he notes, "in Matthew, the demoniac, stricken with terror, deprecates the unwelcome approach of Jesus; in Luke, he accosts Jesus, when arrived, as a suppliant; in Mark, he eagerly runs to meet Jesus, while yet at a distance."[114] Various contradictions and problems are evident be-

---

111. Strauss, *Life of Jesus*, 2:250.
112. Strauss, *Life of Jesus*, 2:251.
113. Strauss, *Life of Jesus*, 2:251.
114. Strauss, *Life of Jesus*, 2:258.

tween the versions and within each version. For example, Strauss considers it implausible that the demoniac would both be in mortal fear of Jesus and run toward Jesus (Mark 5:6–7).

Strauss deems Matthew's version to be the original one or the "purest."[115] He argues at some length that Mark's version does not work, and he takes Mark 5:8 to be evidence (as Schleiermacher thought) that the original story lacked Jesus' words. In Matthew's version there are two demoniacs, not one, and Jesus does not ask the name of the demon(s) or receive the answer "Legion." Strauss proposes that perhaps Mark and Luke added the detail of the presence of many demons in order to account for how, when the demons (whether two or many) entered the pigs, all the pigs ran down the steep bank and drowned.

With regard to the detail of the pigs, Strauss asks why an intelligent demon, let alone a group of intelligent demons, would want to enter into pigs. He notes Olshausen's reply that this entrance into the pigs merely signified "an influence of all the evil spirits on the swine collectively."[116] If it was just an influence, Strauss observes, then the demons' relation to the demoniac would also be just an influence. Regarding the statement in Mark 5:12—"Send us to the swine, let us enter them"—Strauss therefore concludes that it is ludicrous. Such a plea "cannot possibly have been offered by real demons."[117] He is willing to grant that the demoniac, filled with the cultural notions of his day, might have said something of the kind. He knows that according to some Second Temple Jewish notions of demons, "it is a torment to evil spirits to be destitute of a corporeal envelopment, because without a body they cannot gratify their sensual desires."[118] In the Jewish worldview of the day, the idea that demons would wish to enter into pigs (unclean spirits entering into unclean animals) might make some sense, but we cannot make sense of it in modern terms.

Strauss does not stop there, but continues further in the same vein. How, he asks, could demons actually enter into pigs? Not only is such an event impossible, but also, says Strauss, we can make nothing of the idea that the demons would proceed to destroy the very bodies they had entered, by compelling them to rush into the sea. Besides, presumably Jesus could have healed the demoniac without causing the death of the pigs.

Strauss's conclusion is that the story of the healing of the Gerasene demoniac "is a tissue of difficulties"; the story resists any attempt to make

---

115. Strauss, *Life of Jesus*, 2:259.
116. Strauss, *Life of Jesus*, 2:262.
117. Strauss, *Life of Jesus*, 2:262.
118. Strauss, *Life of Jesus*, 2:262.

sense of it.[119] As Strauss notes, modern exegetes therefore "began to doubt the thorough historical truth of this anecdote earlier than that of most others in the public life of Jesus, and particularly to sever the connexion between the destruction of the swine and the expulsion of the demons by Jesus."[120] Among the theories proposed was that the storm during the crossing of the Sea of Galilee had fatally swept the pigs into the water before Jesus arrived. On this view, the evangelist's sources mixed up the details. What happened instead—so this theory goes—was that Jesus "healed" the man by persuading him that the demons plaguing him had all gone into the dead pigs. Another theory was that the swineherds went to meet Jesus when his boat landed, and their herds of pigs got out of hand and drowned. At the very same time, Jesus happened to heal a demoniac, and so the evangelist's sources conflated the two events. Theories such as these rightly strike Strauss as absurd.

Strauss's solution to all the problems caused by the story of the Gerasene demoniac is simply to point to the Jewish worldview of the day. Taking up a contemporaneous story from Josephus, Strauss observes that at least in some cases in Jesus' day, "the agitation of some near object, without visible contact, was held the surest proof of the reality of an expulsion of demons."[121] It fit the purpose of the evangelists and their sources to have Jesus perform an exorcism that had strong evidence in its favor. By sending the demons into the pigs so that they rushed down the bank and drowned, Jesus demonstrated to his contemporaries that he really did have the power of exorcism. Moreover, Jesus exorcised not merely one demon but a large number, thereby further demonstrating his strength. Of course, the narrative is false in Strauss's view, but he shows how the narrative would have been attractive and intelligible to a first-century audience.[122]

In light of Strauss's work, one can see why Johnson places so much emphasis on reframing the meaning of "myth" and on viewing the miracle narratives as narratives rather than trying to probe first into the historicity of each. One can see why Johnson focuses so strongly on the context of

---

119. Strauss, *Life of Jesus*, 2:265.

120. Strauss, *Life of Jesus*, 2:265.

121. Strauss, *Life of Jesus*, 2:267.

122. See also MacDonald, *Mythologizing Jesus*, 37–44, where MacDonald argues that Mark 5:1–20 on the Gerasene demoniac borrows from Homer's story of Polyphemus the Cyclops in Book IX of the *Odyssey* and also from Homer's story of Circe in Book X of the *Odyssey*. MacDonald provides a chart to show that the literary "similarities between these Homeric episodes and Mark's demon-infested man are too dense and distinctive to be accidental" (*Mythologizing Jesus*, 42), but closer inspection shows MacDonald's claim to be a stretch, based upon superficial similarities.

the Creator God, in which context miracles make sense. Although a plausible defense of the historicity of the exorcism of the Gesarene demoniac is possible (as we have seen), and although much more can be said against Strauss's perspective, Strauss had much success in catching his opponents on the horns of a dilemma: either defend every detail as literally what happened, or else grant that the whole story is false.

There is no need to fall into Strauss's trap.[123] Miracles of exorcism, as Wright and Johnson show, serve to display the eschatological battle that Jesus' mission involves and to display how Jesus' miraculous work aims to restore fallen humans to true life—just as the life of the troubled "young man" who fled after Jesus' arrest was restored to that "young man" by Jesus' resurrection. For Johnson and Wright, it is not so much a matter of defending the historicity of a particular miracle story, although they demonstrate the story's intelligibility. They begin with a worldview that allows for the existence of the Creator God and for the existence of demons, as well as for God's redemptive battle against the forces of evil, sin, and death. In this light, the fact that Jesus did exorcisms in fulfillment of Old Testament figuration is plausible. So long as Jesus' performance of supernatural miracles is affirmed, particular miracle narratives (or details) can be read symbolically, along lines that are relatively close to medieval readings of such narratives in the spiritual sense.[124]

In sum, we are not stuck between biblical literalism and the collapse of biblical truth. Scripture communicates its judgments of truth in a complex fashion, along lines that allow for the symbolism highlighted by the spiritual sense as well. Outside the cramped alternatives that Strauss provides us, there is a plentiful ground for Jesus' powerful words and deeds—including supernatural miracles.

---

123. See my discussion of inspiration and inerrancy in *Engaging the Doctrine of Revelation*, chapter 7; and see also Pidel, *Inspiration and Truth of Scripture*.

124. See also Gordon, *Divine Scripture in Human Understanding*. Gordon challenges "[t]he attempt to achieve the unity of Scripture through the employment of harmonizing strategies," which inevitably are grounded in "a specific set of expectations for Scripture" (242). We should not assume that we have gotten God's intentions in Scripture correct when we try to harmonize the issue of whether there was one Gadarene demoniac or two (Matt 8:28), or whether there were two demons or a vast number. When Jesus is making judgments of truth and revealing God to us in his teaching, parables, commissioning of the twelve, Last Supper, miracles, and so on, he does so with perfect authority and freedom in light of his intimate and perfect communion with his Father. But he does not need to clarify the Jewish people's understanding of exorcism and disease, no more than he needs to resolve questions regarding the authorship of the Pentateuch or how doctors should treat particular diseases.

ENGAGING THE DOCTRINE OF JESUS (AND MARY)

V. Craig Keener, Miracles, and the Virgin Mary

This chapter has sought to explicate and defend Jesus' working of real miracles. As a final step, let me examine how the Pentecostal biblical scholar Craig Keener turns the tables on Strauss by challenging the reasonableness of modern skepticism about God and miracles. Keener's two-volume work *Miracles: The Credibility of the New Testament Accounts* places biblical miracles in the context of the ongoing presence of miracles in the Church as the Spirit-filled inaugurated kingdom. Johnson gestures in this direction, but Keener supports this case with an astounding array of examples.

Let me begin with Luke 7:11–17, where Jesus raises from the dead the widow's son at Nain. To support the credibility of the miracle narratives about Jesus' raising the dead, Keener points out that "we have firsthand accounts of raisings" both in recent decades and in past centuries.[125] Irenaeus, for example, states in Book II of *Against the Heresies* that such miracles of raising (or resuscitation) occur regularly in the Church of his time. Augustine says the same in Book XXII of the *City of God*. Bede and Gregory the Great describe miraculous raisings from the dead. We have multiple attestations to the raising of the dead boy Roger of Conway in 1303. Numerous medieval witnesses attest to the raising of a dead girl through prayers to St. Thomas Cantilupe. John Wesley reported resuscitating a seemingly dead man. Various early twentieth century evangelists claimed to raise the dead, with corroborative evidence. Numerous early twentieth century Christians claimed that their dead infants had been raised by prayer. Katherine Taylor bore witness to the raising from the dead of her mother Elouise Jordan in 1949, through the prayers of the local African American bishop. There are many accounts of miraculous raisings in Africa. Keener describes contemporary examples with living eyewitnesses who include some of his own trusted friends.

As Keener documents, India has seen a number of miraculous raisings through the prayers of both Catholics and Protestants. He cites the historian Philip Jenkins's observation that China, too, has many such reports of the dead being raised.[126] Keener presents a typical example: "after an accident in 1992, Zhao Yu-e was pronounced dead on arrival at a hospital at 10 a.m. Despite ridicule, believers kept praying for her, and at 8 the next morning she recovered, leading to the hospital superintendent asking how to become a follower of Jesus."[127] Keener has interviewed subjects who have

---

125. Keener, *Miracles*, 1:538.
126. See Keener, *Miracles*, 1:567, citing Jenkins, *New Faces of Christianity*, 114.
127. Keener, *Miracles*, 1:567.

been raised through prayer and he argues that their testimony is credible. Keener's wife has a sister who was raised/resuscitated at age two through prayer, and Keener provides the testimony of his mother-in-law.

Keener also describes many other kinds of miracles purported to have been accomplished through intercessory prayer. As Keener knows, modern people are skeptical about such testimonies, not only because miracles normally do not happen in daily life but also because of the cultural dominance of materialist philosophy. He cites the example of the biblical scholar Walter Wink, who began as a firm skeptic about the Gospels' and Acts' miracle narratives, but who later changed his mind after hearing credible testimony to miracles that occurred through prayer.[128] Keener also cites his own experience: he was present when a woman unable to walk began to do so when commanded to rise in Jesus' name. As another example, he mentions that he prayed for a woman to be healed of a cyst and failed kidneys, and he was present when she was instantaneously healed.[129]

Keener remarks, "Roman Catholics have proved most careful about documenting healings, including medical testimony for many hundreds of cases in recent centuries."[130] He does not believe in the Virgin Mary's special intercession after Jesus' lifetime, although in his commentary on the Gospel of John, he states regarding Mary's intercession at the wedding at Cana in John 2:5: "Jesus' mother continues with the 'holy chutzpah' demonstrated in 2:3; in 2:5 she bids the servants to do whatever Jesus says, thus both recognizing Jesus' authority and demonstrating her expectation that he is going to do something . . . [D]espite her shortcomings, Jesus' mother ultimately functions as a model of faith."[131] While not adopting Catholic Mariology, Keener treats the miracles at Lourdes with respect. At Lourdes since Mary's appearance to Bernadette Soubirous in 1858, there have been seventy miracles confirmed by an extremely rigorous process. He examines cases of the healing of cancer, blindness, and paralysis. For instance, there is credible reason to suppose that "a paralyzed and nearly blind man was instantly, permanently, and unexpectedly cured on May 1, 1970."[132] In addition to the ecclesiastically confirmed miracles at Lourdes, there have been numerous healings there that also have credibility in Keener's view.

---

128. See Keener, *Miracles*, 1:103, citing Wink, "Our Stories, Cosmic Stories, and the Biblical Story."

129. See Keener, *Miracles*, 2:752.

130. Keener, *Miracles*, 2:713.

131. Keener, *Gospel of John*, 1:509.

132. Keener, *Miracles*, 2:683. Keener draws upon various sources, including Nichols, "Miracles in Science and Theology."

Skepticism about miracles remains difficult to dislodge. As Keener recognizes, doctors who are philosophical materialists are generally likely to refuse to grant any causal association between praying and the occurrence of a naturally inexplicable healing. Therefore, we need to factor in the power of this skeptical bias when dealing with miracle narratives. Keener states, "while faith is often assumed to be a controlling bias, academic skepticism can also be a controlling and even coercive bias."[133]

Not only does human experience over the centuries indicate strongly that miracles take place, but also it indicates that these miracles take place through people praying. In prayer, people intercede for the good of others. The book of Revelation presents the blessed dead as alive and praying for the consummation of the kingdom and in a state of rest and joy (Rev 6:9–11). Just as we ask our friends to pray for particular persons who are experiencing trials, so we can ask the blessed who are "at home with the Lord" (2 Cor 5:8) to pray for these persons. In making this request, we are asking the blessed to intercede with the Lord.

Let me now draw a Marian conclusion. Mary has an ongoing intercessory role, since her intimacy with her Son does not come to an end. It is an intimacy based not merely on blood, but on the grace by which God made her the most blessed woman ever to live (Luke 1:28, 42).[134] Mary possesses a spiritual motherhood of all believers, in light of Jesus' symbolically rich words to her at the cross: "When Jesus saw his mother, and the disciple whom he loved standing near, he said to his mother, 'Woman, behold, your son!' Then he said to the disciple, 'Behold, your mother!'" (John 19:26–27). Given the profundity of our union with Jesus in his Mystical Body, believers are Jesus' adopted brothers and sisters, sharing the same divine Father and even sharing the same mother.[135] As our mother, Mary intercedes for us.

Some Catholic theologians have employed exaggerated language about Mary. An example is found in the 1955 textbook in which Joseph de Aldama observes, "Theologians dispute whether Mary can be said to be a

---

133. Keener, *Miracles*, 2:688.

134. For a contrasting view, see Brown et al., *Mary in the New Testament*, 135–37. The authors recall Judges 5:24, "Blessed be Jael among women"; and Judith 13:18, "O daughter [Judith], you are blessed by the Most High God above all women on earth." The authors then comment, "On the one hand, such a blessing invoked upon Mary recognizes that God has employed her in His plan of salvation; on the other hand, the fact that such a blessing has been invoked upon others prevents us from taking it too absolutely, as if it meant that Mary was the most blessed woman who had ever lived" (*Mary in the New Testament*, 136). But, given that Luke (and, according to Luke, also Elizabeth and John the Baptist) knows that Mary is the mother of the Messiah and Lord, why would he not portray her as the most blessed woman ever to live?

135. See Moloney, *Gospel of John*, 503–4.

complement of the Trinity, as if Mary, by her maternity, contributed something to the Holy Trinity. Indeed, given the imperfection of the term, which can be understood badly, it is still true that Mary was the reason why new relations *ad extra* were added to the Divine Persons."[136] De Aldama is correct to say that the phrase "complement of the Trinity" can easily be misunderstood, but he thinks that, strictly speaking, the phrase is true because her *fiat* is the reason for new relations *ad extra*. While I agree that Mary enjoys an intimacy with the Trinity, the title "complement of the Trinity" should be ruled out; no mere creature can be a "complement" of the Creator. Just prior to the passage I have quoted, de Aldama cautions against calling Mary "the Spouse of the Holy Spirit," even though this title can be understood in an orthodox way and has been employed by various saints and popes.[137]

---

136. de Aldama, "Treatise 2," 422.

137. For the same caution, see Bouyer, *Seat of Wisdom*, 179. As Robert Fastiggi pointed out to me, these include Francis of Assisi, Pope Leo XIII, Pope Pius XII, and most recently Pope John Paul II. When describing Mary as the "spouse of the Holy Spirit," Thomas Joseph White, OP, takes care to observe, "There is no real likeness to the hypostatic union in the life of the Virgin, as it pertains to the activity of the Holy Spirit. She is just as conformed to the Father and the Son as she is to the Holy Spirit, and she is no more one with the Holy Spirit than she is one with the Father and the Son" (White, "Mariology and the Sense of Mystery," 231–32). White notes that he is here arguing against Boff, *Maternal Face of God*. I should note that Bouyer argues, in my view unpersuasively, that Mary's motherhood reflects an intra-Trinitarian (nonsexual) "femininity" of the Spirit, just as in Hebrew the word for "Spirit" is feminine. He is indebted to Sergius Bulgakov and Matthias Joseph Scheeben. In his "Introduction" to Bulgakov's 1927 work *Burning Bush*, Thomas Allan Smith comments that Bulgakov relies upon "the notion, now regarded as outmoded, that the feminine principle is passive and receptive—both in the relations of husband and wife and in the conceptualization of Sophia herself. Here too Bulgakov remains very close to the thinking of Scheeben concerning the feminine principle" (Smith, "Introduction," xxiv). See Bulgakov, *Burning Bush*, 82–83: "*in His human nature* His male principle is joined inseparably with the female principle of the Mother of God, and the fullness of the Divine image in humankind, or to put it another way, of the human image in God, is expressed through these two, through 'the new Adam' and 'the new Eve.'" Bulgakov goes on to relate these two "principles" to the Trinitarian processions, with the Holy Spirit connected with the feminine principle. With regard to Mary's perfect feminine receptivity, see Scheeben, *Handbook of Catholic Dogmatics* 5.2, 419. Balthasar argues correctly that Mary's "fruitfulness is not a primary fruitfulness: it is an answering fruitfulness, designed to receive man's fruitfulness (which, in itself, is helpless) and bring it to its 'fullness' . . . This yields an analogy for the relationship between God and the creature. We have already indicated that the creature can only be secondary, responsive, 'feminine' vis-à-vis God . . . Insofar as every creature—be it male or female in the natural order—is originally the fruit of the primary, absolute, self-giving divine love, there is a clear analogy to the female principle in the world" (Balthasar, *Theo-Drama* 3:285, 287).

De Aldama also rightly remarks that Mary can be called "Daughter of the Father" but not "Spouse of the Father."[138]

For de Aldama, it is a matter of course that because Mary is the mother of Jesus, she is the mother of his Mystical Body. Mary participates spiritually in the incarnation through her *fiat*, and Mary participates spiritually in the cross through her prayerful presence beneath it. Unceasingly, Mary prays that the human race be united to Christ's redemptive cross and thereby become part of her Son's body. De Aldama also directs attention to the symbolic connections between Christ and Mary/Israel/Church in Revelation 12.[139] When Revelation 12 describes Mary/Israel/Church by stating that "she was with child and she cried out in her pangs of birth" (Rev 12:2), de Aldama suggests these birth pangs are ongoing, as Mary prays for the birthing of the entire Mystical Body of believers in Christ.

According to de Aldama, Mary is Mediatrix because "she brings to men the things that pertain to God and she brings the things that pertain to men to God."[140] She brings to humankind the Son of God, her Son Jesus

---

138. De Aldama, "Treatise 2," 421. For Alphonsus de Liguori's response to Louis Muratori (who wrote under the name Pritanius)—specifically to passages where Muratori charged Alphonsus with making exaggerated statements about Mary—see St. Alphonsus de Liguori, *Glories of Mary*, 684–94. The debated issue was whether it is appropriate to say that "Mary commands in heaven" and that "no grace comes to us from God otherwise than through the hands of Mary" (685). To my mind, although these statements can with enough explanation be rendered reasonable, their plain sense tends to put Mary at the center, whereas only Christ and God are truly at the center. Mary does not command in heaven except insofar as she follows the command of the Lord; Mary no more commands than does a subordinate who, in commanding, obeys and communicates the command of his or her superior. St. Alphonsus has chapters on Mary as "Our Help" and "Our Mediatress" and "Our Advocate," but he exaggerates when he titles a chapter to "Mary, Our Salvation" although his meaning is that Mary leads us to Christ. For discussion of John Henry Newman's helpful response to Marian exaggerations (including by saints), see my *Newman on Doctrinal Corruption*, chapter 4.

139. See also Andrei A. Orlov's argument, regarding Revelation 12 and the complex background to its symbolism: "it is noteworthy that the dragon's exile to the earth coincides in Revelation 12 with the wilderness motif, since upon his exile to earth the dragon pursues the woman clothed with the sun in the desert . . . This is relevant for our study of the imagery of the scapegoat, whose exile in the wilderness represents an important topological marker in many apocalyptic Yom Kippur accounts" (Orlov, *Demons of Change*, 114). To my mind, Orlov is on the wrong track here but his effort to read the New Testament in light of Second Temple Jewish texts is influential and worthy of attention.

140. De Aldama, "Treatise 2," 436. For a contemporary discussion of Mary as Mediatrix, see Nichols, *There Is No Rose*, chapter 6. He brings out the fact that at Vatican II, "the Byzantine rite Catholic bishop Vladimir Malanczuk was instrumental in ensuring that the term 'mediatrix' should be retained in the schema . . . He did so on the ground that the idea of Mary's mediation—in Greek, *mesiteia*—accentuated by specifications that bring out its preeminence and universality when compared with the intercessory

Christ. Christ is the one Mediator because his mediation alone is "necessary and sufficient"; Mary's mediation is willed by God but only as "a mediation participated and subordinate to the mediation of Christ."[141] Pope Leo XIII, in his encyclical *Fidentum Piumque*, likewise portrays Mary as Mediatrix. He explains, "Undoubtedly the name and attributes of the absolute Mediator belong to no other than to Christ, for being one person, and yet both man and God, he restored the human race to the heavenly Father [cf. 1 Tim 2:5] ... And yet, as the Angelic Doctor [Aquinas] teaches, there is no reason why certain others should not be called in a certain way mediators."[142] For example, pastors mediate Christ to the congregation when they proclaim the Scriptures. Far more is this the case for Mary, who gave birth to Jesus Christ for the whole world. De Aldama comments that Mary's mediation is "distinct from the common mediation of the Saints, because it is based on Her maternity, on the special work she contributed to the reconciliation of men, on her association with Christ the Mediator which she accepted from Him, in a moral communion of sufferings and sorrows."[143]

---

activity of other saints, was essential to the integrity of the Oriental tradition ... [H]e was also right to draw attention to the deplorable impression which would have been made on the Eastern Orthodox and other separated Orientals by any refusal of the Second Vatican Council to confirm the legitimacy of the term 'mediatrix' (parallel to its refusal to sanction 'co-redemptrix'). We are sometimes given the impression that all ecumenical dialogues are convergent, such that advance on one front is necessarily advance on all. To the contrary, hard choices must sometimes be made because advance in one direction can well mean regress in another. There can be no question that the major theologians of Byzantine Orthodoxy after the schism with Rome did indeed both preserve and develop a doctrine of Marian mediation of graces" (122–23).

141. De Aldama, "Treatise 2," 436.

142. Pope Leo XIII, *Fidentum Piumque*, in *Acta Sanctae Sedis* 29, 206, cited in de Aldama, "Treatise 2," 437. See https://www.vatican.va/content/leo-xiii/en/encyclicals/documents/hf_l-xiii_enc_20091896_fidentem-piumque-animum.html.

143. De Aldama, "Treatise 2," 438. I concur with Thomas Joseph White, OP, when he remarks that Mary's "cooperation in the mystery of the cross is active, exemplified by her faith, hope, and charity. She lives in union with her Son even in his moment of extraordinary suffering, torment, and eventual death, as well as in his burial and descent into hell. Because she lives in all of this with faith and hope, the Virgin Mary believes however obliquely that the action undertaken by her Son is redemptive; that is, the redemption of the universe is taking place in and through his life, ministry, and now his suffering and death, in an intentional way. She understands however obscurely in faith that what is transpiring is happening in view of the salvation and transformation of the world. Insofar as she bears the sorrow and unspeakable maternal suffering of being subject to this event herself in genuine and profound love for her Son, his mission, and his self-offering to the Father, so too she associates herself willingly in his offering and in his living act of atonement" (White, "Mariology and the Sense of Mystery," 224). White goes on to distinguish between Christ's condign merit and Mary's congruent merit. The latter "is wholly dependent upon and derived from that of Christ crucified,

Let me now return to Keener's observation that Mary, by interceding with Jesus on behalf of the wedding guests (who are symbolically all believers since Jesus has come to inaugurate the marriage of God and his people), "functions as a model of faith."[144] I note that she is a model of faith not only in her confidence that Jesus will act—a confidence shown in her command to the servants to "do whatever he tells you" (John 2:5)—but also in her work of intercession for the wedding guests. Every member of the faithful should be constantly praying to Jesus for the sake of the good of others (Matt 5:44). Paul tells the Colossians that he has never "ceased to pray for you, asking that you may be filled with the knowledge of his will in all spiritual wisdom and understanding" (Col 1:9); and he tells the Thessalonians that he is "constantly mentioning you in [his] prayers" (1 Thess 1:2).

Mary is a model of faith when she prays to her Son on our behalf. She models the practice of intercession—intercessory prayer to Jesus—and does so on behalf of all. In his encyclical *Redemptoris Mater*, Pope John Paul II draws out the broad significance of Mary's intercession at Cana. He remarks that because Mary's is a spiritual and not solely a bodily motherhood, it is marked by *"Mary's solicitude for human beings."*[145] When Mary prays for human needs, Mary serves (in accordance with her Son's will) to bring "those needs within the radius of Christ's messianic mission."[146] John Paul II explains further with respect to what Mary does at Cana in John 2:3–5, "[T]here is a mediation: Mary places herself between her Son and mankind in the reality of their wants, needs, and sufferings. *She puts herself 'in the middle'*, that is to say *she acts as a mediatrix not as an outsider, but in her position as mother."*[147]

Vatican II's Dogmatic Constitution on the Church, *Lumen Gentium*, includes a similar appreciation for Mary's maternal intercession. Much like

---

but it is also a first fruit of the Cross, the life of Christ made manifest and expressed in ecclesial fashion in the life of the Virgin Mary. Her merit and intercession at the Cross are of a maximal extension and intensity because they take place in the hour of the redemption of all human beings in the most perfect unity with Christ in the order of faith, hope, and love, in a human person in a perfection of creation grace ('full of grace'; Lk 1:28), and in a person without sin (characterized symbolically by the notion of the immaculate heart of Mary)" (225). For this distinction between the merit of Christ and the merit of Mary, see also Pope Pius XI, *Ad Diem Illum*, §14.

144. Keener, *Gospel of John*, 1:509.

145. John Paul II, *Redemptoris Mater* §21, 87. For discussion of John Paul II's Mariology, see Hauke, *Introduction to Mariology*, 101–4 and elsewhere.

146. John Paul II, *Redemptoris Mater* §21, 87.

147. John Paul II, *Redemptoris Mater* §21, 88.

Leo XIII and John Paul II, *Lumen Gentium* remarks, "In the words of the apostle there is but one mediator: 'for there is but one God and one mediator of God and men, the man Christ Jesus, who gave himself [as] a redemption for all' (1 Tim. 2:5-6) . . . Mary's function as mother of men in no way obscures or diminishes this unique mediation of Christ, but rather shows its power."[148] I note that in John's Gospel Jesus hardly was ignorant of the lack of wine at the wedding. In John's Gospel, Jesus knows all things. He surely intended to perform "the first of his signs" (John 2:11) at this wedding. Had he wanted to do the sign or miracle without Mary's intercession, he would have done so. Mary acts as the representative of the whole people of God, praying and beseeching the Lord to bestow the "wine" of the new covenant. She intercedes with confidence because her will is aligned with God's will, as shown by her complete trust in her Son (John 2:5). Mary's mediation does not obscure Jesus' salvific power, but rather directs attention to it. John Paul II states in this regard that "the episode at Cana in Galilee offers us *a sort of first announcement of Mary's mediation*, wholly oriented toward Christ and tending to the revelation of his salvific power."[149]

In sum, Jesus performs miracles as part of his eschatological mission of inaugurating the kingdom; but he also intends for his followers to intercede with him on behalf of others, which leads to postbiblical miracles. Keener is correct that when believers pray and beseech the Lord, the Lord works miracles even here and now. Miracles have not ceased; Christ the King still performs them as signs of his sovereignty. He often works through the prayers of his people, because his desires our participation and cooperation in his work of salvation. In the Gospel of John, Mary is the model believer and the mother of the Church because she asks her Son to bless his people and she is confident that he will do so. As *Lumen Gentium* puts it, "This motherhood of Mary in the order of grace continues uninterruptedly from the consent which she loyally gave at the Annunciation and which she sustained without wavering beneath the cross, until the eternal fulfilment of all the elect . . . By her maternal charity, she cares for the brethren of her Son, who still journey on earth."[150]

148. Vatican Council II, *Lumen Gentium* §60, 418.
149. John Paul II, *Redemptoris Mater* §22, 89.
150. Vatican Council II, *Lumen Gentium* §62, 418-19. *Lumen Gentium* continues, "Therefore the Blessed Virgin is invoked by the Church under the titles of Advocate, Helper, Benefactress, and Mediatrix. This, however, is so understood that it neither takes away anything from nor adds anything to the dignity and efficacy of Christ the one Mediator. No creature could ever be counted along with the Incarnate Word and Redeemer; but just as the priesthood of Christ is shared in various ways both by his ministers and the faithful, and as the one goodness of God is radiated in different ways among his creatures, so also the unique mediation of the Redeemer does not exclude

Mary's maternity vis-à-vis Christ's Body means that her mediation differs in scope from that of any other saint. Aidan Nichols emphasizes that "Marian mediation cannot be understood by reference simply to the mode of operation of the communion of saints generally conceived. There is a distinguishing factor which makes her role in the communication of the fruits of the objective redemption more specific—indeed, unique."[151] The distinguishing factor is Mary's unique motherhood of her Son. This has led to some exaggerations, as Nichols shows by citing the efforts of Marie-Joseph Nicolas to curtail them.[152] Among them was the claim that Mary, like Christ, has a *right* to be heard in her intercessory prayer. Nichols also rejects the claim that Mary mediates all *sacramental* graces.[153]

but rather gives rise to a manifold cooperation which is but a sharing in this one source. The Church does not hesitate to profess this subordinate role of Mary, which it constantly experiences and recommends to the heartfelt attention of the faithful, so that encouraged by this maternal help they may the more closely adhere to the Mediator and Redeemer" (*Lumen Gentium* §62, 419).

151. Nichols, *There Is No Rose*, 124.

152. See also, on the "hypostatic order" to which Mary and Joseph belong because their Son is the Son of the Father, Nichols, *There Is No Rose*, 42–43. In rejecting certain Mariological excesses associated with the hypostatic order, Nichols draws upon Nicolas, *On the Incarnation and Redemption*, §447.

153. Here he concurs with the neo-scholastic theologian Edouard Druwé. Nichols states, "Speaking of sacraments brings me to what is probably the chief qualification a sane account of Marian mediation ought to include. The formula 'mediatrix of all graces' reads as though it ought to include sacramental graces as well, but the identity of sacramental acts as acts of the incarnate Word who, in his human nature, is our great High Priest militates against a Marian moment in sacramental engracing *as such*" (*There Is No Rose*, 127). See Druwé, "Mediation universelle de Marie." Nichols also cites, from the same volume, Marie-Joseph Nicolas, OP, "Essai de synthèse mariale." He goes on to observe: "scholastically trained theologians working in a christo-typical idiom in French Catholicism of this period drew back from the assertion that sacramental graces—as distinct from 'providential arrangements' and 'actual' graces—are given through the mediation of Mary. By contrast, [Otto] Semmelroth has absolutely no difficulty at all with the claim that grace in every mode, including the sacramental, is communicated through our Lady. This is because he understands Mary to be, as the primal church, the total recipient, in a single all-encompassing act of acceptance, of all the spiritual good the Savior has to give to the world" (*There Is No Rose*, 146, with reference to Semmelroth, *Mary, Archetype of the Church*. Robert Fastiggi has proposed to me in email correspondence that Mary as the mother of Christ (and therefore the mother of the man who suffered bodily on the Cross for our salvation) can be said to have a remote mediating relation to sacramental grace insofar as it flows from the paschal mystery. Fastiggi pointed me to Pope Benedict XVI's May 11, 2007 homily at Campo de Marte, São Paulo (Brazil) for the canonization of Frei Antônio Sant'Ana Galvão, where Benedict XVI states, "Mary, Mother of God and our Mother, stands particularly close to us at this moment. Frei Galvão prophetically affirmed the truth of the *Immaculate Conception*. She, the *Tota Pulchra*, the Virgin Most Pure, who conceived in her womb the Redeemer of mankind and was preserved from all stain of original sin,

Regarding the fruits of Mary's intercession, Maximus the Confessor imagines the bridegroom and bride at the wedding at Cana as so amazed by the miracle that they drop everything and follow Jesus. He interprets the exchange between Mary and Jesus as exhibiting Mary's humility and confidence in Jesus, and Jesus' humility and love for Mary. According to Maximus, Jesus does not wish to go around exercising divine powers, if such powers distract people from his "hour"—his saving cross. But Jesus fulfills Mary's request both out of love for her and because the time had come to begin to reveal "the power of his divinity."[154] Maximus emphasizes Mary's desire to see her Son manifest himself and his goodness to the world, since "she knew that he was the creator of all things."[155]

From a complementary perspective, Alphonsus de Liguori interprets Mary's intercessory role in the miracle at Cana as exhibiting her love and compassion for those who are in need. Running out of wine would be a great humiliation at a wedding banquet, and so Mary responds to the neediness of those whom she loves by interceding with her Son. Alphonsus comments that at Cana "the compassionate Mother saw the embarrassment in which the bride and bridegroom were, and that they were quite ashamed on seeing the wine fail; and therefore . . . she begged her Son to console them simply by laying their distress before him: *they have no wine* [John 2:3]."[156]

In sum, Mary at Cana plays a role in Jesus' paradigmatic working of a miracle—a sign of the inauguration of the kingdom of God. Jesus' miracles, which continue today through the prayers of believers on earth and in heaven, have an important place in confirming Jesus' teaching about the kingdom. Mary's intercessory prayer for the members of his inaugurated kingdom has always been and continues to be unique in its richness. As Gregory Palamas says, "It is fitting that she, who held Him Who fills all things and is above all things, should herself outstrip all, and become higher than all in her virtues and great honour."[157]

---

wishes to be the definitive seal of our encounter with God our Savior. There is no fruit of grace in the history of salvation that does not have as its necessary instrument the mediation of Our Lady."

154. Maximus the Confessor, *Life of the Virgin*, 96.

155. Maximus the Confessor, *Life of the Virgin*, 96.

156. Alphonsus de Liguori, *Glories of Mary*, 135. For valuable background to the Mariology of Liguori's era, see Fastiggi, "Mariology in the Counter Reformation."

157. Gregory Palamas, *Mary the Mother of God*, 74. For background, see Kappes, "Doctrine of the *Theotokos* in Gregorios Palamas"; and, more broadly, Gambero, *Fede e devozione mariana nell'Impero Bizantino*; and Kappes, *Immaculate Conception*.

VI. Conclusion

In bringing this chapter to a close, let me recall the context of Jesus' greatest miracle, his transfiguration.[158] According to the Gospels, this miracle took place immediately after Jesus informed his disciples about his coming passion and told his disciples that they, too, would have to follow the path of the cross.[159] Aquinas states about the miracle of the transfiguration, "Now in order that anyone go straight along a road, he must have some knowledge of the end . . . Above all is this necessary when hard and rough is the road, heavy the going, but delightful the end."[160] Jesus' miracle of transfiguration has the purpose of strengthening his disciples for the path of the cross, by revealing the glorious "end" of this path. If the miracle of the transfiguration has this purpose, then so do the other miracles done by Jesus. They demonstrate that Jesus' preaching is true: he has indeed inaugurated the kingdom of God by his divine authority. The miracles are eschatological signs of the inbreaking of true life and true power. They are publicly revealed signs of Jesus' conquest of the enemies of God, that is, sin and death as the result of slavery to Satan.

At the same time, because Jesus achieves this conquest by the power of self-sacrificial love, all his miracles must be understood in the sober light of his cross. As Jesus explains in preparation for the miracle of the transfiguration, "If any man would come after me, let him deny himself and take up his cross and follow me. For whoever would save his life will lose it, and whoever loses his life for my sake will find it" (Matt 16:24-25). In the midst of suffering and tribulation, miracles make clear that the self-sacrificial love of Christ is eschatological power and "this power can already be experienced as present."[161] The thirteenth-century Orthodox theologian Nikephoros Choumnos begins his reflection on the miracle of the transfiguration by saying that this miracle makes a person wish "to reach out and seize his own cross, as it were . . . and to lift it on his shoulders and follow Christ himself, as he encourages us to do."[162] Choumnos exhorts his readers to

---

158. For historical-critical background, see Heil, *Transfiguration of Jesus*.

159. Philippians 2:6-11 is relevant here, including Jesus' exaltation. See, for a variety of exegetical and theological perspectives, Hurtado, *How on Earth Did Jesus Become a God?*, chapter 4; Burnett, *Christ's Enthronement at God's Right Hand*, chapter 5; Sonderegger, "Christ," 73-77; and Emery, "Kenosis, Christ, and the Trinity in Thomas Aquinas." For Christ as the new Adam, see Crowe, *Last Adam*; and Reardon, *Reclaiming the Atonement*, 144-56.

160. Aquinas, *Summa theologiae* III, q. 45, a. 1.

161. Feldmeier and Spieckermann, *God Becoming Human*, 370.

162. Choumnos, "On the Holy Transfiguration of Christ," 297.

pattern their lives on the ascent of the disciples up Mount Tabor, so as even now to contemplate the glorious Christ and to shine with the reflection of the divine glory through virtuous and deified hearts and minds. Even in the midst of tribulation, we can join Christ who exorcises the demoniac and frees him from a life of self-mutilation among the tombs. United to Christ in the power of his inaugurated kingdom, we can dare to live as the good Samaritan does, spending our strength in care and compassion even for our enemies when they are in need.

To my mind, it is evident that Jesus, the divine Messiah, did not enter into a world that is a set of locked immanent causes, as imagined by Strauss, foolishly denying God's existence.[163] Rather, Jesus came "to his own home" (John 1:11), because "all things were made through him" and "in him was life" (John 1:3–4).[164] Strauss's worldview is unreasonable; the cosmos has a Creator. This Creator is Love and has revealed himself in a personal and covenantal way among his people Israel, so as to heal and deify his creation, as shown by Jesus' miraculous signs.[165] With the Virgin

163. See my *Proofs of God*.

164. For background, see Klink, "Light of the World," 74–89; Miller, *Salvation History in the Prologue of John*.

165. On the basis of the Old and New Testaments, read in faith with a historical-critical eye, the biblical scholars Feldmeier and Spieckermann argue for the following thesis: "Becoming human is the definitive deed of love on the part of the God who created in his creation, and especially in his most beloved creature, the human being who is God's likeness, the vis-à-vis without which he does not wish to be God" (*God Becoming Human*, 367). Lest this understanding of salvation history as a love story sounds sentimentalized, they observe: "This history of love was not an edifying 'love story.' On the contrary, it is embedded in the history of the creature who is in love with himself, the creature who rebels against his creator and himself wants to be like God—and that is a history that unfolds according to very different laws. From the 'fall' and its lethal consequences onwards, via all the innumerable realizations of the fundamental conflict between the creator and his creature in the prehistory, then in the history of the people of God, and finally in the history of the Son of God, we see the bloody traces of the human arrogance that, according to the visions of the seer in the last book of the Christian Bible, continues until the end of days. Against this background, the biblical writings were interpreted as dramatic stations of a struggle for power between the creator's will to enter into relationship, a will that makes alive, and the deadly urge of the creature to choose the path of non-relationality vis-à-vis God and one's fellow creatures. This is an asymmetrical struggle, because love is a bond to the other, and it therefore cannot retaliate with similar measures. Love is always vulnerable, because it does not compel the other to do what one wants; and what is true of love among human beings is always true of the foundation and model of this love: God's love for human beings" (*God Becoming Human*, 367–68). While I admire their core argument, I think their rejection of ontology causes them difficulties, as when they say, "The theologoumenon of the incarnation affirms in mythical language that the history of the Lord of heaven and earth is inextricably woven into the history of the Galilean craftsman who apparently ended in failure on the cross" (368)—or when they argue earlier, "The human being

Mary at Cana, therefore, let us rejoice in Jesus' provision of the "good wine" (John 2:10) that symbolizes the marriage of the Bridegroom Messiah to his Bride the Church.

Jesus does not want to be like God but instead (as he tells the tempter) adores the Lord alone and serves him (Matt 4:10 par. Luke 4:8). It is precisely therein that he is 'the Son' who belongs wholly to 'the Father,' and the one through whom God becomes present for human beings" (271). These formulations are insufficient to convey a real incarnation with its wondrous divine presence.

Chapter 4

CROSS

I. Introduction

My argument in this chapter is that the Spirit-filled incarnate Son, having proclaimed the coming of the kingdom of God by word and deed, intentionally and freely chose to bear our sorrowful penalty for sin out of supreme love for us, uniting us everlastingly to the divine presence as the new-covenant fulfillment of Israel's sacrificial temple cult.

Elsewhere I have explored Christ's cross as a superabundant act of satisfaction.[1] The present chapter goes further by reflecting upon Christ's cross under the rubric of sacrifice—namely, the covenantal sacrifice that establishes the new covenant.[2] With Aidan Nichols and Matthias Joseph Scheeben, among many others, I propose that the concept of "sacrifice," interpreted in light of worship and offering, is "the key to the death of the Messiah as the congruent climax to his life."[3] As the new Abraham and new Isaac, Jesus obediently surrendered all that he had received, all that was most dear, out of love for God; and his sacrificial path brings about union

---

1. See my *Engaging the Doctrine of Creation*, chapter 7.

2. Both "sacrifice" and "satisfaction" have charity at their center. Since this is so, and since charity entails friendship with God ("founded on the communication of beatitude"), John Emery, OP, argues plausibly that "Christ's charity lends cohesiveness to the ensemble of his saving agency" (Emery, "Aquinas's Christology of Communication," 172). See also Reginald M. Lynch, OP's "Cajetan on Christ's Priestly Sacrifice," where Lynch shows that Aquinas (following Book X of Augustine's *City of God*) "argues that it is the charity of Christ's passion that displays this union between priest, victim, and recipient in a most acceptable way" (237). Lynch's concern, like Cajetan's, is to examine the relationship between the cross and the Eucharist.

3. Nichols, *Chalice of God*, 42.

with God and the forgiveness of sins.[4] Knowing himself to be the divine Messiah, Jesus offered his life as the perfect sacrifice to God in supreme love for the salvation of Israel and the whole world.

This claim makes sense in light of Jesus' Second Temple context and his actions at the Last Supper. N. T. Wright has remarked that if Jesus "believed that the kingdom was about to dawn, in other words that YHWH was about to inaugurate the new covenant, the end of exile, the forgiveness of sins, it becomes very likely that he would distinguish this meal from the ordinary Passover meal, while retaining enough of its form for the symbolism to be effective."[5] It is noteworthy here that, as Gary Anderson has shown, Second Temple Jews understood God's indwelling in the temple and the sacrificial service carried out in the temple as forming a unity.[6] Jesus' perfect sacrifice therefore aimed to secure the divine presence dwelling in his people, through the path of self-surrendering love to which the Old Testament also testifies. Jesus is the conquering "Lion of the tribe of Judah, the Root of David" precisely as the "Lamb standing, as though it had been slain" (Rev 5:5–6), and his sacrifice on the cross established the everlasting communion that is the new covenant.[7] In the words of Cyril

---

4. See Anderson, *That I May Dwell Among Them*, 228; and see also my *Reconfiguring Thomistic Christology*, chapter 3.

5. Wright, *Jesus and the Victory of God*, 557; see also Pitre, *Jesus and the Last Supper*. For a helpful theological summary of Jesus' understanding of his death—influenced heavily by Wright—see Egan, *Rethinking Catholic Theology*, 114–15. Emphasizing Jesus' self-surrendering obedience to the Father in love at all times in his life (a point affirmed by Karl Rahner and countless other theologians across the centuries), Egan goes so far as to argue that "Jesus Messiah not only offers sacrifice; he *is* sacrifice incarnate" (130). I understand what Egan means, but to my mind it is better to distinguish more firmly between the sacrifice of the Cross and the other self-sacrificial dimensions of Jesus' life. I agree with Egan, however, when he writes that "the Son's incarnation, conception, gestation, life, passion, crucifixion, descent into hell, resurrection, ascension, glorification, sending of his Spirit, sitting at the Father's right hand, and his person itself all express his loving obedience as the supreme glorification of God in the world *and in heaven* . . . The righteousness of God is revealed in the cross of Christ. The precious blood of the Son of God is the perfect *sacrifice* for sin. The ransom was paid to deliver captives. The gates of hell were stormed. The Red Sea was crossed and the enemy drowned. God's judgment has been executed upon sin. The kingdoms of the present evil age are passing away. Adam's disobedience is recapitulated in Jesus' obedience; a new creation has come into being" (131).

6. See Anderson, *That I May Dwell Among Them*.

7. For an account of Jesus' sacrificial death that retrieves Bernard Lonergan's "Law of the Cross" in the context of contemporary discussions, see Ryliškytė, *Why the Cross?*. For a historical and sociological study of sacrifice, see Stroumsa, *End of Sacrifice*; and see also the background provided by Heesterman, *Broken World of Sacrifice* and, more pertinent to my chapter, Martin Hengel's observation that "[t]he theme of expiation in the sense of 'purifying the land' from evil and disaster or of 'assuaging' the wrath

of Alexandria, Jesus "was, at it were, a sacrificial victim without blemish, offering himself up as a pleasing aroma to God the Father, slain like a kid on behalf of our sins."[8] The Catholic theologian Charles Journet sums up the point: Jesus "gave to his death on the cross the character of a definitive sacrificial offering."[9]

Admittedly, understanding Jesus' cross as the new covenant sacrifice can cause problems for Jewish-Christian relations, since it emphasizes Jesus' fulfillment of "the Jewish cultic system that revolved around animal offerings."[10] But such fulfillment is fundamental to Christology and to Jesus' own self-understanding as the divine Messiah. Christ has reconfigured the temple cult around himself, as the eschatological temple. But this point need not entail antipathy toward the temple cult, as has been demonstrated from a historical-critical perspective most recently by Michael Patrick Barber in his *The Historical Jesus and the Temple*.[11]

---

of the gods was part of the *lingua franca* of the religions of late antiquity ... In the Graeco-Roman world in particular, the theme of expiation was often connected with a human sacrifice ... The same figures keep on being mentioned in ancient literature for their sacrifices: by his voluntary sacrifice, Menoeceus atones for the ancient blood-guilt of Oedipus; the sacrifice of Iphigenia reconciles angry Artemis and opens up the way for the sack of Troy; the sacrifice of Polyxena appeases the spirit of Achilles and thus guarantees the safety of the victors' return" (Hengel, *Atonement*, 19). In *Engaging the Doctrine of Israel*, I address the work of René Girard on sacrifice, in light of the important critique offered by Jonathan Klawans. See (as a representative work) Girard, *I See Satan Fall Like Lightning*; and see Klawans, *Purity, Sacrifice, and the Temple*. For a helpful appreciation of Girard's theory, without ignoring the critiques, see Johnson, *God's Being in Reconciliation*. See also the background provided in Zachhuber, "Modern Discourse on Sacrifice and Its Theological Background"; as well as, in the same volume, Fiddes's "Sacrifice, Atonement, and Renewal." Fiddes argues that the solution is the expiation of sin through entering into our condition in love—a perspective in this respect much like that of Eleonore Stump: "Sin is an attitude of the creature towards the Creator, a lack of trust and a stance of rejection ... This means that we can only think of the 'expiation' of sin as the transforming of the sinner, or the changing of persons. The objective power of the cross of Jesus is to transform personalities, to enable them to recognize their relatedness to God and neighbour, and to renew that relation which already exists within the space God makes for creation within a triune life" (64). For a critique of Girard that supplements that of Klawans, see Frazier's "From Slaughtered Lambs to Dedicated Lives."

8. Cyril of Alexandria, *Glaphyra on the Pentateuch*, 2:36. Later, commenting on Exodus 24 and drawing out the christological meaning, Cyril observes that Christ "gave his life in exchange for the life of all, and ... offered up the flesh that he had assumed as a pleasing aroma. For he gave himself on our behalf as an offering that was holy and undefiled to God, a spiritual burnt offering" (110).

9. Journet, *L'Église du Verbe incarné*, 3:1447.

10. Moyaert, "Redemptive Suffering after the Shoah," 194.

11. See Barber, *Historical Jesus and the Temple*; and for further discussion see my *Engaging the Doctrine of Israel*. See also Freyne, *Jesus, a Jewish Galilean*, 167: "the

Not surprisingly, numerous contemporary biblical scholars maintain that Jesus intended to institute the new covenant and to constitute the eschatological temple by shedding his blood, bearing Israel's judgment and ending its alienation from the fullness of the divine presence.[12] Scot McKnight states in this vein, "When Jesus sat at table over that last supper and spoke of

---

Pauline theology of the cross was such a powerful influence in Christian theology and devotion in explaining the death of Jesus as an atoning sacrifice for the sins of the world (Rm. 3.21–31, 4.25, 5.1–11). Owing to this influence of later theology, the tendency has been ... to attribute to the historical Jesus a similar understanding of his death. This has had the effect not only that the charge of deicide could be levelled at Jews who are deemed to have murdered God's son, but [also] that the purpose of Jesus' life is viewed as having solely to do with his death." Seeking to displace Paul, Freyne argues that "Q" not only lacked a passion story but also considered that Jesus' death was simply the result of the persecution of a wisdom teacher, along the lines of Wisdom of Solomon 2. I disagree with Freyne's approach and with his claim that the Pauline theology of the cross need implicate the Jewish people as a whole any more than it implicates all other peoples. For Moyaert, the problem is ultimately the Jewish concept of the election of a particular people, signaling that others are non-elect. She remarks, "wrestling with the suffering servant made me realize that this song is susceptible to binary patterns of thinking, pitting us versus them. However consoling it may be that God is on your side and that the others are completely misjudging what is actually happening, it is, in all likelihood, not going to advance the process of restoring the relations between communities who understand their role in God's plan for salvation differently. Both Jewish and Christian commentaries on the suffering servant claim that there is only one beloved people, that the claim projected by the other is fraudulent, and that this will be revealed in the eschaton" ("Redemptive Suffering after the Shoah," 205). I think that the ongoing Jewish people remain God's beloved people and that this is manifested now and will be fully revealed in the eschaton. But I disagree that this means ridding our theologies of the doctrine of election and covenantal fulfillment; to make this move would itself be anti-Jewish and supersessionist. Moyaert attempts "a rethinking of how Christ's new covenant relates to the first covenant never revoked" (205), and she argues that we can conceive of Christ's cross as a "symbolic act" (209) like the symbolic act of the scapegoat. It is indeed a symbolic act (and Moyaert writes eloquently about it as such), but it is also more than this, unless one includes objective efficacy in one's understanding of "symbol." See also Kaminsky, *Yet I Loved Jacob*.

12. See Pitre, *Jesus and the Last Supper*; Pitre, *Jesus, the Tribulation, and the End of the Exile*. In *Jesus and the Last Supper*, Pitre comments (among many other insights in a similar direction) that the Septuagint text of Jeremiah 31:7–9 (Jer 38:7–9 LXX) "places the eschatological restoration of Israel and the establishment of the new covenant during Passover" (388). See also Richard B. Hays's observation that "Jesus and his first followers were Jews whose symbolic world was shaped by Israel's Scripture: their ways of interpreting the world and their hopes for God's saving action were fundamentally conditioned by the biblical stories of God's dealings with the people Israel ... Difficulties for contemporary Christian theology, however, arise wherever this acute awareness of narrative continuity with Israel's Scripture is lost—whether unwittingly forfeited or deliberately rejected" (Hays, *Echoes of Scripture in the Gospels*, 5). I hope to avoid such difficulties by focusing on the category of sacrifice, in light of Matthias Joseph Scheeben's reading of the cross as prefigured by the temple sacrifices, especially the burnt offering.

his blood as a *Pesah*-like event, it would only be a few furious months before his followers would see in that blood, as a result of their pneumatic life, the very reconstitution of God's new covenant with Israel."[13] Paul's letters reflect this perspective. In *Paul, a New Covenant Jew*, Brant Pitre, Michael Patrick Barber, and John Kincaid show that Paul's description of the Last Supper in 1 Corinthians 11:23-26 indicates that for Paul "*Christ's death was a covenant-making sacrifice* . . . [A]s has long been acknowledged, the pairing of 'blood' and covenant' evokes the covenant ratification ceremony described in Exodus 24."[14] Likewise, Harold Attridge has observed that for the Letter to the Hebrews, "Christ's death, traditionally interpreted as an atoning sacrifice, is seen in a new light as Yom Kippur becomes blended with Sinai as a covenant inaugurating event."[15] Attridge says the same about the Gospel of John. He states, "The place where God most manifestly dwells

---

13. McKnight, *Jesus and His Death*, 321. McKnight's repeated reference to Jesus' blood should remind us that, as Eugene F. Rogers Jr. points out—in a book that combines insight with eccentricity—"*The New Testament cites the blood of Christ . . . three times more often than his 'cross,' and five times more often than his 'death'*" (Rogers, *Blood Theology*, 65). Note that for McKnight, "*covenant* probably was not language used by Jesus at that last supper, but was instead language used soon after Pentecost" (339).

14. Pitre, Barber, and Kincaid, *Paul, a New Covenant Jew*, 229–30. The authors continue, "[T]he altar is to be taken as a symbol of God. Moses's act of placing the blood of the sacrifices on both the people and the altar thus symbolically demonstrates their covenant communion with God. With this echo in place, Paul depicts Christ's death as the sacrificial act that establishes the 'new' covenant promised in Jeremiah's famous oracle (cf. Jer 31:33)" (230). For the view that the Petrine circle was responsible for shifting the meaning of Jesus' words and deeds in this direction, see Chilton, *Feast of Meanings*, 86–89. Chilton argues, "The construal of the 'last supper' as a sacrifice of sharings with specifically covenantal meaning suited the practice of daily worship in the Temple together with fellowship at meals, the emblematic pattern of the Petrine circle in Jerusalem (see Acts 2:46, cf. v. 42). The dominical paradigm of the ordinary sacrifice of sharings, however implicit, ran the risk—if simply repeated by Jesus' followers—of being taken as a challenge to the regular practice of sacrificial offerings, which was how the authorities in the Temple had understood Jesus' own meals after his occupation of the outer court. The Petrine modulation of the paradigm to assimilate the meal of Jesus' followers to Exodus 24 enabled regular worship to proceed, while insisting upon the normative value of what Jesus had done" (*Feast of Meanings*, 88).

15. Attridge, "'Heard Because of His Reverence' (Heb 5:7)," 280. Attridge underscores "the requirement that blood is necessary for a covenant," and Jesus' action "accomplish[es] the spiritual cleansing and interior renewal" promised by Jeremiah 31 because Jesus is conformed to the will of God: "Interior and external, heavenly and earthly are united in the action of Christ. Because his sacrifice is made in the body it can, figuratively, cast a shadow (10:1). Less imagistically, it fulfills the requirement for establishing a lasting covenant relationship between human beings of 'blood and flesh' (2:14) and God. Yet because that bodily act is a unique act of conformity to God's will it is the sort of act that establishes the interior and effective covenant promised by Jeremiah" (280).

in Christ, the locus of the New Temple and its worship in spirit and truth, is . . . the cross."[16]

All can agree that the New Testament regularly employs sacrificial imagery for Jesus' death, but in my view the element of *covenant* sacrifice needs special highlighting. In his *Jesus the Sacrifice*, Scott Shauf emphasizes the significance of covenant sacrifice and Exodus 24 in the New Testament accounts of Christ's cross. He offers two reasons for interpreting the cross as the new covenant sacrifice, both of which are persuasive to me: "First, it is the most widespread interpretation of Jesus' death as a sacrifice in the New Testament, appearing in Matthew, Mark, Luke, several of the Pauline letters, 1 Peter, and Hebrews. Second, it is the only sacrificial interpretation of Jesus' death that is attributed to Jesus himself."[17] In fact, numerous New Testament texts treat Jesus as the eschatological Passover lamb, as exemplified by Paul's statement that "Christ, our Paschal Lamb, has been sacrificed" (1 Cor 5:7). James Prothro observes that "Paul . . . saw Christ's death as a new Passover and as a sacrifice like, though surpassing, those of the Levitical system."[18] Similarly, the Gospel of John attributes to John the

---

16. Attridge, "Cubist Principle in Johannine Imagery," 85. Attridge draws a connection here to Romans 6:3–4, and he makes reference to Koester, *Dwelling of God*.

17. Shauf, *Jesus the Sacrifice*, 116. Shauf expands upon the connection to the Old Testament: "the New Testament interpretations of Christ's death as a sacrifice cluster around three occasions in the life of Israel: the covenant sacrifice, Passover, and the Day of Atonement. These interpretations connected the story of Jesus and the early church to the story of Israel, forming the eschatological climax" (189). He points out that interpreting Jesus' death as a sacrifice—on the basis of Jesus' own words at the Last Supper—provided a solution to the question of why God allowed his Messiah to suffer a horrific death upon a Roman cross. He adds, "Even without Jesus's words . . . it is likely that the church would have arrived at this interpretation on its own. There was a long tradition in the Greco-Roman world of interpreting meaningful deaths with sacrificial language" (190). For a theology of the cross that emphasizes the Day of Atonement (and that therefore fits broadly within my emphasis on Jesus' death as a sacrifice, although along lines that I cannot explore in detail in this chapter), see Barry, *Jewish Temple Theology and the Mystery of the Cross*. Barry draws heavily upon Hans Urs von Balthasar's approach and upon the early Old Testament understanding of sin as a burden or a weight, and he concurs with Balthasar's view that sin is ontologically not simply a privation but can be borne by Jesus as "chaff." As Barry notes, I disagree with this claim. Barry's appreciation for Israel's temple theology and for the Akedah, and the exegetically detailed biblical theology he develops around these elements (with attention to Israel's sin and to the divine judgment of exile), enable him to make a distinctive and profound contribution, demonstrating the highly positive meaning of sacrifice and of the Day of Atonement. I treat the Akedah at length in my *Sacrifice and Community*.

18. Prothro, *Apostle Paul and His Letters*, 86. Prothro goes on to say, "Not unlike these sacrifices, the atoning benefit of Christ's death is received through identification with the Victim, whereby his life and death are made one's own. For Paul, this type

Baptist the proclamation that Jesus is "the Lamb of God, who takes away the sin of the world" (John 1:29).[19] Thus the Orthodox theologian Patrick Henry Reardon is on solid ground when he observes that "a concentrated study of Israel's ritual worship, particularly the significance of sacrifice, is of primary importance for a proper theological understanding of *what* was accomplished—and *how* it was accomplished—on the Cross."[20]

I will devote a substantial section of the present chapter to proposing an interpretation of John 19:25–27, a passage that in my view offers John's way of portraying the sacrificial sealing of the new covenant. According to my reading, in John 19:25–27 Mary and the beloved disciple stand at the foot of the cross as the new covenant community. They do so in accordance with the understanding of the new covenant found in Jeremiah 31 and Ezekiel 36 (see John 14:17; 16:7; 19:30), as well as in accordance with a nuptial understanding of the new covenant (see John 2). I propose that John also recognizes Jesus as the new Moses and the cross as the eschatological Sinai that accomplishes the sealing of the new covenant, requiring the presence not only of the covenant sacrifice but also of the faithful people.[21] On this view, Mary and the beloved disciple mirror the role played by the faithful people of God at the foot of Mount Sinai, where Moses sealed the covenant by placing half the sacrificial blood upon the people and half upon the altar. My argument, then, is that John 19 has a sacrificial and covenantal import (consummating the Mosaic covenant by Jesus' perfect sacrificial obedience, and, indeed, bringing God's whole plan to completion [John 19:30]) that has been illuminated, but not yet fully tapped, by recent studies of covenantal themes and patterns in the Gospel of John.[22] The goal of this section is to underline once more the integration of Christology and Mariology.

---

of union is mediated in baptism and endures in one's living faith and loyalty to God" (87). For Paul on the new covenant, in 2 Corinthians, see Prothro, *Apostle Paul and His Letters*, 136–37. For biblical and patristic passages that treat Christ's cross as a sacrifice (often the new covenant Passover sacrifice), see Smith, *Meaning of Jesus' Death*, 51–71.

19. For the Gospel of John on John the Baptist, see Coloe, "John as Witness and Friend."

20. Reardon, *Reclaiming the Atonement*, 24.

21. For Jesus as the new Moses (and thus an eschatologically greater Moses) in the Gospel of John, see especially Wayne Meeks, *Prophet-King*; T. Francis Glasson, *Moses in the Fourth Gospel*; and Marie-Émile Boismard, OP, *Moses or Jesus*.

22. For an exploration of the meaning of the death of Jesus in John's Gospel, showing that many Johannine scholars have significantly downplayed or rejected the view that John understands Jesus' death as sacrificial expiation, see Loader, *Jesus in John's Gospel*, especially his summation on 194–202. Loader concludes that for John, "the task to be completed through Jesus' suffering and death is not seen *primarily* as an expiatory or vicarious sacrifice" (202), but should instead be primarily understood as the climax of the revelation of divine love and of God's judgment upon sin. My argument does not

I will begin the chapter with two preliminary sections, the first addressing Eleonore Stump's critique of sacrificial atonement, and the second adding some further scriptural background regarding the themes of covenant, cross, and sacrifice. I then turn to John 19 with the aid of the biblical scholars Alexander Tsutserov, Rekha Chennattu, and especially Sherri Brown. Although it would take more work to demonstrate all the connections that I wish to make between Jesus' sacrificial shedding of his blood and the presence of Mary at the foot of the cross, I hope to indicate a fruitful path for further reflection on John's crucifixion scene. The fourth section draws out the implications of my overall perspective on the cross as the new covenant sacrifice, by retrieving Matthias Joseph Scheeben's theology of the cross. The final section of the chapter then explores Mary's participation in the cross according to Scheeben.

II. Concerns about a Salvific Bloody Sacrifice

Sacrifice has long been controversial, and in recent years it has become even more controversial as a way of understanding the cross of Jesus.[23] The

---

depend upon giving expiatory sacrifice primacy over love or judgment (and indeed I argue that love is the very heart of expiatory sacrifice, properly understood). I agree with D. Moody Smith that "several passages in the Gospel clearly allude to the primitive Christian interpretation of Jesus' death as a vicarious sacrifice" (Smith, *Theology of the Gospel of John*, 116). Although I hold that love is the core of sacrifice, it will be clear that I am sympathetic with the identification of the cross as an expiatory sacrifice in John's Gospel that is found in Frey, "'Theologia crucifixi' des Johannevangeliums."

23. See also Johnson, *Living Gospel*, 27. Johnson tells the story of meeting two theologically educated women who were repelled when he told them he was working on the topic of sacrifice. He recalls, "So I asked them what immediately came to mind when they heard the word 'sacrifice'. One replied, the slaughter of helpless animals; the other said, the oppression of women" (27). Johnson grants that "sacrifice" meant the slaughter of animals in Jesus' day, and he also grants that Christian preachers have oppressively used the rhetoric of sacrifice in calling upon women to maintain strict gender roles. He goes on to say, however, that the New Testament makes clear that Jesus' death is a "sacrifice." He observes in this regard, "Paul . . . speaks of Jesus' death in terms of the blood that was sprinkled on the 'mercy seat' on the Day of Atonement (Rom 3:25). John writes in his first letter that Jesus makes 'expiation through his blood' (1 John 1:7) and Peter likewise speaks of Jesus' death in terms of a sacrificial 'sprinkling of blood' (1 Pet 1:19)" (28). Johnson adds that "sacrifice" has (or should have) a deeply positive meaning even in modern culture, for example in the raising of children, despite its difficulty: "Authentic parenting is one long sacrificial act that does not end even when children grow up and move away. Even more than in the marriage relationship, parenting reveals the way that sacrifice at once diminishes our life as we knew it . . . while at the same time revealing to us larger and infinitely more fascinating forms of life . . . that are not other than our own life but an enlarged expression of our own life. Parents know experientially that the very process which makes them suffer also makes

Catholic thinker Eleonore Stump, for example, has recently critiqued the understanding of Christ's suffering and death as a sacrifice, at least insofar as "sacrifice" involves expiation for sins.[24] Her viewpoint is worth examining here, because it represents a widely shared contemporary concern about the traditional theology of the cross.

Stump understands the doctrine of satisfaction as follows: "From the point of view of the Anselmian interpretation, something beyond the repentance of sinful human beings is needed if God is to forego rejecting and punishing them, and this something else is the satisfaction made to God by Christ's passion and death . . . Christ pays the debt owed to God or bears the punishment God must mete out to sinners."[25] Rejecting this doctrine, Stump argues that it is more appropriate instead to focus on the fact that Christ on the cross opens his heart in sorrow, love, and mercy to all human beings. She proposes that Christ on the cross receives "within himself the psyches of all post-Fall persons," receiving their shame and guilt and embracing them with the love of God.[26] Christ makes satisfaction not in the sense of paying a penalty, but rather solely in the sense of making "an offer of union of love . . . to each human sufferer of the depredations of others."[27] Thus, for Stump "there is no question of Christ's satisfaction counting as a penalty for human sin or as a payment of debt owed to God," but instead "Christ's atonement *defeats* human evil, by weaving it into union in love with God in a way that removes guilt and shame from wrongdoers

---

them grow. What they give never comes back in the same form. But what they are given in return is a share in a depth of being created by the gifts of knowledge, love and care, that they have given, moment by moment, in the hurly-burly of family turmoil" (33). Note that Johnson's account of how salvation was wrought by Jesus is inadequate in my view: "More fundamental than words and deeds was the heart of the Saviour, his deepest orientation in the world, his most fundamental attitudes, in a word, the disposition of his freedom. Or, to put it another way, it was the *character* of Jesus the human person through which God brought salvation to all humans" (197).

24. For an effort—in part successful, but grounded in some exaggerations—to expand the notion of sacrifice by separating it from "atoning death" and emphasizing its metaphorical character, see Eberhart, *Sacrifice of Jesus*. See also Eberhart, *Kultmetaphorik und Christologie*.

25. Stump, *Atonement*, 101. She adds, "On this Anselmian approach to satisfaction, Christ's atonement constitutes satisfaction because it gives God something due to him; and the point of Christ's satisfaction is to provide a perfectly good God with this needed condition for pardoning human beings. It is true that God arranges for the condition to be met. But the point remains that God's forgiveness and acceptance of reconciliation depends on Christ's making satisfaction to God" (102). For further discussion of Anselm, along helpful lines (quite different from Stump's), see Sonderegger, "Anselmian Atonement."

26. Stump, *Atonement*, 363.

27. Stump, *Atonement*, 369.

and satisfies fully for the suffering of their victims if they will receive what Christ offers them."[28]

As will already be clear, I do not think such an account of Christ's cross suffices. For one thing, it cannot adequately interpret the biblical evidence. According to Mark, Christ gave his "life as a ransom for many" (Mark 10:45). James Dunn suggests that "ransom" here means service rather than being an allusion to Isaiah 53:10-11, but Dunn also thinks it likely that "Jesus spoke of his anticipated death in terms of a *covenant sacrifice*."[29] To my

---

28. Stump, *Atonement*, 371.

29. Dunn, *Jesus Remembered*, 816. Dunn adds, "rather than a sin offering"; but I think the two are unlikely to be mutually exclusive, given that the "long-promised covenant" involved the forgiveness of sins (816). For further discussion, see Pitre, *Jesus, the Tribulation, and the End of the Exile*, 382-455; Bolt, *Cross at a Distance*, 71-75; Barber, *Historical Jesus and the Temple*, 195-200. Pitre interprets Mark 10:45 in light of the restoration of Israel and the ingathering of the ten lost tribes (the end of the exile). He argues that Jesus had in view "the *restoration of Israel in a final Passover*" through the sacrificial offering of himself (bearing the eschatological tribulation or judgment for the sake of his people) in order to "atone for the sins of Israel, set in motion and New Exodus, and bring about the End of the Exile" (*Jesus, the Tribulation, and the End of the Exile*, 448). See also Wright, *Jesus and the Victory of God*, 591-92: "There was no such thing as a straightforward pre-Christian Jewish belief in an Isaianic 'servant of YHWH' who, perhaps as Messiah, would suffer and die to make atonement for Israel or for the world. But there was something else, which literally dozens of texts attest: a large-scale and widespread belief, to which Isaiah 40-55 made a substantial contribution, that Israel's present state of suffering was somehow held within the ongoing divine purpose; that in due time this period of woe would come to an end, with divine wrath falling instead on the pagan nations that had oppressed Israel (and perhaps on renegades within Israel herself); that the explanation for the present state of affairs had to do with Israel's own sin, for which either she, or in some cases her righteous representatives, was or were being punished; and that this suffering and punishment would therefore, somehow, hasten the moment when Israel's tribulation would be complete, when she would finally have been purified from her sin so that her exile could be undone at last . . . Jesus, therefore, was not offering an abstract atonement theology; he was identifying himself with the sufferings of Israel." This seems correct to me, and it also seems to me that (broadened to include, in some way, the sufferings of the whole world under the domination of sin and death) this is what "abstract" atonement theologies such as satisfaction, merit (love), and sacrifice are about. As the Messiah, Jesus is uniquely "Israel's representative" fulfilling "Israel's vocation" (596-97). Wright goes on to say, "Jesus intended that his death should in some sense function sacrificially . . . It is not going beyond the evidence . . . to suggest that Jesus saw his own approaching death in terms of the sacrificial cult. But his would not be one sacrifice among many. The controlling metaphor that he chose for his crucial symbol was not the Day of Atonement, but Passover: the one-off moment of freedom in Israel's past, now to be translated into the one-off moment which would inaugurate Israel's future" (604-5). See also Evans, "Aspects of Exile and Restoration," 292-93: "It is interesting to reflect on Jesus' use of traditions from Daniel, Zechariah, and especially Second Isaiah. All three of these books play a major role in Jesus' theology; and all three reflect periods of exile in the life and history of Israel . . . Jesus' utilization of these books, indeed his being informed

mind, the reference to Isaiah 53 and the suffering servant is clear enough. Certainly there is little doubt that Jesus, in the Gospel of Mark, "sees his death as representative" and "as somehow *vicarious and protecting*"; and Jesus at the Last Supper "suggested that he was the Passover victim whose blood would protect his followers from the imminent judgment."[30] As the Protestant biblical scholar Paul Williamson remarks, "Although the 'new covenant' is mentioned explicitly only in connection with the Last Supper, the Gospels are replete with associated ideas."[31] These covenantal ideas are

and shaped by them, is very revealing. It strongly suggests that Jesus identified himself and his mission with an oppressed Israel in need of redemption and that he himself was the agent of redemption. He was the Danielic 'son of "man' to whom kingdom and authority were entrusted. He was the humble Davidic king of Zechariah's vision who entered the Temple precincts and offered himself to the High Priest and took umbrage at Temple polity. And, of course, he was the eschatological herald of Second Isaiah who proclaimed the 'gospel' of God's reign and the new exodus. All of this suggests that, among other things, Jesus understood his message and ministry as the beginning of the end of Israel's exile."

30. McKnight, *Jesus and His Death*, 339. McKnight goes on to say, "Paul's theory of atonement is more than just a resolution of sin, guilt, and wrath problems. Instead, it is an *actual recreation and empowerment* (cf. 2 Cor 5:14–15). Paul's system is other than Anselm's, whose theory has dominated Christian thinking on the atonement. His system has a different logic: the problem is not how (in an academic, rational, philosophical system) one might cohere belief in an absolutely righteous and holy God who expresses wrath against human sinfulness with a simultaneous belief in forgiveness and reconciliation of human subjects . . . Instead, Paul's logic is the logic of death and life, Adam and Christ, flesh and Spirit, old and new covenant, sin and righteousness, and disobedience and obedience—to name but a few of Paul's possible tension points . . . It is Paul's indissoluble connection of death and resurrection that shatters the cultic and quantitative reductionism in Anselm's theory of the atonement" (349–50). McKnight is far more knowledgeable about Paul than about Anselm, and I think he has misconstrued Anselm's book by thinking of it in terms of traditional substitution theory (as distinct from satisfaction theory). For helpful and appreciative exegetical and theological discussion of "substitution," understood simply as "Jesus' death *for us and in our place*, repeatedly attested in the New Testament," see Rutledge, *Crucifixion*, chapter 11 (quotation from 466)—although Rutledge agrees with McKnight's critique of Anselm. For Rutledge, "Anselm's rationalistic and scholastic way of arguing his case had tremendous influence, and it opened the way to subsequent trends in the interpretation of the cross that eventually led to unfortunate consequences," namely, in the penal substitution theory of late Reformed Scholasticism (*Crucifixion*, 481). As she says, "*rethinking* the substitution motif does not mean *eliminating* it"—and "a good deal of the opposition to the substitution motif is rooted in an aversion to its fundamental recognition of the rule of Sin and God's judgment upon it" (506). She favors Karl Barth's account of the Cross as the Judge (the incarnate Son Jesus) allowing himself to be judged in our place. In my view, Aquinas's satisfaction doctrine of the Cross, which emphasizes that Jesus bears our penalty (but not that God judges Jesus as guilty), is preferable.

31. Williamson, *Sealed with an Oath*, 183.

generally tied to sacrifice, and in this way "covenant is intrinsic to the definition of atonement."[32]

Of course, affirming that Jesus' cross sacrificially sealed the new covenant does not entail that God punished his innocent Son Jesus.[33] God did not punish Jesus; rather, Jesus freely atoned for us, establishing the new covenant and liberating us to dwell with God. Sin wounds our relationship with God and neighbor, and it separates us from the divine giver of life, thereby delivering us to well-deserved death. Jesus bore this penalty, as Aquinas underscores, with supreme sorrow for our sins and with supreme love.[34] The cross does not change God's love for us, but it does change our relationship to God. While God could have restored us without the satisfaction accomplished by Christ, God has deemed it better to restore us to justice by healing us from within our fallen condition.[35]

---

32. Treat, "Covenant," 434. Treat affirms both that "Christ's death must be understood as a covenantal sacrifice" and that Christ's death "ratifies the new covenant" (433). See also Treat, "Atonement and Covenant."

33. Shauf cautions against "a too-easy equation between sacrifice and atonement. Christians are accustomed to thinking of Jesus's death as a sacrifice solely in the sense of an atoning sacrifice, as achieving forgiveness of sins, without even being aware that sacrifice was more commonly performed for purposes other than atonement, especially for the purposes of communion and gift" (*Jesus the Sacrifice*, 195). On the other hand, Jesus' death "was atoning," although it "accomplished much more" as well (196). For the view that Jesus' death was not an atoning sacrifice (though it was a sacrifice), see Rillera, *Lamb of the Free*. Rillera is polemicizing against substitution theory, but the dimension of paying the penalty of sin (by undergoing death for us) needs more attention. For Rillera, "The consistent message throughout the entire NT is not that Jesus died instead of us; rather, it repeatedly indicates that Jesus dies ahead of us so that we can unite with him and be conformed to the image of his death" (*Lamb of the Free*, 274). Rillera works with a strict Old Testament definition of "atoning sacrifice," in which (for example) the Passover sacrifice does not fit. Where there is the imagery of atoning sacrifice, as in the Letter to the Hebrews, Rillera emphasizes that it "is not about Jesus dying 'instead of' us, but rather about Jesus's death and resurrection making it possible for us to pattern our own lives after him in union with his suffering and death and to participate in his resurrection. This is a participatory atonement (*kipper*) theology" (241).

34. See Aquinas, *Summa theologiae* III, q. 46, aa. 5–8.

35. See Aquinas, *Summa theologiae* III, q. 46, aa. 1–2. In q. 46, a. 2, ad 3, Aquinas states that if God "had willed to free man from sin without any satisfaction, He would not have acted against justice . . . But God has no one higher than Himself, for He is the sovereign and common good of the whole universe. Consequently, if He forgive sin, which has the formality of fault in that it is committed against Himself. He wrongs no one, just as anyone else, overlooking a personal trespass, without satisfaction, acts mercifully and not unjustly." The primacy of love in Aquinas's understanding of Christ's Cross is emphasized by many authors, among them Raith, "Thomas Aquinas's Pauline Theology of the Atonement." For a focus on Christ's bearing of all sins by sorrowing for them and by enduring the loss of God's presence that sin entails, see Cantalamessa, "He Was Pierced for Our Sins." See also Cantalamessa's "One Man Has Died for All!"

The Mennonite theologian Denny Weaver, however, denies that in any way "God's modus operandi presumes or depends upon violence," including the violence intrinsic to every bloody sacrifice.[36] For Weaver, therefore, Jesus is simply an innocent victim of Satan's incitement of Jesus' opponents to commit violence, so that in fact "the death [of Jesus] pays God nothing and is not Godward directed."[37] In my understanding of Jesus' sacrificial death, his death pays the penalty of sin for all human beings, as part of uniting us to the divine presence. This penalty is not a payment that God *needs* or that is necessarily required by some divine attribute. The penalty is not a punishment that God inflicts extrinsically upon us—let alone upon Jesus. Rather, the penalty is a debt that humans must pay in order to be healed of the injustice of sin not by divine fiat but from within the broken human condition, so as to share fully in divine worship.[38]

III. Sacrifice and the New Covenant: The Last Supper and Exodus 24

Let me now explore the relationship between sacrifice and the new covenant in detail, focusing on the Last Supper narratives and Exodus 24. In the Gospel of Luke, Jesus at the Last Supper takes the cup of wine after supper and proclaims, "This chalice which is poured out for you is the new covenant in my blood" (Luke 22:20).[39] Commenting on this passage, the Catholic

---

36. Weaver, "Narrative *Christus Victor*," 1. In the same edited volume (*Atonement and Violence*), Hans Boersma responds to Weaver by offering a condensed rendition of his *Violence, Hospitality, and the Cross*, with which I agree only in part: see Boersma, "Violence, the Cross, and Divine Intentionality." See also the book-length critique of sacrificial understandings of atonement by Finlan, *Problems with Atonement*. Representative of Finlan's viewpoint is the following passage: "Redemption-sacrificial doctrine perpetuates intense anxiety about a temperamental and judgmental God, firing a cycle of outbursts of rage or guilt, blame or self-blame. Superstition is a wolf that dons the sheep's clothing of 'selfless sacrifice' and 'innocent blood' and so enters into Christian theology and wreaks havoc in one generation after another. People learn to develop strategies of bargaining, appeasement, diversion, and payment through self-punishment and pain—each of which is manipulative. These strategies were played out in great detail in the Middle Ages in penances, self-flagellations, promises of building chapels, and other attempts at negotiation with God, none of which reflects the simple Gospel teaching that disciples should *trust* God who delights in giving every good thing to God's children (Matt 6:30–33; 7:7–11). This God need not be manipulated" (*Problems with Atonement*, 82). Finlan finds Weaver's approach commendable in certain ways, but Finlan deems that Weaver does not go far enough.
37. Weaver, "Narrative *Christus Victor*," 25.
38. For further background, see R. Jared Staudt, *Primacy of God*.
39. For historical-critical study of the words of institution of Luke 22, arguing for

biblical scholar Joseph Fitzmyer notes that Jesus' words of institution at the Last Supper are firmly tied to his cross. Fitzmyer remarks, "No matter what one would say about the character of the meal that the historical Jesus took with his disciples . . . the reference to Jesus' death and the connection with it of this reinterpreted Passover in the Lucan account is unmistakable."[40] Fitzmyer notes that Luke's description of the cup as "the new covenant in my blood" parallels Mark 14:24, where Jesus says, "This is my blood of the covenant, which is poured out for many." According to Fitzmyer, Jesus' words have in view Exodus 24:3-8, where Moses at Mount Sinai seals the covenant of God with the people of Israel.

The events of Exodus 24 are of central importance. After writing down all the Lord's commandments and explaining them to the people, who promised to obey, Moses constructed an altar at the base of Mount Sinai, with twelve pillars symbolizing Israel's twelve tribes. In sealing the covenant, Moses first offered animal sacrifices—burnt offerings and peace offerings—and then he took the sacrificial blood and spread half of it on the altar and half upon the people. He proclaimed to the people, "Behold the blood of the covenant which the Lord has made with you in accordance with these words" (Exod 24:8). Once the covenant had been sealed, Moses, along with the seventy elders and Aaron, Nadab, and Abihu, ascended Mount Sinai and "saw the God of Israel . . . [T]hey beheld God, and ate and drank" (Exod 24:10-11).[41] The covenant sacrifice was consummated through a meal in God's presence.

Fitzmyer perceives that Luke 22, like Mark 14, connects four realities: the cup at the Last Supper, the cross, the covenant sealed by Jesus' blood, and the covenant sealed through sacrificial blood by Moses at Mount Sinai. At the Last Supper, the twelve disciples stand in the place of the people of Israel at the base of Mount Sinai. Moses seals the covenant and gives the people of Israel a participation in the sacrificial blood; Jesus seals the covenant and gives his messianically reconfigured Israel a participation in his sacrificial blood.

In Fitzmyer's view, therefore, Luke 22 is likely referencing not only Exodus 24 but also the "new covenant" of Jeremiah 31:31. He states, "The

---

the likelihood that they go back to Jesus, see Bradly S. Billings, *Do This in Remembrance of Me*.

40. Fitzmyer, *Gospel According to Luke (X-XXIV)*, 1391. See also Pitre, *Jesus and the Last Supper*, 417-21, indebted to Fitzmyer.

41. For discussion of Nadab and Abihu's sin, for which they died, see Anderson, *That I May Dwell Among Them*, 128-39. Anderson remarks, "The lesson learned at the close of the Ark Narrative in Samuel applies here as well: 'Who is able to stand before the Lord, this holy God?' The implied answer: no one" (138).

allusion to the Sinai pact, when Moses sprinkled the blood of twelve sacrificed oxen, half of it on the altar representative of Yahweh and half of it on the people of the twelve tribes, as a conclusion of the covenant, is still clear . . . Because it is now a 'new covenant,' the pact is concluded not with the blood of sacrificed oxen, but 'with my blood.'"[42] The "new covenant" is the fulfillment of the covenant at Sinai. The covenant at Sinai promised to make Israel a holy people dwelling intimately with God, and Jesus is the one who accomplishes this through his cross. In Exodus 24 Moses pours half the sacrificial blood upon the altar as a symbol of Yahweh's presence. Similarly, Jesus embodies the Lord's presence in spilling his sacrificial blood on the cross. Moses pours the other half of the sacrificial blood upon the people of Israel at the base of the mountain (or at the foot of the altar of Yahweh's presence). Similarly, Jesus shares his sacrificial blood sacramentally with his disciples.[43]

In his commentary on Exodus 24, the Protestant biblical scholar Thomas Dozeman remarks, "The halving of blood and its sprinkling on both the altar and the participants repeats only in the ordination of the Aaronide priesthood in Lev 8:22–30 . . . The sprinkling of blood on the people may also be functioning as a form of purification for the covenant."[44] The fact that the covenant sacrifice involves sharing the sacrificial blood with the people, as part of their (priestly) purification, is important. Dozeman observes that the people's reception of the "blood of the covenant" prepares them to see "the glory of the Lord . . . on the top of the mountain" (Exod 24:17). He also points out that Zechariah 9:9–13 takes up "the theme of purification and theophany" by reference to "the blood of my [God's] covenant with you [Israel]"—a clear influence on the Last Supper accounts in the Synoptic Gospels and Paul.[45] Dozeman emphasizes the purifying di-

42. Fitzmyer, *Gospel According to Luke (X–XXIV)*, 1391.

43. For the arguments that "the historical Jesus' criticism of blood/animal sacrifice was muted into ambivalent and ambiguous prioritizations of 'mercy' over sacrifice" and that "[t]he New Testament does not preserve Jesus' rejection of blood sacrifice because its authors identified Jesus *as* a blood sacrifice," see Joseph, *Jesus and the Temple*, 244. For Joseph, "The Gospels narrated the events that led to Jesus' death in order to proclaim and defend the sacrificial interpretation of Jesus' death. In this process, the historical circumstances, characters, and conflicts that led to Jesus' death were re-imagined as part of a cosmic drama, with Pilate re-described as the reluctant governor and Caiaphas and 'the Jews' as bloodthirsty villains. The Gospels proclaimed the 'good news' of Jesus' atoning death and resurrection, but they also subordinated Jesus' teachings and example as a faithful witness (martyr) to the kingdom of God—the original referent of 'following Jesus'—to secondary status" (244). In my view, Joseph's reconstruction is mistaken.

44. Dozeman, *Commentary on Exodus*, 566, citing Milgrom, *Leviticus 1–16*, 528–29.

45. Dozeman, *Commentary on Exodus*, 566. More broadly—though focused on

mension of the blood in preparation for communion with God, but he also recognizes that "[t]he ritual may function as a way of sealing the covenant," which seems correct to me.[46]

In Matthew 26:27–28, as noted above, Jesus states, "Drink of it, all of you; for this is my blood of the covenant, which is poured out for many for the forgiveness of sins." The Catholic biblical scholar Leroy Huizenga summarizes the Gospel of Matthew's perspective: "Jesus, as willing priest but also victim, imitates God . . . by sacrificing himself, obediently and willingly, and, as a result, secures and also mediates the divine presence for those who would be part of his community."[47] The connection to Exodus 24 is made explicit by Richard Hays, reflecting upon Jesus' words of institution in Matthew 26. Hays first points out that the "blood of the covenant" echoes Exodus 24:8 along lines that suggest "strongly that Jesus' death is a sacrificial offering and that his blood signifies the sealing of a new covenantal relationship between God and the people."[48] He then notes the significance of the fact that Exodus 24:9–11 recounts a covenant meal in the divine presence: the twelve disciples stand in the place of the Israelites who ascend Mount Sinai after the sealing of the Mosaic covenant. Just as in Exodus 24:7 the people profess their obedience to God's commands, so also in the Gospel of Matthew the disciples are expected to obey God's and

---

the Gospel of Matthew—see Moss, *Zechariah Tradition and the Gospel of Matthew*. In chapter 7, she observes, "Both Exod 24.8 and Zech 9.11 have figured in scholarly studies of the 'cup saying' in Mark 14.24 and Matt 26.28. If Zech 9.11 itself is an allusion to Exodus 24, the emphasis in the prophetic context is different from the pentateuchal passage. Exod 23.3–8 describes the ceremony surrounding the giving of the law and the people's vow to obey God's commandments. In Zech 9.11–12, God remembers a covenant which was sealed by blood, and that is the basis upon which prisoners will be set free and recompensed double" (152–53; cf. 212).

46. Dozeman, *Commentary on Exodus*, 566.

47. Huizenga, *New Isaac*, 278. See also the discussion of Jesus as the new Isaac and priestly (sacrificial) Son in Perrin, *Jesus the Priest*, 67–79, 85–88. Perrin argues, "At his baptism, Jesus became aware of his role as one who, in the spirit of David, would reconstitute the temple (Psalm 2); at his baptism, too, Jesus began to reckon on the possibility that he would have to contribute somehow to the consecration of the same sanctuary (Genesis 22). There is no reason to doubt that Jesus saw both these aspects as falling under his identity as the priestly Son of God" (*Jesus the Priest*, 89). Anderson provides some important details regarding the relationship of Genesis 22 to Israel's understandings of sacrifice: see Anderson, *That I May Dwell Among Them*, chapters 8 and 10; and see also Crescas, *Light of the Lord (Or Hashem)*, upon which Anderson draws.

48. Hays, *Echoes of Scripture in the Gospels*, 134. Hays adds that there is also an echo of Zechariah 9:11's reference to "the blood of my covenant." Given that Matthew 21:5 quotes Zechariah 9:9, it is clear that Matthew "is fully cognizant of Zechariah's expectation for a messianic king who will 'command peace to the nations'" through an act of eschatological deliverance (*Echoes of Scripture in the Gospels*, 135).

Jesus' commands. In Hays's view, Jesus on the cross spills his blood upon himself (as the altar/divine presence) and upon his people, uniting God and Israel/Church through his sacrificial blood.[49] Just as the people of Israel bore witness to the sealing of the covenant at Sinai, so do the disciples at the Last Supper bear witness to the soon-to-take-place sealing of the eschatological new covenant on the cross.

The covenant at Sinai is the culmination of the people's exodus from Egyptian slavery, made possible by the blood of the Passover Lamb. Fitzmyer sheds light on the links between the Passover meal as described in Exodus 12 and the Last Supper meal. He remarks, "Among first-century Palestinian Jews the Passover meal was celebrated annually in Jerusalem as a re-presentation and a reliving of the experience of their ancestors described in Exod 12:3–14; Num 9:1–14; Deut 16:1–8 . . . It was a 'memorial' (*anamnēsis*) in a

---

49. Hays makes an important advance here with respect to Jewish-Christian dialogue. He states, "When the people say, 'His blood be on us and on our children!' they are responding to Pilate's hand-washing disclaimer of responsibility for 'this man's blood' (Matt 27:24–25). At the surface level of the narrative, they appear to be bluntly assuming bloodguilt on themselves. But at a deeper level, Matthew's narrative has already tapped into subterranean exegetical currents running the other way, currents that associate outpoured *blood* not with guilt but rather with cleansing, binding commitment, and liberation. If the people of Israel were originally brought into membership in the Mosaic covenant by having blood dashed upon them, and if Jesus has already (in private with twelve disciples who symbolize a restored Israel) declared that the new (or renewed) covenant is sealed by participation in his own blood—if these are the textual precursors of the scene before Pilate—what then can it mean for the people . . . to say, 'his blood be upon us'? They themselves, as characters in the unfolding narrative, certainly do not mean to place themselves under a covenant initiated by Jesus. But as readers we may wonder whether there is a deeper intentionality at work here, not the intentionality of the hostile, fickle crowd, but the intentionality of the God who has sent Jesus to the lost sheep of the house of Israel. If so, surely that intentionality is not to secure their eternal condemnation but rather to bring about the liberation promised by Zechariah and even earlier prefigured by that dreamlike banquet at the foot of Mount Sinai, where the elders of Israel beheld God standing on 'something like a pavement of sapphire stone, like the very heaven for clearness' (Exod 24:10). Perhaps that is the God who, contrary to the intention of the crowd that has been agitated and deceived by false shepherds, will see the blood of Jesus figuratively on the heads of the people of Israel and regard it as blood 'poured out for many for the forgiveness of sins'—that is, as a redeeming sign of the new covenant promised by Jeremiah, in which God will say, 'I will forgive their iniquity, and remember their sins no more' (Jer 31:34). If so, that would be the culmination of the promise foregrounded by Matthew in the very beginning of his Gospel: 'He will save his people from their sins' (Matt 1:21)" (Hays, *Echoes of Scripture in the Gospels*, 135–36). Rather than deeming the crowd to be "fickle," Michael Patrick Barber has remarked to me that the crowd that calls for Jesus' death is likely not comprised of the same people as were in the crowd that welcomed Jesus joyfully on Palm Sunday: the latter were likely Galileans, whereas the former were likely the aristocratic people who live in Jerusalem and were aligned with the high priests.

pregnant sense."⁵⁰ Jesus' command to his disciples at the Last Supper, "Do this in remembrance of me" (Luke 22:19), is a clear instruction regarding liturgical *anamnēsis*. Jesus is replacing the *anamnēsis* or liturgical remembrance of the Passover meal with the *anamnēsis* or liturgical remembrance of the Last Supper, thereby making present in the liturgical here-and-now the saving sacrifice by which the definitive liberation from slavery to sin and death took place.

Indeed, Brant Pitre has argued that Jesus, and not only (some of) the evangelists, understood himself to be establishing the eschatological new Passover as the new Passover Lamb. Pitre makes a strong case that "Jesus, by explicitly identifying the bread as his body, is . . . implicitly identifying himself with the sacrificial body of the Passover lamb."⁵¹ The Passover Lamb's blood brings about the protection and liberation of God's people, as demonstrated by the Passover meal which sustains the people on their new Exodus journey to dwell with God.

Inquiring into what Jesus meant by identifying the cup "as his blood and tying it to the establishment of a covenant," Pitre examines Jesus' status as the new Passover Lamb.⁵² First and foremost, Jesus' death is a cultic, Passover sacrifice. As the eschatological Lamb, his death brings about the eschatological Passover, accomplishing all that the original Passover sought to accomplish. Pitre recalls that the exodus from Egypt (made possible by the Passover) was ordered from the outset toward "offering the covenant sacrifice on Mount Sinai."⁵³ God intended the exodus to culminate in the sealing of God's covenant with his people.

Pitre remarks that in Zechariah 9:11, the phrase "blood of the covenant" also appears. In Zechariah, God connects this blood with liberation of his people from Sheol or the "waterless pit," that is, from the power of death. Zechariah prophesies an eschatological new Exodus, leading to everlasting life with God. Pitre concludes that at the Last Supper, "Jesus is

---

50. Fitzmyer, *Gospel According to Luke (X–XXIV)*, 1390. See also Barber, *Historical Jesus and the Temple*, 201, 203. While in general agreement with Fitzmyer, Barber shows that caution is needed regarding the specific resonances of *anamnēsis*, a word that is never actually used for Passover. In the LXX, the Greek word used in connection with the Paschal Lamb is *mnēmosynon*, not *anamnēsis* (Exod 12:14 LXX). In Barber's view, the word *anamnēsis* is nevertheless broadly linked to Israel's liturgical life (*Historical Jesus*, 201), and so it can be connected broadly to the Passover. The language is specifically evocative—especially but not exclusively in 1 Corinthians—of the bread of the presence traditions: see Barber, *Historical Jesus and the Temple*, 202–3; Pitre, Barber, and Kincaid, *Paul, A New Covenant Jew*, 232–35, building on Mary Douglas's work.

51. Pitre, *Jesus and the Last Supper*, 409.

52. Pitre, *Jesus and the Last Supper*, 412.

53. Pitre, *Jesus and the Last Supper*, 415.

performing a sign of the new Passover and the new covenant, the constitutive elements of a new exodus."[54] It is also worth noting, as Michael Barber (with Pitre and Kincaid) has done, that covenant-making sacrifices and sacrifices effecting atonement were edible. Arguably, Jesus identified the Eucharist not simply as the new Passover sacrifice but also as a covenant-making sacrifice and a sin offering.[55]

A final point will assist my transition to the Gospel of John. This point is what Anthony Giambrone—drawing especially upon the work of the Catholic biblical scholar John Paul Heil—describes as the "Johannine construction of Jesus as the new high priest."[56] The contrast between the high priest Caiaphas and Jesus plays a central role in this regard. In John 11:51–52, as Giambrone observes, the evangelist makes clear that "Caiaphas's entire priestly ministry is intimately bound to the atonement offering of Jesus"—and yet (as Jesus underscores many times, including in John 10:18) "in a more eminent way this high priestly offering is the work of Jesus himself. The laying down of his life is a free self-offering, not a sacrifice forced upon him."[57] The new covenant sacrifice is accomplished by the eschatological "great priest over the house of God," who has "offered

---

54. Pitre, *Jesus and the Last Supper*, 416. For another (complementary) angle on the new exodus, see Perrin, *Jesus the Priest*, 14: "Just as the trials (*peirasmoi*) of the exodus would be the means by which Israel, precisely as son of god (Exod. 4.22–23), would actualize its elect role as a 'kingdom of priests' (19.6); so too, Jesus' followers were to realize their sonship and priesthood through suffering." See also *Jesus the Priest*, 38, 52–53, drawing upon Davies, *Royal Priesthood*. Perrin sums up, "Much as the first exodus looked ahead to the establishment of the temple and the consequent reign of God (Exod. 15:17–18), this new exodus would likewise look forward to the inauguration of the eschatological temple and the uninterrupted reign of God ... Jesus' kingdom vision, like that of the prophets as a whole, revolved around the renewal of sacred space, populated by a new guild of priests, sustained by the Spirit and purged of idols. Yet for Jesus the path to this kingdom was to be paved by suffering" (*Jesus the Priest*, 143).

55. See Barber, *Historical Jesus and the Temple*, 197–98; Pitre, Barber, and Kincaid, *Paul, A New Covenant Jew*, 236–37.

56. Giambrone, *Bible and the Priesthood*, 176; see Heil, "Jesus as the Unique High Priest in the Gospel of John."

57. Giambrone, *Bible and the Priesthood*, 178. Giambrone adds, "For John, Jesus is at once the innocent Lamb and the Good Shepherd. He at once presides over the *aulē* and offers the great atonement sacrifice" (180). Elsewhere, Giambrone draws a connection to the Transfiguration, which he interprets as follows: "Jesus' experience on Mount Tabor is thus an exaltation in the Johannine sense—a simultaneous revelation of cross and heavenly glorification—for it is precisely as the glorified heavenly high priest that Christ must perfect his sacrificial journey to Jerusalem to die (Heb 7–9)" (Giambrone, "*Scientia Christi*," 284).

for all time a single sacrifice for sins" (Heb 10:12, 21), a priest who is also the new Moses.[58]

IV. Covenant and the Gospel of John

Given the above foundations, let me now turn to a detailed inquiry into John 19:25-27. My argument in this section will be that the Gospel of John, too, presents Jesus' crucifixion as the sealing of the eschatological new covenant. Just as the people in Exodus 24 are at the foot of Mount Sinai and at the foot of the twelve-pillared altar (symbolic of divine presence) when they receive the sacrificial blood that seals the Mosaic covenant with its promise of a holy people, so also at the foot of the cross—the altar of the new covenant sacrifice—are Mary the mother of Jesus, her sister, Mary Magdalene, and the beloved disciple. These persons represent the community of Jesus' disciples, the reconfigured messianic people of God. As noted above, my contention is that even in John's Gospel, Jesus seals a divine covenant with his people by his blood of the covenant, that is, by his perfect sacrificial self-offering. The fruit of the new covenant is that his followers are now his brothers and sisters who share, as adopted sons and daughters, in his inheritance as the Son of the Father. Just as after the ceremony at the altar Moses and Aaron and the seventy-two elders "beheld God, and ate and drank" (Exod 24:11), so also the community of Jesus' disciples at the foot of the cross behold the Lord and commune in him eucharistically, through the "blood and water" that flow from Jesus' pierced side.[59] The fruit of the new

---

58. For Jesus as the high priest, see also Barber, *Historical Jesus and the Temple*, 219-20; and see the works of Meeks et al. (noted above) for Jesus as the new Moses.

59. The symbolism here is not only eucharistic and baptismal, but also arguably relates, as the church fathers emphasized, to Jesus' status as the new Adam from whose side comes the new Eve, the Church: see *Gospel According to John (xiii-xxi)*, 949, although Brown in fact denies "that the Genesis story was in John's mind here" (949), underestimating John's fertile typological mind. For Brown, the blood signifies Jesus' death, and the water signifies the Spirit's outpouring (cf. John 7:38-39). Brown concludes that "at most we can give a probability to the double sacramental reference of xix 34b (on a secondary level), with better proof for the baptismal than for the Eucharistic reference" (952). By contrast, Francis D. Moloney, SDB, has argued at length—and persuasively in my view—in favor of the eucharistic (and baptismal) reference of John 19:34. As Moloney powerfully puts it in the conclusion of his "When Is John Talking about the Sacraments?," 130: "The Passion account has culminated with the exaltation of Jesus as King on his cross (19:17-21). There he has founded his Church (19:25-27) and brought to perfection the task the Father had given him (19:28-30). That is the Johannine understanding of past event, but how is it to become part of the experience of the Church now? The answer is found in 19:34 as the blood and water, the life-giving sacraments of Eucharist and baptism, are described as flowing down upon the

covenant—adoptive sonship—then appears when Jesus says to his mother, "Woman [new Eve], behold your son!" and to the beloved disciple, "Behold, your mother!" (John 19:26).[60] Jesus' mother becomes our mother, because we become members of his Body, his adoptive brothers and sisters (see John 20:17).[61] This event of adoptive filiation accords with Jesus' prayer in his (Mosaic) Farewell Discourse, "The glory which you have given me I have given to them, that they may be one even as we are one, I in them and you in me.... Father, I desire that they also, whom you have given me, may be with me where I am, to behold my glory which you have given me in your love before the foundation of the world" (John 17:22–24).[62]

As already noted, scholars recognize that the Synoptic Gospels connect the Eucharist and the cross with the sacrificial sealing of the Mosaic covenant that took place at Sinai in Exodus 24, but scholars have seen no parallel to this in the Gospel of John.[63] John 19's portrait of Jesus on the cross has not been understood to be a portrait of the sacrificial sealing of the new covenant between Jesus and his holy people.

Nevertheless, some scholars have come somewhat close to this viewpoint. For example, Richard Bauckham comments that the Gospel of John's "narrative of the death of Jesus itself suggests a sacrificial interpretation (19:34)."[64] Still closer, Francis Moloney has remarked, "As a result of the

---

nascent Church from the King lifted up on his throne." See also Malatesta, "Blood and Water from the Pierced Side of Christ (Jn 19,34)," to which Moloney directs attention. For background regarding the topic (up through the 1960s), see Klos, *Sakramente im Johannesevangelium*.

60. For reflections upon the identity of the beloved disciple, see for example Bauckham, *Jesus and the Eyewitnesses*, chapters 15 and 20; Bauckham, *Testimony of the Beloved Disciple*, chapter 3; Bernier, *Quest for the Historical Jesus after the Demise of Authenticity*, 83–86.

61. See the commentary on this passage by Martin and Wright, *Gospel of John*, 337–38: "Jesus' death and resurrection has radically changed the relationship between human beings and God. By completing the Father's saving work, Jesus gives his disciples a share in his own relationship with the Father—his sonship—by making them God's children ([John] 1:12–13). For the first time, Jesus speaks of the disciples as 'brothers' because, on account of Jesus' saving act of love, they now share the same Father (see Rom 8:14–17)." The full verse includes Jesus' instruction "Do not hold me, for I have not yet ascended to the Father." On this portion of the verse, which has been interpreted in a wide variety of ways, see Attridge, "'Don't Be Touching Me,'" 159: "the verse does not indicate a problem with Mary, but with the situation of Jesus' transitional state. On his way back on high, he was simply not fit to be touched."

62. See Meeks, *Prophet-King*, 304n3. For theological analysis of the prayer of the incarnate Son, see Legge, "Christ's Prayer to the Father (and Ours)."

63. Representative here is Smith's *Theology of the Gospel of John*, which does not mention covenant at all.

64. Bauckham, "Sacraments and the Gospel of John," 94. Bauckham disagrees with

lifting up of Jesus on the cross the Beloved Disciple and the Mother become one . . . Because of the cross and from the moment of the cross a new family of Jesus has been created."[65] Surely this is a *covenantal* "new family," and the moment of its formation is none other than Jesus' sacrificial death on the cross as the "Lamb of God" (John 1:29), in Johannine new Passover terms. Yet, Moloney does not draw these links in commenting on John 19. In addition, he warns against what he deems to be the "[e]xaggerated mariological claims" that people have made with respect to John 19:25-27.[66] Regarding the identification of Jesus as the "Lamb of God," Moloney thinks it can be connected with Isaiah 53 and "the Passover link is undeniable."[67] While af-

---

Francis Moloney that John 19:34, or indeed any passage in the Gospel of John, intends primarily to refer to the sacraments. His argument is rooted in part in his understanding of Mark's Gospel. He states, "John presupposes his readers know Mark's Gospel and deliberately does not repeat what could be read in Mark unless he has a specific reason for doing so . . . To call Mark 14:22-25 and Matthew 26:26-29 accounts of 'the institution of the Eucharist' is misleading because, unlike Luke (22:19) and Paul (1 Cor 11:25), they contain no indication that what Jesus does is to be repeated by his disciples. The *function* of these accounts in Mark and Matthew is to provide readers, in advance of the narrative of Jesus' death, with a sacrificial interpretation of that death" ("Sacraments and the Gospel of John," 94). I think that the argument from silence regarding Mark 14 and Matthew 26 is not convincing, nor is Bauckham's minimizing of the sacramental reference in the Gospel of John, as when with regard to John 6 Bauckham holds, "John used eucharistic language to speak, not of the Eucharist, but of faith in the crucified Jesus and participation in his life" (93). I agree that John is speaking of faith-filled "participation" in the life of the crucified Jesus, but this participation is precisely what the Eucharist (the sacrament known to John) delivers. Bauckham introduces an unnecessary dichotomy. Indeed, he recognizes in his essay that "John is not opposing sacraments or an over-emphasis on sacraments or a mistaken reliance on the outward rite as such," and he affirms that in fact "the sacraments represent those central realities of salvation in Christ to which this Gospel gives memorable expression" (95). For an approach to John 6 that allows for *both* faith and the Eucharist, see Brown, *Gospel According to John (i–xii)*.

65. Moloney, *Gospel of John*, 503-4. Without reference to Jesus' death as new covenant sacrifice, Weinandy similarly observes (in light of John 2) that "Mary, as the ecclesial woman who embodies ancient Israel and is the icon of the future church, has *everything* 'to do' with Jesus, for only in the fulfillment of his 'hour' will the church, of which she is the icon, come to be . . . For the ecclesial woman, the hour has come, not only for Jesus but also for her, and it is time for Jesus, the son whom she so named, to become Jesus—YHWH-Saves . . . [T]hus Cana becomes . . . the hermeneutical lens through which we must interpret what is now being fulfilled" in John 19 (Weinandy, *Jesus Becoming Jesus*, 3:245-46). On the cross, Jesus establishes "his church, the conjoined union of Mary and the beloved disciple to himself" (249).

66. Moloney, *Gospel of John*, 504.

67. Moloney, *Gospel of John*, 59. On Isaiah's suffering servant, see Anatolios, *Deification through the Cross*, 129-38. New Testament scholars debate whether the New Testament's references to Isaiah 52-53 derive from Jesus or from the early Christians. James D. G. Dunn argues that "a convincing case cannot be made that Jesus saw himself

firming the significance of the use of sacrificial animals to symbolize and establish divine communion, however, he underscores that Jesus "is not a cultic offering" and "is not a cultic victim."[68] Instead, Jesus is God coming to earth and offering forgiveness and communion.

No doubt Moloney is right that "an old symbol is being used in a new way"[69]—in other words, Jesus is not a sacrificial animal offered within Israel's cult. But I cannot see why the Johannine Jesus is not, in accordance with his eschatological mission, the supreme "cultic offering" or "Lamb," whose blood is received by his faithful people.[70]

For his part, the usually perceptive Johannine commentator Craig Keener focuses attention in John 19 upon John's emphasis on the positive role played by Jesus' female followers by comparison to his male disciples. Keener maintains that we should not think of the women as literally by the cross; they would have had to be standing some ways off, though able somehow to hear what was being said by Jesus. In Keener's view, the sister of Mary the mother of Jesus may be different from "Mary the wife of Clopas," so there may have been four women present. Keener rejects the notion that Mary the mother of Jesus is here unnamed because John is identifying her as the new Eve; as he remarks, "less than convincingly, some even connect Jesus' title 'man' (19:5) with a new Adam, and his

---

as the suffering Servant. That is not to deny that he might have reflected on the Servant passages, as he evidently did on other Scriptures. Indeed, the more Isaiah 53 was already seen to be part of the more extensive motif of the suffering righteous, the more likely it is that Jesus did reflect on what the Servant passages might contribute to his understanding of his own role. The point, however, is that the Jesus tradition does not allow us to draw that as a firm conclusion. That may simply be a reminder of the inadequacy of our critical tools" (Dunn, *Jesus Remembered*, 817). In my view, Jesus recognized himself as the suffering servant but, indeed, historical-critical tools may well be inadequate to show this. See also Freyne, *Jesus, a Jewish Galilean*, 168, for the argument that "the suffering servant of Isaiah and the *maskilim* of Daniel were likely background figures for Jesus' public ministry." Freyne adds, "Even those earlier scholars who maintained direct influence on Jesus' understanding of his death of Isa. 53, especially v. 10f., with its reference to the servant's death as a 'sin offering', have had to acknowledge that instances of direct verbal links are rare and uncertain. What is being proposed in this study is that such images provided significant analogues for Jesus' public ministry, and that there are sufficient indicators in its broad contours for the claim that they played a decisive role in shaping key aspects of that ministry, including, I believe, acceptance of the inevitability of his death" (168; cf. 114).

68. Moloney, *Gospel of John*, 59.

69. Moloney, *Gospel of John*, 59.

70. Moloney, *Gospel of John*, 59. It is likely that Moloney is making a point against the Catholic doctrine of eucharistic sacrifice. His understanding of the purposes of Israel's cult seems too narrow; for a broader portrait see Anderson, *That I May Dwell among Them*.

mother's title, 'woman,' her with a new Eve."[71] I think Keener is mistaken here. The evangelist John does nothing without import and he loves typology, and closer attention to John 2 and 19 makes the reference to the new Eve clear enough.[72]

In Keener's opinion, the identification of Mary as mother of the new family of believers, with the beloved disciple representing that family in John 19, is also unlikely. He argues, "had John intended such allegorical allusion, one would have expected stronger clues in the narrative, particularly more parallels with Eve or with Israel."[73] Instead, he supposes that Jesus is here teaching Mary that she is merely a disciple and ensuring that another disciple will care for her after Jesus' death. He sums up his view: "because Jesus' brothers did not believe . . . Jesus entrusted his believing mother to a disciple" and thereby completed the work of honoring his parents.[74] Keener's position mistakenly reduces John 19:25–27 to Jesus' difficulties with his "brothers," difficulties that Mary never shared.

Raymond Brown notes that in John 19:23–24, the evangelist goes out of his way to describe Jesus' seamless tunic and to observe that the soldiers do not tear it. According to Brown, this may be a reference to the tunic of the high priest (Exod 28:4, 32) and may therefore be a sign that Jesus' cross is a priestly action, in addition to being a royal action as indicated by John 19:19. The fact that the tunic was not torn may be a link to the expectation that a priest must not rend his clothing. This priestly link is underlined powerfully by Heil's essay "Jesus as the Unique High Priest in the Gospel of John." Heil points out, "by not tearing his unified tunic, the soldiers unwittingly advance the goal of Jesus as the good shepherd-high priest to

---

71. Keener, *Gospel of John*, 2:1143.

72. For further discussion of this point, see my *Mary's Bodily Assumption*; and see also Raymond Brown's comments on John 2 and 19 below.

73. Keener, *Gospel of John*, 2:1143.

74. Keener, *Gospel of John*, 2:1145. See also the position of Amy-Jill Levine that the Gospel of John is simply correcting the Synoptics: "Mark made it clear that at Jesus's arrest in Gethsemane, 'All of them [i.e., the disciples] deserted him and fled' (Mark 14:50), and Matthew agrees. Luke begins the process of rehabilitating the male disciples: 'But all his acquaintances, including the women who had followed him from Galilee, stood at a distance, watching these things' (Luke 23:49). These 'acquaintances' include the men who fled from the arrest. John's Gospel, conversely, insists that they did not all forsake him and flee. They did not all stay at a distance. The Beloved Disciple stayed the course and remained at the cross, close enough for Jesus to see him and to talk with him. Jesus is most definitely not alone as he dies" (Levine, *Witness at the Cross*, 81). At the same time, Levine agrees with other scholars that Jesus is "setting up a new family, not based in biology and not based in marriage or adoption but based on another new commandment"—namely, love grounded in relationship to Jesus and in caring for and comforting each other (83).

unify all sheep (people) into a believing community, so that there will be one flock and one shepherd."[75] For Moloney (and for Aquinas, indebted to the church fathers[76]), the seamlessness of the tunic and the fact that the soldiers do not tear it symbolize the unity of the community of believers established by Jesus' cross. This too makes sense, but it does so in light of Jesus' *priestly* action.

On the basis of John 19:28, Raymond Brown comments, "The action of Jesus in relation to his mother and the Beloved Disciple completes the work that the Father has given Jesus to do and fulfills the Scripture."[77] Brown surmises that Jesus' action from the cross must be deeply significant, far more than solely taking care of his mother. He notes that Catholic interpreters have long perceived in John 19:25-27 an affirmation of Mary's spiritual motherhood of all believers and/or of Mary's symbolic representation of the Church. In his view, given the language of the Johannine episode of the wedding at Cana (John 2, where Jesus calls Mary "woman"), it is in fact correct to say, "The sorrowful scene at the foot of the cross represents the birth pangs by which the spirit of salvation is brought forth (Isa xxvi 17-18) and handed over (John xix 30). In becoming the mother of the Beloved Disciple (the Christian), Mary is symbolically evocative of Lady Zion who, after the birth pangs, brings forth a new people in joy."[78] Brown affirms that in John's Gospel, as in the book of Revelation, Mary is the new Eve. She is the mother of the new divine community, the people united by her Son's (the new Adam's) cross. Mary thus cooperates in Jesus' "hour," his cross. Thus, Brown comes somewhat close to the viewpoint that I advocate in this chapter. Mary at the foot of the cross, along with the beloved disciple, specially represents the covenant community, participating in Jesus' establishment of the new covenant.[79]

---

75. Heil, "Jesus as the Unique High Priest in the Gospel of John," 743. For shepherd themes in Ezekiel 34 and the Gospel of Matthew—themes connected with Jesus' teaching and healing—see Zacharias, *Matthew's Presentation of the Son of David*, 95-101.

76. See Aquinas, *Commentary on the Gospel of John: Chapters 13-21*, pp. 240-41, §§2428-29.

77. Brown, *Gospel According to John (xiii-xxi)*, 923.

78. Brown, *Gospel According to John (xiii-xxi)*, 925.

79. On the beloved disciple's role, see Pope Leo XIII, *Adiutricem*, §6: "The mystery of Christ's immense love for us is revealed with dazzling brilliance in the fact that the dying Saviour bequeathed His Mother to His disciple John in the memorable testament: 'Behold thy son.' Now in John, as the Church has constantly taught, Christ designated the whole human race, and in the first rank are they who are joined with Him by faith." Leo XIII distinguishes Mary as Mother of the Church.

Immediately after his exchange with Mary and the beloved disciple, Jesus proclaims, "It is finished" (John 19:30).[80] He has completed the new covenant sacrifice—consummating the earlier covenants—and has established the messianic people of God. Moloney comments that Jesus by the end of John 19 "has fulfilled the Scriptures in two ways," first as "the perfect Paschal Lamb," and second as the one who makes God's presence available to all who desire to see God and to commune with God as forgiven sinners.[81] No wonder that, in Moloney's words, "[c]limaxing these indications of fulfillment, Jesus cries out '*tetelestai*' (v. 30a), an exclamation of achievement, almost of triumph. The task given to him by the Father (cf. 4:34; 5:36; 17:4) has now been consummately brought to conclusion."[82]

The Orthodox theologian John Behr has these texts in view in the exegetical portion of his *John the Theologian and His Paschal Gospel*, and he too comes somewhat close to sharing the perspective that I am advocating. Drawing upon the work of the Catholic biblical scholar Mary Coloe, Behr notes that John presents Jesus as "the priest of this new sacrifice," namely, the sacrifice of laying down his life out of love for his people—the sacrifice

---

80. See Pryor, *John*, 82: "the 'it is finished' means not just that the earthly work of Jesus, given to him by the Father, has been completed (cf. 4:34; 17:4), but also that the Scriptures have been fulfilled, not only in the incidental details of Jesus' death but in the death itself as the end to which they [the Scriptures] have been fulfilled." Despite his emphasis on the covenant people, Pryor's commentary on John 19:25-27 is disappointing. He merely states, "Jesus' giving over of his mother to the B[eloved] D[isciple], unique to our gospel, is clearly a symbol of something important for John, but its meaning is not immediately apparent. Some would see it as a symbol of Jew (Mary) and Gentile (the BD) in the new community, as each is given to the other. But the problem here is with seeing the BD as a symbol of Gentile Christianity ... Many Roman Catholic scholars have seen in the segment the church as given over to the care of Mary its mother" (*John*, 81). Similarly, I find disappointing (or frustratingly close) the perspective on John 19:25-27 of Schuchard, *Word from the Beginning*, 98: "For the time has come for Jesus as Temple, as place of the glory and of sacrifice, to become the sacrifice to end all sacrifice. In the company of the Beloved Disciple, the women receive also. They receive an emblematic indication of what Jesus's work will mean for those who are of his house ... Jesus entrusts his mother to the care of the disciple (19:27-27). For the future responsibility of caring for Jesus's house (8:35; 14:2-3) is to be that of his sent ones (20:21-23)."

81. Moloney, *Gospel of John*, 506. In her discussion of the scenes of "prophetic drama" in the Gospel of John, Morna D. Hooker similarly mentions that "in 19.32f. the soldiers refrain from breaking Jesus' legs—a sign, we are surely meant to understand, that he is the true passover lamb, since he was crucified at the time the passover lambs were sacrificed" (Hooker, *Signs of a Prophet*, 75).

82. Moloney, *Gospel of John*, 504. Aquinas himself is very modest in what he draws from this scene, and indeed, like Keener (and Augustine), Aquinas thinks that the main significance is that Jesus is caring for his mother by asking the beloved disciple to care for her. See Aquinas, *Commentary on the Gospel of John: Chapters 13–21*, 243, §2441.

of love.[83] Behr highlights the importance of the beloved disciple standing by the cross. He suggests that there may be a reference here to Zechariah 6:13, which prophesies that the eschatological Davidic (priest-)king "shall build the temple of the Lord, and shall bear royal honor, and shall sit and rule upon his throne. And there shall be a priest by his throne." Arguably, John 19:26 portrays the beloved disciple as this priest. Behr comments, "We have seen other instances where aspects of the Temple and its feasts are shared by the believer . . . So perhaps also here, Christ's priesthood is shared by the disciple who stands by the cross unashamed, ministering at the throne."[84] When Jesus speaks to the beloved disciple and to his mother Mary ("woman"), he establishes a mother-son relationship between them. The beloved disciple becomes a true "son" in the "Son," thereby sharing intimately in Jesus' Sonship.

Regarding the figure of Mary, Behr emphasizes that the "woman," as it were, gives birth to the body of Christ only at the cross, through her Son's death.[85] Behr uses this point to support his overarching argument that human beings only become fully human by dying.[86] He recognizes that the Bridegroom Messiah here constitutes, through Mary (and the beloved disciple), the Bride or Church. He contrasts this with the Reformed theologian Peter Leithart's mistaken claim that at the conclusion of John's Gospel, Christ "might as well be a jilted Groom, because there is no Bride."[87] Behr concludes that at the cross, Christ establishes the family of God, a "household of God" comprised of believers who are indwelt by the Trinity and who, having shared in Christ's passion (his dying), are "the assembly of faithful witnesses, martyrs, who are also enthroned and reign with Christ."[88]

---

83. Behr, *John the Theologian*, 183, with reference to Coloe, *God Dwells with Us*, 205.

84. Behr, *John the Theologian*, 183.

85. See Behr, *John the Theologian*, 185, with reference to Lieu, "Mother of the Son in the Fourth Gospel." Levine suggests that John simply aims to show (in a manner that clarifies the Synoptics) "that the mother of Jesus was a faithful follower, and that Jesus specifically recognized her fidelity" (*Witness at the Cross*, 92).

86. See also, for the same argument about dying, Behr, *Mystery of Christ*; and Behr, *Becoming Human*; and for background to Behr's perspective in the work of Panayiotis Nellas, see Kariatlis, "Deification as Christification," as well as Nellas, *Deification in Christ*.

87. Leithart, "'You Shall Judge Angels,'" 196, quoted in Behr, *John the Theologian*, 187.

88. Behr, *John the Theologian*, 189. Behr here draws appreciatively upon Leithart, "'You Shall Judge Angels,'" 197–200, which argues that the book of Revelation completes the Gospel of John in this respect.

For Behr, however, while John clearly depicts Jesus as "the Lamb of God who takes away the sin of the world" (John 1:29), John does not portray Jesus' cross as a sacrificial sin offering. Behr states, "Christ's life-giving death on the cross, although understood by others as an atoning death for sin (cf. Rom. 4:25), is not understood by John as a response to sin but rather as principally deriving from the love that God himself is (cf. 1 John 4:8) and has for the world (3:14-16)."[89] In my view, Behr has created a false alternative, because Christ's sacrifice can be a response to sin and also, simultaneously, a cultic act principally reflective of divine communion. After all, First John affirms *both* that God is love, and that "if we walk in the light, as he is in the light, we have fellowship with one another, and the blood of Jesus his Son cleanses us from all sin" (1 John 1:7; cf. 2:2).

Thus, although Behr offers helpful insights, his approach needs supplementing along the covenantal and sacrificial lines that I have set forth above. Behr himself points out with respect to John 2:1-12 (the miracle at Cana) that Irenaeus identified Mary as a symbol of the Church and identified the wine as "'the cup of recapitulation' . . . , the cup that is filled with the blood that flowed, together with water, from Christ's side (19:34), and

---

89. Behr, *John the Theologian*, 192. Behr continues (quite beautifully and insightfully), "It is precisely this love, shown in this way, that has liberated human beings from the condition of being slaves to that of being friends (15:15), members of the household of God, enthroned in the Temple as sons alongside the Son, and the commandment that Jesus gives as his own is simply 'that you love one another as I have loved you' (15:12). Now, however, we know what is involved in such love" (192). Behr goes on to draw heavily upon Leithart's insights into John's imagery: "John thus gives us a very rich understanding of Jesus as the Temple and the fulfilment of its feasts . . . However, as Leithart notes, to get the full effect of what John has done, we must also recognize that he has presented Jesus 'as a new Moses assembling and furnishing the new tabernacle that he is', and doing so as a 'tour of the tabernacle' by 'moving from the outer courts to the holy place, so that, by the time we arrive at the crucifixion we are in the inner sanctuary, the most holy place'. We are given a spring of living water (4:5-15; 7:37-39) resembling the bronze laver between the door of the tabernacle and the altar (Exod. 30:17-21); the heavenly bread (6:22-71), as the manna which was kept in a jar in the ark (Exod. 16:33) and the bread of Presence lying on the golden altar (Exod. 24:29[30]); the light of the world (8:12), as the golden lamp-stand (Exod. 25:30[31]); and Jesus himself, offering prayer for his disciples to the Father (17:1-26) as the priest before the altar. However, whereas we might have expected the cross to be presented as one of the butcher blocks where the animals were slaughtered, we are, at the end of the tour, instead at the most holy place itself" (Behr, *John the Theologian*, 192-93, quoting Leithart, "'You Shall Judge Angels'," 192). The sacrificial sealing of the new covenant—grounded in Exodus 24 with Moses throwing the sacrificial blood upon the altar and upon the people—has its place within this new temple imagery. See also Behr, *John the Theologian*, chapter 2 (on "'The Temple of His Body'") for a full and rich account, drawing upon the work of Mary Coloe and Paul Hoskins, of Jesus as "the new and true Temple of God" according to the Gospel of John (Behr, *John the Theologian*, 139).

which alone 'cleanses us from all sin' (1 John 1:7)."[90] The sealing of the new covenant sacrifice and Mary's role as "woman" or new Eve can unite the diverse theologies of the cross. As the Catholic theologian Robert Barron says, "covenant and sacrifice are always linked. Therefore when, in the Gospel of John, John the Baptist spies Jesus, he turns to a group of his disciples and says, 'Look, here is the Lamb of God' (John 1:36)."[91] The evangelist John, Barron observes, knows that the new covenant has come about in the perfect sacrificial self-offering of the incarnate Son. The Reformed theologian Brandon Crowe, similarly, has noted: "Especially clear in John are the exodus contours of Jesus's death as a Passover sacrifice . . . The blood of Jesus sealed the new covenant in his blood."[92]

The Gospel of John, however, never mentions covenant in connection with the cross, unlike the Last Supper narratives in the Synoptic Gospels. Fortunately, two students of Francis Moloney have recently done important work on covenant in the Gospel of John: Rekha Chennattu in *Johannine Discipleship as Covenant Relationship*, and Sherri Brown in *Gift upon Gift: Covenant through Word in the Gospel of John*. Before turning to their findings, I will very briefly discuss Alexander Tsutserov's *Glory, Grace, and Truth: Ratification of the Sinaitic Covenant according to the Gospel of John*. These three works will help to display the covenantal-sacrificial elements that are present in the Gospel of John and are relevant for interpreting John 19:25–27.

Alexander Tsutserov

The thesis of Tsutserov's book is that "three key concepts—1) *hē charis kai hē alētheia*, 2) *charis*, and 3) *doxa*—of the Gospel's account of the revelation of God as Jesus (John 1:14–18ff.) allude to the covenant of God's presence

---

90. Behr, *John the Theologian*, 142, quoting Irenaeus, *Against Heresies*, 3.16.7. Behr adds that the miracle at Cana, which occurs "on the third day" (John 2:1), "alludes backwards to the descent of the Lord upon Mount Sinai to give the Law to Moses and manifest his glory (Exod. 19:16-20; 24:16-17), and forward to the raising of Christ's body, the true temple, on the third day (2:19–21)" (Behr, *John the Theologian*, 142).

91. Barron, *Eucharist*, 78–79. Barron construes this sacrifice as involving Jesus entering into the bitterest and most sorrowful consequences of our sin and, through the power of his love, turning the darkness of our alienation into the merciful light of his divine life. See also the excellent study, focused on the inseparable connection of cross and Eucharist in the early Church—and rightly critical of contemporary understandings of the Eucharist primarily as a meal—by Cardó, *Cross and the Eucharist in Early Christianity*.

92. Crowe, *Lord Jesus Christ*, 81.

originated in the revelation of God at Sinai (Exod 33:12—34:10 LXX)."[93] On this view, both at Sinai and in Jesus the purpose of the covenant is to make available God's presence. The covenant in both cases has the same "matter," but the degree of intensity differs: Jesus reveals and bestows God's presence much more fully.

Recall that during the exodus journey, after the episode of the golden calf, Moses received the covenantal privilege of speaking to God in the tent of meeting. The pillar of cloud, a symbol of the divine presence, would "descend and stand at the door of the tent," and in this way "the Lord would speak to Moses" (Exod 33:9). Whenever this happened, the people would come to their own tent doors and worship God who was manifesting his presence through Moses. The narrator explains, "Thus the Lord used to speak to Moses face to face, as a man speaks to his friend" (Exod 33:11).

From within this unique relationship, Moses interceded with God on behalf of the people. He first asked God to assure him that the divine presence would be with him as he led the people on the remainder of the exodus journey. He then asked God to show him the divine glory.[94] God responds, "I will make all my goodness pass before you, and will proclaim before you my name 'The Lord'; and I will be gracious to whom I will be gracious, and will show mercy on whom I will show mercy" (Exod 33:19). God permits Moses to see his glory—but only his "back," not his "face" (Exod 33:23). God calls Moses up to the top of Mount Sinai where Moses receives a new copy of the Ten Commandments, to replace the tablets broken because of the worship of the golden calf. To Moses, the Lord reveals himself as "a God merciful and gracious, slow to anger, and abounding in mercy and faithfulness, keeping merciful love for thousands, forgiving iniquity and transgression and sin, but who will by no means clear the guilty" (Exod 34:6–7). The Lord then renews his covenant with Israel.

---

93. Tsutserov, *Glory, Grace, and Truth*, 243.

94. On the theology of δόξα in the New Testament, with a focus on Paul, see Newman, "God and Glory and Paul, Again"; Newman, *Paul's Glory-Christology*; Newman, "Resurrection as Glory." Newman observes, "Paul used something that was uniquely Israel's, the glory, to mark the boundaries between the new movement that he led and the faith community of his former co-religionists. Identifying Jesus as the glory of God either outright breached, or dangerously and recklessly flirted with breaching, what was permissible. It was one thing to report a heavenly journey in which a seer saw glory—be it God's, a throne's, or an angel's. It was altogether something new to say that a recently crucified Jewish prophet, who was also being hailed as both the Christ and the Lord, is the glory of God, God's divine presence . . . Paul's choice to identify the risen Jesus as the glory of Israel's god was 'becoming Christian' by 'transgressing monotheism'" ("God and Glory and Paul, Again," 138).

Tsutserov calls this "the covenant of God's presence (*charis*)" inaugurated at Sinai.[95] Jesus is the incarnate Word who is "full of grace and truth" and who manifests the Father's "glory" and from whose fullness comes "grace upon grace" (John 1:14, 16; cf. 1:17).[96] In Tsutserov's view, John's Gospel presents Jesus as the Word of God and as the greater (eschatological) Moses perfecting and ratifying the Mosaic covenant of divine presence. Jesus acts as the new Moses above all when "Jesus is glorified on the cross," so that "believers receive the Spirit of *(hē) charis kai (hē) alētheia* (1:32-33; 3:34; 7:39; 20:22)."[97] God's glory, the same glory that Moses asked to see, is "continuously seen in the Word made flesh," and Jesus' signs and acts of power display what is "required by the Sinaitic covenant to ratify the covenant of the presence (*charis*) of God."[98] Jesus pours out this glory upon his

95. Tsutserov, *Glory, Grace, and Truth*, 243.

96. For an instructive discussion of these verses—influenced by Tsutserov—see Bauckham, *Who Is God?*, 80-85. Bauckham notes that John 1:14 ("full of grace and truth") makes an allusion to Exodus 34:6-7. Bauckham explains, "As in many of the Old Testament's allusions to the divine character description, John has summed up the five qualities by selecting two of them. But he has imitated the structure of the last part of the description—'abounding in steadfast love and faithfulness' [Exod 34:6]—in his phrase 'full of grace and truth.' The Hebrew word for 'faithfulness' (*emet*) is often translated in the Greek Bible as *alētheia*, 'truth.' Faithfulness is being true to one's word. Faithfulness is truth as a personal characteristic. For *ḥesed*, 'steadfast love,' John seems to use the Greek word *charis*, 'grace,' which is an unusual translation, though certainly not impossible [it is found in Esther and in Sirach]. John may have chosen it not simply to translate *ḥesed* but to summarize all four of the first four qualities: merciful, gracious, slow to anger, steadfast love. All four of these amount to God's generosity to his people, which is the meaning of 'grace'" (82). For his part, Moloney renders the final clause of John 1:14 as "the fullness of a gift that is truth [*plērēs charitos kai alētheias*]." He explains that the words "*kai alētheias*" are "an example of an epexegetical *kai* or a so-called *hendiadys*, where the second noun is not something added to the former, but explains it" (Moloney, *Gospel of John*, 45). The translation of John 1:14 as "the fullness of *a gift that is truth*" should lead us to recall that Jesus in the Gospel of John describes the Spirit as "the Spirit of *truth*" (Jn 14:17; 15:26; 16:13; emphasis added). Likewise, John 1's references to Christ's possessing the fullness of "grace," and to Christ as the source of our grace, also seem to suggest the Spirit's presence. A connection of this kind is made by Thomas Aquinas, who comments on John 1:14 ("full of grace and truth") by applying John 3:34 to Jesus' *Spirit-filled* humanity: "in his soul there was the fullness of all graces without measure: 'God does not bestow the Spirit in fractions'" (Aquinas, *Commentary on the Gospel of John: Chapters 1-5*, §189, p. 77).

97. Tsutserov, *Glory, Grace, and Truth*, 247. I note that Tsutserov argues that the Gospel of John "holds the Law in high regard," notably the Decalogue and the Shema (248). According to the Gospel of John, says Tsutserov, "The Law is a revelation of the Divine (1:17). Jesus acknowledges that 'the Scripture cannot be broken' (10:35). His new commandment provides the proper insight into the Law (13:34 cf. Lev 19:18)" (248).

98. Tsutserov, *Glory, Grace, and Truth*, 252.

disciples. Tsutserov states, "This conformity of the character of the faithful with God enables believers to continue performing covenantal *endoxa* (*erga*, *sēmeia*) in the Spirit (6:14; 14:12; 21:19) to glorify God."[99]

Rekha Chennattu

The value of Tsutserov's book for my purposes consists in making a strong connection between John's Gospel and the covenant of Sinai as mediating the divine presence—although Tsutserov does not connect this back to Exodus 24. Moloney's students Rekha Chennattu, writing prior to Tsutserov, and especially Sherri Brown push this covenantal theme forward by making a connection to the cross. Chennattu, who is particularly concerned to explore discipleship according to John's Gospel, focuses her attention upon John 13–17 (the Farewell Discourse) and John 20–21 (the resurrection appearances). Although she mentions John the Baptist's identification of Jesus as the "Lamb of God" (John 1:36), she does not inquire into the sacrificial connections.[100]

Chennattu first sets forth the various kinds of covenants in the Old Testament and the ancient Near East. She attends to the "communion sacrifices" by which a covenant is confirmed, as in Exodus 24.[101] A covenant establishes the people permanently as God's and assures them of God's presence so long as they are faithful. She notes that Yves Simoens, in his *La gloire d'aimer*, has argued that the Farewell Discourse conforms to the covenantal pattern of Deuteronomy, with its great commandment, stipulations, and blessings and woes.[102]

---

99. Tsutserov, *Glory, Grace, and Truth*, 253. See also Caneday, "Glory Veiled in the Tabernacle of Flesh." According to Caneday, "John's fourfold use of χάρις in his prologue but not elsewhere in the Gospel suggests that it refers to the Lord's 'covenant presence' which is now realized in the person of Christ Jesus, the 'Covenant Presence.' It is for this presence that Moses petitioned the Lord: 'And how will it be truly known that I have found *favor* with you, both I and your people, other than if you go along with us? And we shall be *glorified*, both I and your people, above all the nations that are on the earth.' The Lord assured Moses, 'Even this *word* that you have spoken, I will do for you. For you have found *favor* before me, and I know you above all others' (Ex 33:17). It is at this point that Moses requests, 'Show me your own *glory*!' . . . The Lord provided many marvelous manifestations of his presence with ancient Israel, but now John announces, 'And the Word was made flesh and tented among us, and we have seen his glory, glory as of the only Son from the Father, full of grace and truth' (John 1:14)" (59). For his appreciation of covenant in John's Gospel and his focus on Exodus 33–34, Caneday is indebted both to Tsutserov and to John W. Pryor.

100. See Chennattu, *Johannine Discipleship as a Covenant Relationship*, 29.

101. Chennattu, *Johannine Discipleship as a Covenant Relationship*, 57.

102. See Simoens, *Gloire d'aimer*.

Among the points Chennattu makes is that the disciples, in John 16:29–30, offer a confession of faith that reflects the traditional pattern of the oaths preceding covenant renewals. She observes, "In Exod 24:8 and Josh 24:25–28, this declaration of commitment to Yahweh is followed by a covenant making ritual."[103] She then reads John 17 as a covenant-sealing prayer on the part of Jesus, establishing the disciples as his people and promising them the divine presence. In her view, the setting of a meal and the symbolic action of footwashing in John 13 can be understood to be analogous to the Last Supper and the institution of the Eucharist in the Synoptic Gospels. Just as the Eucharist gives the disciples a participation in Christ, so explicitly does the footwashing. Chennattu argues that the footwashing has an eschatological meaning going beyond simple service, since in Ezekiel's prophecy of the new covenant, God's "washing and cleansing" of the people is "a necessary condition for the people to return to their land ... and to re-establish their covenant relationship."[104] The footwashing gives believers a share in the incarnate Lord of the new covenant, and thus a share of his divine, priestly inheritance.

The washing of the feet is followed by Jesus' new commandment of love. The new commandment is in continuity with the Mosaic covenant, which required the people to love God and each other (see Deuteronomy 6:5 and Leviticus 19:18). The new commandment is new, however, because it is centered around Jesus and his perfect sacrifice on the cross. He is both the fullness of the divine presence and the fullness of human obedience. As he says with reference to his coming cross, "A new commandment I give to you, that you love one another; even as I have loved you, that you also love one another" (John 13:34). Chennattu notes that in John 13, three ways of relating to the perfect covenant are exemplified: Judas' rejection, Peter's misunderstanding and denial followed by acceptance, and the beloved disciple's wholehearted acceptance.[105]

The covenantal themes of John 13 are amplified, as Chennattu shows, by John 14. The main purpose of John 14 is to convey the promise of Jesus that God's presence will dwell permanently with his people. Not only does Jesus promise to send "the Spirit of truth" to dwell with his disciples forever, but also Jesus promises, "If a man loves me, he will keep my word, and my Father will love him, and we will come to him and make our home with him" (John 14:17, 23). Chennattu points out that according to Ezekiel 8–11,

103. Chennattu, *Johannine Discipleship as a Covenant Relationship*, 86.

104. Chennattu, *Johannine Discipleship as a Covenant Relationship*, 95.

105. For further background, see Brown, "'Follow Me,'" 173–74; Gorman, *Abide and Go*. See also such works as Lee, *Hallowed in Truth and Love*; and the essays in Brown and Skinner, *Johannine Ethics*.

God abandoned the temple due to Israel's sins; and she adds that "God's presence in the sanctuary or tabernacle . . . signals both God's faithfulness to the covenant relationship (e.g., Lev 26:11; Ezek 37:27) and Israel's obedience to the commandments of God (Exod 31:12–17)."[106] In John 14, Jesus promises that the divine presence will dwell within all believers who obey the new covenant commandment of cruciform love, exemplified by the cross.[107] John 14 also involves the knowledge of God, in accord with Exodus 29:46's promise that when God dwells with his people, they will "know that I [God] am the Lord their God." Jesus makes clear that his disciples will know his Father, will know the Spirit of truth, and will know the relationship that the Son has with the Father. This is a perfected and intensified covenantal bond.

Chennattu comments upon John 14:26–27, where Jesus states that the Spirit will "bring to your remembrance all that I have said to you. Peace I leave with you; my peace I give to you." The theme of covenantal remembrance, as Chennattu notes, "permeates the whole OT."[108] Just as the people of Israel must liturgically bring to remembrance the events of the exodus (preeminently the Passover Lamb), so must Christians bring to remembrance all that Jesus, the true Lamb of God, accomplishes in his sacrificial love for the establishment of the people as a community of God's intimate presence. Jesus' gift of peace harkens back to such passages as Ezekiel 36:26, "I will make a covenant of peace with them; it shall be an everlasting covenant with them; and I will bless them and multiply them, and will set my sanctuary in the midst of them for evermore." In the Gospel of John, Jesus, the prophesied Davidic servant-king (Ezek 36:25), brings about this "covenant of peace" by his cross.[109]

John 15 emphasizes the need for obedience to Jesus' new covenant commandment of love in imitation of Jesus' covenant-sealing love on the cross. Lest there be any doubt about the reference to the cross, Jesus reiterates his new commandment and then explains, "Greater love as no man than this, that a man lay down his life for his friends" (John 15:13). Chennattu argues that John 16:10, where Jesus describes the righteousness to

---

106. Chennattu, *Johannine Discipleship as a Covenant Relationship*, 102. See also Mary Coloe's point that in the Gospel of John, when Jesus leaves the Temple for the final time (John 10:40), he crosses the Jordan, heading East, thereby tracing "the path of God's glory when it left the Solomonic Temple prior to its destruction by the Babylonians" (Coloe, *God Dwells with Us*, 155).

107. For helpful background, emphasizing the theme of Jesus as the eschatological Temple, see Behr, *John the Theologian*, 172–76. Behr draws upon Coloe's *God Dwells with Us*, 160–63; Kerr, *Temple of Jesus' Body*, 278–92; and (to a much lesser extent) Gärtner, *Temple and the Community in Qumran and the New Testament*, 16–46.

108. Chennattu, *Johannine Discipleship as a Covenant Relationship*, 109.

109. For background, see Daly-Denton, *David in the Fourth Gospel*.

which the Spirit will testify, has to do with the fact that the cross itself "is the vindication and ratification of Jesus' life by the Father."[110] The cross manifests God's righteousness, God's fidelity to his covenantal promises. Jesus is the one who fulfills the covenantal commandments on behalf of all human beings and who fulfills the covenantal promises as the incarnate Lord.[111]

After quoting Raymond Brown's trenchant comment that "John xvii 19 has Jesus consecrating himself, seemingly as a [sacrificial] victim," Chennattu remarks: "It is Jesus' death that ultimately seals the new covenant and consecrates the disciples, the new people of God."[112] This observation, which goes to the heart of the matter, indicates that the entirety of the Farewell Discourse (John 13–17) is, as we should expect, a preparation for the Cross and its sealing of the new covenant. Chennattu draws a link here to the understanding of consecration or sanctification found in Hebrews 10:10, "we have been sanctified through the offering of the body of Jesus Christ once for all."[113]

The key point that Chennattu makes with regard to Christ's cross in relation to Jesus' prayer in John 17 is that it is "Jesus' death, revealing God's love and redemptive power, that consecrates and empowers the disciples to be the new covenant community."[114] This indicates why the salvific efficacy of Christ's cross should be studied under the rubric of a covenant sacrifice

110. Chennattu, *Johannine Discipleship as a Covenant Relationship*, 125.

111. I am here filling out what Chennattu leaves mostly implicit. I am drawing upon Moloney, *Gospel of John*, 446, as well as adding my own emphasis.

112. Chennattu, *Johannine Discipleship as a Covenant Relationship*, 134, quoting Brown, *Gospel According to John (xiii-xxi)*, 767.

113. For the Letter to the Hebrews on Jesus' death as sacrifice and as the sealing of the new covenant (marked by the forgiveness of sins), see Smith, *Meaning of Jesus' Death*, 27–33; Dunnill, *Covenant and Sacrifice in the Letter to the Hebrews*. For the argument, with which I disagree, that "[f]or the writer of Hebrews, it is God *as human*—not the human Jesus alone but *God* as human—who is the subject of the 'loud cries and tears' [Heb 5:7]. No separation of the divine from the human is permitted," see McCormack, *Humility of the Eternal Son*, 219.

114. Chennattu, *Johannine Discipleship as a Covenant Relationship*, 134–35. See also Bauckham, *Testimony of the Beloved Disciple*, 253–69 (a study of "The Holiness of Jesus and His Disciples in the Gospel of John"). Bauckham states, "The holiness of the disciples relates to that of Jesus in two ways. First, it is because Jesus has accomplished his self-offering that the disciples can also be consecrated. Second, they are consecrated in order to continue Jesus' own mission in the world. There is a difference in that the disciples' mission is not to atone for the sin of the world, but it is similar in its demand for costly dedication to the service of God. As holy, the disciples are set apart from the world but, as in Jesus' case, this consecration is in the service of God's self-giving love for the world. They are distinguished from the world both for God's sake and for the world's sake" (*Testimony of the Beloved Disciple*, 269).

and in light of the community's role in receiving the blood of the sacrifice. As Richard Bauckham says, Jesus is "the one God has consecrated for the offering of sacrifice," or the one who has been consecrated "as the new altar of burnt offering" and thus as "the eschatologically new altar on which the final sacrifice is to be offered."[115]

Sherri Brown

Last but not least, let me turn to Sherri Brown's *Gift upon Gift*. Brown treats the crucifixion scene in John 19. She notes that "Jesus' last breaths on the cross establish the church, as symbolized by the garment that cannot be torn apart" and also as symbolized by the fact that "[t]he first to believe [the Virgin Mary] and the beloved model disciple are given to each other to establish a new community in faith and love."[116] She perceives how deep the theme of sacrifice is in John's crucifixion scene—as befits the one introduced by John the Baptist as the "Lamb of God, who takes away the sins of the world" (John 1:29).

Brown points out that immediately after Jesus' death, the evangelist adds the following detail: "Since it was the day of Preparation [for the Passover], in order to prevent the bodies from remaining on the cross on the sabbath . . . the Jews asked Pilate that their legs might be broken, and that they might be taken away" (John 19:31). In Jesus' case, the soldiers do not break his legs but pierced his side. Zechariah 12:10 speaks of the eschatological day of the Lord, when divine forgiveness is poured out and the people of Jerusalem sorrowfully "look on him whom they have pierced." But the more important allusions for my purposes may instead be Exodus 12:10 regarding the Passover Lamb: "you shall let none of it remain until the morning"; and, even better, Exodus 12:46's instruction regarding the Lamb, "you shall not break a bone of it." The point that Jesus' cross is in fact the covenant sacrifice of the true Passover Lamb could hardly be clearer. Brown states, "Jesus' side is pierced to confirm his death on the Day of Preparation,

---

115. Here is the full quotation from Bauckham, *Testimony of the Beloved Disciple*, 264: "We must therefore reject the interpretation of John 10:36 offered by Mary Coloe, that, just as 'in the Tabernacle and the Temple, God's glory dwells in [Jesus], consecrating him as a new House of God.' The thought here is not of Jesus as God's presence but of Jesus as the one God has consecrated for the offering of sacrifice. Probably we should think not of his consecration to be the temple as the place of sacrifice, but more specifically of his consecration as the new altar of burnt offering. Just as the altar installed by Judas Maccabaeus was a new one, so is Jesus the eschatologically new altar on which the final sacrifice is to be offered." See Coloe, *God Dwells with Us*, 153.

116. Brown, *Gift upon Gift*, 195.

the day of the sacrifice of the Passover Lamb."[117] The flow of blood and water from Jesus' side (John 19:34) pertains to the establishment of the new covenant community by means of his sacrifice, likely with reference to baptism and the Eucharist.[118]

Brown observes that at the cross, the sacrifice of the true Lamb (Jesus) establishes the covenantal community as "the family of the new community of God."[119] However, Brown does not specify that Jesus' death is the new covenant sacrifice, and she does not relate the role of Mary and the beloved disciple at the foot of the cross to that of the people of Israel at the foot of the altar at the base of Mount Sinai.

As her book's subtitle indicates, Brown is focused not on covenant through sacrifice but on "covenant through word" in John's Gospel. Her treatment of the Sinai covenant in Exodus 24 exemplifies her approach. Whereas above I emphasized Moses' throwing half the blood upon the altar (the divine presence) and half upon the people—in accordance with the Last Supper narratives in the Synoptics—Brown emphasizes the words and promises of God and the people at Sinai. She recalls that when the Israelites reach Mount Sinai, God calls to Moses and commands him to speak the following words to the people: "You have seen what I did to the Egyptians, and how I bore you on eagles' wings and brought you to myself. Now therefore, if you will obey my voice and keep my covenant, you shall be my own possession among all peoples . . . and you shall be to me a kingdom of priests and a holy nation" (Exod 19:4-6). In the Gospel of John, Jesus' new covenant sacrifice brings to full fruition this divine promise. For Brown, it is particularly noteworthy that as Exodus 19–24 unfolds, the people three times say to God in response to his words: "All that the Lord has spoken we will do" (Exod 19:8; 24:3; and 24:7). In Exodus 24:7, they also add the phrase, "and we will be obedient." Recall that as soon as the people say these words, Moses "took the blood and threw it upon the people, and said, 'Behold the blood of the covenant which the Lord has made with you in accordance with all these words'" (Exod 24:8).

---

117. Brown, *Gift upon Gift*, 196.

118. Aidan Nichols, OP, puts the matter well: "The blood and water of beasts already flowed out from the altar of the Temple, the sole place where sacrificial worship could lawfully be carried out. But now a new Sacrifice is offered. The opening of Jesus's side in the nineteenth chapter of St. John's Passion narrative accords with this: the Temple, site of the myriad sacrifices of beasts, is replaced by the sacrificial body of the Lord, from which blood and water also flow. What began in the upper room is completed, the Temple's purpose fulfilled, Jesus's own Temple identity revealed" (Nichols, *Deep Mysteries*, 80).

119. Brown, *Gift upon Gift*, 196.

In Brown's view, the evangelist John set up his Gospel to portray Jesus as the one "who fulfills the Torah of the Sinai covenant and gives the new covenant."[120] Brown's emphasis on Jesus' fulfillment of the Mosaic covenant informs her portrait of Mary in John 2. John's narration of this profoundly symbolic wedding begins with the phrase, "On the third day" (John 2:1). As Brown observes, one might here think of the Israelites' arrival at Mount Sinai in Exodus 19. God commands Moses, "Go to the people and consecrate them today and tomorrow, and let them wash their garments, and be ready by the third day; for on the third day the Lord will come down upon Mount Sinai in the sight of all the people" (Exod 19:10–11). The fact that God will reveal his glory to the people of Israel "on the third day" resonates with John's narration and "brings the revelatory event of the covenant at Sinai to the fore as its guiding force."[121]

At the center of the wedding festivities in John 2 is Mary. She is the first character introduced, and in the story she is referred to repeatedly as "mother" and "woman." She is the one who tells Jesus, "They have no wine" (John 2:3). Behind this lack of "wine" stands the eschatological promise of covenantal fulfillment. Brown states, "if the messianic era is marked by a wedding banquet and an abundance of wine (Amos 9:13–14; Hos 2:19–20, 14:7; Isa 25:6–8, 54:4–8, 62:4–5; Jer 2:2, 31:12; Song of Songs), her direct testimony of the lack of wine highlights this symbolism."[122] Against the view that Jesus' terse reply (in which he refers to Mary as "woman" and references his "hour") is a rebuke of Mary, Brown points out that in fact Jesus rectifies the situation to which she alerts him, and Brown also observes that Mary makes no request of Jesus but instead simply describes the situation and says to the servants, "Do whatever he tells you" (John 2:5). Once we perceive that the evangelist records neither a request nor a rebuke, we can understand that what Mary is actually articulating is "a symbolic statement

---

120. Brown, *Gift upon Gift*, 95. Indebted to Francis Moloney, she states, "The giving of the gift of the Law was God's covenantal activity at Sinai. The incarnation of the Word that is full of the gift which is truth is God's covenantal activity in Jesus" (Brown, *Gift upon Gift*, 94). See Moloney, *Gospel of John*, 46.

121. Brown, *Gift upon Gift*, 114.

122. Brown, *Gift upon Gift*, 116. I note that Nicholas Perrin interprets the verse from the Lord's Prayer, "Give us this day our daily bread" (Matt 6:11), in terms of the messianic banquet and also in terms of the eschatological manna (cf. John 6:32–33). Perrin states, "Jesus may intend either the bread that accompanies the longed-for messianic banquet, which is supported by the Jesus tradition (Matt. 8.11–12; 22.1–14; 25.1–13; Luke 12.35–37; 13.28–29), or the fresh outpouring of manna expected to accompany the eschatological rest, on the model of Exodus 16. It is not impossible that both are simultaneously in view, that is, on the assumption that the messianic feast would be supplied by heaven-sent manna" (Perrin, *Jesus the Priest*, 47).

signaling that the people are bereft of the essential components for the messianic wedding banquet within the further symbolic context of Pentecost— the revelation of the glory of God."[123]

Brown translates the colloquial phrase used by Jesus in John 2:4— which the RSV translates as "O woman, what have you to do with me?"—as "what belongs [in common] to me and to you?"[124] Although Brown is going against the grain here, I think her broader point is insightful: the exchange may be in the genre of a covenantal challenge. This fits with the symbolism of the "third day" and of the eschatological "wedding" and "wine." Mary's words, "Do whatever he tells you," are not the words of an offended party. Rather, they are words that the people of Israel accepted in promising to keep covenant with God: "All that the Lord has spoken we will do" (Exod 24:7). Mary's words "confirm her acceptance" of Jesus' will regarding his eschatological hour.[125] She stands in relation to Jesus as one who fully makes her own the obedience expressed by the Israelites during the covenant-sealing sacrifice at the base of Mount Sinai.

The evangelist concludes this story, "This, the first of his signs, Jesus did at Cana in Galilee, and manifested his glory; and his disciples believed in him" (John 2:11). According to Brown, the reference to Jesus' divine "glory" connects the scene even more strongly to Exodus 19–24, which contains many references to the manifestation of God's glory at Mount Sinai. Brown also thinks that Mary embodies at Cana the covenantal relationship into which the disciples are to be drawn. In John 2, Mary is already anticipating the glorification of Jesus on the cross through his perfect covenant sacrifice in love, and she is already representing the people of Israel who obediently assent to God's will and participate in the sacrificial sealing of the covenant at the foot of Mount Sinai.

For Brown, the covenantal "symbolic framework" of the story of the miracle at Cana and of the Gospel of John as a whole is "presented through the dialogue between Jesus and his mother and the relationship that is established."[126] On this view, Mary is the model disciple, the model believer in God and his Messiah. Even prior to seeing any miraculous signs, she stands in a covenantal relationship of faith toward Jesus. She embodies the stance of the faithful Israelites at the sealing of the covenant at Sinai. She already anticipates, Brown suggests, the uniqueness of the "hour" or the

---

123. Brown, *Gift upon Gift*, 118. On the imagery of the eschatological banquet, see also Wright, *Lord's Prayer*, 123–24.
124. Brown, *Gift upon Gift*, 119.
125. Brown, *Gift upon Gift*, 120.
126. Brown, *Gift upon Gift*, 126.

fact that "[t]he revelation of God in Jesus must always be anchored in the historical event of the cross and the glorification that can only be revealed upon the belief in that word of Jesus."[127] In her acceptance of the coming hour of the cross toward which all Jesus' signs point, Mary "becomes the paradigmatic disciple in the time before Jesus' 'hour.'"[128] With the beloved disciple at the foot of the cross, Mary forms the new family or people of God constituted by the new covenant sacrifice of love. Mary shows us how "to live as the Word's own even at the foot of the cross," obediently doing God's will as expressed in the covenant of cruciform love.[129]

In her more recent book *God's Promise: Covenant Relationship in John*, Brown repeats much of her earlier book, but she examines more closely the crucifixion scene in John 19. By means of a performative action, Brown argues, Jesus here causes the beloved disciple and Mary to be his covenantal "new family."[130] This new-covenant kinship relationship points back to the promise given at the beginning of the Gospel (John 1:12) and forward to the ongoing new covenant community of Jesus' followers, who share in Jesus' family as adopted sons and daughters. The obedience of Mary and the beloved disciple at the foot of the cross enable them to be the chosen core of God's new covenant family in his Son, "as the true children of God living in covenant relationship through the gift of truth, which is life in the name of Jesus."[131]

Although Brown never makes this connection explicitly, it is but a short logical step to the conclusion that for John the purified community, led by Mary and the beloved disciple, is present obediently at the foot of the cross, sharing interiorly and exteriorly in the new covenant sacrifice— just as the obedient Israelites in Exodus 24 did in the Mosaic covenant sacrifice. It is through the blood of Christ's sacrifice that seeing and knowing God and his glory will be fully opened up for the new covenant people of God. The words of Michael Gorman in his *The Death of the Messiah and the Birth of the New Covenant* are apropos: "The purpose of Jesus' death was to effect, or give birth to, the new covenant, the covenant of peace; that is, to create a new-covenant community of Spirit-filled disciples of Jesus who would fulfill the inseparable covenantal requirements of faithfulness

---

127. Brown, *Gift upon Gift*, 127.

128. Brown, *Gift upon Gift*, 138.

129. Brown, *Gift upon Gift*, 140. For discussion of covenant as familial kinship, see Hahn, *Kinship by Covenant*. Hahn builds upon Cross's "Kinship and Covenant in Ancient Israel." See also Jon D. Levenson's instructive emphasis in his *Love of God* that the crucial element is love; and for further insight see Barber, *Salvation*, 25–27.

130. Brown, *God's Promise*, 73.

131. Brown, *God's Promise*, 97.

to God and love for others through participation in the death of Jesus."[132] This new covenant sacrifice is related in the Synoptics to the sealing of the Mosaic covenant in Exodus 24, and, arguably, the same can be said of the Gospel of John.

V. Matthias Joseph Scheeben's Contribution

One might still ask, however, whether covenant sacrifice is today a viable way of depicting the cross of Christ—even if it is determinative for the Synoptics, Paul, Hebrews, and John. As already indicated, there are plenty of people who say no. In a recent essay, the Catholic theologian Johannes Zachhuber describes the rise of strongly "antisacrificial attitudes" in the eighteenth century.[133] Paradigmatically, Voltaire condemned "religion as inherently cruel: no religion without sacrifice, no sacrifice without the immolation of a victim and thus, ultimately, without the killing of human beings."[134] Thus, it is one thing to show that the cross is a covenant sacrifice in which Jesus' saving blood is received by his new covenant family, participating in the sealing of the new covenant; but it is quite another thing to claim that this should be positively received today. Here, I think, Matthias Joseph Scheeben's *Handbook of Catholic Dogmatics* can be very helpful, and so I will devote this section to surveying his approach, which was penned with the anti-sacrificial attitude at least partly in view.

Discussing Christ's "atoning sacrifice," Scheeben begins by affirming the obvious: the language of sacrifice has biblical justification that has been taken up doctrinally by the Church, well before the Council of Trent. Ephesians 5:2 teaches, "Christ loved us and gave himself up for us, a fragrant offering and sacrifice to God"; and the Council of Ephesus drew upon Ephesians 5:2 in expressing Christ's saving work. Similarly, 2 Corinthians 5:21 teaches, "For our sake he made him to be sin who knew no sin, so that in him we might become the righteousness of God"; and the Creed of Toledo (400 AD) interpreted the phrase "made him to be sin" as meaning that Christ became a sacrificial sin offering.[135]

---

132. Gorman, *Death of the Messiah and the Birth of the New Covenant*, 203. This passage is italicized by Gorman as a summary of his book's proposal.

133. Zachhuber, "Modern Discourse on Sacrifice and Its Theological Background," 25.

134. Zachhuber, "Modern Discourse on Sacrifice and Its Theological Background," 26. For background in Catholic eucharistic theology, see David L. Augustine, "Two Paradigms on the Eucharist as Sacrifice."

135. See Scheeben, *Handbook of Catholic Dogmatics* 5.2, 219.

Although the Letter to the Hebrews emphasizes Christ's action in heaven, Scheeben argues that the cross is the locus of atonement.[136] It is the cross that *"independently* and *in the first place* establishes salvation."[137] Christ, needing no propitiation for himself, accomplishes it for us as our head.[138] Scheeben describes Christ as offering a "payment" of superabundant love. Sin incurs a debt, and that Christ settles this debt for us by his free dying out of love for us.[139] Scheeben cites Hebrews 9:15 and Matthew

---

136. For a contrasting viewpoint, see Moffitt, *Atonement and the Logic of Resurrection in the Epistle to the Hebrews*; Moffitt, *Rethinking the Atonement*. In *Atonement and the Logic of Resurrection in the Epistle to the Hebrews*, drawing heavily upon Second Temple literature outside the New Testament in support of a close reading of Hebrews, Moffitt concludes that "the death/suffering of Jesus can ... be seen as the event that puts into motion the process that results in atonement. The suffering of Jesus leads to his resurrection, an event that makes it impossible for him to die again. His resurrection means he has crossed over into the existence that characterizes the coming world/age. Entering heaven, he appeared before God (9:24, 26) and obtained atonement. His death sets the sequence into motion. His appearance before God in heaven effects atonement. The bridge between the two is his resurrection" (294). David L. Augustine has brought Moffitt and Scheeben together, demonstrating that Scheeben concurs with Moffitt in a certain respect while adding necessary insights that Moffitt lacks: see his "Atonement, Cross, and Heavenly Sacrifice." David Augustine sums up: "Scheeben's flexible use of typology and nuanced conceptual reading of Christ's sacrifice allow him to effectively integrate the existentialist and post-resurrection sequentialist readings of Hebrews' blood-presentation language, which Moffitt opposes one to the other ... By first doubling back and identifying Christ's divinity and capital grace/charity (in different ways) as the NT equivalent of the altar fire and then proceeding to graft it on top of the Yom Kippur imagery of Hebrews, Scheeben has a way to speak of the acceptability before God of Christ's earthly acts and crucifixion in a hieratic/sacrificial framework, while (1) holding on to the realism of the epistle's language of Christ's heavenly priesthood, but also (2) preventing it from tipping over into the Socinian reading, which denies that Christ accomplishes atonement or is in any way a priest on earth. More broadly, this is how Scheeben overcomes the difficulty in principle of applying a sacrificial theology like that held by himself, Milgrom, Eberhart, or Moffitt to Christ's redemptive work without at the same time falling into the trap of mitigating the Cross's role in procuring redemption" (326–27). For further discussion, see David L. Augustine's PhD dissertation, "Christ and the Altar Fire." Exegetically, see also Jamieson, *Jesus' Death and Heavenly Offering in Hebrews*; and see the principles laid down by Crowe, *Lord Jesus Christ*, 124–25. For the notion that Jesus' sacrifice includes not only the cross but also his actions at the Last Supper—a proposal of Maurice de la Taille, SJ, that I find unpersuasive—see Matthiesen, *Sacrifice as Gift*, chapter 2.

137. Scheeben, *Handbook of Catholic Dogmatics* 5.2, 220.

138. See Emile Mersch, SJ's remarks on Christ's headship and juridical satisfaction, in Mersch, *Whole Christ*, 451–54 and elsewhere.

139. See Pomplun, "Matthias Joseph Scheeben and the Controversy over the *Debitum Peccati*," which focuses on Mary and explains the ways in which the post-Tridentine "debate about Mary's *debitum peccati* takes us deep into the heart of our understanding of the Incarnation and original sin" (458).

18:30, which refer to redemption from the debt of sin, and he also points to Colossians 2:13–14, where Paul describes God as "having forgiven us all our trespasses, having canceled the bond which stood against us with its legal demands; this he set aside, nailing it to the cross." As Scheeben observes, the language of debt goes back to the Old Testament; sacrifices can serve as a surety to cover the debt of sin.[140] The language of debt appears strikingly in 1 Corinthians 6:20, "you were bought with a price."[141] In Scheeben's view, this language correlates with the concept of "satisfaction," which involves "the cancellation of a debt of honor and of a debt to the Holy God."[142]

In the payment of the debt, says Scheeben, love is primary. The goal is not simply averting God's wrath, but becoming God's friends. Christ's cross

---

140. For further background, going into much more detail and focusing more closely upon the biblical meaning of "debt," see Anderson, *Sin*. See also Sri, "Release from the Debt of Sin."

141. For analysis of this verse (among other texts), in the context of arguing for a strong connection between atonement and covenant love, see Pitre, Barber, and Kincaid, *Paul, A New Covenant Jew*, 129–61.

142. Scheeben, *Handbook of Catholic Dogmatics* 5.2, 224. According to Anatolios, Scheeben develops a notable "doxological transformation" of Anselm's account of satisfaction (*Deification through the Cross*, 320). Scheeben does so, says Anatolios, "by enfolding the Anselmian language of honor and satisfaction into his doxological framework while also making some decisive modifications to the Anselmian framework" (321). Specifically, Scheeben uses "'satisfaction' language to denote his own understanding of the salvific efficacy of Christ's glorification of the Father," and Scheeben extends "the content of Christ's satisfaction from merely his death, as in Anselm, to all Christ's acts and sufferings" (321). The result is that "the primarily negative Anselmian definition of satisfaction as what is 'not owed' is simply set aside and replaced by the positive conception of satisfaction as an active human adoration and glorification of God that achieves commensuration with the divine glory through humanity's union with the hypostasis of the Word . . . In the work of Christ as High Priest, God's communication of his infinite glory establishes a corresponding human capacity to offer a proportionate adoration and glorification of the divine glory" (321–22). I agree with Anatolios's emphasis on Christ's cross as glorifying God, while at the same time I note (as Anatolios recognizes) that the aspect of payment of the debt retains a central place in Scheeben. See also the insights of Marshall, "Debt, Punishment, and Payment." It will be clear that I do not agree with Robert M. Doran, SJ's argument in favor of "a transposition of the familiar but timeworn and exhausted theological category of 'satisfaction' from the Anselmian, Thomist, and Lonerganian discussions into 'social reparation and restitution.' 'Satisfaction' is redeemable (pun intended) as a theological category if it is conceived as offered not to God but to the historical victims of basic sin and moral evil and/or to their descendants and associates, whether physical, cultural, or social" (Doran, *Trinity in History*, 3:96). This denies that the order of justice inscribed in creation involves an ordering toward (and duties toward) God, and it neglects the fact that satisfaction needs to be offered not only on behalf of certain oppressive humans toward their victims, but on behalf of all sinners, since we are all caught up in the sorrowful history of active evildoing and its consequences.

reconciles us to God primarily by way of Christ's love and obedience. This is the formal condition of "satisfaction," and paying the penalty of death is the material condition. When satisfaction is understood as subordinate to merit—when, in other words, Christ's paying of the debt is primarily seen in terms of love and obedience—then, for Scheeben, we have arrived at the true concept of "sacrifice." In a proper sacrifice, love and satisfaction are united, with love (and thus communion with God) having pride of place.[143]

In this context, Scheeben attends to Psalm 22, Isaiah 53, and Daniel 9. Jesus quotes Psalm 22:1 from the cross, "My God, my God, why have you forsaken me?" (Mark 15:34).[144] Isaiah 53 describes the suffering servant; and Daniel 9 begins with a prayer confessing God's righteousness and Israel's sin, and then turns to God's plan "to atone for iniquity" and "to bring in everlasting righteousness" (Dan 9:24). Daniel 9:27 speaks in eschatological language about the establishment of "a strong covenant" and the cessation of "sacrifice and offering."[145]

---

143. See Hütter, "Debt of Sin and the Sacrifice in Charity."

144. For Mark 15's use of Psalm 22, see especially Ahearne-Kroll, *Psalms of Lament in Mark's Passion*, 197-213; and—indebted to Ahearne-Kroll—Botner, *Jesus Christ as the Son of David in the Gospel of Mark*, 182-88. See also Ahearne-Kroll's important critique of Joel Marcus's *Way of the Lord*, a critique summarized in *Psalms of Lament in Mark's Passion*, 216-19. Ahearne-Kroll argues that Psalm 22 "is a carefully crafted attempt to elicit the saving response of God by (1) appealing to God's past relationship with Israel and with the psalmist, (2) vividly depicting the psalmist's sufferings, and (3) vowing praise that will bring untold glory to God. With this in mind, Mark 15:34 takes on a significance that does not fall into the either/or categories of despair or hope that have given rise to the polarization of scholarship on this issue" (*Psalms of Lament in Mark's Passion*, 209). For further discussion, see Hays, *Echoes of Scripture in the Gospels*, 78-87. Hays observes that Mark, by contrast to Luke, John, and Paul, does not appeal to Isaiah 53. Instead, for Mark "it is chiefly the psalms of the suffering righteous one, along with the apocalyptic visions of Zechariah and Daniel, that provide the hermeneutical framework for interpreting the death of Jesus, the crucified Messiah" (*Echoes of Scripture in the Gospels*, 87). For a strong argument that Mark does in fact appeal to Isaiah 53, however, see J. Christopher Edwards, *Ransom Logion in Mark and Matthew*. On the cry of abandonment, see also Senior, *Passion of Jesus in the Gospel of Matthew*, 136-37; as well as Zacharias, *Matthew's Presentation of the Son of David*, 186: "As Matthew's passion narrative unfolds, it is evident that David's passion in Ps 22 looms large in the background. Its influence went beyond Jesus' quotation from the cross to color much of the passion narrative. Jesus' cry from the cross echoes the emotion of Ps 22 while at the same time paralleling the temporary abandonment of the righteous sufferer. But Matthew is unique when compared with the other Gospel authors by going beyond this citation to add numerous parallels in order to create a sustained typological connection with David. It is clear that the whole of Ps 22 was in the mind of the evangelist."

145. For a more recent discussion of Daniel 9:27's import for Jesus and the evangelists, see Pitre, *Jesus, the Tribulation, and the End of the Exile*.

Turning to the New Testament, Scheeben highlights the fact that it consistently presents Christ as having died for our sins, so that "His death and His blood are the cause of our salvation."[146] He cites a long list of passages that portray Christ's cross in sacrificial terms. In a number of these passages, Christ is depicted as a sacrificial sin offering, while other passages speak more generally of a redemption or a cleansing from sin accomplished by Christ's shedding his blood.[147]

Scheeben also clears up misunderstandings of "satisfaction," especially the anthropomorphic notion that God is angry and his anger has to be quenched. Instead, the divine justice recognizes a debt owed in justice by sinners. In Christ, "God Himself in His mercy gives to the sinner the means by which to comply with the demands of His justice."[148] This does not entail that God punishes the innocent Christ; rather, as I discussed above, Christ freely takes on a penalty owed by others.[149] Christ does this out of love, and for this reason his action on the cross is a true (priestly) sacrificial offering of himself to God the Father.

Discussing Christ's priestly office, Scheeben explores "priest" and "sacrifice" as they are depicted in the Old Testament and Hebrews, as well as in the documents of the Council of Trent. In offering a sacrifice, he says, the worshipper desires "to be shaped, by a sanctification and transfiguration of his life and being that is as perfect, radical, and comprehensive as possible, into a living and eternal gift for God's honor that reflects God's holiness and glory in itself, and in this form to be brought into God's sight as a 'pleasing fragrance.'"[150] The offering of animal sacrifices had in view the

---

146. Scheeben, *Handbook of Catholic Dogmatics* 5.2, 242.

147. For further background, see Hengel, *Atonement*, 45–55.

148. Scheeben, *Handbook of Catholic Dogmatics* 5.2, 255.

149. Scheeben adds, "Making satisfaction is of course *imposed by God* on Christ, whether by a formal and strict command or else by a wish or an order that is practically equivalent to a command. But this by no means entails a violation of Christ's right or of the love due to Him, in other words, an injustice or a cruelty. For God demanded of Christ only an act of virtue that would redound to the greatest honor of Christ Himself and would be richly rewarded, an act which corresponded anyway to Christ's supreme love for God and for mankind, so that Christ was willing to perform it by Himself even without an order" (Scheeben, *Handbook of Catholic Dogmatics* 5.2, 258). For a strong affirmation that Christ takes on himself the penalty due to sin, see Anatolios, *Deification through the Cross*, 417–18.

150. Scheeben, *Handbook of Catholic Dogmatics* 5.2, 332. See Anatolios, *Deification through the Cross*, citing Scheeben's *Mysteries of Christianity*. Anatolios states, "Scheeben contends that propitiation and satisfaction for sin are not themselves the ultimate goals of Christ's work and suffering. Rather, the ultimate aim of Christ's suffering was to glorify God and to humanly manifest his infinite divine love for the Father ... [T]he most essential content of Christ's salvific work is his own glorification of God, and the

reconciliation and sanctification of the offerer through communion with the living God. Scheeben refers to Book X of the *City of God*, where Augustine highlights the primary goal of being united to God in fellowship and communion, so that a sacrifice done in love involves the configuration of the soul to divine love. At the same time, Scheeben warns against supposing that it is only the offering of the soul that is "spiritual." A bodily offering is also spiritual or sacred, as is clearest with respect to Christ's offering of his sacred humanity, and as is also expressed by Paul's exhortation "to present your bodies as a living sacrifice, holy and acceptable to God, which is your spiritual worship" (Rom 12:1).

In light of the above clarifications, Scheeben's understanding of the Old Testament's burnt offerings or altar fire deserves special attention.[151] He holds that the altar fire represents "the pious latreutic worship of sanctified man, which is the *goal* of atoning worship; at the same time, however, it represents, in organic unity with the shedding of blood, the holy love as such which theoretically should underlie the atoning worship."[152] In the altar fire, therefore, one finds satisfaction and merit united in such a way as to embody "sacrifice" most perfectly. Scheeben also examines the meaning of Israel's "sin offering," "burnt offering," and "peace offering," along with the function of the purification sacrifices, the sacrifices of firstfruits, the meal offering, and the incense offering. Turning to Christ's priesthood, he sets forth various elements of comparison with the priest-king Melchizedek, as

---

ultimate content of human salvation is its glorification of God in Christ" (Anatolios, *Deification through the Cross*, 316).

151. Scheeben comments, "Generally in Scholastic writings, especially in the later destruction theologians, this consideration of the altar fire in the case of unbloody sacrifices is precisely what was very deficient. Instead of the burning on the altar, many of them, particularly Vasquez, bring into the sacrifice itself the preparation of the bread through grinding, roasting, baking as destructive actions, although they were not performed at a holy place; moreover we can hardly view the baking of bread as a destructive action" (Scheeben, *Handbook of Catholic Dogmatics* 5.2, 342). Thomas Aquinas argued that a sacrifice—including the eucharistic sacrifice—required that something be done to the thing that is offered.

152. Scheeben, *Handbook of Catholic Dogmatics* 5.2, 346. See the superb discussion of Scheeben's theology of sacrifice in Nichols, *Romance and System*, 368–82. Nichols remarks, "Doxology, glorifying God, is as central to Scheeben's theology of Christ's perfect sacrifice as that theology is itself central—and from its central position overwhelmingly dominant—in his presentation of the *tria munera Christi* [priest, prophet, king]. To Scheeben's mind, Christ's sacrifice is first and foremost 'latreutic,' a word formed from the Greek *latria*, 'adoration': i.e. it is an offering of adoring praise to the Father. And as this is the God-man we are talking about, his sacrifice is, more specifically, 'a latreutic sacrifice of infinite value'" (369). For Scheeben's theology of sacrifice in general, see also Anatolios, *Deification through the Cross*, 324–35.

well as the way in which Christ fulfills the roles of David and Solomon.[153] On the basis of Hebrews, he argues that "the *true sanctuary*, absolutely speaking, in which Christ as priest presents and asserts His sacrifice, is to be understood as the *spiritual throne and bosom of God* or *God Himself*, insofar as He is able and willing to accept creation into the most intimate communion with Himself."[154] Indeed, Christ himself, in his divinity, is the true altar of divine presence and divine fire upon which Christ's bodily sacrifice on the cross rests.[155]

Scheeben therefore warns that we must avoid the notion that the Roman soldiers performed a sacrificial slaying. Nor does Christ's free decision to accept crucifixion function like a slayer's knife. Instead, says Scheeben, Christ's sacrifice "*occurs in the form of disintegration and transformation through spiritual altar fire.*"[156] The point that Scheeben is making here is that Christ's act of satisfaction for sin—his suffering and dying—is grounded in and suffused by "the expansive and diffusive force of His love."[157] His bodily death takes on its meaning as a "sacrifice" through his love, which flows from the "altar fire" *within him* that is the indwelling "fire of the eternal

---

153. On David and Solomon's royal *and priestly* status, see Perrin, *Jesus the Priest*, 152–64, citing Hahn, *Kinship by Covenant*, 187–94. For Perrin, Jesus claimed the title "Son of David" as a way of "signalling an eschatological identity involving his priestly oversight of Israel's restoration . . . If the bulk of Second-Temple Judaism expected the eschatological Son of David to install a monarchic hagiocracy (i.e. rule by a royal priest) . . . then Jesus' claim to be 'son of David' implies an agenda that is fundamentally oriented to the temple" (*Jesus the Priest*, 164–65).

154. Scheeben, *Handbook of Catholic Dogmatics* 5.2, 377. Anatolios comments, "For Scheeben, while Christ's doxological stance encompasses his every action, it comes to complete fruition in his sacrificial death, which is thus to be understood primarily as a doxological, or 'latreutic,' sacrifice . . . In contrast to the unassuming manner by which Scheeben transposes the Anselmian notion of satisfaction into a doxological key, he is much more deliberate and explicit in his prioritization of the doxological meaning of Christ's sacrifice . . . Scheeben's prioritization of the doxological significance of Christ's sacrifice is based on the same radically theocentric principle by which he elsewhere insists on the primacy of the doxological telos of all divine activity. Simply put, the benefit of the creature is always derivative from and dependent on the glory of God" (*Deification through the Cross*, 323).

155. Scheeben adds, "Of course Christ's humanity too and specifically His flesh, as well as His cross, is in a certain sense an altar, but not as a principle of the sanctification of His sacrifice, but rather as a substrate and organ/instrument of His priestly activity that is sanctified by Christ Himself" (Scheeben, *Handbook of Catholic Dogmatics* 5.2, 385).

156. Scheeben, *Handbook of Catholic Dogmatics* 5.2, 389. In my view, this is the path for responding to the concerns raised by Lombardo, *Father's Will*. Scheeben's perspective can be joined to Anatolios's on doxological contrition, and it also fully integrates the relational order of justice that I underscore in *Engaging the Doctrine of Creation*.

157. Scheeben, *Handbook of Catholic Dogmatics* 5.2, 389.

Spirit."[158] Since this is so, Christ's sacrifice fulfills Israel's peace and sin offerings but is preeminently related to the burnt offering. Scheeben explains this point with special attention to the Spirit and the altar fire. Just as a burnt offering is utterly consumed and given over to God, Christ's bodily sacrifice on the cross is utterly consecrated to God through the fiery indwelling of the Spirit.[159] No wonder that this offering has the power, in the Spirit, to deify all those who are united to Christ's Body.

Scheeben sums up his perspective by describing Christ on the cross not only as sacrifice and priest, but also as the altar and the altar fire. He remarks in this vein that Christ's "*offering is found from the beginning on the altar and in the altar fire.*"[160] The altar is the divine presence, and Christ is God. The hypostatic union and the fullness of the Spirit's presence in Christ's humanity ensure that his sacrifice on the cross is not a mere sacrifice of the kind where a priest violently slays a cultic victim; rather it is quite the opposite. His sacrifice on the cross is the action of the divine Son and is fueled by the fire of the Spirit's Love, and so there is no need for a slayer or for an extrinsic altar. It is Christ's sacrifice understood in this sense that has "atoning-meritorious force and significance."[161] Again, Christ's sacrifice is ultimately "the effect of spiritual fire" grounded in "[t]he glowing love for God kindled in Christ's soul by the fire of the Holy Ghost," and manifesting itself in an interior suffering or sorrow that Scheeben describes as "a process

---

158. Scheeben, *Handbook of Catholic Dogmatics* 5.2, 389. The myth that pneumatology was dead in the centuries prior to Vatican II is confounded by Scheeben's work.

159. On the Spirit's indwelling (in us and in Christ), see Staudt, "Substantial Union with God in Matthias Scheeben," 519–21 (and see 531–36 for some important criticisms of Scheeben's understanding of "substantial union"). Scheeben adds in light of the hypostatic union that "by dint of that unity with God, Christ in His sacrifice represents God in such a way that the shedding of His divine blood in the name of mankind to the glory of God is no less a gift of this blood given by God for the salvation of mankind and in this regard an image, pledge, and means of the gift of the Holy Spirit" (Scheeben, *Handbook of Catholic Dogmatics* 5.2, 391).

160. Scheeben, *Handbook of Catholic Dogmatics* 5.2, 390. I owe thanks to David Augustine for drawing my attention to this element of Scheeben.

161. Scheeben, *Handbook of Catholic Dogmatics* 5.2, 394, 398. Anatolios comments, "Scheeben presents Christ as surrendering his body in a perfect symbolic offering of love and esteem for God and accomplishing the transference of this body into the divine realm, while being himself both priest and victim in the same person. A mere human being cannot make such a sacrifice. If a human being offers in sacrifice a material object other than his own body, such a sacrifice would not actualize a real consummation and realization of spiritual surrender and glorification of God. Such a complete surrender and glorification can be effected only by offering up one's own body, which is the primary symbolic representation of the human soul. But if a human being were to initiate the offering of one's own body to death as a sacrifice to God, such an act would be merely suicide" (*Deification through the Cross*, 325).

of being consumed by the ardor of His love for God."[162] Christ's cross involves a "spiritual sacrificial conflagration" of love.[163]

Scheeben also underscores the fact that Christ offers himself as a representative of God's people. In Christ the head, this people shares in Christ's sacrifice. Indeed, this people "*is sacrificed and sacrifices in Him and through Him.*"[164] There is a participation of the people in the (new covenant) sacrifice of Christ, just as—and indeed far more than—the people of Israel participated in the covenantal sacrifices offered by the mediator Moses. Scheeben points out that on the Day of Atonement, the sacrificial goat was given to the high priest who then performed the sacrifice on behalf of the people. Christ's holy humanity, by contrast, is the highest fruit of the people of Israel and of the human race. Christ therefore can truly represent all people in his

---

162. Scheeben, *Handbook of Catholic Dogmatics* 5.2, 396. See Anatolios's summation of his treatment of Scheeben's theology of the cross, in Anatolios, *Deification through the Cross*, 329–30. For Anatolios—focusing on the *Mysteries of Christianity*, though with a footnote recognizing that the *Dogmatics* places Christ's cross more firmly within the context of original sin and its consequences—Scheeben provides "a clear affirmation that suffering and self-abdication need no other rationale than the glorification of God and have an intrinsic capacity to render that glorification. One of the consequences of this logic is that it seems to at least come close to glorifying suffering and death as such, as if they were intrinsically doxological and not rather the negative ream that the glory of God can invade and colonize. As applied to Christ, one gets the impression that he would have needed to suffer and die simply to render the greatest honor to God, apart from the consideration of human sin. When one compares Scheeben's soteriological logic in this regard with Anselm's, we see that, on the one hand, Scheeben has a much more robust account of the positive content of Christ's glorification of God. For Scheeben, the 'honor' that Christ renders to God is a much less abstract notion than it seems to be in Anselm and is filled with concrete trinitarian and christological content: Christ honors the Father through his perfect human adoration of God, throughout his life and death, which flows out of the hypostatic union. But, on the other hand, Scheeben seems to be still beholden to the Anselmian logic in which the relation between the 'honor' that Christ pays to God and the sin that is thereby canceled is fairly extrinsic. As in Anselm so with Scheeben, Christ's honoring of God seems to cancel sin simply by outweighing sin on some great metaphysical scale" (329–30). Anatolios's solution is that Christ "gains this grace for us in himself, by condemning sin in his *own* flesh (cf. Rom 8:3) and by subsuming the rejection of sin, in the form of a vicarious contrition, into his glorification of God ... Christ's suffering and death were part of his drawing human sin and its consequences into the glorification of God and, as such, constituted Christ's own perfect 'doxology of judgment' in which he accepted the consequences of human sin as a means of rejecting and condemning sin itself" (330).

163. Scheeben, *Handbook of Catholic Dogmatics* 5.2, 396. For his understanding of the "sacrificial fire" in relation to the cross (by comparison to his earlier view that the "sacrificial fire" has to do with his resurrection), Scheeben gives credit to the work of Thalhofer, *Opfer des Alten und Neuen Bundes*.

164. Scheeben, *Handbook of Catholic Dogmatics* 5.2, 391.

sacrifice and do so as their Head. In his human nature, the Son of God offers himself in such a way that all people are taken up in his sacrifice.[165]

For Scheeben, in accordance with Hebrews, Christ's "priestly offering-up of the sacrifice of Cross" does not end with his death, because Christ continues to offer up this sacrifice in his heavenly intercession with the Father.[166] The resurrection and the ascension of Christ are therefore not cut off from Christ's sacrifice, even if the cross has a pride of place. The cross, Scheeben specifies, contains the fullness of the "atoning-meritorious power" of the sacrifice.[167] But the sacrifice is nevertheless "completed" in a certain way by Christ's resurrection and ascension. On the cross, the "altar fire" of divine presence and divine love is already there. Yet, says Scheeben, the resurrection and the ascension make Christ's sacrificed body into an eternally and gloriously alive body, and thus into "a constantly burning sacrificial flame" in love.[168] Scheeben compares the resurrection and ascension to a burnt offering's ascending to God in flame and smoke, and he cites Revelation's image of "the *standing of the Victim Lamb, transfigured after His bloody immolation, upon God's throne.*"[169] The resurrection and ascension add to our understand-

---

165. Nichols comments, "This sacrifice is 'exclusive' inasmuch as only the Mediator, the Second Adam, the immaculate Lamb, could offer it. That statement excludes, and is meant to. It excludes all other possible candidates as offerers of sacrifice fully pleasing to God . . . But Christ's sacrifice is also 'inclusive' because in him and through him, in Scheeben's words, '[T]he whole human race . . . took from its own substance and offered to God the pledge of an infinite worship, and sent it up to heaven.' The sacrifice which is exclusively his is also inclusively that of the human community in and through him" (Nichols, *Romance and System*, 373). Nichols adds that Scheeben's "key idea of the organicity of the relation between Christ and the *humanum* in its total (quantitative as well as qualitative) extent" means that "no human being in their earthly life is excluded beforehand from the scope of Christ's sacrificial death" (381).

166. Scheeben, *Handbook of Catholic Dogmatics* 5.2, 400. See Nichols, *Romance and System*, 380.

167. Scheeben, *Handbook of Catholic Dogmatics* 5.2, 405.

168. Scheeben, *Handbook of Catholic Dogmatics* 5.2, 406. In Anatolios's view, it is the "emphasis on donation and adoration as integral to genuine sacrifice that impels Scheeben to stress that Christ's resurrection and exaltation are intrinsic moments of Christ's sacrifice and not merely the consequences or 'reward' for this sacrifice" (*Deification through the Cross*, 326). For the view (with which I disagree) that it is "more biblically coherent and theologically persuasive" to "focus on the resurrection as the primary saving event," see Ralston, "Judgment on the Cross," 234. I should add that Ralston's essay is nevertheless a brilliant and very helpful exemplar of constructive Christian theological dialogue with Muslims. See also Madigan, "Who Needs It?," arguing, in significant part on the basis of the Qur'ān (but also drawing upon Karl Rahner, Eleonore Stump, Scot McKnight, Matthew Bates, and others), against standard Muslim criticisms of the Christian doctrine of the atonement.

169. Scheeben, *Handbook of Catholic Dogmatics* 5.2, 408.

ing of Christ's sacrifice by demonstrating that it is an everlasting sacrifice of love, glorifying God, since Christ lives to intercede forever.[170]

Scheeben notes that in order to make an "appeasing satisfaction," Christ must be holy; Christ must perform a morally just action; and Christ's satisfaction must be centered in love for God. Because sin is fundamentally arrogant, an act of satisfaction must be fundamentally humble and obedient. As such, the act of satisfaction must exhibit deep sorrow over sin, rather than imagining sin to be something minor. A true act of satisfaction must, therefore, take "the form of a *spiritual sacrifice* of suffering that burns with the fire of love, resigned obedience, and sorrow for sin, which compensates for the *injury and offense to God* inherent in sin or the *dishonor of God through denial of the respect and love that are owed to Him.*"[171]

Scheeben adds that although satisfaction aims to pay a debt whereas merit aims to gain a good, nevertheless an act of satisfaction must preeminently be suffused with love. Satisfaction is not a mere legal payment of a penalty. Rather, Christ's act of satisfaction is a sorrowful surrender of his bodily life out of love and obedience to God's will. Our turning away from the life-giver has as its intrinsic punishment "the dissolution and destruction of ... being and life."[172] By freely bearing this penalty without owing it, Christ destroys the claims of sin. As a work of supreme love, this act of satisfaction "represents the *most complete compensation* for the dishonor of God contained in sin," since Christ not only bears the just penalty owed by sinners, but also gives to God the love and obedience (or glorification) that should have been given by sinners.[173] Because satisfaction and love are here perfectly

---

170. Scheeben goes on to explain: "If therefore God's heavenly throne, prefigured by the propitiatory (throne of grace) over the Ark of the Covenant, as bearer of the Victim-Lamb is also an altar to the highest power and as such takes up into itself specifically the altar of the light offering together with that sacrifice, then self-evidently it is also the altar of the heavenly incense offering, in which Christ Himself is at the same time altar and victim and the one who sacrifices" (Scheeben, *Handbook of Catholic Dogmatics* 5.2, 410).

171. Scheeben, *Handbook of Catholic Dogmatics* 5.2, 226. Anatolios draws upon Scheeben for an account of "Christ's vicarious glorification of God," while drawing upon Aquinas "for an affirmation of Christ's vicarious contrition for human sin" (Anatolios, *Deification through the Cross*, 339). I think Anatolios could have equally drawn upon Scheeben for the latter as well. Anatolios observes that "contrition is the form that the human glorification of God takes in the face of human sin. Inasmuch as sin itself should be considered ultimately a 'disglorification' of God, contrition is the disavowal of that disglorification and the repentant 'return' (*shub*) to the true glorification of God" (339).

172. Scheeben, *Handbook of Catholic Dogmatics* 5.2, 229.

173. Scheeben, *Handbook of Catholic Dogmatics* 5.2, 229. For Scheeben on intra-Trinitarian glorification, see Anatolios, *Deification through the Cross*, 241–52, relying

joined, Christ's cross is a true sacrifice. And because Christ died for all sinners as the head of the human race, all sinners can share in offering his sacrifice to God.[174] Although Scheeben does not focus upon the covenantal dimension of Christ's sacrifice, it is implicit in his discussion. The covenants consistently involved the dwelling of the people with God and their enjoyment of the divine presence, which is what Christ's sacrifice brings about.

I note that in John 14:30, with reference to his coming passion, Jesus states, "I do as the Father has commanded me, so that the world may know that I love the Father." In John 15:12–13, we find Jesus' commandment to his followers to share in his sacrificial love. Jesus' followers will belong to the new covenant family, sharing in the glory of the Father and Son, if they actively obey Jesus' commandment to "love one another as I have loved you," by laying down their lives for their friends.[175] Since this is so, it makes

---

mainly upon the *Mysteries* but quoting a lengthy passage from the *Handbook of Catholic Dogmatics* on page 251 (as well as another passage on page 248n29). Anatolios states on page 250: "Scheeben conceives of the rationale, so to speak, of the Father's begetting of the Son and breathing forth the Spirit in terms of glorification. The Father generates the Son and breathes forth the Spirit in order to manifest, express, glorify, and bear testimony to the fruitfulness of his self-knowledge and self-love. These formulations recall the conceptions we have seen earlier in patristic theology of the trinitarian circle of mutual glory, which is the source and goal of the human worship of God. Indeed, we also find in Scheeben the understanding that the human glorification of God is grounded and enfolded in the mutual glorification of the divine persons, by which they eternally 'bear witness' and 'give testimony' to the glory of one another." See also Minz, *Pleroma Trinitatis*.

174. Anatolios draws out this dimension in *Deification through the Cross*, 326.

175. The depth-dimensions of "sacrifice" present here tend to be missing in feminist approaches to sacrifice as "self-sacrifice": see for instance Pamela Sue Anderson, "Sacrifice as Self-destructive 'Love.'" Anderson focuses on "the psychological, ethical, and political dangers for women in religious rituals and acts of sacrifice. The fundamental problem is that gender oppression can reinforce painful burdens of attending to the suffering of others, when the woman who attends to the pain of others is already suffering under domination. Under oppressive conditions, religious practices requiring asymmetrical acts of sacrificing/non-sacrificing love (especially for women and other sacrificing subjects who are socially constructed as an inferior gender) merely make a bad situation worse... [A]ddressing sacrificial practices from a standpoint of gendered confidence is necessary in order to transform the masochism and the sadomasochism damaging religious practices: the new vision is to equalize relations between human subjects, exposing how it is that God as male (i.e. Father) has meant male is divine and so, superior to female and other non-Fathers who face ineluctable sorrow" ("Sacrifice as Self-destructive 'Love,'" 46). Of course, more issues than "sacrifice" are at work here, including theological anthropology, male-female differences, the image of God, marriage and children, the nature of power, and so on. But Christ's bearing our sins and their penalty in sorrowful love, and our sharing in his sacrifice, is not about domination but about doxological liberation. For a sometimes quite helpful analysis of power in Christ, in dialogue with an array of feminist scholarship and kenotic theologies (and

quite a difference that the new covenant family of Christ, at the foot of the cross, shares in his sorrowful suffering as he seals his new covenant by his blood. As Jean-Hervé Nicolas says, "Man cannot be a mere spectator of the redemption. He is implied in it. Mary's role at the foot of the cross, as a prolongation of the role that she had to play and that she did play at the annunciation, is to represent mankind before Christ so that she may consent to His sacrifice and make it her own."[176] Nicolas is aware of the objection that Christ, not Mary, represents humankind before God. But he explains that Mary represents humankind before Christ, and "she does so precisely at the moment when He takes this humanity into Himself in order to bring it back to the Father—and speaks in its name, consenting to this undertaking performed by the Savior for humanity."[177] For this reason, as a final step in this chapter, let me turn again to Mary's role—the role of the embodiment of faithful Israel sharing in the sealing of the new covenant in Christ's blood.

---

falling into some serious mistakes about God and humanity, under the influence of queer theology as advocated by, among others, Althaus-Reid, *Queer God,* and by the contributors to *Queer Theology*), see Mercedes, *Power For.* See also Crysdale, *Embracing Travail* and Biviano, *Paradox of Christian Sacrifice*; and see the reductionist portrait of deification offered by Brock and Parker, *Saving Paradise,* as well as the overview of feminist Christology in Guðmundsdóttir, *Meeting God on the Cross.*

176. Nicolas, *On the Incarnation and Redemption,* §523.

177. Nicolas, *On the Incarnation and Redemption,* §523. For a salutary perspective that complements Nicolas's from a different direction, focusing on what it means for Christ to be male, see Gondreau, "Aquinas on Christ's Male Sexuality as Integral to His Full Humanity." For a starkly opposed viewpoint to Nicolas's, see Kearns, *Virgin Mary, Monotheism and Sacrifice,* indebted to Julia Kristeva's perspective as found for instance in "Stabat Mater." Anderson sums up (along lines that in my view fail to do justice to Catholic theology of Mary, or, for that matter, to the lived experience of Catholic women who understand and live the Church's faith), "The damage done to women by the ethical formation of traditional Roman Catholicism in emulation of Marian sacrifice focuses upon Mary's purity, but also Mary's suffering in complete acceptance of her passive role as the Virgin Mother in her son's conception, his birth, earthly life, suffering in death and resurrection to eternal life. If Kant had a difficulty in comprehending Christ's innocent sacrifice as non-autonomous, feminists have an even more difficult problem in trying to comprehend the story of a heteronomous virgin-mother whose purity renders impossible any sense of freedom or responsibility: her life is one of submission to her predetermined role in life and in relation to God the Father. Kearns offers some constructive background here, while Kristeva directs her (and us) to the damaging psycho-sexual problems suffered by those women who have been taught to be 'virtuous' like the Virgin Mary and to seek solace from Marian suffering, when they fail—necessarily!—to be virgin mothers. But indirectly Marian sacrifice re-enforces the dominant roles of the Father and of the blood of the victim (the Son) in religious sacrifice" (Anderson, "Sacrifice as Self-destructive 'Love,'" 42).

VI. Mary's Participation in Christ's Sacrifice

In *The Gospel According to John*, Raymond Brown argues, "The action of Jesus in relation to his mother and the Beloved Disciple completes the work that the Father has given Jesus to do and fulfills the Scripture."[178] Although he does not make all the connections that I made above in my discussion of John 19:25-27, Brown holds that Mary and the beloved disciple are representative of faithful Israel and that the cross is the "birth pangs" of "a new people."[179]

In my view, as suggested above, the missing piece in Johannine scholarship on John 19 is the identification of Jesus' cross as the new Exodus sacrifice that seals the new covenant, with Jesus the new Moses standing in the place of Moses (the Mediator), of the altar (the divine presence), and of the sacrificial victim. Again, at the foot of the cross Mary and the beloved disciple stand in the place of the faithful people of Israel, and they participate in obedience and love in the blood of Christ as God's new covenant people, fulfilling the covenantal promises of Israel in Exodus 24.[180]

Mary's role comes through the grace of the Holy Spirit. As Scheeben says, without neglecting the transcendent uniqueness of the hypostatic union, "The grace of Motherhood is indeed in the Mary the principle of a *supernatural efficacy specifically peculiar to her*, much as in Christ the grace

---

178. Brown, *Gospel According to John (xiii-xxi)*, 923.
179. Brown, *Gospel According to John (xiii-xxi)*, 925.
180. With regard to John 2:4, Brown warns against the fact that "most Protestant commentators pass over the verse as if it were unthinkable that Mary played a role in Johannine theology," although Brown also warns that Catholics often fall into "pious exegesis" of the verse (Brown, *Gospel According to John (i-xii)*, 107). See also the discussion of John 2 and John 19 in Brown, *Death of the Messiah*, where Brown observes: "These are the only two Johannine passages in which the mother of Jesus appears; that same designation is used for her in both instances (with no personal name); in each she is addressed as 'Woman,' an address perfectly proper for a man to a woman, but never found for a son to his mother; and while Cana occurred before the hour had come (2:4), this episode [in John 19:25-27] occurs after the hour has come (13:1)" (1020). Backing away from his earlier interest in the new Eve (which he now considers to be a possible but doubtful interpretation), Brown argues regarding the meaning of John 19:26-27, "the significance of this episode lies in the new relationship between the mother of Jesus and the beloved disciple, not in symbolism attached to Mary through the history of interpretation. My contention that this new relationship involves the issue of how Jesus' natural family was related to a family created by discipleship (in Johannine language, through birth from above) gains support from the fact that this precise issue was one that the Synoptic evangelists struggled with" (2:1024-25). This interpretation fits with Brown's focus in his intervening work, *Community of the Beloved Disciple*; and see Brown et al., *Mary in the New Testament*, 188-90, 212 (where the authors claim, rather obtusely in my view, that Jesus uses the title "woman" "for all women" and so it has no special meaning in John 19), and 215-18. For further discussion along these lines, see McHugh, *Mother of Jesus in the New Testament*, 361-87.

of union is for His humanity, in that it lends to her activity an altogether singular dignity and power."[181] Scheeben is able to balance this praise of Mary's vocation with the affirmation that the "efficacy of Mary's actions as well as their inner value is essentially different from the value and the efficacy of Christ's actions and has an entirely different character."[182]

According to Scheeben, Mary and her Son are dynamically related in such a way that Mary is never a competitor but always drawn into cooperation with her Son. He specifies that "Mary *cannot be a principle coordinated with Christ and independent of Him that is authorized and called to complete His redeeming power and might.* On the contrary she is subordinated to Christ as to *the* Redeemer."[183] Mary is redeemed by Christ, and Mary's cooperation in his redemptive work comes about only insofar as she herself is redeemed by him and insofar as she receives grace through him. Mary does not add anything to Christ's redemptive power. Mary's cooperation with Christ, says Scheeben, is "only a *ministerial cooperation* with Christ's redemptive deed—the real act of Redemption which is in itself independent."[184]

Thus, Scheeben cautions that the title "Coredemptrix" can only be used in a highly qualified manner and generally should not be used at all, given that Mary does not contribute anything to Christ's redemptive power or act.[185] Mary does not coordinate with Christ or supplement his work.

---

181. Scheeben, *Handbook of Catholic Dogmatics* 5.2, 605. I do not fully agree with the direction Scheeben takes this valid insight into Mary's bridal Motherhood. Connecting the Word with the humanity of Christ and the Spirit with the humanity of Mary, he states, "since the personal character of the Bride of Christ in Mary is fully understood only in her capacity as bearer and sanctuary of the Holy Ghost, therefore the reason for the singular dignity and power of her activity is also to be traced back to this capacity of her person and thus to be posited formally in the fact that Mary *is analogously an organ of the Holy Ghost* working in her and through her, *as Christ's humanity is an organ of the Logos*, and indeed in a fuller and higher sense than this can take place with another created person" (Scheeben, *Handbook of Catholic Dogmatics* 5.2, 605). Scheeben recognizes that the Holy Spirit perfects and deifies the humanity of Christ. Scheeben speaks, for example, of "the efficacy which Christ Himself as Incarnate Word exercises through His own 'eternal Spirit' and in which His flesh too as flesh of the Word participates in the form of a physical vehicle of the power of the 'eternal Spirit'" (Scheeben, *Handbook of Catholic Dogmatics* 5.2, 606). For discussion of Scheeben's Mariology, see especially Nichols, *Romance and System*, 425–83; Hoffmann, "Zur 'Perichorese' von Maria und Kirche in der Sicht M. J. Scheebens"; and Nepil, *Bride Adorned*, 33–58; and for Scheeben's Mariology in the context of that of his Roman School teachers, see Boss, "Original Holiness," 492–98; and Carola, *Engaging the Church Fathers in Nineteenth-Century Catholicism*, 457–67.

182. Scheeben, *Handbook of Catholic Dogmatics* 5.2, 608.
183. Scheeben, *Handbook of Catholic Dogmatics* 5.2, 611.
184. Scheeben, *Handbook of Catholic Dogmatics* 5.2, 612.
185. He comments, "The term Coredemptrix is set forth by many recent, even

That said, Mary's cooperation entails that she contributes to the effects of redemption; the new Eve cooperates with the new Adam. She does so especially through her presence at the foot of the cross, where the (covenant-sealing, sacramental) blood and water comes forth from Christ's wounded side (John 19:34) and recapitulates the creation of Eve from Adam's side. While Christ's sacrifice is superabundantly sufficient for our salvation, it requires to be received and ratified by the covenantal people for whom he dies. Scheeben puts it this way: the participation of Mary in Christ's redemptive sacrifice, as "*the spiritual Mother* of the other redeemed persons," is fitting "not in order to constitute or complete the internal power of the work of Redemption, but rather only to complete comprehensively its beauty and loveliness and in particular its *organic union with the mankind*

---

learned theologians as if it were a classical expression sanctioned by the language of the Fathers of the Church or of 'the Saints.' Some think, accordingly, that the expression is indeed '*surprising*,' but by no means '*daring*'; the offense that the Protestants took at it is only one of their usual misunderstandings; for Catholics there is only scandal taken here, no scandal given ... Yet despite all our research we have found this expression *nowhere before the 16th c.* ... [N]either and even less does it follow from the fact that Mary is called in a broader sense cause, servant, mediatrix of Redemption and therefore is sometimes even called Redemptrix, that we are justified in saying that she is Co-redemptrix, because in Christ's case we always understand 'redeeming' formally as bringing about the freedom of human beings through His divine, priestly, and royal power and through a ransom which He Himself is" (Scheeben, *Handbook of Catholic Dogmatics* 5.2, 613–14). For a strong defense of Mary as "co-redemptrix," as well as a helpful historical overview, see Nichols, *There Is No Rose*, chapter 4. He argues, "It was the Son who meritoriously caused the distinguishing role she was to play ... Her supportive contribution consists ... of the costing ratification of the offering of Christ by a human person. It took the form of a dolorous offering of the offering—and so can be called a co-oblation, always understanding that we use the term 'co-oblation' analogically, to mark the subordinate, dependent, and participatory character of her involvement. Whereas the first Eve by her disobedience solicited the old Adam to total soteriological ruin, the New Eve, in her perfect obedience, ratifies the Second Adam in his achieving of all saving good" (*There Is No Rose*, 87). This is theologically correct, but I think the gist of the doctrine can be communicated without using the title "co-redemptrix." See also Jean-Hervé Nicolas's concerns about the title "co-redemptrix": Nicolas, *On the Incarnation and Redemption*, §523; as well as, for the opposite side, the vigorous defense of "co-redemptrix" (and "Mediatrix") in the essays that comprise Peter Damian Fehlner, OFM Conv.'s *Systematic Mariology*. For a historical survey of Mary as co-redemptrix, joined to a theological defense of this title, see Fastiggi, "Mary in the Work of Redemption"; and Miravalle, '*With Jesus*'. It is clear that Scheeben was mistaken to suppose that there are no references to Mary as "co-redemptrix" prior to the sixteenth century, although the term was rare. The first pope to use the term was Pope Pius XI, and Pope John Paul II did so six times. In correspondence with me, Fastiggi has remarked that Christ's sacrifice was absolutely sufficient for the redemption of humanity, but Christ decided to include the members of his Mystical Body in the paschal mystery, just as the faithful join themselves to Christ's sacrifice at Mass.

that is to be redeemed."[186] This union is the new covenant union of Christ and the Church, sealed by Christ and, as I would put it, ratified at the foot of the cross by the participation of Mary and the beloved disciple in the sacramental blood and water that comes forth from Christ.

Again, Scheeben warns against imagining that Mary joined to Christ's sacrifice her own distinct sacrifice, as though there was "a twofold sacrifice through which the world was redeemed."[187] There was only one redemptive sacrifice: Christ's. But Scheeben aptly describes Mary's intense sorrow and prayer at the foot of the cross as "the moaning of the Dove," and he notes that it "proceeded from a heart that through its loving participation in the Passion of the Lamb was itself a spiritual sacrifice," united to the one redemptive sacrifice of Christ.[188]

The way that Scheeben depicts Mary's cooperation in Christ's sacrifice on the cross is broadly similar to—though not identical with—what I have identified above with respect to John 19 in light of Exodus 24. Scheeben states that "in the *redemptive sacrifice*, the object and content of which is Christ's flesh, Mary, representing mankind, for which the sacrifice was performed and offered, *acted jointly in the most proper and fullest sense of the word as the Woman bringing the sacrifice and jointly offered it as her sacrifice.*"[189] I take this to describe something similar to how the people of Israel brought the sacrifice that Moses offered, even though Moses alone undertook the sacrifice at the altar. Scheeben has in view Mary's act of interiorly handing over her own Son, rather than clinging to him or opposing his sacrificial intention. She consented to his action, and she joined in his sorrow for sin. Her consent was already present at the annunciation, as manifested by her *fiat* in consenting to bear the Messiah; and her consent was amplified at the infant Jesus' presentation in the temple, when Simeon proclaimed, "Behold, this child is set for the fall and rising of many in Israel, and for a sign that is spoken against (and a sword will pierce through your own soul also)" (Luke 2:34–35).[190] As Scheeben maintains, the presentation at the temple was already "a formal sacrificial dedication."[191]

---

186. Scheeben, *Handbook of Catholic Dogmatics* 5.2, 619.
187. Scheeben, *Handbook of Catholic Dogmatics* 5.2, 625.
188. Scheeben, *Handbook of Catholic Dogmatics* 5.2, 625.
189. Scheeben, *Handbook of Catholic Dogmatics* 5.2, 627.
190. For a helpful recent Protestant exegetical treatment of Simeon's prophecy, see Peeler, *Women and the Gender of God*, 54–56. Without going so far as does Scheeben, Peeler observes, "What she [Mary] has learned in this exchange is that her heart, too, will be exposed for all to see, that she will suffer at his suffering" (55).
191. Scheeben, *Handbook of Catholic Dogmatics* 5.2, 628.

Scheeben compares Mary's activity with that of Abraham in acceding to the sacrifice of Isaac (Genesis 22). Like Abraham, the faith-filled disciple Mary is willing to give up her Son, the Son of the promise, knowing that God will be faithful. Scheeben also compares Mary to the faithful covenantal people of the Mosaic era. The task of the people in the Mosaic sacrifices was to bring the animals to be ritually slaughtered. Mary consented to the offering not merely of one of her flock, but of her Son. Scheeben's identification of Mary with the *"bringer of the sacrifice,"* in terms drawn from the Old Testament, surely puts the covenantal context front and center, despite Scheeben's lack of explicit reference to the covenant.[192] This point becomes clearer when he turns to another Marian title, the "Ark of the Covenant." The Ark of the Covenant both bears the divine presence and is the seat of the "throne of atonement."[193] Although other humans participate in Christ's sacrifice, Mary's participation is unique in degree and scope.

Scheeben argues that Christ's sacrifice becomes, in and through Mary's cooperation, a "sacrifice of humanity"—thereby (in my terms) involving both parties of the new covenant, the God-man and the merely human members of the Church.[194] Indeed, Scheeben presses so far as to say that the fruits of Christ's sacrifice are mediated to all humanity by Mary, insofar as her soul is the privileged "bearer of his sacrifice" (just as it was the privileged bearer of the Incarnation through her *fiat*) through her interior consent to and cooperation with his sacrificial self-offering at the cross.[195] To my mind, explicit appeal to the covenantal relationship between Christ and his Bride the (Marian) Church, as sealed by the blood of his new covenant sacrifice, would help Scheeben here to avoid any hint of exaggeration. Scheeben comes close to such an explicit appeal when he adds, "Christ poured out all His redemptive blood into the heart of His Mother standing beneath the cross."[196] This statement resonates with Moses' pouring of half the sacrificial blood upon the people in Exodus 24. Scheeben's image makes clear that Mary, at the foot of the cross, embodies the relation of the people of the new covenant toward Christ the new Moses who has sacrificially sealed the covenant as the one Priest and Mediator.

For Scheeben, Mary's cooperative mediation of the fruits of Christ's sacrifice cannot be demonstrated solely from Christ's words to Mary and John.[197]

192. Scheeben, *Handbook of Catholic Dogmatics* 5.2, 630.
193. Scheeben, *Handbook of Catholic Dogmatics* 5.2, 630.
194. Scheeben, *Handbook of Catholic Dogmatics* 5.2, 638.
195. Scheeben, *Handbook of Catholic Dogmatics* 5.2, 638.
196. Scheeben, *Handbook of Catholic Dogmatics* 5.2, 639.
197. Scheeben adds somewhat later, "it can of course be concluded with *a high degree of probability* that the Savior intended to refer to this motherhood in those solemn

Instead, Scheeben employs a spousal analogy that depicts Christ (the father/husband) as begetting spiritual children by pouring out his sacrificial blood, and Mary (the mother/bride) as begetting spiritual children "by receiving Christ's sacrifice into herself as the seed of the new humanity, by means of her most intimate bodily and spiritual union with that sacrifice."[198] This imagery can be easily transposed to reflect the participation of the faithful people in the sealing of the Mosaic covenant, now with Christ (a better Moses and a better sacrifice) and Mary (God's perfectly faithful people). Scheeben does not want to make identical Mary's motherhood and the Church's motherhood, since he conceives of Mary as greater than the Church due to her concrete and personal childbearing of her Son. But he recognizes that the two motherhoods are intimately and inextricably united.[199]

words [John 19:26–27]. But for this reason the words by no means contain for us a proof *for Mary's motherhood generally*, but rather, *presupposing the latter*, contain only a *presumptive proof* for Christ's will that Mary *should care for and nourish* the children conceived by her; and to this extent it is logically quite correct when in the use of the words by ascetical writers they generally derive *from* them only an instruction for Mary to take the redeemed into her care, and for the redeemed to honor Mary and to entrust themselves to her care. Apoc 12 and generally Mary's relation to the Church suggest also the application of the magnificent passages Is 54:8 ff. and 66:7 ff., which prophesy Jerusalem's supernatural fruitfulness after painful trials, to Mary's spiritual motherhood, at least in the form of an illustration. But it goes too far when sometimes it is asserted in the form of a proof" (Scheeben, *Handbook of Catholic Dogmatics* 5.2, 643–44). For a path taken by recent exegesis, minimizing Mary's role and replacing it with Israel (on tenuous grounds), see Brown et al., *Mary in the New Testament*, 216–17: "Now John was not interested in the mother of Jesus as the mother of the messiah king with a natural claim on him, since the Johannine Jesus is the messianic Son of God not because of his earthly birth from Mary but because of his heavenly pre-existence with the father. This would mean that the evangelist would not be interested in the symbolic possibilities of Mary as Israel giving birth *to Jesus*; yet he might be interested in the symbolism of Israel giving birth *to the Christian community* through discipleship and acceptance of Jesus. If the beloved disciple was the special model for the Johannine Christians and if they were of Jewish Christian origin, then John would see Israel as the true mother of (Johannine) Jewish Christianity; and it would be among such Jewish Christians that the genuine heritage of Israel would find a home. As a support for this symbolism, Rev 12:1–5, 17 has been invoked."

198. Scheeben, *Handbook of Catholic Dogmatics* 5.2, 640.

199. Scheeben remarks toward the end of a lengthy discussion, "insofar as the *effective new birth of individual redeemed persons* is considered from the viewpoint of the *birth of the members of the Mystical Body of Christ* or *of the Church*, Mary's spiritual motherhood plainly appears *immediately as motherhood with respect to the Church*, so that in its relation to the individual redeemed members her motherhood is mediated by the motherhood of the Church itself" (Scheeben, *Handbook of Catholic Dogmatics* 5.2, 649). For further discussion of Scheeben's understanding of Mary's bridal motherhood, see Nepil, *Bride Adorned*, 55–58. He emphasizes Scheeben's use of *perichoresis* to understand the Mary-Church relationship: "The maternal *perichoresis* of Mary and the Church is here [in Scheeben's *Handbook of Catholic Dogmatics*] described in two ways.

VII. Conclusion

This chapter has ranged widely in support of the claim that Jesus, on the cross, offered the new covenant sacrifice, in a manner that contains a mariological element. As the Synoptics and John (and Paul) agree, Jesus' sacrifice on the cross established the new covenant, marked by the forgiveness of sins and entrance into the family of God. This sacrifice is a sin offering, since Jesus bears the penalty of our sin in his sorrowful dying. Even more, the sacrifice is a burnt offering, which means that it is not death, but rather the fiery power of divine and human love, that stands at the heart of the sacrifice and establishes perfect communion between God and all who share in this sacrifice through faith and love.

In his *Deification through the Cross*, Khaled Anatolios observes that "the proposition that Christ took upon himself the penalty due to our sin, considered simply in its objective and literal sense and apart from any other accoutrements . . . , must be affirmed as true."[200] As depicted biblically—and

---

First, it is an inner and total mutual relationship (*innige und allseitige wechselseitige Beziehung*)—a maternal partnership. Second, it is an inner bond and similarity (*innere Verbindung und Ähnlichkeit*)—a maternal fastening. From this inner, total, and mutual relationship, rooted in an inner bond and similarity, we see Scheeben's important conclusion: 'Each can be completely understood only in and with the other.' Mary and the Church point to the Trinitarian *perichoresis* in an analogical way; by being themselves in a perichoretic relationship, they image the Trinity insofar as they themselves cannot be distinguished apart from relation. The two mothers are in fact one, bound together and similar, deriving their fecundity and animation from the Holy Spirit. Working together in coordination with Christ, they aim at a single purpose: the communication of a holy spiritual life" (57).

200. Anatolios, *Deification through the Cross*, 417. Anatolios affirms, too, "the ontological inescapability of the negative consequences of sin, which include both physical and spiritual death," as well as the "dialectic between an objective aspect, according to which sin leads to the diminishment of humanity's being by virtue of the fundamental terms of the ontological relation between God and creation, and a subjective and personalist aspect, according to which God personally pronounces the law of this ontological relation and proclaims the consequences of the breaking of this law as a self-manifestation and self-affirmation of the glory of his own holiness" (418). He goes on to say, "From the perspective of a soteriology of doxological contrition, the fundamental premise that Christ pays the penalty for human sins must be interpreted in terms of a dialectic between the *transference* of the penalty from sinful humanity to the sinless Christ and the *transformation* of that penalty at the point of this transference . . . In the case of the penalty for human sin, Christ assumes that penalty, not in the form of a visitation of divine wrath on a sinful humanity, but rather in the form of a communication to Christ's contrite and thankful humanity of both God's absolute rejection of sin and his forgiving love. It is precisely this element of the transformation of the penalty that we can characterize, from the point of view of Christ's humanity, as doxological contrition . . . Christ takes the place of sinners as the ideal penitent who lovingly accepts God's rejection of sin as an inalienable element of the adorable glory of

as understood by Scheeben—Jesus' sacrifice contains "satisfaction" within it, since Jesus bears sin's penalty, out of love. Yet, Anatolios rightly highlights the interpersonal, glorifying, and deifying elements of Christ's cross, in light of Scheeben's understanding of sacrifice and the altar fire. The incarnate Son Jesus Christ, suffused by the Holy Spirit, is the fulfillment not only of the altar of the divine presence, but also of the altar fire and smoke by which the entirety of the sacrifice ascends to God, giving God glory and incorporating us into the Trinitarian life of interpersonal glorification.

In foregrounding the notion of sacrifice in this chapter, I have more than once referred to the fact that sacrifice is sharply contested in modern Western culture, where sacrifice is associated with victimization and bloodlust. Indeed, there have always been problems with cultic sacrifice, as seen for instance in the prevalence of human sacrifice within many cultures.[201] Peter Leithart therefore warns against the temptation toward what he calls a "quasi-stoicheic politics, a politics of sacred/profane, clean/unclean, a political order that redraws and maintains sacred boundaries and cleanses out pollutions. A stoicheic order, inevitably, encourages fleshly violence, the sacred violence of sacrifice."[202] Cultic sacrifice can be used as a mark of exclusion, a political tool for the worldly gains of those deemed worthy to share in the sacrifice.

Leithart, however, is not opposed to sacrifice and sacred boundaries as such. On the contrary, he argues that Jesus' death is a sanctifying sacrifice that fulfills the Levitical sacrifices and constitutes the true temple, and he

---

God" (418–19). In my view, the penalty is simply death (which, indeed, is not simple): Jesus Christ undergoes death, a death suffused by supreme love and sorrow.

201. For the horrific practice of human sacrifice in religious ritual, including (what she reconstructs as) the free sacrifice of the "god impersonator," see Rival, "Aztec Sacrificial Complex"—and see David Brown's attempt, which I find to be a failure, to argue (in light of Aztec poetry) that the religious ritual of human sacrifice in Mesoamerican cultures nevertheless conduced to real experience of the divine, just as Abraham (commanded to offer his son Isaac) had an experience of the divine: Brown, "Human Sacrifice and Two Imaginative Worlds, Aztec and Christian" (similarly, Bettina E. Schmidt comes close to defending pre-colonial human sacrifice in Benin, West Africa, in her "Blood Sacrifice as a Symbol of the Paradigmatic Other," 198). For human sacrifice in ancient Greece and ancient Israel—and for later related developments—see Hughes, *Culture and Sacrifice*; Levenson, *Death and Resurrection of the Beloved Son*; Day, *Molech*. For the deeply unfortunate way in which some modern Catholic political thinkers such as Joseph de Maistre and Carl Schmitt celebrate the spilling of blood as the root of social order—and for the misguided anti-sacrificial attitude of other modern thinkers—see Palaver, "Sacrificial Cults as 'the Mysterious Centre of Every Religion.'" See also Halbertal, *On Sacrifice*, 105–7, cited by Palaver. Intriguingly, Palaver draws a connection between Girard's viewpoint and the work of Weil, as for instance her *Intimations of Christianity among the Ancient Greeks*.

202. Leithart, *Delivered from the Elements of the World*, 278.

maintains that baptism establishes the sacred boundaries of the ecclesial body of Christ. But he firmly separates Jesus' death, on the one hand, from "the elemental spirits of the universe [*ta stoicheia tou kosmou*]" (Gal 4:3), including the Levitical sacrifices themselves, on the other.[203] Insofar as the Levitical sacrifices pertained to what Leithart calls a "stoicheic" order of purity/defilement and clean/unclean—from which exclusion inevitably results—Jesus' fulfillment of the Levitical sacrifices establishes a Spirit-constituted order of absolute inclusion.[204]

203. For further interpretations of "*ta stoicheia tou kosmou*," a phrase whose precise meaning is unclear, see Wright, *Paul and the Faithfulness of God*, 976; Witherington, *Grace in Galatia*, 286; Matera, *Galatians*, 155–56; Martyn, *Galatians*, 393–406; Pitre, Barber, and Kincaid, *Paul, a New Covenant Jew*, 77–82. Wright holds that "what Paul seems to be indicating is a Jewish version of paganism, the concentration on 'days, months, seasons and years' which would put Gentile converts back under the rule of the *stoicheia* from which they had so recently escaped" (*Paul and the Faithfulness of God*, 976). For Witherington, "It would appear that Paul's view is as follows. There are elementary teachings that are found throughout the world, and one form of these elementary teachings is the Mosaic Law. Jews were under one form of these elementary teachings while Gentiles were under another, but both shared a common condition of being enslaved and under subjection because of these teachings" (*Grace in Galatia*, 286). After detailing four widely varied interpretative options, Martyn takes a position closely similar to Leithart's: "the cosmos that was crucified on the cross is the cosmos that was founded on the distinction between Jew and Gentile, between sacred and profane, between the Law and the Not-Law" (Martyn, *Galatians*, 406). Pitre, Barber, and Kincaid, indebted to Robert Ewusie Moses's *Practices of Power*, offer a solution that I find preferable. They remark, "While many think Paul is simply speaking about the material elements of the world, a more likely reading is that Paul is conflating such elements with the angelic powers who were seen as governing them... [I]n early Jewish texts the heavenly bodies were identified with the angels, the ones who governed the nations of the world, the seasons, and the liturgical calendar" (*Paul, a New Covenant Jew*, 78–79). Since Paul holds that the Law was "ordained by the angels" (Gal 3:19), it is reasonable to suppose, as do Pitre, Barber, and Kincaid, that before Christ's coming both Jews and (in a different way) Gentiles were "under" or in "slavery" to the angels. Pitre, Barber, and Kincaid conclude, "In the old creation the angels ruled over human beings... In the new creation those who are 'in Christ' have been exalted above the angels, precisely because they now belong to the 'new creation' (cf. Gal 6:15)" through faith and baptism (*Paul, a New Covenant Jew*, 80).

204. For Leithart, Paul's key claim is that there is now "no holy space other than the human being and human community indwelt by the Spirit of Jesus" (*Delivered from the Elements of the World*, 41). Leithart adds that "Torah is holy, righteous and good, but its purpose and achievements are limited: it enables communion with Yahweh and promotes peace among nations *under the conditions of flesh*" (104; cf. 116–18 for further important reflections on this point). Note also Leithart's remark, "Augustine's definition of sacrifice (*City of God* 10.6) as any act by which the actors seek to be united to God in holy society captures the sense of Levitical sacrifice. Augustine's definition is teleological, and thus includes not only the moment of death but also the ascent and incorporation that follows. Sacrifice traverses the boundary between sacred and profane space, as the animal serves in a priestly capacity to enter the sanctuary on the worshiper's behalf.

Although I do not agree with some aspects of Leithart's argument—for instance, he criticizes Catholic eucharistic practice on the grounds that it excludes non-Catholic Christians, and he associates Torah and Judaism with the "stoicheic order" as though the messianic reconfiguration of Israel was an utter abolition of cultic boundaries, which it was not (Leithart, grounding himself in certain Pauline texts, is too critical of the Jewish cult and of Judaism)—I appreciate his emphasis on Jesus' faithful embodiment of life in the Spirit, Jesus' refusal to live out of fear with its patterns of exclusion and violence, and Jesus' sacrificial self-offering on behalf of his people as the true King of Israel.[205] To have a positive sacrificial meaning, Jesus'

It includes a moment of substitutionary death, but the point is that the animal dies in the process of drawing near to God . . . Every sacrifice is a meal, offered on Yahweh's altar-table and often involving human beings in table fellowship with Yahweh" (107–8).

205. Leithart therefore considers Jesus to be the one "who does Torah as it was meant to be done" (*Delivered from the Elements of the World*, 158). Regarding Jesus' death as a sacrifice, Leithart specifies: "He fulfilled the sacrificial system because he did what all the sacrifices signified . . . Every faithful Israelite worshiper offered himself, or the 'son' of his herd or flock, to Yahweh at the altar. Jesus did this in fact when he offered *himself*, passing through death into union with God like an animal sacrifice. Jesus was not the first martyr to give his life to the God of Israel, but none of the earlier martyrs ended the stoicheic system or brought in a new covenant. What made Jesus' death different? The answer is, his *identity* and his *life*" (159). Leithart goes on to say, "As head of the body, Jesus went to the cross for his body" (160), by offering himself to the Roman soldiers in the place of his disciples and by accepting condemnation and punishment "as the rebellious son when they [the Jews who accused him of blasphemy and Torah-breaking] were Yahweh's rebellious but beloved son, Israel" (163). For Leithart, "Jesus' death at the hands of wicked men ransomed and redeemed because Jesus was the Davidic king, Israel embodied in one person . . . Jesus the King took on the penalty that Israel deserved, and so released Israel from the capital penalty for her blasphemy. If Jesus did not step in to take Israel's punishment, wrath would come to the uttermost, Israel would be scattered and die, the Abrahamic promise would not be fulfilled" (164). This is a good description of penal substitution, but not of satisfaction—and to my mind the latter fits equally well and in certain ways better with the biblical portraits; see Turek, *Atonement*, 64–70 for God's wrath as a modality of his love. In my view, Leithart needs to pay more attention to the relational order of creation, to the relationship of Torah to this order, and to the full scope of Jesus' cultic actions. Leithart is compelled to hold that it is Jesus' resurrection that makes his cross "sufficient to save" (167). He states that his "sacrificial 'theory' of atonement depends *entirely* on the resurrection and exaltation of Jesus . . . A dead Jesus does not fulfill the Abrahamic promise; he does not reverse either the Edenic or the Babelic curse. If Jesus remained dead, his *way* was also dead, and we are *still* under elementary things, still under the law, still under the Adamic curse . . . The sacrificial story *cannot* end with sacred violence, even *ultimate* sacred violence. Death must be swallowed up in victory, or there is no atonement, no release from the curse (1 Cor 15). Jesus must die *and rise* to be a sacrifice, because that is what sacrifices do: they are slaughtered in flesh in order to rise in smoke and Spirit" (168–69). Without separating Jesus' cross and resurrection and ascension and pouring out of the Spirit, however, it is possible to understand more richly the salvific

death must (as the Catholic theologian Julia Meszaros says) be grounded in Jesus' love, his trust in God's plan for eschatological consummation, and his Torah-based "recognition of the human self as an intrinsically relational reality, whose good—and flourishing—is intertwined with that of others."[206]

Let me also mention the Protestant theologian Mark Heim's recent book *Crucified Wisdom*, which, although it adopts René Girard's critique of sacrifice, articulates a position quite close to my own in certain important ways. As he says, the cross must embody for humankind not only humility, love, judgment, and forgiveness, but also the fact that in Christ there is "one who suffered what they [humankind] have suffered on account of sin, and one who delights in their humanity for all it has proved to be in Christ and can become in each person's distinctive life."[207] The cross is good news about God, who stands at the deepest center of the horrors caused by sin and enables his people to be his friends and to be members of his family in true (covenantal) flourishing.

This valuation of Jesus' covenantal family explains why I pay so much attention to Mary and the beloved disciple at the foot of the cross in John 19. As suggested in this chapter, the Gospel of John's crucifixion scene is a sealing of the new covenant, in accordance with what we find at the Last Supper in the Synoptic Gospels. As portrayed by John, the cross reveals Jesus' love, his trust in his Father's plan, his mission as the new Moses to consummate the covenants, and his relation to his faithful people. Leithart underlines that Jesus never seeks to "effect salvation *without the church*."[208] Jesus' salvific sacrifice

---

power of the cross (as such)—beginning with a fuller account of 1 Corinthians. Even so, Leithart's perspective is generally close to my own (and to Scheeben's) and is always instructive. In an appendix, Leithart provides a superb and appreciative summary of Aquinas's theology of Christ's saving work (313–18), and he suggests that his own account of Torah "is an effort to perfect Thomas's treatment of the atonement by incorporating recent work on sacrifice and Levitical law into atonement theology" (317fn56).

206. Meszaros, "Sacrifice and the Self," 69, indebted to Marcel, *Faith and Reality*, 150 and elsewhere. See also my *Sacrifice and Community*, which differs in some notable ways (while agreeing in others) with another book to which Meszaros is indebted, Daly's *Sacrifice Unveiled*. For exposition of these differences in the context of the various streams of contemporary Catholic theology, arguing that the diversity is in certain ways valuable, see Philip McCosker, "Sacrifice in Recent Roman Catholic Thought."

207. Heim, *Crucified Wisdom*, 257. Heim's dialogue regarding atonement with Buddhist thought is exemplary, although he does not differentiate along the lines that I would wish between satisfaction and substitution, and therefore observes critically: "Among Christian theories of the cross, substitutionary or satisfaction views stand closest to the idea of karma: every magnitude of sin/offense has to be balanced out by an equal magnitude of negative consequence before sinners can be saved" (254).

208. Leithart, *Delivered from the Elements of the World*, 172; note that Leithart and I agree on this point.

is constitutive of true covenantal flourishing, which includes his people, the Church—that is, the messianically fulfilled and reconfigured Israel.[209]

Anatolios defines doxological contrition as "the recognition of estrangement from divine glory and the setting out on the path of return to that glory," but he generally does not articulate this in covenantal terms.[210] He does, however, discuss Jeremiah's prophesied new covenant, which he describes as "a covenant of repentance, a new capacity for repentance" in the hearts of the people of Israel.[211] On this view, the new covenant consists in God's gift of the new heart that is able to repent. A repentant people will glorify God for his mercy and will receive "divine forgiveness and a resumption of the communication of divine glory."[212]

The sealing of this new covenant happens in and through Jesus' sacrifice on the cross, fueled by his love. Recall Pitre's observations regarding the Last Supper. In light of Exodus 24:8, Pitre notes, "by identifying the wine of the covenant at the Last Supper with *his* blood, Jesus is by definition

---

209. Meszaros continues (still indebted to Marcel), "Even from the perspective of its own selfhood and good, the intersubjective human being will want to subordinate and at times sacrifice certain immediate personal gods to those commitments which more explicitly bind him to other subjects . . . As a free giving and receiving between subjects, self-sacrifice properly manifests and builds a bond or relationship between these subjects that lies at the root of the very subjectivity and, thus, the individual being of the partners in relation. In a sense, then, self-sacrifice is the occasional cost of those commitments to others that are definitive also for one's own self. As such, it is an act of fidelity both to oneself and to the other. This does not, however, mean that self-sacrifice is adequately described as the result of rational *calculation* about what best serves one's own good. If we follow Marcel's identification of intersubjectivity and love, self-sacrifice much rather emerges out of and promotes love. The rootedness of self-sacrifice in love runs counter to the kind of abstract *ethic* or 'doctrine' of self-sacrifice that would seem to promote oppressive self-victimization" ("Sacrifice and the Self," 72–74). See also Rosati, "Self-Interest and Self-Sacrifice," cited by Meszaros; and Gathercole, *Defending Substitution*, including his remark that "Paul and Plato. . . are in some agreement that vicarious death is something of a rarity. Paul imagines someone might be willing to die for a good or righteous person; Plato's character Phaedrus thinks that only lovers would consider it . . . For Seneca, 'to have someone for whom to die' is the very reason for friendship" (97, 100). With Paul, Gathercole emphasizes that Christ died for sinners: his death enables our friendship with him. In this sense, Christ's death involves "a death that averts death" and so can be called a "substitutionary" death, although it is necessary to distinguish satisfaction from the doctrine of substitution insofar as the latter entails that God punishes or pours out his wrath upon his innocent Son.

210. Anatolios, *Deification through the Cross*, 95.

211. Anatolios, *Deification through the Cross*, 123. He adds, "Jeremiah's announcement of a new covenant . . . by no means annuls the Deuteronomic association of human repentance and divine forgiveness. It simply reverses the order of causality: instead of human repentance bringing about divine forgiveness, it is now divine forgiveness that gives rise to human repentance" (124).

212. Anatolios, *Deification through the Cross*, 127.

speaking of the *new covenant* that Jeremiah and the other prophets had foretold . . . Jesus' actions at the Last Supper are a kind of 'new Sinai,' in which he inaugurates a new union between God and his people."[213] The eschatological center of the new covenant sacrifice is the marriage of God and his people (John 2), which Anatolios describes as our inclusion in God's tripersonal glorification. Pitre argues that the Last Supper functions as a "prophetic sign whose symbolism would have been recognized by any Jew familiar with the prophecies of God's future wedding. Just as YHWH wed himself to the twelve tribes of Israel at Mount Sinai through the blood of the old covenant, so now Jesus unites himself to the twelve disciples through the blood of the new covenant."[214]

If the new covenant is the heart of the matter, then Anatolios's deeply insightful emphasis on Jesus' doxological contrition on the cross has its full power within an understanding of the cross as the *new covenant sacrifice* whose love (and contrition) and satisfaction glorify God and draw us into the glory of the triune life, through the marriage of God and his faithful people.[215] Leithart puts the matter well, with reference to the Levitical sac-

---

213. Pitre, *Jesus the Bridegroom*, 50. Importantly, Pitre directs attention here to another work of Johannine commentary: Ronning, *Jewish Targums and John's Logos Theology*.

214. Pitre, *Jesus the Bridegroom*, 51. See also Hahn, *Kinship by Covenant*, 336: "Atonement theology would do well to take into account the necessity of sacrifice and curse-bearing for the establishment of covenant. Christ's atoning self-sacrifice, then, should not be understood simply in ancient or modern legal/judicial categories, but in light of its function to fulfill the terms of a familial bond established by covenant oath between God and his people, the ultimate goal of which was the restoration of the filial relationship with all humanity. Thus, the atonement is ordered to kinship by covenant."

215. Anatolios's emphasis on Christ's doxological contrition does not mean that he evacuates the significance of Christ's actual death. In reflecting upon the Letter to the Hebrews, he states, "The interiority of Christ's sacrifice corresponds to the interiority of the new covenantal relation to God which this sacrifice brings about. Thus, the Epistle to the Hebrews cites Jeremiah's prophecy of the new covenant (Heb 8:8–12), which is written on people's hearts and brings about the definitive forgiveness of Israel's sins, as being fulfilled through Christ's self-offering. This emphasis on the interior and concretely existential dimensions of Christ's sacrifice, as self-dedication and obedience, should inform our conception of Christ's salvific work as one of representative contrition. At the same time, Hebrews also sets a limit over against the psychologizing and interiorizing of the notion of sacrifice to the point where the physical and bodily dimensions are simply denied any value or efficacy. The perfection of Christ's self-offering and obedience does not detract from but rather informs the superlative efficacy of the physical shedding of his blood . . . The superiority of this mode of access to divine glory over that which was available in the old covenant is that the latter kept witnesses at a distance of dread, while now earthly and heavenly worshipers are gathered together before the divine throne itself" (*Deification through the Cross*, 161). On Christ's obedience, see also—in critical dialogue with Karl Barth—White, *Incarnate Lord*, chapter 6. White holds that "the 'obedience' of the Son [is] a figurative expression of his eternal reception of the divine will from

rifices: "Jesus offered his life to establish a new covenant that remits sins, when God put Jesus forth publicly as a *hilastērion* in blood (Rom 3), when he brought Jesus as a sin offering to purify the people and temple once and for all (Rom 8:3). Jesus became the first full human worshiper of Yahweh, the first Torah-keeper, who passed through death into Eden *as a man*."[216] Jesus did this in order to bring his people with him into the eschatological Eden, the new creation—infinitely greater than the original Eden.

Put otherwise, on the cross Jesus sealed the nuptial new covenant presaged at the wedding of Cana. The Catholic biblical scholars Francis Martin and William Wright observe the following about John 2:1 ("On the third day there was a marriage at Cana in Galilee"): "Beyond being the simple report of a wedding banquet, this notice recalls the biblical prophets' likening of the covenant relationship between God and Israel to a marriage . . . : God is the groom, and his people Israel are the bride."[217] Martin and Wright trace this imagery to Hosea and Isaiah, especially Isaiah 54 and its prophecy of redemption and mercy after the Babylonian exile: "For your Maker is your husband, the Lord of hosts is his name; and the Holy One of Israel is your Redeemer, the God of the whole earth he is called . . . In overflowing wrath

---

the Father . . . The Son proceeds eternally from the Father and therefore possesses his divine will from the Father. This eternal relativity of being permits him to receive from the Father his temporal mission to become man for our salvation. The existence of the Son as a human being in temporal history in turn reflects his personal relativity toward the Father in all that the incarnate Logos does as man. In this way the obedience of God the Son in his human nature reveals the essence of his temporal mission, the truth that he is sent by the Father. It also reveals, however, something of his relation to the Father in his divine nature: that the Son is eternally relative to the person of the Father from whom he proceeds. It does not, however, teach us that there is an obedience in the divine nature itself. Nor does it oblige us to posit a relation of commandment and obedience as constitutive of the immanent life of the Trinitarian persons" (306). For a fruitful inquiry into the obedience of the incarnate Son in light of the Confucian understanding of *xiao* or filial piety, see Brown, *Balthasar in Light of Early Confucianism*.

216. Leithart, *Delivered from the Elements of the World*, 171; for further discussion of *hilastērion*, see 338–40, where Leithart also offers an account of God's "wrath": "Scripture nowhere polarizes wrath and love. Wrath is, on the contrary, the *expression* of offended love, love bewildered and grieved that it is not reciprocated . . . Jesus' death overcomes God's wrath. But that does not mean that the Father is angry with *Jesus* or that the divine communion is torn apart at the cross. It *cannot* be the case that the gentle Son propitiates his angry Father, because the Son is on the cross only because 'God so loved the world that he sent' him. If Jesus' Father is angry with sin, he is angry with the same passionate Spirit that breathes the Word" (338–39). To my mind, it is good that Leithart rejects the dreadful notion that the Father pours out his anger (against sin) upon Jesus, but Leithart's account of divine wrath remains too anthropomorphic. For an overly brief defense of the patristic-medieval understanding of divine wrath, see my "Trinity and Suffering."

217. Martin and Wright, *Gospel of John*, 56.

for a moment I hid my face from you, but with everlasting mercy I will have compassion on you, says the Lord, your Redeemer" (Isa 54:5, 8).

As we saw, at the foot of the cross, Mary stands as the preeminent representative of faithful Israel participating in her divine Son's redemptive blood of the new covenant. With her, the entire people of God—here represented by the beloved disciple—enters into the new covenant sacrifice of Jesus.[218] Just as Moses in Exodus 24 led the representatives of the people up the mountain to see God and to eat and drink (after the sacrificial sealing of the covenant), Jesus poured forth blood and water from his side, and he calls us to share in his body and blood and in the water of the Spirit. The sacramental blood and water display the manner in which the new covenant people of God ascend, through Jesus' sacrificial death, to nuptial union with God.[219] Believers share in Christ's death and resurrection by baptism and the Eucharist, and Jesus' body is the eschatological temple (see John 2:21).[220]

To sum up: Christ offers the perfect sacrifice of fiery love and manifests himself gloriously to his new covenant family—his eschatological bride—as

---

218. See also Brown et al., *Mary in the New Testament*, 212: "It has often been remarked that for John the elevation of Jesus on the cross is already part of his return to his Father and that Pentecost is anticipated on the cross in symbolic references to the Spirit. Accordingly the crucified Jesus does not die alone but leaves behind him at the foot of the cross a small community of believing disciples—the kind of community that in other NT works is called into being in the post-resurrectional or pentecostal period. This may be the reason why after the scene involving Jesus' mother and the beloved disciple, John says that Jesus knew that all was now completed (*telein* in 19:28)—the completion of his work involves the bringing into existence of the Christian community."

219. See Martin and Wright, *Gospel of John*, 327: "In John's Gospel, the other references to blood and water allude to the sacraments of baptism and the Eucharist ... By drinking his blood, believers grow in communion with Jesus and share in his eternal, resurrected life ... These gifts of mercy, re-creation, and eternal life in the Spirit have been made available to us through the sacraments and through Jesus' death on the cross." This covenantal, sacrificial, and sacramental vision differs from the reparative understanding of atonement offered by Vernon White, *Atonement and Incarnation*, who proposes that the atonement can be understood as universal because Christ, "having achieved in his own particular space and time the reshaping of appalling evil into greater good, takes that recreative activity throughout the whole universe" (105). Christ does turn evil (the evil of the cross) into great good, and he does spread this work throughout all creation, but he does so within the covenantal-sacrificial (and sacramental) framework of justice, mercy, and new creation in the overcoming of sin and death.

220. See Hoskins, *Jesus as the Fulfillment of the Temple*; Rahner, "*Er aber sprach vom Tempel seines Leibes*," especially 305–11, emphasizing the direct immediacy of God's holy presence in Christ, in fulfillment of Zechariah 14:20–21; Hays, *Echoes of Scripture in the Gospels*, 308–23; and Chanikuzhy, *Jesus, the Eschatological Temple*. More broadly, see Beale, *Temple and the Church's Mission*. See also the multiple Old Testament prophecies about "the life-giving waters of mercy and regeneration flowing from God's temple on the day of salvation" (Martin and Wright, *Gospel of John*, 327).

the incarnate Son, calling us to share in his glory.[221] He proclaims in his last discourse in the Gospel of John, preparing the disciples for his crucifixion: "Father, the hour has come; glorify your Son that the Son may glorify you ... Father, I desire that they also, whom you have given me, may be with me where I am, to behold my glory which you have given me in your love for me before the foundation of the world" (John 17:1, 24).[222] Through baptism and the Eucharist received in faith, sharing in Christ's new covenant sacrifice with Mary and the beloved disciple, we enter into this eternal circle of glorification. "Know that the Lord is God! It is he that made us, and we are his; we are his people" (Ps 100:3).

---

221. For background, see Meeks, *Prophet-King*; and see also the extensive treatment of Christ as new Moses in Pitre, *Jesus and the Last Supper*, chapter 2, as well as my *Reconfiguring Thomistic Christology*, chapter 4. Morna D. Hooker notes that Luke 9:51—18:14 is presented as Jesus' new exodus: Luke "wished to present Jesus, not simply as a new and greater Elijah, but as a new and greater Moses" (Hooker, *Signs of a Prophet*, 61).

222. In highlighting the cross, resurrection, and ascension, I am aware that I am leaving out the "descent into hell" of Christ's soul during the period between his death and his resurrection. Theologians such as Karl Barth, Hans Urs von Balthasar, and some Barthians and Balthasarians give a central soteriological importance to Christ's descent into hell. See Lauber, *Barth on the Descent into Hell*; Brotherton, *One of the Trinity Has Suffered*, chapter 1; and for a far too critical, but informative, perspective, Pitstick, *Light in Darkness*. Soteriologically, I consider Christ's descent to be important but firmly secondary (by comparison to his cross, resurrection, and ascension). My perspective accords with White, *Incarnate Lord*, chapter 9. As White notes, perhaps surprisingly "Balthasar is quite ambivalent about the theological possibility of an interim state of the immaterial soul separated from the body" (391). For Balthasar the main soteriological significance of Christ's descent into hell is that Christ, taking the most alienated place (as the one who bears all sins, the substitute who endures the divine wrath out of love for sinners), embraces in his love even the most alienated sinner, with the result that (in White's words) "[a]ll human beings, ... *even after the time of death in the body*, are invited into a new possibility of choice for the grace of Christ" (392). My understanding of the intermediate state, by contrast, is that of Aquinas, as set forth by White in his chapter.

Chapter 5

RESURRECTION

I. INTRODUCTION

In reflecting upon Jesus' glorious resurrection, I strive to join in Paul's conversation with the Athenians in the book of Acts, where Paul proclaims that God "will judge the world in righteousness by a man whom he has appointed, and of this he has given assurance to all men by raising him from the dead" (Acts 17:31). The Athenians at the Areopagus respond to Paul's claim in diverse ways, reflective of how people today still respond: "when they heard of the resurrection of the dead, some mocked; but others said, 'We will hear you again about this'" (Acts 17:32). Elsewhere, I have defended the historicity and theological centrality of Jesus' resurrection.[1]

---

1. See my *Did Jesus Rise from the Dead?*; and my *Jesus and the Demise of Death*. See also Moloney, *Resurrection of the Messiah*. Moloney sums up his viewpoint: "What happened in the post-Easter appearances? It is impossible to describe 'what happened' in any concrete sense. We simply have no parameters within which we can judge what might have happened when someone who was crucified and buried appeared to women (all the Gospels), to two disciples on the road to Emmaus (Luke 24:13–35), to Peter (1 Cor 15:5; Luke 24:34), to a variety of gatherings of the disciples (Matt 16:16–20; Luke 24:35–53; John 20:19–23; 21:4–23), to the Twelve, to the more than five hundred, to James, to all the apostles, and to Paul (1 Cor 15:5–9). How can we decide whether or not Jesus suddenly appeared in locked rooms (see Luke 24:36; John 20: 19, 26), or describe what sort of 'risen body' the women and the disciples actually 'saw'? We can only speculate, but we cannot extend anything from measurable human experience to affirm historically certain answers to these questions" (147). Moloney is here speaking about historical judgments made according to the standard of contemporary historiography, and his point is that the mystery (rooted in the claim of glorious resurrection, and amplified by the diversity of the narratives) cannot be pinned down. While I agree with Moloney's sense of mystery, I agree more fully with Moloney when he continues, "One thing is certain: the witness of the earliest Church that Jesus 'appeared' is firm. We are

From an angle that I hope will prove fruitful, this chapter focuses on the link between Jesus' resurrection and ours, and therefore on issues pertaining to the nature of resurrected flesh and glorified bodiliness.

Thomas Joseph White says in *The Incarnate Lord*, "Christ in his glorified humanity is the exemplary cause of our resurrection from the dead."[2] White probes Aquinas's discussion of Christ's resurrection in his *Summa theologiae*, where Aquinas makes manifest the instrumental efficient causality of Christ's risen humanity. Drawing upon the sixteenth-century Protestant theologian Peter Martyr Vermigli (who was influenced by Aquinas), the Protestant theologian Steven Harris adds that Jesus' resurrection is the cause of ours specifically through the power of the Spirit. Harris notes persuasively that the Spirit "is participant, first, with the Father in raising Christ, then in being sent by the living Lord upon his followers to conform them to his death and risen life, and, finally, in conforming their bodies to Christ's risen body [cf. 2 Cor 4:16; Rom 8:11]."[3]

In this chapter, complementing and supplementing the above insights, I will ask what it might mean to have our bodies conformed to Christ's risen and glorified body. After all, a human body is comprised of cells and organs that are fit for temporal existence but not for eternal existence.[4] It seems clear that an everlastingly alive body, which cannot suffer, decay, or die, must be extraordinarily different from earthly bodies. Furthermore, when we die, our bodies—unlike Jesus'—turn to dust and become

---

not in a situation to describe the *physical* experience of these encounters, but that they took place should not be questioned. *What* took place is hard to determine, but *that* these encounters took place is affirmed across many traditions (Paul, Mark, Matthew, Luke, John, and other New Testament witnesses)" (147). For further discussion, see Hengel, *Four Gospels*; and Hengel, "Jesus, the Messiah of Israel," 8–10.

2. White, *Incarnate Lord*, 439. See also, from the standpoint of biblical theology (unfolded with systematic rigor and insight), Steven Edward Harris's *Refiguring Resurrection*. Harris is concerned to retrieve the significance of the miraculous raising of persons such as Lazarus from the dead, on the grounds that these raisings are instructive figures of Jesus' resurrection. But he differentiates these figures from Jesus' own resurrection in part because, as he says, "Christ's resurrection is both efficient and exemplary cause of Christian resurrection; the prefigurative miracles are only exemplary" (165).

3. Harris, *Refiguring Resurrection*, 166. See Vermigli, *Loci Communes*, 3.15.12, 776.

4. As I will emphasize in this chapter, I agree with Stephen T. Davis when he says that for there to be real resurrection, "our lives after death will be physical lives, embodied lives. It [resurrected life] will not be an immaterial existence in a world of pure mind or spirit" (Davis, "Resurrection, Personal Identity, and the Will of God," 23). Davis recognizes, of course, that our resurrection will involve not only "bodily continuity" but also "bodily change" (23). Davis's essay replies to Peter van Inwagen's problematic "Possibility of Resurrection," as do a number of essays in Gasser's volume. See also the defense of soul-body dualism—in which the soul grounds personal identity across the gap between death and resurrection—in Davis, *Risen Indeed*.

a material source for future generations of living things. Since this is so, it hardly seems that our risen and glorified body at the end of time could really be the same body that we now have.

Such issues have always been pressing ones for Christians seeking to understand Jesus' resurrection in light of our resurrection hope. That these issues remain central today is evident from recent books.[5] In *Refiguring Resurrection*, Harris devotes a chapter to "The Same Body or Another Body?"[6] Similarly, the Protestant theologian Jürgen Moltmann emphasizes in his *Resurrected to Eternal Life* that our glorious resurrection will not entail "the infinite extension of this life"; rather our bodies will be *glorified*, not only raised from the dead, and we will share in the life of the Triune God, "a life in the eternal present."[7] Although there is no way of adequately conceiving glorified bodiliness, inquiry into this mystery remains urgent. The Catholic theologian Thomas Weinandy points out, "When a mystery has been clarified, it has not become fully comprehensible, and so it remains open to further clarification and development."[8] Belief in glorified bodiliness requires faith in a mystery, but such faith cannot be sustained if glorified bodiliness is consigned to a domain inaccessible to thought, incapable of any real clarification or intellectual illumination.

---

5. See for example Moss, *Divine Bodies*. Moss notes that scholars of early Christianity, along with classicists, tend to "treat discussions of the afterlife"—specifically, hope for bodily resurrection in Christ—"as fundamentally irrational," arguing that "bodily resurrection is a by-product of social and political alienation" (7). While Moss distances herself from this perspective, she also distances herself from a theological perspective that holds (as I do) that the early Christians believed that bodily resurrection was indeed bodily and that this belief can rightly be characterized as "orthodox" in the classical sense of that term. Moss warns, "The institutionalization of corporeal resurrection at the expense of other, more ethereal forms of postmortem subsistence has served both as a cipher for the triumph of 'orthodoxy' over 'heresy' and as an emblem of Christianity's theological distinctiveness" (8). I agree with Moss, however, that for second- and third-century Christians (Gnostic and otherwise), "The resurrection of the body could mean many things; it did not always mean resurrection of the flesh. Aspects of the arguments of the so-called gnostics at times overlap with those of the self-proclaimed orthodox" (10). Moss also draws attention to the fact that bodily resurrection includes resurrection to bodily punishment, a point that I hope to address in a future book.

6. See Harris, *Refiguring Resurrection*, chapter 9.

7. Moltmann, *Resurrected to Eternal Life*, 2, 4. Moltmann rightly envisions "a profound discontinuity between this world and the hereafter" (43). See also Frey, "Bodiliness and Resurrection."

8. Weinandy, *Does God Suffer?*, 36. Undeniably, the realities disclosed by Jesus Christ are marked by the "excess" of meaning that characterizes a "saturated phenomenon," to use Jean-Luc Marion's terms. See Marion, *In Excess*. For a more recent, related work by Marion, see Marion, *D'ailleurs, la revelation*.

Richard Hays rightly cautions that what our "new embodied state" will be in the new creation is far "beyond our limited powers of imagination."[9] But at the same time, Hays bemoans the fact that "many Christians at the turn of the millennium have lost sight of the fundamental apocalyptic doctrine of the resurrection of the body. Those who continue to hope for some sort of postmortem existence more often imagine a disembodied salvation of the soul."[10] This situation necessitates retrieving glorified *bodiliness* as an intelligible human destiny; otherwise disembodied salvation will inevitably dominate the eschatological imagination of Christians. I second the observation of the Catholic philosopher Caitlin Smith Gilson: "When we do not pant like the deer for heaven, we unknowingly reduce the Christ-event to a narrative of wishes and ideals."[11] My point is that we can avoid such a reduction only if the mystery of risen and glorified bodiliness—a constitutive component of "heaven" in the sense of the term intended by Gilson—is intelligible.

In what follows, therefore, I investigate how Christian thinkers over the centuries have understood the mystery of risen and glorified bodiliness, in hopes of providing resources and guideposts for a contemporary account of glorified bodiliness, combining both continuity and discontinuity.

First, I will offer a broad introduction to what I deem to be the two main lines of Christian theologies of glorified bodiliness, grounded in the thought of Origen and Augustine, respectively. In this section, I will briefly treat the biblical testimony along with some contemporary voices skeptical of the possibility of speaking about risen flesh. As representative of the two main lines, I set forth Origen and Sergius Bulgakov, on the one hand, and

---

9. Hays, "Eschatology," 385.

10. Hays, "Eschatology," 385. For an apocalyptic approach to the cross—building upon the "apocalyptic Paul" of Ernst Käsemann, J. Louis Martyn, and others—see Rutledge, *Crucifixion*, chapter 9. Rutledge appreciates the apocalyptic approach but also seeks to make room for "the *whole cluster* of images surrounding the death of Christ, within *the overarching apocalyptic drama* that consistently presents God as the acting subject while at the same time enlisting even the humblest Christian (*especially* the humblest Christian) in God's band of resistance fighters" (*Crucifixion*, 393). I agree with Rutledge (as surely Hays would also agree) when she states, "The 'apocalypse' of the cross and resurrection . . . was not an inevitable final stage in an orderly process, or an accumulation of progressive steps toward a goal; it was a dramatic rescue bid into which God has flung his entire self" (355). For a critique of "apocalyptic antinomies" especially with regard to the relationship of creation and new creation, see R. David Nelson, "Creation and the Problem of Evil after the Apocalyptic Turn." Hays does not fit into the "apocalyptic Paul" stream of thought, although he agrees with a number of aspects of it (as do I).

11. Gilson, *As It Is in Heaven*, 12. See also Allen, *Grounded in Heaven*; and Morales, "'With My Body I Thee Worship.'"

Johann Gerhard and Kathryn Tanner, on the other. Second, I turn in more detail to three patristic and medieval approaches to glorified bodiliness, reflecting the philosophical and scientific discourses prevalent in these epochs: Gregory of Nyssa, Augustine, and Albert the Great. Gregory and Augustine respond in fascinating ways to problems regarding the risen and glorified body that continue to resonate today, while Albert's Augustinian-Aristotelian approach shows both the promise and the risks of engaging with scientific discourse.[12] Third, I will discuss some recent approaches to glorified bodiliness in conversation with post-Newtonian science.[13] My goal is to affirm *both* bodily continuity and the radical strangeness of glorified bodiliness, always keeping in view that Jesus' Resurrection is "the exemplar and the cause of ours."[14]

The fourth and final section of the chapter, then, treats Mary's Assumption—the glorification and exaltation of her body after her death. The doctrine of Mary's bodily assumption, which emerged in the Church in the fifth century through liturgical and typological contemplation of Scripture's testimony to Mary, concretizes the connection between Christ's resurrection and ours.[15] In confessing Mary's assumption, the Church confesses that

---

12. For further background, see Lehtipuu, *Debates Over the Resurrection of the Dead*, 120–57; Adams, "Resurrection of the Body according to Three Medieval Aristotelians." See also Davenport, "Locating Heaven."

13. Schmisek cautions that "even though the term 'glory' itself may not conjure up any physical notion, once it becomes an attribute of 'body,' the imagination becomes easily drawn to the earth once again" (Schmisek, *Resurrection of the Flesh or Resurrection from the Dead*, 82). But I think this is necessary at least to a certain respect, or else "body" will cease to mean "body" in any sense. Gilson has put it well: "We do not recover earth and earthly flesh, that is not the way of salvation ... Viewing paradise as a mere continuation of earth undermines the resurrection, just as conceiving it to be something so far beyond the senses, alienated from all incarnational meaning" (*As It Is in Heaven*, 214). It is necessary to retain the earthy dimension even while transcending it.

14. Aquinas, *Summa theologiae* III, q. 54, a. 2. Aquinas adds that the risen Christ's bodily glory is far greater than ours will be. For extensive background, see Thomas Marschler, *Auferstehung und Himmelfahrt Christi in der scholastischen Theologie bis zu Thomas von Aquin*.

15. On the evidences for Mary's Assumption, see Nichols, *There Is No Rose*, 89–94. Nichols and I agree that there is biblical evidence in Revelation 12 for Mary's bodily assumption, but we disagree somewhat about the value of the earliest *Transitus Mariae* literature, which some scholars have dated to as early as 300 AD, in which, Nichols suggests tentatively, "the church had externalized an interior memory in tangible monuments" (*There Is No Rose*, 90). I think the liturgical practices associated with the emerging belief in Mary's assumption came about due to liturgical and typological contemplation of the biblical testimony, but I am agnostic about the testimonial value of the earliest texts (as distinct from texts from the mid-fifth century onward, which clearly reflect liturgical and typological contemplation of the biblical testimony).

Christ, having inaugurated his kingdom, never wills to be alone in his risen flesh. The new Adam calls the new Eve to himself; the kingdom is already truly inaugurated. As Brant Pitre puts it, Jesus "bring[s] the true Ark of the Covenant—his mother—into the heavenly Temple."[16] In making this point about Mary's assumption, I highlight the bond between the resurrection of Christ the head and the resurrection of his members, with Mary as the first due to her unique role.

II. Introducing Glorified Bodiliness

The Protestant biblical scholar Patrick Schreiner rightly remarks in his *The Body of Jesus*, "The new world and the new body go hand in hand. Jesus cannot reign in the new world without a new body. The new world and

---

Nichols directs attention to the background provided by such studies as Jugie, "Assomption de la Sainte Vierge"; Shoemaker, *Ancient Traditions of the Virgin Mary's Dormition and Assumption*. For the relation of the doctrine of Mary's assumption to other Marian doctrines, Nichols draws upon the study by Healey, "Assumption among Mary's Privileges." Nichols contends, "The peculiarity (in the pejorative sense) of the Neo-Scholastic theology of the assumption was, surely, its comparative lack of interest in historical enquiry, as though the deep consciousness of the Church could only contain a sense of the inner coherence of revelation and not any actual memory of revelational events. Of course it was understood that, at any rate by spiritual exegesis, and if possible by literal, Scripture had to be invoked in some way. Here the twelfth chapter of the Apocalypse was pertinent—though, surprisingly, the pope would make no reference to it in the bull [1950's *Munificentissimus Deus*]. The materials from tradition were, however, kept distinctly at arm's length ... The marked aversion of modern Scholastics, like some of their early mediaeval predecessors, to the *Transitus* accounts which, despite their naïveté, vehicled, for the most part, the basic paschal pattern of salvation and so preserved a strong Christological reference, was perhaps understandable given the legendary cast of these texts and their contradictions with one another ... But what the *Transitus Mariae* texts did in the history of the church was to stimulate the development of a faith intuition and the consecration of that intuition in the liturgies of both East and West ... Catholic theology has to dare to take seriously the signs of that sporadically reviviscent ecclesial memory: in the Book of the Apocalypse, in the beginnings of the festal commemoration, in the *Transitus* accounts, in the homilies of Oriental bishops both Melchite and Miaphysite (Monophysite), and—not least—the intriguing fact that the only Marian relics known to the patristic Church were here robe and her girdle" (*There Is No Rose*, 107–9). This seems right, but it would be necessary firmly to distinguish this approach from the effort (found among some neo-scholastics and some contemporary theologians) to claim a basis for the truth of Mary's assumption in an unbroken chain of memories of the event, handed on hiddenly and then (later) explicitly.

16. Pitre, *Jesus and the Jewish Roots of Mary*, 66. Here Pitre has in view Jesus' status as the new David, since David was the one who brought the ark of the covenant to Jerusalem. See also Sri, *Rethinking Mary in the New Testament*, 87–90, drawing links between Mary and the ark of the covenant in 2 Samuel 6.

the resurrected body of Jesus cannot be disjoined."[17] Jesus' risen and glorified body belongs to the "new world" of the new creation. This fact comes through strongly in the resurrection narratives of the Gospels, which describe the body of the risen Jesus as being able to do things that no earthly body could do, such as "being able to appear physically in a room without needing to traverse an open door."[18] But such radically new abilities show that Jesus' glorified body is "not fully comprehensible," to say the least, as human flesh.[19]

Indeed, as indicated above, it is hard to exaggerate the difficulty of understanding how a glorified and immortal body can really be *material*. Unlike any kind of materiality that we now know, Jesus' glorified body cannot suffer diminishment or harm. Jesus also teaches that "in the resurrection they neither marry nor are given in marriage, but are like angels in heaven" (Matt 22:30).[20] If so, then resurrected and glorified men and women will no

17. Schreiner, *Body of Jesus*, 140. Schreiner emphasizes that the members of Jesus' body, while not yet risen or glorified, are united with Jesus so that "[t]he world is infused with the presence of Jesus through the community" (149). See also Lemna, "'O Christ, Ever Greater'," 780: "There can be no risen body without its cosmological milieu. However, the risen body in its universal extension in and through human bodies will radiate—in its perfect union with the Father, in Christ the head, and filled with the glory of the Spirit—with a splendor that is only vaguely anticipated by the most incandescent effusions of light and energy in the universe of evolutionary duration as we now know it or even as we can imagine it." Lemna helpfully demonstrates Henri de Lubac's "interpretive recalibrating of Teilhard" (580). For de Lubac's critique of Pierre Teilhard de Chardin's eschatology, in the course of arguing for its general value, see de Lubac, *Religion of Teilhard de Chardin*, 164. For Karl Rahner's variation on this Teilhardian theme, see for example his "Christology in the Setting," 218: "We must assume here the concept of an essential self-transcendence on the part of an existing creature sustained by God as its ultimate cause, and on the basis of this assumption we can freely assert that the development of biologically organized materiality is orientated in terms of an ever-increasing complexity and interiority towards spirit, until finally, under the dynamic impulse of God's creative power, and through a process of self-transcendence of this kind, it becomes spirit."

18. Weinandy, *Jesus Becoming Jesus*, 3:291.

19. Weinandy, *Jesus Becoming Jesus*, 3:291.

20. See Wright, *Resurrection of the Son of God*, 421–23. Discussing Mark and Matthew's version of this verse, Wright argues (quite reasonably when the verse is viewed in the context of the whole Gospel), "The 'likeness' in question is meant, not in the *ontological* sense that the resurrected ones are now the same sort of creature as the angels, nor in the *locational* sense that they are sharing the same space, but in the *functional* sense that the angels do not marry" (422). He adds, "Neither here nor anywhere else in the early Christian literature is it suggested that resurrected people have turned into angels" (422). Wright goes on to examine the parallel verse in Luke: "Instead of saying that the resurrected are *like* angels, he has Jesus say that they are *equal* to angels, using the rare word *isangeloi* . . . [H]e does not say that they are like, or equal to, angels in all respects; only in this respect . . . that they are immortal" (423).

longer have the desire to marry, and will no longer have procreative desires or the need to sustain life by means of food and drink. How can this be, given the central place of such desires and needs in the human experience of bodiliness? In addition, the risen Jesus appeared and disappeared at will (Luke 24:31) and entered the upper room through closed doors (John 20:26). The point is that glorified humans who are "like angels," and who defy the limits and needs of corporeality, hardly seem to be *bodily* creatures anymore.

Addressing the questions "How are the dead raised? With what kind of body do they come?" (1 Cor 15:35), Paul responds along lines that seem to exacerbate these problems still more, even if they also suggest a solution: "What you sow does not come to life unless it dies. And what you sow is not the body which is to be, but a bare kernel" (1 Cor 15:36-37).[21] The trouble is that if our earthly body is like "a bare kernel" in comparison to our glorified body, then there does not seem to be much (if any) real bodily continuity. Paul emphasizes that risen bodies are glorified.[22] He states, "What is sown is perishable, what is raised is imperishable. It is sown in dishonor, it is raised in glory. It is sown in weakness, it is raised in power. It is sown a physical

---

21. See most recently James Ware's valuable "Paul's Understanding of the Resurrection." For a lengthy discussion, citing a range of scholarly literature, see Wright, *Resurrection of the Son of God*, 312–60. Wright comments that Paul in verses 35–41 "is setting up categories from the created order to provide a template of understanding for the new creation ... The new, resurrected body will be in continuity and discontinuity with the present one, not least because the present one is 'corruptible' whereas the new one will be 'incorruptible' ... This is because the new body will be brought into being, and held in incorruptible being, by the Spirit of the creator God, as a result of the life-giving work of the final Adam" (341). See also Malcolm, "Resurrection of the Dead in 1 Corinthians," which connects 1 Corinthians 15 with 1 Corinthians 1–4. For a response to certain elements of Wright's reading of John's Gospel in *Resurrection of the Son of God*—a response that helpfully explores "how the future of resurrected life is a present reality" (namely, by "abiding in the Son who abides in the Father," and doing so through self-sacrificial love and mercy thanks to the power of the Spirit, within the Spirit-filled community)—see Attridge, "From Discord Rises Meaning," 173.

22. For the argument that Paul has in view a pneumatic state that is quite the opposite from fleshly, see Engberg-Peterson, "Complete and Incomplete Transformation in Paul." Moss nicely sums up Engberg-Peterson's position, which she favors: "what was previously a body made up of flesh and blood is now a pneumatic body. The model for this process of transformation ... is the conflagration: the physical transformation of the entire world into a pneumatic state. Christians will be fully transformed into pure *pneuma*, and as a result of this change, they might lose the kind of individual identity and self-consciousness that they had before" (Moss, *Divine Bodies*, 12). For Engberg-Peterson, Paul holds that glorified bodies are fleshless; this is the meaning of "flesh and blood cannot inherit the kingdom" (1 Cor 15:50). I disagree with this interpretation, although I affirm that (for Paul and for the New Testament, as for instance Luke 24) bodily resurrection—while bodily—involves a radical transformation.

body, it is raised a spiritual body" (1 Cor 15:42–44). Again, however, what could it mean to have a "spiritual body"—still recognizably somehow a human "body"—that is "imperishable" and marked by glory and power?[23]

In the Gospels, of course, there is no doubt that Jesus' glorified body is in continuity with his earthly body. When the risen Jesus encounters his disciple Thomas, who had refused to believe unless he saw and touched Jesus' wounds, Jesus shows Thomas his wounded hands and side (John 20:27). But such bodily continuity is also somewhat undermined in the Gospels. Shortly after Jesus shows himself to Thomas, a very different event occurs: "Just as day was breaking, Jesus stood on the beach; yet the disciples did not

---

23. Outi Lehtipuu contends, "Paul is as little interested in the resurrection of Jesus' earthly body as he is in his earthly life" (Lehtipuu, *Debates Over the Resurrection of the Dead*, 43)—but numerous scholars, including Allison in *Constructing Jesus*, 392–403, and Holzbrecher, *Paulus und der historischen Jesus*, have shown how interested and informed Paul is about Jesus' earthly life. See Lehtipuu's further discussion of 1 Corinthians 15 in *Debates over the Resurrection of the Dead*, 53–61, where Lehtipuu grants, "All along, Paul is talking about *bodies* that will be resurrected, not only about immortal souls or ascending spirits" (56; see also 113: "resurrection will take a bodily form, but the resurrection body is a 'spiritual body' which resembles the earthly body as little as a seed that is sown in the ground resembles the plant that will sprout"). Lehtipuu puts the matter somewhat more controversially when she points to "the outright rejection of the resurrection of the flesh found . . . in the letters of Paul, most explicitly in his declaration that 'flesh and blood will not inherit the kingdom of God'" (113). For a comparison between Paul's theology of (eucharistic and mystical) union with the risen Christ and Luke 24's resurrection appearances, in light of Luke's eucharistic theology, see Tappenden, "Luke and Paul in Dialogue." Tappenden remarks regarding Paul's theology of resurrection, "On the one hand, it cannot be denied that Paul insists on a *bodily* resurrection (15, 42–44). As Dale Martin has skillfully illuminated, Paul's entire somatic mapping in 1 Cor 15 is premised upon a hierarchical scale of low-level earthly substances and high-level celestial substances. Thus, Paul understands resurrected bodies as being comprised of high- rather than low-level substance, which results in such bodies being much different than regular human bodies. On the other hand, Paul insists that Christ is the *firstfruits* of those who will be raised at the eschaton (15,20.23; cf. 15,45–49). Given this connection between Christ (who *has been* raised) and those who believe in Christ (i.e., those who *will one day be* raised), the apostle understands Jesus' risen body as a precursor, similar in both kind and substance, to that which is described in 15,35–50. Elsewhere Paul insists that believers' bodies will one day be 'conformed to his [Christ's] body of glory' [Phil 3:21] . . . , a passage that, in light of budding Jewish mysticism, suggests Paul may have understood Christ's risen existence in relation to the *kabod* of God" (203). In my view, there is no need to suppose that Paul literally identifies the (celestial) substance out of which risen bodies are made; and in this respect I agree with Wedderburn, *Beyond Resurrection*, 74, also cited by Tappenden. See also Martin, *Corinthian Body*, 117–29. I have no doubt that Paul conceives of glorified bodies (Christ's and, in some way, ours) as somehow participating in the divine glory or presence—though not literally becoming divine as such. Tappenden directs attention in this regard to Segal, "Paul's Thinking about Resurrection in Its Jewish Context."

know that it was Jesus" (John 21:4).[24] Even when he conversed with them, his own disciples did not recognize him! It was only when they hauled in a miraculous catch of fish that one of them, the beloved disciple, suddenly proclaimed, "It is the Lord!" (John 21:7). Likewise, Mary Magdalene does not recognize the risen Jesus at first, despite directly conversing with him (John 20:11-16). In the Gospel of Luke, when the risen Jesus encounters two of his followers on the road to Emmaus, they do not recognize him despite talking with him for quite some time. They recognize him only when he allows them to do so, namely, when he breaks bread for them in a eucharistic fashion. What kind of real body can sometimes be recognized and sometimes not, depending upon the wish of the glorified person?[25]

A further complicating factor is that in the Gospel of Luke the risen Jesus, in order to demonstrate that it really is he and not a ghost, eats "a piece of broiled fish" (Luke 24:42) in the company of his disciples. Presumably, if one eats something, then it must go to the stomach and be digested (and so forth), unless it is miraculously vaporized. But if glorified bodies

---

24. See Keener, *Gospel of John*, 2:1189-90. Keener comments on 21:4 by pointing back to 20:14-15, where Mary Magdalene does not recognize Jesus. He states, "Mary's encounter with Jesus in 20:14-16 is one of several 'recognition scenes' in the Gospel, reflecting a dramatic-type scene in ancient literature ... That Mary at first does not recognize Jesus (20:14) reflects early tradition that Jesus was not immediately recognized by all who saw him after the resurrection ... This tradition may also imply something about the character of the resurrection body, analogous to the early Jewish belief that angels could appear in different forms" (1189). For further discussion, see Culpepper, *Gospel and Letters of John*, 72-86.

25. Without doubt, Luke-Acts presents Jesus' risen body as physical or material. Brittany E. Wilson remarks aptly with regard to Jesus' ascension in Acts, "Luke depicts Jesus physically ascending into heaven, and he offers assurances of his physical return (delayed though it may be). Jesus does not dissolve into the ether and become an omnipresent, cosmic being, for Luke depicts him as a human journeying into heaven in a manner that can be seen ... Luke presses us to see the continuity of Jesus's corporeality, and with the ascension, he indicates that this corporeal continuity extends to the Parousia. Because of his ascent, Jesus is now in heaven as an embodied being" (Wilson, *Embodied God*, 263). Even in the epiphanies described in Acts, Wilson notes, "Jesus's form ... is not necessarily physical, but it is visibly perceptible and concretely present" (264). For Wilson, I should make clear, God is "bodily," along the lines sketched by Sommer (with whom I disagree) in his *Bodies of God and the World of Ancient Israel*. Wilson also claims that Luke blurs "the boundaries between Jesus, angels, the Spirit, and even God" (*Embodied God*, 273)—whereas I think that the notion of "blurring the boundaries" is here a postmodern distortion, although of course Luke challenges the boundary between Jesus and God. For an effort to locate Luke-Acts within Hellenistic culture and its stories of the assumption into heaven of mythical (divine or divinized) heroes, see van Tilborg and Counet, *Jesus' Appearances and Disappearances in Luke 24*, 263-64. Van Tilborg and Counet, who employ cognitive linguistics and sociology in their analysis, do not take seriously the possibility that Jesus actually did what the narratives depict him as doing.

still have functional digestive organs, then it seems that the blessed will get hungry and thirsty. And if our bodily organs remain operational in the state of glory, then it is somewhat hard to see how suffering and disease will not continue, as well.[26]

As noted above, a central tenet of Christian faith is that Jesus rose from the dead in his glorified flesh so that we too might, at the general resurrection, receive glorified bodies and live with him in the new creation. Since this is so, doubts about whether a glorified body is even possible are highly consequential. Such doubts undermine faith in bodily resurrection—Jesus' and ours.

Some theologians, however, have argued that we must simply eschew questions about the glorified body, even to the point of avoiding the phrases "resurrection of the body" and "resurrection of the flesh" in favor simply of "resurrection of the dead." For theologians who adopt such a strategy, "questions about the appearance of the resurrected body do not contribute to the profundity of the resurrection; rather, they drag it into the mire of the ridiculous."[27] On this view, resurrection to glorified life is "a metaphor" for a reality that is beyond human ken, and "[f]ailure to understand this will result in nonsensical notions of life after death that will be easily dismissed by today's educated audience."[28] Seeking to avoid such disreputable speculation, saints such as Jerome and Pope John Paul II have cautioned against

---

26. In Outi Lehtipuu's view, "The writer of Luke-Acts . . . seems to treat Jesus' resurrection as a special case . . . [T]he bodily resurrection of believers is not a necessary conclusion to be drawn from the belief in Jesus' bodily resurrection. There is no clear indication that Luke believes that the general resurrection might involve a body. All in all, the author does not reveal much about the more precise form of the resurrection life of believers" (Lehtipuu, *Debates Over the Resurrection of the Dead*, 50). I think Luke-Acts assumes as a given the bodily character of "resurrection," as in Luke 22:34-38 where Jesus rejects the viewpoint of the Sadducees, who denied that there would be a resurrection. Without doubt, however, Luke links resurrection and spiritual ascent.

27. Schmisek, *Resurrection of the Flesh or Resurrection from the Dead*, 117.

28. Schmisek, *Resurrection of the Flesh or Resurrection from the Dead*, 119. In *Refiguring Resurrection*, Steven Harris similarly warns against much speculation about the risen and glorified state. Harris notes appreciatively that in Calvin's *Institutes of the Christian Religion*, "attention is focused on the risen Christ and his future coming throughout; the description of the future resurrection is restrained; and useless or harmful questions are avoided" (191). Rightly, Harris criticizes the speculations of a number of analytic theologians, including Peter van Inwagen and Dean Zimmermann, who (lacking an account of the soul—a lack that characterizes Harris's perspective as well) end up making absurd claims when trying to defend the intelligibility of the future resurrection of the dead. He also rightly criticizes Thomas Flint's view that the blessed will literally come to share in the hypostatic union: see Flint, "Possibilities of Incarnation."

speculation about what glorified bodies will look like.[29] In his *Eschatology*, Joseph Ratzinger similarly warns that "the detailed particularities of the world of the resurrection are beyond our conceiving. First Corinthians 15, 50 and John 6, 63 bar the doors against such misconceived ventures."[30] For his part, Steven Harris maintains that speculation about glorified bodiliness must be strictly limited to what can be ascertained directly from Scripture and from Jesus' risen body. On these grounds, he rules out answering such questions as whether there will be male and female bodies in the new creation and whether disabilities will be removed.[31]

Debates about what should be said about glorified bodiliness date back to the early fathers. In the second century, Ignatius of Antioch, Justin Martyr, and Clement of Rome emphasized that our resurrection, like Jesus', will be a "resurrection of the flesh."[32] They sought to insist upon the strong continuity of the risen and glorified body with the body that dies. Their emphasis caused some controversy—and not only with Gnostic Christians. Cutting against this early line of thought, the third-century theologian Origen held that the bodies that we now have are the result of the fall, and so our glorified bodies will be radically different from the bodies we now have. In fact, according to Origen's extant writings and other writings by Origen that we know today from his adversaries, our bodies will be so spiritualized as to be more pure spirit than flesh, to the point that the phrase "resurrection of the flesh" may be misleading.[33] Origen states, "[I]n the life-principle of human bodies, there are certain, already-existing principles of rising ... but they are not restored to the same bodily flesh nor to the same forms

---

29. See Schmisek, *Resurrection of the Flesh or Resurrection from the Dead*, 117–18, citing Jerome's *Epistula* 84.5 (CSEL 55, 127) and Pope John Paul II's General Audience for July 21, 1999.

30. Ratzinger, *Eschatology*, 192.

31. See Harris, *Refiguring Resurrection*, 196–202.

32. See Lehtipuu, *Debates Over the Resurrection of the Dead*, 112. See also Setzer, *Resurrection of the Body in Early Judaism and Early Christianity*, 72–75.

33. See Lehtipuu, *Debates Over the Resurrection of the Dead*, 117, 153–56, and elsewhere. After citing various patristic texts, including Origen's work, Lehtipuu states: "all these writings on resurrection from the 2nd to the 4th century show that the subject was highly controversial. Moreover, it was widely discussed, in practically all parts of the Christian world" (Lehtipuu, *Debates Over the Resurrection of the Dead*, 17). Lehtipuu engages with Gnostic and apocryphal texts in addition to works by the recognized church fathers. Much like Moss, Lehtipuu emphasizes that these writings are rooted in "an interest in securing identity, drawing boundaries around what [is] construed as Christianity, and ... [a preoccupation] with the contest for power" (20). Lehtipuu also notes that controversy already appears in 1 Corinthians 15 and 2 Timothy 2:17–18—the latter of which reads, "Among them are Hymenaeus and Philetus, who have swerved from the truth by holding that the resurrection is past already."

which they had before ... Now we see with our eyes, hear with our ears, act with our hands, walk with our feet; but in that spiritual body we will see as a whole, act as a whole, walk as a whole."[34] Origen insists that this spiritual body is nevertheless a "body," in at least *some* continuity with our earthly body. To this extent at least, as Outi Lehtipuu observes, all parties in the early Church conceived of the resurrected body as "a manifestation of both continuity and change."[35]

I will return in the next section to the church fathers, specifically the perspectives of Gregory of Nyssa, whom Origen influenced, and of Augustine, who carries forward the outlook of the second-century fathers as well as of Tertullian. Augustine's perspective informs the Aristotelian approach of Albert the Great, whom I treat in the next section. A notable example of the Augustinian perspective can be found in the 1622 work of the Lutheran Scholastic theologian Johann Gerhard, published as the ninth volume of his *Theological Commonplaces*.

Gerhard begins by discussing "the complete restoration of the divine image,"[36] and he affirms a strong doctrine of deification: "Since the divine image is perfectly reflected in the blessed, they can rightly be called the children of God and, in fact, 'gods' of a certain kind."[37] He provides various deification texts from the fathers, including Irenaeus, Gregory of Nazianzus, and Augustine. Gerhard then divides the goods of eternal life into goods of the soul and goods of the body. At the top of the list of the goods of the soul comes the knowledge of God through beatific vision—a knowledge that Gerhard finds foreshadowed in Isaiah 54:13 and Jeremiah 31:34, and that Paul teaches in 1 Corinthians 13:9–10. Beatific knowledge, says Gerhard, is attested in texts by Origen, Gregory of Nazianzus, Ambrose, Augustine, Gregory the Great, Anselm, and Bernard of Clairvaux. In every way, the will, emotions, and appetites of the blessed will be in conformity with right reason. There will be no "difficulty, boredom, or satiety"; the blessed will be in a condition that is "most pleasant, relaxed, serene, and sincere."[38]

---

34. Origen, *Spirit and Fire*, 143, §346.

35. Lehtipuu, *Debates Over the Resurrection of the Dead*, 21. See also the highly critical (in my view appropriately so) discussion of Origen on male and female in Mitchell, *Origen's Revenge*, 112–16. Mitchell notes that "Methodius, Theophilus of Alexandria, Epiphanius, and Jerome all accused Origen of identifying the 'coats of skin' [Gen 3:21] with our present bodies and thus impugning both marriage and resurrection" (*Origen's Revenge*, 119).

36. Gerhard, *On Eternal Life*, 137.
37. Gerhard, *On Eternal Life*, 138.
38. Gerhard, *On Eternal Life*, 148.

As Gerhard notes, Paul makes clear in Romans 8 that the body will be redeemed from slavery to corruption, to disease and death. In 1 Corinthians 15 and Philippians 3:21, among other passages, Paul promises the absolute transformation of our bodies to become like Jesus' glorified body. Gerhard pauses to reject the Photinian position that this transformation involves passing beyond bodiliness altogether—even though Gerhard grants (in accord with Matthew 22:30) that human bodies will receive "angelic properties."[39] While accepting that glorified bodiliness is a mystery, Gerhard observes that various patristic and medieval authors appropriately suggested various attributes of glorified bodies. Anselm, for example, provides a list of seven such attributes, including agility, beauty, strength, pleasure, freedom, health, and longevity. Later medievals, among them Aquinas (Gerhard cites chapter 168 of Aquinas's *Compendium theologiae*), focused on bodily subtlety, agility, impassibility, and splendor. Gerhard grounds these four attributes biblically: subtlety insofar as Jesus' body ascended; agility in his power to walk on water; impassibility in the Eucharist; and splendor in his transfiguration. Gerhard also appreciatively quotes Bonaventure defending these four attributes with arguments from reason.

The attributes that Gerhard, indebted to Martin Chemnitz, determines to have clear biblical and patristic grounds are spiritualness (for example, no longer needing food or desiring sex); immortality; impassibility; clarity or brightness; strength and health; beauty and the absence of deformity; agility or the ability to move rapidly and easily; subtlety; illocality or the condition of not being "circumscribed by any corporeal place"; invisibility or the ability not to be seen by non-glorified eyes; and impalpability or the ability not to be felt by non-glorified persons.[40] These eleven attributes—each of which Gerhard defends extensively—provide a striking portrait of what glorified bodiliness entails.

In modern theology, the Orthodox theologian Sergius Bulgakov and the Protestant theologian Kathryn Tanner have offered accounts of glorified bodiliness that show how the two "lines" have continued. Indebted to the tradition that follows from Origen, Bulgakov argues, "While remaining a mystery of God, the resurrection of the dead is explained to a certain

39. Gerhard, *On Eternal Life*, 150.

40. Gerhard, *On Eternal Life*, 179. Steven Harris, in *Refiguring Resurrection*, offers further insight while rejecting (for reasons that are unpersuasive to me) some aspects found in portraits such as Gerhard's. Harris states that "the spirituality of the resurrection body has nothing to do with its transformation into spirit, not even the increased 'subtlety' of the body with its freedom from the so-called lower bodily functions . . . Rather, it will stand in perfect and unhindered relationship with God's Spirit. It will, as it were, be fully receptive to the Spirit's donation of eternal life and pliable to the Spirit's impulsion and influence" (183).

degree by its effects, and to this extent it can be understood on the basis of revelation."[41] In light of 1 Corinthians 15:37–42, Bulgakov suggests that the ensouled body that dies contains the "energy" (or "idea" or "entelechy" or "quickening power") from which will come forth, not a body precisely like the one that died, but an incorruptible and immortal body. He adds that the "spiritual" body about which Paul speaks in 1 Corinthians 15:44 refers to a new state "of human corporeality in its relation to the spirit" of the person.[42] The glorified or "spiritual" body will be entirely transparent to and obedient to the spirit. Although Bulgakov opposes the notion that the distinction of gender—male and female—will be erased in the glorified body, he holds that the bodily organs devoted to food and procreation will be transformed. Every glorified body will "express with perfect clarity the [eternal, divine] idea of each person."[43]

The connection with Origen becomes clearer when Bulgakov hypothesizes that every glorified body will share in a universal spiritualized corporeality, so that each human being will participate far more deeply in other human beings (and in all matter) than at present. All glorified bodies will be utterly permeable and weightless, no longer bound in any way by space or time or by anything comparable. Bulgakov maintains that texts such as 1 Corinthians 15:42–49, 2 Corinthians 3:18, and Philippians 3:21 presage "the universal resurrection of spiritual bodies in power and glory, in the image of the glorious body of the resurrected Christ, with which they are even identified, so that all resurrected humanity is included in the glorified body of Christ."[44] This will be transformed—spiritualized—bodiliness indeed.

---

41. Bulgakov, *Bride of the Lamb*, 438. As he notes—and as this chapter will explore in some detail—"a question arises that was much debated in the patristic literature (by Origen, St. Gregory of Nyssa, St. Ephraem, St. Augustine, and others): In what state, at what age, and in what appearance is the body of a resurrected individual restored? To what degree does it retain the individual features that distinguished it in earthly life? The main difficulty here is that the body of the resurrection must possess fullness, perfection, and permanent stability, whereas the earthly body does not have these features. St. Gregory of Nyssa asked, If the goal is fullness, will there not be a whole crowd of bodies for each resurrected individual, with different ages and bearing the traits of these ages? If the goal is the exact repetition of earthly bodies, with what bodies will children, the sick, the handicapped, and so on be resurrected? Let us skip the details of the dispute, all of which reduce to a single general question: Will the resurrected body be an exact as possible reproduction of all the empirical states proper to it in this world of sin and death, or will it be their general adequate form that fully and perfectly expresses the ideal image of a human being as a person and that therefore does not have an exact physical correspondence with his different aspects?" (441).

42. Bulgakov, *Bride of the Lamb*, 447.

43. Bulgakov, *Bride of the Lamb*, 445.

44. Bulgakov, *Bride of the Lamb*, 447. For historical-critical background to 2

For Tanner, by contrast, the resurrected body is not, in its bodiliness, changed radically. Taking a strongly (indeed supercharged) Augustinian line inflected by Barthian concerns, she argues that the resurrected body will not be immortal in itself. Rather, the resurrected body will be immortal because God freely draws it into his life; God becomes its life principle, so that it no longer depends upon its own (mortal) life principle. Tanner clarifies, "This immortality is properly considered ours, despite the fact that we remain mortal in and of ourselves, in so far as, living in God, we are no longer our own but God's."[45] Just as the risen Jesus continues to have his mortal body—as his wounds indicate[46]—so also we will have our mortal bodies. In her view, the only possible bodies that humans *can* have are mortal bodies. God does not change our human nature, and bodiliness as such is vulnerable and mortal. We are material organisms, and all such "structures are prone to fail"; finitude, including temporal finitude, belongs to human nature.[47] But we are nevertheless glorified and receive immortality when we are taken up by Christ. In Christ, "God's own animating eternity shines through or suffuses the very mortal being of those who hold their existence in God."[48] Immortality, then, is always a gift and never becomes something that glorified bodies intrinsically have in themselves. On this view, glorified bodies differ from earthly bodies only inasmuch as the former are suffused in every way with "the life-giving powers of the Word."[49]

The above perspectives introduce the two most influential traditional lines of reasoning about glorified bodiliness—one somewhat more spiritual, the other somewhat more corporeal. But of course both lines are concerned to maintain the corporeal dimension in some way, so as to make clear that a real resurrection has taken place. In this light, let me now turn to Gregory of Nyssa, Augustine, and Albert the Great, in order to assess more fully the options regarding glorified bodiliness, and in order to begin to build up the broadly Augustinian approach, appreciative of modern science about

---

Corinthians 3:18, along lines that seem close to Bulgakov's (although the author writes from a quite different theological perspective), see Bernard, *Glory of God in the Face of Jesus Christ*, 167–73.

45. Tanner, *Jesus, Humanity, and the Trinity*, 118.

46. For the argument that Jesus shows Thomas his scars, not his open wounds—and that this matters—see Moss, *Divine Bodies*, 26–40. Moss also argues, mistakenly I think, that Mark 9:43–47, with its reference to self-amputation, "is nudging us toward the preservation of perceived disability in the afterlife" (61; cf. 73–75). I agree, however, with her point that "Mark subverts the idea that able bodies are virtuous bodies" (64).

47. Tanner, *Jesus, Humanity, and the Trinity*, 114.

48. Tanner, *Jesus, Humanity, and the Trinity*, 116.

49. Tanner, *Jesus, Humanity, and the Trinity*, 119.

human bodiliness and human flourishing, that I will advocate on the basis of the biblical testimony.

III. Gregory of Nyssa, Augustine, and Albert the Great

Gregory of Nyssa

When Gregory of Nyssa grapples with bodily resurrection—Jesus' and ours—he arrives at some striking, and at times strikingly strange, conclusions about our glorified bodies.[50] For Gregory, as Sarah Coakley says, "We are on a continuum . . . from this 'body' to our 'angelic' future 'bodies,'" and at the final judgment we will "be de-genitalized"—returning to what Gregory conceives of as the Edenic condition—"and so receive that angelic status that was our lot originally."[51] At the same time, however, Gregory insists upon the absolute material identity of our risen body with the body that we now possess.

In *On the Soul and the Resurrection*, Gregory first points out that Scripture teaches that the created order as we know it, with its cycles of birth and death, will at the eschaton give way to the new creation in which the processes of generation and corruption will be no more. At the final judgment, all human souls will once again inhabit their bodies. Time will be no more, replaced by an indescribable sharing in the life of the Trinity. Gregory rejects the notions of the transmigration of souls and reincarnation, both of which were relatively common ideas in the pagan philosophical culture

---

50. For broad background, see Daley, *Hope of the Early Church*. See also Harrison, "Male and Female in Cappadocian Theology," showing that Gregory of Nyssa's views about resurrected bodies being neither male nor female are found also in some texts by Basil of Caesarea and Gregory of Nazianzus; and see the discussion of the Cappadocians (focusing on Gregory of Nyssa) in Mitchell, *Origen's Revenge*, 124–31. Mitchell recognizes that Gregory "defends the bodily resurrection, arguing that God creates souls and bodies at the same time, that both are dependent upon the other for what they are meant to be, and that soul and body will be brought back together in the resurrection" (127). But Mitchell also posits (persuasively), "The abandonment of male and female seems to be the veiled meaning of Gregory's *On the Making of Man* . . . The 'making of man' in his title is not the story of Adam and Eve, whom he barely mentions, but the creation of a sexless ideal of divine humanity and then the realization of that sexless ideal in the resurrection" (128, 131; see also Mitchell's discussion of Maximus the Confessor's similar "eradication of male and female" as fit only for fallen human nature [146; cf. 148]). For further discussion, siding with Mitchell's concerns, see Boersma, *Embodiment and Virtue in Gregory of Nyssa*, 100–108.

51. Coakley, *Powers and Submissions*, 163.

of his day, and the former of which had been advocated by Origen.[52] For Gregory, the soul and body are separated at death, but at the general resurrection "the same body is constructed again around the same soul, fitted together from the same elements."[53] The soul knows its own matter and is attracted to union with its own matter.[54] The disembodied soul, by its intellectual power, is in a real sense present to each material element that once belonged to its body. The soul remains with all of these elements, no matter how much the elements are spatially separated from each other, until at the general resurrection the soul's power will recombine all the original elements and reconstitute the same body, now in a glorified condition.

Gregory's main concern in this section of his work is to show that the resurrection of the body differs from the formation of a mere replica—a glorified body that was never really the body of the dead person. Gregory sums up this problem: "For if it should not recover its own exactly, but should use some material of the same kind instead of its very own, it will become a different one in place of the one it was before. Such an event would no longer be resurrection but the fashioning of a new man."[55] He is aware, of course, that the bodily elements of a person who has died can be scattered widely and can mingle with all sorts of other bodily elements. But the power of the spiritual soul is not impeded by spatial distance or material recombinations. Rather, as indicated above, the spiritual soul can "follow" its body's elements wherever they may go. Gregory remarks, "When the elements mix with their own kind, the soul does not let go of its own in the subtlety and nobility of its intellectual power. It is not deceived by the small particles of the elements, but it slips away together with its own when they are mixed with their kind."[56] Gregory adds that it is not only the soul's intelligence that ensures the connection to each of the material elements of the soul's (decomposed) body; rather, there are also marks or signs persisting in the material elements themselves. These marks identify the particular elements as belonging to the body of a particular soul.

Gregory takes up some additional problems regarding bodily resurrection. One such problem has to do with the fact that many people are displeased with their bodies and hardly want them to be resurrected, at least not in their present form. If we are raised from the dead with ugly

52. Since Gregory is the author of this dialogue, I will not differentiate between his comments and Macrina's, but instead will attribute the whole to Gregory—with apologies to Macrina!

53. Gregory of Nyssa, *On the Soul and the Resurrection*, 90.

54. See Gregory of Nyssa, *On the Soul and the Resurrection*, 67.

55. Gregory of Nyssa, *On the Soul and the Resurrection*, 67.

56. Gregory of Nyssa, *On the Soul and the Resurrection*, 68.

or misshapen bodies, we will be dismayed. But if the body that we now know is not recognizably the same as our risen body, how will the latter have real continuity or identity with our present body? Gregory sums up the quandary: "So if our bodies will be revived the same in all respects, what we expect is a misfortune; but if they will not be the same, the one who is being raised will be a different person from the one who was dead."[57] If God will simply make for each of us a new and better model of our body, this could not suffice for a real resurrection.

A second problem consists in the fact that our body is in constant flux. Our body may seem to be the same each day, but it is not. Just as a person cannot touch the same flame twice, so also one never possesses the same body twice. Each moment and each day, we are changing in our bodily constitution. How, then, can there be identity or sameness between the resurrected body and our own, given that our body undergoes constant material change and, indeed, might be better described as an ever-changing stream of bodies?

An even more troubling problem is the one Gregory sketches next. Most of a human body is devoted to managing life within this condition of temporality and flux. Blood must circulate, organs must digest and process food, sexual desire must make itself manifest so that the species can continue. What, then, will such organs as the heart, stomach, genitals, and even the lungs do in eternal life? Gregory denies that eternal life will involve the needs served by these organs, and I think he is right. But this position seems to rule out the need for our actual bodies with their various organs. As he puts the matter, "the hands are for work, the feet for running, the mouth for the reception of food, the teeth for the service of nourishment, the bowels for digestion, and the outlet passages for the elimination of what has been used. So when these functions do not exist, how or for what purpose will the organs which came to be because of them still exist?"[58]

Christians often assume that after the general resurrection we will still look like humans. But so many of our body parts are ordered to things that we will not do after the resurrection. If so, then in raising and glorifying our bodies, God will be turning our bodies—or at least most of our

---

57. Gregory of Nyssa, *On the Soul and the Resurrection*, 109. See Lehtipuu, *Debates Over the Resurrection of the Dead*, 122, describing the concern to which many church fathers responded: "Flesh is weak and contemptible; it is inclined to sinning and drags down the soul along with it. If it rises, its infirmities will rise, too. Who would want the body back and to continue an imperfect life in it? The soul is incorruptible, as God is, and God will save what is like him."

58. Gregory of Nyssa, *On the Soul and the Resurrection*, 112.

body parts—into useless decorations. Such a resurrection would seem to be unfitting.

In response to the challenges he has sketched, Gregory first observes that the dimension of mystery must be respected. Theologians should attempt to show the suitability of the resurrection of the body, but no one cannot really conceive of the state of glory or of the glorified body. It is rather like talking about light before one has ever seen it. One can talk about it with reasonable adequacy, but the reality will so far outpace one's words that the reality will make the words seem worthless. The most that can be done, says Gregory, is to show that the doctrine of the bodily resurrection (Christ's and ours) is intelligible.

The intelligibility of resurrection rests partly upon God's work as the good Creator. Gregory holds that God did not make human death and that original sin is the ultimate cause of bodily corruption and defect. The resurrection of the body, Gregory argues, restores human bodily life to what God first intended it to be. Gregory considers that at the outset, humans were not subject to the pain of disease, hunger, sexual desire, and so on. He states in *On the Soul and the Resurrection*, "Since whatever was added to human nature from the irrational life was not in us before humanity fell into passion, we shall also leave behind [at the resurrection] all the conditions which appear along with passion"—including whatever pertains to "sexual intercourse, conception, childbearing, dirt, lactation, nourishment, [and] evacuation."[59]

---

59. Gregory of Nyssa, *On the Soul and the Resurrection*, 114. The biblical scholar Dale C. Allison Jr. says, along somewhat similar lines, though without an appeal to Eden: "Natural selection has designed us for life on earth. Teeth are for chewing food, and lungs are for breathing air, and all for the purpose of keeping us alive. Christians hold, however, that, once we rise, death will be no more. The exegetical justification is 1 Corinthians 15, where Paul foresees an imperishable body, a spiritual body, a glorious body . . . Why, then, with death passé, would resurrected saints need to eat? Or why would they need to breathe? If they're invested with immortality, death won't be able to touch them, so eating or not eating and breathing or not breathing should be matters of indifference. What could be the purpose, in an immortal state, of organs that evolved in the struggle for survival, organs designed to keep us alive on earth for a few decades? Gregory of Nyssa inferred that, when Jesus rose, he didn't take his intestines with him and that, in the world to come, we won't need ours either . . . It takes only a little reflection to hollow out resurrected bodies entirely. If, as Jesus teaches, we'll neither marry nor be given in marriage but will be like the angels in heaven, then we won't require ovaries or fallopian tubes, prostate glands or seminal vesicles. And if, as 4 Ezra avows, illness will be banished, we won't need white blood cells, antibodies, and the rest of the immune system. And if, as Revelation promises, we'll neither hunger nor thirst any longer, then we won't require kidneys to reabsorb water. Nor will we, if immortal, need blood, veins, arteries, and a pumping heart to circulate nutrients and remove waste products . . . Everything about us has been fashioned for life on earth, so that we

Thus, Gregory presents our eschatological future as a return to the original condition of human nature. Interpreting Genesis 1:27, he argues in his *On the Making of Man* that the distinction of male and female was added due to human sin. In his foreknowledge of human sin, God "formed for our nature that contrivance for increase which befits those who had fallen into sin, implanting in mankind, instead of the angelic majesty of nature, that animal and irrational mode by which they [human beings] now succeed one another."[60] For this reason, our risen and glorified bodies will no longer be sexually differentiated.[61]

Regarding the other problems sketched above, Gregory appeals in *On the Soul and the Resurrection* primarily to the divine power. God has the power to accomplish a continuity and identity that nevertheless involves great difference as well. In answer to the problem about which of our ever-changing bodies is raised from the dead, Gregory suggests it may be a combination of our bodies across the years.[62] Indebted to Paul in 1

---

might grow, repair, and reproduce ourselves; but if, in the future, we no longer grow, repair, or reproduce, won't stomachs, intestines, and the rest necessarily be vestigial, so that glorified bodies will be, their entirety, akin to our irrelevant tailbone, that is, eternal relics of a one-time utility? Or should we look forward to something like what biologists call 'exaptation,' the process by which a trait serving one function comes to serve another function, such as bird feathers evolving from temperature regulators into instruments for flight? This sounds a bit like Tertullian, who did in fact hazard that maybe old organs might take on new functions. He asked: 'What will be the use of the entire body when the entire body will become useless?' He answered by observing that organs may have more than one function—the mouth, for instance, not only chews food but makes speech—and by affirming, rather cryptically, that 'in the presence of God there will be no idleness'" (Allison, *Night Comes*, 23–24; for further discussion of Tertullian's viewpoint, and for Athenagoras's response, see Moss, *Divine Bodies*, 78–88).

60. Gregory of Nyssa, *On the Making of Man*, XVII.4, 407. This treatise also defends the intelligibility of bodily resurrection on various grounds, most of which are repeated in *On the Soul and the Resurrection*.

61. Gregory also makes this point in his *Discourse on the Dead*.

62. He states, "So if a person is not the same as he was yesterday but becomes another by alteration, it follows that when the resurrection restores our body again to life, the one man will have to become a whole people. In this way no aspect of the one raised will be missing: the infant, the toddler, the child, the youth, the husband, the father, the old man, and all the intermediate stages" (Gregory of Nyssa, *On the Soul and the Resurrection*, 111). See also Guardini, *Last Things*, 68–69: "Each phase is the man, and each is indispensable to his life as a whole. That endless series of configurations which is the human body must be included in the resurrected body . . . Man's deeds and his destiny are part of him, and, set free from the restrictions of history, will remain for all eternity, not by any power of his own, not as a final phase of an inner development, but at the summons of the Almighty, and in the strength of his Spirit" (cited in O'Callaghan, *Christ Our Hope*, 111). I note that sometimes modern scholars conceive of Gregory's position as more naïve than it actually is, as for instance when John Polkinghorne criticizes "Gregory of Nyssa's notion of the reassembly of the atoms

Corinthians 15, Gregory offers an organic metaphor to defend risen bodiliness. Under the right conditions, a seed can become an ear of corn which "differs completely from its former self in size, beauty, variety, and form," yet is in demonstrable continuity.[63] Glorified by God's power, our bodies will receive an immutable, perfected condition that is quite different from their previous temporal and fallen condition. The glorified body will have powers that go far beyond its natural powers, and it will no longer have any properties that are needed only for temporal life. But it will still be an instance of human nature, just as the ear of corn—radically different from the seed—receives its nature from the seed.

In sum, Gregory argues in two directions. First he suggests that resurrection is a restoration to our pre-fall condition; and second he suggests that resurrection involves a glorification far beyond any natural condition even prior to the fall. He joins the two together by proposing that our pre-fall condition was quite graced, since we were not subject to death or (in Gregory's view) to passion of any kind. As Gregory says of Adam and of risen human beings, "Incorruptibility, glory, honor, and power, which are agreed to be characteristic or the divine nature, formerly belonged to the one made in God's image, and are expected to be ours as well."[64] Gregory compares human beings to a beautiful ear of corn (Adam) that is killed by the heat and drought of sin and turned into a dry seed (us) and that soon will be raised to its glorious beauty as a fully perfect ear of corn (our resurrected bodies).

I think that Gregory's portrait of risen human beings mistakenly discards our sexed biology. I also think that real bodily resurrection, as distinct from the formation of a replica, need not require that the precise matter of our body (the body that died) be reunited to our soul. But I agree with much of what Gregory says, including his insistence that our glorified bodies will be vastly different than our present bodies.

Augustine

A generation younger than Gregory of Nyssa, Augustine in *City of God* addresses many of the same issues about our risen bodies. Augustine often

---

that 'belong' to the body of an individual human soul—an idea that makes no sense to us with our knowledge of the material flux that sustains biological life" (Polkinghorne, "Eschatological Credibility," 48).

63. Gregory of Nyssa, *On the Soul and the Resurrection*, 118.
64. Gregory of Nyssa, *On the Soul and the Resurrection*, 119.

reaches different conclusions, influenced by a different stream of pre-Nicene theological literature.[65]

Augustine begins by remarking that in pagan cultures, a general resurrection was typically not envisioned. Even supposedly deified humans such as Hercules were not thought to have been taken up to heaven in the flesh. As he points out, furthermore, the Platonists contend that no earthly body can exist in heaven, since an earthly body would be too heavy.

Augustine responds that God has the power to enable the glorified body to dwell where it will. He also notes that the Platonic view is unable to account for the dwelling of birds in the air, or, indeed, for the dwelling of immaterial souls in earthly bodies. Besides, if the elements are really so sharply divided, then no "higher" or less heavy element could dwell in the regions of the earth, and so we would have no fire. Since there is in fact fire on earth, the Platonists face a quandary. One solution is to hold that earthly fire is not the *pure* element of fire but has been mixed in some way so as to enable it to exist on earth. If so, says Augustine, then God could likewise adapt earthly bodies in order to enable them to dwell in the higher regions.[66]

Augustine goes on to address other reasons that people give for rejecting the notion of bodily resurrection. Can aborted fetuses, for instance, rise from the dead, and if so, in what shape would they rise? And how will bodies that have been burned or turned to dust or eaten by wild animals be restored in such a way that real continuity and identity are sustained? Opponents of Christianity seize especially upon Jesus' promise, "not a hair of your head will perish" (Luke 21:18), which echoes Jesus' statement in another context that "even the hairs of your head are all numbered" (Matt 10:30). These opponents claim that Christians must maintain that the risen

65. For discussion see, most recently, Reisenauer, *Augustine's Theology of the Resurrection*. For criticisms of Augustine's position for overemphasizing physical continuity, see for example Bynum, *Resurrection of the Body in Western Christianity, 200–1336*, 101–9; O'Collins, "Augustine on the Resurrection," 72; Greshake and Kremer, *Resurrectio Mortuorum*, 213. John J. O'Meara points out that Augustine's viewpoint was firmly critiqued by John Scotus Eriugena in the ninth century: see O'Meara, "Parting from Porphyry." I owe these references to Fletcher, *Resurrection Realism*, 53. Fletcher observes that "Augustine initially denied a material resurrection, yet later not only allowed this but suggested that this material, risen body will be so glorified and enlivened by spirit that it will be capable of the divinizing *visio Dei*" (*Resurrection Realism*, 181). Writings from the early-to-mid 390s in which Augustine argued that our risen bodies will not be physical flesh (but instead will be angel-like) include *De Fide et Symbolo*, *Contra Adimantum*, *De Agone Cristiano*, and Sermon 264. The mature Augustine distinguished between corruptible flesh and incorruptible flesh, and holds that glorified bodies will be the latter. Fletcher directs appreciative attention to Börresen, "Augustin, interprète du dogme de la resurrection"; and Alfeche, "Rising of the Dead in the Works of Augustine (1 Cor 15:35–57)."

66. See Augustine, *City of God*, XXII.11, p. 1052.

body will be extraordinarily hairy! Moreover, since Christ's risen body retained his wounds, it seems that someone born with a terrible deformity will necessarily retain this deformity in his or her risen body. Another issue is what happens in the case of cannibalism, where two people may end up possessing some of the same bodily elements.

One aspect of Augustine's reply to the above problems is his view that every human body has, in potentiality if not in actuality, a perfect state of that body. Each risen body, then, will express the perfect state appropriate to it. Since the risen body will express its perfect actualization, it will neither be too old nor too young (let alone too hairy), but rather will be in the prime of life as was Christ when he died. Augustine also appeals to the divine power. God can fix our deformities without compromising the continuity of the risen body with the person's body on earth.

On the basis of Paul's statement that believers are "predestined to be conformed to the image of his Son" (Rom 8:29), some Christians known to Augustine denied that the female sex will be present at the general resurrection. Instead, female bodies will be turned into male bodies, in accord with the Lord's male body. On this view, the female reproductive system and breasts have served their purpose and will not be present in resurrected bodies. In reply, Augustine insists that female bodies, just as much as male bodies, will be present at the general resurrection, since "a woman's sex is not a defect; it is natural."[67] He states that female bodiliness "will be part of a new beauty," not one that excites the lust of the male gaze but one that "will arouse the praises of God" who is the Creator of human beauty.[68] His point is that the Creator "who established the two sexes will restore them both."[69]

What about Jesus' teaching that there will be no marriage in heaven because humans will be like angels? Augustine notes that in resurrection life, humans will be like angels by possessing immortality, happiness, and so on.[70] But humans will remain corporeal. Humans will therefore retain their

---

67. Augustine, *City of God*, XXII.17, p. 1057.

68. Augustine, *City of God*, XXII.17, p. 1057.

69. Augustine, *City of God*, XXII.17, p. 1058.

70. Gilson adds some important clarifications in this regard: "What becomes of sexual intimacy in paradise is glorious completion. Our glorified bodies possess sexual organs not because we *need* them to complete something lacking in us. Our whole bodies are glorified because each aspect is a critical indicator of our desire for our permanent home. Love-*making* emphatically distinguishes us from the angels. It confirms that our intentionality desires union that befits the soul and body. The resurrected state completes the glorious waitingness of the virginal as it completes the relentless incompleteness of every earthly striving, every frenetic sexual union, every weaving of ourselves, in and towards the other, which could never outwit time, sin, weakness, and death . . . There would not be sex in paradise because such an action would not be

sexed bodies. Moreover, according to Augustine, our bodies at the resurrection will continue to have hair, fingernails, and so forth—although nothing that disfigures our bodies will be present in a disfiguring way. Whatever belongs to our bodies but cannot be present without disfiguring us—such as extra hair or fingernail clippings—could be present, says Augustine, in some other way as part of the substance of the body.

At the same time, Augustine grants that God will significantly remold our bodies. Whatever pertains to our body's essential nature will be present but will be "recast" so as to express the perfection of our body's potentialities. There will be no disharmony, ugliness, or imperfection.

Augustine reflects carefully upon Christ's risen body. It seems evident, says Augustine, that Christ had the power to ensure that his glorious clarity or splendor did not overpower the apostles' eyes. He also had the power to eat, even though no longer driven by the need for nourishment. He kept his scars, not because he was suggesting that our risen bodies would retain the deformities caused by injuries or disease, but because his apostles needed to know it was him. Augustine grants that the martyrs may retain their scars in their risen bodies, since such wounds give glory to Christ and (like Christ's wounds) reveal the dignity and beauty of the soul.[71] But martyrs who lost arms, legs, or head will not be missing these body parts in their risen bodies. On the contrary, the risen body will be perfectly whole.

---

paradisal. All union, intimacy, completion is accomplished and held in full *Actus* in the incarnational climax as beatific vision. In the resurrected state, one's entire body and soul would be bathed in union with the bridegroom. There would be no parting, no separation, no need to enter the other, to renegotiate a union, everything would be *ad fontes*. This definitively contrasts to all earthly sexual intimacy, whether it be the virginal and chaste, erotic, or mystical. All earthly *eros*, no matter how transcendent, must find itself incomplete, unable incarnationally and entirely to self-empty into the beloved and be wholly infixed by the beloved" (*As It Is in Heaven*, 226–27). Along similar lines, see also Lewis, *Miracles*, 165–66.

71. Gilson puts it this way, rightly emphasizing the resurrection's integral connection to the cross: "Without Christ's martyrological and *kenotic* love, there would be only fantasy and disoriented desire for our immortality and for the glorified body" (Gilson, *As It Is in Heaven*, 192). She goes on to say, "Christ resurrects with his scars, this signifies that death paradoxically dilates our understanding of the glorified body ... The human body in the resurrected state would be a living art form, with the keys to understanding the manifold layers of each story illuminating from the skin, shining from the face, transmitted in the warmth of touch, and in the gaze that does not hide ... The God-man's *kenosis* overflows into his infixion: heaven as Christ's body is now ours, suffused with his in the resurrected state. This filling up of our scars does not cover over our imperfections, for like Christ we too rise with our scars, but perfuses them with the radiant Truth, Goodness, Beauty, and Being" (*As It Is in Heaven*, 194, 196–97). Gilson's depiction is richly evocative. I would add that I hope that the glorified body truly will be perfected (i.e., with its imperfections taken away or transformed)— as a body radiant with Goodness, Beauty, and Being would be.

What about people whose bodies were burned to ashes or disintegrated into the soil or eaten by cannibals? God, says Augustine, knows everything; therefore, God knows where the elements of our bodies are, and God can bring them together no matter how they have been dispersed or seemingly obliterated. As for flesh eaten by cannibals, it belongs to the person in which it originally was, and at the general resurrection it will be restored to his or her body.

It should be emphasized that Augustine knows he is only offering surmises. In general, he does not insist upon his answers, although he insists that "all ugliness must disappear, all weakness, all sluggishness, all corruption, and anything else that is inconsistent with that kingdom in which the sons of the resurrection and of the promise will be equal to the angels of God, in felicity if not in body or in age."[72] After setting forth a brief summary of the various kinds of miseries and trials of human life after the fall, Augustine argues that these trials will not be present in the life of glory. There will be no toil, no pedagogy, no attacks, and no vulnerability to demons or disease.

In light of 1 Corinthians 15, Augustine explores what it might mean to have a "spiritual" body. In his view, it means that one's body is incorruptible and immortal. The glorified body will be fully "subject to the spirit."[73] At present, our soul is in many ways subject to our body—we need sleep, we get hungry, we need a well-functioning brain in order to think, and so on. Our glorified body will be flesh but fully subject to our glorified soul. The glorified or spiritual body will be so grace-filled that it is not possible to imagine it, says Augustine.

Augustine quotes Porphyry's claim that souls in bliss cannot be in contact with bodies. In response, Augustine points out that Plato himself describes the gods as dwelling in the heavenly bodies. Even Plato recognizes that God has the power to make people immortal, and it is but a short step to granting that God has the power to raise and transform our bodies. Besides, Plato thinks the souls of the wise eventually return to dwell in bodies. For his part, Porphyry denies that wise souls could ever wish to descend once more into mortal bodies. Augustine suggests that the ideas of the two thinkers should be brought together: our souls will dwell in bodies again, but not in perishable bodies since our bodies will be glorified. The souls of the blessed will be united to glorified, immortal bodies—and not just to any bodies, but to our own bodies, the same bodies (now glorified) in which we suffered in the present life. Augustine remarks that Varro believes that "the

---

72. Augustine, *City of God*, XXII.20, p. 1064.
73. Augustine, *City of God*, XXII.21, p. 1064.

soul returns to the same body as before," and so the solution is to combine the best insights of Varro, Plato, and Porphyry and to arrive at Christian truth about the resurrection.[74]

Augustine concludes by attempting once more to describe what our risen bodies will be like. Again, he grants that he does not know; he speaks from a perspective of faith, not sight. He measures his words by Paul's statement, "For now we see in a mirror dimly, but then face to face. Now I know in part; then I shall understand fully, even as I have been fully understood" (1 Cor 13:12). Obviously, we cannot simply transpose our current bodily life to the glorified bodily life that the blessed will receive. For instance, glorified persons will not need sleep and will constantly behold the face of God. Thus, it is not clear what shutting one's eyelids would do, even though glorified bodies will presumably have eyelids that open and close. Moreover, bodily eyes will not be necessary for the seeing that we will do in the state of glory; the glorified soul will be able to see everything in God. But bodily eyes "will have their own function and the spirit will make use of them through the spiritual body."[75] Augustine even suggests that the eyes of our resurrected bodies will be able to see spiritual realities—a radical transformation indeed! Ultimately, however, he accepts that "we do not know what new qualities the spiritual body will have, for we are speaking of something beyond our experience."[76] We know simply that our glorified bodily members and movements will be caught up entirely in active and joyful praise of God, in perfect obedience to our glorified soul.

To my mind, there is no need to insist upon the ongoing presence of all our bodily organs or things such as hair, fingernails, and eyelids. After all, Augustine grants that our risen bodies are unimaginable in their glory. Since this is so, and since there is going to be a great transformation, I think that we do not need to imagine risen bodies as possessing everything that earthly bodies possess. But male and female will persist, since this difference belongs to the goodness of creation and it images the union of Christ and his Church, being inscribed even in our very cells.[77] I also agree with Augustine that the transformation of our bodies will not negate our individuality or our recognizable corporeality. We will not be as spiritualized as Origen supposes, nor will we be united in a universal nonspatial corporeality as Bulgakov supposes.

---

74. Augustine, *City of God*, XXII.28, p. 1081.
75. Augustine, *City of God*, XXII.29, p. 1083.
76. Augustine, *City of God*, XXII.29, p. 1085.
77. For further defense of this position, see Beth Felker Jones's *Marks of His Wounds*.

Albert the Great

Let me now jump forward eight centuries to the high medieval period. Albert the Great wrote his *On Resurrection* in response to the rise of medieval Aristotelian philosophical skepticism about the intelligibility of such paradoxes as an "impassible body" or "incorruptible matter."[78] In Albert's day, there were not only increasing philosophical challenges to glorified bodiliness (resulting in ecclesiastical condemnations in Paris in 1241 and 1277), but also sectarian communities that stood outside the Catholic Church and that held, among other things, that Christ did not rise from the dead and so neither will we.[79] Among the propositions condemned at Paris in 1277 were that the resurrected body is not one and the same with the body that has died; that philosophers cannot affirm the general resurrection because reason cannot prove it; and that a corruptible earthly body cannot receive everlasting existence from God.[80]

For Albert, the full power of Christ's resurrection will only be revealed in our resurrection. He compares the relation of Christ's resurrection and ours to the relation of heat in fire and heat in other things. Heat belongs to fire per se, whereas heat belongs to other things through fire (that is, through that which has heat per se). Albert explains that "if something is found in which different things participate in various ways, and it exists in

---

78. Resnick and Harkins, "Introduction," 3. For background in the medieval period, see also Kromholtz, *On the Last Day*; Frasseto, "Resurrection of the Body"; Niederbacher, "The Same Body Again?"; Brown, "Aquinas on the Resurrection of the Body." Niederbacher follows Robert Pasnau's viewpoint, to which I am attracted as well: "The question of whether the resurrected body is the same body or merely a replica does not arise, because sameness of body is accounted for in terms of sameness of form" (Pasnua, *Thomas Aquinas on Human Nature*, 393). Yet I agree with Josef Quitterer—who draws upon Aquinas—that the ongoing existence of the soul could not suffice, by itself, for the ongoing existence of the human person, since a human being is a hylomorphic creature: see Quitterer, "Hylomorphism and the Constitution View." For a different view, also indebted to Aquinas's hylomorphic anthropology and contending that resurrection occurs immediately after death (with no intermediate state), see James T. Turner Jr., *On the Resurrection of the Dead*. Caroline Walker Bynum treats the high scholastics, including some brief attention to Albert, in *Resurrection of the Body*, 232–78. She also takes up the impact of the 1277 condemnations. For a fascinating study, though one that goes beyond my focus here, see McMichael, "Resurrection of Jesus and Human Beings."

79. See Resnick and Harkins, "Introduction," 4–5.

80. See Resnick and Harkins, "Introduction," 4–5. Resnick and Harkins comment, "While earlier theologians may have been satisfied with suggestive metaphors in defense of their understanding of the resurrected body, by the thirteenth century discussions of resurrection had become far more technical . . . as Christian thinkers sought to assimilate Aristotelian concepts regarding matter, generation and corruption, and natural bodies" (5).

one of them *per se* but it exists in the others from another (*ab alio*), the one that exists *per se* will be the cause of the others."[81] Christ's resurrection exists in Christ per se, because of his power as the incarnate Word. Our (future) resurrection is therefore related to Christ's resurrection as to a cause from which our resurrection flows.

According to Albert, all will be raised by the power of Christ's resurrection to incorruptible life. Even those who are damned will receive their bodies, now incorruptible, in the resurrection of the dead caused by Christ's resurrection. In Albert's view, this is the meaning of 1 Corinthians 15:52, "For the trumpet will sound, and the dead will be raised imperishable." This statement describes not simply the blessed but all the dead; and this fits with Christ's teachings about the final judgment. Albert also argues that resurrection, in the proper sense (as distinct from resuscitation), means a change from a state of corruption—that is, being a corpse or having decomposed entirely—to a state of incorruption. When human beings are raised from the dead, they are raised incorrupt, to a condition of immortality (*pace* Tanner).

Why is not everyone resurrected shortly after death, as Christ was? Albert answers in terms of fittingness. Just as all matter was given form at the same instant at the beginning of creation, so all matter should (allowing for exceptions) be resurrected to immortal life at the same time. It is fitting that matter as we know it, with its laws of generation and corruption, should continue to exist rather than having portions of matter transformed on a daily basis into resurrected bodies. Since the earthly generation of new bodies will continue until the end of time, the material realm with its principles of generation and corruption should continue to be ordered by these twin principles until the end of time.

Albert believes that some saints of Israel rose from the dead at Christ's passion and also that Mary's assumption has likewise preceded the general resurrection. In his view, the resurrection of these persons proceeded from a special *ratio* that does not apply to other human beings. Among those who rose from the dead prior to the general resurrection, some did so because of their reception of divine covenantal promises, some as a sign of Christ's coming resurrection, and some because of a special connection to Christ's body. The last-named reason applies to the case of the Virgin Mary. But the fact that there are some exceptions—some persons who are raised prior to the general resurrection—does not negate the truth that bodily resurrection will and should occur en masse at the end of time.

Like Augustine, Albert maintains that human resurrected bodies will be what they would have been at age thirty, in the fullness of the actualization

---

81. Albert, *On Resurrection*, Tractate 2, q. 1, p. 77.

of their potencies. He argues that Christ's humanity is the measure for all other instances of human nature, and this explains why we will rise in the form we would have had at age thirty, with all potencies realized.

Asking whether a glorified body is movable, Albert notes that it seems that the answer is no. To move from place to place, or to move or change in any other way, requires a desire to be somewhere different or to attain something new. Something movable would therefore not have received the fulfillment of all desire. Such could not be true of a glorified body, since a person in the state of glory has received the fulfillment of all desire.[82] Besides, no nature suited to the empyrean realm—where Albert deems glorified bodies presently dwell—is able to dwell in the earthly realm.[83] In addition, because glorified bodies are fully actualized, it seems that they cannot exist in time. Nor, it seems, can a glorified body exist in a place, since a glorified body depends upon God but not upon any other body.[84] If the above points are true, then the risen and glorified Christ would not have been able to make real appearances on earth. Albert faces head-on the possibility that the resurrection of Christ, as reported in the Gospels, is scientifically impossible on Albert's terms—and "if Christ has not been raised, your faith is futile and you are still in your sins" (1 Cor 15:17).[85]

Albert's solution is that, despite the difficulties, "[o]ne must say that a glorious body has the perfect power for progressive motion."[86] He defends this claim vigorously, showing that the objections noted above do not in fact apply. Regarding whether a glorified body can move, Albert observes that while motion or change caused by desire or need is not possible, nevertheless "motion will exist as a demonstration of the motive power, according to which the power is directed by eternal wisdom to act."[87] The state of glory will not be marked by permanent bodily stillness; quite the contrary. Progressive motion will not be tiresome for the glorified human body. In the realm of glory, we will not be constrained by anything, but will be able to

---

82. See Albert, *On Resurrection*, Tractate 2, q. 8, p. 111.

83. Regarding the notion of the empyrean realm, see Davenport, "Locating Heaven," 104, with reference to Thomas Aquinas (*Summa theologiae* I, q. 66, a. 3) and to the work of Grant, "Cosmology."

84. Yet another problem is whether two bodies can exist in the same place at the same time. This problem arises due to the risen Christ's entering through closed doors in John 20:19. In Book IV of his *Physics*, Aristotle proves that this is impossible. Nor can the problem be solved by supposing that a glorified body could squeeze through a tiny space.

85. Albert does not quote this biblical text at this juncture, but proceeds instead to his solution.

86. Albert, *On Resurrection*, Tractate 2, q. 8, p. 114.

87. Albert, *On Resurrection*, Tractate 2, q. 8, p. 114.

move anywhere. Glorified bodies will not move randomly, but will move in accordance with the divine wisdom.

Furthermore, the notion that bodies can only exist in the place proper for them—earthly bodies on earth, heavenly bodies in heaven—may be true for bodies that depend upon the place that contains them but cannot be true for glorified bodies, which do not depend upon place. Christ's glorified body has the freedom to move and manifest itself. A glorified body is not *fully* actual but retains some potency, because "there is a certain potency that is not opposed to a body's perfection, as is the potency to a [particular] position (*ad situm*) in local motion."[88]

Similarly, Albert holds that a certain kind of time exists for a glorified body, although that body is also outside time. Glorified persons do not experience the kind of time characterized by "changes in the emotions" or "changes in punishments," whereas the damned will forever endure this kind of time.[89] But time as related to change of place can exist in something that (according to its nature) does not exist in time. A nontemporal entity can possess motion that is temporal.[90]

---

88. Albert, *On Resurrection*, Tractate 2, q. 8, p. 115.

89. Albert, *On Resurrection*, Tractate 2, q. 8, p. 116.

90. Albert's account—arguing for temporality and nontemporality—is more complex than I can convey here. For a liturgical and christological effort to contrast time as we now experience it and time in everlasting life, see Griffiths, *Decreation*, 81–108. Griffiths argues that "there must be a kind of temporality that is not subject to the law of measure" (95), and he calls this kind of time "systolic" as distinct from "metronomic." He thinks that metronomic time no longer exists "in the liturgy of heaven: there will only be the time of the systole, the time in which human action is fully enfolded into the life of the Trinity ... Systolic time, the time proleptically present in the liturgy, cannot be measured by metronomic time" (104, 106). He grounds "systolic" time in Christ: "Time ... has been systolated, ingathered or infolded, by the events of the incarnation and of the passion; this systolation of time is in every significant way opposed to and transformative of the linear timespace of the metronome, which can be mapped on a grid and timed by a clock ... The systolation of timespace around the LORD reaches its acme in heaven, so that the LORD, triune and incarnate, is the timespace in which the resurrected find themselves" (217). For further the view that there will be no succession of time in eternal life (a view that Griffiths shares, since "metronomic" time involves succession), see Thomas Aquinas, *Summa contra gentiles*, III, ch. 61; as well as Scheeben, *Mysteries of Christianity*, 663–65. Paul O'Callaghan states with his typical clarity of expression, "It is clear that the blessed do not experience the perfect and ineffable coming together of past, present, and future that characterizes the eternity of God, for they are creatures whose actions take place necessarily one after another, in succession, in such a way that each action is incapable of expressing the entirety of their being. Nonetheless, they do participate in God's eternity, and do not experience time as earthly wayfarers do" (O'Callaghan, *Christ Our Hope*, 179). It seems to me that Griffiths is rightly seeking to articulate a heavenly (liturgical) action of the blessed that does express "the entirety of their being." O'Callaghan may be seeking the same when

In Albert's view, too, glorified bodies actually do exist in a place. "Place" can be understood in various ways: as one of Aristotle's categories; as a kind of immobile quantity; or as a principle of motion. When "place" is understood as a container that gives form to an imperfect thing, "place" is not applicable to glorified bodies. But place as a kind of immobile quantity does have application to glorified bodies, since place understood in this way has to do simply with measuring something by external boundaries. Glorified bodies have external boundaries and in this sense have "place." Albert concludes that "the noblest body does not exist in a place in such a way that it is contained by place; but it can have a boundary."[91] Insofar as a glorified body has width, length, and depth, it has extrinsic quantity and thereby has boundaries. This is the kind of place that glorified bodies have.[92]

What about the ability of a glorified body can go through a closed door (as the risen Christ did), given the fact that two bodies cannot be in the same place at the same time? Albert grants that a glorified body requires a place that fits its quantity. But he thinks that a glorified body is not comprised of "gross matter." A glorified body is spiritual and "subtle" rather than earthly. In Albert's view, this means that a glorified body has the capacity to exist in the same place as an earthly body, because the glorified body does not compete with the gross matter of the earthly body.[93]

---

he quotes Karl Barth: "It may be said that as creatures the blessed in heaven partake of 'eternity as an inner possession of the totality of life'" (*Christ Our Hope*, 180, quoting Barth, *CD* 2/1:610–11).

91. Albert, *On Resurrection*, Tractate 2, q. 8, p. 117.

92. As noted above, Griffiths describes heaven as a "timespace," "a *locus-tempus* in which defect, lack, damage, and distance are all absent to the extent compatible with (particular varieties of) creaturehood. It is a timespace in which creatures capable of heaven, in their various kinds, find the damage that separated them ... from the LORD and from other creatures finally and irreversibly healed" (Griffiths, *Decreation*, 5). In my view, Albert's way of putting it is more helpful, since "timespace" sounds too similar to our present state.

93. On this topic, Denys Turner remarks that Aquinas disagrees (see *Summa theologiae* III, q. 54, a 1; Suppl., q. 83, a. 4): "Thomas rejects the view taken by some theologians of his time that Jesus' being able to walk through the closed door of the upper room where the disciples are meeting (John 20:19) is a natural consequence of his body's being raised—a raised body can do just that sort of thing as a matter of course, such theologians supposed. Not so, says Thomas. If in effect you strip the raised body of Jesus of all those properties that belong to bodies as such, then your theology of resurrection in consequence entails the denial of the resurrection of the human person who is Jesus. Human bodies are material objects, and no two material objects can naturally occupy the same place at the same time as one another. It follows that a raised body is not a material body if it can of its nature walk through closed doors, and Jesus' body is not a human body if it is not material—indeed, if it is not material it is simply not a body at all, just a ghost ... The key point is that, raised or not, the essential properties of

Albert next takes up whether, in order for people on earth to see a glorified body, a miracle is necessary. As he says, a glorified body is on a significantly higher ontological level than are our eyes—and the earthly eye's power of vision is not even strong enough to look directly upon the sun, let alone upon a glorified body. Albert also quotes Alpetragius's *Astrology* to the effect that the highest heaven (beyond the fixed stars) is invisible because its light is so subtle that human eyes cannot perceive it.

Yet, Christ manifested his glorified body and his disciples saw it. It seems, then, that it is within the power of a glorified body to make itself visible; but if so, does this visibility require a miracle? Another question is whether a person possessed of a glorified body can make this body visible or invisible at will—as the risen Christ seems to have done with the two disciples he met on the road to Emmaus (Luke 24:31). Another question is whether the risen Christ was seen in the way that his glorified body really is, as opposed to inventing an appearance that had less luminosity. A final related question has to do with why Christ's glorified body, in his resurrection appearances, was less luminous than at his transfiguration.

Albert responds to these questions as follows. He argues that "a glorious body is not visible to a non-glorious [eye] without a miracle, but . . . it is visible to a glorious [eye] without a miracle."[94] When the risen Christ appeared to his disciples, therefore, it required a miracle for them to see him. The miracle consisted in elevating their non-glorified eyes to be able to see him. Christ could become invisible by withdrawing this miracle. When his disciples saw Christ's glorified body, furthermore, they saw color rather than sheer luminosity. Albert argues on the basis of Aristotle that whenever light is "perceived in a bounded body"—as was the case with Christ's glorified body—then the light will be bounded light, "perceived as color and not as light."[95] This is how the risen body of Christ could be seen as something other than sheer light, which explains the difference between the resurrection appearances and the transfiguration.

---

human bodies remain continuously the same between their pre- and post-resurrection conditions. For otherwise, how could it be said that the raised body of Jesus is the *same* body as that of the Jesus dead on the Cross if, in the relevant sense, the raised person of Jesus lacks the essential properties of a *body* in the first place?" (Turner, *Thomas Aquinas*, 247–48). I disagree with this position, since it seems to me that a glorified body—imbued with subtlety—could indeed pass through a closed door, especially given what we now know about matter. Besides, glorified materiality (which is unimaginable in its glory) does not need to conform strictly to the laws of non-glorified matter, as Albert makes clear.

94. Albert, *On Resurrection*, Tractate 2, q. 8, p. 124.
95. Albert, *On Resurrection*, Tractate 2, q. 8, p. 125.

Albert takes a similar approach to how it could be possible to touch a glorified body, as the disciple Thomas does in John 20. A glorified body is not defined by its elemental qualities; rather, a glorified body possesses brightness, subtlety, and so on. Therefore, Albert deems that to be able to touch (and palpate) a glorified body requires a miracle. A person with a glorified body can certainly touch another person with a glorified body, but for a person with a non-glorified body to do so requires a miracle. Touch is normally oriented toward such things as hot or cold, hard or soft, and so on. But touch is also about "the perception of an indivisible continuous [body] or a divided non-continuous [body]."[96] Because it is incorruptible and spiritual (or "non-elemental"), a glorified body transcends the categories of hot or cold and hard or soft, but it is still an indivisible, continuous, and therefore tangible body.[97]

Another problem stems from the fact that the risen Jesus ate food. Here, Albert agrees with Augustine's distinction between power and need. Glorified bodies retain the power to eat, but not the need to do so (and thus not the processes by which we become full when we eat and hungry when we do not). What then happened to the fish that the risen Jesus ate? Albert maintains that, just as an earthly body converts food into nourishment, a spiritual or glorified body can convert food into "a subtle, airy matter"—clearly going far beyond what digestive organs do.[98]

Let me add that Albert carefully avoids the notion that the risen Jesus deceived the people who did not recognize him—for example, Mary Magdalene in John 20 and the two disciples on the road to Emmaus in Luke 24. Albert insists that the risen Jesus "revealed himself to them in his own proper form," and they did not recognize him because they were not expecting to see him and because they saw him in strange circumstances.[99]

In sum, Albert engages the intelligibility of bodily resurrection from the perspective of Aristotelian philosophy, but he does not reduce the glorified body to the level of the bodies known to Aristotle. On the contrary, Albert's understanding of glorified bodiliness renders it both intelligible and radically mysterious. A glorified body is so luminous as to be utterly beyond the natural ability of earthly eyes to see, as well as so subtle as to be utterly beyond the laws of physics. A glorified body has marvelous agility and thus movement, but not in the sense that we do, since we move due to unfulfilled desire and neediness. A glorified body is tangible and can

---

96. Albert, *On Resurrection*, Tractate 2, q. 8, p. 128.
97. Albert, *On Resurrection*, Tractate 2, q. 8, p. 128.
98. Albert, *On Resurrection*, Tractate 2, q. 8, p. 129.
99. Albert, *On Resurrection*, Tractate 2, q. 8, p. 135.

consume food, but its tangibility and digestion are radically different from what are found in an earthly body. A glorified body is temporal and spatial in a certain sense, but not in the sense that applies to earthly bodies. A glorified body is immortal and cannot suffer in any way. Thus, with Christ's risen and glorified body as the measure, Albert puts his Aristotelian philosophy to work both to defend the intelligibility of revealed glorified bodiliness and to show that it is a mystery beyond our ken.

IV. Post-Newtonian Science and Bodily Resurrection

I consider exemplary the work that Albert does to address basic questions regarding Christ's glorified body and ours. He goes beyond simply asking how a dead body can be reconstituted. He seeks understanding of what bodily glorification might mean, especially given the presence of Christ's glorified body in time and space prior to his ascension. He helps deepen an appropriate sense of the glorified body's strangeness, without rendering it unintelligible.

That said, let me now move beyond Albert's Aristotelian scientific worldview and also beyond the Newtonian one that replaced it. As the Reformed theologian T. F. Torrance says, today we have "a profounder and more differential view of reality in which energy and matter, intelligible structure and material content, exist in mutual interaction and indetermination. This is a dynamic view of the world as a continuous integrated manifold of fields of force in which relations between bodies are just as ontologically real as bodies themselves."[100] What then might it mean to say that Christ's glorified body, prior to his ascension, was present within the created cosmos's "manifold fields of force" and "relations between bodies"?

I note first that post-Newtonian science ensures that the universe is not viewed as a container in which bodies operate.[101] This strengthens Albert's case regarding the transcendence of Christ's glorified body over any spatial container, even while affirming (as Albert does) that Christ's glorified body can be measured. Post-Newtonian science also does not see space and time as constants but rather recognizes them to be contingent on particular states of affairs. Arguably, this opens up room for the entrance of a glorified body upon the stage of space and time, as exemplified by Jesus' resurrection appearances.

---

100. Torrance, *Space, Time and Resurrection*, 185.

101. Torrance thinks that John Philoponos anticipated this in the patristic era but his insights were not taken up. See *Space, Time and Resurrection*, 186.

Contemporary Christian thinkers have grappled with the intelligibility of bodily resurrection in light of post-Newtonian science. Briefly, I will set forth the ideas of three such thinkers: Ted Peters, John Polkinghorne, and Jeffrey Schloss. Peters's essay "Resurrection: The Conceptual Challenge" focuses on the problem of the identity or continuity of the resurrected body and the earthly body. He reflects upon Paul's understanding of the "spiritual body," arguing that "[t]he *sōma pneumatikon* is the resurrected body that is determined by the Holy Spirit."[102] He then inquires into the issue of continuity, which was not a problem for Jesus' corpse but is a major problem for the long-dead and disintegrated bodies of his followers.

Peters recognizes that the most important task in this regard is to distinguish resurrection from reincarnation or from the creation of a mere replica. He sets forth Gregory's argument about the coming together of bodily elements from all stages of the person's existence, so as to reproduce our Edenic "essential nature" rather than simply being a carbon copy of the post-fall human being that we are now. For Peters, however, Gregory's argument fails. Peters gives the example of a shark that eats a swimmer and then in turn is eaten by a family, who thereby consume some elements of the swimmer as transformed into shark flesh. In Peters's view, such a situation is fatal for Gregory's position regarding the recombination of our bodily elements, especially in light of contemporary science's recognition "of the interrelatedness of elements in the ongoing life cycle" so that "[w]e all share ... the same physical elements."[103] This emphasis on the human race sharing the same physical elements strikes me as a good reason for doubting that the continuity of our risen bodies depends upon reconstituting the same material elements that were present in our earthly bodies.

Peters agrees with the Protestant theologian Arthur Peacocke that the bodily resurrection of all human beings is intelligible only if God newly creates or re-creates our bodily elements. Otherwise, since we share them with others, there would be insufficient bodily material to fund the general resurrection.[104] But rather than following Peacocke's perspective as a whole, Peters directs attention to the work of John Polkinghorne. For Polkinghorne, Peters observes, the continuity of the resurrected body with the earthly body that died depends not on the material elements but on two things: the divine power, and the "soul" as the form or "information-bearing pattern"

---

102. Peters, "Resurrection," 303.

103. Peters, "Resurrection," 313.

104. For a fuller articulation of Peacocke's view, see Peacocke, *Theology for a Scientific Age*, 285.

of the body.[105] Polkinghorne does not think the soul is immortal; in his view, it dissolves with the body, just as Aquinas thinks happens to the souls of nonrational animals. But the "soul" is retained firmly in the divine memory, and so God is able to resurrect the person's body. God will do this by reconstituting, on the basis of the "soul" or pattern, the person's body out of "new material" that (as immortal and glorified) obeys "new laws of nature, laws of life rather than laws of death."[106] Although I think the soul does not dissolve when the body dies, I consider Peters (and Polkinghorne) to be correct that the solution to the problem of material continuity rests with the spiritual soul.

In his essay "Eschatological Credibility," Polkinghorne begins with the cosmic anthropic principle. There would have been no human life had it not been for a set of fine-tuned cosmic variables that could have been otherwise. On this basis, it is reasonable to suppose that the cosmos reflects a teleological order, given the "strong propensity for the emergence of pattern" or "emergent properties of complexity."[107] Yet, there is also strong scientific evidence that the universe will end either in a fireball (the big crunch) or in cold cosmic waste (endless expansion). In either case, the human race has no future and the cosmos seems to be the very opposite of teleologically ordered.

For Polkinghorne, the evidence for teleology at the outset (the anthropic principle) and the inability of the cosmos to be the site of its own teleological fulfillment indicate, when taken together, the plausibility of the Christian understanding of the new creation as the God-orchestrated consummation of all things. He points to Paul's argument in Romans 8:19–23 that the whole creation is longing to be freed from its bondage to decay, a liberation that will happen at the end of time.[108] The fulfillment of the cosmos, from a Christian perspective, will involve both continuity and discontinuity—just as can be seen in Jesus' glorified body, which is a real body and bears his scars, but which also "possesses wholly new properties, so that he appears and disappears within locked rooms."[109] The resurrected body of Jesus and our future resurrection are best understood within a cosmic fulfillment or new creation.

---

105. Peters, "Resurrection," 319, drawing upon Polkinghorne, *Science and Christian Belief*, 162–67.

106. Peters, "Resurrection," 320.

107. Polkinghorne, "Eschatological Credibility," 45. Polkinghorne cites Barrow and Tipler, *Anthropic Cosmological Principle*.

108. For rich background, see Hays, "Pneumatology."

109. Polkinghorne, "Eschatological Credibility," 49.

Thus, Polkinghorne adds a much-needed cosmic dimension to theological consideration of Christ's resurrection and ours. As I have noted above, he is also right that the soul is the bearer of continuity, even this requires (in my view) that the soul not perish with the body in death.[110] If both soul and body perished, resurrection could only be a divinely made replica, not a real resurrection of the earthly body that died.

Yet, assuming that the soul is the bearer of continuity, one may still ask how the risen body and the body that died are the same, if the risen body is not made of the same identical matter. In response, Polkinghorne emphasizes that there is no pure "body": a living human body is always matter informed by soul, and the matter is always changing.[111] Matter, then, is not really the principle of continuity even during the person's life, let alone between a person's corpse and his or her risen body. At the same time, Polkinghorne does not exclude matter from a role in serving the continuity between our present life and the life of the new creation. In his view, existing cosmic matter will be transformed to make the new creation.

Surprisingly, Polkinghorne draws from this point the conclusion that eternal life must be temporal, in accordance with the evolutionary character of the material cosmos. He arrives at this position partly on the basis of the fact that matter, space, and time are mutually integrated in the theory of general relativity. But I note that if glorified bodies continue to exist in "time," eternal life would be an endless and tedious extension. It is better to adopt the nuanced position of Aquinas, who holds (in Bryan Kromholtz's words) that "risen human persons will not be subject to time, but they will have certain temporal operations. They will not be eternal, but the just will participate in God's eternity."[112]

---

110. See my chapter on the spiritual soul, engaging with various biblical scholars, philosophers, and theologians, in *Jesus and the Demise of Death*. For a recent Thomistic account of the soul with which I agree, see Cunningham, "Thomas Aquinas's Anthropology."

111. See Polkinghorne, "Eschatological Credibility," 51: "What could be the carrier of continuity that links me today with the young schoolboy in the photograph of sixty years ago? It is certainly not the matter of my body that plays that role. That is changing all the time, through wear and tear, eating and drinking. None of us has many atoms in our bodies today that were there even two years ago. Materially, we are in a state of flux."

112. Kromholtz, *On the Last Day*, 490; see the discussion of this point in Kromholtz's chapter 6. Kromholtz states astutely, "The notion that various forms of durational measure may apply to humans, whether they be persons *in via*, separated souls, or risen persons, is an idea of which theology today should take note. Human life is certainly an especially complex phenomenon; given that it may involve a life of grace, and is believed to involve a spiritual dimension, a created permanence, a bodily existence, and the possibility of all these kinds of existence in an after-life, it is altogether

Lastly, in his essay "From Evolution to Eschatology," Jeffrey Schloss raises a crucial question regarding the risen and glorified body: What is "life," and what does it mean to be living? If the risen and glorified body does not have normal biological processes, is it really a *living* body?

Schloss first notes that individual living organisms on earth are "embedded in a larger creation" of interdependence—an environment.[113] Scripture attests that our glorified bodies will likewise be embedded in an environment, the new creation. But this should not lead us to believe that the new creation will simply be a glorified replica of the natural vistas and forests of our world. According to Scripture, there will be no death in the world to come, and no hunger or thirst or any kind of lack. The book of Revelation suggests that there will not even be any night or any sun or moon. Schloss is aware that Revelation's imagery is metaphorical, but he points out that when dealing with the domain of the new creation or "heaven," the difference between "literal" and "metaphorical" is relativized since no literal description could do justice to the reality. The point is that the new creation will be vastly different.

In life on earth, Schloss observes, creatures are plagued not only by disease and death, but also by competition for scarce resources. Moreover, the optimal performance of an individual organism often does not correspond to the maximal abundance of the organism. Every organism must deal with trade-offs, seeking an optimal situation in the midst of competition. Each ecosystem will be suboptimal for one species while optimal for another. These kinds of trade-offs and competitions will, Schloss argues, no longer exist in the life of the new creation. But at present, it is still the case that *"life* is not describable in terms that do not invoke the tensions

---

reasonable and consonant with the faith to suppose that the durational measures for these aspects should vary in nuanced ways. We would not suggest that St. Thomas has the last word on these types of duration. However, his conception of the kinds of duration that apply to humans in the various stages of life that are implied in his teaching on the time of the resurrection is not only valid, but promising in its explanatory power . . . Aquinas's idea that different kinds of duration apply at once, in different respects, to a given soul or risen human person, could help to overcome extreme antinomies among time, eternity, and other forms of duration that have been conceived. Some more recent conceptions of the temporality of the risen, such as Lohfink's 'transfigured time,' seem to labor under the supposition that a single kind of duration must apply to the risen" (498). See also Christina Van Dyke's emphasis on the unchanging character of the beatific vision, although Van Dyke should pay more attention to Aquinas's understanding of "sempiternal" and to Aquinas's discussion of the dimensions of bodily beatitude: Van Dyke, *Hidden Wisdom*, 202–4.

113. Schloss, "From Evolution to Eschatology," 58.

between telos and chaos, desire and denial, flourishing and attrition, being and non-being."[114]

Schloss emphasizes that an individual organism exists always in relation to its environment. For example, a beaver would hardly be a beaver if there were no trees or rivers, since a beaver's particular mode of being is oriented to such an environment.[115] To be a beaver, then, involves not merely an individual beaver, but rather includes the environment in which a beaver does beaver-like things, that is, the things that a beaver's physical characteristics have been evolutionarily formed to do. It follows that a beaver's body "may be considered to extend beyond the skin, to include all its fitness-enhancing influences on the environment."[116]

As Schloss says, this may be helpful for reflection on Christ's risen body, a body that has an intrinsic relation to the kingdom of God and thus to the resurrection of other bodies. But the point that Schloss highlights first is simply that the body of a particular organism (e.g. a beaver) is related to, and serves, the flourishing of other organisms. Genetic information is operative both inside the organism and via external organisms, inasmuch as genes in other bodies assist in the reproduction of genes in a particular body. Schloss therefore emphasizes "collective identity or symbiotic cooperation rather than individual competition."[117] This emphasis on the communal character of "life" is highly beneficial for the project of conceiving of risen and glorified bodiliness. Everlasting life or the new creation includes the fullness of such collective identity and symbiotic cooperation. This fits with the collective dimension of risen or glorified bodiliness as the body of Christ. A glorified body—whether Christ's or someone else's—must be viewed in light of other glorified bodies, since it is the whole that makes for the environment in which each individual body plays its role.

Schloss thinks in terms of a scale or hierarchy of being, according to which some living things have a greater degree of livingness or "ability to engage and freely respond to the environment" through sensation, movement, and cognition.[118] On this basis, Schloss reflects on what having "more life" might mean, so as to understand better what glorified life is. He identifies two aspects: the ability to avoid corruption of being, and the ability to extend oneself more profoundly into the exterior world. Both these things

---

114. Schloss, "From Evolution to Eschatology," 63. He is drawing upon a wide variety of works, including Jonas, *The Phenomenon of Life*, and Rosen, *Essays on Life Itself*.

115. See Schloss, "From Evolution to Eschatology," 64–65, drawing upon Dawkins, *The Extended Phenotype*.

116. Schloss, "From Evolution to Eschatology," 65.

117. Schloss, "From Evolution to Eschatology," 65.

118. Schloss, "From Evolution to Eschatology," 68.

are associated with Jesus' risen body, which is immortal and not bound to earthly limitations in engaging with the world. Like Jesus, we will have our bodies in the new creation, but they will not be corruptible and they will enjoy intimate communion with each other and with God.

Schloss notes that some natural scientists see life as the great exception to nature's laws, whereas others see organic systems as instructive for understanding all natural systems. Whether life can emerge from nonliving matter is still an open question. In Schloss's view, the fact that this is an open question should serve to answer those who argue that this or that aspect of Christian eschatology is impossible. He cautions against treating life as "a mechanistic subset of nonlife."[119] The reduction of life to nonlife, he argues, flies in the face of the extraordinary reality of life. It makes death primary, when in fact what we actually experience as living creatures is not death but life. He proposes in this vein that "resurrection is a promise because life is the ultimate unit of cosmic ontology," as befits the God who is infinite Life.[120]

When death is no more, therefore, this does not mean that life will be no more. On the contrary, God stands as an infinite source of energy that fuels life. Glorified life thus strikes Schloss as intelligible, even if beyond our imagination and dependent upon the divine power. He concludes with the hope that resurrection does not merely continue or extend, but radically intensifies, human life in its positive characteristics.

In sum, these contemporary thinkers have much to add regarding the cosmic and collective dimensions of glorified life. They provide further building blocks for a contemporary "Augustinian" position. Gregory and Augustine help us to ponder glorified bodiliness, both in its strangeness and its real continuity with our bodily identity; Albert enables us to contemplate questions such as how a glorified body could be present and visible within the limits of space and time, as distinct from the state of glory; and the above engagements with modern science help us to think further about the nature of matter, the soul, life, and the interdependence of all glorified bodies in the new creation.

V. Mary's Bodily Assumption

It is fitting to conclude with Mary's bodily assumption. Catholics and Orthodox believe that Jesus is not the only human whose body has been glorified. Like many others, Brant Pitre has defended this belief on the grounds of Revelation 11–12. Revelation 11:19 portrays a vision of "God's temple in

---

119. Schloss, "From Evolution to Eschatology," 81.
120. Schloss, "From Evolution to Eschatology," 82.

heaven" containing "the ark of his covenant," and Revelation 12:1–6 contains explicit allusions to Mary. On the basis of these texts, Pitre makes an argument of fittingness: "if Mary is the new Ark of the Covenant, then it makes sense that Jesus, the new David, would bring her up into heaven to be with him forever."[121]

A similar argument of fittingness is based upon First Corinthians. Paul states, "For as in Adam all die, so also in Christ shall all be made alive. But each in his own order: Christ the first fruits, then at his coming those who belong to Christ" (1 Cor 15:23). If Christ is the new Adam and Mary the new Eve, then the phrase "each in his own order" indicates the fittingness of recognizing an order in which Mary comes after Christ but before us, given Mary's unique vocation as the Mother of God. Furthermore, for patristic and medieval Christians (as noted above), it was evident biblically that people were taken up bodily into heaven even prior to Christ. An example is Genesis 5:24, "Enoch walked with God; and he was not, for God took him." Another instance is the fate of Elijah, who "went up by a whirlwind into heaven" (2 Kgs 2:11).

For the neo-scholastic theologian Joseph Pohle, the main theological reason in favor of the assumption of Mary is "the doctrine of the incorruptibility of her body,"[122] which is connected with Mary's holy motherhood and her perpetual virginity, both of which, in his view, tell firmly against her body corrupting in the grave. He makes much of her sinlessness, arguing that given the connection that Genesis 3 and Paul (Romans 6:23) make between sin and death, Mary "could not possibly be subject to the dominion of death up to the time of the general resurrection."[123] Grace and holiness, Pohle suggests, prepare for bodily glorification—so that a *perfectly* holy human being such as Mary does not owe the debt of death (even if she freely pays it in configuration to her Son) and is ready to be taken up in glory. In holy human beings, we already find the translucence to the divine light of love that characterizes the glorified body. We know that a glorified body is possible not least because we have seen holy persons radiant with love and grace. Among mere humans, Mary has preeminence in this regard.[124]

---

121. Pitre, *Jesus and the Jewish Roots of Mary*, 66. On new David typology in the Gospels, see Zacharias, *Matthew's Presentation of the Son of David*; Botner, *Jesus Christ as the Son of David in the Gospel of Mark*; Miura, *David in Luke-Acts*; Daly-Denton, *David in the Fourth Gospel*.

122. Pohle, *Mariology*, 109.

123. Pohle, *Mariology*, 112.

124. As noted above, Aidan Nichols in his *There Is No Rose* criticizes this kind of argument for the truth of Mary's assumption. He thinks more attention needs to be paid to Scripture and the patristic tradition. I agree with him, even though my own

In his first homily for the Feast of Mary's Assumption (which he terms her dormition), the eighth-century bishop and theologian Andrew of Crete focuses upon the connection between Christ's resurrection and ours. He suggests that Mary's assumption is Christ's way of assuring us that his resurrection was not merely the exaltation of himself, but was about the marriage of God and his people. Christ the new Adam desires to bring the new Eve into the life of glory, as a pledge or representative of the whole body and Bride of Christ, "that he might present the Church to himself in splendor, without spot or wrinkle or any such thing" (Eph 5:27). Andrew puts it this way: "Christ himself—the pure sacrifice, the ever-living light who shines forth from the Father like a sun from the sun, a ray gleaming out without beginning and without motion in distance—Christ wishes to gather us together as our host. He shows this clearly by taking up his ever-virgin mother from this earth today as Queen of human nature."[125]

Note that Andrew does not describe Mary's being taken up from the tomb into glorified life as her "resurrection." The reason for this is *not* that he thinks she never died. The Catholic theologian Brian Daley has proposed that perhaps the reason is that "it seemed more appropriate to reserve the term 'resurrection' for what happened to Jesus, and for the eschatological hope of all Christians for the end of time."[126] Mary's bodily assumption cannot be understood if it is perceived as a competitor to Jesus' resurrection, or if it is perceived as in competition with the general resurrection. Mary's assumption simply underscores the reality that Jesus did not rise for himself but for his people, his Bride. He rose to unite his people to himself. Although the full victory awaits his second coming, the new Adam and the new Eve are already present together in their glorified flesh in the inaugurated kingdom at the right hand of the Father.

In his own first homily on Mary's dormition (or assumption), John of Damascus begins by expressing awe at the mystery of Mary's receiving "the super-essential Word of God" into her womb.[127] He deems that it is hardly possible to speak words worthy of the dignity of Mary's exaltation

---

Mary's Bodily Assumption—due to my concerns about Réginald Garrigou-Lagrange's claim that there must have been a hidden and continuous oral tradition about Mary's bodily Assumption—neglects the patristic tradition except inasmuch as it shows the emergence of a liturgical and typological contemplation of the biblical testimony about Mary. I should also mention that my *Mary's Bodily Assumption*, in some (though not all) respects, fails to appreciate the wide diversity of neo-scholastic approaches.

125. Andrew of Crete, "On the Dormition of Our Most Holy Lady, the Mother of God: Homily I," 108.

126. Daley, "Introduction," 28.

127. John of Damascus, "On the Dormition of the Holy Mother of God: Homily I," 183.

in her earthly life, since it was through Mary that the incarnate Word entered the world. On this basis, Damascene imagines the separation of her soul and body at death, and the welcome that her holy soul received from Christ, the angels, and the blessed. He imagines her burial as a gathering of the apostles, who carry to the grave her dead body as "the true ark of the Lord God."[128] The apostles represent the fullness of Christ's holy people, while Christ and Mary (once the latter has been bodily taken up) represent the inauguration of the new creation—the new Adam and new Eve now united in glory through the work of Christ. Damascene comments, "Your immaculate, completely spotless body was not left on earth, but you have been transported to the royal dwelling-place of heaven as queen, as lady, as mistress, as Mother of God, as the one who truly gave God birth."[129]

Damascene makes this point even more clearly in his second homily on Mary's dormition. Indebted to Revelation 11:19, he first describes her as the ark of the covenant: "Today the holy, living ark of the living God, the one who carried her own maker within herself, comes to her rest in the temple of the Lord not made by hands."[130] He then describes the establishment of the new creation, the new Eden that Christ died and rose to establish. He proclaims, "Today the Eden of the new Adam welcomes the spiritual Paradise where our condemnation has been cancelled, where the tree of life is planted, where our nakedness is clothed again."[131] Having inaugurated the kingdom of God, the new Adam draws to himself the new Eve in her glorified flesh. Christ thereby establishes the bulwark of the new creation and points the whole Church in yearning toward the fullness of the general resurrection to come.

Damascene also presents the idea that Mary's body in her earthly life, filled with the Holy Spirit, was prepared for glorified life. In his view, Mary's connection to her Son and her extraordinary fullness of grace entail that Mary in her earthly life "was filled with the energy of the Spirit" and "was wholly united with God" by grace.[132] She was thereby prepared in her flesh to be glorified in the flesh. Damascene asks, "How shall death consume her?

---

128. John of Damascus, "On the Dormition of the Holy Mother of God: Homily I," 198.

129. John of Damascus, "On the Dormition of the Holy Mother of God: Homily I," 198.

130. John of Damascus, "On the Dormition of the Holy Mother of God: Homily II," 205.

131. John of Damascus, "On the Dormition of the Holy Mother of God: Homily II," 205.

132. John of Damascus, "On the Dormition of the Holy Mother of God: Homily II," 207.

How shall the realm of death receive her? How shall corruption dare to assault that body once filled with life?"[133] He knows that she died, but he thinks it fitting that her graced body did not corrupt in the tomb but was instead assumed into heaven and glorified, so that her profound cooperation with her Son does not end with her death.

Without doubt, the homilies of John of Damascus and Andrew of Crete are intensely imaginative. They are not reporting what they have seen, nor are they reporting New Testament history. Celebrating the liturgical feast of Mary's dormition, a feast that had been celebrated for generations, they are trying to paint a picture for their congregations. What they are praising is the reality, known liturgically by the Church in the Holy Spirit, that Christ's resurrection is for the sake of ours. Christ has not allowed the great woman of faith who conceived him in her womb to corrupt and turn to dust. Having risen gloriously from the dead, Christ the new Adam has lifted up the "woman" (John 2:4), the new Eve who pronounces the words Eve should have spoken ("Behold, I am the handmaid of the Lord; let it be to me according to your word" [Luke 1:38]). The marriage of God and his people, for which Adam and Eve were originally created, has begun in earnest.

VI. Conclusion

Jesus' resurrection only makes sense in light of ours: the glorious resurrection of the Bridegroom is for the glorious resurrection of (all the members of) the Bride.[134] His saving sacrifice in wondrous love has for its purpose the reconciliation and deification of humanity, and this cannot occur without resurrection and glorified bodiliness, since humans are hylomorphic creatures. As Joseph Ratzinger remarks with 1 Corinthians 15 in view, "Christ's Resurrection is either a universal event, or it is nothing . . . And only if we understand it as a universal event, as the opening up of a new dimension of human existence, are we on the way toward any kind of correct understanding of the New Testament Resurrection testimony."[135]

In his Letter to the Romans, Paul maintains that by sharing in Christ's death through baptism, we can be assured that we will share in his glorious resurrection in the world to come.[136] Paul states, "For if we have been united with him in a death like his, we shall certainly be united with him

---

133. John of Damascus, "On the Dormition of the Holy Mother of God: Homily II," 207.
134. For background, see McWhirter, *Bridegroom Messiah and the People of God*.
135. Ratzinger/Benedict, *Jesus of Nazareth*, 2:244.
136. See Snodgrass, "Baptized into Christ," 106–22.

in a resurrection like his ... For if we have died with Christ, we believe that we shall also live with him" (Rom 6:5, 8). In his Second Letter to the Corinthians, Paul presents the connection between Jesus' resurrection and ours in a similar way. He reminds the Corinthians that in faith we know "that he who raised the Lord Jesus will raise us also with Jesus and bring us with you into his presence" (2 Cor 4:14). The connection between our resurrection and Jesus' begins now, through self-sacrificial lives that manifest the power of Christ and that unite us with Christ's crucified and risen life. Paul notes that Jesus' risen life is already apparent in his (Paul's) own life. He states, "For while we live we are always being given up to death for Jesus' sake, so that the life of Jesus may be manifested in our mortal flesh" (2 Cor 4:11).[137]

The Corinthian Christians belonged to a Greco-Roman culture in which the immortality of the soul was widely accepted but the resurrection of the body was not. According to the biblical scholar Raymond Collins, some Corinthian Christians thought of themselves as "spiritual men" (1 Cor 3:1) who, having been united to the Wisdom of God, no longer needed the flesh.[138] Some Corinthian Christians seem to have supposed that they could believe in the risen Jesus, without believing in a future general resurrection of the dead.[139] Shocked by this supposition, Paul emphasizes the relationship between Christ's resurrection and ours. Logically, says Paul, "if there is no resurrection of the dead, then Christ has not been raised" (1 Cor 15:13); and if there is no resurrection of dead, then believers will never be raised. But if Christ's resurrection is true (as it is), then our resurrection too will happen; and so the risen Christ is "the first fruits of those who have fallen asleep" (1 Cor 15:20). For Paul as for the whole New Testament, these two eschatological realities must be thought through together.[140]

137. See Gorman, "Paul's Corporate, Cruciform, Missional *Theosis* in 2 Corinthians." Grant Macaskill has noted critically that for some interpreters (in light of Paul's comparison of Christ and Adam in 1 Corinthians 15), "the Pauline idea of the glory of Christ and of the glorification of believers is understood to represent a recovery of Adam's glory" (Macaskill, *Union with Christ in the New Testament*, 130). With Macaskill, I hold that resurrection life is much more than the "recovery of Adam's glory."

138. Collins, *First Corinthians*, 541.

139. Collins, *First Corinthians*, 543n12.

140. See the summary given by Chilton, *Resurrection Logic*, 4: "Believers claimed (1) that God has raised Jesus from the dead and (2) that his resurrection swept up humanity as a whole within the process of resurrection." For Chilton, the differing accounts of the risen Jesus in the New Testament indicate that there are multiple ways of understanding Jesus' resurrection—what Chilton calls "resurrection sciences"—in the New Testament. He notes, "Two lines of reasoning are deployed within the New Testament in order to coordinate these accounts. In one, the characteristic idiom is that of prophecy, so that those who see Jesus are empowered by a spiritual vision that enables them to pursue their own resurrection sciences. In the other, an arc of

In the Gospel of John, Jesus promises the disciples at his Farewell Discourse that his resurrection will ensure their glorious resurrection. That the disciples will suffer for his sake, Jesus well knows (John 16:2). But he is preparing an everlasting habitation for his disciples with God. He exhorts, "Let not your hearts be troubled; believe in God, believe also in me. In my Father's house are many rooms; if it were not so, would I have told you that I go to prepare a place for you? And when I go and prepare a place for you, I will come again and will take you to myself, that where I am you may be also" (John 14:1–3).[141] Jesus' resurrection is surety for ours; and our suffering configures us to his cross and prepares us to dwell fully with him, just as even now the Father and Son interiorly dwell in those who obey the new commandment of self-sacrificial love (John 14:23).

Where glorified bodiliness is no longer intelligible, however, Jesus' resurrection seems absurd. Caroline Walker Bynum has pointed out that post-Christian Western culture still "consider[s] any survival that really counts to entail survival of body"; few people imagine existing as pure spirits after their death.[142] But at the same time, Bynum says that today "the

---

narrative, including the various descriptions of disciples visiting Jesus' tomb, grounds the resurrection more in the Jesus who is seen than in the disciples whose gift is to see" (Chilton, *Resurrection Logic*, 6). This suggestion about the "two lines" is reasonable, but Chilton goes on to deem "Fundamentalist" the claim that "'the empty tomb' has to have been believed for any statement about the resurrection to have been made" (184). The problem here, though, is the alternative: if Jesus' corpse was still in the tomb—if the tomb was not empty—then the claim of "resurrection" is not believable, either in Jesus' day or in ours. Chilton continues by warning that the logic of the empty tomb "is then deployed to make the tomb in all the narratives equally 'empty,' despite the crucial variations from passage to passage. The problems of essentializing the resurrection to the point of identification with the account of the 'empty' tomb are not only exegetical but logical" (184). In Chilton's view, the risen Jesus at least was experienced consistently as "embodied consciousness" and probing such a reality will enrich "current controversies concerning physics, the status of embodiment, and how consciousness relates to meaning" (201)—but I have significant doubts about the viability of his approach.

141. Craig S. Keener interprets this passage as "realized eschatology" rather than "future eschatology," but I think the latter is intended as well. See Keener, *Gospel of John*, 2:932. Keener notes that in 1 Enoch 91:13, "the righteous in the final time receive 'houses' as rewards" (935). My position accords with that of Gundry, "'In My Father's House Are Many Monai' (John 14:2)," noted by Keener. For Keener, "Jesus' 'coming' in this context can represent only his postresurrection coming to impart to them the Spirit (14:16–18), and the 'dwelling places' in the Father's presence can refer only to God dwelling in believers (14:23). Although both John (e.g., 5:28–29; 6:39–40, 44, 54; 11:24; 12:48) and his audience (cf., e.g., 1 John 2:28–3:3; Rev 1:7) accept future eschatology, the emphasis of this passage is clearly realized rather than future eschatology" (*Gospel of John*, 2:939). This may well be the emphasis, but the fullness of dwelling with God—resurrection life—is also inevitably in view.

142. Bynum, *Resurrection of the Body in Western Christianity, 200–1336*, 15. Bynum

resurrection of the body is a doctrine that causes acute embarrassment, even in mainstream Christianity."[143] Moreover, bodiliness itself is contested in contemporary Western culture, due to a widespread notion that real freedom entails liberation from all biological givens. Many people in the West experience, in Candida Moss's words, "anxieties about the identity, nature, and continuity of the self."[144]

It is therefore necessary to recover the doctrine of glorified bodiliness, but the question is how to do this. Influenced by Pierre Teilhard de Chardin and Karl Rahner, the young Ratzinger argued in 1968 that the order of creation contains a cosmic evolutionary movement in which "matter and its evolution form the prehistory of spirit or mind."[145] At this early stage in his career, he even granted that Christ's bodily glorification may be seen simply as the apex of matter's spiritualization, its movement away from the biological realm. For Ratzinger in 1968, mind—not matter—"*is* reality."[146] He contended that in the glorified Christ—and thus in his whole glorified body—matter will be fully spirit. Responding to these Ratzingerian texts, Patrick Fletcher has correctly voiced concerns: "In such a view it must be asked whether matter can really be fulfilled *as matter*, since it appears as a stage in the evolution of spirit."[147]

Fortunately, in *Eschatology*, originally published in 1977, Ratzinger indicates more clearly that materiality retains a place in the state of glory. Of course, "the detailed particularities of the world of the resurrection are beyond our conceiving."[148] But he insists that it is not absurd to say that

---

is speaking here specifically of America, but I think it applies more widely. Of course, in many Western countries, death is now generally considered to be annihilation, and glorified bodily existence is considered absurd.

143. Bynum, *Resurrection of the Body in Western Christianity, 200–1336*, 14.

144. Moss, *Divine Bodies*, 3. To some degree, Moss aims to enlarge those anxieties, in various ways. She concludes her book by warning against forgetting the "thought-provoking uncanniness of the resurrection of the dead" (121)—an uncanniness that is indeed crucial to remember.

145. Ratzinger, *Introduction to Christianity*, 320.

146. Ratzinger, *Introduction to Christianity*, 321.

147. Fletcher, *Resurrection Realism*, 187. For valuable critiques of Teilhard's position, see O'Callaghan, *Christ Our Hope*, 122–23; Farrow, *Ascension and Ecclesia*, 198–220. Farrow notes that Rahner's position, while influenced by Teilhard (since Rahner "adopts an evolutionary worldview as the starting point for christology"), should be distinguished from Teilhard's in important ways, including due to Rahner's emphasis that matter, even as glorified and spiritualized, remains matter. Ratzinger would certainly agree with Rahner on this point. See Farrow, *Ascension and Ecclesia*, 215.

148. Ratzinger, *Eschatology*, 192. See Rahner, "Unity of Spirit and Matter in Christian Faith"; Rahner, *Foundations of Christian Faith*, 190; Teilhard de Chardin, *Christianity and Evolution*; Teilhard de Chardin, *Heart of Matter*.

matter will be glorified. Adapting Teilhard's insight to his own purposes, he notes that the cosmos has been "in steady ascent toward ever more complex unities," and Christ is the key to this dynamism.[149] His point is that glorified bodiliness is not an irrational idea given the dynamism we perceive in the cosmos. The eschaton will consist in "a situation in which matter and spirit will belong to each other in a new and different fashion," far more intimate than we can imagine.[150]

149. Ratzinger, *Eschatology*, 194. He states earlier that Rahner "noted that in death the soul becomes not acosmic but all-cosmic. This means that its essential ordination to the material world remains, not in the mode of giving form to an organism as its entelechy, but in that of an ordering to this world as such and as a whole. It is not difficult to connect up this thought to ideas formulated by Teilhard de Chardin. For it might be said in this regard that relation to the cosmos is necessarily also relation to the temporality of the universe. The universe, matter, is as such conditioned by time. It is a process of becoming. This temporality of the universe, which knows being only in the form of becoming, has a certain direction, disclosed in the gradual construction of 'biosphere' and 'noosphere' from out of physical building blocks which it then proceeds to transcend. Above all, it is a progress to ever more complex unities. This is why it calls for a total complexity, a unity that will embrace all previously existing unities. From the cosmic standpoint, the appearance of each individual spirit in the world of matter is an aspect of this history in which the complex unity of matter and spirit is formed. For, significantly enough, the exigence for unity found in matter is fulfilled precisely by the nonmaterial, by spirit. Spirit is not, then, the splintering of unity into a duality. It is that qualitatively new power of unification absolutely necessary to what is disintegrated and disunited if ever it is to be one" (191).

150. Ratzinger, *Eschatology*, 194. In Fletcher's view, "it must be admitted that within *Eschatologie* there is inconsistency in Ratzinger's thought on the risen body. Two different anthropological ideas are being held in tension" (*Resurrection Realism*, 199); and he notes that "when Ratzinger argues against Greshake, he reverts to what could be called a more physicalist, indeed, a more Augustinian view of resurrection" (*Resurrection Realism*, 194). As Fletcher points out, although Ratzinger disagrees with Gisbert Greshake's thesis of "resurrection in death," Ratzinger himself employs Greshake's categories at various points, especially the distinction between "Leib" and "Körper," although Ratzinger eventually "abandoned the *Leib-Körper* distinction due to the polemic with Greshake" (*Resurrection Realism*, 194). See Greshake, "Auferstehung im Tod"; Greshake, "Leib-Seele-Problematik und die Vollendung der Welt." For a helpful contribution to the discussion, see, in addition to Fletcher's significant work, Marschler, "Perspektiven der Eschatologie bei Joseph Ratzinger." For a critique of Greshake's (and Rahner's) perspective on resurrection in death, see also Kromholtz's *On the Last Day*, 63–66 (and elsewhere). As Fletcher observes, "what we are dealing with in Greshake's theology is a risen embodiment which is a property of the soul, deriving from its relation to the world and history during its life, but not necessarily requiring the ongoing existence of matter *qua* matter ... Greshake asserts that the concept of a bodiless soul waiting in an 'intermediate state' is nonsensical. He suggests that man 'interiorizes' his body and his world throughout life. Thus, if in death man is not annihilated but saved by God, then that body and world also come to fulfillment ... Greshake, then, holds the eternal preservation of matter's *finality*, but not of its existence *as matter*" (*Resurrection Realism*, 205–6, 211). Or, to quote Ratzinger's concerns in *Eschatology*, 195: "Greshake's

The Teilhardian approach risks making it seem that Christ's resurrection and his glorified body simply reveal what the evolutionary cosmic process was bound to achieve at some point. As evidence of Ratzinger's change of mind, Fletcher points especially to Ratzinger's 1990 Afterword to the sixth German edition of his *Eschatology*, as well as to the nuanced criticisms that Ratzinger mounts against Teilhard's position in his 1998 essay "The End of Time."[151] But Ratzinger's line nevertheless remains somewhat more like Origen's than Augustine's. In his 2011 *Jesus of Nazareth: Part Two: Holy Week. From the Entrance into Jerusalem to the Resurrection*, Ratzinger comments that Christ's resurrection "bursts open" and "transcends" history's dimensions, and is comparable "to a radical 'evolutionary leap', in which a new dimension of life emerges."[152] Again referring to the radical transformation of bodiliness that Christ's resurrection entails, Ratzinger contends that "matter itself is remolded into a new type of reality," one that expresses the soul's immortality.[153] Jesus' transformed body becomes the cosmic locus of communion with God for all humanity. We cannot conceive of this bodiliness, "[s]ince we ourselves have no experience of such a renewed and transformed type of matter, or such a renewed and transformed kind of life."[154] But it will remain bodily; it is transformed matter, but matter nonetheless.

Ratzinger's core argument is simple. Jesus' resurrection opens up for all of us the hope of glorified bodiliness, the fullness of eschatological existence, by "creating for all of us a new space of life, a new space of being in union with God," due to the "ontological leap" that Jesus' resurrection constitutes.[155] Most important for my purposes is that Ratzinger regularly

---

idea that the soul receives matter into itself as an 'ecstatic aspect' of the realization of its freedom, while leaving it for ever to the clutches of the necessarily imperfectible precisely in its quality as matter, would be unthinkable for Thomas [Aquinas]. If it belongs to the very essence of the soul to be the form of the body then its ordination to matter is inescapable. The only way to destroy this ordering would be to dissolve the soul itself."

151. See Ratzinger, "Nachwort zur 6. Auflage," 191–92; Ratzinger, "End of Time," 14–15; cf. 24.

152. Ratzinger/Benedict, *Jesus of Nazareth*, 2:273–74.

153. Ratzinger/Benedict, *Jesus of Nazareth*, 2:274. Note that, as Bryan Kromholtz remarks, Aquinas "believes that his doctrine concerning the immortality of the soul amounts to an argument for the resurrection. Given that humans by nature are to be a unity of soul and body, such a disembodied soul should not exist in the separated state forever, without coming to completion. So if the soul is such that it will subsist forever, then it ought eventually to be rejoined to the body" (Kromholtz, *On the Last Day*, 498). See also Denys Turner, "Human Person"; and Kromholtz, "Spirit of the Letter."

154. Ratzinger/Benedict, *Jesus of Nazareth*, 2:274.

155. Ratzinger/Benedict, *Jesus of Nazareth*, 2:274.

returns—like all the theologians surveyed in this chapter—to the task of demonstrating that the concept of a glorified body is not irrational.

In dialogue with this diverse set of theologians, this chapter has addressed some difficulties that arise in trying to conceive of bodily resurrection and glorification. First and foremost, it must be the person's body—the body that died—that is gloriously raised from the dead, from corruption to incorruption. Unlike Gregory and Augustine, I do not think this requires the material elements to be identical, given that the soul is the unifying form of the body and that the body's material elements can be entirely different at different stages of bodily life.[156] I disagree with Dale Allison's

---

156. O'Callaghan agrees, if I understand him correctly: "Affirmation of the identity of the risen body with the earthly one, however, does not require a strict *material identity* between the physical elements of our earthly condition and those of the risen state ... In effect, as Origen explained in his commentary on Jeremiah's image of the potter, the matter of our risen bodies is not numerically identical to that of our earthly body ... Besides, it is now well known that the human metabolism is such that the physical and chemical elements of the human composite are cyclically replaced over a limited span of years" (O'Callaghan, *Christ Our Hope*, 106). Yet O'Callaghan distances himself from the view that "*formal identity*, involving merely the identity of the human soul (which is the 'only form of the body'), would be sufficient to ensure human identity at resurrection. In other words, the same soul that informs matter would ensure the identity of the same person, independently of the physical matter people had in this life. This theory was put forward during the Middle Ages by Durandus, and has been followed in recent times by several neo-Thomists [e.g., F. Hettinger, H. Schell, L. Billot, A. Michel, and D. Feuling]. In the same direction, Origen, who takes up Paul's representation of resurrection in terms of a sprouting seed (1 Cor 15:35), spoke of a spiritual *eidos* (image) in humans that remains unchanged throughout all the mutations of life and after glorification ... It would seem that this position does not give sufficient weight to the realism and objectivity of Jesus' resurrection, which by no means excludes the earthly and bodily existence of Jesus. Neither does it take sufficiently into account the eschatological implications of the liturgical praxis of venerating bodily relics of the saints ..., and the dogma of the assumption of Our Lady into heaven. In fact, Durandus's explanation of identity in formal terms could be read as an equivalent to the doctrine of transmigration of souls, or reincarnation" (*Christ Our Hope*, 107). For these concerns, see also O'Callaghan, "Formula 'Resurrección de la carne' y su significado para la moral Christian"; Nicolas, "Corps humain et sa resurrection." In my view, the identity or continuity of the human soul does in fact suffice, although this does not take away from the holiness attached to the bodily remains of the saints or from the power of the resurrection of Jesus' actual body (and the assumption of Mary's). The issue is simply whether there is a "resurrection of the body" if, at the final judgment, the matter of a person's body is (for evident reasons, including dispersion of the atoms) not the same matter as the person's body possessed during the person's lifetime. I think the answer is yes, because the person's soul informing the matter enables the new matter to be the person's *own* body and thus in real continuity with the prior bodiliness of the person (just as my matter today is in real continuity with the matter I possessed fifty years ago). As Ratzinger says, "the material elements from out of which human physiology is constructed receive their character of being 'body' only in virtue of being organized and formed by the expressive power of soul ... This is what Origen was getting at with

claim that there is "no adequate solution to the problem of shared matter."[157] Pointing out that the Fourth Lateran Council (1215) taught that all people will rise in the same bodies that they now possess, the Catholic theologian Bryan Kromholtz notes that Aquinas supports this conciliar teaching while emphasizing that matter depends upon form in order to be a particular body. The separation of soul and body in death turns the body into a corpse, which means that the material remains of the person's body are *no longer* the person's body per se. As Kromholtz remarks, Aquinas maintains that "the matter that had last been informed by the soul before death (or at least some of it) will rise in the resurrection. But the form's survival [i.e. the soul's survival] is what assures that the numerically identical body will rise."[158] For Aquinas, the amount of matter from the person's earthly body included in the risen body can be minimal. This material minimalism (if indeed any of the same matter is needed at all[159]) seems reasonable to me, given a proper

his idea of the characteristic form, but the conceptual tools at his disposal did not allow him to formulate it. The individual atoms and molecules do not as such add up to the human being. The identity of the living body does not depend upon them, but upon the fact that matter is drawn into the soul's power of expression. Just as the soul is defined in terms of matter, so the living body is wholly defined by reference to the soul. The soul builds itself a living body, a self-identical living body, as its corporeal expression. And since the living body belongs so inseparably to the being of man, the identity of that body is defined not in terms of matter but in terms of soul. In Thomas [Aquinas], these insights find their determinate expression" (*Eschatology*, 179–80). I can agree, however, with O'Callaghan's point that what is needed for continuity and a real resurrection is not only the soul but also an emphasis on "the eternal projection and value of historical human actions carried out in a limited, temporal, material context" (*Christ Our Hope*, 108).

157. Allison, *Night Comes*, 39.

158. Kromholtz, *On the Last Day*, 92. Kromholtz explains further: "In most cases, over the course of a lifetime, a person who dies will have left behind more matter than is needed to make up an adult body in the resurrection. Thomas notes that not all this matter—or even most of it—needs to be reassembled in order to assure that the identical body is restored. This 'flow' of matter—that results in a surplus of matter being identified with a given individual over the period of his lifetime—is no obstacle to the numerical identity of the body before death, so it is no obstacle after death, either. However, there is an even trickier problem: in at least some cases, more than one person will have shared the same matter. Thomas asserts that it is not necessary for all or even most of the matter that had been part of the person at the moment of death to make up the risen body. *Some* amount of matter will remain that was associated most closely with only one person, even if it is only the seed by which that person was conceived" (93). John Duns Scotus and later Scotists have argued that Aquinas's perspective does not comport with the Church's veneration of saints' bodily relics and, more generally, does not recognize the true significance of a person's corpse. For discussion, see Ward, *Ordered by Love*, 58–63. In my view, the veneration of relics can be justified without needing to suppose that a corpse remains a "human body."

159. Kromholtz adds, "Thomas generally maintains that at least some portion of

understanding of what it means to have the "same" body as the body that one previously had.

Augustine proposes that in the glorified body, all bodily organs and components will give glory to God in some way. While I am doubtful that such things as fingernails and guts need to remain, it seems plausible that all the parts of the glorified body can be transformed so as to give God glory. According to Albert, the glorified body will be subtle, no longer bound by physical laws. The glorified body will no longer be contained by space and time, even though it will be tangible (and bounded) and will be temporal in some sense. Glorified bodies will remain male or female, a distinction that is intrinsic to the created human person, and bodily defects will be healed.[160]

---

these [bodily] remains, however small, will be reunited with the soul in the resurrection—otherwise, it would not be resurrection but a union to a new body . . . [Yet] some have said that Thomas did not with complete consistency follow out the implications of his own anthropology of the unicity of the human form, an anthropology that would have allowed the soul to be understood as the sole principle of personal identity enduring through life and death to the resurrection, such that the bodily remains would be abandoned (or at least *could* be abandoned) at the resurrection. In fact, Thomas *did* make use of this possibility in part, saying that in problematic cases, God could make up for whatever is lacking in material—though Thomas claims that some small quantity of the remains must be reunited with the soul . . . For Thomas, the world as we know it will participate in the final restoration, just as bodily remains are to participate in the resurrection. This doctrine reaffirms that man is not completely an alien to the world in which he has been born. The material world is in need of repair, but it is not to be abandoned completely. Many recent conceptions of resurrection, such as resurrection in death, in which remains are considered unimportant—or are even thoroughly excluded from the possibility of participation in the final restoration—imply, even if they do not always state, that matter and the world in themselves will not be perfected. Concomitantly, such conceptions may involve a spiritualized understanding of resurrection, since the body to be received must be one whose materiality is completely other-worldly in origin. However, the promise of a new heaven and a new earth is not one that excludes the world as it now is, but transforms it . . . This truth is better preserved by a position that presumes that bodily remains are to participate in the resurrection" (Kromholtz, *On the Last Day*, 499–500). This seems reasonable to me, even if arguably not strictly necessary in every case.

160. See O'Callaghan's helpful summary: "some Christian writers have suggested [in light of Matthew 22:30] that no sexual distinction will obtain among humans in the risen state. This position was held for example by Origen, although it was rejected by the Synod of Constantinople in AD 543. According to Cassiodorus the same idea was taught by Pope Vigilius I. Likewise, both Basil and Gregory of Nyssa held that the human body would be sexless at resurrection. The majority of Church Fathers, however, took it that men and women will remain as such in the risen state, because the sexual distinction belongs, according to the book of Genesis (1:27), to human nature itself, and may not be considered a result of the primitive fall, to be redeemed by Christ" (O'Callaghan, *Christ Our Hope*, 103). See also chapter 4 of Anderson, *When Harry Became Sally*, including with respect to intersex bodies (known to ancient authors as "hermaphrodites"). Anderson notes that persons with intersex conditions "do

Given the absence of sexual desire, however, a significant part of the meaning of maleness and femaleness will be transformed. The measure of the transformation of earthly bodiliness is—as Gerhard makes especially clear, but as is equally true for the Fathers and medievals (whose work Gerhard takes up)—Christ's risen and glorified body as described in the New Testament.

The radical transformation wrought by resurrection and glorification fits with Paul's sharp contrast between our earthly body and the spiritual body that we will receive. It will not be the case that "bodies designed for earthly life are, with only modest revision, equally designed for life eternal."[161] Allison correctly affirms, "The discontinuity between now and then must be extreme."[162] The state of glory will not leave in place the bodily

---

not constitute a third sex; they are either male or female, but with a disorder in their development" (91).

161. Allison, *Night Comes*, 39. O'Callaghan, drawing upon Aquinas's *Summa contra gentiles* (IV, ch. 86) and the Supplement of the *Summa theologiae*, observes: "Thomas says that the properties of the risen body are three: spiritualization, immortality, and incorruptibility" (*Christ Our Hope*, 102). All three properties come from 1 Corinthians 15 in light of Jesus' glorified body. O'Callaghan recounts, "In the first place, *spiritualization*, for 'it is sown a physical body, it is raised a spiritual body' (1 Cor 15:44). Of course the human being does not become a spirit (an 'angel'); rather the human body takes on to some degree the properties of the soul. With the resurrection, Aquinas says, the soul (which is the *forma corporis*) becomes perfectly united with the body, and so 'the body becomes totally subject to the soul, not only in respect of its being, but also in respect of its actions and passions and movements.' . . . As a result of spiritualization, *immortality*: 'For this perishable nature must put on the imperishable, and this mortal nature must put on immortality . . .' (1 Cor 15:53–54). . . . And finally, according to Aquinas, the risen body is *incorruptible*: 'What is sown is corruptible, what is raised is incorruptible' (1 Cor 15:42)" (*Christ Our Hope*, 102–3).

162. Allison, *Night Comes*, 39. For an emphasis on discontinuity between earthly life and the life to come, in response to biblical scholars and theologians who highlight continuity, see the final chapter of my *Dying and the Virtues*. For Allison, however, "resurrection language must be a way of suggesting an eschatological future that transcends prosaic description, a future that can only be intimated through sacred metaphor and sanctified imagination. In other words, resurrection, like the parables of Jesus, characterizes God's future for us via an analogy, in recognition of the fact that we can't do any better. We see dimly" (*Night Comes*, 40). I hold that bodily resurrection is more than a "sacred metaphor": it really will happen, even if glorified bodiliness goes beyond our ability to conceive. As Jürgen Moltmann says, "Jesus's body—which had been killed, buried, and preserved—was raised from the dead by God, his Father, through the vitality of the Holy Spirit" (Moltmann, *Resurrected to Eternal Life*, 23). We too will have our bodies raised—even though Moltmann obscures this somewhat by saying, "Unlike Jesus, our corpse decays quickly, or our ashes are scattered over the earth. It is not our corpse that is raised from the grave but the entirety of our lived life that is resurrected in the hour of death to eternal life" (25). Note that Moltmann also believes (and here I disagree with him, believing instead in an intermediate state) that we die into resurrection, a position that entails, for him, supposing that our corpse simply rots and we receive a new glorified body as soon as we die: "Our hour of death is

defects and limits that impede our fullest possible actualization, as indicated by Gerhard's eleven attributes of glorified bodiliness.[163] Augustine *may* be right that our glorified bodies will have hair and fingernails and all our bodily organs will remain. But hair and fingernails and organs that are utterly luminous, no longer bound by space and time, capable of operations impossible for earthly bodies, no longer serving their original purposes, and fully obedient to the glorified soul, have clearly been radically transformed!

Matter itself, and the spatio-temporal framework, no longer seems absolute in an Einsteinian framework. Matter's openness to glorification seems more scientifically plausible, given the teleological ordering that the anthropic principle suggests. The new creation of all things reflects the fact that the cosmos as a whole, and certainly life on earth, constitutes a collective and symbiotic environment. The connection between Christ's resurrection and ours fits with the unity of all organisms. Life, not nonlife, should have epistemic primacy, as Schloss insists. To my mind, true bodily resurrection (as distinct from a bodily replica) requires the existence of the spiritual and immortal soul, although Polkinghorne stops just short of this.

Mary's assumption displays the power of Jesus' resurrection vis-à-vis his people. Her assumption teaches us to contemplate the Bridegroom's glory in such a way as to remember its *telos*: the glorification of the Bride.[164] Here we perceive our own bodily future—and the cosmic future—flowing from the saving work and glorified bodiliness of the risen Jesus on behalf of the

---

the hour of our resurrection. When we die, we wake to eternal life. The pains of death are the birth pains into eternal life. While our body with the 'sum' of its limbs lies dead and decays, the entirety of our life, the 'whole' of our living soul, will rise again with a new body to everlasting life. The new body in the resurrection—the *soma pneumatikon*—will be a body intensely alive in the divine life force in accordance with the body of the resurrected Christ, which was 'transfigured' in the majesty of God" (26; cf. 34–37 for Moltmann's change of mind since his earlier *Coming of God*). For Moltmann, the new glorified body has continuity with our earthly body, but only in the sense that in the new body one's *"entire life* is resurrected, healed, and transfigured" (28). See also Lehtipuu, *Debates Over the Resurrection of the Dead*, 162–73, for debates in the patristic era that are similar to the current debate about dying into resurrection.

163. See Yong, *Theology and Down Syndrome*, 259–92; Eisland, *Disabled God*, 98–100.

164. Allison comments along helpful lines, though without Mary's assumption in view and without making explicit that the iconography depicts the opening of the gates of heaven to separated souls: "Even Jesus, in the old icons of his resurrection, isn't alone. As he departs from Hades and rises from the dead, he hauls others up with him, including Adam and Eve, representatives of fallen and redeemed humanity. His defeat of death is their defeat of death. His victory is their victory. So resurrection is about the human collectivity. It puts everyone in the same story by giving us all the same ending . . . Resurrection isn't about you or me but about us, and about a kingdom" (*Night Comes*, 41).

whole body of Christ. Yet, our embodied life at present is terribly marked by suffering, just as Jesus' was. In faith, we are "heirs with Christ, provided we suffer with him in order that we also may be glorified with him" (Rom 8:17). Thus we look forward to the unimaginable, but intelligible, perfecting of our embodied life and love through the power of God, being assured in faith that "the sufferings of this present time are not worth comparing with the glory that is to be revealed to us" (Rom 8:18).

Chapter 6

Ascension

I. Introduction

The argument of this final chapter is that the Spirit-filled incarnate Son, having proclaimed the kingdom by word and deed, and having offered to God the new covenant sacrifice on the cross and been raised from the dead to glorious life, now reigns as king at the right hand of the Father, pouring forth his Spirit in preparation for the final consummation of the kingdom of God. The ascension is Christ's royal enthronement.

Let me begin this chapter with a common complaint. Patrick Henry Reardon has pointed out, "The Lord's Ascension into heaven . . . goes often unmentioned in treatises of soteriology; there is frequently no sense that the Ascension was an act integral to our salvation. It is amazing how rarely—or in what a cursory manner—the Ascension is mentioned at all."[1] This situation is indeed unfortunate, for in fact Jesus' ascension to the right hand of the Father signals his fully becoming the priest-king of creation, in the transcendent fulfillment of Adam's royal and priestly vocation. The Ascension is integral to the plan of God described by the Catholic theologian David Fagerberg: "Man and woman were created as royal priests to rule over creation and under God in the cosmic hierarchy," a ladder "down

---

1. Reardon, *Reclaiming the Atonement*, 19. Admittedly, Reardon also says, "What an Orthodox Christian should find especially distressing is the total omission of the Lord's Transfiguration from some modern soteriological studies" (19). I have not totally omitted it in this book, but—for reasons of space—I have sadly not been able to devote a chapter to it. I should add that Reardon falls into some overgeneralizations, as for instance when he writes, "Orthodox soteriology does not start—as Saint Anselm did—with fallen man. It commences, rather, with man completely restored and transformed in Christ" (17).

which flows God's creative love and up which flows creation's eucharistic response."[2] Christ's vocation as priest-king and eschatological new Adam, however, is not a mere repristination of Adam's original vocation. As the *ascended* Lord, Christ calls human beings into the intimate communion of the Trinitarian life itself. As Brant Pitre remarks, "Jesus ascends 'into heaven' *in his body* to show us that the earthly promised land is not the ultimate destination of his 'exodus' (Luke 9:31)."[3]

The image of Adam as an Edenic priest-king has a long history. As Robert Barron observes, "The first man was presented by the rabbis of the intertestamental period and by the church fathers as priest as well as king."[4]

---

2. Fagerberg, *Consecrating the World*, 32, 37. Fagerberg adds, "The sort of nature that men and women were given at their creation is a nature designed for committing liturgy. A perfect human being is a liturgist; that is their place in the hierarchical ladder. Hierarchy exists for the purpose of agape descending creatively, and glorification ascending eucharistically: hierarchy is a liturgical thoroughfare. And the reason for every being in the hierarchy—both heavenly [i.e. angels] and earthly—is to pass love from Creator to creation, and glory from creation to Creator . . . When Lucifer willed to take glory to himself, he was rebelling against his liturgical status. Sin is idolatrous from the start: it is a failure to give right adoration, to rightly glorify, to worship righteously" (*Consecrating the World*, 34–35). For his understanding of hierarchy, Fagerberg directs attention to Bouyer, *Meaning of Monastic Life*, 28–29. See also the essays collected in Fagerberg, *Liturgical Cosmos*.

3. Pitre, *Jesus and the Jewish Roots of Mary*, 69. For reflection on Jesus' messianic fulfillment of the Abrahamic land promise, see my forthcoming essay "Christian Bible and the Land." See also Collins and Collins, *King and Messiah as Son of God*, 152, where Adela Yarbro Collins (who wrote this section) interprets the parable of the weeds (Matthew 13) and emphasizes the parable's "explicit teaching that the Son of Man has a kingdom (13:38, 41). Since the field is interpreted as 'the world' (13:38), the kingdom of the Son of Man is also the whole world." Here may also be the place to mention J. R. Daniel Kirk's argument: "The mystery of the Synoptic Gospels is that the Christ who rules all things in God's name came into his throne only by a cruciform path. It is that the human messiah sits literally where his predecessors sat only metaphorically: at the right hand of God, executing God's reign from a heavenly throne. These claims are each, in their own ways, just as radical, if not more radical, than the claim that God himself fulfills each of these roles as incarnate preexistent son" (Kirk, *Man Attested by God*, 580). I think it is incorrect to say that the adoption of a mere human to the right hand of God—without that human being ontologically God—is as "radical" as the incarnation. Nor does the New Testament as a whole fail to attest to the incarnation, even if Kirk were correct about the Synoptics (which, especially in the case of Matthew and Luke, I think he is not). Kirk urges that we "must fully embrace the human Jesus and not think that this dimension of his person is a husk to be beaten off in hopes of discovering within some divine mystery that truly unlocks the story" (581). Of course we must embrace the human Jesus; no Christian can suppose that Jesus' humanity is "a husk to be beaten off." But the New Testament also reveals the "divine mystery" of the Incarnation, which reverberates through the mysteries of Christ's human life, death, Resurrection, and Ascension.

4. Barron, *2 Samuel*, 50.

On this view, prior to the fall, Adam was a priest insofar as he offered true worship on behalf of all creation, and Adam was a king insofar as he obeyed God's words and did not seize "for himself the prerogative of determining the difference between good and evil."[5] Barron notes that King David is presented as a new Adam in Scripture.[6] Given that David unified the tribes as a priest-king—dancing before the ark and planning for the building of the temple—David enjoyed an Adamic role, although David's vocation, like Adam's, was wounded and distorted by pride.

The Lutheran theologian Ian McFarland adds some further elements to this picture.[7] On the cross, argues McFarland, Christ is preeminently king—as made clear by Pilate's inscription "The King of the Jews" (Matt 27:37 and parallels).[8] The cross is where Christ supremely performs the task of the king, establishing justice and unifying the people in righteousness by conforming them to God's law. McFarland considers that the resurrection, for its part, reveals or makes manifest Christ's royal enthronement on the

---

5. Barron, *2 Samuel*, 64.

6. See Barron, *Light from Light*, 44–45.

7. See McFarland, *Word Made Flesh*. McFarland mounts a broader argument for a "Chalcedonianism without reserve" that contends that "because the divine nature is inherently invisible and so not capable of perception (1 Tim. 1:17; cf. Col. 1:15; 1 John 4:12), when we look at Jesus, what we see is his humanity only. It follows that no aspect of that which we perceive in Jesus—his miracles, his faith, his obedience, or anything else—are to be equated with his divinity; all are fully and exclusively human, and thus created, realities" (McFarland, *Word Made Flesh*, 6). I recognize that Jesus never does or says anything that bypasses the instrumentality of his human nature—which of course would be impossible for a human action, and Jesus is fully human. But whether, when Jesus forgives sins (for example), this action is "fully and exclusively" a human reality, seems doubtful to me. Surely only God can forgive sins. Jesus' divine nature is here working through his human nature in such a way as to make the phrase "fully and exclusively"—or at least "exclusively"—an exaggeration. See also Hägerland's *Jesus and the Forgiveness of Sins*. Hägerland argues on the basis of his historical-critical research that Jesus likely forgave sins but that it is also "likely that Jesus acknowledged that God was the ultimate source of forgiveness and that his own role was that of an agent. Accordingly, he 'forgave sins' in the sense of mediating God's forgiveness" (*Jesus and the Forgiveness of Sins*, 250). I am not persuaded by Hägerland's use of criteria (he focuses especially on Mark 2:1–12) to distinguish what counts as historical and what not.

8. See McFarland, *Word Made Flesh*, 151–53. See also the exegetical connections between cross and kingdom (and the new covenant) in Treat, *Crucified King*, especially his summary in chapter 5. Treat describes Jesus' royal "victory through sacrifice" and explains that "[t]he kingdom is established at the cross, where Jesus sheds his blood as the mediator of the new covenant, thereby restoring the right relationship between the divine king and his servants" (*Crucified King*, 129–30). For a discussion of other first- and early second-century claimants to Jewish kingship, see Evans, "From Anointed Prophet to Anointed King," 437–41. As Evans notes, Josephus describes three claimants to Jewish kingship, all of whom "were quasi-military figures at the head of large followings" (438).

cross.⁹ McFarland's linking the cross and resurrection with Christ's kingship is supported by numerous biblical scholars, among them Richard Hays, who states that the crucified and risen Jesus of Matthew 28 is portrayed "as the triumphant Son of Man figure—representing Israel—who exercises ἐξουσία over all the nations of the world in a kingdom that will not pass away," built upon love rather than worldly power.¹⁰ Another biblical scholar, Helen Bond, remarks that for both the Gospels of Mark and of John, "Jesus' shameful death is indeed the triumph of the king."¹¹

If Christ's cross and resurrection have to do with his *royal* vocation, then for McFarland the ascension is where Christ preeminently accomplishes his *priestly* vocation. The Letter to the Hebrews indicates that the ascended Christ offers his bloody sacrifice as perfect atonement in the heavenly sanctuary, thereby acting as priest in his ascension.¹² McFarland clarifies that "it would be wrong to limit Jesus' priestly work to his ascension and session, just as it would be to limit his exercise of the office of king to the cross."¹³ Jesus is a priest already in his earthly ministry, as for instance in his priestly prayer on behalf of his disciples in John 17. McFarland grants, too, that the ascended Jesus is not only priest but also king. In this regard, he appreciatively recalls the Lutheran tradition's insistence "that 'the right hand of God' refers to God's effective power as Creator and Lord of the universe,

---

9. See McFarland, *Word Made Flesh*, 167; and see also Treat, *Crucified King*, 110: "The resurrection [in Mark] is the confirmation that Jesus is who he said he was and that on the cross he truly was reigning as king."

10. Hays, *Echoes of Scripture in the Gospels*, 184.

11. Bond, "Triumph of the King," 254; and for further background see Bond, *First Biography of Jesus*; and Treat, *Crucified King*, chapter 3 (on "Crucified King in Mark"). Bond observes that John draws "out themes already present in Mark and heighten[s] their dramatic quality—both the motifs of kingship and triumph, for example, can be found in Mark, but it is in John's masterly treatment that they reach their full artistic potential" ("Triumph of the King," 266). For the cross as exaltation according to the Gospel of John, see also Hays, *Echoes of Scripture in the Gospels*, 334–35, including his argument that "John's single word ὑψωθῆναι ('lifted up') echoes and evokes Isaiah's culminating Servant song and that John is hinting that the 'glory' Isaiah saw was a vision of the crucified Jesus (Isa 52:13—53:12)" (335, drawing upon Brendsel, *"Isaiah Saw His Glory,"* 123–34); and see Senior, *Passion of Jesus in the Gospel of John*, 34–39. For Luke-Acts, see Beverly Roberts Gaventa's point that "Luke's story, then, both insists that Jesus is king and acknowledges that he does not become king, at least not in the usual sense of that word . . . Jesus' kingship radically undermines the authority of every empire. His kingship in Luke-Acts is not an escape from the world of flesh and blood; instead, it is larger than that world, encompassing it but not limited to it" (Gaventa, "Learning and Re-Learning the Identity of Jesus from Luke-Acts," 156–57).

12. See McFarland, *Word Made Flesh*, 173. McFarland draws here upon Moffitt, *Atonement and the Logic of Resurrection in the Epistle to the Hebrews*.

13. McFarland, *Word Made Flesh*, 173.

so that the claim that Jesus ascended to God's right hand (Mark 16:19; cf. Acts 2:34) is simply a means of affirming that the crucified participates fully in God's governance of the world."[14] Nevertheless, McFarland associates the ascension primarily with Christ's *priestly* bridging of the separation between God and creatures. He sums up the ascended Jesus' priestly role: "because this creature now lives God's own life before God, no creature's life can finally be separated from God's (Rom. 8:38–39)."[15]

It seems to me that McFarland's association of the cross primarily with Jesus' kingship and the ascension primarily with his priesthood, while warranted by Scripture in certain ways, still leaves room for a different approach. In chapter 4, I argued that Jesus' cross is best understood as the new covenant sacrifice, a primarily priestly act (even if also a royal one). In the present chapter, I will therefore treat the ascension primarily in *royal* terms.

As McFarland recognizes, this approach to the ascension has biblical warrant. In the book of Revelation, the Seer proclaims the ascended Jesus to be "the ruler of kings on earth" (Rev 1:4–5).[16] When Jesus appears in the Seer's vision of the final apocalyptic battle, the Seer states that "on his robe and on his thigh he has a name inscribed, King of kings and Lord of lords" (Rev 19:16). Emphasizing the royal dimension of the ascension, the *Catechism of the Catholic Church* comments that to sit at the Father's right hand—sharing the Father's divine glory—is to reign as king: "Being seated at the Father's right hand signifies the inauguration of the Messiah's kingdom, the fulfillment of the prophet Daniel's vision concerning the Son of man: 'To him was given dominion and glory and kingdom, that all peoples, nations, and languages should serve him; his dominion is an everlasting dominion' [Dan 7:14]."[17]

---

14. McFarland, *Word Made Flesh*, 170.

15. McFarland, *Word Made Flesh*, 175. For McFarland, the difference between the resurrection and the ascension is not a temporal one but rather a logical one: the resurrection means that the corpse of the crucified Jesus is no longer a corpse, because Jesus has gloriously risen from the dead; the ascension means that at the instant of his resurrection, Jesus has lived in the presence of God—that is, Jesus has not been merely resuscitated but has been glorified.

16. For background, see Hays, "Christology." Hays directs (critical) attention to such works as Huber, *Einer gleich einem Menschensohn*; and Johns, *Lamb Christology of the Apocalypse of John*. For the argument that John's Gospel is itself an "apocalypse in mode" even while retaining the genre of "gospel," see Reynolds, *John among the Apocalypses*, 116; and Boxall, "From the Apocalypse to the Johannine 'Apocalypse in Reverse."

17. *Catechism of the Catholic Church*, §664. For some background in historical-critical scholarship, addressing portions of the Synoptic Gospels (along with John 1:51) that I have not been able to treat, see Perrin, *Jesus the Priest*, chapters 5 and 6, with reference in chapter 5 to (among others) Bergsma, "Cultic Kingdoms in Conflict"; Angel,

In his discussion of the ascension of Christ, Thomas Aquinas argues that it causes our salvation in three ways. First, the ascension opens the way to the fullness of the kingdom or the fullness of the divine presence, as Aquinas shows by quoting John 14:2–3, "In my Father's house are many rooms; if it were not so, would I have told you that I go to prepare a place for you? And when I go and prepare a place for you, I will come again and will take you to myself, that where I am you may be also." Aquinas points out that in his ascension, Christ took with him the holy souls who had awaited his passion in order to be freed of original sin. Second, the ascension makes possible the high-priestly work of Christ, who "holds his priesthood permanently" and who "is able for all time to save those who draw near to God through him, since he always lives to make intercession for them" (Heb 7:24–25). Third, in accord with the above royal and priestly offices, Christ's ascension (to which Aquinas here joins his session) enables Christ to send forth divine gifts upon the human race, constituting the Church or "body of Christ" so that people might grow into "the measure of the stature of the fulness of Christ" (Eph 4:12–13). The passage Aquinas quotes here is Ephesians 4:10, "He who descended is he who also ascended far above all the heavens, that he might fill all things."[18]

The ascended Jesus, then, is by all accounts the eschatological priest-king. My first section will briefly sketch the Second Temple Jewish context of messianic Christology, showing how royal and priestly figures were present and how the royal role was expanded to include suffering. My second and lengthier section examines two recent exegetical studies of the royal dimension of Jesus' ascension: Timo Eskola's *Messiah and the Throne: Jewish Merkabah Mysticism and Early Christian Exaltation Discourse* and Félix Cortez's *With the Veil: The Ascension of the Son in the Letter to the Hebrews*. Both these books place Jesus' ascension within the context of the Messiah's royal enthronement, and I think they are correct. Third, I will offer my own biblical-theological account of Jesus' ascension. I contend that Jesus' ascension primarily has to do with Jesus' royal reign in his Church, which is his body, through his "ongoing activity of teaching, healing, and forgiving" and his sending of the Spirit.[19] His reign does not prevent his followers' sufferings, since it is by suffering that we are configured to the cruciform love constitutive of his kingdom.[20] He is enthroned as the eucharistic (self-

---

Otherworldly and Eschatological Priesthood in the Dead Sea Scrolls, 196–202; and the works of Crispin Fletcher-Louis.

18. Aquinas, *Summa theologiae* III, q. 57, a. 6.

19. McFarland, *Word Made Flesh*, 197.

20. With regard to suffering, Kindalee Pfremmer De Long observes that "Luke holds apocalyptic glory in tension with Messianic suffering. Jesus possesses the glory

surrendering) king, as distinct from the worldly model of power that we tend to expect from rulers.

Christ the ascended king is joined by Mary as "queen," as I will discuss in the chapter's final section. Jesus Christ "is the only one who, having risen from the dead, ascends to the right hand of the Father, for he alone among human beings is Lord and God, and thus he shares in the divine rule of the universe."[21] In the Gospels, however, Christ promises his disciples that they will receive a share in his reign and in his governance. Since this is so, it is fitting that the new Adam chooses to reign always with the new Eve. Although the whole Church is the bride of Christ, Mary is uniquely the new Eve, the "woman." Christians have long hailed Mary as queen with her divine King and Son. As the Catholic theologian Thomas Ward remarks, Mary "was selected to be the Mother of Jesus. It is an inconceivably lofty honor, to be so close to Christ. Her blood in his veins; his blood in hers. To have such high rank in the realm of Christ the King—literally, the Queen Mother!"[22]

II. Messianic Ideas in Second Temple Judaism

Let me begin with a brief examination of the diversity of Second Temple messianic ideas, inclusive of royal and priestly dimensions—and with the royal dimension expanded to include suffering and seeming weakness, rather than immediate glorious conquest.

In his *Christ among the Messiahs*, Matthew Novenson points out that many scholars today argue that there are in fact numerous possible meanings for the term "Messiah," given the wide diversity of Second Temple Judaism.[23] This observation bears upon whether the Messiah is conceived

---

of the Father and the angels (Luke 9:26), but as Messiah, he suffers and dies. When heaven and earth meet in Jesus, power meets humility. In the same way, his disciples receive heavenly power and authority; yet, they too are called to take up their cross (Luke 9:23). This tension continues in Acts, where the disciples suffer even as the narrative's apocalyptic scenes reveal God's eschatological redemption moving powerfully across the Mediterranean world, triumphing over evil" (De Long, "Angels and Visions in Luke-Acts," 106–7).

21. McFarland, *Word Made Flesh*, 184.

22. Ward, *Ordered by Love*, 143.

23. See Novenson, *Christ among the Messiahs*, 44–45. Novenson cites, for example, Charlesworth, "From Messianology to Christology." I note that in a 1993 essay, H. J. de Jonge goes so far as to implore: "Would theology and the church not do better, when putting into words the meaning of Jesus for a present-day audience, to refrain from using such unclear, misleading functional terms as 'Christ', 'Messiah' and 'Son of Man'? Jesus' message and the message about Jesus could be well communicated without those obscure and ambiguous terms. He himself had no need of them to describe his own

as a king or a priest. Some of Jesus' contemporaries seem to have expected two Messiahs, a priestly (Levitic) one and a royal Davidic one. Anthony Giambrone remarks that "the duties of the two agents stand in an apparently complementary relation, even if certain confusions and tensions are also apparent, which at times seem to fuse the two figures as one."[24] In Qumran's *Priestly Blessings for the Last Days*, for example, two Messiahs are mentioned, one a priest and the other a Davidic prince.[25] Somewhat similarly, Qumran's *War of the Messiah* describes a final eschatological battle, with the messianic "Branch of David" bringing about the conquest and the high priest also having a role.[26] Discussing Qumran's *Priestly Blessings for the Last Days* and related Qumranic texts, the Protestant biblical scholar Bernardo Cho deems that the Qumran community envisioned that "the Davidic Branch or the Prince of the Congregation would rule alongside a priest" and that "the Aaronic ruler should be likewise called messiah."[27]

---

role" (de Jonge, "Historical Jesus' View of Himself and of His Mission," 37). Along lines similar to H. J. de Jonge's, see Meeks, "Asking Back to Jesus' Identity." Marinus de Jonge explores the term "Messiah" in the New Testament and in other Second Temple literature, in his "Earliest Christian Use of *Christos*," and also in his *God's Final Envoy*. In the latter book, he argues that "Jesus may have understood himself as a prophetic Son of David called to proclaim the gospel and exorcise demons in order to inaugurate God's kingdom, and destined to hold full royal power in the near future. If so, he could regard himself as the Lord's anointed like David, not only in the future, but already during his prophetic work in Galilee. This is how his disciples saw him, as Mark's clearly stylized, prototypical story of Peter's confession seeks to make clear. Jesus' messiahship could be and indeed was misunderstood by some of his followers and many of his opponents alike, but there is no reason to deny that he probably did regard himself as the Lord's anointed in the sense indicated" (*God's Final Envoy*, 103; cf. 144–45). See also Marinus de Jonge's *Jesus, the Servant-Messiah*.

24. Giambrone, "'Why Do the Scribes Say?,'" 308.

25. See Wise et al., *Dead Sea Scrolls*, 142–43 (1QSb [1Q28b] Col. 4 and 5). For further background, see Xeravits, *King, Priest, Prophet*; Zimmermann, *Messianische Texte aus Qumran*.

26. See Wise et al., *Dead Sea Scrolls*, 370 (4Q285 Frag. 7 + 11Q14 Frag. 1 Col. 1). For discussion, see Knohl, *Messiah Confrontation*, 114–15. I should note here that I do not accept the authenticity of "The Gabriel Revelation," a text purported to be from the time around Jesus' birth that speaks of the death and resurrection of the messiah. For interpretation of and advocacy for this text, see Knohl, *Messiahs and Resurrection in The Gabriel Revelation*, which argues that according to "The Gabriel Revelation," the Son of man's "shed blood" will be "the catalyst for the coming of salvation" and so "the death of the Messiah is not a sign of the falsehood of the messianic claim, but rather an essential stage in the redemptive process," in which "the dying Messiah would be resurrected by the angel Gabriel 'by three days'" (92). For evidence that "Gabriel Revelation" is a forgery, see Klawans, "Deceptive Intentions"; Atkinson, "Gabriel Revelation (Hazon Gabriel)." See also Klawans, *Heresy, Forgery, Novelty*.

27. Cho, *Royal Messianism and the Jerusalem Priesthood in the Gospel of Mark*, 41. Cho sums up, "From the perspective of the Dead Sea sect . . . the sphere of authority

Christianity has often been thought to be the only place where a *suffering* Messiah was conceived.[28] However, the Qumran documents have at least somewhat complicated this claim. For instance, in a fragment from Qumran that scholars have titled the "Self-Glorification Hymn," the speaker proclaims, "[Wh]o has been considered contemptible like me? Who is comparable to me in my glory? . . . Who has born[e] troubles like me? . . . Who can endure the utterance of my lips?"[29] The biblical scholar Israel Knohl contends, albeit unpersuasively in my view, that this text refers to a suffering, quasi-divine Messiah, though he grants that its meaning is not certain.[30] Similarly, Knohl observes that in the Isaiah scroll found at

---

exercised by the royal messiah would be limited in terms of the preeminence of the messiah of Aaron in ceremonial procedures. Yet, it was still the task of the eschatological king to judge the wicked and to vindicate the community as the true sons of Zadok. This means that, so far as the idealized portrayal of the last days in the Scrolls is concerned, the view advocating an alleged rivalry between the royal and the priestly offices should be put to rest, not least since both king and high priest would exercise complementary functions in the eschaton" (51).

28. See for instance Stanton, *Jewish and the Christian Messiah*; Klausner, *Messianic Idea in Israel*.

29. Wise et al., *Dead Sea Scrolls*, 169 (4Q491 Manuscript C Frag. 11 Col. 1). For a comparison of the Self-Glorification Hymn to Philippians 2:6–11, see Bühner, *Messianic High Christology*, 23–63—though to my mind the similarities are not nearly as pronounced as Bühner believes and the dissimilarities are more pronounced than he grants. With some important qualifications (but in full agreement that Philippians 2 belongs within a Second Temple Jewish context even if it goes beyond that context in certain ways), I can agree with Bühner that "Paul's high Christology in Phil 2:6–11 is 'within reach' of other messianic expectations and is therefore not an alien or un-Jewish idea" (*Messianic High Christology*, 63). See also the discussion of 11QMelch in Aschim, "Melchizedek and Jesus."

30. See Knohl, *Messiah Confrontation*, 122; and Knohl, *Messiah before Jesus*, 1–26, 75–86. Indebted to David Flusser, Knohl argues that Jesus could have imbibed these Qumranic ideas (about a suffering Messiah) from John the Baptist, who, according to Flusser, was a former member of the Qumran sect. Discussing Luke 3:22, Knohl connects Jesus's self-understanding to Qumran: "The combination of a quasi-divine glorification as the 'son of God' with physical weakness and power of judgment is reminiscent of the figures in the Qumran documents that we have discussed earlier. Both the hero of the document in Aramaic and the hero of the self-glorification hymn combine glorification ('who is like me among the gods?') and a wonderful capacity for teaching and judgment ('no teaching is like my teaching') with weakness and suffering ('who is despised like me who is like me rejected of men')" (*Messiah Confrontation*, 146). For Flusser's hypothesis, see his *Judaism and the Origins of Christianity*, 141–49; and see also the similar perspective offered by John Bergsma and Otto Betz regarding John the Baptist and Qumran, as well as Bergsma's argument that the evangelist/apostle John may have been a disciple of John the Baptist: Bergsma, *Jesus and the Dead Sea Scrolls*, 37–42, 65; and Betz, "Was John the Baptist an Essene?" For the opposite view, see Chilton, "John the Purifier," 217: "Once it is appreciated that John is not known to have shared the cultic program of the Essenes, the argument that he is to be associated

Qumran, in the text for Isaiah 52:14 "an additional letter is added to *mshhat* ('marred') so the word becomes *mshhahti* ('I have anointed')."[31] Overly speculatively but nevertheless in a manner not without influence, Knohl argues that this addition was intentional and had the purpose of depicting the suffering servant as the Messiah.[32]

Another portrait of the Messiah is found in Qumran's *11QMelchisedek*, which envisions an eschatological Day of Jubilee brought about by the return of Melchizedek, a godlike figure who rewards the Sons of Light with the gift of the forgiveness of sins and who enacts vengeance upon the wicked.[33] Joined by all "the divine beings"—perhaps angels?—this eschatological Melchizedek will deliver Israel from the power of the wicked.[34] God's messenger, anointed by the Spirit, proclaims this salvation.[35] Additionally, in Qumran's *Redemption and Resurrection*, a Messiah is described who will be manifested to the whole world and who will place the blessed upon "the th[ro]ne of His eternal kingdom, setting prisoners free, opening the eyes of the blind, raising up those who are bo[wed down]."[36] All will be raised from the dead and judged, and the righteous will receive everlasting life and the wicked everlasting death. The righteous will dwell in the new Jerusalem, with its walls, gates, towers, and temple service.[37]

---

with the covenanters of Qumran loses its foundation." Regarding the speaker in the Self-Glorification Hymn, Joseph Angel comments: "The identity of this mysterious figure has been a perennial flashpoint in scholarship. Numerous proposals have been put forward, but based on the comparative evidence the most likely explanation is that he is an extraordinary priest" (Angel, "Enoch, Jesus, and Priestly Tradition," 301). Angel refers to Collins, *Scepter and the Star*, 146-64; Fletcher-Louis, *All the Glory of Adam*, 199-216; Zimmermann, *Messianische Texte aus Qumran*; and Angel, "Liturgical-Eschatological Priest of the *Self-Glorification Hymn*."

31. Knohl, *Messiah Confrontation*, 119.

32. See also Brooke, "4QTestament of Levid(?) and the Messianic Servant High Priest," which concludes that 4QTestament of Levid employed "the servant passages of Isaiah to support the understanding that there was to be an eschatological priest who would suffer, possibly even that the suffering involved death, death that would lead to joyous benefits for others" (96). For the relationship of this Qumranic text to the *Testaments of the Twelve Patriarchs*, see de Jonge, "Testament of Levi and 'Aramaic Levi.'"

33. Wise et al., *Dead Sea Scrolls*, 592 (11Q13 Col. 2).

34. Wise et al., *Dead Sea Scrolls*, 592 (11Q13 Col. 2).

35. Wise et al., *Dead Sea Scrolls*, 592 (11Q13 Col. 2).

36. Wise et al., *Dead Sea Scrolls*, 531 (4Q521 Frags. 2 + 4 Col. 2).

37. Wise et al., *The Dead Sea Scrolls*, 558-62 (4Q554-555. 5 Q15. 11Q18, 1Q32, 2Q24). See also Qumran's "Son of God" text, published in Puech, "Fragment d'une apocalypse en Araméen (4Q246=psDand) et le 'Royaume de Dieu.'" This text has some parallels with the angel Gabriel's promises regarding Jesus in Luke 1:32 and with Gabriel's statement that Jesus "will be called . . . the Son of God" in Luke 1:35. There are also echoes of the War Scroll. For discussion, see Collins, "*Son of God* Text from

ENGAGING THE DOCTRINE OF JESUS (AND MARY)

Some parts of *1 Enoch*, likely also dating from the early first century AD (pre-Christian), also merit attention. In a heavenly ascent, Enoch sees a vision of the Son of Man, who is the predestined "Chosen One" and who will receive the worship of all the righteous on earth, both Jew and gentile (1 Enoch 48:4-6).[38] The Son of Man will reveal the divine wisdom to the blessed on earth, and he will save all those who have hated the world and

---

Qumran"; Bühner, *Messianic High Christology*, 114-20, making connections to Luke 1:26-38 while granting that 4Q246 may in fact be describing "an evil figure who blasphemously boasts to be of divine origin" (119). Bühner comments, "Whereas some Jews, such as the apocalyptic group behind 4 Ezra, readily called their hoped-for messiah 'son of God,' others, like the group behind 4Q246, rejected the use of such titles for any earthly rulers. Since, regardless of the historical reliability of their claims, all four Gospels within the New Testament provide Jesus' claim of divine sonship as the reason he is charged with blasphemy, it is reasonable to understand the portrayals of the Gospels in light of such messianic discourses and debates. That is to say, within the diverse discourse of Second Temple messianism, some Jews had no reservations about calling their hoped-for messiah 'son of God' or even depicting him as divinely begotten. Other Jews, however, considered such messianic claims as blasphemy" (*Messianic High Christology*, 119-20).

38. *Book of Enoch*, 35. For the heavenly ascent in 1 Enoch, see Reynolds, "Apocalyptic Revelation in the Gospel of John," 115-16; Rowland and Morray-Jones, *Mystery of God*, 33-61 in relation to Jesus' ascension. For discussion of the Enochic Son of Man, see—in addition to the texts I noted in chapter 3—the essays in Boccaccini, *Enoch and the Messiah Son of Man*; Moloney, "*Parables of Enoch* and the Johannine Son of Man"; and Grabbe, "'Son of Man,'" 182-88. Bühner sums up (keeping in view the fact that this portion of 1 Enoch is available only in Ethiopian manuscripts from the late Middle Ages that are not fully trustworthy), "is the elect son of man addressed with 'cultic' worship due to the one God alone? Scholarly opinion is divided on this issue. While there is a consensus that the veneration of the elect son of man in the Parables of Enoch goes beyond the veneration offered to any other figure but the one God in Second Temple Judaism, its precise nature remains debated. Some interpret the evidence as a veneration that approaches, but is not the same as, 'cultic' worship. Others understand it as the kind of worship that is due only to the one God" (*Messianic High Christology*, 138). Bühner essentially sides with the latter viewpoint, although with the caveat that he rejects systematizing claims about kinds of worship. He states, "in 1 Enoch, it is quite clear that the elect son of man is worshipped in the same way as the one God is worshipped in the immediate context. See especially 1 En. 48:5, where it says that all who dwell on the earth will fall down and worship before the elect son of man and simultaneously glorify the name of the Lord of Spirits. Moreover, in 1 En. 62 the worship of the elect son of man is explicitly linked with his characterization as sitting on the Divine throne. In 62:3 it is said that the kings mighty on earth 'will see and recognize that he sits on the throne of his glory,' and from this follows in v. 6 that they 'bless and glorify and exalt him.' If, therefore, the elect son of man's act of sitting on the throne of God is the reason for him being worshipped, then this enforces the conclusion that the elect son of man is indeed worshipped in the same line as God" (138). I note that Bühner grants that 1 Enoch does not explicitly say that God and the Son of Man share the divine throne, and he finds that this aspect is accentuated more by Revelation, "whereas 1 Enoch focuses more on the distinction between God and the elect son of man" (140).

have not "denied the Lord of the Spirits and his Messiah" (1 Enoch 48:10).[39] At the final judgment, the Son of Man will sit on the divine throne and will speak all the divine wisdom which he has received from the Father God. The judgment will take place; and all the wicked, both humans and fallen angels, will be thrown into the everlasting fire. The righteous will reign forever, shining with the glorious "light of eternal life" (1 Enoch 58:3).[40] The "Lord of the Spirits" will take his throne, in the fullness of the spirit, and will judge all people by his powerful word. The Lord of the Spirits or "the Most High One" (1 Enoch 62:7) will reveal to everyone the Son of Man.[41] All the rulers of the world will see the "Son of Man sitting on the throne of his glory," and they will "bless, glorify, [and] extol him" (1 Enoch 62:5-6).[42] The resurrection of the dead will occur and the blessed will "eat and rest and

---

39. *Book of Enoch*, 36.
40. *Book of Enoch*, 39.
41. *Book of Enoch*, 43.
42. *Book of Enoch*, 43. In light of 1 Enoch 48:5's depiction of the simultaneous worship of God and the son of man, Bühner points out a difference: "whereas [in 1 Enoch] the elect son of man is depicted as being worshipped by all humanity in the future, Christ in Rev 5 is said to be the recipient of worship by the angels already in the present. Moreover, this heavenly worship in Rev 5 is surely meant to be joined by the readers of the Apocalypse of John. Therefore, only Rev 5 gives us evidence for an actual religious practice of 'cultic' worship of a figure other than God, whereas the Parables of Enoch only reveal a similar idea without the implication of an actual practice" (*Messianic High Christology*, 140). Yet Bühner warns against exaggerating this difference, as he thinks Hurtado does. Bauckham agrees that the son of man receives worship in 1 Enoch, but he draws a different conclusion from that of Bühner. Bauckham states, "A series of texts concerned with Jesus' enthronement in heaven portray the worship given him specifically by all the heavenly beings (Heb. 1:6; *Ascen. Isa.* 10:15; *Ap. Jas.* 14:26-30), while others portray his worship by all creation (Phil. 2:10-11; Rev. 5:12-14 . . .). That this is the worship due to God alone is clear from the context of Jesus' enthronement on God's own heavenly throne, the symbol of the uniquely divine sovereignty over all things. It should be noted that it goes much further than the very limited worship accorded the Son of Man in the *Parables of Enoch*, who is worshipped neither by angels nor by any other part of the non-human creation, but only by the wicked at the day of judgement. The Christian texts draw out the full consequences of Jesus' exaltation to the divine throne, and deliberately deploy the strongest Jewish theological means of placing Jesus emphatically [on] the divine side of the line between the one God of Israel and the rest of reality, his creation. It is worship by the angels that differentiates God absolutely from them; it is worship by the whole creation that differentiates God absolutely from all other reality. However we may evaluate the evidence adduced for some kind of veneration of angels in some parts of Second Temple Judaism, no angel is worshipped by other angels in Second Temple Jewish literature. These texts do not place Jesus in some ambiguous semi-divine position on a spectrum" (Bauckham, "Throne of God and the Worship of Jesus," 178).

rise with that Son of Man forever" in the presence of the Lord of the Spirits (1 Enoch 62:14).⁴³

The above examples are instructive regarding the eschatological hopes and speculations of Jesus' day. As Novenson shows, then, scholarly appreciation of diversity within Second Temple Judaism has been largely helpful. Yet, it has also sometimes suffered from a tendency to exaggerate, as though the term "Messiah" had no identifiable meaning at all. The Protestant biblical scholar William Horbury proposes that even if the term "Messiah" has no one clear meaning, there was a coherent "messianic" hope among the Jewish populace in the Second Temple period.⁴⁴ To this notion of a widely shared messianic hope, Novenson adds the important observation that the diverse messianic portraits often draw upon the same passages from Israel's Scriptures. As he says, late Second Temple Jews frequently cited Genesis 49:10, Numbers 24:17, 2 Samuel 7:12-13, Isaiah 11:1-2, Amos 9:11, and Daniel 7:13-14 as messianic texts, even though none of these texts explicitly uses the term "Messiah."⁴⁵ According to Novenson, late Second Temple Jews "take the word itself from one set of scriptures and the imagery with which they interpret the word from a different set of scriptures"; and the latter set of Scriptures (which does not contain the word "Messiah") consistently contains "the promise, either in oracular or in visionary form, of an indigenous ruler for the Jewish people."⁴⁶

Another point worth noticing is that Simon bar Kokhba, proclaimed Messiah by Rabbi Akiba in the early 130s during the second Jewish war against Rome, lacked Davidic ancestry.⁴⁷ If the Messiah did not have to be

43. *Book of Enoch*, 44.

44. See Horbury, *Jewish Messianism and the Cult of Christ*; Horbury, *Messianism among Jews and Christians*.

45. Novenson, *Christ among the Messiahs*, 57-58. Novenson draws upon Oegema, *Anointed and His People*, 294-99.

46. Novenson, *Christ among the Messiahs*, 58. For Novenson, each Messianic notion is shaped by a particular political context: "all ancient messiah texts, Jewish or Christian, are the product of the reinterpretation of scriptural oracles in the light of the experience of their respective authors" (Novenson, *Grammar of Messianism*, 184). For further discussion, see Oegema, *Anointed and His People*; Stuckenbruck, "Messianic Ideas in the Apocalyptic and Related Literature of Early Judaism"; and Novenson draws upon Collins, *Scepter and the Star*, 74-101.

47. See Novenson, *Grammar of Messianism*, 66-67. Israel Knohl argues that Jesus was not a Davidide. Highlighting Mark 12:35-37 and parallels, Knohl observes, "Scholars have suggested that Jesus used this verse from the book of Psalms to show that although he did not descend genealogically from the house of David, he was the Messiah nevertheless" (Knohl, *Messiah Confrontation*, 148; cf. Fredriksen, *Jesus of Nazareth, King of the Jews*, 141). On this basis, Knohl builds a further argument: "Jesus' sermon denying that the Messiah would be descended from the house of David also

royal (a Davidide), did the Messiah have to be a political or military leader? Simon bar Kokhba was a military leader, as were Barabbas and certain other messianic pretenders of Jesus' day. Still other messianic pretenders were not military leaders or revolutionaries. But Novenson warns against sharply dividing a Jewish (political) messianic conception from a Christian one.[48] For example, Paul backs up his claim that Jesus is the Messiah largely by appeal to Davidic scriptural texts such as 2 Samuel 7:12, Psalm 110:1, and Isaiah 11:10, with the result that Paul's Messiah is hardly apolitical.[49] Novenson states, "Like the *Psalms of Solomon*, Paul conceives the messiah as a Davidide whose job it is to rule over the pagan nations."[50] Faced with the fact that Jesus does not at present visibly reign over the nations, Paul and other early Christians held that Jesus fulfills these political aspects in other ways that will be fully manifested at his second coming. Novenson adds that there are some passages in the New Testament that suggest that Jesus may

---

represented an ideological rejection of Davidic messianism, which expected the arrival of a fighting Messiah who would liberate the Jews from Roman rule. To Jesus, the Messiah was not cast in the mold of the warlike David, but was the son of God" (149).

48. See Fitzmyer, *One Who Is to Come*, 182–83; Zetterholm, "Introduction," xxiv; Cohn-Sherbok, *Jewish Messiah*, 77–79. Novenson observes critically, "To a certain supersessionist Christian line of reasoning, less popular now than a generation ago but by no means obsolete, the Christian messiah is so different from the Jewish messiah as to be morally or religiously superior to it. On such a view, the early Jewish concept 'messiah' suffers from some perceived deficiency (e.g., carnality or this-worldliness or ethnocentrism or a tendency to violence), but Jesus purges, spiritualizes, redefines, or revolutionizes the concept . . . Contrariwise, to a certain apologetic Jewish line of reasoning, the Christian messiah is so different from the Jewish messiah as to be, well, not a messiah at all. On such a view, Christian talk about a spiritual messiah is really so much wishful thinking. To resort to the idea of a spiritual messiah is, effectively, to concede that the person in question is simply not a messiah" (*Grammar of Messianism*, 214). For concerns similar to Novenson's in this regard, see Bühner, *Messianic High Christology*, 193.

49. See also Joshua W. Jipp's instructive *Christ Is King*, as well as a work upon which Jipp draws, Julien Smith's *Christ the Ideal King*.

50. Novenson, *Christ among the Messiahs*, 177. In this context Novenson disagrees with E. P. Sanders's remark, "Paul's principal conviction was not that Jesus *as the Messiah* had come, but that God had appointed Jesus Christ *as Lord*" (Sanders, *Paul and Palestinian Judaism*, 514). For his part, James D. G. Dunn argues that the early Christian proclamation of Jesus as Messiah—which in Paul's letters is not the focal point of controversy—may not have been "so controversial as a point of issue between Christian Jews and their fellow Jews" (Dunn, "How Controversial Was Paul's Christology?," 152). Dunn goes on to say, "Perhaps we should ask, therefore, whether the messianic status accorded to Jesus was any more controversial than the significance accorded to the Teacher of Righteousness at Qumran or to Phinehas by the Zealots or to bar Kokhba in the second Jewish revolt" (152).

not have been a Davidide (see Mark 12:35–37; John 7:40–44)—even though Novenson grants that Jesus most likely was one.[51]

Rather surprisingly to me, beginning with William Wrede's early twentieth-century *Das Messiasgeheimnis in den Evangelien*, many scholars have denied that Jesus understood himself to be the Messiah.[52] Against such scholarly views, Martin Hengel shows that Paul and the first Christians, in the face of persecution, firmly proclaimed "Jesus of Nazareth as the crucified Messiah whom God had raised from the dead."[53] Hengel and others have persuasively criticized various arguments that suppose that Jesus laid no claim to messianic status.[54] As the Messiah, Jesus exercised both royal and priestly functions.

Anthony Giambrone notes that "[t]he Dead Sea Scrolls and other Second Temple traditions were . . . captivated by the luminous power of the priestly clothes," so that in one instance—in the thirteenth text in the *Songs of the Sabbath Sacrifice*—"the high priest possesses, through his gleaming vestments, 'the appearance of splendor and the likeness of the spirit of glory' (4Q405 23 ii 9)."[55] The point that Giambrone draws from his lengthy and instructive discussion of such texts, which includes a detailed examination of the imagery and terms employed in the transfiguration narrative of Mark

---

51. Against this reading of Mark 12:35–37, see the persuasive case made by Gray, *Temple in the Gospel of Mark*, 79–80; Barber, *Historical Jesus and the Temple*, 142.

52. See Wrede, *Messiasgeheimnis in den Evangelien*. For recent exponents of the view that Jesus himself did not claim (or likely did not claim, at least before the passion) to be the Messiah, see for example Brown, *Death of the Messiah*; Dunn, *Jesus Remembered*, 653; Dahl, *Crucified Messiah and Other Essays*; Sanders, *Historical Figure of Jesus*, 242. For a critique of Wrede's study insofar as it bears upon Mark's understanding of Jesus as the Davidic Messiah, see Botner, *Jesus Christ as the Son of David in the Gospel of Mark*.

53. Hengel, "Jesus, the Messiah of Israel," 8. Hengel goes on to say, "that a righteous man via resurrection from the dead is appointed as Messiah, is absolutely without analogy. Neither resurrection nor translation have anything to do with messiahship. Indeed, the suffering righteous man attains a place of honour in Paradise or Heaven, or in certain circumstances in the very presence of God, but there is never any question of messianic majesty and the transfer of eschatological functions in this connection. Enoch and Elijah are exceptions, but then death and resurrection are not part of their tradition: God translated them alive (cf. Josephus, *Ant.* 9:28). At most one might mention the identification of Enoch with the Son of Man in 1 En. 71, but in the Similitudes of the Ethiopic Eunuch no trace at all is found of suffering and death, despite certain references to the Servant of God in Deutero-Isaiah" (12).

54. See for example Hengel, "Jesus, the Messiah of Israel"; Wright, *Jesus and the Victory of God*, 477–539; Bockmuehl, *This Jesus*, 51–58; and Bird, *Are You the One Who Is to Come?*.

55. Giambrone, "'Why Do the Scribes Say?,'" 325. See also Fletcher-Louis, "Revelation of the Sacral Son of Man," 247–98.

9, is that Jesus is presented both as the true high priest and as the "Davidic Temple Builder," given that the title "Son of Man" had a "strong Davidic/royal valence."[56] Giambrone therefore emphasizes Jesus' status as the messianic priest-king, concluding that "the Gospels . . . [fuse] together priestly and royal figures in Jesus."[57] The background to this eschatological fusion of priest and king includes 1 Samuel 2:35 ("And I will raise up for myself a faithful priest, who shall do according to what is in my heart and in my mind; and I will build him a sure house, and he shall go in and out before my anointed for ever") and, even more, Zechariah 4:6–14, with its vision of "the two anointed who stand by the Lord of the whole earth" (Zech 4:14).

---

56. Giambrone, "'Why Do the Scribes Say?,'" 315. For the phrase "Davidic Temple Builder," see Barber, "Jesus as the Living Temple Builder and Peter's Priestly Role in Matt 16:16–19"—and for an expansion of this research (focused on Matthew) see Barber, *Historical Jesus and the Temple*, especially chapter 5 on "Jesus, David, and the Temple" and chapter 6 on "The Son of David and the Temple-Community" (the latter of which reprises the earlier essay). Giambrone speculates that Jesus understood John the Baptist as a priestly Elijah figure and believed that his own "role was to take up John's mantle to share his fate and complete the priestly mission" (Giambrone, "'Why Do the Scribes Say?,'" 332; see also Perrin, *Jesus the Temple*, 37–44, emphasizing John the Baptist's critique of the temple; and Chilton, "John the Purifier," taking the opposite view from that of Perrin). Giambrone thinks that his approach assists in the interpretation of the Letter to the Hebrews as well. He also remarks, "The priestly-clad 'Son of Man' who appears in Revelation 1:13, glorious in the midst of the celestial cult and radiant in his long robe and golden sash, provides an important link to the Gospel accounts both via his vestments and via his title" ("'Why Do the Scribes Say?,'" 333; see also Reynolds, *Apocalyptic Son of Man in the Gospel of John*. Giambrone relies upon pseudepigrapha such as the *Testament of Levi*, which in Giambrone's view retains "a substantial and fundamentally Jewish core" ("'Why Do the Scribes Say?,'" 306), despite the fact that, as James Davila observes, this text displays a heavy Christian imprint—see Davila, *Provenance of the Pseudepigrapha*, 81. For contrasting views of the dating and provenance of this text, see deSilva, "*Testaments of the Twelve Patriarchs* as Witnesses to Pre-Christian Judaism"; Kugler, *Testaments of the Twelve Patriarchs*; de Jonge, "Testaments of the Twelve Patriarchs." On John the Baptist and Jesus, see also Allison, *Constructing Jesus*, 204–20, arguing that "the historical Jesus related himself to John's ministry and expectations in positive ways" and that "Jesus' very self-conception was informed by his predecessor's vision of a judge baptizing with fire" (219).

57. Giambrone, "'Why Do the Scribes Say?,'" 308; see also 319: "After the Baptism [of Jesus by John], Second Temple 'diarchic messianism' is radically simplified, at least as far as the Gospels are concerned." On eschatological or messianic priestly figures in Second Temple Judaism, and on Jesus as a priestly Messiah, see also Heil, "Jesus as the Unique High Priest in the Gospel of John"; Angel, "Enoch, Jesus, and Priestly Tradition"; Fletcher-Louis, "Jesus as the High Priestly Messiah: Part 1"; Fletcher-Louis, "Jesus as the High Priestly Messiah: Part 2."

III. Jesus' Royal Ascension in Jewish Context

On the basis of Jesus' identity as the messianic priest-king, whose arrival was anticipated in various ways within Second Temple Judaism, let me now turn to Jesus' ascension in its royal dimensions. According to the Gospels, when facing his death, Jesus prophesied that (after his death) he would "be enthroned at the right hand of God as the rightful king of the nation," as the triumphant Messiah and Son, ascended or exalted to the Father's right hand.[58] This theme of royal enthronement has Second Temple Jewish roots that underscore the royal dimension of Jesus' ascension. I will make this case largely through the work of Timo Eskola and Félix Cortez, with attention to some other scholars as well in reflecting upon Jesus' preexistence. While Eskola and Cortez have Hebrews particularly in view, they range widely through the Scriptures and Second Temple literature.

Timo Eskola's Messiah and the Throne

In his *Messiah and the Throne: Jewish Merkabah Mysticism and Early Christian Exaltation Discourse*, the Protestant biblical scholar Timo Eskola advocates for the importance of Second Temple merkabah mysticism for discussion of Christ's ascension. Merkabah mysticism involves journeys of ascent to the divine realm or throne and the enthronement or inclusion of a human figure or "son of man" on the divine throne.[59] The various themes of heavenly enthronement, heavenly journeys or ascents, the messianic role of a Davidide, the resurrection of the dead, and angelomorphic figures are generally kept distinct in Jewish merkabah mysticism.[60] Eskola points out,

---

58. Cho, *Royal Messianism and the Jerusalem Priesthood in the Gospel of Mark*, 190.

59. Eskola, *Messiah and the Throne*, 11, describing Hengel's "'Sit at My Right Hand!'" See also Burnett, *Christ's Enthronement*, which argues that "the sharing of a deity's temple and throne, which were rewards that Greco-Roman communities bestowed on pious, beneficent, and divinely approved rulers, explicate the widespread use of Ps 110:1 and enthronement imagery in earliest Christianity" (135).

60. For discussion of angels in relation to Christology, see for example Stuckenbruck, *Angel Veneration and Christology*; Hannah, *Michael and Christ*; Gieschen, *Angelomorphic Christology*; Garnett, *No Ordinary Angel*; Fossum, "Kyrios Jesus as the Angel of the Lord in Jude 5–7"; Fossum, *Name of God and the Angel of the Lord*; and Fletcher-Louis, *Luke-Acts*. For background, exploring particular angelic figures who embodied the deity, mediated the divine name, sustained creation, and stood as heavenly high priest in early Jewish mysticism, see Orlov, *Yahoel and Metatron*; and see also Boyarin, "Beyond Judaisms"; Boyarin, "Is Metatron a Converted Christian?" It seems clear that the first Christians connected various "unnamed angelomorphic figures intimately identified with YHWH (i.e., the Angel, the Glory, the Name, the Word, Wisdom) to the fleshly Jesus who had ascended and was now enthroned" (Gieschen, *Angelomorphic*

"In no [apocalyptic Jewish] writing is the resurrection considered a premise for the enthronement of the Shoot of David."[61] Furthermore, even when his eschatological enthronement is described in Second Temple Jewish texts, the Davidide is not divine and his kingship remains fundamentally an earthly one.

For this reason, Eskola therefore aims to distinguish a specifically "Christian merkabah tradition."[62] At the center is Jesus' resurrection, which results in his heavenly enthronement. On this view, Jesus' resurrection and the ascension to the Father's right hand are essentially the same. Jesus Christ gloriously rises to sit upon the divine throne as the ruler and savior of the entire creation. The heavenly throne is now the throne of Christ, not solely

---

Christology, 350). But Bühner is quite right to critique the maximalism of most of the above authors; and Bühner sums up, "although the term 'angelomorphic' is helpful in describing the relation between some New Testament christological texts and angelic traditions, one should not infer from these angelomorphic descriptions an identification of Christ as an angel . . . An angelic Christology in the sense that Christ was explicitly called and identified with an 'angel' certainly existed in the second century CE, but nowadays most scholars rightly deny that it existed as early as the first century CE" (*Messianic High Christology*, 179). See also Pitre, Barber, and Kincaid, *Paul, a New Covenant Jew*, 121–22, pointing out that Galatians 3:19 tells strongly against the possibility that Paul understood Jesus as an angel. Garnett offers an inspiring conclusion pertinent to faith in Jesus' ascension: "Christ's way of humility and love unmasks the powers, including the power of death, and shows them for the idols that they are. The radical claim of Christian discipleship is that it is Christ's way of humility and love (and not death marshaled against death) that will lead to the ultimate redemption of the powers. Christ has been raised above the angels. He has been victorious over the powers. Still, 'we do not yet see everything in subjection to him' (Heb 2:8). We see the world still mired in the Fall and it is hard to fend off cynicism or even despair. But let our cynicism be a virtue: disabused of our delicate sensibilities, let us stop shielding our eyes from the brokenness of the world. When we place ourselves in solidarity with those who suffer—watching with them, and acting in their interest—we will find that the Spirit has room to move and work in our lives. The flame of the Spirit will kindle love, and hope for a New Creation—across the world, or in our tiny corner of it . . . Through Jesus we are enabled to enter into God's presence, trusting that the one who sees all faults will neither mock nor condemn but offer us mercy and grace to help in time of need. By accepting us as we are, Jesus in turn enables us to give of ourselves in love—to come to know God by serving God" (*No Ordinary Angel*, 242).

61. Eskola, *Messiah and the Throne*, 377.

62. Eskola, *Messiah and the Throne*, 384. See the critique of Eskola (focusing upon an earlier section of his book) offered by Bühner, *Messianic High Christology*, 141: "scholars such as Timo Eskola deny the high messianism found in 1 Enoch. Eskola creates separate categories for angels, exalted patriarchs, and heavenly messianic figures. This attempt to create clearly defined and differentiated categories allows him to emphasize the innovative character of the early Christian ideas about the enthronement of Christ. However, in contrast to Eskola, the early Jewish sources themselves do not think in such separate and clear-cut categories" (*Messianic High Christology*, 141).

the throne of God, and the throne has thereby become the cultic mercy seat of the heavenly temple.

Eskola identifies three kinds of discourse regarding the ascended Christ: enthronement discourse, cultic discourse, and judicial discourse. The risen and ascended Jesus is enthroned as the Davidic Messiah and king over the whole cosmos. Cultically, the risen and ascended Jesus is the new Melchizedek, the perfect high priest who presides in the heavenly sanctuary or temple. And judicially, as the Son of Man, Jesus is the eschatological judge of all humankind. Eskola concludes, "The throne metaphor . . . is understood in a slightly different way in different contexts. In the enthronement discourse it is the royal throne of the heavenly Messiah. In cultic discourse it is the mercy seat in the heavenly debir. And finally, in the judicial discourse, the throne is Christ's tribunal on the day of the last judgment."[63] As the conqueror of death, Jesus is the Davidic Messiah, the risen one. As the priest-king whose sacrifice is for the whole human race, Jesus is the new Melchizedek who ascends to the heavenly temple and even to the holy of holies that transcends the cosmos. As the judge, Jesus is "the Exalted King . . . who is able to enter upon his own throne and execute the judgment when the last day arrives."[64]

63. Eskola, *Messiah and the Throne*, 386.

64. Eskola, *Messiah and the Throne*, 387. For background to Jesus' (and John the Baptist's) preaching of the coming eschatological judgment—and for background in the Old Testament and Second Temple literature as well—see Reiser, *Jesus and Judgment*. Reiser concludes, "If the unique center of Jesus' preaching is the reign of God, understood as impending and already present in his own work, what about the *presence of judgment*? For formative Judaism, the coming of the reign of God meant likewise the judgment of all the enemies of God . . . For Jesus, that judgment had already begun. He had seen Satan fall like lightning from heaven (Luke 10:18). With that, the 'rule of Belial' is ended; the stronger one has overcome the strong (Mark 3:27). Therefore the reign of God 'has come' when he drives out demons (Matt. 12:28// Luke 11:20). Thus, for Jesus, the judgment has already begun in his own work, not only in the sense that the completion of the end time event of judgment has begun, at least as far as Satan and the demons are concerned" (320). Reiser adds that it is characteristic of Jesus' preaching of judgment to call for the repentance of sinners rather than to announce vengeance upon sinners. Reiser states, "The depictions of judgment in the early Jewish writings are quite often dictated by an unconcealed hatred and thirst for revenge: the hatred of the pious against the godless, of the righteous against the wicked, of the tortured against their torturers . . . [Jesus'] words about judgment are not inspired by hatred of sinners, but solely by love for them. In fact, he has come especially to call them to the eschatological banquet. Of course, a rejection of the invitation would mean nothing other than self-imposed judgment. Hence the call to repentance, which is equally valid for the righteous and for sinners, plays a central role in Jesus' preaching. The danger that is anticipated can still be averted. Jesus proclaims judgment to 'this generation,' because he wants to preserve them from it" (321-22). See also the section on Jesus' preaching of judgment in Dunn, *Jesus Remembered*, 420-25; as well as the salutary warning of

In the narratives of Jesus' exaltation, Eskola finds that the symbols and metaphors of the Old Testament and Second Temple Jewish literature are present but in a significantly altered form. Jesus is the Son of David who reigns cosmically, not only (or specifically) in Jerusalem. Jesus is the high priest, but not in the typical Jewish understanding of that term. Jesus "is a God-chosen king-priest whose priesthood replaces that of the first covenant," and Jesus is the divine Davidide.[65] These various ways of describing Jesus form a coherent unity due to Jesus' exaltation—his resurrection and ascension.

According to Eskola, the first Christians coupled together the Jewish notions of the resurrection of the dead and the enthronement of the Messiah to articulate an account of Jesus' unique resurrection and ascension.[66] In Second Temple Jewish literature the enthronement of the Davidide does not entail his divinity; but, when coupled with his resurrection/ascension, it does so in the New Testament. In the latter, "the Davidic prince in his transcendent post-resurrection enthronement, has become κύριος on the throne of Glory. Now he reigns in the kingdom of God as Lord."[67] The ascension makes clear that it is the Lord Jesus who fulfills for the people the royal role of YHWH. Believers in Christ are called to place their faith in God, present as Redeemer in the exalted and all-powerful King Jesus.[68]

Bruce D. Marshall regarding the contemporary Western Catholic loss of (filial) fear of God, joined to a presumption that God will not everlastingly condemn the unrepentant wicked: see Marshall, "God Almighty in the Flesh." Daria Spezzano addresses many of the same issues in her valuable "Is Jesus Judgmental?" For the soteriological centrality of Jesus' battle against Satan, joined to a warning not to employ "the figure of Satan in order to project evil outside our own group onto others," see Rutledge, *Crucifixion*, 435–39.

65. Eskola, *Messiah and the Throne*, 388.

66. See especially Martin Hengel, "'Sit at My Right Hand!'"; and see also Lee, *From Messiah to Preexistent Son*, 202–39. Lee draws upon the work of Hengel and also upon Hay, *Glory at the Right Hand*. Lee maintains that "one of the most significant christological implications from the early Christian messianic exegesis of Ps 110:1 was that they came to interpret Jesus' resurrection as his exaltation to God's right hand, through which his status as the pre-existent Lord saw its confirmation" (*From Messiah to Preexistent Son*, 239).

67. Eskola, *Messiah and the Throne*, 389.

68. Larry W. Hurtado challenges Eskola in this regard. In *How on Earth Did Jesus Become a God?*, Hurtado comments, "Eskola proposes that the key factor which explains the worship of Jesus was the belief that Jesus had been enthroned in heaven. Drawing comparisons with Jewish *merkavah* mysticism, Eskola contends that early Christians came to the conviction about Jesus' heavenly enthronement. Then, having come to believe that Jesus shared the divine throne, it seemed to them that worshipping him was the proper thing to do" (22). As Hurtado says, however, "devout Jews of Second-Temple time were often quite ready to portray this or that figure in astonishingly exalted terms (whether divine attributes such as divine Wisdom or the divine Word,

This worldview, Eskola argues persuasively, contains within it the cosmology and symbolic world of merkabah mysticism, since Jesus now sits upon the divine "throne" as the royal Messiah, endowed with the divine power. Jesus, descended from David, has become the Lord Christ at the right hand of God, and has therefore taken on the role of perfect high priest approaching the mercy seat. He is the "glorified king-priest who is exalted above the cherubim" and who will judge the whole world.[69]

Does this mean that the New Testament's divine Christology is adoptionist, that is, dependent upon Jesus' resurrection/ascension? Eskola's answer is no. He notes that the adoptionist theory contends, often on the basis of Romans 1:3–4, that "the first Christians and apostles thought that, as regards the nature of Jesus, he was not a true Son of God but that he only became a 'son' in the resurrection."[70] The fundamental question then is this: "Did the first Christians believe that the exalted Christ was merely a human Davidide who has ascended to heaven, or did they ascribe to him divine features that reach beyond the theocratic hierarchy?"[71] Eskola considers the latter to be the case. Christ does not simply mediate God's rule. Christ is God ruling; he is the authoritative ruler of his people. He is exalted to the throne of God (as in Jewish merkabah mysticism) but not as a mere divine agent under God. Eskola argues, "the exalted Christ was indeed a messianic Davidide who was enthroned on the throne of Glory. His factual status, however, is unique in respect of Jewish messianology. He is revered as God on his throne, and he is the source of salvation for those who call upon his name."[72]

Eskola knows, of course, that the Qumran documents refer to the enthronement of messianic figures and that intertestamental texts describe the eschatological enthronement of various patriarchs of Israel—to which can be

---

or principal angels such as Michael or Yahoel, or revered ancestors such as Enoch of Moses). Indeed, a number of the specific claims about Jesus in the New Testament have precedents and analogies in some of the claims made for these figures in sources that derive from or reflect Second-Temple Jewish circles. But what we do not find in the Second-Temple Jewish tradition is the further, momentous step of treating any such figure as the recipient of cultic devotion that in any way parallels the devotion given to Jesus in earliest Christianity" (24). The point is that belief in Jesus' heavenly enthronement would not likely have been sufficient to prompt worship of Jesus. Hurtado argues that Jesus was worshipped because of his followers' "powerful revelatory experiences" of the risen Jesus (30). For the view that the devotional practices highlighted by Hurtado do not actually amount to "worship" of Jesus, see Dunn, *Did the First Christians Worship Jesus?*.

69. Eskola, *Messiah and the Throne*, 390.
70. Eskola, *Messiah and the Throne*, 295.
71. Eskola, *Messiah and the Throne*, 315.
72. Eskola, *Messiah and the Throne*, 320. Here Eskola rightly goes beyond the position found in Bühner's work.

added texts such as 1 Enoch 48 that describe an enthroned "Son of Man" who will judge the world and who receives worship, as noted above. While appreciating the importance of the symbolism of the divine throne, he argues that Jesus' case is unique, for reasons that I will discuss further below.[73]

Félix Cortez's Within the Veil

For his part, Cortez proposes that Jesus' ascension—his heavenly exaltation—reflects the elements that one finds in the narratives of Israel's righteous kings. These elements include ascending the throne, renewing the covenant, cleansing the land of idolatry, repairing (or building) the temple, reforming the cult, working toward the unification of Israel, defeating Israel's enemies, and working with a faithful priest. According to Cortez, it is

---

73. Here may be the place to mention that Eskola considers the theory of "divine agents" to be a problem with Hurtado's *One God, One Lord*; and he critiques Alan Segal's argument that Jesus is an angelic figure. See Segal, "Heavenly Ascent in Hellenistic Judaism, Early Christianity and Their Environment"; as well as, more broadly, Segal, *Two Powers in Heaven*; Barker, *Great Angel*; and Orlov, *Glory of the Invisible God*. Orlov focuses on the transfiguration and baptism narratives, comparing them to Second Temple Jewish texts about Moses and about the divine *Kavod*. In my view, Orlov assimilates Jesus too completely with the earlier texts, as does Segal, rather than fully allowing that Jesus and the evangelists employ shared symbolic elements in certain ways that go beyond their religio-cultural matrix. Representative of Orlov's approach is the following passage: "in both the baptism and transfiguration accounts, Jesus appears along with the invisible deity, whose revelations are conveyed through aural discourse. It is significant that in Jesus' baptism account, as in the transfiguration story, the 'two powers' appear together. Likewise, in both accounts the ocularcentric theophanic profile of the second power appears juxtaposed and contrasted with the aural manifestation of the deity. Furthermore, as in the transfiguration account, in some synoptic renderings of the baptism story the construction of Jesus' upper identity as the second power/person coincides with his visionary experience. Yet, unlike the transfiguration story, where Jesus' role as an ocularcentric seer remained rather hidden, in the baptism vision he is openly portrayed as a visionary. Jesus' role as a seer, however, does not diminish his unique mediatorial position as the second power and heir of the glorious attributes of the deity. As we already noted in our investigation of various Jewish two powers in heaven accounts, in these materials the second powers often begin their initiation as beholders of the divine theophanies, in order that later they themselves might become the very centers of these theophanic events . . . Within this conceptual framework, the initiate first sees what he will later become . . . This conceptual tendency was further perpetuated in the Christian two powers in heaven accounts. In the baptism narratives Jesus appears to be portrayed not only as the recipient of the vision, but also as the theophanic manifestation, thus undergoing in the course of his vision a momentous transition from a beholder of a theophany to the embodiment of the theophany himself" (*Glory of the Invisible God*, 148-49; cf. for further background see Orlov's *Embodiment of Divine Knowledge in Early Judaism*). Despite its insights, this passage exaggerates what is happening in the baptism narratives.

the ascension or enthronement of Jesus that, for the Letter to the Hebrews, makes it possible for King Jesus to accomplish the above tasks in an eschatological way. In Cortez's view, however, Hebrews 1:5 and 5:5 express an adoptionist Christology: God adopts Jesus as his Son.[74]

Cortez holds that "Jesus's exaltation in heaven involves his enthronement as king."[75] He observes that in the Old Testament, all the righteous Davidic kings—Solomon, Asa, Joash, Hezekiah, and Josiah—renew the covenant with God. In Ezekiel 37 and Jeremiah 31–33, the prophecy of a wondrous Davidic king is tied to the inauguration of a new covenant. With regard to Jesus' appointment as priest, Cortez suggests that a parallel can be found in Zechariah 6:12–13, which contains the prophecy: "Thus says the Lord of hosts, 'Behold, the man whose name is the Branch: for he shall grow up in his place, and he shall build the temple of the Lord. It is he who shall build the temple of the Lord, and shall bear royal honor, and shall sit and rule upon his throne. And there shall be a priest by his throne." Of course, Jesus is not a Levitical priest and he combines the royal and priestly offices in himself, but this simply means that the royal ascension of Jesus includes his status as priest.

---

74. For a contrasting view, with which I agree, see Bauckham, "Monotheism and Christology in Hebrews 1." Bauckham comes right to the edge of Chalcedon and then retreats due to (a mistaken) fear of ontology: "Although we have given detailed attention in this essay to ch. 1 of Hebrews, a final comment concerns the Christology of chs. 1 and 2 taken together. These chapters are perhaps the closest the New Testament texts come to the conceptuality of the Chalcedonian Christology that emerged in the fifth century from the patristic christological controversies. Jesus is identified both with God (ch. 1) and with humanity (ch. 2). In the one case he is in every respect like God ('the reflection of God's glory and the exact imprint of God's being': 1.3), in the other case he is in every respect like us ('he had to become like his brothers and sisters in every respect': 2.17). In him, as Chalcedon insisted, true divinity and true humanity are both to be recognized. One might even speak of two natures in these two chapters: the divine nature which is unchangeably eternal (1.10–12) and the flesh-and-blood mortal nature of humanity (2.14). But to call the Christology of these chapters a two-natures Christology would not be adequate. Nature is here subordinate to narrative identity. Just as the God of Israel is who he is in the story the Hebrew Bible tells, so Jesus Christ is who he is in the narrative that includes him in the unique divine identity (notably, creation and exaltation to divine rule) and in the narrative that tells of his human experience of identifying with his human brothers and sisters, learning obedience through suffering, tested but without sin, dying and being exalted to heaven" (Bauckham, "Monotheism and Christology in Hebrews 1," 185). On the issue of "narrative identity," one might see the cautionary notes sounded by Murphy, *God is Not a Story*; and for succinct background to Chalcedon and the other early christological councils, see Oakes, *Infinity Dwindled to Infancy*, chapter 4. See also Bauckham's helpful defense of divine eternity and immutability in Hebrews, even while he continues to insist that "identity" should be the central category: Bauckham, "Divinity of Jesus in the Letter to the Hebrews."

75. Cortez, *Within the Veil*, 306. See also Cortez, "Atonement and Inauguration."

Thus, Cortez describes the ascended Jesus as "the heavenly king-priest" who reorganizes Israel's cult around himself in accordance with the new covenant that he inaugurates.[76] Cortez sees connections here with the Davidic kings. According to 1 Chronicles 28:13, it is David who receives (and delivers to Solomon) the plan for the construction of the temple and "for the divisions of the priests and of the Levites, and all the work of the service in the house of the Lord." Kings Hezekiah and Josiah further reform the priestly cult. Josiah not only gathered the people together to read the book of the Law and to make "a covenant before the Lord, to walk after the Lord and to keep his commandments and his covenants and his statutes" (2 Chron 34:31), but also he took away the idols and "appointed the priests to their offices and encouraged them in the service of the house of the Lord" (2 Chron 35:2). Josiah demonstrates his authority over the priests, instructing them upon how to fulfill their duties in the temple. For Cortez, this authority presages the uniting of royal and priestly offices in the enthroned (ascended) Davidic Messiah.

As the exalted priest-king ascended to the right hand of the Father, Jesus also performs a temple-work: his consecration of the sanctuary not "made with hands" (Heb 9:24) by his offering of the perfect sacrifice. Ezekiel had prophesied that the coming of the eschatological Davidic king would entail the construction of a vast and glorious new temple. Various kings (including Josiah and Hezekiah) had re-consecrated or repaired the temple. The ascended Jesus' temple-work therefore is both royal and priestly.[77]

With respect to the priestly dimension of the ascension, Cortez comments, "A majority of expositors consider that Jesus's ascension in Hebrews in structured in three stages that correspond to the Day of Atonement ritual."[78] The three stages are Jesus' passion and death (the victim's immolation), Jesus' ascension (the high priest entering into the holy of holies), and Jesus' purification of believers (the high priest's purification of the sanctuary). At the heart of this viewpoint is Hebrews 9:1–14, which begins with a description of the Mosaic cult and ends with Jesus' priestly work in the heavenly temple. Hebrews 9:24–25 contains a similar comparison, as does Hebrews 10:1–10. Many scholars argue that these comparisons stand behind Hebrews' understanding of Jesus' ascension.

By contrast, in Cortez's view, the author of Hebrews "envisioned a more restricted use of Day of Atonement imagery for Jesus's ascension than has

---

76. Cortez, *Within the Veil*, 308.
77. For further discussion, see Church, *Hebrews and the Temple*.
78. Cortez, *Within the Veil*, 9.

been allowed by contemporary scholars."⁷⁹ Cortez makes this case on four grounds. First, on the Day of Atonement, the priest must engage in fasting and self-affliction prior to entering into the holy of holies, whereas in Hebrews 9 Jesus enters into the heavenly sanctuary with rejoicing because he has expiated all sins. If he has done so prior to his entrance into the holy of holies, then the model of the Day of Atonement is not being followed here. Second, Hebrews does not mention the scapegoat. It is only when the scapegoat bears the people's sins and is driven into the desert that the people are purified. But if Jesus is still in the holy place when the purification of the sanctuary takes place, then the scapegoat rite has not yet taken place. Instead of mentioning the scapegoat, Hebrews mentions burning the sacrificial animals outside the camp, a ritual that is not confined to the Day of Atonement.⁸⁰ Third, when Hebrews mentions the sprinkling of Jesus' blood in the heavenly sanctuary, it describes this in terms of new covenant inauguration or ratification rather than in terms of the Day of Atonement. Hebrews focuses on the fact of the broken covenant—broken by the people's sins—that is rectified by "the death of the one who made [the covenant]" (Heb 9:16).⁸¹ Fourth, the emphases of Hebrews are distinct from the Day of Atonement ritual. For instance, Jesus' sacrifice is once-and-for-all, whereas the Day of Atonement ritual is annual.

79. Cortez, *Within the Veil*, 13.

80. For the argument that Jesus represents the two goats, see Richard J. Barry's insightful *Jewish Temple Theology and the Mystery of the Cross*. Barry's work undermines some of what Cortez is saying here, but I agree with Cortez that the Day of Atonement is not the primary framework in Hebrews' understanding of Christ's ascension.

81. Here Cortez draws especially upon articles by Scott W. Hahn, including Hahn's "Broken Covenant and the Curse of Death." I would direct attention, as well, to Hays's "Covenant." Hays sums up: "(1) *First, there is not a trace of anti-Judaism in these texts*, or any sense that God has rejected Israel in favor of gentile believers in Jesus. All of the warnings about Israel's faithlessness and failure are expressed in the language and imagery of Deuteronomy, the Psalms, and the Prophets. In this respect, Hebrews is no more supersessionist than Jeremiah. The identity of the implied reader of Hebrews appears to be thoroughly Jewish . . . (2) *Israel's Scripture is read as a living and active word* in and through which God continues to speak directly to his people. Nowhere do we find anything analogous to Paul's denigration of the 'letter' or the merely written form of Israel's sacred text . . . (3) When the old covenant is contrasted unfavorably to the new, *the specific deficiency of the old is described exclusively in terms of the ancient sacrificial cult as a means of atonement for sins*. At no point does Hebrews suggest that the OT is legalistic, that it leads to self-righteousness, that its moral laws are in any way inadequate, or that its conception of God stands in need of correction. (4) . . . The persistent emphasis in Hebrews on the *new* results not from an evolutionary idea of progress, but from the conviction that God has acted through the death and resurrection of Jesus to do something unprecedented—that is, to inaugurate a new covenant for Israel, precisely as Israel's ancient Scripture had anticipated" (Hays, "Covenant," 316–17). Hays is correcting his own earlier work, *Echoes of Scripture in the Letters of Paul*, where he deemed Hebrews to be "relentlessly supersessionist" (98).

The Day of Atonement's sacrifices do not provide forgiveness, whereas Jesus' sacrifice does. In Hebrews, too, "Jesus is compared positively to the sacrifice for the ratification of the covenant."[82] Like a covenant-ratification sacrifice (such as Exodus 24), Jesus' sacrifice is unique and not intended to be repeated, and Jesus' sacrifice provides forgiveness.

Cortez therefore affirms that the Day of Atonement framework is present the mind of the author of Hebrews in connection with Jesus' ascension, but it is not the primary framework. According to Cortez, Hebrews understands Jesus' ascension as the enthronement of the Davidic king. Hebrews mentions Jesus' ascension explicitly in six places—1:6; 4:14–16; 6:19–20; 9:11–14, 24; 10:19–22—and these references associate Jesus' ascension with his royal enthronement, his priesthood, and his new covenant inauguration. Cortez contends that "all of these events form part of Jesus's exaltation at the right hand of God (1:3, 13; 8:1; 10:12; 12:2) and contribute to his identity as 'Son.'"[83] The title "Son" is a royal title in Hebrews. In this sense, Jesus' ascension inaugurates his royal office as "Son." He is the Davidic king foretold by the Old Testament prophecies and promises. Ascended to the right hand of the Father, he is able to accomplish in an eschatological fashion what a righteous king is supposed to do. The ascended Jesus, enthroned as king, "has defeated 'death,' the enemy (2:14–16), built the 'house of God' (3:1–6; 8:1–5), and provided 'rest' for his people (4:1–10)."[84] He has mediated the new covenant, cleansed the people, and reordered the cult around his single sacrifice. Just as when a righteous king did these things in Jerusalem, so also Jesus' ascension or enthronement is greeted with joy. Hebrews urges believers to recognize that they have come to the eschatological feast, "to Mount Zion and to the city of the living God, the heavenly Jerusalem, and to innumerable angels in festal gathering" (Heb 12:22).

For Cortez, then, the subtext in Hebrews is the stories about David and the righteous Davidic kings, in light of the prophecies and promises regarding the eschatological Davidide. Jesus does indeed ascend to consecrate or inaugurate the heavenly sanctuary, and Jesus fulfills the symbolism of the Day of Atonement by his sacrifice. But he does so as the righteous Davidic king who has ascended to the right hand of the Father. Of course, his enthronement as king cannot be separated from his appointment as high priest (in the order of Melchizedek) or from his inauguration of the new covenant.[85]

82. Cortez, *Within the Veil*, 19.
83. Cortez, *Within the Veil*, 27.
84. Cortez, *Within the Veil*, 28.
85. Again, however, Cortez holds that "Hebrews 9:11–14 describes Jesus's ascension to heaven as an entrance into the heavenly sanctuary," specifically as "the inauguration of Jesus's ministry in heaven and—therefore—of the new covenant" rather than as the

Preexistent Son or Adopted Son?

As noted above, Cortez maintains that it is only as the *adopted* Son that is Jesus enthroned at the right hand of the Father. He argues, "Hebrews 1:6 refers to the ascension of Jesus into heaven as an act of God in which he introduces the Son to the heavenly court as their ruler . . . God has fulfilled in Jesus his purpose of crowning humanity with 'glory and honor' (Heb 2:6-9)."[86] In Cortez's reading, Hebrews 4:14 describes Jesus' ascension as a heavenly journey by which Jesus arrives at the divine throne.[87] Because Jesus has taken this journey, he is now the high priest able to help others on the (new exodus) journey. Having entered into the heavenly sanctuary, Jesus has the fullness of priestly power, able to fulfill the promises of the new covenant.

The view that Jesus' ascension constitutes a royal enthronement that brings the man Jesus into the divine realm by *adoption* accords in certain ways with the perspective on Hebrews offered by Eskola. Eskola affirms, "In many respects the letter to the Hebrews is a perfect example of the use of enthronement Christology in the New Testament letters . . . Exaltation Christology appears to be the backbone of the theology of the writer."[88] Like Cortez, Eskola connects the title Son with Davidic kingship.[89] Cortez's emphasis on enthronement is also present in Eskola with regard to Jesus' ascension, even if Eskola does not draw the links to the Old Testament portraits of the righteous Davidic kings. Eskola states, "Christ is here a Davidide that is enthroned to power in his resurrection. Christ's exaltation resembles a heavenly journey that leads to the holy throne of Glory in the heavenly Temple."[90]

Cortez and Eskola agree, then, that the resurrection/ascension is the enthronement of the prophesied Davidide. But Eskola sees this enthronement as more than a mere adoption of a human Davidic king into the divine realm. If the latter were the case, then Jesus, even as enthroned, would simply be an exalted mediating figure under the reign of God, as in the case

---

eschatological Day of Atonement (Cortez, *Within the Veil*, 258). He thinks that "the Day of Atonement in Heb 9:6-10 functions as a parable that illustrates the transition from the first covenant to the new covenant" (267).

86. Cortez, *Within the Veil*, 301.

87. See also Richard Ounsworth, OP's rich discussion of Hebrews 4 in his *Joshua Typology in the New Testament*; and Attridge, "'Let Us Strive to Enter That Rest.'" For further background, see Wray, *Rest as a Theological Metaphor*.

88. Eskola, *Messiah and the Throne*, 202.

89. In this regard Eskola cites Rissi, *Theologie des Hebräerbriefs*, 48.

90. Eskola, *Messiah and the Throne*, 207.

of Jewish merkabah mysticism. In such a case, the adoption of the Davidic kings in the Old Testament to be mediators between God and his people would be fully parallel to Jesus' adoption. As Eskola says, "According to the adoptionist theory, Jesus was merely an ordinary Jewish man or perhaps a prophet in his resurrection to power."[91] But in the Jewish context, adoption as such does not suffice for one to be the source of salvation and truly the enthroned deity.

Let me explain Eskola's viewpoint a bit further. He notes, "The first Christians presented a transcendental interpretation of the enthronement of the Davidide. His power is heavenly power and his reign is eternal reign in the kingdom of God."[92] Jesus receives worship in a manner that would be unacceptable for an Old Testament Davidic king or ruler, no matter how great that king or ruler was and no matter how closely bound to God. When the first Christians developed their understanding of the enthroned Jesus in light of his resurrection, they employed the Jewish merkabah-mysticism framework—even while going beyond it—in which Jesus ascended to become enthroned and worthy of worship as "the Lord of the whole universe."[93] This sounds like adoptionism, insofar as the Davidic king truly is radically exalted in his resurrection, but it is not mere adoptionism. As Eskola puts it, "The enthroned Christ sits where the King of Israel should be sitting."[94]

Eskola maintains that Jewish accounts of the Davidic king and of messianic figures were indeed adoptionist: these figures, no matter how exalted, were created beings raised up to be exalted servants of God. For various strands of intertestamental and rabbinic Judaism, there can be said to be "two" Gods in the sense that (in the words of Peter Schäfer) "one of the two is the ancestral 'first' (as a rule, older) God of higher rank, who generously makes space in heaven next to and beneath him for the second (as a rule, younger) God. The 'divinity' of this second God can be expressed in different degrees."[95] The question then is whether Hebrews' Christology is adoptionist in this Jewish sense. To this question, Eskola answers no. In fact, as Schäfer admits, in the Jewish texts "a clear reference to a second 'God' in the fullest sense of the word is avoided," because the "second godlike figure" is only godlike, not actually God.[96]

91. Eskola, *Messiah and the Throne*, 315.
92. Eskola, *Messiah and the Throne*, 349.
93. Eskola, *Messiah and the Throne*, 351.
94. Eskola, *Messiah and the Throne*, 362.
95. Schäfer, *Two Gods in Heaven*, 135.
96. Schäfer, *Two Gods in Heaven*, 135. As Giambrone remarks, "metaphysically considered, it seems to me that we have a problem ... *Two Gods in Heaven* is certainly no award-winning description of anything truly analogous to the Christian dogmatic

Eskola concludes that there are no prototypes of truly divine figures prior to Jesus, but what there is instead is Jewish merkabah mysticism (and texts such as Psalm 110:1), taken in a fundamentally new direction by the first Christians.[97] The claim that Jesus was to be worshipped came about through "the combining of the theme of Messiah's enthronement and the eschatological event of the resurrection of the dead."[98] If Jesus is the risen one, and if Jesus is the Davidic Messiah, then he is enthroned as Lord and shares in the divine Glory of the Father. The resurrection/ascension is the key event prompting the claim that the Davidic Messiah is truly divine. Rather than being under the reign of God, the exalted Christ is the source of salvation and worthy of all worship. Enthroned at the right hand of the Father, Christ is king over all creation, just as Israel confessed YHWH to be king over all creation.

In this context, further attention should be given to the early Christian passages that depict Christ's preexistence, including 1 Corinthians 8:6's reference to "one Lord, Jesus Christ, through whom are all things and through whom we exist." Jesus Christ is here the Creator, which entails preexistence. As Simon Gathercole points out, such passages as Romans 8:3 ("sending his own Son in the likeness of sinful flesh") and Galatians 4:4 ("God sent forth his Son, born of woman") likewise imply preexistence.[99] Gathercole argues

---

conception of the Trinity" (Giambrone, *Scientia Christi*," 279). See also Idel, "Righteousness, Theophorism and Sonship."

97. Martin Hengel points out, "The most important christological titles and predications such as 'Son of God' (Ps 2:7, cf. 89:28: firstborn), 'Lord' (Ps. 110:1), even 'God' (Ps 45:7) and the pre-existence (Ps. 110:3 LXX in relation to Prov. 8:22ff.) were already given or prefigured in the hymnbook of Israel" (Hengel, "Song about Christ," 290). For discussion, see also Lee, *From Messiah to Preexistent Son*, chapters 6–7; as well as Bühner's observation that "in light of 11QMelch and the messianic rereading of Ps 45, it is possible to imagine a line of development from the earlier Jewish messianic language to the terminology found in 1 John" (*Messianic High Christology*, 161).

98. Eskola, *Messiah and the Throne*, 366.

99. See Gathercole, *Preexistent Son*, 27–28. Gathercole responds to perspectives such as that of Dunn, *Theology of Paul the Apostle*, 274–75. For a critique of Gathercole's view of the Synoptic Gospels (as well as the positions of Richard Bauckham, Kavin Rowe, and Richard B. Hays), see Kirk, *Man Attested by God*, 17–31 and elsewhere. Kirk grants that "[d]ivine and preexistence Christologies can be found in the New Testament, including John's Gospel, the Christ hymn of Colossians 1, and the opening salvo of Hebrews" (16; note that Kirk does not treat 1 Corinthians 8:6). But Kirk argues that the Synoptic Gospels present Jesus instead as an exalted man like other figures in Second Temple Judaism who can be said to be "made like God and even stand in for God, but are not divine with the same ontology as the one God of Israel" (*Man Attested by God*, 36). See also Bauckham, "Confessing the Cosmic Christ"; and the discussion of 1 Corinthians 8:6 (among other texts) in Tilling, *Paul's Divine Christology*, chapter 5. Bauckham concludes, "1 Corinthians 8:6, as a Christian version of the Shema,

that Christ's preexistence is a central theme of the Letter to the Hebrews as well. In Hebrews 1:2, Christ's preexistence is signaled when the author states that "in these last days he [God] has spoken to us by a Son, whom he appointed the heir of all things, through whom also he created the ages." The Son is Jesus Christ, and he is the Creator (or the one through whom God created). Hebrews 1:10 is similarly speaking about the Son when it quotes Psalm 102:25, "You, Lord, founded the earth in the beginning, and the heavens are the work of your hands."[100] In his commentary on Hebrews, Harold Attridge observes that Hebrews 1:10 presents Christ as "eternally sovereign over all things."[101] Other indications of Christ's preexistence include Hebrews 2:14, "Since therefore the children share in flesh and blood, he himself likewise partook of the same nature"; Hebrews 5:8, "Although he was a Son, he learned obedience through what he suffered"; and perhaps especially Hebrews 7:3, where Melchizedek is compared to the Son of God with respect to everlasting existence: "He is without father or mother or

---

incorporates Jesus Christ within the Shema's definition of the one Lord God of Israel. This is indicated not only on the surface level, by the way that the words of the Shema are apportioned to God the Father and to Jesus Christ, but also by means of numerical composition. Each of the two sections consists of thirteen words, the numerical value of the Hebrew word 'one,' as used in the Shema and duplicated in this Christian version, while the twenty-six words of the complete unit correspond to the numerical value of the divine Name. Not only does Christ himself bear the divine Name, but also he is included in the unique divine identity of the God who is so named. This version of the Shema also expands it by specifying the relationship of the one God and the one Lord to the whole of creation ('all things'). It adapts a Jewish confessional statement that uses three prepositions to specify God's relationship to all things—as effective cause, final cause and instrumental cause. Just as the words of the Shema are apportioned to God and Jesus Christ, so the prepositions are apportioned to them. In this way Jesus Christ is included in the unique divine activity of creation as the instrumental cause or agent through whom God created all things" ("Confessing the Cosmic Christ," 169; for similar analysis, see Bauckham, "God Crucified," 26–30, and Bauckham, "Biblical Theology and the Problems of Monotheism," 97–104). Although Bauckham's point about the Shema is well taken, it is insufficient if taken alone. See Philo's ambiguous Logos theology, including in relation to 1 Corinthians 8:6, in Giambrone, "Primitive Christology as Ancient Philosophy." Laying emphasis upon John 1 and Hebrews 1, Giambrone emphasizes the necessity of doctrinal development after Paul (though not against Paul), arguing that "[n]o amount of creative agency or even *latreia* accorded by Christians to Christ can successfully assert his divinity without some idea of divine homo-*ousia*. And that requires some proto-Dionysian grammar of transcendent being or Thomistic notion of *ipsum esse subsistens*. Otherwise, the *Logos* will remain an Arian Artisan and worshipful super-angel: above all things, but merely atop and not entirely beyond" (53).

100. See, more broadly, Vall, "Psalms and the Christ Event in the Epistle to the Hebrews"; Attridge, "Giving Voice to Jesus"; and the essays in Human and Steyn, *Psalms and Hebrews*.

101. Attridge, *Epistle to the Hebrews*, 68, cited in Gathercole, *Preexistent Son*, 34.

genealogy, and has neither beginning of days nor end of life, but resembling the Son of God he continues a priest for ever."[102]

Gathercole remarks that some scholars have granted the preexistence of the Son in Hebrews but have denied that this means "*personal* preexistence."[103] But he rightly considers this to be implausible, since, from Hebrews 1 onward, the "Son" who is described as eternally existing is quite clearly Jesus Christ, not only in his ascended and enthroned state but also in his earthly life, as the one who "learned obedience through what he suffered" precisely as "a Son." Hebrews does not simply associate Jesus' ascension with his royal (and priestly) enthronement, but also recognizes him to be the preexistent divine Son, the Creator, prior to his ascension.

The Protestant biblical scholar Sean McDonough has developed these considerations further. In McDonough's reading of Hebrews, "when the author thinks about the creation of the world [cf. Heb 11:3], he chooses to associate it with God's speaking rather than with God's Wisdom"—and thus with God's Word.[104] McDonough deems Hebrews 1:10-12 to be an extraordinary statement of Christ's role in God's creative work—a clear assertion that "what YHWH did, Christ did."[105] For McDonough, reflection on Christ's powerful

---

102. For background to Hebrews 5:8 from a different angle, see Aune, "Historical Jesus Traditions in Hebrews."

103. Gathercole, *Preexistent Son*, 35.

104. McDonough, *Christ as Creator*, 198. McDonough argues, "there is little question that the author of Hebrews was comfortable in the milieu of Hellenistic Judaism. His palette shows marked similarities to the hues of Sirach or the Wisdom of Solomon, and like them he uses Hellenistic rhetorical conventions to depict traditional Jewish beliefs. But Hebrews' focus on Jesus the Messiah as God's final Word leads him in some very different directions" (199). See also, more broadly, Laansma, "Cosmology of Hebrews"; and see the remark of Martin Hengel in "Jesus as Messianic Teacher of Wisdom," 102 (cf. 113-17): "If we seek a pre-Christian-Jewish key to understanding the development of post-Easter christology we will most probably find it in the Wisdom of Solomon, where Palestinian traditions of apocalyptic and Wisdom provenance have combined in unique fashion with typically Hellenistic vocabulary. However, the preconditions for this influence of Wisdom and Spirit teaching on Christology are not to be found first in the post-Easter early Church with its exaltation Christology, but go back rather . . . to Jesus' activity itself as messianic teacher and Spirit-bearer."

105. McDonough, *Christ as Creator*, 206. He goes on to say that Hebrews 1:10-12's use of Psalm 101 has the following import: "If Jesus was understood as the eschatological deliverer of Israel (and the nations), as he surely was by the author of Hebrews, then the logic of the psalm would demand that the eternal, saving Lord of Ps. 101:13-14 be the eternal, creating Lord of verses 26-28" (207). Regarding Hebrews 3:1-6, McDonough observes: "in view of the strong assertions of Jesus' role in creation in chapter 1 [of Hebrews], I think it likely that 'the builder' in 3:3 is in fact Christ, the creator of the universe . . . [T]he juxtaposition of Jesus as builder in verse 3 with God as the builder of all things in verse 4 is yet another instance of Hebrews' remarkably high Christology" (209).

works of new creation—preeminently his resurrection—led the first Christians to identify him as the everlasting Creator.[106]

By contrast, the Protestant biblical scholar G. B. Caird supposes that Hebrews only ascribes a creative work to Jesus Christ because of Jesus' exaltation; in the *exalted* Jesus, Wisdom dwells. In Caird's view, Hebrews 1:2–3's ascription to Jesus of a role in creation simply echoes Wisdom 7–9, and does so solely with reference to the exalted Lord, in an adoptionist fashion.[107] Similarly, some other scholars propose that Hebrews "calls Jesus Son while on earth in anticipation of his exaltation when he will truly become the Son."[108]

---

106. Daniel Boyarin rejects the resurrection of Jesus (and his divinity) partly on the grounds that Second Temple Jews had a worldview that presupposed them to believe in such things without real evidence. He argues, "It may have been necessary that Jesus was so extraordinary for such a compelling narrative of divine being and function to have developed, but it was hardly sufficient. Even more so, the notion that some kind of experience of the risen Christ preceded and gave rise to the idea that he would rise seems to me so unlikely as to be incredible. Perhaps his followers saw him arisen, but surely this must be because they had a narrative that led them to expect such appearances, and not that the appearances gave rise to the narrative . . . A people had been for centuries talking about, thinking about, and reading about a new king, a son of David, who would come to redeem them from Seleucid and then Roman oppression, and they had come to think of that king as a second, younger, divine figure on the basis of the Book of Daniel's reflection of that very ancient tradition. So they were persuaded to see in Jesus of Nazareth the one whom they had expected to come: the Messiah, the Christ. A fairly ordinary story of a prophet, a magician, a charismatic teacher is thoroughly transformed when that teacher understands himself—or is understood by others—as this coming one. Details of his life, his prerogatives, his powers, and even his suffering and death before triumph are all developed out of close midrashic reading of the biblical materials and fulfilled in his life and death. The exaltation and resurrection experiences of his followers are a product of the narrative, not a cause of it. This is not to deny any creativity on the part of Jesus or his early or later followers, but only to suggest strongly that such creativity is most richly and compellingly read within the Jewish textual and intertextual world, the echo chamber of a Jewish soundscape of the first century" (Boyarin, *Jewish Gospels*, 159–60). In my view, Boyarin offers a false alternative. Of course the New Testament and the figure of Jesus are related, in a profound way, to Israel's Scriptures and to late-Second Temple receptions of those Scriptures. Jesus and the New Testament texts do not attempt to hide their Jewishness, and they also teach that God has been providentially preparing for Jesus' life, death, and resurrection. This providential preparation includes the intertestamental period. Indeed if Jesus had not been prepared for, then he could not have been truly the Messiah. Boyarin's view that because some intertestamental texts indicate that the Messiah will suffer and be vindicated, Jesus' followers must have concluded without external evidence that Jesus rose from the dead is rather a stretch. If they had had to invent his vindication, his followers could have proclaimed him vindicated through a heavenly ascent, without needing to posit his resurrection.

107. See Caird, "Son by Appointment."

108. Eskola, *Messiah and the Throne*, 179, referencing Thompson, *Beginnings of*

Eskola identifies the problems with such proposals, beginning with the fact that the evident parallels between the ascended Lord and personified Wisdom should not obscure the point that Hebrews is speaking about a historical person, Jesus.[109] Jesus may be a new Solomon, a bearer of Wisdom, but not in the sense of having to ask God for Wisdom; and the "Solomon" of the Wisdom of Solomon is manifestly a literary character, not the actual King Solomon. Eskola observes, too, that Hebrews 5:8—"Although he was a Son, he learned obedience through what he suffered"—makes clear enough that Jesus was the Son of God in his earthly life and not merely proleptically or solely at his ascension.[110]

Christian Philosophy. Eskola directs attention also to the position of Lincoln D. Hurst, which builds upon Caird's: Hurst, "Christology of Hebrews 1 and 2."

109. For further discussion of Hebrews 1 and other texts from Hebrews, emphasizing the connections to Jewish apocalyptic literature, see Mason, "Heavenly Revelation in the Epistle to the Hebrews"; Barnard, *Mysticism of Hebrews*.

110. For various positions regarding when Jesus became "Son," Eskola references Attridge, *Epistle to the Hebrews*, 55nn47-49. Eskola notes more broadly, "It is usually understood that Christian understanding of Jesus as the Son of God experience development throughout time (evidenced in the different uses of the title in the NT) from a functional understanding (Son of God = the messianic Son of David) to an ontological one (Son of God = pre-existent divine sonship) that was already formulated at the end of the 1st century but became dominant centuries later" (Eskola, *Within the Veil*, 177n133). Eskola adds with particular reference to the work of James Dunn (and, to a degree, also that of Attridge): "Some scholars believe that Hebrews incorporates two different sonship traditions without any attempt at reconciliation; therefore, we should not try to reconcile them either. They note that both early Jewish and Christian writings independently combined traditions about exaltation and pre-existence that seem contradictory"—as for instance Luke who "saw no difficulty in including assertions that seem to set the decisive moment of Jesus's divine sonship at three different moments: conception or birth (Luke 1:32, 35; cf. 2:49), baptism (Luke 3:22; cf. 3:23-28), and resurrection (Acts 13:33)" (Eskola, *Messiah and the Throne*, 178; he also cites Romans 1:3 as an example of Jesus becoming Son at his Ascension and 1 Corinthians 8:6 as a pre-existence text). See Dunn, *Christology in the Making*, 50-53. See also Hengel, *Four Gospels*, 151: "already for Paul a basic presupposition of the saving event was the sending of the pre-existent Son of God into the world, i.e. his real incarnation. Already for him the eternal Son of God had become a real man in space and time, in Judaea, and only a few years previously." Hengel is quite right to add: "Some theologians do not want to perceive the *vere homo* and others—who are in the majority—deny the *vere deus*. For a third group, basically there is no longer either one or the other, but only a shadow, the 'Christ idea', which can no longer be identified. Fundamentally they all take offence at the real 'kenosis', the incarnation of the Son of God which is completed on the cross. It is remarkable how much the motif of the 'exaltation to the right hand of God' and any speculative apocalyptic elaboration of his heavenly glory fades into the background in Paul; in the foreground is the crucified, i.e. human Jesus, 'who paradoxically—as "God incarnate"—became obedient to death, death on the cross'" (*Four Gospels*, 152).

Eskola differentiates between royal office and filial identity. In terms of filial identity, Jesus was always the eternal Son, the Creator, at every moment of his earthly life; and this is what Hebrews 5:8 expresses. In terms of royal-priestly office, Jesus was "appointed" Son at his ascension.[111] This is conveyed by Hebrews 5:5, "Christ did not exalt himself to be made a high priest, but was appointed by him who said to him, 'You are my Son; today I have begotten you.'" Eskola summarizes the key point, which preserves the Son's preexistence while affirming that he becomes king preeminently at his ascension: "The Son, in his filial identity, participates with the Father in the creation of the universe (Heb 1:2); but in his royal identity, he assumes the rulership of the universe (cf. Ps 2:8)."[112]

IV. Jesus' Reign and the Outpouring of the Spirit

To the question of when Jesus became king, one might add the question of whether Jesus was (and is) a failed king.[113] As we saw above, Jesus in his public ministry already possessed royal authority over Satan and the demons, and his teaching already bore the marks of royal authority (Mark 1:22, 27). When Jesus asks the disciples, "Who do you say that I am?," Peter receives praise for answering that Jesus is the Messiah, the eschatological Davidide (Mark 8:29; Matt 16:16–17).[114] But Jesus ended his life on the

111. For background to Eskola's argument here, see Schenck, "Keeping His Appointment"; Johnson, *Hebrews*, 67.

112. Eskola, *Messiah and the Throne*, 180. For a similar perspective, indebted to Eskola, see Jamieson, *Paradox of Sonship*; and see also, more broadly but equally definitively, Peeler, *You Are My Son*; and Pierce, *Divine Discourse in the Epistle to the Hebrews*. Eskola adds, "Paul probably held a similar view. I have already mentioned Paul's assertion that Jesus 'was declared to be Son of God with power according to the spirit of holiness by resurrection from the dead' (Rom 1:4). It is commonly accepted that the qualification 'with power' should be taken with the noun (υἱοῦ θεοῦ) in the sense that the role Jesus assumed after the resurrection was 'Son of God with power.' This suggests that in Paul's view Jesus did not become Son of God at the resurrection but that he acquired royal or executive power at the resurrection" (180; for this view Eskola references Dunn, *Romans 1–8*, 14).

113. For the Gospel of Matthew on Jesus' (Davidic) kingship, see Barber, *Historical Jesus and the Temple*, 137–39; Zacharias, *Matthew's Presentation of the Son of David*; Chae, *Jesus as the Eschatological Davidic Shepherd*; Verseput, *Rejection of the Humble Messianic King*; Novakovic, *Messiah, the Healer of the Sick*. See also the viewpoint of William R. Herzog II that Jesus, while a political (anti-Roman) and religious (anti-Temple priests) subversive, never claimed to be the messianic king: see Herzog, *Jesus, Justice and the Reign of God*.

114. See also the theophany at Jesus' baptism in Mark 1. For the argument that Mark's depiction of Jesus' baptism describes the inauguration of the new exodus and the revelation of the Trinity, see Bauckham, *Who Is God?*, 91–110. See also McKnight,

cross—not normally the mark of royal power!—and even after his resurrection and ascension, both the Church and the world remain plagued by sin and suffering. Has his reign failed or been postponed until the eschaton?

The Marks of Jesus' Kingdom

The first point to emphasize is that the ascended Jesus clearly does not presently reign in the way that a powerful earthly king would. The unique character of Jesus' kingdom is expressed in his beatitudes, when he states, "Blessed are the poor in spirit, for theirs is the kingdom of heaven" and "Blessed are the meek, for they shall inherit the earth" (Matt 5:3, 5). Similarly, he teaches, "If any one strikes you on the right cheek, turn to him the other also" and "Love your enemies and pray for those who persecute you" (Matt 5:39, 44).[115] In Mark 10:42-44, Jesus further instructs his disciples about the way in which to share in his reign: "You know that those who are supposed to rule over the Gentiles lord it over them, and their great men exercise authority over them. But it shall not be so among you; but whoever would be great among you must be your servant, and whoever would be first among you must be slave of all."

To follow King Jesus, reigning at the Father's right hand, means to obey his commandment to "love one another as I have loved you" (John 15:12); it is here we can perceive his inaugurated kingdom or temple. Michael Patrick Barber observes that, in accordance with the prophecy of Zechariah 4:7-8, "Jesus's Davidic role has a necessary implication: *he will*

"Jesus' New Vision within Judaism," 81: "John baptized in the Jordan in order to reenact the foundational story of ancient Israel, the Entry into the Land. John asked his followers, and Jesus was one of them at this point, to leave Israel by crossing the Jordan, stand with him at the edge of the Transjordanian bank, confess the sin of Israel, enter into the water as a baptismal act of repentance, and then reenter the Land as a purified people ready to take the message of an eschatological repentance to the whole Land." McKnight goes on to argue that Jesus acts as an eschatological new Moses—and, I would add, new Joshua.

115. Peter J. Leithart comments aptly, "Jesus' instructions to his disciples detail a way of life that achieves what the *lex talionis* aimed at. Jesus' commands, though, go beyond an attempt to curb the effects of fleshly violence. Jesus taught a way to overcome flesh and to redeem human relationships. It seeks reconciliation and reunion in love, rather than simply trying to control the evil effects of sin and flesh. If enacted, the instructions of the Sermon would unravel the dynamics of flesh. Jesus did not dismiss the *lex talionis* so much as suggest a paradoxical, surprising fulfillment of the law, a fulfillment that surpasses the fulfillment of the law by the scribes and Pharisees, a fulfillment that participates in the coming of the kingdom of God that brings harmony and peace and justice into the world. By following the Torah of Jesus, the disciples *are* that coming of the kingdom" (Leithart, *Delivered from the Elements of the World*, 140-41).

establish a sanctuary. For Matthew, however, this is understood in terms of the *ekklēsia*."[116] Those who belong to this temple-Church will suffer and will even endure martyrdom, and precisely through this suffering the "gospel of the kingdom will be preached throughout the whole world" (Matt 24:14; cf. 24:9), for the salvation of many. The Catholic biblical scholar Andrew Dalton sums up the Gospel of Matthew's perspective, emphasizing the royal character of the cross: "If the shepherd-king's enthronement came through the cross, the disciple-shepherds will not be exempt from similar suffering (cf. [Matt] 10:38). They too will endure hatred, persecution, and death."[117]

In his own proclamation of the gospel of the kingdom, Paul sounds similar notes. He remarks that we Christians must "rejoice in our sufferings, knowing that suffering produces endurance, and endurance produces character, and character produces hope, and hope does not disappoint us" (Rom 5:3–5).[118] The reason why believers can suffer without losing hope is that "God's love has been poured into our hearts through the Holy Spirit who has been given to us" (Rom 5:5). The Gospel of John likewise speaks about the kingdom of Christ as constituted by the Holy Spirit's presence—to which John adds the indwelling of the Father and the Son, so that believers become the eschatological temple, configured to the cruciform Lord and filled with his presence. As Jesus promises his disciples in John 14:23, "If a man loves me, he will keep my word, and my Father will love him, and we will come to him and make our home in him."

The great kingdom- and temple-building gift that the ascended King Jesus provides is the Holy Spirit. Jesus proclaims at the Feast of Tabernacles in the Gospel of John, "If any one thirsts, let him come to me and drink. He who believes in me, as the Scripture has said, 'Out of his heart shall flow rivers of living water'" (John 7:37–38).[119] In this vein, Paul sharply differentiates between those who live by the Spirit and those who live by the flesh. The latter have committed themselves to the temporal kingdoms of this world, whereas belonging to Christ's cruciform kingdom requires a different way of life. Paul states, "For those who live according to the flesh set

---

116. Barber, *Historical Jesus and the Temple*, 160. For further discussion, see Shauf, *Jesus the Sacrifice*, 192–93.

117. Dalton, *Fulfilled Israel*, 308.

118. For discussion of these verses of Romans 5, see especially Gorman, *Romans*.

119. For background, see Coloe, *God Dwells with Us*, 115–43; Behr, *John the Theologian*, 160–66. See also Guilding, *Fourth Gospel and Jewish Worship*. Behr sums up, "Jesus himself is the Temple, providing water and light, given through the gift of the Spirit bestowed upon the disciples in the resurrection on the eighth day (20:19–23)" (Behr, *John the Theologian*, 166).

their minds on the things of the flesh, but those who live according to the Spirit set their minds on the things of the Spirit" (Rom 8:5).

According to John, the Spirit convicts us of sin and leads us into the fullness of the truth of Christ. According to Paul, the Spirit enables us to pray as we ought. The Spirit enables us to persevere in love as we endure suffering and wait for the consummation of all things. The Spirit makes us temples of God who glorify God in our bodies. The Spirit enables us to say in faith, "Jesus is Lord" (1 Cor 12:3). The Spirit provides the Church with "varieties of gifts," all in service to the common good: wisdom, knowledge, faith, gifts of healing, the working of miracles, and so forth (1 Cor 12:4). The Spirit unifies and builds up the body of Christ, the eschatological Temple and Kingdom of the ascended Davidic King, who pours out his Spirit upon his people.[120]

Jesus Becoming King

As noted above, Jesus was always king, from the very moment of the incarnation. At his birth, according to the Gospel of Luke, the angel of the Lord proclaimed to the shepherds around Bethlehem that "to you is born this day in the city of David a Savior, who is Christ the Lord" (Luke 2:11). He is the Davidic Messiah, the Christ, at his birth. He is certainly king on the cross. His cross is a royal and priestly act of love, by which he makes his people righteous and establishes justice once and for all.

Yet, there is a certain dynamic progression toward the fullness of his royal reign, a way in which he can be said to "become" king fully. At the annunciation, the angel Gabriel tells Mary about the son whom she will conceive: "He will be great, and will be called the Son of the Most High; and the Lord God will give to him the throne of his father David, and he will reign over the house of Jacob for ever; and of his kingdom there will be no end" (Luke 1:32–33).[121] It seems clear that this reign begins in earnest when, at the culmination of his Pasch, he ascends to the right hand of the Father from whence he pours out the Spirit. Thus, as Michael Patrick Barber observes, in Luke's account of the Last Supper, "Jesus is depicted as the king

---

120. See the background in my *Engaging the Doctrine of the Holy Spirit*; and see also, on the tasks of believers and on "spiritual warfare," Zoltán Dörnyei's *Progressive Creation and the Struggles of Humanity in the Bible*, chapters 6 and 7.

121. For discussion, see Hays, *Echoes of Scripture in the Gospels*, 195, emphasizing the allusion to 2 Samuel 7:12–14. Edward Sri persuasively connects Luke 1:32–33 with 2 Samuel 7:9–16: see Sri, *Rethinking Mary in the New Testament*, 34–35.

anticipating his enthronement."[122] This occurs in his cross but even more, in certain ways at least, in his resurrection and ascension.

Recall Paul's words at the outset of his Letter to the Romans, where he announces "the gospel concerning his Son, who was descended from David according to the flesh and designated Son of God in power according to the Spirit of holiness by his resurrection from the dead" (Rom 1:3–4). Cortez interprets this passage as adoptionist, but, as noted above, there is another way to read it. Just prior to the ascension, in response to the disciples' question about when the kingdom of God will come, the risen Jesus explains that the disciples are not to know the time of the consummation of the kingdom, but they will soon experience the power of that kingdom and they will be commissioned to spread this good news. Jesus tells them, "It is not for you to know times or seasons which the Father has fixed by his own authority. But you shall receive power when the Holy Spirit has come upon you; and you shall be my witnesses in Jerusalem and in all Judea and Samaria and to the end of the earth" (Acts 1:7–8). The power to which Jesus refers is the power of the inaugurated kingdom, the power of his Spirit. It is the power of grace-filled charity in opposition to the ways of worldly power.[123]

When Jesus ascends to the Father, the crucified one is glorified. The man who died on the cross out of supreme love stands before the Seer of the book of Revelation as "one like a Son of man, clothed with a long robe and with a golden sash across his chest; . . . in his right hand he held seven stars, from his mouth issued a sharp two-edged sword, and his face was like the sun shining in full strength" (Rev 1:13, 16).[124] As the Catholic theologian Anscar Vonier says, "The Spirit is essentially and unalterably the radiation in this world of Christ's glorification."[125] This is what the kingdom is: the "radiation" throughout the world of the supreme love of the one "who died,

---

122. Barber, *Historical Jesus and the Temple*, 207. Barber goes on to suggest that "Jesus saw himself as the Davidic king in waiting" and as the one who would "appoint the priestly leaders of the eschatological regime" (233).

123. See Rowe, *World Upside Down*.

124. As Ruben Bühner comments, "there are aspects of an angelomorphic Christology within the New Testament, in the sense that characteristics that typically describe angelic figures are attributed to Christ . . . In Rev 1:13–16 Christ is described in ways astonishingly similar to those used to describe the mighty angel in Rev 1:1–3, when it is said that 'his face was shining like the sun shining in its strength' (cf. Rev 1:16 with 10:1). When Christ is depicted 'with a long robe and wish a golden sash across his chest' in Rev 1:13, this certainly reflects the same angelomorphic tradition that can be found with respect to the angels in Rev 15:6, who are likewise 'clothed in linen, clean and bright, with golden sashes across their chests'" (Bühner, *Messianic High Christology*, 178). Bühner directs attention here to Carrell, *Jesus and the Angels*.

125. Vonier, *Spirit and the Bride*, 44.

yes, who was raised from the dead, who is at the right hand of God, who indeed intercedes for us" (Rom 8:34).

In his speech at Pentecost in the book of Acts, Peter identifies the fullness of Jesus' kingship with Jesus' ascension, along lines that support Vonier's insight. Speaking on behalf of all the apostles, Peter tells the gathered crowd: "This Jesus God raised up, and of that we all are witnesses. Being therefore exalted at the right hand of God, and having received from the Father the promise of the Holy Spirit, he has poured out this which you see and hear" (Acts 2:32–33). The Davidic King Jesus, unlike David, has ascended to God's right hand in fulfillment of David's prophetic words in Psalm 110:1. Peter states, "For David did not ascend into the heavens; but he himself [David] says, 'The Lord said to my Lord, Sit at my right hand, till I make your enemies a stool for your feet'" (Acts 2:34–35). Peter concludes by affirming Jesus' fullness of messianic kingship through his resurrection and ascension: "Let all the house of Israel therefore know assuredly that God has made him both Lord and Christ, this Jesus whom you crucified" (Acts 2:36).[126] The ascended Jesus reigns through his cross, configuring believers to his cruciform love by his Spirit in the communion of the Church. If, for the Gospel of Luke, "the resurrection is the moment when Israel's Messiah 'comes into his glory' [Luke 24:26]," the ascension definitively establishes Jesus as king in the sense that "[t]he one who sits in heaven is the one who rules on earth"—who rules by the grace of the Spirit, liturgically uniting his people to himself and sending them out to spread the good news and to live in his love.[127]

At his ascension, Jesus, though always the divine Son and always king, is enthroned. Having followed the path of the cross, he now shares in the divine throne at the right hand of the Father and receives "all authority in heaven and on earth" (Matt 28:18). His exercise of authority retains the form of radical self-giving love rather than adopting the kinds of power that

---

126. Joshua W. Jipp nicely explains the shift that occurs at Jesus' ascension, making a comparison to David's shift from being the anointed king to being the reigning king: "Just as David was God's elected king even while King Saul was alive but only entered into his role as King of Israel upon Saul's death (1 Sam 15—2 Samuel 5), so it is only at his resurrection and heavenly enthronement to God's right hand that Jesus, as the incarnate, crucified, true human, is installed as messianic king." See Jipp, *Messianic Theology of the New Testament*, 334.

127. Wright, *How God Became King*, 246–47. Joshua Jipp has recently argued that it is in light of the "scriptural Davidic-sonship framework that Paul makes sense of Jesus' resurrection and enthronement (see 2 Sam. 7:12–14; Pss. 2:7; 89:26–27)" (Jipp, *Christ Is King*, 5). Paul teaches his congregations to understand their communal life as centered around the ascended King Jesus. Christians are intimately related "to the resurrected and living body of the enthroned king" (*Christ Is King*, 12). See also Hays, "Paul's Use of an Early Christian Convention"; Campbell, "Story of Jesus in Romans and Galatians."

we associate with earthly kingdoms. He reigns by pouring out his Spirit, whose graces configure God's people—though we are still sinners and can repel the Spirit—to the wisdom and love of Christ. Jesus' inaugurated kingdom, visible and apostolically structured in the world, proclaims and lives the truth of Jesus' Pasch by the grace of the "Spirit of truth" (John 15:26).

V. The Queenship of Mary

In this final section, let me turn to the Marian complement to Christ's kingship. Catholics and Orthodox believe that Mary has been taken up by Christ to reign with him as queen—united to her Son by his grace and configured to his self-surrendering love and humility. As Brant Pitre has argued in light of Matthew 1, Luke 1, and Revelation 12, Mary is the queen mother in the kingdom of God that her Son has inaugurated. Pitre observes, "the woman clothed with the sun and wearing a crown of stars is standing *above* the moon and the stars 'in heaven' (Revelation 12:1). Her location matters because it presents a strong parallel with Jesus' being 'caught up' to the 'throne' of God in heaven . . . Just as Jesus is a *heavenly* king who reigns over a *heavenly* kingdom, so Mary, Jesus' mother, is a *heavenly queen*."[128]

---

128. Pitre, *Jesus and the Jewish Roots of Mary*, 88. In support of the claim that the Book of Revelation presents Mary as "the queen of the cosmos," Pitre cites Aune, *Revelation*, 2:713. Pitre directs attention also to Sri, *Queen Mother*, as well as (among many other scholarly works) Ackerman, "Queen Mother and the Cult in the Ancient Near East," 196. Pope Pius XII's 1954 encyclical on Mary as Queen, *Ad Caeli Reginam*, also deserves mention. I note that Pitre is well aware of the polyvalence of Revelation 12's "woman." He comments, "On the one hand, the woman can be seen as an individual. For one thing, she is explicitly identified as the mother of the Messiah: She gives birth to the 'male child' who is 'to rule all the nations' (Revelation 12:5; compare Psalm 2:7–9). On the other hand, the woman can be interpreted as a collective figure—a symbol for the people of God. One reason for seeing her this way is that in the Old Testament, Jerusalem is often depicted as the 'bride' of God (Isaiah 62:1–6; Hosea 2:16) and the sufferings of the people to a 'woman with child' who 'cries out in her pangs' (Isaiah 26:17; Jeremiah 4:31—5:1; Micah 4:10). In fact, the book of Revelation describes the Church as the 'Bride' of Christ and as a new 'Jerusalem' (Revelation 19:7–8; 21:1–9). For these reasons, many interpreters conclude that the woman in John's vision is a symbol for Israel, or the Church, or both . . . In this case, the best explanation is not either/or but both/and. There are good reasons to conclude that the 'woman clothed with the sun' is *both an individual figure and a symbol for the Church*" (*Jesus and the Jewish Roots of Mary*, 31). Pitre points the reader not only to recent literature on this topic but also to Le Frois, *Woman Clothed with the Sun (Ap. 12)*.

Gregory of Palamas

St. Gregory Palamas does not hesitate to describe Mary as Queen. In his second homily on Mary's dormition (or assumption)—titled "On the Entry of the Mother of God into the Holy of Holies"—Palamas applies the title "Queen" to Mary. How does he arrive at this title?

His first step is to ponder Mary's motherhood. Utterly awestruck by what it is to be the mother of the divine Son incarnate, he makes clear that this unique motherhood elevates Mary in dignity over any other creature and indeed over all creation. He comments, "The whole Creation would fall short of offering her the glory that befits her, for she has become the mother of the Creator of all."[129] He tries to express the dignity that the creature Mary has, but, while fully recognizing that she is just a creature, he contends that words fall short in praising the dignity of being the Mother of God. He states, "How could any words of ours adequately express the great things done for her by her Son, even taking all of us together? Would our words not be as the tiniest drop of water compared with the inexpressible abyss of her glory?"[130] For Palamas, of course, Mary's motherhood is not something solely physical. To be mother of such a Son means to be a temple in which the incarnate Son dwells and therefore to be a supremely holy temple.[131] Mary's motherhood involves not just conception and giving birth but also virtue and holiness by God's grace.

At the outset of his homily, Palamas's favorite moniker for Mary—other than Mother of God—is "Bride." This is because of what Mary symbolizes when she enters body and soul into the holy of holies of the heavenly temple, just as her Son did. Palamas relies upon his audience to recall that Christ "entered once for all into the Holy Place, taking not the blood of goats and calves but his own blood, thus securing an eternal redemption" (Heb 9:12). When Christ secured this redemption, he inaugurated the marriage of God and his people. By calling Mary to join him body and soul after her death, Christ ensured the ongoing presence of his Church in union with him in the new creation. Just as many New Testament texts describe Christ as the Bridegroom and the Church as the Bride, so Mary stands in for the whole Church. Mary can do this, Palamas explains, because she is the exemplar

---

129. Palamas, "On the Entry of the Mother of God into the Holy of Holies II," 17.

130. Palamas, "On the Entry of the Mother of God into the Holy of Holies II," 17.

131. See the exegetical comments (on Luke 1) of Peeler, *Women and the Gender of God*, 74–75: "Zechariah [John the Baptist's father] had been given the privilege of entering the holy of holies; but now the presence in the holy of holies is poised to enter Mary herself."

and "sacred starting point" of the Church or "spiritual Israel."[132] In giving birth to her Son by God's power, "she made God the Son of man, and men the sons of God."[133]

Because Christ is the king of all creation, Mary is not only "Bride" (new Eve) but also "Queen of the entire Creation."[134] The one who bears in her womb the king of all creation—the king "through whom" (Heb 1:2) God created all things—must be creation's queen. Palamas describes the "signs of her rule."[135] She is not known by jewels, crowns, or royal clothes. Such signs of royal dignity are mere outward signs or substitutes for true dignity, which resides in the soul and which can only be manifested spiritually. Mary's signs of royal dignity or "tokens of her royal power" are "indescribable graces beyond our comprehension, abilities and energies surpassing nature and directed heavenwards."[136] Her royal dignity as queen comes from the Spirit of her Son, the Spirit in whose grace she partakes. As Palamas says, she receives "the coming of the divine Spirit, the overshadowing by the power of the Highest."[137] His reference here is to Luke 1:35, where the angel Gabriel foretells that Mary will conceive the Christ child when the Holy Spirit overshadows her. In Palamas's view, Mary's virginal conception and *virginitas in partu* already indicate her royal power as queen of creation, since her childbearing is extraordinary in every way.

Palamas goes on to cite Psalm 45:13–15, widely applied by Christians over the centuries to Mary: "The daughter of the king is decked in her chamber with gold-woven robes; in many-colored robes she is led to the king, with her virgin companions, her escort, in her train. With joy and gladness they are led along as they enter the palace of the king." Mary is the virginal queen of creation. From Mary, an inexpressibly (interiorly) beautiful woman, God created "an image sharing His divine nature"—namely, Christ.[138] Commenting on her "gold-woven robes," Palamas observes that her clothing is royal. Although royal, she is certainly not divine. Yet she stands higher than her fellow creatures, because of what God has done for her. In return, she shows her royal dignity by living for her fellow creatures in service to the Lord. In her childbearing and in her devotion, she participates decisively in the exaltation of the human race.

---

132. Palamas, "On the Entry of the Mother of God into the Holy of Holies II," 19.
133. Palamas, "On the Entry of the Mother of God into the Holy of Holies II," 19.
134. Palamas, "On the Entry of the Mother of God into the Holy of Holies II," 19.
135. Palamas, "On the Entry of the Mother of God into the Holy of Holies II," 19.
136. Palamas, "On the Entry of the Mother of God into the Holy of Holies II," 19.
137. Palamas, "On the Entry of the Mother of God into the Holy of Holies II," 19.
138. Palamas, "On the Entry of the Mother of God into the Holy of Holies II," 21.

Palamas praises God's gifts to her and her use of these gifts: "Partaking of higher honour, superior power and heavenly election, she became the highest Queen of all and the most blessed Sovereign of a blessed race, sending out all around her, from both body and soul, bright and holy rays of light."[139] She is queen because, by God's grace, she so perfectly reflects the rays of charity and humility that stream from her Son, the divine King. She is an icon of God's Light insofar as, by her natural and supernatural gifts, she shows what a human being who shares in the life of her Son can be. The marriage of God and his people has Mary as the supreme representative of those to whom the divine Son comes. Palamas states, "He [God] made her supremely lovely, uniting all the separate components with which He had adorned the universe, showing us an extraordinary aspect of that creative power which is exclusively His, as was truly fitting for the Mother of the Light."[140]

The Light, of course, is her Son—he is "the Sun, Who rose marvellously upon men from her."[141] Palamas shows that her Son is infinitely greater than she is. Yet, Mary is queen because her Son creates her and bestows such blessings upon her. Mary's queenship arises because, as Palamas says in praise of Mary, "you alone held mysteriously in your womb Him in Whom are the treasures of all these spiritual gifts, and became inexplicably His tabernacle."[142] God prepared Mary to be his earthly throne, to be his temple or tabernacle or ark in which he was to dwell; and thus Mary was prepared to be queen "with all the virtues appropriate to the great King."[143] Palamas states, "She was the Tabernacle in which He Who is seated above the whole Creation rested, the true King, the Lord of all rulers, Who is marvellously clad in the many-colored kingly robe woven from both created and uncreated natures."[144]

Much more could be said about Palamas's Mariology, but I hope to have made clear why he thinks Mary is queen in her earthly life and, even more fully, as the one who is assumed body and soul into heaven to be

139. Palamas, "On the Entry of the Mother of God into the Holy of Holies II," 21.

140. Palamas, "On the Entry of the Mother of God into the Holy of Holies II," 21.

141. Palamas, "On the Entry of the Mother of God into the Holy of Holies II," 22.

142. Palamas, "On the Entry of the Mother of God into the Holy of Holies II," 23. Palamas goes on to say, "This is why He Who adorned the lilies of the field more excellently than Solomon's royal attire (Matt. 6:28–29; Luke 12:27), also arrayed the Virgin, from Whom He would be clothed in human flesh, in this extraordinary fashion, making her admirable in the eyes of all, as she is the divine repository of every single noble and good attribute" (24).

143. Palamas, "On the Entry of the Mother of God into the Holy of Holies II," 25. For a similar perspective grounded in biblical exegesis, see Anderson, "Mariology."

144. Palamas, "On the Entry of the Mother of God into the Holy of Holies II," 25–26.

united with her Son, sharing in his throne—as, to varying degrees, all the blessed will do.

Hans Urs von Balthasar

Hans Urs von Balthasar, in his meditations on the rosary, also praises Mary's queenship. The angle that he takes is instructive, reflecting ecumenical sensitivity. Commenting on Mary's being crowned queen after being assumed body and soul into heaven, Balthasar advises that we should "look less at the Crowned than at the hand of the Crowner—the triune God himself."[145] What is Mary's glory, and what is her queenship? Fundamentally, says Balthasar, it is simply that the holy Trinity indwells her profoundly: this is what it means to be dignified or glorified in the order of salvation. In all that she is and does, the "crown" that is the Trinity makes himself manifest.

Mary's is a largely hidden life, even though, as Balthasar points out, we know more about her than about any other woman in Scripture. Mary reveals preeminently that God "has put down the mighty from their thrones, and exalted those of low degree" (Luke 1:52). Mary's absolute humility and self-surrender exhibit the truth about her Son and show us the path of following her Son. As queen, Mary "is raised up precisely as the lowly one."[146]

It may seem that the apostles knew Jesus better and did more work for him; surely their heavenly thrones will be higher than Mary's. Balthasar denies that this is the case. He observes that Mary "committed herself to the work of her Son—the Church—more deeply, earlier and more thoroughly than they."[147] Her *fiat* goes beyond any of the disciples' responses, and she was present at the incarnation and the cross, as well as at Pentecost. Mary stands before God as the representative of the whole Church (and all Israel), and she says yes on behalf of all. She is the embodiment of humility and absolute faith or surrender of self to God. Balthasar argues that her humility is, in the economy of salvation, true power. Because all followers of Jesus have Mary for their mother (John 19:27), Mary is a symbol of the Church—and all believers have the Church as their spiritual mother. Balthasar explains, "we receive all personal graces from God and Christ always as members of the holy Church—and, therefore, as children of Mary."[148] In this sense, Mary's mediation of grace is always present; and this is her "power" as queen, as she intercedes for the whole Church. Her intercession does not compete

---

145. Balthasar, *Threefold Garland*, 133.
146. Balthasar, *Threefold Garland*, 135.
147. Balthasar, *Threefold Garland*, 135.
148. Balthasar, *Threefold Garland*, 136.

with or stand on the same level as Christ's (Heb 7:25), but it participates preeminently in Christ's. As Balthasar says, "it is the King himself who is the almighty intercessor for sinners before the Father (Heb 8:6f; 1 Jn 2:1)"—but this means that the body of Christ participates in his work, so that in a certain sense "Christ and his Body, the holy Church, constitute one single principle of mediation."[149]

Balthasar emphasizes that the queen shares in the power of the King, a power that is merciful love. Otherwise, the impression could be given that Mary, the merciful queen, begs Christ the Judge to have mercy—as though Christ were stern and needed to be persuaded by his mother or by the Church to relent. No doubt, Christ is judge and possesses the fullness of power in a unique way, as befits his redemptive work and his status as the incarnate Lord. Balthasar emphasizes, however, that Christ "will never divide his function as Judge from his function as Redeemer," and so "Mary and the interceding Church will never take a position against him but will always stand on his side."[150]

As queen, Mary is preeminent among the communion of saints, but Balthasar notes that she belongs firmly within the communion of saints rather than occupying a separate, intermediate position. The saints commune in Christ, and they share the gifts of Christ with each other in the Spirit. Mary is unique among the saints because in her the creaturely reception of the gift and the will to share the gift are one. Balthasar states that "in Mary ... the correspondence between gift and self-giving, reception and thanksgiving attains perfection."[151]

God's power is not something that God hoards, even though only God is God. God's very life, his very power, is self-giving love. For Balthasar, as we have seen, Mary is queen because she is preeminent in her sharing in God's utterly humble love and his pouring out of himself for the good of the other. To be "full of grace" (Luke 1:28) is to be "capable of being fruitful along with the eternal fruitfulness of God"; the human person is meant to receive the self-surrender of God in Christ and to become a gift for others, by surrendering the self in turn for the good of others.[152] As Balthasar says, "Mary-the-Church keeps no grace for herself; she receives grace in order to transmit it."[153] Just as Christ's kingship is profoundly misunderstood if it is conceived along the lines of earthly power, so also Mary's queenship

---

149. Balthasar, *Threefold Garland*, 136.
150. Balthasar, *Threefold Garland*, 136.
151. Balthasar, *Threefold Garland*, 137.
152. Balthasar, *Threefold Garland*, 137.
153. Balthasar, *Threefold Garland*, 137.

consists not in earthly power but in her unique role and extraordinary configuration to her Son. Balthasar comments, "We are the children of Mary's fruitfulness, and her fruitfulness has been given her that she might receive and fulfill the fruitfulness of her Spouse," Jesus Christ.[154]

Balthasar sums up his perspective on Mary in light of Revelation 12. Recall that in Revelation 11:15, the seventh angel blows the trumpet and announces, "The kingdom of the world has become the kingdom of our Lord and of his Christ, and he shall reign for ever and ever." And in Revelation 12:5, we find that Mary (representing Israel) has brought forth "a male child, one who is to rule all the nations with a rod of iron"; and when Satan tries to destroy this Messianic child, the "child was caught up to God and to his throne." For Balthasar, if one reflects upon Revelation 12, one can perceive that the "fullness of Israel's faith was a particular human being called Mary, who bore the Messiah in the flesh and shared in experiencing and suffering his entire fate up to the crucifixion and being raised to the throne of God."[155]

In sum, through being raised up to the divine throne (deification), Mary presently shares as Queen Mother in her Son's royal-priestly intercession, without compromising the fact that he is the one Mediator. Jesus wills the participation of Mary and the Church in his power of love and mercy, through his Spirit.

Joseph de Aldama, SJ's Contributions

In his neo-scholastic treatise on Mariology, the Catholic theologian Joseph de Aldama draws upon a wide range of texts from Scripture and Tradition to reflect upon Mary's queenship. He first defines what he means by the term "queen." Metaphorically one can be called a "queen" if one is preeminent in a certain order of things; but properly "a woman is called a queen who either by herself, or by reason of her husband or of her son participates in the supreme dignity and power in a perfect society."[156] De Aldama thinks that Mary is both properly and metaphorically "queen," but he points out that we need to be very careful in asserting this point. The reason is that Mary is not queen in the same way that Jesus is King. Jesus, in the supernatural order, is

---

154. Balthasar, *Threefold Garland*, 137.

155. Balthasar, *Mary for Today*, 10. For much fuller discussions of Balthasar's Mariology, see Nepil, *Bride Adorned*, 97–152; and Leahy, *Marian Principle in the Ecclesiology of Hans Urs von Balthasar*. As Nepil says, "The hermeneutical key for unlocking von Balthasar on the relationship of Mary and the Church is the Marian act of *fiat*" (*Bride Adorned*, 101). For Balthasar on Revelation 12, see Nepil, *Bride Adorned*, 131–32.

156. De Aldama, "Mariology or On the Blessed Virgin Mary," 490.

"completely, properly, and absolutely" King; and he is the only King.[157] By comparison, Mary is queen only "in a limited and analogical way."[158] To acclaim Mary as queen of heaven is something that we Christians should do, but not if by so doing we are imagining Mary to be at the level of the divine King, the incarnate Lord and Savior.

De Aldama cites a number of councils and popes that identify Mary as "lady" or "queen"—a title that becomes much more frequent as the centuries progress. Pope Pius XI instituted a liturgical feast of Christ the King in 1925, and Pope Pius XII instituted a liturgical feast of Mary as queen in 1954. Scripturally, de Aldama contents himself with Luke 1:30–35, which makes clear that Mary's Son will be the divine Davidic king—and if so, then Mary, as the king's mother, is a queen. De Aldama finds that some of the church fathers call Mary not only mother of the Lord but also "mother of the king." Beginning with Andrew of Crete and including Germanus of Constantinople and John of Damascus, the Fathers call her "queen." The title of "lady" (meaning "queen") is employed by Ildephonsus of Toledo, who also employs "queen." Medieval doctors also named Mary "queen." De Aldama's list includes (among others) Anselm, Bernard, Bonaventure, and Albert the Great. In addition, he offers a brief accounting of Mary's queenship among the post-Tridentine theologians: Francisco Suárez, Alphonsus de Liguori, and others. He adds that the liturgies of both East and West hail Mary as "queen," as does the rosary.

The ground of Mary's queenship is her motherhood. In standard understandings of royalty, if the son is royal, then the son's mother shares in this royal dignity. But there is also the fact that Jesus is king especially in his redemptive work, and Mary participates uniquely in that redemptive work. Thus, Mary can also be called "queen" through her unique role in serving her Son's mission. Specifically, her Son is the new Adam and Mary cooperates with him as the new Eve.

One of the most important parts of de Aldama's treatment of Mary's queenship consists in his examination of the efforts of post-Tridentine theologians to develop more fully the theological understanding of Mary as queen. Various post-Tridentine theologians argued that Mary's queenship must involve executive, judicial, and legislative elements, just as Jesus' kingship demonstrably does. Other post-Tridentine theologians looked toward the relation of a queen to a king in an earthly court: the king is the supreme ruler, but the queen also has much power due to the fact that "by her requests and the amiableness of her person, she can influence the heart

---

157. De Aldama, "Mariology or On the Blessed Virgin Mary," 490.
158. De Aldama, "Mariology or On the Blessed Virgin Mary," 490.

and mind of the king for the benefit of his subjects."[159] On this view, Mary is queen because, as the mother of the king and as the new Eve, she is influential upon him in the distribution of graces. Still other post-Tridentine theologians held that Mary's queenship should be understood in terms of her matriarchal role in the family of Christ. She has a maternal royal power insofar as she acts "in favor of her children, by conferring supernatural perfection on them."[160]

Addressing these post-Tridentine perspectives, de Aldama rejects the first one—the notion that just as Christ's kingship involves executive, judicial, and legislative elements, so also must Mary's queenship. In his view, the fact that Mary is mother of God and new Eve (and therefore queen) implies nothing about a threefold queenly power. Similarly, de Aldama rejects the effort to understand Mary's queenship as that of a familial matriarch. His reason is that although Mary is both mother and queen, nevertheless the two are distinct concepts rather than co-defining. Mary's queenship cannot be explained simply in terms of her matriarchal role. For de Aldama, it is more fitting to probe the reality of Mary's queenship through reflecting on the ways in which an earthly queen influences an earthly king. Admittedly, Mary's queenship is only analogous in certain ways to earthly queenship, but Mary does possess a deep association with Christ the King.

As the mother of Christ the King, says de Aldama, Mary intrinsically has "a royal splendor and eminence that surpasses the excellence of all creatures."[161] Her unique relation to Christ ensures that she has the greatest possible dignity for a mere creature. Indeed, the dignity of all creation (including all other mere human beings) could not add up to a degree of dignity equivalent to being the mother of the Son of God. She is therefore rightly called queen of the world, and she has "a true, though subordinate, preeminence in the kingdom of Christ."[162] As the new Eve cooperating with the new Adam in his mission of redemption, she has a right (in the order of grace) to share in the dispensing of the "treasures of the kingdom" won by Christ with her cooperation.[163] In this sense, too, she is correctly hailed as queen. She is much more queen than is a queen of a mere earthly kingdom, just as Christ is much more King than is a king of a mere earthly kingdom. The greatness of her queenship stems from the fact that "she has a closer association with the King and so both possesses a great splendor and power

---

159. De Aldama, "Mariology or On the Blessed Virgin Mary," 494.
160. De Aldama, "Mariology or On the Blessed Virgin Mary," 494.
161. De Aldama, "Mariology or On the Blessed Virgin Mary," 495.
162. De Aldama, "Mariology or On the Blessed Virgin Mary," 495.
163. De Aldama, "Mariology or On the Blessed Virgin Mary," 495.

and exercises an influence on subjects that is more true and intimate."[164] Mere earthly queens are far less close to the will of their kings than Mary is to Jesus, since Mary's will is fully configured to that of Jesus; and mere earthly queens can have an influence regarding external things but cannot intercede in the interior order of grace.

VI. Conclusion

I began the present chapter with Ian McFarland's contention that, theologically and exegetically, Jesus is king preeminently in his cross, while being priest preeminently in his ascension. McFarland's position is echoed by numerous biblical scholars and theologians who perceive the ways in which the letter to the Hebrews emphasizes the ascended Lord's priestly intercession. Indeed, inspired by the Protestant biblical scholar L. Michael Morales, I have elsewhere explored Jesus' ascension as part of his priestly "ascension offering"—Jesus' burnt offering or total self-surrender, by which he ascends to God (and establishes the new creation) and by which he enables us to ascend to God.[165] This perspective, which correlates in important ways with Scheeben's understanding of sacrifice, emphasizes the priestly dimension of Jesus' Ascension. For Morales, the cross itself already embodies the priestly ascension offering that culminates in Jesus' sitting at the right hand of the Father.

Inspired by the Catholic theologian Douglas Farrow and by Brant Pitre, I have also previously reflected upon Jesus' ascension in light of the (priestly) sacrament of the Eucharist.[166] As Farrow says, "the eucharist is left behind [by Jesus] as a witness to the world of what actually happens in the ascension, namely, that the entire cosmos is fundamentally reordered to God in Christ."[167] Not surprisingly, Farrow's understanding of Jesus' Ascension is primarily priestly.[168] Farrow nonetheless insists upon Jesus'

164. De Aldama, "Mariology or On the Blessed Virgin Mary," 495. For further discussion of Mary's queenship, see Hauke, *Introduction to Mariology*, 295–301.

165. See Morales, *Who Shall Ascend the Mountain of the Lord?*, 135–36. For discussion see chapter 7 of my *Did Jesus Rise from the Dead?*.

166. See *Did Jesus Rise from the Dead?*, chapter 7.

167. Farrow, *Ascension Theology*, 65.

168. Farrow emphasizes that "the church becomes with Jesus a community of ascension and oblation, sharing in his heavenly offering to the Father, and manifesting the Spirit who reorganizes created reality around him" (*Ascension Theology*, 64). See also 122: "The ascension of Jesus Christ is an act of saving grace accomplished by the triune God. It is an act of Jesus the Son, who for our sake presents himself before the Father in his priestly role as offerer and offering. It is an act of the Father who receives Jesus, and so also receives us; and who also says to him, 'Sit here, while I make your enemies a footstool for your feet.' It is an act of the Holy Spirit, who places Jesus at

establishment, by his ascension, of the eschatological kingdom—the marriage of God and creation and the reconstitution of creation by the Holy Spirit. Farrow makes clear that this kingdom, in its inaugurated but not yet consummated form, is the Church visibly constituted on earth by Christ around Peter and the apostles.[169]

Thus, Jesus is always the priest-king, as indicated by the fusion of these roles in other Second Temple messianic texts. The Catholic theologian Robert Imbelli has pointed out, "The Ascension is not postscript but recapitulation: taking up the whole history of Christ into the eternal life of God."[170] When Christ ascends to the right hand of the Father, he is able to be present to all times and places in a way that he was not able to be during his earthly life. He is present liturgically in the Eucharist, and he is present by pouring out his Spirit so as to unite believers to himself in eucharistic love. He is present as priest, and it is his priestly "eternal self-offering" that is "enacted in time and space at every Eucharist."[171]

My point in this chapter has been that by ascending, Christ has entered fully into his royal reign; and, if we remain faithful, we "will reign together with him in his kingdom, even sharing his throne."[172] Recall John's vision of the ascended Christ in the book of Revelation, where John sees "one like a Son of man, clothed with a long robe and with a golden sash across his chest; . . . in his right hand he held seven stars, from his mouth issued a sharp two-edged sword, and his face was like the sun shining in full strength" (Rev 1:13, 16). *This* Christ promises the church at Thyatira that whoever holds fast and rejects immorality will receive "power over the nations . . . even as I myself have received power from my Father" (Rev 2:26–27). The point is that the kingdom of God has been inaugurated; Christ is now reigning, and

---

God's right hand by reorganizing all things around him, beginning with the church, which is the first and greatest consequence of his ascension and heavenly session. In all these ways the ascension is salvific, finishing what was begun in the baptism of Jesus, namely, the defeat of sin, the overthrow of Satan, the reconciliation of Israel to God, and the founding of a royal priesthood that is catholic in scope. But the ascension of Jesus Christ is also an act of perfecting grace, completing what was begun when the Spirit, who long ago brooded over the waters and brought forth life on earth, hovered over Mary, who brought forth a son. Not only does it fully erase the alienation between God and man introduced by the fall, it fully establishes the communion between God and man at which God was already aiming in the creation itself . . . The ascension . . . is atonement: the 'one-ing' of God and man that is the goal of the incarnation."

169. See Farrow, *Ascension Theology*, 47–49, 155–56 and elsewhere.
170. Imbelli, *Rekindling the Christic Imagination*, 48.
171. Imbelli, *Rekindling the Christic Imagination*, 49.
172. Jipp, *Messianic Theology of the New Testament*, 404.

we must obey him (and emulate his love) in order to reign with him in the power of his Spirit.

Commitment to the ascended Christ reigning as Lord even now is needed in order to endure the difficulties that believers face in the fallen world and as members of a Church that can too easily become "lukewarm" or even, in certain manifestations, "dead" (Rev 3:1, 15). It is Christ's ascension as King (the eucharistic King, whose path is the Cross) that enables his Spirit-guided Church to perdure under external and internal trial. Joshua Jipp comments, "Those who resist evil and actively pursue truth-telling, loyalty to Christ, and hope are promised the eschatological reward of vindication whereby, with their resurrected bodies, they will rule in Christ's kingdom where the powers of Satan, Sin, and Death have all been subjected to Christ's messianic kingship."[173] It is this reward and this rule that Mary has already received in a unique fashion and that the whole Church must yearn to receive in fullness.

With Mary queen of heaven, let us rejoice in God and his Messiah, of whose "kingdom there will be no end" (Luke 1:33). For we know in faith the truth of Mary's proclamation: "He has shown strength with his arm, he has scattered the proud in the imagination of their hearts, he has put down the mighty from their thrones, and exalted those of low degree" (Luke 1:33, 51–52).

---

173. Jipp, *Messianic Theology of the New Testament*, 404.

General Conclusion

Let me very briefly recapitulate the central arguments of my book—that is, the portrait of Jesus (and Mary) that I have set forth in conversation with theologians and biblical scholars. I began by taking up the issues surrounding the testimony in the Gospels of Matthew and Luke to the virgin birth. Not only can the infancy narratives be defended historically, along lines laid out especially well by Amy Peeler, but also the virgin birth is of crucial importance for understanding Christ's entrance into the world as the inauguration of the new creation. I also suggested that when theologians fail to pay attention to the virgin birth (and virginal conception), Christology loses its concreteness. Mary is necessary for a theology of the Incarnation that avoids Nestorianism and its offshoots. As the Congregation for Catholic Education remarked in a 1980 letter, attention to Mary serves as "a guarantee against everything which would tend to eradicate the historicity of the mystery of Christ."[1]

Second, I examined Jesus' teaching. In academic and even some ecclesiastical circles, it is not uncommon to run into descriptions of Jesus that reduce his teaching to a few challenging wisdom sayings and the illusory claim that the literal end of the world was about to happen. I argued that his teaching has far more content and far deeper truth than such portraits suppose. Not only did Jesus teach his own divinity, but also much of his teaching expresses a claim to divine and messianic authority. He taught about God, himself, his community of followers, the life of discipleship, salvation and eternal life, and much more. His words are authoritative and life-giving, and we should listen to and obey them.

Third, I examined Jesus' miracle-working. Drawing upon contemporary biblical scholars and Bonaventure, I sought to carve out a position between a biblical literalism that insists upon the historicity of every detail

---

1. Congregation for Catholic Education, *Circular Letter Concerning Some of the More Urgent Aspects of Spiritual Formation in Seminaries*, 619.

of every miracle story, on the one hand, and a Strauss-like skepticism about Jesus' supernatural miracle-working, on the other. Given the existence of the Creator God, the biblical testimony to Jesus' miracle-working is plausible. Jesus comes as the one who conquers the powers of sin and death, and his miracles reflect this divine authority and eschatological purpose.

Fourth, I investigated Jesus' cross. In accordance with much recent biblical scholarship, I presented the cross as a covenantal sacrifice, indeed, as the definitive new covenant sacrifice. I showed how this works in the Gospel of John, where the sealing of the Mosaic covenant in Exodus 24 may help make sense of the presence of Mary and the beloved disciple at the foot of the cross. I retrieved Matthias Joseph Scheeben's understanding of (covenantal) sacrifice, on the fiery altar of God, as inclusive of supreme love and sorrowful "satisfaction" for sin. In my view, understanding Jesus' cross as the new covenant sacrifice provides the best possibility of understanding the atonement in the way that Jesus himself, in fulfilling Israel's temple cult and the covenants of Israel in the midst of the crippling sins of Israel and the world,[2] likely understood it.

Fifth, I treated an aspect of Jesus' resurrection, namely, the nature of risen and glorified bodiliness. Jesus rose from the dead so that we, too, will rise with him in glory. There are a number of difficulties, however, with conceiving of an immortal bodiliness in which suffering is no more, and with understanding how bodies that have long since turned to dust can be raised (as distinct from God creating replicas of us). After comparing the Origenist and Augustinian lines of resurrection theology, I argued for a middle ground between accounts of glorified bodiliness that spiritualize away all sexed and tangible corporeality, on the one hand, and accounts of glorified bodiliness that insist upon the reconstitution of all the body's matter and all hair, fingernails, and organs, on the other. The glorified body is profoundly different from bodies in this-worldly time and space, but the glorified body is nevertheless intelligible as a risen human body, grounded in the continuity provided by the spiritual soul. I also highlight the relationship of the glorified body to the glorification of the cosmos and of the whole body of Christ.

Lastly, I inquired into whether the ascended Jesus not only intercedes in a priestly fashion for his people and for the salvation of the world, but also truly reigns even now in this world. I argued that the ascension should

---

2. See Eskola, *Theodicy and Predestination in Pauline Soteriology*, 311: "As regards the 'plight' of man, we have argued that it was precisely this concept which Paul *shared* with other Second Temple theologians. The general form of theology of that time was the theology of crisis. According to practically all theologians of that period, the plight of Israel was sin, because it was sin that brought the wrath of God on the people from one century to another."

primarily be understood as Jesus' royal enthronement at the right hand of the Father—even in the Letter to the Hebrews with its extensive priestly motifs. This reign should not be understood in terms of power exercised in a worldly way. Rather, Christ's reign in the Spirit involves the radiation in the world of the communion of cruciform love, a communion that may or may not, in particular instances, manifest itself in an increased justice of earthly societies. Martyrdom, after all, is a prime sign of Christ's reign.

Overall, my book contends that the apostolic witness to Jesus, prepared for by the centuries of God's relationship to his people Israel and by Israel's Scriptures (and by Second Temple Judaism), is in tune with the Church's dogmatic Christology. Jesus is the incarnate "Word [who] was with God, and . . . was God" (John 1:1); and "in him the fullness of God was pleased to dwell" (Col 1:19). He is the one "who baptizes with the Holy Spirit" (John 1:33) because he has the fullness of the Spirit and came into the world to bestow the Spirit.[3] He is the one who was born of a virgin who "was found to be with child of the Holy Spirit (Matt 1:18). He caused the crowds to be "astonished at his teaching, for he taught them as one who had authority" (Matt 7:28–29); and his authority is such that he could rightly say, "Every one then who hears these words of mine and does them will be like a wise man

---

3. In Thomistic terms: As the human nature of the person of the Word, the human nature of Christ receives the fullness of grace, and Christ can thereby act as man for our salvation. Of course, habitual grace is a created effect that is caused by the three persons acting as one. Yet the charity produced by habitual grace "terminates in and conforms the soul to the Holy Spirit himself," who proceeds distinctly as Love in the Trinity (Legge, *Trinitarian Christology*, 158). Legge adds, "the important thing is not to distinguish different actions belonging to different divine persons, but to distinguish the divine persons within the one divine action" (158). Legge directs attention here to no. 1775 (ch. 17, lect. 5) of Aquinas's *Commentary on the Gospel of John*, and to the discussion of this passage in Marshall, "What Does the Spirit Have to Do?," 69. As Legge says, "In eternity *and* in time, the Word proceeds from the Father, breathing forth Love" (*Trinitarian Christology*, 149). On the same page, he confirms this point with a marvelous passage, attributed by Aquinas to Athanasius, from *Contra errores Graecorum* II, c. 1: "Christ himself as God the Son sent the Spirit from above, and as man below he received the Spirit; from himself to himself, therefore, the Spirit dwells in his humanity from his divinity." Yet another summation along these lines by Legge deserves to be quoted for its clarity and insight: "When the Word is personally united to the human nature of Christ, that Word breathes forth or bursts Love—that is, the Word bestows the Holy Spirit on that human nature in the gift of habitual grace, which blossoms in wisdom and love, so that Christ knows and loves God perfectly in that nature and according to a properly human mode" (*Trinitarian Christology*, 152). The same conclusion is reached by Weinandy, *Jesus Becoming Jesus*, 1:20: "The Spirit resides within the humanity of Jesus, then, not as an anointing bestowed from without, but as an anointing that flows necessarily from within his coming to be and so existing as the incarnate Son."

who built his house upon the rock" (Matt 7:24).[4] He performed miraculous signs of the arrival of the new creation, so that "wherever he came, in villages, cities, or country, they laid the sick in the market places, and begged him that they might touch even the fringe of his garment; and as many as touched it were made well" (Mark 6:56). He is the sacrificial and priestly "Lamb of God, who takes away the sin of the world" (John 1:29). He is the risen one, "the first-born from the dead" (Col 1:18), the one whom the Seer of the book of Revelation describes in visionary language as having a "face . . . like the sun shining in full strength" (Rev 1:16). He is the glorious king of all creation, having established his people in justice and righteousness by his cross, presently "seated at the right hand of God" (Col 3:1) and pouring forth the Spirit of truth in preparation for the fullness of the new creation. He is the "Lamb who was slain" who receives divine worship (Rev 5:12–13).[5] He reigns not like an earthly king, but by the eucharistic power of self-sacrificial love, so that "grace . . . might reign through righteousness" (Rom 5:21) in those whom Christ royally configures to cruciform love by his Spirit.

The people of Israel, with whom God had made covenant and whose Scriptures testify to God's work of creation and covenantal redemption, were expecting a Redeemer; and a Redeemer came, establishing the promised new covenant and pouring out the promised Spirit. The wisdom of the Word turned out to be: "love one another as I have loved you" (John 15:12), which means nothing less than "Love your enemies and pray for those who persecute you" (Matt 5:44). The Spirit's outpouring has fueled charity and courage on the path of the cross: "For all who are led by the Spirit of God are sons of God. For you did not receive the spirit of slavery to fall back into fear, but you have received the spirit of sonship," which means that believers are "heirs of God and fellow heirs with Christ, provided we suffer with him in order that

---

4. For Matthew 7 on Jesus' authority or kingdom power, see Dalton, *Fulfilled Israel*, 71–73. As Dalton says, in this chapter "either Jesus evinces blasphemous audacity, or he is the most authoritative being on earth" (73).

5. For historical-critical discussion of this passage, see Bühner, *Messianic High Christology*, 123–42, with the background provided by Gallusz, *Throne Motif in the Book of Revelation*; Frey, "'Mystical' Traditions in an Apocalyptic Text?"; Hannah, "Throne of His Glory"; and Morton, *One upon the Throne and the Lamb*. Bühner comments, "the context of the Apocalypse of John reveals that the author considered withholding worship from other figures but the one God as crucial for monotheism. In Rev 19:10 and 22:8–9, we find in two instances aspects of a tradition within early Judaism that prohibited worship of angels. This is especially clear in Rev 19:10, where the seer falls down at the feet of the angel in order to worship him, but the angel replies, 'You must not do that! I am a fellow servant with you and your comrades who hold the testimony of Jesus. Worship God!' . . . Therefore . . . the worship of Christ as Lamb alongside God in Rev 4–5 is surely meant to depict Christ as belonging to the side of the one God" (*Messianic High Christology*, 130).

we may also be glorified with him" (Rom 8:14–15, 17). The beloved Father "put forward" his incarnate Son to bear the penalty of sin "as an expiation by his blood, to be received by faith" (Rom 3:25), and every follower of Christ must "take up his [or her] cross" and recognize that "whoever would save his life [rather than follow Christ] will lose it" (Matt 16:24–25).

The eschaton, or glorious kingdom, that the risen and ascended Christ has inaugurated is one whose governing wisdom is self-sacrificial charity. As Eugene Schlesinger puts it, summing up the theological vision of Henri de Lubac: "We are brought into salvation by Christ's sacrifice on the cross, which has charity as its inmost content. This charity informs the life of Christ's body, the church... His saving sacrifice is the fulcrum and meaning of history, and history's fulfillment will likewise be this same sacrifice, as the body of Christ is offered, in union with its head, to the Father as a supreme act of loving worship."[6]

At present, the Spirit within us impels us to yearn for the fulfillment of history, because sin and suffering continue and because we do not yet see God face to face. Paul says, "We know that the whole creation has been groaning with labor pains together until now; and not only the creation, but we ourselves, who have the first fruits of the Spirit, groan inwardly as we wait for adoption as sons, the redemption of our bodies. For in this hope we were saved" (Rom 8:22–24). In Colossians and many other places, the same note is sounded. Colossians 3:4 looks forward to the glorious consummation: "When Christ who is our life appears, then you also will appear with him in glory."[7] The yearning for God to set all things to rights, for the perfect peace and justice of the final consummation, appears in the vision of the Seer of the book of Revelation: "When he [the Lamb] opened the fifth seal, I saw under the altar the souls of those who had been slain for the word of God and for the witness they had borne; they cried out with a loud voice, 'O Sovereign Lord, holy and true, how long before you will judge and avenge our blood on those who dwell upon the earth?'" (Rev 6:9–10). Clearly, sin and death still run amuck everywhere. We yearn for the fullness of Christ's reign, for his coming in glory.

Even so, if our yearning is grounded in love, then we will already experience a taste of the reign of the ascended Christ. Insofar as we have faith, hope, and love, we will recognize that we have already "come to Mount Zion and to the city of the living God, the heavenly Jerusalem, and to innumerable angels in festal gathering, and to the assembly of the first-born who are

---

6. Schlesinger, *Salvation in Henri de Lubac*, 155.

7. For discussion, with reference to Psalm 110:1 (and in light of traditional Greco-Roman practices), see Burnett, *Christ's Enthronement at God's Right Hand and Its Greco-Roman Cultural Context*, chapter 6.

enrolled in heaven, and to the spirits of the just men made perfect, and to Jesus, the mediator of a new covenant" (Heb 12:22-24). Christ has already delivered his people, "who through fear of death were subject to lifelong bondage" (Heb 2:15). In the inaugurated kingdom of Christ, nourished by his sacraments, we already "live in him" and are "rooted and built up in him and established in the faith," so that we are "abounding in thanksgiving" (Col 2:6-7). We already experience what Paul calls "the riches of the glory of this mystery, which is Christ in you, the hope of glory" (Col 1:27). No wonder Paul commands, in the midst of serious suffering, "Rejoice in the Lord always; again I will say, Rejoice" (Phil 4:4); and no wonder Paul assures his flock that, if they remain constant in prayer, "the peace of God, which passes all understanding, will keep your hearts and your minds in Christ Jesus" (Phil 4:7).

The reign of the ascended Christ is the reign of the one who pours out his Spirit upon the inaugurated kingdom, a Spirit of mercy, love, justice, and humility. The Spirit builds up Christ's body the Church. Paul describes how this upbuilding operates: "Now there are varieties of gifts, but the same Spirit; and there are varieties of service, but the same Lord; and there are varieties of working, but it is the same God who inspires them all in every one. To each is given the manifestation of the Spirit for the common good" (1 Cor 12:4-7). Configured to Christ by the Spirit, believers make Christ manifest in the world. We "are a chosen race, a royal priesthood, a holy nation, God's own people, that you may declare the wonderful deeds of him who called you out of darkness into his marvelous light" (1 Pet 2:9).

Sadly, however, we Christians often fail to witness to Christ, despite the graces that we have been given. The New Testament does not describe an idealized Church. The above-quoted passage from 1 Peter continues, "Beloved, I beg you as aliens and exiles to abstain from the passions of the flesh that wage war against your soul" (1 Pet 2:11). In the second letter attributed to Peter, we read the dire warning, "But false prophets also arose among the people [Israel], just as there will be false teachers among you, who will secretly bring in destructive heresies, even denying the Master who bought them. . . . And many will follow their licentiousness, and because of them the way of truth will be reviled" (2 Pet 2:1-2). Paul issues a very similar warning in the book of Acts. He instructs the elders of the church in Ephesus, "Take heed to yourselves and to all the flock, in which the Holy Spirit has made you guardians, to feed the Church of the Lord which he obtained with his own blood. I know that after my departure fierce wolves will come in among you, not sparing the flock; and from among your own selves will arise men speaking perverse things, to draw away the disciples after them" (Acts 20:28-30).

Paul in Corinth finds himself struggling with boastful and licentious Christians who do not even believe in bodily resurrection, and Paul in Galatia finds himself struggling with Christians who do not recognize the covenantal fulfillment and reconfiguration that Christ has accomplished. Thus, the ascended Lord has inaugurated his kingdom and poured out his Spirit, but we may repudiate and undermine it. He has "all authority in heaven and on earth" (Matt 28:18), and yet we can turn away. We are only too often like those in Jesus' parable "who, when they hear the word, immediately receive it with joy," but "when tribulation or persecution arises"—or when encountering "the cares of the world, and the delight in riches, and the desire for other things"—soon turn away from Christ (Mark 4:16–17, 19).

The truth of Christology, then, is intimately bound up with the truth of the Church. In this Engaging the Doctrine series, ecclesiology is my next topic. Among those who have borne true testimony to Christ and embodied his Church, Mary is most blessed. Her words are true: "For behold, henceforth all generations will call me blessed; for he who is mighty has done great things for me, and holy is his name" (Luke 1:48–49). She makes manifest the inaugurated kingdom of her Son through the grace of the Holy Spirit; she is the Mother of God; she is the model of the Church in mediating her Son's saving work and in pondering of his mysteries; she stands in sorrow at the foot of the cross, sharing in the sealing of the new covenant as the representative of the new Israel; she is elevated by Christ the new Adam to reign as the new Eve in her glorified flesh. She is the virgin who conceived and bore a son (Matt 1:23); she is "full of grace" (Luke 28); she is the one who exemplified the hearer of the Word when she "kept all these things, pondering them in her heart" (Luke 2:19); she is the one who interceded at the miracle at Cana, saying, "Do whatever he tells you" (Luke 2:5); she is the new Eve, "woman," cooperating with the work of the new Adam (John 19:26–27); she is "the ark of his [God's] covenant" present in "God's temple in heaven" (Rev 11:19); she is the queen of creation, the "woman clothed with the sun, with the moon under her feet, and on her head a crown of twelve stars" (Rev 12:1). In all these ways, she is an eschatological sign of the inaugurated kingdom. She exemplifies the Spirit-filled reception in faith of the saving Lord. As the Catholic theologian John Nepil says, "No other person traversed the entire life of Christ—from conception to death, and from Resurrection to Ascension—his mother was there."[8]

In Jesus' eschatologically charged era, the people of Israel were awaiting the spectacular fulfillment of God's covenantal history with Israel. John the Baptist was "preaching a baptism of repentance for the forgiveness of

---

8. Nepil, *Bride Adorned*, 254–55.

sins" (Luke 3:3). The Qumran community was filled with eschatological expectation for a coming Messianic figure or figures who would renew temple and restore Israel. John the Baptist proclaimed of the coming Messiah, "he who is mightier than I is coming, the thong of whose sandals I am not worthy to untie; he will baptize you with the Holy Spirit and with fire. His winnowing fork is in his hand, to clear his threshing floor and to gather the wheat into his granary" (3:16–17). The Jewish people were in a state of apocalyptic fervor, imagining (after John's beheading) that Jesus might be John the Baptist risen from the dead or else might be Elijah or another one of the prophets (Luke 9:7–8). Jesus planned to undergo the eschatological tribulation or judgment for the sake of sinners, to renew the temple (and indeed to be the eschatological temple), to establish the new Passover and to be the new Passover Lamb, to lead his followers on the new exodus, and to constitute the new (messianic) Israel of God by calling his twelve disciples.

Of course, there is no way for a historian (qua historian) to know whether Jesus was the incarnate Lord, or whether Jesus was born of a virgin, or whether Jesus ascended to the right hand of the Father. That Jesus was crucified is a fact that is historically demonstrable; and converging reasons of probability, available to historians, point firmly toward the truth of Jesus' resurrection.[9] The works that Jesus did, his embodiment of supreme love on the cross, his teachings and miracles, his fulfillment of the covenants and promises of Israel, his priestly and prophetic and royal mission—all these tell in favor of the Church's testimony to the mysteries of Jesus.

In faith, Catholic believers affirm that God reveals himself in the two-testament Scripture as handed on in tradition. Scripture both contains a record of divine revelation and *is* divine revelation.[10] Scripture is Spirit-governed, and its handing on is guided faithfully (though not in a manner that excludes internal and external troubles!) by the Spirit in the community of Christ, the Church. Patrick Henry Reardon speaks aptly of "Holy Scripture ... as it is read, proclaimed, understood, chanted, and prayed-over *in the Church*. Holy Scripture is the text of a proclamation; it is the *Word*, spoken and listened to. It is not a mere book of record; it is God's living and dynamic Word."[11] Scriptural words and prophecies are employed by Jesus and the New Testament authors to make Jesus known, and so "the Bible not only

9. See my *Did Jesus Rise from the Dead?*

10. See Dauphinais, "Place of Christ and the Biblical Narrative," 3: "Aquinas has a thoroughly biblical and Christological theology of revelation. Christ communicates to his followers and to the Church the saving truth about God and his plan for the salvation of the human race. Furthermore, the Bible itself is both witness to and part of Christ's saving and revealing action. The full phenomenon of revelation as saving truth includes its communication and reception."

11. Reardon, *Reclaiming the Atonement*, 35.

records salvation history; it also transmits and creates salvation history," in the sense that the Bible "influences and directs the course of salvation history," including salvation history's unfolding in our own lives.[12]

Thus, Paul exhorts Timothy, "Follow the pattern of the sound words which you have heard from me, in the faith and love which are in Christ Jesus; guard the truth that has been entrusted to you by the Holy Spirit that dwells within us" (2 Tim 1:13-14). Paul perceives Christ in all the Scriptures, and he recognizes that the apostles and their successors are commissioned to guard this truth. Timothy knows "the Sacred Writings" (which we call the Old Testament) that instruct him "for salvation through faith in Christ Jesus"; and Paul reminds Timothy that "[a]ll Scripture is inspired by God and profitable for teaching, for reproof, for correction, and for training in righteousness" (2 Tim 3:15-16). Paul takes joy in "the revelation of the mystery which was kept secret for long ages but is now disclosed and through the prophetic writings is made known to all nations, according to the commandment of the eternal God, to bring about the obedience of faith" (Rom 16:25-26). This mystery and the obedience of faith continue to be powerfully present in our salvific encounters with the ascended Jesus today.

Christians know that God makes manifest the truth of the gospel in "the demonstration of the Spirit and power, that your faith might not rest in the wisdom of men but in the power of God" (1 Cor 2:4-5).[13] In the Spirit, the living Jesus makes himself personally present and known, in a wide variety of ways.[14] Paul testifies to the Corinthians that it is God himself "who has shone in our hearts to give the light of the knowledge of the glory of God in the face of Christ" (2 Cor 4:6).[15]

Let me end this book, then, with a simple confession of faith. Guided by the work of many biblical scholars and theologians, I have pondered the mysteries of Jesus Christ, in whom, with countless other believers across space and time, I place my hope. "For I am not ashamed of the gospel: it is the power of God for salvation to every one who has faith, to the Jew first and also to the Greek" (Rom 1:16).

---

12. Reardon, *Reclaiming the Atonement*, 35.

13. For historical-critical background, making connections to Daniel 2 and 7, see Perrin, *Jesus the Priest*, 252-55, with reference to various studies including Kwon, "Critical Review of Recent Scholarship."

14. See Johnson, *Living Jesus*, which emphasizes that "[t]he process of learning Jesus is *continuous* because Jesus, as a living person, continues to act and speak in the world through the Holy Spirit and through a variety of embodiments" (195).

15. For background, see chapter 7 of Griffiths, *Preaching in the New Testament*.

Bibliography

Ackerman, Susan. "The Queen Mother and the Cult in the Ancient Near East." In *Women and Goddess Traditions in Antiquity and Today*, edited by Karen L. King, 179–209. Minneapolis: Fortress, 1997.

Adams, Marilyn McCord. "The Resurrection of the Body according to Three Medieval Aristotelians: Thomas Aquinas, John Duns Scotus, William Ockham." *Philosophical Topics* 20 (1992) 1–33.

Ahearne-Kroll, Stephen P. *The Psalms of Lament in Mark's Passion: Jesus' Davidic Suffering*. Cambridge: Cambridge University Press, 2007.

Albert the Great. *On Resurrection*. Translated by Irven M. Resnick and Franklin T. Harkins. Washington, DC: Catholic University of America Press, 2020.

Alexander, Philip. "From Son of Adam to a Second God: Transformation of the Biblical Enoch." In *Biblical Figures Outside the Bible*, edited by M. E. Stone and T. A. Bergren, 102–11. Harrisburg, PA: Trinity, 1998.

Alfeche, Mamerto. "The Rising of the Dead in the Works of Augustine (1 Cor 15:35–57)." *Augustiniana* 39 (1989) 54–98.

Allen, Michael. *Grounded in Heaven: Recentering Christian Hope and Life on God*. Grand Rapids: Eerdmans, 2018.

Allison, Dale C., Jr. *Constructing Jesus: Memory, Imagination, and History*. Grand Rapids: Baker Academic, 2010.

———. "The Historians' Jesus and the Church." In *Seeking the Identity of Jesus: A Pilgrimage*, edited by Beverly Roberts Gaventa and Richard B. Hays, 79–95. Grand Rapids: Eerdmans, 2008.

———. *Jesus of Nazareth: Millenarian Prophet*. Minneapolis: Fortress, 1998.

———. "Memory, Methodology, and the Historical Jesus: A Response to Richard Bauckham." *Journal for the Study of the Historical Jesus* 14 (2016) 13–27.

———. *The New Moses: A Matthean Typology*. Minneapolis: Fortress, 1993.

———. *Night Comes: Death, Imagination, and the Last Things*. Grand Rapids: Eerdmans, 2016.

Alphonsus de Liguori. *The Glories of Mary*. Edited by Eugene Grimm. Brooklyn: Redemptorist Fathers, 1931.

Althaus-Reid, Marcella. *Queer God*. London: Routledge, 2003.

Anatolios, Khaled. *Deification through the Cross: An Eastern Catholic Theology of Salvation*. Grand Rapids: Eerdmans, 2020.

Anderson, Gary A. "Mariology: The Mother of God and the Temple." In *Christian Doctrine and the Old Testament: Theology in the Service of Biblical Exegesis*, 121–33. Grand Rapids: Baker Academic, 2017.

———. *Sin: A History*. New Haven: Yale University Press, 2009.
———. *That I May Dwell Among Them: Incarnation and Atonement in the Tabernacle Narrative*. Grand Rapids: Eerdmans, 2023.
Anderson, Pamela Sue. "Sacrifice as Self-destructive 'Love': Why Autonomy Should Still Matter to Feminists." In *Sacrifice and Modern Thought*, edited by Julia Meszaros and Johannes Zachhuber, 29–47. Oxford: Oxford University Press, 2013.
Anderson, Paul N. "John and Mark: The Bi-Optic Gospels." In *Jesus in Johannine Tradition*, edited by Robert T. Fortna and Tom Thatcher, 175–88. Louisville: Westminster John Knox, 2001,
Anderson, Ryan T. *When Harry Became Sally: Responding to the Transgender Moment*. New York: Encounter, 2019.
Andrew of Crete. "On the Dormition of Our Most Holy Lady, the Mother of God: Homily I." In *On the Dormition of Mary: Early Patristic Homilies*, translated by Brian E. Daley, SJ, 103–16. Crestwood, NY: St Vladimir's Seminary Press, 1998.
Angel, Joseph L. "Enoch, Jesus, and Priestly Tradition." In *Enoch and the Synoptic Gospels: Reminiscences, Allusions, Intertextuality*, edited by Loren T. Stuckenbruck and Gabriele Boccaccini, 285–316. Atlanta: SBL, 2016.
———. "The Liturgical-Eschatological Priest of the *Self-Glorification Hymn*." *Revue de Qumran* 96 (2010) 585–605.
———. *Otherworldly and Eschatological Priesthood in the Dead Sea Scrolls*. Leiden: Brill, 2010.
Annen, Franz. *Heil für die Heiden. Zur Bedeutung und Geschichte der Tradition vum besessenen Garasener (Mk 5, 1–20 parr.)*. Frankfurt: Knecht, 1976.
Appold, Mark L. *The Oneness Motif in the Fourth Gospel*. Tübingen: Mohr Siebeck, 1976.
Aquinas, Thomas. *Commentary on the Gospel of John: Chapters 1–5*. Translated by Fabian Larcher, OP and James Weisheipl, OP. Edited by Daniel Keating and Matthew Levering. Washington, DC: Catholic University of America Press, 2010.
———. *Commentary on the Gospel of John: Chapters 13–21*. Translated by Fabian Larcher, OP and James Weisheipl, OP. Edited by Daniel Keating and Matthew Levering. Washington, DC: Catholic University of America Press, 2010.
———. *Commentary on Isaiah*. Translated by Louis St. Hilaire. Green Bay, WI: Aquinas Institute, 2021.
———. *Commentary on the Letter of Saint Paul to the Hebrews*. Translated by Fabian Larcher, OP. Edited by J. Mortensen and E. Alarcón. Lander, WY: The Aquinas Institute for the Study of Sacred Doctrine, 2012.
———. *Light of Faith: The Compendium of Theology*, translated by Cyril Vollert, SJ. Manchester, NH: Sophia Institute Press, 1993.
———. *Summa theologiae*. Translated by the Fathers of the English Dominican Province. Westminster, MD: Christian Classics, 1981.
Aristotle. *Physics*. Translated by Robin Waterfield. Oxford: Oxford University Press, 2008.
Aron, Robert. *Jesus of Nazareth: The Hidden Years*. London: Morrow, 1962.
Aschim, Anders. "Melchizedek and Jesus: 11QMelchizedek and the Epistle to the Hebrews." In *The Jewish Roots of Christological Monotheism: Papers from the St. Andrews Conference on the Historical Origins of the Worship of Jesus*, edited by Carey C. Newman, et al., 129–47. Leiden: Brill, 1999.
Ashton, John. *Understanding the Fourth Gospel*. Oxford: Oxford University Press, 2007.

Aslan, Reza. *Zealot: The Life and Times of Jesus of Nazareth*. New York: Random House, 2013.
Assefa, Daniel. "Matthew's Day of Judgment in the Light of 1 Enoch." In *Enoch and the Synoptic Gospels: Reminiscences, Allusions, Intertextuality*, edited by Loren T. Stuckenbruck and Gabriele Boccaccini, 199–213. Atlanta: SBL, 2016.
Athanasius. *On the Incarnation*. Translated and edited by a Religious of CSMV. Crestwood, NY: St Vladimir's Seminary Press, 1993.
Atkinson, Kenneth. "The Gabriel Revelation (Hazon Gabriel): A Reused Masseba Forgery?" *Qumran Chronicle* 26 (2018) 113–27.
Attridge, Harold W. "The Cubist Principle in Johannine Imagery: John and the Reading of Images in Contemporary Platonism." In *Essays on John and Hebrews*, 79–91. Grand Rapids: Baker Academic, 2012.
———. "'Don't Be Touching Me': Recent Feminist Scholarship on Mary Magdalene." In *Essays on John and Hebrews*, 137–59. Grand Rapids: Baker Academic, 2012.
———. *The Epistle to the Hebrews*. Minneapolis: Fortress, 1989.
———. "From Discord Rises Meaning: Resurrection Motifs in the Fourth Gospel." In *Essays on John and Hebrews*, 160–76. Grand Rapids: Baker Academic, 2012.
———. "Genre Bending in the Fourth Gospel." In *Essays on John and Hebrews*, 61–78. Grand Rapids: Baker Academic, 2012.
———. "Giving Voice to Jesus: Use of the Psalms in the New Testament." In *Essays on John and Hebrews*, 320–30. Grand Rapids: Baker Academic, 2012.
———. "'Heard Because of His Reverence' (Heb 5:7)." In *Essays on John and Hebrews*, 268–80. Grand Rapids: Baker Academic, 2012.
———. "'Let Us Strive to Enter That Rest': The Logic of Hebrews 4:1–11." In *Essays on John and Hebrews*, 260–67. Grand Rapids: Baker Academic, 2012.
———. "Philo and John: Two Riffs on One Logos." In *Essays on John and Hebrews*, 46–59. Grand Rapids: Baker Academic, 2012.
Augustine. *City of God*. Translated by Henry Bettenson. New York: Penguin, 1984.
———. *Homilies on the Gospel of John 41–124*. Translated by Edmund Hill, OP, edited by Allan D. Fitzgerald, OSA. Hyde Park, NY: New City, 2020.
———. *Enchiridion on Faith, Hope, and Charity*. Translated by Bernard M. Peebles. In vol. 2 of *The Fathers of the Church*, 369–472. New York: Fathers of the Church, 1947.
———. *The Trinity*. Translated by Edmund Hill, OP. Brooklyn: New City, 1991.
Augustine, David L. "Atonement, Cross, and Heavenly Sacrifice: Matthias Scheeben and David Moffitt in Dialogue." In *Engaging Catholic Doctrine: Essays in Honor of Matthew Levering*, edited by Robert Barron, et al., 275–327. Steubenville, OH: Emmaus Academic, 2023.
———. "Christ and the Altar Fire: Sacrifice as Deification in the Theology of Matthias Scheeben." PhD diss., Catholic University of America, 2021.
———. "Two Paradigms on the Eucharist as Sacrifice: Scheeben and Journet in Dialogue." *Nova et Vetera* 16 (2018) 401–37.
Aune, David E. "Historical Jesus Traditions in Hebrews." In *The Figure of Jesus in History and Theology: Essays in Honor of John Meier*, edited by Vincent T. M. Skemp and Kelley Coblentz Bautch, 223–43. Washington, DC: Catholic Biblical Association of America, 2020.
———. *Prophecy in Early Christianity and the Ancient Mediterranean World*. Grand Rapids: Eerdmans, 1983.
———. *Revelation*. 3 vols. Nashville: Thomas Nelson, 1998.

Austin, Michael. "The Hypocritical Son." *Evangelical Quarterly* 57 (1985) 307–15.
Balthasar, Hans Urs von. *Mary for Today*. Translated by Robert Nowell. San Francisco: Ignatius, 1988.
———. *Seeing the Form*. Vol. 1 of *The Glory of the Lord: A Theological Aesthetics*. Translated by Erasmo Leiva-Merikakis. Edited by Joseph Fessio, SJ, and John Riches. San Francisco: Ignatius, 1982.
———. *Theo-Drama: Theological Dramatic Theory*. Vol. 3, *The Dramatis Personae: The Person in Christ*. Translated by Graham Harrison. San Francisco: Ignatius, 1992.
———. *Theo-Drama: Theological Dramatic Theory*. Vol. 4, *The Action*. Translated by Graham Harrison. San Francisco: Ignatius, 1994.
———. *The Threefold Garland: The World's Salvation in Mary's Prayer*. Translated by Erasmo Leiva-Merikakis. San Francisco: Ignatius, 1982.
Banks, Robert. *Jesus and the Law in the Synoptic Tradition*. Cambridge: Cambridge University Press, 1975.
Barber, Michael Patrick. *The Historical Jesus and the Temple: Memory, Methodology, and the Gospel of Matthew*. Cambridge: Cambridge University Press, 2023.
———. "Jesus as the Living Temple Builder and Peter's Priestly Role in Matt 16:16–19." *Journal of Biblical Literature* 132 (2013) 935–53.
———. "The New Temple, the New Priesthood, and the New Cult in Luke-Acts." *Letter and Spirit* 8 (2013) 101–24.
———. *Salvation: What Every Catholic Should Know*. Denver: Augustine Institute, 2019.
Barclay, John M. G. *Paul and the Gift*. Grand Rapids: Eerdmans, 2015.
Barker, Margaret. *The Great Angel: A Study of Israel's Second God*. Louisville: Westminster John Knox, 1992.
Barnard, Jody A. *The Mysticism of Hebrews: Exploring the Role of Jewish Apocalyptic Mysticism in the Epistle to the Hebrews*. Tübingen: Mohr Siebeck, 2012.
Barnes, Corey L. *Christ's Two Wills in Scholastic Thought: The Christology of Aquinas and Its Historical Contexts*. Toronto: Pontifical Institute of Mediaeval Studies, 2012.
Barron, Robert. *And Now I See . . . : A Theology of Transformation*. New York: Crossroad, 1998.
———. *Eucharist*. Maryknoll, NY: Orbis, 2008.
———. *Light from Light: A Theological Reflection on the Nicene Creed*. Park Ridge, IL: Word on Fire Academic, 2021.
———. *The Priority of Christ: Toward a Postliberal Catholicism*. Grand Rapids: Brazos, 2007.
———. *2 Samuel*. Grand Rapids: Brazos, 2015.
Barrow, John, and Frank Tipler. *The Anthropic Cosmological Principle*. Oxford: Oxford University Press, 1986.
Barry, Richard J., IV. *Jewish Temple Theology and the Mystery of the Cross: Atonement and the Two Goats of Yom Kippur*. Washington, DC: Catholic University of America Press, 2023.
Barth, Karl. *Church Dogmatics*. 4 vols. Edited by G. W. Bromiley and T. F. Torrance. Translated by G. W. Bromiley, et al. Edinburgh: T. & T. Clark, 1936–1975.
———. *Dogmatics in Outline*. Translated by G. T. Thomson. London: SCM, 1955.
Barton, Stephen C. *Discipleship and Family Ties in Mark and Matthew*. Cambridge: Cambridge University Press, 1994.

Bastero, Juan Luis. "La *Virginitas in Partu* en la Reflexión Teológica del Siglo XX." *Scripta Theologica* 32 (2000) 835–62.

Bates, Matthew. *The Birth of the Trinity*. Oxford: Oxford University Press, 2016.

Bauckham, Richard. "Biblical Theology and the Problems of Monotheism." In *Jesus and the God of Israel: God Crucified and Other Studies on the New Testament's Christology of Divine Identity*, 60–106. Grand Rapids: Eerdmans, 2008.

———. "Confessing the Cosmic Christ (1 Corinthians 8:6 and Colossians 1:15–20)." In *Monotheism and Christology in Greco-Roman Antiquity*, edited by Matthew V. Novenson, 139–71. Leiden: Brill, 2020.

———. "The Divinity of Jesus in the Letter to the Hebrews." In *Jesus and the God of Israel: God Crucified and Other Studies on the New Testament's Christology of Divine Identity*, 233–53. Grand Rapids: Eerdmans, 2008.

———. "The Family of Jesus." In *Jesus among Friends and Enemies: A Historical and Literary Introduction to Jesus in the Gospels*, edited by Chris Keith and Larry W. Hurtado, 103–25. Grand Rapids: Baker Academic, 2011.

———. "The General and the Particular in Memory: A Critique of Dale Allison's Approach to the Historical Jesus." *Journal for the Study of the Historical Jesus* 14 (2016) 28–51.

———. "God Crucified." In *Jesus and the God of Israel: God Crucified and Other Studies on the New Testament's Christology of Divine Identity*, 1–59. Grand Rapids: Eerdmans, 2008.

———. *Gospel Women: Studies of the Named Women in the Gospels*. Grand Rapids: Eerdmans, 2002.

———. *Jesus and the Eyewitnesses: The Gospels as Eyewitness Testimony*. 2nd ed. Grand Rapids: Eerdmans, 2017.

———. *Jesus and the God of Israel: God Crucified and Other Studies on the New Testament's Christology of Divine Identity*. Grand Rapids: Eerdmans, 2008.

———. *Jude and the Relatives of Jesus in the Early Church*. Edinburgh: T. & T. Clark, 1990.

———. "Monotheism and Christology in Hebrews 1." In *Early Jewish and Christian Monotheism*, edited by Loren T. Stuckenbruck and Wendy E. S. North, 167–85. London: T. & T. Clark, 2004.

———. "Sacraments and the Gospel of John." In *The Oxford Handbook of Sacramental Theology*, edited by Hans Boersma and Matthew Levering, 82–96. Oxford: Oxford University Press, 2015.

———. "The Scrupulous Priest and the Good Samaritan: Jesus' Parabolic Interpretation of the Law of Moses." *New Testament Studies* 44 (1998) 475–89.

———. *The Testimony of the Beloved Disciple: Narrative, History, and Theology in the Gospel of John*. Grand Rapids: Baker Academic, 2007.

———. "The Throne of God and the Worship of Jesus." In *Jesus and the God of Israel: God Crucified and Other Studies on the New Testament's Christology of Divine Identity*, 152–81. Grand Rapids: Eerdmans, 2008.

———. *Who Is God? Key Moments of Biblical Revelation*. Grand Rapids: Baker Academic, 2020.

Bauer, Walter. *Orthodoxy and Heresy in Earliest Christianity*. Edited by Robert A. Kraft and Gerhard Krodel. Philadelphia: Fortress, 1971.

Beale, G. K. *The Temple and the Church's Mission: A Biblical Theology of the Dwelling Place of God*. Downers Grove, IL: InterVarsity, 2004.

Beasley-Murray, George Raymond. *Jesus and the Kingdom of God*. Grand Rapids: Eerdmans, 1986.
Becker, Eve-Marie, Helen K. Bond, and Catrin H. Williams, eds. *John's Transformation of Mark*. London: T. & T. Clark, 2021.
Beers, Holly. *The Followers of Jesus as the 'Servant': Luke's Model from Isaiah for the Disciples in Luke-Acts*. London: Bloomsbury, 2015.
Begasse de Dhaem, Amaury, SJ. *Mysterium Christi: Cristologia e soteriologia trinitaria*. 2nd ed. Assisi: Cittadella Editrice, 2022.
Behr, John. *Becoming Human: Meditations on Christian Anthropology in Word and Image*. Crestwood, NY: St Vladimir's Seminary Press, 2013.
———. *John the Theologian and His Paschal Gospel: A Prologue to Theology*. Oxford: Oxford University Press, 2019.
———. *The Mystery of Christ: Life in Death*. Crestwood, NY: St Vladimir's Seminary Press, 2006.
Behr-Sigel, Elisabeth. *The Ministry of Women in the Church*. Translated by Steven Bigham. Crestwood, NY: St Vladimir's Seminary Press, 1991.
Beiser, Frederick C. *David Friedrich Strauß, Father of Unbelief: An Intellectual Biography*. Oxford: Oxford University Press, 2020.
———. *The German Historicist Tradition*. Oxford: Oxford University Press, 2011.
Benedict XVI. "May 11, 2007 Homily at the Canonization of Frei Antônio Galvão." https://www.vatican.va/content/benedict-xvi/pt/homilies/2007/documents/hf_ben-xvi_hom_20070511_canonization-brazil.html.
Bergsma, John. "Cultic Kingdoms in Conflict: Liturgy and Empire in the Book of Daniel." *Letter and Spirit* 5 (2009) 47–83.
———. *Jesus and the Dead Sea Scrolls: Revealing the Jewish Roots of Christianity*. New York: Random House, 2019.
Bernard of Clairvaux. "Sermon for the Sunday within the Octave of the Assumption." In *St Bernard's Sermons on the Blessed Virgin Mary*. Translated by A Priest of Mount Melleray, 206–7. Chumleigh: Augustine, 1984.
Bernard, David K. *The Glory of God in the Face of Jesus Christ: Deification of Jesus in Early Christian Discourse*. Blandford Forum, UK: Deo, 2016.
Bernier, Jonathan. *The Quest for the Historical Jesus after the Demise of Authenticity: Toward a Critical Realist Philosophy of History in Jesus Studies*. London: Bloomsbury, 2016.
Betz, Otto. "Was John the Baptist an Essene?" In *Understanding the Dead Sea Scrolls: A Reader from the Biblical Archeology Review*, edited by Hershel Shanks, 205–14. New York: Random House, 1992.
Billings, Bradly S. *Do This in Remembrance of Me: The Disputed Words in the Lukan Institution Narrative (Luke 22:19b–20): An Historico-Exegetical, Theological and Sociological Analysis*. London: T. & T. Clark, 2006.
Bingemer, Maria Clara, et al. "Editorial: What Is at Stake in Christology." In *Jesus as Christ: What Is at Stake in Christology?*, edited by Andrés Torres Queiruga et al., 7–10. *Concilium* 2008/3. London: SCM, 2008.
Bird, Michael F. *Are You the One Who Is to Come? The Historical Jesus and the Messianic Question*. Grand Rapids: Baker Academic, 2009.
Bird, Michael, ed. *How God Became Jesus*. Grand Rapids: Zondervan, 2014.
Bird, Michael F., and Joel Willitts, eds. *Paul and the Gospels: Christologies, Conflicts and Convergences*. London: T. & T. Clark, 2011.

Biviano, Erin Lothes. *The Paradox of Christian Sacrifice: The Loss of Self, the Gift of Self.* New York: Crossroad, 2007.

Blinzler, Josef. *Die Brüder und Schwestern Jesu.* Stuttgart: Katholisches Bibelwerk, 1967.

Boccaccini, Gabriele. "From Jewish Prophet to Jewish God." In *Reading the Gospel of John's Christology as Jewish Messianism: Royal, Prophetic, and Divine Messiahs*, edited by Benjamin Reynolds and Gabriele Boccaccini, 335–57. Leiden: Brill, 2018.

———. "How Jesus Became Uncreated." In *Sibyls, Scriptures, and Scrolls: John Collins at Seventy*, vol. 1, edited by Joel S. Baden et al., 185–208. Leiden: Brill, 2017.

———. "Jesus the Messiah: Man, Angel, or God? The Jewish Roots of Early Christianity." *Annali di Scienza Religiose* 4 (2011) 193–220.

Boccaccini, Gabriele, ed. *Enoch and the Messiah Son of Man: Revisiting the Book of Parables.* Grand Rapids: Eerdmans, 2007.

Bockmuehl, Markus. "God's Life as a Jew: Remembering the Son of God as Son of David." In *Seeking the Identity of Jesus: A Pilgrimage*, edited by Beverly Roberts Gaventa and Richard B. Hays, 60–78. Grand Rapids: Eerdmans, 2008.

———. *This Jesus: Martyr, Lord, Messiah.* Edinburgh: T. & T. Clark, 1994.

———. "Reno Contra Mundum." https://www.firstthings.com/article/2023/05/reno-contra-mundum.

Boersma, Hans. *Embodiment and Virtue in Gregory of Nyssa: An Anagogical Approach.* Oxford: Oxford University Press, 2013.

———. *Five Things Theologians Wish Biblical Scholars Knew.* Downers Grove, IL: IVP Academic, 2021.

———. "Sacramental Interpretation: On the Need for Theological Grounding of Narratival History." In *Exile: A Conversation with N. T. Wright*, edited by James M. Scott, 255–72. Downers Grove, IL: IVP Academic, 2017.

———. "Violence, the Cross, and Divine Intentionality: A Modified Reformed View." In *Atonement and Violence: A Theological Conversation*, edited by John Sanders, 47–69. Nashville: Abingdon, 2006.

———. *Violence, Hospitality, and the Cross: Reappropriating the Atonement Tradition.* Grand Rapids: Baker Academic, 2004.

Boff, Leonardo. *The Maternal Face of God: The Feminine and Its Religious Expressions.* London: Collins, 1989.

Boismard, Marie-Émile, OP. *Moses or Jesus: An Essay in Johannine Christology.* Translated by Benedict T. Viviano, OP. Minneapolis: Fortress, 1993.

Bolt, Peter G. *The Cross at a Distance: Atonement in Mark's Gospel.* Downers Grove, IL: InterVarsity, 2004.

———. *Jesus' Defeat of Death: Persuading Mark's Early Readers.* Cambridge: Cambridge University Press, 2003.

Bonaventure. *Commentary on the Gospel of Luke: Chapters 1–8.* Translated by Robert J. Karris, OFM. Saint Bonaventure, NY: Franciscan Institute Publications, 2001.

Bond, Helen K. *The First Biography of Jesus: Genre and Meaning in Mark's Gospel.* Grand Rapids: Eerdmans, 2020.

———. "The Triumph of the King: John's Transformation of Mark's Account of the Passion." In *John's Transformation of Mark*, edited by Eve-Marie Becker et al., 251–67. London: T. & T. Clark, 2021.

Bonino, Serge-Thomas, OP. *Angels and Demons: A Catholic Introduction.* Washington, DC: Catholic University of America Press, 2016.

———. *Reading the Song of Songs with St. Thomas Aquinas*. Translated by Andrew Levering with Matthew Levering. Washington, DC: Catholic University of America Press, 2023.

The Book of Enoch. In *The Old Testament Pseudepigrapha*. Vol. 1, *Apocalyptic Literature and Testaments*, edited by James H. Charlesworth, 13–89. New Haven: Yale University Press, 1983.

Borg, Marcus J. *The Heart of Christianity: Rediscovering a Life of Faith*. New York: HarperCollins, 2003.

———. *Meeting Jesus Again for the First Time: The Historical Jesus and the Heart of Contemporary Faith*. New York: HarperOne, 1994.

———. "Was Jesus God?" In *The Meaning of Jesus: Two Visions*, edited by Marcus Borg and N. T. Wright, 145–56. San Francisco: HarperSanFrancisco, 1999.

Borgman, Erik. "Opening up New History: *Jesus of Nazareth* as the Beginning of a New History." In *Jesus as Christ: What Is at Stake in Christology?*, edited by Andrés Torres Queiruga et al., 64–72. *Concilium* 2008/3. London: SCM, 2008.

Börresen, Kari Elisabeth. "Augustin, interprète du dogme de la resurrection: Quelques aspects de son anthropologie dualiste." *Studia Theologica* 23 (1969) 141–55.

Boss, Sarah Jane. *Empress and Handmaid: Nature and Gender in the Cult of the Virgin Mary*. London: Cassell, 2000.

———. "Original Holiness: The Blessed Virgin Mary in the Catholic Theology of Nineteenth-Century Europe." In *The Oxford Handbook of Mary*, edited by Chris Maunder, 486–502. Oxford: Oxford University Press, 2019.

Botner, Max. *Jesus Christ as the Son of David in the Gospel of Mark*. Cambridge: Cambridge University Press, 2019.

Bougerol, J. G. "Bonaventure as Exegete." In *A Companion to Bonaventure*, edited by J. M. Hammond, J. A. W. Hellmann, and J. Goff, 167–88. Leiden: Brill, 2014.

Bouyer, Louis. *The Church of God: Body of Christ and Temple of the Spirit*. Translated by Charles Underhill Quinn. San Francisco: Ignatius, 2011.

———. *Le consolateur: Esprit-Saint et vie de grâce*. Paris: Cerf, 1980.

———. *Le Fils éternel*. Paris: Cerf 1974.

———. *The Meaning of Monastic Life*. Translated by Kathleen Pond. London: Burns & Oates, 1955.

———. *The Seat of Wisdom: An Essay on the Place of the Virgin Mary in Christian Theology*. Translated by A. V. Littledale. New York: Pantheon, 1962.

Boyarin, Daniel. "Beyond Judaisms: Metatron and the Divine Polymorphy of Ancient Judaism." *Journal for the Study of Judaism in the Persian, Hellenistic and Roman Period* 41 (2010) 323–65.

———. *The Jewish Gospels: The Story of the Jewish Christ*. New York: The New Press, 2012.

———. "A Jewish Reader of Jesus: Mark, the Evangelist." In *Jesus Among the Jews: Representation and Thought*, edited by Neta Stahl, 6–17. London: Routledge, 2012.

———. "Is Metatron a Converted Christian?" *Judaïsme Ancien—Ancient Judaism* 1 (2013) 13–62.

Boxall, Ian. "From the Apocalypse to the Johannine 'Apocalypse in Reverse': Intimations of Apocalyptic and the Quest for a Relationship." In *John's Gospel and Intimations of Apocalyptic*, edited by Catrin H. Williams and Christopher Rowland, 58–78. London: T. & T. Clark, 2013.

Braine, David. "The Virgin Mary in the Christian Faith: The Development of the Church's Teaching on the Virgin Mary in Modern Perspective." *Nova et Vetera* 7 (2009) 877–940.

Brendsel, Daniel J. *"Isaiah Saw His Glory": The Use of Isaiah 52–53 in John 12.* Berlin: De Gruyter, 2014.

Brock, Rita N., and Rebecca Ann Parker. *Saving Paradise: How Christianity Traded Love of This World for Crucifixion and Empire.* Boston: Beacon, 2008.

Brooke, George J. "4QTestament of Levid(?) and the Messianic Servant High Priest." In *From Jesus to John: Essays on Jesus and New Testament Christology in Honour of Marinus de Jonge*, edited by Martinus C. De Boer, 83–100. Sheffield: Sheffield Academic, 1993.

Brotherton, Joshua R. *One of the Trinity Has Suffered: Balthasar's Theology of Divine Suffering in Dialogue.* Steubenville, OH: Emmaus Academic, 2020.

Brown, David. "Human Sacrifice and Two Imaginative Worlds, Aztec and Christian: Finding God in Evil." In *Sacrifice and Modern Thought*, edited by Julia Meszaros and Johannes Zachhuber, 180–96. Oxford: Oxford University Press, 2013.

Brown, Joshua R. *Balthasar in Light of Early Confucianism.* Notre Dame: University of Notre Dame Press, 2020.

Brown, Montague. "Aquinas on the Resurrection of the Body." *The Thomist* 56 (1992) 165–207.

Brown, Raymond E., SS. *The Birth of the Messiah: A Commentary on the Infancy Narratives in the Gospels of Matthew and Luke.* 2nd ed. New York: Doubleday, 1993.

———. *A Coming Christ in Advent: Essays on the Gospel Narratives Preparing for the Birth of Jesus. Matthew 1 and Luke 1.* Collegeville, MN: Liturgical, 1988.

———. *The Community of the Beloved Disciple.* New York: Paulist, 1979.

———. *The Death of the Messiah: From Gethsemane to the Grave: A Commentary on the Passion Narratives in the Four Gospels.* 2 vols. New York: Doubleday, 1994.

———. *The Gospel According to John (i–xii): Introduction, Translation, and Notes.* Garden City, NY: Doubleday, 1966.

———. *The Gospel According to John (xiii–xxi): Introduction, Translation, and Notes.* Garden City, NY: Doubleday, 1970.

———. *The Virginal Conception and Bodily Resurrection of Jesus.* New York: Paulist, 1973.

Brown, Raymond E., et al., eds. *Mary in the New Testament.* Philadelphia: Fortress, 1978.

Brown, Sherri. "'Follow Me': The Mandate for Mission in the Gospel of John." In *Cruciform Scripture: Cross, Participation, and Mission*, edited by Christopher W. Skinner et al., 163–83. Grand Rapids: Eerdmans, 2021.

———. *Gift upon Gift: Covenant through Word in the Gospel of John.* Eugene, OR: Pickwick, 2010.

———. *God's Promise: Covenant Relationship in John.* New York/Mahwah, NJ: Paulist, 2014.

Brown, Sherri, and Christopher W. Skinner, eds. *Johannine Ethics: The Moral World of the Gospel and Letters of John.* Minneapolis: Fortress, 2017.

Brunner, Emil. *The Mediator: A Study of the Central Doctrine of the Christian Faith.* Translated by Olive Wynn. Philadelphia: Westminster, 1947.

Bryan, Steven M. "Jesus and Israel's Eschatological Constitution." In *Handbook for the Study of the Historical Jesus*, edited by Tom Holmén and Stanley E. Porter, 3:2833–853. Leiden: Brill, 2010.

———. *Jesus and Israel's Traditions of Judgement and Restoration*. Cambridge: Cambridge University Press, 2002.

Buckwalter, H. Douglas. *The Character and Purpose of Luke's Christology*. Cambridge: Cambridge University Press, 1996.

Bühner, Ruben A. *Messianic High Christology: New Testament Variants of Second Temple Judaism*. Waco, TX: Baylor University Press, 2021.

Bulgakov, Sergius. *The Bride of the Lamb*. Translated by Boris Jakim. Grand Rapids: Eerdmans, 2002.

———. *The Burning Bush: On the Orthodox Veneration of the Mother of God*. Translated and Edited by Thomas Allan Smith. Grand Rapids: Eerdmans, 2009.

Bullard, Collin Blake. *Jesus and the Thoughts of Many Hearts: Implicit Christology and Jesus' Knowledge in the Gospel of Luke*. London: Bloomsbury, 2015.

Burkett, Delbert. *The Son of Man Debate: A History and Evaluation*. Cambridge: Cambridge University Press, 1999.

Burkitt, F. C. "Preface." In *The Quest of the Historical Jesus: A Critical Study of Its Progress from Reimarus to Wrede*, by Albert Schweitzer, translated by William Montgomery, v–vii. London: A. & C. Black, 1910.

Burnett, D. Clint. *Christ's Enthronement at God's Right Hand and Its Greco-Roman Cultural Context*. Berlin: de Gruyter, 2021.

Burridge, Richard A. *Four Gospels, One Jesus? A Symbolic Reading*. 2nd ed. Grand Rapids: Eerdmans, 2005.

Byrne, Brendan, SJ. "Christ's Preexistence in Pauline Soteriology." *Theological Studies* 58 (1997) 308–30.

Bynum, Caroline Walker. *The Resurrection of the Body in Western Christianity, 200–1336*. New York: Columbia University Press, 1995.

Byrskog, Samuel. "Introduction." In *Jesus in Memory: Traditions in Oral and Scribal Perspectives*, edited by Werner H. Kelber and Samuel Byrskog, 1–20. Waco, TX: Baylor University Press, 2009.

———. *Story as History—History as Story: The Gospel Tradition in the Context of Ancient Oral History*. Leiden: Brill, 2002.

Cadenhead, Raphael A. *The Body and Desire: Gregory of Nyssa's Ascetical Theology*. Berkeley: University of California Press, 2018.

Caird, G. B. "Son by Appointment." In *The New Testament Age*, edited by William C. Weinrich, 73–82. Macon, GA: Mercer University Press, 1984.

Calkins, Arthur B. "Mariology at and after the Second Vatican Council." In *The Oxford Handbook of Mary*, edited by Chris Maunder, 516–30. Oxford: Oxford University Press, 2019.

Campbell, Douglas A. "The Story of Jesus in Romans and Galatians." In *Narrative Dynamics in Paul: A Critical Assessment*, edited by Bruce W. Longenecker, 97–124. Louisville: Westminster John Knox, 2002.

Campbell, Joan C. *Kinship Relations in the Gospel of John*. Washington, DC: Catholic Biblical Association of America, 2007.

Caneday, Ardel B. "Glory Veiled in the Tabernacle of Flesh: Exodus 33–34 in the Gospel of John." *Southern Baptist Journal of Theology* 20 (2016) 55–72.

Cantalamessa, Raniero. "He Was Pierced for Our Sins." In *The Power of the Cross: Good Friday Sermons from the Papal Preacher*, edited by Raniero Cantalamessa, 70–76. Elk Grove Village, IL: Word on Fire, 2023.

———. "One Man Has Died for All!." In *The Power of the Cross: Good Friday Sermons from the Papal Preacher*, edited by Raniero Cantalamessa, 137–44. Elk Grove Village, IL: Word on Fire, 2023.

Capes, David B. "Jesus' Unique Relationship with YHWH in Biblical Exegesis: A Response to Recent Objections." In *Monotheism and Christology in Greco-Roman Antiquity*, edited by Matthew V. Novenson, 85–98. Leiden: Brill, 2020.

Capps, Donald. *Jesus the Village Psychiatrist*. Louisville: Westminster John Knox, 2008.

Cardó, Daniel. *The Cross and the Eucharist in Early Christianity: A Theological and Liturgical Investigation*. Cambridge: Cambridge University Press, 2019.

Carola, Joseph, SJ. *Engaging the Church Fathers in Nineteenth-Century Catholicism: The Patristic Legacy of the Scuola Romana*. Steubenville, OH: Emmaus Academic, 2023.

Carrell, Peter R. *Jesus and the Angels: Angelology and the Christology of the Apocalypse of John*. Cambridge: Cambridge University Press, 1997.

Carreño, Juan Eduardo. "Theology, Philosophy, and Biology: An Interpretation of the Conception of Jesus Christ." *Nova et Vetera* 22 (2024) 71–102.

Casey, Maurice. *An Aramaic Approach to Q: Sources for the Gospels of Matthew and Luke*. Cambridge: Cambridge University Press, 2002.

Catechism of the Catholic Church. 2nd ed. Vatican City: Libreria Editrice Vaticana, 1997.

Cavadini, John C. "The Sex Life of Mary and Joseph." *Nova et Vetera* 13 (2015) 365–77.

Chae, Young S. *Jesus as the Eschatological Davidic Shepherd*. Tübingen: Mohr Siebeck, 2006.

Chanikuzhy, Jacob. *Jesus, the Eschatological Temple: An Exegetical Study of Jn 2,13–22 in the Light of the Pre-70 C.E. Eschatological Temple Hopes and the Synoptic Temple Action*. Leuven: Peeters, 2012.

Charlesworth, James H. "From Messianology to Christology: Problems and Prospects." In *The Messiah: Developments in Earliest Judaism and Christianity*, edited by James H. Charlesworth, 3–35. Minneapolis: Fortress, 1992.

Chemnitz, Martin. *The Two Natures of Christ*. Translated by J. A. O. Preus. St. Louis: Concordia, 1971.

Chennattu, Rekha M. *Johannine Discipleship as a Covenant Relationship*. Peabody, MA: Hendrickson, 2006.

Chenu, Marie-Dominique, OP. "Une Constitution Pastorale de l'Église." In *Peuple de Dieu dans le monde*, 11–34. Paris: Cerf, 1966.

Chidgzey, Aaron. "Subjugating Subjectivity: Why Wright's Critical Realism Is Not Critical Enough." *Journal for the Study of the Historical Jesus* 21 (2023) 203–27.

Chilton, Bruce D. "E. P. Sanders and the Question of Jesus and Purity." In *Jesus in Context: Temple, Purity, and Restoration*, edited by Bruce Chilton and Craig A. Evans, 221–30. Leiden: Brill, 1997.

———. *A Feast of Meanings: Eucharistic Theologies from Jesus through Johannine Circles*. Leiden: Brill, 1994.

———. *The Herods: Murder, Politics, and the Art of Succession*. Minneapolis: Fortress, 2021.

———. "Jesus within Judaism." In *Jesus in Context: Temple, Purity, and Restoration*, edited by Bruce Chilton and Craig A. Evans, 179–201. Leiden: Brill, 1997.

———. "John the Purifier." In *Jesus in Context: Temple, Purity, and Restoration*, edited by Bruce Chilton and Craig A. Evans, 203–20. Leiden: Brill, 1997.
———. *Pure Kingdom: Jesus' Vision of God*. Grand Rapids: Eerdmans, 1996.
———. *Resurrection Logic: How Jesus' First Followers Believed God Raised Him from the Dead*. Waco, TX: Baylor University Press, 2019.
———. *The Temple of Jesus: His Sacrificial Program within a Cultural History of Sacrifice*. University Park: Pennsylvania State University Press, 1992.
Chilton, Bruce, and Jacob Neusner, eds. *In Quest of the Historical Pharisees*. Waco, TX: Baylor University Press, 2007.
Cho, Bernardo. *Royal Messianism and the Jerusalem Priesthood in the Gospel of Mark*. London: T. & T. Clark, 2019.
Choumnos, Nikephoros. "On the Holy Transfiguration of Christ." In *Light on the Mountain: Greek Patristic and Byzantine Homilies on the Transfiguration of the Lord*, translated by Brian E. Daley, SJ, 297–315. Yonkers, NY: St Vladimir's Seminary Press, 2013.
Church, Philip. *Hebrews and the Temple: Attitudes to the Temple in Second Temple Judaism and in Hebrews*. Leiden: Brill, 2017.
Coakley, Sarah. *Powers and Submissions: Spirituality, Philosophy and Gender*. Oxford: Blackwell, 2002.
Cohn-Sherbok, Dan. *The Jewish Messiah*. London: T. & T. Clark, 1997.
Collins, Adela Yarbro, and John J. Collins. *King and Messiah as Son of God: Divine, Human, and Angelic Messianic Figures in Biblical and Related Literature*. Grand Rapids: Eerdmans, 2008.
Collins, John J. *The Scepter and the Star: The Messiahs of the Dead Sea Scrolls and Other Ancient Literature*. New York: Doubleday, 1995.
———. "The *Son of God* Text from Qumran." In *From Jesus to John: Essays on Jesus and New Testament Christology in Honour of Marinus de Jonge*, edited by Martinus C. De Boer, 65–82. Sheffield: Sheffield Academic, 1993.
Collins, Raymond F. *First Corinthians*. Collegeville, MN: Liturgical, 1999.
Coloe, Mary L. *God Dwells with Us: Temple Symbolism in the Fourth Gospel*. Collegeville, MN: Liturgical, 2001.
———. "John as Witness and Friend." In *John, Jesus, and Historicity*, vol. 2: *Aspects of Historicity in the Fourth Gospel*, edited by Paul N. Anderson et al., 45–61. Atlanta: SBL, 2009.
Compton, Jared. *Psalm 110 and the Logic of Hebrews*. London: Bloomsbury, 2015.
Congar, Yves, OP. *La Parole et le Souffle*. Paris: Desclée, 1984.
———. "Theology's Tasks after Vatican II." In *Renewal of Religious Thought: Proceedings of the Congress on the Theology of the Renewal of the Church*, edited by L. K. Shook, CSB, 47–65. Montreal: Palm, 1968.
———. *Tradition and Traditions: An Historical and a Theological Essay*. Translated by Michael Naseby and Thomas Rainborough. New York: Macmillan, 1967.
Congregation for Catholic Education. *Circular Letter Concerning Some of the More Urgent Aspects of Spiritual Formation in Seminaries*. January 6, 1980. https://www.usccb.org/beliefs-and-teachings/vocations/priesthood/priestly-formation/upload/spiritual.pdf.
Cortez, Félix H. "Atonement and Inauguration at the Heavenly Sanctuary: A Wider Perspective to Jesus's Ascension in Hebrews." In *Earthly Shadows, Heavenly Realities: Temple/Sanctuary Cosmology in Ancient Near Eastern, Biblical, and Early*

Jewish Literature, edited by Kim Papaioannou and Ioannis Giantzaklidis, 175–88. Berrien Springs, MI: Andrews University Press, 2016.

———. *Within the Veil: The Ascension of the Son in the Letter to the Hebrews*. Dallas: Fontes, 2020.

Council of Chalcedon. "Definition of the Faith." In *Decrees of the Ecumenical Councils*, vol. 1: *Nicaea I to Lateran V*, edited by Norman P. Tanner, 83–86. Washington, DC: Georgetown University Press, 1990.

Cover, Michael Benjamin. "Historically, Was Jesus's Mother from a Priestly Family?" In *The Figure of Jesus in History and Theology: Essays in Honor of John Meier*, edited by Vincent T. M. Skemp and Kelley Coblentz Bautch, 127–42. Washington, DC: Catholic Biblical Association of America, 2020.

Craig, William Lane. "Who Was Jesus? A Christian Perspective." In *Who Was Jesus? A Jewish-Christian Dialogue*, edited by Paul Copan and Craig A. Evans, 21–28. Louisville: Westminster John Knox, 2001.

Crescas, Hasdai. *Light of the Lord (Or Hashem)*. Translated by R. Weiss. Oxford: Oxford University Press, 2018.

Crisp, Oliver. *Analyzing Doctrine: Toward a Systematic Theology*. Waco, TX: Baylor University Press, 2019.

———. *God Incarnate: Explorations in Christology*. London: T. & T. Clark, 2009.

Cross, Frank Moore. "Kinship and Covenant in Ancient Israel." In *From Epic to Canon: History and Literature in Ancient Israel*, 3–21. Baltimore: Johns Hopkins University Press, 1998.

Cross, Richard. *Duns Scotus*. Oxford: Oxford University Press, 1999.

———. *The Metaphysics of the Incarnation: Thomas Aquinas to Duns Scotus*. Oxford: Oxford University Press, 2002.

Crowe, Brandon D. *The Last Adam: A Theology of the Obedient Life of Jesus in the Gospels*. Grand Rapids: Baker Academic, 2017.

———. *The Lord Jesus Christ: The Biblical Doctrine of the Person and Work of Christ*. Bellingham, WA: Lexham Academic, 2023.

Croy, N. Clayton. *Escaping Shame: Mary's Dilemma and the Birthplace of Jesus*. Leiden: Brill, 2020.

Crump, David. *Encountering Jesus, Encountering Scripture: Reading the Bible Critically in Faith*. Grand Rapids: Eerdmans, 2013.

Crysdale, Cynthia S. W. *Embracing Travail: Retrieving the Cross Today*. London: Continuum, 1999.

Cuddy, Cajetan, OP. "Sixteenth-Century Reception of Aquinas by Cajetan." In *The Oxford Handbook of the Reception of Aquinas*, edited by Matthew Levering and Marcus Plested, 144–58. Oxford: Oxford University Press, 2021.

Culpepper, R. Alan. *The Gospel and Letters of John*. Nashville: Abingdon, 1998.

Cunningham, Conor. "Thomas Aquinas's Anthropology: Stuck in the Middle with You." In *Theological Anthropology in Interreligious Perspectives*, edited by Mujadad Zaman et al., 220–40. Tübingen: Mohr Siebeck, 2022.

Cyril of Alexandria. *Commentary on John*, vol. 2. Translated by David R. Maxwell. Edited by Joel C. Elowsky. Downers Grove, IL: IVP Academic, 2015.

———. *Glaphyra on the Pentateuch, Volume 2: Exodus through Deuteronomy*. Translated by Nicholas P. Lunn. Washington, DC: Catholic University of America, 2019.

———. *On the Unity of Christ*. Translated by John Anthony McGuckin. Crestwood, NY: St Vladimir's Seminary Press, 1995.

Dabney, D. Lyle. "Starting with the Spirit: Why the Last Should Be First." In *Starting with the Spirit: Task of Theology II*, edited by G. Preece and S. Pickard, 3–27. Hindmarsh, SA: Australian Theological Forum, 2001.

Dahl, Nils A. *The Crucified Messiah and Other Essays*. Minneapolis: Augsburg, 1974.

Dales, Douglas. *Divine Remaking: St Bonaventure and the Gospel of Luke*. Cambridge: James Clarke, 2018.

Daley, Brian E., SJ. *God Visible: Patristic Christology Reconsidered*. Oxford: Oxford University Press, 2018.

———. *The Hope of the Early Church: A Handbook of Patristic Eschatology*. 3rd ed. Cambridge: Cambridge University Press, 1995.

———. "Introduction." In *On the Dormition of Mary: Early Patristic Homilies*, 1–45. Crestwood, NY: St Vladimir's Seminary Press, 1998.

———. "'One Thing and Another': The Persons in God and the Person of Christ in Patristic Theology." *Pro Ecclesia* 15 (2005) 17–46.

Dalman, Gustaf. *Jesus-Jeshua: Studies in the Gospels*. Translated by Paul P. Levertoff. London: SPCK, 1929.

Dalton, Andrew D., LC. *Fulfilled Israel according to Matthew's* Plerosis *Paradigm*. Tübingen: Mohr Siebeck, 2024.

Daly, Robert, SJ. *Sacrifice Unveiled: The True Meaning of Christian Sacrifice*. London: T. & T. Clark, 2009.

Daly-Denton, Margaret. *David in the Fourth Gospel: The Johannine Reception of the Psalms*. Leiden: Brill, 2000.

Daniélou, Jean, SJ. *The Infancy Narratives*. Translated by Rosemary Sheed. Providence, RI: Cluny, 2022.

Dauphinais, Michael A. "Creation Is Not Incarnation: Responding to a Contemporary Crisis in Catholic Christology in Light of Aquinas's Teaching on Participation." In *Thomas Aquinas and the Crisis of Christology*, edited by Michael A. Dauphinais et al., 251–78. Ave Maria, FL: Sapientia, 2021.

———. "The Divine *Communicatio* as the Formal and Material Principle of Aquinas's *Summa Theologiae*." In *Thomas Aquinas as Spiritual Teacher*, edited by Michael A. Dauphinais et al., 177–208. Ave Maria, FL: Sapientia, 2023.

———. "The Place of Christ and the Biblical Narrative in Aquinas's Theology of Revelation." In *Thomas Aquinas, Biblical Theologian*, edited by Roger W. Nutt and Michael Dauphinais, 1–34. Steubenville, OH: Emmaus Academic, 2021.

Davenport, Thomas, OP. "Locating Heaven: Modern Science and the Place of Christ's Glorified Body." *Nova et Vetera* 21 (2023) 93–114.

Davies, John A. *A Royal Priesthood: Literary and Intertextual Perspectives on an Image of Israel in Exodus 19:6*. London: T. & T. Clark, 2004.

Davies, W. D., and Dale C. Allison, Jr. *A Critical and Exegetical Commentary on the Gospel according to Saint Matthew*. 3 vols. London: T. & T. Clark, 2004.

Davila, James R. "Of Methodology, Monotheism and Metatron: Introductory Reflections on Divine Mediators and the Origins of the Worship of Jesus." In *The Jewish Roots of Christological Monotheism: Papers from the St. Andrews Conference on the Historical Origins of the Worship of Jesus*, edited by Carey C. Newman et al., 3–20. Leiden: Brill, 1999.

———. *The Provenance of the Pseudepigrapha: Jewish, Christian, or Other?* Leiden: Brill, 2005.

Davis, Stephen T. "Resurrection, Personal Identity, and the Will of God." In *Personal Identity and Resurrection: How Do We Survive Our Death?*, edited by Georg Gasser, 19–32. Aldershot: Ashgate, 2010.

———. *Risen Indeed: Making Sense of the Resurrection*. Grand Rapids: Eerdmans, 1993.

Day, John. *Molech*. Cambridge: Cambridge University Press, 1989.

Dawkins, Richard. *The Extended Phenotype: The Gene as the Unit of Selection*. Oxford: Oxford University Press, 1996.

de Aldama, Joseph A., SJ. "Treatise 2: Mariology or On the Blessed Virgin Mary." In *Sacrae Theologiae Summa*, IIIA: On the Incarnate Word and On the Blessed Virgin Mary, by Iesu Solano, SJ, and J. A. de Aldama, SJ; translated by Kenneth Baker, SJ, 347–503. Saddle River, NJ: Keep the Faith, 2014.

DeHart, Paul J. *Unspeakable Cults: An Essay in Christology*. Waco, TX: Baylor University Press, 2021.

DeJong, David N. *A Prophet Like Moses (Deut 18:15, 18): The Origin, History, and Influence of the Mosaic Prophetic Succession*. Leiden: Brill, 2022.

de Jonge, H. J. "The Historical Jesus' View of Himself and of His Mission." In *From Jesus to John: Essays on Jesus and New Testament Christology in Honour of Marinus de Jonge*, edited by Martinus C. De Boer, 21–37. Sheffield: Sheffield Academic, 1993.

de Jonge, Marinus. "The Earliest Christian Use of *Christos*: Some Suggestions." In *Jewish Eschatology, Early Christian Eschatology and the Testaments of the Twelve Patriarchs: Collected Essays of Marinus de Jonge*, 102–24. Leiden: Brill, 1991.

———. *God's Final Envoy: Early Christology and Jesus' Own View of His Mission*. Grand Rapids: Eerdmans, 1998.

———. *Jesus, the Servant-Messiah*. New Haven: Yale University Press, 1991.

———. "The Testament of Levi and 'Aramaic Levi.'" In *Jewish Eschatology, Early Christian Eschatology and the Testaments of the Twelve Patriarchs: Collected Essays of Marinus de Jonge*, 244–62. Leiden: Brill, 1991.

———. "The Testaments of the Twelve Patriarchs: Christian and Jewish. A Hundred Years after Friedrich Schnapp." In *Jewish Eschatology, Early Christian Eschatology and the Testaments of the Twelve Patriarchs: Collected Essays of Marinus de Jonge*, 233–43. Leiden: Brill, 1991.

De Long, Kindalee Pfremmer. "Angels and Visions in Luke-Acts." In *The Jewish Apocalyptic Tradition and the Shaping of New Testament Thought*, edited by Benjamin E. Reynolds and Loren T. Stuckenbruck, 79–107. Minneapolis: Fortress, 2017.

de Lubac, Henri, SJ. *The Splendor of the Church*. Translated by Michael Mason. San Francisco: Ignatius, 1999.

———. *The Religion of Teilhard de Chardin*. Translated by René Hague. Garden City, NY: Image, 1968.

Del Colle, Ralph. "Spirit-Christology: Dogmatic Foundations for Pentecostal-Charismatic Spirituality." *Journal of Pentecostal Theology* 3 (1993) 91–112.

Delio, Ilia, OSF. *The Emergent Christ: Exploring the Meaning of Catholic in an Evolutionary Universe*. Maryknoll, NY: Orbis, 2011.

deSilva, David A. "The *Testaments of the Twelve Patriarchs* as Witnesses to Pre-Christian Judaism: A Re-assessment." *Journal for the Study of the Pseudepigrapha* 22 (2013) 21–68.

Detweiler, Robert, and William G. Doty, eds. *The Daemonic Imagination: Biblical Texts and Secular Story*. Atlanta: Scholars, 1990.

Dewey, Arthur J. "The Eyewitness of History: Visionary Consciousness in the Fourth Gospel." In *Jesus in Johannine Tradition*, edited by Robert T. Fortna and Tom Thatcher, 59–70. Louisville: Westminster John Knox, 2001.

Dicken, Frank E. "Luke and the Cross: A Vision of Crucicentric Discipleship." In *Cruciform Scripture: Cross, Participation, and Mission*, edited by Christopher W. Skinner et al., 37–55. Grand Rapids: Eerdmans, 2021.

The Divine Liturgy of St. Basil the Great. Service Books of the Orthodox Church, vol. 2. South Canaan, PA: St. Tikhon's Seminary Press, 1984.

Donneaud, Henri, OP. "La constitution dialectique de la théologie et de son histoire selon M.-D. Chenu." *Revue Thomiste* 96 (1996) 41–66.

Doran, Robert M., SJ. "The Nonviolent Cross: Lonergan and Girard on Redemption." *Theological Studies* 71 (2010) 46–61.

———. *The Trinity in History: A Theology of the Divine Missions*. Vol. 3, *Redeeming History*. Edited by Joseph Ogbonnaya. Milwaukee, WI: Marquette University Press, 2022.

Dorner, Isaac August. *Entwicklungsgeschichte der Lehre von der Person Christi von den ältesten Zeiten bis auf die neueste dargestellt*. 2 vols. Berlin: Gustav Schlawitz, 1851–56.

Dörnyei, Zoltán. *Progressive Creation and the Struggles of Humanity in the Bible: A Canonical Narrative Interpretation*. Eugene, OR: Pickwick, 2018.

Douglas, Mary. *Leviticus as Literature*. Oxford: Oxford University Press, 1999.

Dozeman, Thomas B. *Commentary on Exodus*. Grand Rapids: Eerdmans, 2009.

Drago, Augusto. "L'esegesi di S. Bonaventura nei suoi commentari." *Incontri Bonaventuriani* 7 (1972) 121–45.

Druwé, Edouard, SJ. "La mediation universelle de Marie." In *Maria: Études sur la sainte Vierge*, vol. 1, edited by Hubert du Manoir, 417–52. Paris: Beauchesne, 1948.

Duby, Steven J. *Jesus and the God of Classical Theism: Biblical Christology in Light of the Doctrine of God*. Grand Rapids: Baker Academic, 2022.

Dunn, James D. G. *Christology in the Making: A New Testament Inquiry into the Origins of the Doctrine of the Incarnation*. 2nd ed. London: SCM, 1989.

———. *Did the First Christians Worship Jesus? The New Testament Evidence*. Louisville: Westminster John Knox, 2010.

———. "How Controversial Was Paul's Christology?" In *From Jesus to John: Essays on Jesus and New Testament Christology in Honour of Marinus de Jonge*, edited by Martinus C. De Boer, 148–67. Sheffield: Sheffield Academic, 1993.

———. *Jesus and the Spirit*. London: SCM, 1975.

———. *Jesus Remembered*. Vol. 1 of *Christianity in the Making*. Grand Rapids: Eerdmans, 2003.

———. *Romans 1–8*. Dallas: Word, 1988.

———. *The Theology of Paul the Apostle*. Grand Rapids: Eerdmans, 1998.

Dunnill, John. *Covenant and Sacrifice in the Letter to the Hebrews*. Cambridge: Cambridge University Press, 1992.

Duns, Ryan G., SJ. "Reconfigured Through the Word: Jesus' Parables and Metaxological Theopoetics." In *A Heart of Flesh: William Desmond and the Bible*, edited by Steven E. Knepper, 85–103. Eugene, OR: Cascade, 2023.

Durand, Emmanuel, OP. "Christ's Mission Implies His Preexistence: A Scriptural Argument." In *Divine Speech in Human Words: Thomistic Engagements with Scripture*, translated by Matthew K. Minerd, 343–77. Washington, DC: Catholic University of America, 2022.

---. *Jésus contemporain. Christologie brève et actuelle*. Paris: Cerf, 2018.
East, Brad. *The Church's Book: Theology of Scripture in Ecclesial Context*. Grand Rapids: Eerdmans, 2022.
Eberhart, Christian A. *Kultmetaphorik und Christologie: Opfer- und Sühneterminologie in Neuen Testament*. Tübingen: Mohr Siebeck, 2013.
---. *The Sacrifice of Jesus: Understanding Atonement Biblically*. Minneapolis: Fortress, 2011.
Edwards, J. Christopher. *The Ransom Logion in Mark and Matthew: Its Reception and Its Significance for the Study of the Gospels*. Tübingen: Mohr Siebeck, 2012.
Egan, Harvey D., SJ. *Rethinking Catholic Theology: From the Mystery of Existence to the New Creation*. New York: Paulist, 2023.
Ehrman, Bart D. *How Jesus Became God: The Exaltation of a Jewish Preacher from Galilee*. New York: HarperCollins, 2014.
Eisland, Nancy L. *The Disabled God: Toward a Liberatory Theology of Disability*. Nashville: Abingdon, 1994.
Elder, Nicholas A. "Of Porcine and Polluted Spirits: Reading the Gerasene Demoniac (Mark 5:1–20) with the Book of Watchers (*1 Enoch* 1–36)." *Catholic Biblical Quarterly* 78 (2016) 430–46.
Elders, Leo J., SVD. *Thomas Aquinas and His Predecessors: The Philosophers and the Church Fathers in His Works*. Washington, DC: Catholic University of America Press, 2018.
Elledge, C. D. *Resurrection of the Dead in Early Judaism 200 BCE–CE 200*. Oxford: Oxford University Press, 2017.
Emery, Gilles, OP. "The Holy Spirit in Aquinas's Commentary on Romans." In *Reading Romans with St. Thomas Aquinas*, edited by Matthew Levering and Michael Dauphinais, 127–62. Washington, DC: Catholic University of America Press, 2012.
---. "Kenosis, Christ, and the Trinity in Thomas Aquinas." *Nova et Vetera* 17 (2019) 839–69.
---. *The Trinity: An Introduction to Catholic Doctrine on the Triune God*. Translated by Matthew Levering. Washington, DC: Catholic University of America Press, 2011.
Emery, John, OP. "Aquinas's Christology of Communication." In *Thomas Aquinas and the Crisis of Christology*, edited by Michael A. Dauphinais et al., 171–94. Ave Maria, FL: Sapientia, 2021.
Engberg-Peterson, Troels. "Complete and Incomplete Transformation in Paul: A Philosophical Reading of Paul on Body and Spirit." In *Metamorphoses: Resurrection, Body and Transformative Practices in Early Christianity*, edited by Turid Karlsen Seim and Jorunn Økland, 123–46. Berlin: de Gruyter, 2009.
Erickson, Millard J. *Christian Theology*. 3rd ed. Grand Rapids: Baker Academic, 2013.
Eskola, Timo. *Messiah and the Throne: Jewish Merkabah Mysticism and Early Christian Exaltation Discourse*. Tübingen: Mohr Siebeck, 2001.
---. *A Narrative Theology of the New Testament: Exploring the Metanarrative of Exile and Restoration*. Tübingen: Mohr Siebeck, 2015.
---. *Theodicy and Predestination in Pauline Soteriology*. Tübingen: Mohr Siebeck, 1998.
Eubank, Nathan. Review of *Jesus of Nazareth: The Infancy Narratives*, by Joseph Ratzinger. *Nova et Vetera* 13 (2015) 617–21.

———. *Wages of Cross-Bearing and Debt of Sin: The Economy of Heaven in Matthew's Gospel*. Berlin: De Gruyter, 2013.

Evans, Craig A. "Aspects of Exile and Restoration in the Proclamation of Jesus and the Gospels." In *Jesus in Context: Temple, Purity, and Restoration*, edited by Bruce Chilton and Craig A. Evans, 263–93. Leiden: Brill, 1997.

———. "From Anointed Prophet to Anointed King: Probing Aspects of Jesus' Self-Understanding." In *Jesus and His Contemporaries: Comparative Studies*, 437–56. Leiden: Brill, 1995.

———. "From Gospel to Gospel: The Function of Isaiah in the New Testament." In *Writing and Reading the Scroll of Isaiah: Studies of an Interpretive Tradition*, edited by Craig C. Broyles and Craig A. Evans, 651–91. Leiden: Brill, 1997.

———. "In What Sense 'Blasphemy'? Jesus before Caiaphas in Mark 14:61–64." In *Jesus and His Contemporaries: Comparative Studies*, 407–34. Leiden: Brill, 1995.

———. "Jesus and Jewish Miracle Stories." In *Jesus and His Contemporaries: Comparative Studies*, 213–43. Leiden: Brill, 1995.

———. "Jesus and Rabbinic Parables, Proverbs, and Prayers." In *Jesus and His Contemporaries: Comparative Studies*, 251–97. Leiden: Brill, 1995.

———. "Messianic Claimants of the First and Second Centuries." In *Jesus and His Contemporaries: Comparative Studies*, 53–81. Leiden: Brill, 1995.

———. "Parables in Early Judaism." In *The Challenge of Jesus' Parables*, edited by Richard N. Longenecker, 51–75. Grand Rapids: Eerdmans, 2000.

———. "Reconstructing Jesus' Teaching: Problems and Possibilities." In *Jesus in Context: Temple, Purity, and Restoration*, edited by Bruce Chilton and Craig A. Evans, 145–76. Leiden: Brill, 1997.

———. "The Twelve Thrones of Israel: Scripture and Politics in Luke 22:24–30." In *Jesus in Context: Temple, Purity, and Restoration*, edited by Bruce Chilton and Craig A. Evans, 455–79. Leiden: Brill, 1997.

———. *Words and Glory: On the Exegetical Background of John's Prologue*. Sheffield: Sheffield Academic, 1993.

Eve, Eric. *The Healer from Nazareth: Jesus' Miracles in Historical Context*. London: SPCK, 2009.

———. *The Jewish Context of Jesus' Miracles*. Sheffield: Sheffield Academic, 2002.

———. "Meier, Miracle and Multiple Attestation." *Journal for the Study of the Historical Jesus* 3 (2005) 23–45.

Fagerberg, David W. *Consecrating the World: On Mundane Liturgical Theology*. Kettering, OH: Angelico, 2016.

———. *The Liturgical Cosmos: The World through the Lens of the Liturgy*. Steubenville, OH: Emmaus Academic, 2023.

Farrow, Douglas. *Ascension and Ecclesia: On the Significance of the Doctrine of the Ascension for Ecclesiology and Christian Cosmology*. Edinburgh: T. & T. Clark, 1999.

———. *Ascension Theology*. London: T. & T. Clark, 2011.

Fastiggi, Robert. "Fr. Peter Damian Fehlner on Divine Maternity." In *The Spirit and the Church: Peter Damian Fehlner's Franciscan Development of Vatican II on the Themes of the Holy Spirit, Mary, and the Church*, edited by J. Isaac Goff et al., 79–87. Eugene, OR: Pickwick, 2018.

———. "Francisco Suárez, SJ. (1548–1617) on Mary's *Virginitas in Partu* and Subsequent Doctrinal Development." *Marian Studies* 58 (2007) 26–45.

———. "Mariology in the Counter Reformation." In *The Oxford Handbook of Mary*, edited by Chris Maunder, 454–67. Oxford: Oxford University Press, 2019.
———. "Mary in the Work of Redemption." In *The Oxford Handbook of Mary*, edited by Chris Maunder, 303–19. Oxford: Oxford University Press, 2019.
Feldmeier, Reinhard, and Hermann Spieckermann. *God Becoming Human: Incarnation in the Christian Bible*. Translated by Brian McNeil. Waco, TX: Baylor University Press, 2021.
Fehlner, Peter Damian, OFM Conv. *Systematic Mariology*. Edited by J. Isaac Goff. Eugene, OR: Wipf & Stock, 2023.
Feuillet, André. "Les trois grandes prophéties de la Passion et de la Résurrection." *Revue Thomiste* 68 (1968) 41–75.
Fiddes, Paul S. "Sacrifice, Atonement, and Renewal: Intersections between Girard, Kristeva, and Balthasar." In *Sacrifice and Modern Thought*, edited by Julia Meszaros and Johannes Zachhuber, 48–65. Oxford: Oxford University Press, 2013.
Finlan, Stephen. *Problems with Atonement: The Origins of, and Controversy about, the Atonement Doctrine*. Collegeville, MN: Liturgical, 2005.
Fitzmyer, Joseph A., SJ. *The Gospel According to Luke (X–XXIV)*. Garden City, NY: Doubleday, 1985.
———. *The One Who Is to Come*. Grand Rapids: Eerdmans, 2007.
———. "Qumran Literature and the Johannine Writings." In *Life in Abundance: Studies of John's Gospel in Tribute to Raymond E. Brown, S.S.*, edited by John R. Donahue, SJ, 117–33. Collegeville, MN: Liturgical, 2005.
Fletcher, Patrick J. *Resurrection Realism: Ratzinger the Augustinian*. Eugene, OR: Cascade, 2014.
Fletcher-Louis, Crispin. *All the Glory of Adam: Liturgical Anthropology in the Dead Sea Scrolls*. Leiden: Brill, 2002.
———. *Christological Origins: The Emerging Consensus and Beyond*. Vol. 1 of *Jesus Monotheism*. Eugene, OR: Cascade, 2015.
———. "Jesus as the High Priestly Messiah: Part 1." *Journal for the Study of the Historical Jesus* 4 (2006) 155–75.
———. "Jesus as the High Priestly Messiah: Part 2." *Journal for the Study of the Historical Jesus* 5 (2007) 57–79.
———. *Luke-Acts: Angels, Christology and Soteriology*. Tübingen: Mohr Siebeck, 1997.
———. "The Revelation of the Sacral Son of Man: The Genre, History of Religions Context and the Meaning of the Transfiguration." In *Auferstehung—Resurrection*, edited by Friedrich Avemarie, 247–98. Tübingen: Mohr Siebeck, 2001.
———. "The Worship of Divine Humanity and the Worship of Jesus." In *The Jewish Roots of Christological Monotheism: Papers from the St. Andrews Conference on the Historical Origins of the Worship of Jesus*, edited by Carey C. Newman et al., 112–28. Leiden: Brill, 1999.
Flint, Thomas P. "The Possibilities of Incarnation: Some Radical Molinist Suggestions." *Religious Studies* 37 (2001) 307–20.
Flusser, David. *Judaism and the Origins of Christianity*. Jerusalem: Magnes, 1998.
Fornberg, Tord. "The Annunciation: A Study in Reception History." In *New Testament as Reception*, edited by Mogens Müller and Henrik Tronier, 158–80. London: Continuum, 2002.
Fossum, Jarl E. "Kyrios Jesus as the Angel of the Lord in Jude 5–7." *New Testament Studies* 33 (1987) 226–43.

---. *The Name of God and the Angel of the Lord: Samaritan and Jewish Concepts of Intermediation and the Origins of Gnosticism*. Tübingen: Mohr Siebeck, 1985.

Franks, Angela. "Thomistic-Balthasarian Comments on Thomas Joseph White's *The Incarnate Lord*." *Nova et Vetera* 20 (2022) 575–600.

Frasseto, Michael. "Resurrection of the Body: Eleventh-Century Evidence from the Sermons of Ademar of Chabannes." *Journal of Religious History* 26 (2002) 235–49.

Frazier, Jessica. "From Slaughtered Lambs to Dedicated Lives: Sacrifice as Value-Bestowal." In *Sacrifice and Modern Thought*, edited by Julia Meszaros and Johannes Zachhuber, 100–114. Oxford: Oxford University Press, 2013.

Fredriksen, Paula. *Jesus of Nazareth, King of the Jews*. New York: Knopf, 1999.

Freed, Edwin D. *The Stories of Jesus's Birth: A Critical Introduction*. London: Bloomsbury, 2004.

Frey, Jörg. "Between Jewish Monotheism and Proto-Trinitarian Relations: The Making and Character of Johannine Christology." In *Monotheism and Christology in Greco-Roman Antiquity*, edited by Matthew V. Novenson, 189–221. Leiden: Brill, 2020.

---. "Bodiliness and Resurrection in the Gospel of John." In *The Glory of the Crucified One: Christology and Theology in the Gospel of John*, translated by Wayne Coppins and Christoph Heilig, 199–236. Waco, TX: Baylor University Press, 2018.

---. "Die 'theologia crucifixi' des Johannevangeliums." In *Die Herrlichkeit des Gekreuzigten. Studien zu den Johanneischen Schriften I*, edited by J. Schlegel, 485–554. Tübingen: Mohr Siebeck, 2013.

---. "'Mystical' Traditions in an Apocalyptic Text? The Throne Vision of Revelation 4 within the context of Enochic and Merkavah Texts." In *Apocalypticism and Mysticism in Ancient Judaism and Early Christianity*, edited by John J. Collins et al., 103–27. Berlin: de Gruyter, 2018.

Freyne, Sean. *Galilee and Gospel: Collected Essays*. Leiden: Brill, 2002.

---. *Jesus, a Jewish Galilean: A New Reading of the Jesus Story*. London: T. & T. Clark, 2004.

Fuller, Michael E. *The Restoration of Israel: Israel's Re-gathering and the Fate of the Nations in Early Jesus Literature and Luke-Acts*. Berlin: de Gruyter, 2006.

Gaine, Simon Francis, OP. *Did the Saviour See the Father? Christ, Salvation and the Vision of God*. London: Bloomsbury, 2015.

---. "Jesus Christ." In *The Oxford Handbook of the Reception of Aquinas*, edited by Matthew Levering and Marcus Plested, 673–88. Oxford: Oxford University Press, 2021.

---. "*Must* an Incarnate Divine Person Enjoy the Beatific Vision?" In *Thomas Aquinas and the Crisis of Christology*, edited by Michael A. Dauphinais et al., 126–38. Ave Maria, FL: Sapientia, 2021.

---. "Some Recent Arguments for Christ's Earthly Beatific Vision and Aquinas's Own Argument in *Summa theologiae* III, qq. 9 and 34." *The Thomist* 88 (2024) 77–97.

---. "The Veracity of Prophecy and Christ's Knowledge." *New Blackfriars* 98 (2017) 44–62.

Gallusz, Laszlo. *The Throne Motif in the Book of Revelation*. London: T. & T. Clark, 2014.

Gambero, Luigi. *Fede e devozione mariana nell'Impero Bizantino: Dal periodo post-patristico all caduta del 'Impero (1453)*. Milan: San Paolo, 2012.

———. *Mary in the Middle Ages: The Blessed Virgin Mary in the Thought of Medieval Latin Theologians*. Translated by Thomas Buffer. San Francisco: Ignatius, 2005.

Gardner, Lucy. "Balthasar and the Figure of Mary." In *The Cambridge Companion to Hans Urs von Balthasar*, edited by Edward T. Oakes, SJ, and David Moss, 64–78. Cambridge: Cambridge University Press, 2006.

Garnett, Susan R. *No Ordinary Angel: Celestial Spirits and Christian Claims about Jesus*. New Haven: Yale University Press, 2008.

Garrigou-Lagrange, Réginald, OP. *Christ the Savior: A Commentary on the Third Part of St. Thomas' Theological Summa*. Translated by Bede Rose, OSB. St. Louis: Herder, 1957.

———. *The Mother of the Saviour*. Translated by Bernard J. Kelly, CSSp. Charlotte, NC: TAN, 1993.

———. *Our Saviour and His Love for Us*. Translated by A. Bouchard. N.p.: Aeterna, 2016.

Garrigues, Jean-Miguel. "The 'Natural Grace' of Christ in St. Thomas." In *Surnaturel: A Controversy at the Heart of Twentieth-Century Thomistic Thought*, edited by Serge-Thomas Bonino, OP, translated by Robert Williams, revised by Matthew Levering, 103–15. Ave Maria, FL: Sapientia, 2009.

Gärtner, Bertil. *The Temple and the Community in Qumran and the New Testament: A Comparative Study in the Temple Symbolism of the Qumran Texts and the New Testament*. Cambridge: Cambridge University Press, 1965.

Gathercole, Simon. *Defending Substitution: An Essay on Atonement in Paul*. Grand Rapids: Baker Academic, 2015.

———. *The Preexistent Son: Recovering the Christologies of Matthew, Mark, and Luke*. Grand Rapids: Eerdmans, 2006.

Gaventa, Beverly Roberts. "Learning and Re-Learning the Identity of Jesus from Luke-Acts." In *Seeking the Identity of Jesus: A Pilgrimage*, edited by Beverly Roberts Gaventa and Richard B. Hays, 148–65. Grand Rapids: Eerdmans, 2008.

———. *Mary: Glimpses of the Mother of Jesus*. Minneapolis: Fortress, 1999.

Gerhard, Johann. *On Eternal Life*. Translated by Richard J. Dinda. Edited by Joshua J. Hayes and Heath R. Curtis. St. Louis: Concordia, 2022.

———. *On the Person and Office of Christ*. Translated by Richard J. Dinda. Edited by Benjamin T. G. Mayes. St. Louis: Concordia, 2009.

Gerhardsson, Birger. *The Mighty Acts of Jesus according to Matthew*. Lund: Gleerup, 1979.

———. "Mighty Acts and Rule of Heaven: 'God Is with Us.'" In *To Tell the Mystery: Essays on New Testament Eschatology in Honor of Robert H. Gundry*, edited by Thomas E. Schmidt and Moisés Silva, 34–48. Sheffield: Sheffield Academic, 1994.

———. "The Secret of the Transmission of the Unwritten Jesus Tradition." *New Testament Studies* 51 (2005) 1–18.

Giambrone, Anthony, OP. "Aquinas between Abelard and Erasmus: A Brief Ressourcement Thomistic Theology of Biblical Translation." In *Engaging Catholic Doctrine: Essays in Honor of Matthew Levering*, edited by Robert Barron et al., 107–63. Steubenville, OH: Emmaus Academic, 2023.

———. *The Bible and the Priesthood: Priestly Participation in the One Sacrifice for Sin*. Grand Rapids: Baker Academic, 2022.

———. "The German Roots of Historical Jesus Research." In *A Quest for the Historical Christ: Scientia Christi and the Modern Study of Jesus*, 51–71. Washington, DC: Catholic University of America Press, 2022.

———. "*Interpretatio iudaica*: Le monothéisme juif à l'époque du second Temple." *Communio* [French edition] 45 (2020) 43–60.

———. "Introduction." In *A Quest for the Historical Christ: Scientia Christi and the Modern Study of Jesus*, 1–15. Washington, DC: Catholic University of America Press, 2022.

———. "The 'Lying Historians' and Luke 1–2." In *A Quest for the Historical Christ: Scientia Christi and the Modern Study of Jesus*, 72–91. Washington, DC: Catholic University of America Press, 2022.

———. "Memorializing Miracles in the World of the Gospels." In *A Quest for the Historical Christ: Scientia Christi and the Modern Study of Jesus*, 92–106. Washington, DC: Catholic University of America Press, 2022.

———. "Primitive Christology as Ancient Philosophy." In *Thomas Aquinas and the Crisis of Christology*, edited by Michael A. Dauphinais et al., 33–55. Ave Maria, FL: Sapientia, 2021.

———. *A Quest for the Historical Christ: Scientia Christi and the Modern Study of Jesus*. Washington, DC: Catholic University of America Press, 2022.

———. *Sacramental Charity, Creditor Christology, and the Economy of Salvation in Luke's Gospel*. Tübingen: Mohr Siebeck, 2017.

———. "*Scientia Christi*: Three Theses." In *A Quest for the Historical Christ: Scientia Christi and the Modern Study of Jesus*, 265–85. Washington, DC: Catholic University of America Press, 2022.

———. "*Vera et Sincera de Iesu*." In *A Quest for the Historical Christ: Scientia Christi and the Modern Study of Jesus*, 19–50. Washington, DC: Catholic University of America Press, 2022.

———. "'Why Do the Scribes Say?': Scribal Expectations of an Eschatological High Priest and the Interpretation of Jesus' Transfiguration." In *A Quest for the Historical Christ: Scientia Christi and the Modern Study of Jesus*, 301–34. Washington, DC: Catholic University of America Press, 2022.

Gibson, Jeffery B. *The Temptations of Jesus in Early Christianity*. Sheffield: Sheffield Academic, 1995.

Gieschen, Charles A. *Angelomorphic Christology: Antecedents and Early Evidence*. Leiden: Brill, 1998.

———. "The Divine Name as a Characteristic of Divine Identity in Second-Temple Judaism and Early Christianity." In *Monotheism and Christology in Greco-Roman Antiquity*, edited by Matthew V. Novenson, 61–84. Leiden: Brill, 2020.

Gilson, Caitlin Smith. *As It Is in Heaven: Some Christian Questions on the Nature of Paradise*. Eugene, OR: Cascade, 2022.

Girard, René. *I See Satan Fall Like Lightning*. Translated by James G. Williams. Maryknoll, NY: Orbis, 2001.

———. *The Scapegoat*. Baltimore: Johns Hopkins University Press, 1986.

Glasson, T. Francis. *Moses in the Fourth Gospel*. London: SCM, 1963.

Gondreau, Paul. "Aquinas on Christ's Male Sexuality as Integral to His Full Humanity: Anti-Docetism in the Angelic Doctor." In *Thomas Aquinas and the Crisis of Christology*, edited by Michael A. Dauphinais et al., 195–232. Ave Maria, FL: Sapientia, 2021.

Gooch, Paul W. *Paul and Religion: Unfinished Conversations*. Cambridge: Cambridge University Press, 2022.

Gordon, Joseph K. *Divine Scripture in Human Understanding: A Systematic Theology of the Christian Bible*. Notre Dame: University of Notre Dame Press, 2019.

Gorman, Michael. *The Metaphysics of the Hypostatic Union*. Cambridge: Cambridge University Press, 2017.
Gorman, Michael J. *Abide and Go: Missional Theosis in the Gospel of John*. Eugene, OR: Cascade, 2018.
———. *The Death of the Messiah and the Birth of the New Covenant*. Eugene, OR: Cascade, 2014.
———. "Paul's Corporate, Cruciform, Missional *Theosis* in 2 Corinthians." In *"In Christ" in Paul: Explorations in Paul's Theology of Union and Participation*, edited by Michael J. Thate et al., 181–208. Grand Rapids: Eerdmans, 2018.
———. *Romans: A Theological and Pastoral Commentary*. Grand Rapids: Eerdmans, 2022.
Grabbe, Lester L. "'Son of Man': Its Origin and Meaning in Second Temple Judaism." In *Enoch and the Synoptic Gospels: Reminiscences, Allusions, Intertextuality*, edited by Loren T. Stuckenbruck and Gabriele Boccaccini, 169–97. Atlanta: SBL, 2016.
Graebe Brian A. *Vessel of Honor: The Virgin Birth and the Ecclesiology of Vatican II*. Steubenville, OH: Emmaus Academic, 2021.
Graef, Hilda. *Mary: A History of Doctrine and Devotion*. Notre Dame: Ave Maria, 2009.
Grant, Edward. "Cosmology." In *Science in the Middle Ages*, edited by David C. Lindberg, 274–80. Chicago: University of Chicago Press, 1978.
Gray, Timothy C. *The Temple in the Gospel of Mark*. Tübingen: Mohr Siebeck, 2008.
Gregory of Nyssa. *A Discourse on the Dead*. In Gregory of Nyssa, *On Death and Eternal Life*, translated by Brian E. Daley, SJ, 1–36. Yonkers, NY: St Vladimir's Seminary Press, 2022.
———. *On the Making of Man*. In *Select Writings and Letters of Gregory, Bishop of Nyssa*, translated by William Moore and Henry Austin Wilson, edited by Henry Wace, 387–427. Nicene and Post-Nicene Fathers 5. Peabody, MA: Hendrickson, 1995.
———. *On the Soul and the Resurrection*. Translated by Catharine P. Roth. Crestwood, NY: St Vladimir's Seminary Press, 1993.
Gregory Palamas. "On the Entry of the Mother of God into the Holy of Holies II." In *Mary the Mother of God: Sermons by Saint Gregory Palamas*, edited and translated by Christopher Veniamin, 16–50. South Canaan, PA: Mount Thabor, 2005.
———. *Mary the Mother of God: Sermons by Saint Gregory Palamas*. Edited and translated by Christopher Veniamin. South Canaan, PA: Mount Thabor, 2005.
Greshake, Gisbert. "Auferstehung im Tod: Ein 'parteiischer' Rückblick auf eine theologische Diskussion." *Theologie und Philosophie* 73 (1998) 538–57.
———. "Die Leib-Seele-Problematik und die Vollendung der Welt." In *Naherwartung—Auferstehung—Unsterblichkeit: Untersuchungen zur christlichen Eschatologie*, 4th ed., edited by Gisbert Greshake and Gerhard Lohfink, 156–84. Freiburg im Breisgau: Herder, 1982.
Greshake, Gisbert, and Jacob Kremer. *Resurrectio Mortuorum: Zum theologischen Verständnis der leiblichen Auferstehung*. Darmstadt: Wissenschaftliche Buchgesellschaft, 1986.
Griffiths, Jonathan I. *Preaching in the New Testament: An Exegetical and Biblical-Theological Study*. Downers Grove, IL: InterVarsity, 2017.
Griffiths, Paul J. *Decreation: The Last Things of All Creatures*. Waco, TX: Baylor University Press, 2014.
Grindheim, Sigurd. *God's Equal: What Can We Know about Jesus' Self-Understanding in the Synoptic Gospels?* London: Continuum, 2011.

Guardini, Romano. *The Last Things*. New York: Pantheon, 1954.
———. *The Lord*. Washington, DC: Regnery, 2021.
Guðmundsdóttir, Arnfríður. *Meeting God on the Cross: Christ, the Cross, and the Feminist Critique*. Oxford: Oxford University Press, 2010.
Guilding, Aileen. *The Fourth Gospel and Jewish Worship: A Study of the Relation of St John's Gospel to the Ancient Jewish Lectionary System*. Oxford: Clarendon, 1960.
Gundry, Robert H. "'In My Father's House Are Many Monai' (John 14:2)." *Zeitschrift für die neutestamentliche Wissenschaft* 58 (1967) 68–72.
Gutiérrez, Gustavo. *A Theology of Liberation: History, Politics, and Salvation*. Rev. ed. Translated and edited by Caridad Inda and John Eagleson. Maryknoll, NY: Orbis, 1988.
Habets, Myk. *The Anointed Son: A Trinitarian Spirit Christology*. Eugene, OR: Pickwick, 2010.
Hägerland, Tobias. *Jesus and the Forgiveness of Sins: An Aspect of His Prophetic Mission*. Cambridge: Cambridge University Press, 2012.
Hagner, Donald A. "Jesus: Bringer of Salvation to Jew and Gentile Alike." In *Who Was Jesus? A Jewish-Christian Dialogue*, edited by Paul Copan and Craig A. Evans, 45–58. Louisville: Westminster John Knox, 2001.
———. "Matthew's Eschatology." In *To Tell the Mystery: Essays on New Testament Eschatology in Honor of Robert H. Gundry*, edited by Thomas E. Schmidt and Moisés Silva, 49–71. Sheffield: Sheffield Academic, 1994.
Hahn, Scott W. "A Broken Covenant and the Curse of Death: A Study of Hebrews 9:15–22." *Catholic Biblical Quarterly* 66 (2004) 416–36.
———. *Kinship by Covenant: A Canonical Approach to the Fulfillment of God's Saving Promises*. New Haven: Yale University Press, 2009.
Halbertal, Moshe. *On Sacrifice*. Princeton: Princeton University Press, 2012.
Hannah, Darrell D. "The Elect Son of Man of the Parables of Enoch." In *"Who Is This Son of Man?" The Latest Scholarship on a Puzzling Expression of the Historical Jesus*, edited by Larry W. Hurtado and Paul L. Owen, 130–58. London: Bloomsbury, 2011.
———. *Michael and Christ: Michael Tradition and Angel Christology in Early Christianity*. Tübingen: Mohr Siebeck, 1999.
———. "The Throne of His Glory: The Divine Throne and Heavenly Mediators in Revelation and the Similitudes of Enoch." *Zeitschrift für Neutestamentliche Wissenschaft* 94 (2003) 68–96.
Harrigan, John P. *The Gospel of Christ Crucified: A Theology of Suffering before Glory*. 2nd ed. Fayetteville, AR: Paroikos, 2019.
Harris, Steven Edward. *Refiguring Resurrection: A Biblical and Systematic Eschatology*. Waco, TX: Baylor University Press, 2023.
Harrison, Verna. "Male and Female in Cappadocian Theology." *Journal of Theological Studies* 41 (1990) 441–71.
Hart, David Bentley. *You Are Gods: On Nature and Supernature*. Notre Dame: University of Notre Dame Press, 2022.
Harvey, John E. *Faithful History: True Myth in the Scriptures*. Eugene, OR: Cascade, 2023.
Hauke, Manfred. *Introduction to Mariology*. Translated by Richard Chonak. Washington, DC: Catholic University of America Press, 2021.
Havukainen, Tuomas. *The Quest for the Memory of Jesus: A Viable Path or a Dead End?* Leuven: Peeters, 2020.

Hay, David M. *Glory at the Right Hand: Psalm 110 in Early Christianity.* Nashville: Abingdon, 1973.
Hays, Christopher M. "By Almsgiving and Faith Sins Are Purged? The Theological Underpinnings of Early Christian Care for the Poor." In *Engaging Economics: New Testament Scenarios and Early Christian Reception,* edited by Bruce W. Longenecker and Kelly D. Liebengood, 260–80. Grand Rapids: Eerdmans, 2009.
Hays, Christopher M., et al. *When the Son of Man Didn't Come: A Constructive Proposal on the Day of the Parousia.* Minneapolis: Fortress, 2016.
Hays, Richard B. "Christology: Jesus in the Apocalypse of John." In *Reading with the Grain of Scripture,* 285–302. Grand Rapids: Eerdmans, 2020.
———. *The Conversion of the Imagination: Paul as Interpreter of Israel's Scriptures.* Grand Rapids: Eerdmans, 2005.
———. "Covenant: New Covenantalism in Hebrews." In *Reading with the Grain of Scripture,* 303–24. Grand Rapids: Eerdmans, 2020.
———. *Echoes of Scripture in the Gospels.* Waco, TX: Baylor University Press, 2016.
———. *Echoes of Scripture in the Letters of Paul.* New Haven: Yale University Press, 1989.
———. "Eschatology: 'Why Do You Stand Looking Up into Heaven?'" In *Reading with the Grain of Scripture,* 368–91. Grand Rapids: Eerdmans, 2020.
———. "Figural Interpretation of Israel's Story." In *Reading with the Grain of Scripture,* 70–86. Grand Rapids: Eerdmans, 2020.
———. "Paul's Use of an Early Christian Convention." In *The Future of Christology: Essays in Honor of Leander E. Keck,* edited by Abraham J. Malherbe and Wayne A. Meeks, 122–36. Minneapolis: Fortress, 1993.
———. "Pneumatology: The Spirit in Romans 8." In *Reading with the Grain of Scripture,* 204–18. Grand Rapids: Eerdmans, 2020.
———. *Reading Backwards: Figural Christology and the Fourfold Gospel Witness.* Waco, TX: Baylor University Press, 2014.
———. "Reading Scripture in Light of the Resurrection." In *Reading with the Grain of Scripture,* 47–69. Grand Rapids: Eerdmans, 2020.
———. "Soteriology: Christ Died for the Ungodly." In *Reading with the Grain of Scripture,* 166–81. Grand Rapids: Eerdmans, 2020.
———. "Story, History, and the Quest for Jesus." In *Reading with the Grain of Scripture,* 104–22. Grand Rapids: Eerdmans, 2020.
Hayward, C. T. R. "'The Lord is One': Reflections on the Theme of Unity in John's Gospel from a Jewish Perspective." In *Early Jewish and Christian Monotheism,* edited by Loren T. Stuckenbruck and Wendy E. S. North, 138–54. London: T. & T. Clark, 2004.
Healey, Kilian. "The Assumption among Mary's Privileges." *The Thomist* 14 (1951) 72–92.
Hector, Kevin. *The Theological Project of Modernism: Faith and the Conditions of Mineness.* Oxford: Oxford University Press, 2015.
Heesterman, Jan. *The Broken World of Sacrifice: An Essay in Ancient Indian Ritual.* Chicago: University of Chicago Press, 1993.
Hegel, Georg Wilhelm Friedrich. *Lectures on the Philosophy of Religion: The Lectures of 1827,* vol. 3: *The Consummate Religion.* Edited by Peter C. Hodgson. Translated by Robert F. Brown, Peter C. Hodgson, and J. Michael Stewart. Berkeley: University of California Press, 2006.

Heil, John Paul. "Jesus as the Unique High Priest in the Gospel of John." *Catholic Biblical Quarterly* 57 (1995) 729–45.

———. *Jesus Walking on the Sea: Meaning and Gospel Functions of Matt. 14:22–33, Mark 6:45–52, and John 6:15b–21*. Rome: Biblical Institute, 1981.

———. *The Transfiguration of Jesus: Narrative Meaning and Function of Mark 9:2–8, Matt 17:1–8 and Luke 9:28–36*. Rome: Biblical Institute, 2000.

Heiligenthal, Roman. "Werke der Barmherzigkeit oder Almosen? Zur Bedeutung von ἐλεημοσύνη." *Novum Testamentum* 25 (1983) 289–301.

Heim, S. Mark. *Crucified Wisdom: Theological Reflection on Christ and the Bodhisattva*. New York: Fordham University Press, 2019.

Heintz, Michael. "Mariology as Theological Anthropology: Louis Bouyer on Mary, Seat of Wisdom." In *Mary on the Eve of the Second Vatican Council*, edited by John C. Cavadini and Danielle Peters, 204–25. Notre Dame: University of Notre Dame Press, 2017.

Henderson, Suzanne Watts. *Christology and Discipleship in the Gospel of Mark*. Cambridge: Cambridge University Press, 2006.

Hengel, Martin. *The Atonement: The Origins of the Doctrine in the New Testament*. Translated by John Bowden. Minneapolis: Fortress, 1981.

———. "The Dionysiac Messiah." In *Studies in Early Christology*, 293–331. Edinburgh: T. & T. Clark, 1995.

———. *The Four Gospels and the One Gospel of Jesus Christ: An Investigation of the Collection and Origin of the Canonical Gospels*. Translated by John Bowden. Harrisburg, PA: Trinity Press International, 2000.

———. "Jesus, the Messiah of Israel." In *Studies in Early Christology*, 1–72. Edinburgh: T. & T. Clark, 1995.

———. "Jesus as Messianic Teacher of Wisdom and the Beginnings of Christology." In *Studies in Early Christology*, 73–117. Edinburgh: T. & T. Clark, 1995.

———. "'Sit at My Right Hand!': The Enthronement of Christ at the Right Hand of God and Psalm 110:1." In *Studies in Early Christology*, 119–225. Edinburgh: T. & T. Clark, 1995.

———. "The Song about Christ in Earliest Worship." In *Studies in Early Christology*, 227–91. Edinburgh: T. & T. Clark, 1995.

Heringer, Seth. *Uniting History and Theology: A Theological Critique of the Historical Method*. Minneapolis: Fortress, 2018.

Herrmann, Wilhelm. *Systematic Theology (Dogmatik)*. Translated by Nathaniel Micklem and Kenneth A. Saunders. London: Macmillan, 1927.

Herzog, William R., II. *Jesus, Justice and the Reign of God: A Ministry of Liberation*. Louisville: Westminster John Knox, 2000.

Hill, Harvey. *The Politics of Modernism: Alfred Loisy and the Scientific Study of Religion*. Washington, DC: Catholic University of America Press, 2002.

Hill, Wesley. *Paul and the Trinity: Persons, Relations, and the Pauline Letters*. Grand Rapids: Eerdmans, 2015.

Hillebert, Jordan. *Henri de Lubac and the Drama of Human Existence*. Notre Dame: University of Notre Dame Press, 2021.

Hipp, Stephen A. *The Doctrine of Personal Subsistence: Historical and Systematic Synthesis*. Fribourg: Academic, 2012.

———. *"Person" in Christian Tradition and the Conception of Saint Albert the Great: A Systematic Study of Its Concept as Illuminated by the Mysteries of the Trinity and the Incarnation*. Münster: Aschendorff, 2001.

Hoffmann, Norbert. "Zur 'Perichorese' von Maria und Kirche in der Sicht M. J. Scheebens. Grundelemente systematischer Interpretation." In *Geist und Kirche: Studien zur Theologie im Umfeld der beiden Vatikanischen Konzilien. Gedenkschrift für Heribert Schauf*, edited by Herbert Hammans, 247–75. Paderborn: F. Schöningh, 1991.

Holmén, Tom. *Jesus and Jewish Covenant Thinking*. Leiden: Brill, 2001.

Holtz, Gudrun. *Jungfrauengeburt und Greisinnengeburt. Zur Rezeptionsgeschichte von Gen 21,1f im antiken Judentum und im frühen Christentum*. Göttingen: Vandenhoeck & Ruprecht, 2017.

Holzbrecher, Frank. *Paulus und der historische Jesus: Darstellung und Analyse der bisherigen Forschungsgeschichte*. Tübingen: Francke, 2007.

Homolka, Walter. *Jewish Jesus Research and Its Challenge to Christology Today*. Leiden: Brill, 2016.

Hooker, Morna D. *The Signs of a Prophet: The Prophetic Actions of Jesus*. London: SCM, 1997.

Horbury, William. *Jewish Messianism and the Cult of Christ*. London: SCM, 1998.

———. *Messianism among Jews and Christians: Twelve Biblical and Historical Studies*. London: T. & T. Clark, 2003.

Horsley, Richard. *Galilee: History, Politics, People*. Valley Forge, PA: Trinity Press International, 1995.

Horsley, Richard A., and John S. Hanson. *Bandits, Prophets, and Messiahs: Popular Movements at the Time of Jesus*. San Francisco: Harper & Row, 1988.

Hoskins, Paul M. *Jesus as the Fulfillment of the Temple in the Gospel of John*. Eugene, OR: Wipf & Stock, 2007.

Howard, Thomas Albert. *Religion and the Rise of Historicism: W. M. L. de Wette, Jacob Burckhardt, and the Theological Origins of Nineteenth-Century Historical Consciousness*. Cambridge: Cambridge University Press, 2000.

Huber, Konrad. *Einer gleich einem Menschensohn: Die Christusvisionen in Offb 1.9–20 und Offb 14,14–20 und die Christologie der Johannesoffenbarung*. Münster: Aschendorff, 2007.

Hughes, Derek. *Culture and Sacrifice: Ritual Death in Literature and Opera*. Cambridge: Cambridge University Press, 2007.

Huizenga, Leroy A. *The New Isaac: Tradition and Intertextuality in the Gospel of Matthew*. Leiden: Brill, 2009.

Hultgren, Arland J. *The Parables of Jesus: A Commentary*. Grand Rapids: Eerdmans, 2000.

Human, Dirk J., and Gert Jacobus Steyn, eds. *Psalms and Hebrews: Studies in Reception*. London: T. & T. Clark, 2010.

Hunter, Justus H. *If Adam Had Not Sinned: The Reason for the Incarnation from Anselm to Scotus*. Washington, DC: Catholic University of America Press, 2020.

Hurst, Lincoln D. "The Christology of Hebrews 1 and 2." In *The Glory of Christ in the New Testament: Studies in Christology*, edited by Lincoln D. Hurst and N. T. Wright, 151–64. Oxford: Clarendon, 1987.

Hurtado, Larry W. *Ancient Jewish Monotheism and Early Christian Jesus-Devotion: The Context and Character of Christological Faith*. Waco, TX: Baylor University Press, 2017.

———. *How on Earth Did Jesus Become a God? Historical Questions about Earliest Devotion to Jesus*. Grand Rapids: Eerdmans, 2005.

———. *Lord Jesus Christ: Devotion to Jesus in Earliest Christianity*. Grand Rapids: Eerdmans, 2003.

———. *One God, One Lord: Early Christian Devotion and Ancient Jewish Monotheism*. London: SCM, 1988.

Hütter, Reinhard. "The Debt of Sin and the Sacrifice in Charity: A Thomistic Echo to Gary Anderson's *Sin: A History*." *Nova et Vetera* 9 (2011) 133–48.

Idel, Moshe. "Righteousness, Theophorism and Sonship in Rabbinic and Heikhalot Literatures." In *Ben: Sonship and Jewish Mysticism*, 108–93. London: Continuum, 2007.

Imbelli, Robert P. *Rekindling the Christic Imagination: Theological Meditations for the New Evangelization*. Collegeville, MN: Liturgical, 2014.

Irenaeus of Lyons. *Against Heresies*, Book 3. Translated by Dominic J. Unger, OFM Cap., revised by Irenaeus M. C. Steenburg. New York: Paulist, 2012.

———. *Demonstration of the Apostolic Preaching*. Translated by John Behr. Crestwood, NY: St Vladimir's Seminary Press, 1997.

Jamieson, R. B. *Jesus' Death and Heavenly Offering in Hebrews*. Cambridge: Cambridge University Press, 2019.

———. *The Paradox of Sonship: Christology in the Epistle to the Hebrews*. Downers Grove, IL: IVP Academic, 2021.

Jenkins, Philip. *The New Faces of Christianity: Believing the Bible in the Global South*. Oxford: Oxford University Press, 2006.

Jensen, Matthew D. *Affirming the Resurrection of the Incarnate Christ: A Reading of 1 John*. Cambridge: Cambridge University Press, 2012.

Jipp, Joshua W. *Christ Is King: Paul's Royal Ideology*. Minneapolis: Fortress, 2015.

———. *The Messianic Theology of the New Testament*. Grand Rapids: Eerdmans, 2020.

John of Damascus. "On the Dormition of the Holy Mother of God: Homily I." In *On the Dormition of Mary: Early Patristic Homilies*, translated by Brian E. Daley, SJ, 183–201. Crestwood, NY: St Vladimir's Seminary Press, 1998.

———. "On the Dormition of the Holy Mother of God: Homily II." In *On the Dormition of Mary: Early Patristic Homilies*, translated by Brian E. Daley, SJ, 203–23. Crestwood, NY: St Vladimir's Seminary Press, 1998.

———. *On the Orthodox Faith*. Translated by Norman Russell. Yonkers, NY: St Vladimir's Seminary Press, 2022.

John Duns Scotus. *Ordinatio* III (*Opera Omnia*, vol. 9). Vatican City: Typis Vaticanis, 2006.

John Paul II. Encyclical Letter *Redemptoris Mater*. In *Mary: God's Yes to Man*, 41–158. San Francisco: Ignatius, 1988.

———. Encyclical Letter *Veritatis Splendor*. https://www.vatican.va/content/john-paul-ii/en/encyclicals/documents/hf_jp-ii_enc_06081993_veritatis-splendor.html.

Johns, Loren L. *The Lamb Christology of the Apocalypse of John: An Investigation into Its Origin and Rhetorical Force*. Tübingen: Mohr Siebeck, 2003.

Johnson, Adam J. *God's Being in Reconciliation*. New York: T. & T. Clark, 2012.

Johnson, Luke Timothy. *Among the Gentiles: Greco-Roman Religion and Christianity*. New Haven, CT: Yale University Press, 2009.

———. *Hebrews: A Commentary*. Louisville: Westminster John Knox, 2006.

———. *The Living Gospel*. New York: Continuum, 2004.

———. *Living Jesus: Learning the Heart of the Gospel*. New York: HarperCollins, 1999.

---. *Miracles: God's Presence and Power in Creation*. Louisville: Westminster John Knox, 2018.

---. *The Real Jesus: The Misguided Quest for the Historical Jesus and the Truth of the Traditional Gospels*. New York: HarperCollins, 1996.

Johnson, Luke Timothy, and William S. Kurz, SJ. *The Future of Catholic Biblical Scholarship: A Constructive Conversation*. Grand Rapids: Eerdmans, 2002.

Johnson, Sara R. "Third Maccabees: Historical Fictions and the Shaping of Jewish Identity in the Hellenistic Period." In *Ancient Fiction: The Matrix of Early Christian and Jewish Narrative*, edited by Jo-Ann Brant et al., 185–98. Atlanta: SBL, 2005.

Jonas, Hans. *The Phenomenon of Life: Toward a Philosophical Biology*. New York: Harper & Row, 1966.

Jones, Beth Felker. *Marks of His Wounds: Gender Politics and Bodily Resurrection*. Oxford: Oxford University Press, 2007.

---. *Practicing Christian Doctrine: An Introduction to Thinking and Living Theologically*. Grand Rapids: Baker Academic, 2014.

Joseph, Simon J. *Jesus and the Temple: The Crucifixion in Its Jewish Context*. Cambridge: Cambridge University Press, 2016.

Journet, Charles. *L'Église du Verbe incarné. Essai de théologie speculative*. Vol. 2, *Sa structure interne et son unité catholique (Première partie)*. Saint-Maurice, Switzerland: Éditions Saint-Augustin, 1999.

---. *L'Église du Verbe incarné. Essai de théologie speculative*. Vol. 3, *Sa structure interne et son unité catholique (Deuxième partie)*. Saint-Maurice: Editions Saint-Augustin, 2000.

Judge, Thomas A. *Other Gods and Idols: The Relationship Between the Worship of Other Gods and the Worship of Idols within the Old Testament*. London: T. & T. Clark, 2019.

Jugie, Martin. "Assomption de la Sainte Vierge." In *Maria: Études sur la sainte Vierge*, vol. 1, edited by Hubert du Manoir, 619–58. Paris: Beauchesne, 1948.

Jung, Chang-Wook. *The Original Language of the Lukan Infancy Narrative*. London: T. & T. Clark, 2004.

Kahl, Werner. *New Testament Miracle Stories in Their Religious-Historical Setting: A Religions-geschichtliche Comparison from a Structural Perspective*. Göttingen: Vandenhoeck & Ruprecht, 1994.

Kaminsky, Joel S. *Yet I Loved Jacob: Reclaiming the Biblical Concept of Election*. Nashville: Abingdon, 2007.

Kappes, Christiaan. "The Doctrine of the *Theotokos* in Gregorios Palamas." In *The Oxford Handbook of Mary*, edited by Chris Maunder, 168–82. Oxford: Oxford University Press, 2019.

---. *Immaculate Conception: Why Thomas Aquinas Denied, While John Duns Scotus, Gregory Palamas, and Mark Eugenicus Professed the Absolute Immaculate Existence of Mary*. New Bedford, MI: Academy of the Immaculate, 2014.

Kariatlis, Philip. "Deification as Christification and Human Becoming." In *Faith, Reason, and Theosis*, edited by Aristotle Papanikolaou and George E. Demacopoulos, 72–92. New York: Fordham University Press, 2023.

Karris, Robert J., OFM. "St. Bonaventure as Biblical Interpreter. His Methods, Wit, and Wisdom." *Franciscan Studies* 60 (2002) 159–208.

Käsemann, Ernst. *The Testament of Jesus: A Study in the Gospel of John in the Light of Chapter 17*. Translated by Gerhard Krodel. London: SCM, 1968.

Kasper, Walter. *Jesus the Christ*. Translated by V. Green. New York: Paulist, 1976.
Kazen, Thomas. *Jesus and Purity Halakhah: Was Jesus Indifferent to Impurity?*. Stockholm: Almqvist & Wiksell, 2002.
Kearns, Cleo McNelly. *The Virgin Mary, Monotheism and Sacrifice*. Cambridge: Cambridge University Press, 2008.
Keating, Daniel A. *The Appropriation of Divine Life in Cyril of Alexandria*. Oxford: Oxford University Press, 2004.
———. "The Baptism of Jesus in Cyril of Alexandria: The Re-creation of the Human Race." *Pro Ecclesia* 8 (1999) 201–22.
———. "Christology in Cyril and Leo: Unnoticed Parallels and Ironies." *Studia Patristica* 48 (2010) 59–64.
———. "Exegesis and Christology in Thomas Aquinas." In *Reading Sacred Scripture with Thomas Aquinas. Hermeneutical Tools, Theological Questions and New Perspectives*, edited by Piotr Roszak and Jörgen Vijgen, 507–30. Turnhout, Belgium: Brepols, 2015.
———. "The Twofold Manner of Divine Indwelling in Cyril of Alexandria: Redressing an Imbalance." *Studia Patristica* 37 (2001) 543–49.
Kee, Howard C. *Medicine, Miracle and Magic in New Testament Times*. Cambridge: Cambridge University Press, 1986.
Keener, Craig S. *Christobiography: Memory, History, and the Reliability of the Gospels*. Grand Rapids: Eerdmans, 2019.
———. *The Gospel of John: A Commentary*. 2 vols. Grand Rapids: Baker Academic, 2012.
———. *Miracles: The Credibility of the New Testament Accounts*. 2 vols. Grand Rapids: Baker Academic, 2011.
Keith, Chris. *Jesus Against the Scribal Elite: The Origins of the Conflict*. Grand Rapids: Baker Academic, 2014.
———. *Jesus' Literacy: Scribal Culture and the Teacher from Galilee*. London: Bloomsbury, 2011.
Kelber, Werner H., and Samuel Byrskog, eds. *Jesus in Memory: Traditions in Oral and Scribal Perspectives*. Waco, TX: Baylor University Press, 2009.
Kelsey, Catherine L. *Schleiermacher's Preaching, Dogmatics, and Biblical Criticism: The Interpretation of Jesus Christ in the Gospel of John*. Eugene, OR: Pickwick, 2007.
Kereszty, Roch, OCist. "Historical Research, Theological Inquiry, and the Reality of Jesus: Reflections on the Method of J. P. Meier." *Communio* 19 (1992) 576–600.
Kerr, Alan R. *The Temple of Jesus' Body: The Temple Theme in the Gospel of John*. Sheffield: Sheffield Academic, 2002.
Kerr, Fergus, OP. "Questioning the Virgin Birth." *New Blackfriars* 75 (1994) 132–40.
Kessler, Gwynn. *Conceiving Israel: The Fetus in Rabbinic Narratives*. Philadelphia: University of Pennsylvania Press, 2009.
Kilgallen, John. "Luke 15 and 16: A Connection." *Biblica* 78 (1997) 369–76.
Kim, Yung Suk. *Messiah in Weakness: A Portrait of Jesus from the Perspective of the Dispossessed*. Eugene, OR: Cascade, 2016.
Kirk, Alan, and Tom Thatcher. "Jesus Tradition as Social Memory." In *Memory, Tradition, and Text: Uses of the Past in Early Christianity*, edited by Alan Kirk and Tom Thatcher, 25–43. Atlanta: SBL, 2005.
Kirk, J. R. Daniel. *A Man Attested by God: The Human Jesus of the Synoptic Gospels*. Grand Rapids: Eerdmans, 2016.

Klausner, Joseph. *The Messianic Idea in Israel: From Its Beginning to the Completion of the Mishnah*. Translated by W. F. Stinespring. New York: Macmillan, 1955.

Klawans, Jonathan. "Deceptive Intentions: Forgeries, Falsehoods, and the Study of Ancient Judaism." *The Jewish Quarterly Review* 108 (2018) 489–501.

———. *Heresy, Forgery, Novelty: Condemning, Denying, and Asserting Innovation in Ancient Judaism*. Oxford: Oxford University Press, 2019.

———. *Impurity and Sin in Ancient Judaism*. Oxford: Oxford University Press, 2000.

———. *Purity, Sacrifice, and the Temple: Symbolism and Supersessionism in the Study of Ancient Judaism*. Oxford: Oxford University Press, 2006.

Klink, Edward W., III. "Light of the World: Cosmology and the Johannine Literature." In *Cosmology and New Testament Theology*, edited by Jonathan T. Pennington and Sean M. McDonough, 74–89. London: T. & T. Clark, 2008.

Klos, Herbert. *Die Sakramente im Johannesevangelium: Vorkommen und Bedeutung von Taufe, Eucharistie und Besse im vierten Evangelium*. Stuttgart: Katholisches Bibelwerk, 1970.

Klutz, Todd E. *The Exorcism Stories in Luke-Acts: A Sociostylistic Reading*. Cambridge: Cambridge University Press, 2004.

———. "The Grammar of Exorcism in the Ancient Mediterranean World: Some Cosmological, Semantic, and Pragmatic Reflections on How Exorcistic Prowess Contributed to the Worship of Jesus." In *The Jewish Roots of Christological Monotheism: Papers from the St. Andrews Conference on the Historical Origins of the Worship of Jesus*, edited by Carey C. Newman et al., 156–65. Leiden: Brill, 1999.

Knohl, Israel. *The Messiah before Jesus: The Suffering Servant of the Dead Sea Scrolls*. Translated by David Maisel. Berkeley: University of California Press, 2000.

———. *The Messiah Confrontation: Pharisees versus Sadducees and the Death of Jesus*. Translated by David Maisel. Philadelphia: The Jewish Publication Society, 2022.

———. *Messiahs and Resurrection in 'The Gabriel Revelation.'* London: Continuum, 2009.

Kocian, Pierre, OSB. *Marie et l'Église. Compénétration des deux mystères*. Paris: Parole et Silence, 2018.

Koester, Craig. *Dwelling of God: The Tabernacle in the Old Testament, Intertestamental Jewish Literature, and the New Testament*. Washington, DC: Catholic Biblical Association, 1989.

Kristeva, Julia. "Stabat Mater." In *The Kristeva Reader*, edited by Toril Moi, 160–86. Oxford: Blackwell, 1987.

Kromholtz, Bryan, OP. *On the Last Day: The Time of the Resurrection of the Dead according to Thomas Aquinas*. Fribourg: Academic Press Fribourg, 2008.

———. "The Spirit of the Letter: St. Thomas's Interpretation of Scripture in His Reading of Job's Eschatology." In *Reading Job with St. Thomas Aquinas*, edited by Matthew Levering, et al., 364–83. Washington, DC: Catholic University of America Press, 2020.

Ku, John Baptist, OP. "The Fittingness of Mary's Virginity in Birth." *The Thomist* 87 (2023) 451–62.

Kugler, Robert. *The Testaments of the Twelve Patriarchs*. Sheffield: Sheffield Academic, 2001.

Kuhner, Matthew. "Ignatius of Antioch's *Letter to the Ephesians* 19.1 and the Hidden Mysteries: A Trajectory of Interpretation from Origen to Thomas Aquinas." *Journal of Theological Studies* 68 (2017) 93–120.

Kupp, David D. *Matthew's Emmanuel: Divine Presence and God's People in the First Gospel*. Cambridge: Cambridge University Press, 1996.

Kuschel, Karl-Josef. *Geboren vor aller Zeit? Der Streit um Christi Ursprung*. Munich: Piper, 1990.

Kwon, Oh-Young. "A Critical Review of Recent Scholarship on the Pauline Opposition and the Nature of Its Wisdom (σοφία) in 1 Corinthians 1–4." *Currents in Biblical Research* 8 (2010) 386–427.

Laansma, Jon. "The Cosmology of Hebrews." In *Cosmology and New Testament Theology*, edited by Jonathan T. Pennington and Sean M. McDonough, 125–43. London: T. & T. Clark, 2008.

Ladaria, Luis, SJ. *Gesù Cristo, salvezza di tutti*. Bologna: Edizioni Dehoniane, 2009.

Lagrange, Marie-Joseph, OP. *Le messianisme chez les Juifs*. Paris: Gabalda, 1909.

———. *Le sens du christianisme d'après l'exégèse allemande*. Paris: Gabalda, 1918.

Lauber, David. *Barth on the Descent into Hell: God, Atonement, and the Christian Life*. Aldershot: Ashgate, 2004.

Laurentin, René. *A Short Treatise on the Virgin Mary*. Washington, NJ: Ave Maria Institute, 1991.

LaVerdiere, Eugene, SSS, and Paul Bernier, SSS. *The Firstborn of God: The Birth of Mary's Son, Jesus. Luke 2:1–21*. Chicago: Liturgical Training Publications, 2007.

Leahy, Brendan. *The Marian Principle in the Ecclesiology of Hans Urs von Balthasar*. Hyde Park, NY: New City, 2000.

Le Donne, Anthony. *The Historiographical Jesus: Memory, Typology, and the Son of David*. Waco, TX: Baylor University Press, 2009.

———. "The Jewish Leaders." In *Jesus among Friends and Enemies: A Historical and Literary Introduction to Jesus in the Gospels*, edited by Chris Keith and Larry W. Hurtado, 199–217. Grand Rapids: Baker Academic, 2011.

Lee, Aquila H. I. *From Messiah to Preexistent Son: Jesus' Self-Consciousness and Early Christian Exegesis of Messianic Psalms*. Tübingen: Mohr Siebeck, 2005.

Lee, Dorothy. *Hallowed in Truth and Love: Spirituality in the Johannine Literature*. Eugene, OR: Wipf & Stock, 2012.

Lefebvre, Philippe, OP. *Comment tuer Jésus? Abus, violences et emprises dans la Bible*. Paris: Cerf, 2021.

Le Frois, Bernard J. *The Woman Clothed with the Sun (Ap. 12): Individual or Collective?*. Rome: Orbis Catholicus, 1954.

Legaspi, Michael C. *Wisdom in Classical and Biblical Tradition*. Oxford: Oxford University Press, 2018.

Legge, Dominic, OP. "Christ's Prayer to the Father (and Ours)." In *Thomas Aquinas as Spiritual Teacher*, edited by Michael A. Dauphinais et al., 261–74. Ave Maria, FL: Sapientia, 2023.

———. "Incarnate *De Spiritu Sancto*: Aquinas on the Holy Spirit and Christ's Conception." *The Thomist* 84 (2020) 173–205.

———. "The Remedy for Confused Kenoticism: Aquinas as a Kenotic Theologian." In *Thomas Aquinas and the Crisis of Christology*, edited by Michael Dauphinais et al., 56–69. Ave Maria, FL: Sapientia, 2021.

———. *The Trinitarian Christology of St Thomas Aquinas*. Oxford: Oxford University Press, 2017.
Le Guillou, M. J., OP. *Christ and Church: A Theology of the Mystery*. Translated by Charles E. Schaldenbrand. New York: Desclee, 1966.
Lehtipuu, Outi. *Debates Over the Resurrection of the Dead: Constructing Early Christian Identity*. Oxford: Oxford University Press, 2015.
Leithart, Peter J. *Delivered from the Elements of the World: Atonement, Justification, Mission*. Downers Grove, IL: IVP Academic, 2016.
———. "'You Shall Judge Angels': A Response to Fr. Behr." In *The Gospel of John: Theological-Ecumenical Readings*, edited by Charles Raith II, 192–201. Eugene, OR: Cascade, 2017.
Lemna, Keith. "'O Christ, Ever Greater': De Lubac on Teilhard and the Cosmic Scope of Jesus Christ's Humanity." *Communio* 49 (2022) 751–80.
Leo XIII. Encyclical Letter *Adiutricem*. https://www.vatican.va/content/leo-xiii/en/encyclicals/documents/hf_l-xiii_enc_05091895_adiutricem.html.
———. Encyclical Letter *Fidentum Piumque*. https://www.vatican.va/content/leo-xiii/en/encyclicals/documents/hf_l-xiii_enc_20091896_fidentem-piumque-animum.html.
———. Encyclical Letter *Octobri Mense*. https://www.vatican.va/content/leo-xiii/en/encyclicals/documents/hf_l-xiii_enc_22091891_octobri-mense.html.
Lettsome, Raquel S. "Mary's Slave Songs: The Tensions and Turnarounds of Faithfully Reading *Doulē* in the Magnificat." *Interpretation* 75 (2021) 6–18.
Levenson, Jon D. *The Death and Resurrection of the Beloved Son: The Transformation of Child Sacrifice in Judaism and Christianity*. New Haven: Yale University Press, 1993.
———. *The Love of God: Divine Gift, Human Gratitude, and Mutual Faithfulness in Judaism*. Princeton: Princeton University Press, 2016.
Levering, Matthew. *The Achievement of Hans Urs von Balthasar*. Washington, DC: Catholic University of America Press, 2019.
———. *Aquinas's Eschatological Ethics and the Virtue of Temperance*. Notre Dame: University of Notre Dame Press, 2019.
———. *The Betrayal of Charity: The Sins that Sabotage Divine Love*. Waco, TX: Baylor University Press, 2011.
———. "The Christian Bible and the Land." In *The Challenges of Catholic-Jewish Dialogue*, edited by Matthew Tapie, Alan Brill, and Matthew Levering. Washington, DC: Catholic University of America Press, forthcoming.
———. *Christ's Fulfillment of Torah and Temple: Salvation According to Thomas Aquinas*. Notre Dame: University of Notre Dame Press, 2002.
———. *Did Jesus Rise from the Dead? Historical and Theological Reflections*. Oxford: Oxford University Press, 2019.
———. *Dying and the Virtues*. Grand Rapids: Eerdmans, 2018.
———. *Engaging the Doctrine of Creation: Cosmos, Creatures, and the Wise and Good Creator*. Grand Rapids: Baker Academic, 2017.
———. *Engaging the Doctrine of the Holy Spirit: Love and Gift in the Trinity and the Church*. Grand Rapids: Baker Academic, 2016.
———. *Engaging the Doctrine of Israel: A Christian Israelology in Dialogue with Ongoing Judaism*. Eugene, OR: Cascade, 2021.

———. *Engaging the Doctrine of Marriage: Human Marriage as a Sign and Sacrament of the Marriage of God and Creation*. Eugene, OR: Cascade, 2020.

———. *Engaging the Doctrine of Revelation: The Mediation of the Gospel through Church and Scripture*. Grand Rapids: Baker Academic, 2014.

———. *Jesus and the Demise of Death: Resurrection, the Afterlife, and the Fate of Christians*. Waco, TX: Baylor University Press, 2012.

———. *Mary's Bodily Assumption*. Notre Dame: University of Notre Dame Press, 2015.

———. *Newman on Doctrinal Corruption*. Park Ridge, IL: Word on Fire Academic, 2022.

———. *Participatory Biblical Exegesis: A Theology of Biblical Interpretation*. Notre Dame: University of Notre Dame Press, 2008.

———. *Proofs of God: Classical Arguments from Tertullian to Barth*. Grand Rapids: Baker Academic, 2016.

———. *Reconfiguring Thomistic Christology*. Cambridge: Cambridge University Press, 2023.

———. *Sacrifice and Community: Jewish Offering and Christian Eucharist*. Oxford: Blackwell, 2005.

———. *Scripture and Metaphysics: Aquinas and the Renewal of Trinitarian Theology*. Oxford: Blackwell, 2004.

———. "Trinity and Suffering." In *T&T Clark Handbook on Suffering and the Problem of Evil*, edited by Matthias Grebe and Johannes Grössl, 267–76. London: Bloomsbury, 2023.

———. "Variations on a Theme by Paul: Romans 1:20 in the *Summa Theologiae*." *Pro Ecclesia* 22 (2013) 153–66.

Levering, Matthew, and Michael Dauphinais. *Holy People, Holy Land: A Theological Introduction to Scripture*. Grand Rapids: Brazos, 2005.

———. *The Wisdom of the Word: Biblical Answers to Ten Pressing Questions about Catholicism*. Park Ridge, IL: Word on Fire Institute, 2021.

Levine, Amy-Jill. *The Difficult Words of Jesus: A Beginner's Guide to His Most Perplexing Teachings*. Nashville: Abingdon, 2021.

———. *Entering the Passion of Jesus: A Beginner's Guide to Holy Week*. Nashville: Abingdon, 2018.

———. *The Misunderstood Jew: The Church and the Scandal of the Jewish Jesus*. New York: HarperCollins, 2006.

———. *Sermon on the Mount: A Beginner's Guide to the Kingdom of Heaven*. Nashville: Abingdon, 2020.

———. *Short Stories by Jesus: The Enigmatic Parables of a Controversial Rabbi*. New York: HarperCollins, 2014.

———. *Witness at the Cross: A Beginner's Guide to Holy Friday*. Nashville: Abingdon, 2021.

Lewis, C. S. *Miracles*. London: Sheed and Ward, 1947.

Lewis, Jody Vaccaro. "The Inn, the Manger, the Swaddling Clothes, the Shepherds, and the Animals." In *The Oxford Handbook of Christmas*, edited by Timothy Larsen, 224–38. Oxford: Oxford University Press, 2020.

Lieu, Judith. "The Mother of the Son in the Fourth Gospel." *Journal of Biblical Literature* 117 (1998) 61–77.

Lincoln, Andrew T. "The Bible, Theology, and the Virgin Birth: Continuing a Conversation?" *Journal of Theological Interpretation* 14 (2020) 267–85.

———. *Born of a Virgin? Reconceiving Jesus in the Bible, Tradition, and Theology.* Grand Rapids: Eerdmans, 2013.
Lindars, Barnabas. "Re-enter the Apocalyptic Son of Man." *New Testament Studies* 22 (1975) 52–72.
Litwa, M. David. *How the Gospels Became History: Jesus and Mediterranean Myths.* New Haven: Yale University Press, 2019.
———. *Iesus Deus: The Early Christian Depiction of Jesus as a Mediterranean God.* Minneapolis: Fortress, 2014.
———. *We Are Being Transformed: Deification in Paul's Soteriology.* Berlin: de Gruyter, 2012.
Loader, William. *Jesus in John's Gospel: Structures and Issues in Johannine Christology.* Grand Rapids: Eerdmans, 2017.
Lohfink, Gerhard. *The Forty Parables of Jesus.* Translated by Linda M. Maloney. Collegeville, MN: Liturgical Press Academic, 2021.
Loisy, Alfred. *The Gospel and the Church.* Translated by Christopher Home. London: Isbister, 1903.
Loke, Andrew Ter Ern. *The Origin of Divine Christology.* Cambridge: Cambridge University Press, 2017.
Lombardo, Nicholas, OP. *The Father's Will: Christ's Crucifixion and the Goodness of God.* Oxford: Oxford University Press, 2013.
———. "Where Does the Holy Spirit Proceed To?" *International Journal of Systematic Theology* 23 (2021) 473–501.
Lonergan, Bernard J. F., SJ. *The Incarnate Word.* Translated by Charles C. Hefling Jr. Edited by Robert M. Doran, SJ, and Jeremy Wilkins. Toronto: University of Toronto Press, 2016.
———. *The Redemption.* Translated by Michael G. Shields. Edited by Robert M. Doran, H. Daniel Monsour, and Jeremy D. Wilkins. Toronto: University of Toronto Press, 2018.
———. "Revolution in Catholic Theology." In *A Second Collection*, edited by Robert M. Doran, SJ, and John D. Dadosky, 195–201. Toronto: University of Toronto Press, 2016.
Long, Phillip J. *Jesus the Bridegroom: The Origin of the Eschatological Feast as a Wedding Banquet in the Synoptic Gospels.* Eugene, OR: Pickwick, 2013.
Loon, Hans Van. *The Dyophysite Christology of Cyril of Alexandria.* Leiden: Brill, 2009.
Loughlin, Gerard, ed. *Queer Theology: Rethinking the Western Body.* Oxford: Blackwell, 2007.
Louth, Andrew. "Mary in Modern Orthodox Theology." In *The Oxford Handbook of Mary*, edited by Chris Maunder, 231–43. Oxford: Oxford University Press, 2019.
Lüdemann, Gerd. *Virgin Birth? The Real Story of Mary and Her Son Jesus.* Translated by John Bowden. Harrisburg, PA: Trinity Press International, 1998.
Lynch, Reginald M., OP. "Cajetan on Christ's Priestly Sacrifice: *Ressourcement* Thomism in the Sixteenth Century." In *Thomas Aquinas and the Crisis of Christology*, edited by Michael A. Dauphinais et al., 233–48. Ave Maria, FL: Sapientia, 2021.
Macaskill, Grant. *Union with Christ in the New Testament.* Oxford: Oxford University Press, 2013.
Macchia, Frank D. *Jesus the Spirit Baptizer: Christology in Light of Pentecost.* Grand Rapids: Eerdmans, 2018.

MacDonald, Dennis R. *Mythologizing Jesus: From Jewish Teacher to Epic Hero*. Lanham, MD: Rowman & Littlefield, 2015.

Macquarrie, John. *Christology Revisited*. London: SCM, 1998.

Madigan, Daniel A., SJ. "Who Needs It? Atonement in Muslim-Christian Theological Engagement." In *Atonement and Comparative Theology: The Cross in Dialogue with Other Religions*, edited by Catherine Cornille, 11–39. New York: Fordham University Press, 2021.

Madigan, Kevin. *The Passions of Christ in High-Medieval Thought: An Essay on Christological Development*. Oxford: Oxford University Press, 2007.

Malatesta, Edward. "Blood and Water from the Pierced Side of Christ (Jn 19,34)." In *Segni e Sacramenti nel Vangelo à Giovanni*, edited by Pius-Ramon Tragan, 165–81. Rome: Anselmiana, 1977.

Malcolm, Matthew R. "The Resurrection of the Dead in 1 Corinthians." In *Resurrection of the Dead: Biblical Traditions in Dialogue*, edited by Geert Van Oyen and Tom Shepherd, 275–88. Leuven: Peeters, 2012.

Mansini, Guy, OSB. "The Authority and Charity of Christ." In *Thomas Aquinas and the Crisis of Christology*, edited by Michael A. Dauphinais et al., 139–70. Ave Maria, FL: Sapientia, 2021.

———. "Christology in Context: Review Essay of Thomas Joseph White, OP, *The Incarnate Lord*." *Nova et Vetera* 14 (2016) 1271–91.

Marcel, Gabriel. *Faith and Reality*. Vol. 2 of *The Mystery of Being*. South Bend, IN: St. Augustine's, 2001.

Marcus, Joel. *The Way of the Lord: Christological Exegesis of the Old Testament in the Gospel of Mark*. Louisville: Westminster John Knox, 1992.

Margelidon, Philippe-Marie. *Études thomistes sur la théologie de la redemption. De la grace à la resurrection du Christ*. Perpignan: Artège, 2010.

Marion, Jean-Luc. *D'ailleurs, la revelation*. Paris: Grasset, 2020.

———. *In Excess: Studies of Saturated Phenomena*. Translated by Robyn Horner and Vincent Berraud. New York: Fordham University Press, 2002.

Marshall, Bruce D. "The Absolute and the Trinity." *Pro Ecclesia* 23 (2014) 147–64.

———. *Christologies in Conflict: The Identity of a Saviour in Rahner and Barth*. Oxford: Blackwell, 1987.

———. "Debt, Punishment, and Payment: A Meditation on the Cross, in Light of St. Anselm." *Nova et Vetera* 9 (2011) 163–81.

———. "God Almighty in the Flesh: Christology and the Crisis of Faith." In *Thomas Aquinas and the Crisis of Christology*, edited by Michael A. Dauphinais et al., 345–67. Ave Maria, FL: Sapientia, 2021.

———. "What Does the Spirit Have to Do?" In *Reading John with St. Thomas Aquinas: Theological Exegesis and Speculative Theology*, edited by Michael Dauphinais and Matthew Levering, 62–77. Washington, DC: Catholic University of America Press, 2005.

Marshall, I. Howard. *The Origins of New Testament Christology*. 2nd ed. Downers Grove, IL: InterVarsity, 1990.

Marschler, Thomas. *Auferstehung und Himmelfahrt Christi in der scholasticschen Theologie bis zu Thomas von Aquin*. 2 vols. Münster: Aschendorff, 2003.

———. "Perspektiven der Eschatologie bei Joseph Ratzinger." In *Joseph Ratzinger: Ein theologisches Profil*, edited by Peter Hofmann, 161–91. Munich: Ferdinand Schöningh, 2008.

Martens, Allan W. "'Produce Fruit Worthy of Repentance': Parables of Judgment against the Jewish Religious Leaders and the Nation (Matthew 21:28—22:14 par.; Luke 13:6–9)." In *The Challenge of Jesus' Parables*, edited by Richard N. Longenecker, 151–76. Grand Rapids: Eerdmans, 2000.

Martin, Dale B. *The Corinthian Body*. New Haven, CT: Yale University Press, 1995.

Martin, Francis, and William M. Wright IV. *The Gospel of John*. Grand Rapids: Baker Academic, 2015.

Martyn, J. Louis. *Galatians: A New Translation with Introduction and Commentary*. New York: Doubleday, 1997.

Marxsen, Willi. *Die Auferstehung Jesu als historisches und theologisches Problem*. Gütersloh: 1964.

Mason, Eric F. "Heavenly Revelation in the Epistle to the Hebrews." In *The Jewish Apocalyptic Tradition and the Shaping of New Testament Thought*, edited by Benjamin E. Reynolds and Loren T. Stuckenbruck, 277–91. Minneapolis: Fortress, 2017.

Matera, Frank J. *Galatians*. Collegeville, MN: Liturgical, 1992.

———. *New Testament Christology*. Louisville: Westminster John Knox, 1999.

———. *New Testament Theology: Exploring Diversity and Unity*. Louisville: Westminster John Knox, 2007.

———. *The Sermon on the Mount: The Perfect Measure of the Christian Life*. Collegeville, MN: Liturgical, 2013.

Matthiesen, Michon M. *Sacrifice as Gift: Eucharist, Grace, and Contemplative Prayer in Maurice de la Taille*. Washington, DC: Catholic University of America Press, 2013.

Mattison, William C., III. *The Sermon on the Mount and Moral Theology: A Virtue Perspective*. Cambridge: Cambridge University Press, 2017.

Maunder, Chris. "Introduction." In *The Oxford Handbook of Mary*, edited by Chris Maunder, 1–17. Oxford: Oxford University Press, 2019.

Maunder, Chris, ed. *The Oxford Handbook of Mary*. Oxford: Oxford University Press, 2019.

Maximus the Confessor. *The Life of the Virgin*. Translated by Stephen J. Shoemaker. New Haven: Yale University Press, 2012.

McArthur, Harvey K., and Robert Morris Johnston. *They Also Taught in Parables: Rabbinic Parables from the First Centuries of the Christian Era*. Grand Rapids: Zondervan, 1990.

McClellan, Daniel O. *YHWH's Divine Images: A Cognitive Approach*. Atlanta : SBL, 2022.

McCollough, Ross. *Freedom and Sin: Evil in a World Created by God*. Grand Rapids: Eerdmans, 2022.

McCormack, Bruce. *The Humility of the Eternal Son: Reformed Kenoticism and the Repair of Chalcedon*. Cambridge: Cambridge University Press, 2021.

———. "Kenoticism in Modern Christology." In *The Oxford Handbook of Christology*, edited by Francesca Aran Murphy, 444–58. Oxford: Oxford University Press, 2015.

McCosker, Philip. "Sacrifice in Recent Roman Catholic Thought: From Paradox to Polarity, and Back Again?" In *Sacrifice and Modern Thought*, edited by Julia Meszaros and Johannes Zachhuber, 132–46. Oxford: Oxford University Press, 2013.

McCready, Douglas. *He Came Down from Heaven: The Preexistence of Christ and the Christian Faith*. Downers Grove, IL: InterVarsity, 2005.

McDonough, Sean M. *Christ as Creator: Origins of a New Testament Doctrine*. Oxford: Oxford University Press, 2009.
McFarland, Ian A. *The Word Made Flesh: A Theology of the Incarnation*. Louisville: Westminster John Knox, 2019.
McGrath, James F. *John's Apologetic Christology: Legitimation and Development in Johannine Christology*. Cambridge: Cambridge University Press, 2001.
———. *The Only True God: Early Christian Monotheism in Its Jewish Context*. Urbana, IL: University of Illinois Press, 2009.
McHugh, John. *The Mother of Jesus in the New Testament*. Garden City, NY: Doubleday, 1975.
McIver, Robert K. *Memory, Jesus, and the Synoptic Gospels*. Atlanta: SBL, 2011.
McKinion, Steven A. *Words, Imagery, and the Mystery of Christ: A Reconstruction of Cyril of Alexandria's Christology*. Leiden: Brill, 2000.
McKnight, Scot. *Five Things Biblical Scholars Wish Theologians Knew*. Downers Grove, IL: IVP Academic, 2021.
———. *Jesus and His Death: Historiography, the Historical Jesus, and Atonement Theory*. Waco, TX: Baylor University Press, 2005.
———. "Jesus' New Vision within Judaism." In *Who Was Jesus? A Jewish-Christian Dialogue*, edited by Paul Copan and Craig A. Evans, 73–96. Louisville: Westminster John Knox, 2001.
McMichael, Steven J. "The Resurrection of Jesus and Human Beings in Medieval Christian and Jewish Theology and Polemical Literature." *Studies in Christian-Jewish Relations* 4 (2009) 1–8, http://escholarship.bc.edu/scjr/vol4.
McWhirter, Jocelyn. *The Bridegroom Messiah and the People of God: Marriage in the Fourth Gospel*. Cambridge: Cambridge University Press, 2006.
Meeks, Wayne A. "Asking Back to Jesus' Identity." In *From Jesus to John: Essays on Jesus and New Testament Christology in Honour of Marinus de Jonge*, edited by Martinus C. De Boer, 38–50. Sheffield: Sheffield Academic, 1993.
———. *The Prophet-King: Moses Traditions and the Johannine Christology*. Leiden: Brill, 1967.
Meier, John P. *A Marginal Jew: Rethinking the Historical Jesus*. 5 vols. New York: Doubleday/Yale University Press, 1991–2016.
Menzies, Robert Paul. *The Development of Early Christian Pneumatology with Special Reference to Luke-Acts*. Sheffield: Sheffield Academic, 1991.
Mercedes, Anna. *Power For: Feminism and Christ's Self-Giving*. London: T. & T. Clark, 2011.
Mersch, Emile, SJ. *The Whole Christ: The Historical Development of the Doctrine of the Mystical Body in Scripture and Tradition*. Translated by John R. Kelly, SJ. Milwaukee, WI: Bruce, 1938.
Meszaros, Julia. "Sacrifice and the Self." In *Sacrifice and Modern Thought*, edited by Julia Meszaros and Johannes Zachhuber, 66–82. Oxford: Oxford University Press, 2013.
Meyer, Barbara U. *Jesus the Jew in Christian Memory: Theological and Philosophical Explorations*. Cambridge: Cambridge University Press, 2020.
Milgrom, Jacob. *Leviticus 1–16*. New York: Doubleday, 1991.
Miller, Ed L. *Salvation History in the Prologue of John: The Significance of John 1:3/4*. Leiden: Brill, 1989.
Miller, Richard C. *Resurrection and Reception in Early Christianity*. London: Routledge, 2015.

Miller, Robert J. *Born Divine: The Births of Jesus and Other Sons of God*. Santa Rosa, CA: Polebridge, 2003.

Minz, Karl-Heinz. *Pleroma Trinitatis. Die Trinitätstheologie bei Matthias Joseph Scheeben*. Frankfurt: Peter Lang, 1982.

Miravalle, Mark. *'With Jesus': The Story of Mary Coredemptrix*. Goleta, CA: Queenship, 2003.

Mitchell, Brian Patrick. *Origen's Revenge: The Greek and Hebrew Roots of Christian Thinking on Male and Female*. Eugene, OR: Pickwick, 2021.

Mitchell, Stephen. *The Gospel According to Jesus: A New Translation and Guide to His Essential Teachings for Believers and Unbelievers*. New York: HarperCollins, 1991.

Miura, Yuzuru. *David in Luke-Acts: His Portrayal in the Light of Early Judaism*. Tübingen: Mohr Siebeck, 2007.

Moffitt, David M. *Atonement and the Logic of Resurrection in the Epistle to the Hebrews*. Leiden: Brill, 2011.

―――. *Rethinking the Atonement: New Perspectives on Jesus's Death, Resurrection, and Ascension*. Grand Rapids: Baker Academic, 2022.

Mohrlang, Roger. *Matthew and Paul: A Comparison of Ethical Perspectives*. Cambridge: Cambridge University Press, 1984.

Moloney, Francis J., SDB. *The Gospel of John*. Collegeville, MN: Liturgical, 1998.

―――. "The Gospel of John as Scripture." *Catholic Biblical Quarterly* 67 (2005) 454–68.

―――. *Love in the Gospel of John: An Exegetical, Theological, and Literary Study*. Grand Rapids: Baker Academic, 2013.

―――. "The *Parables of Enoch* and the Johannine Son of Man." In *Parables of Enoch: A Paradigm Shift*, edited by Darrell L. Bock and James H. Charlesworth, 296–93. London: Bloomsbury, 2013.

―――. *The Resurrection of the Messiah: A Narrative Commentary on the Resurrection Accounts in the Four Gospels*. New York: Paulist, 2013.

―――. *Signs and Shadows: Reading John 5–12*. Minneapolis: Fortress, 1996.

―――. "When Is John Talking about the Sacraments?" In *"A Hard Saying": The Gospel and Culture*, 109–30. Collegeville, MN: Liturgical, 2001.

Moltmann, Jürgen. *The Coming of God: Christian Eschatology*. Translated by Margaret Kohl. Minneapolis: Fortress, 1996.

―――. *Resurrected to Eternal Life: On Dying and Rising*. Translated by Ellen Yutzy Glebe. Minneapolis: Fortress, 2021.

―――. *The Way of Jesus Christ: Christology in Messianic Dimensions*. Translated by Margaret Kohl. London: SCM, 1990.

Morales, Isaac Augustine. "'With My Body I Thee Worship': New Creation, Beatific Vision, and the Liturgical Consummation of All Things." *Pro Ecclesia* 25 (2016) 337–56.

Morales, L. Michael. *Who Shall Ascend the Mountain of the Lord? A Biblical Theology of the Book of Leviticus*. Downers Grove, IL: InterVarsity, 2015.

Morton, Russell S. *One upon the Throne and the Lamb: A Tradition Historical/Theological Analysis of Revelation 4–5*. New York: Peter Lang, 2007.

Moscicke, Hans M. *Goat for Yahweh, Goat for Azazel: The Impact of Yom Kippur on the Gospels*. Lanham, MD: Lexington, 2021.

Moser, J. David. "The Flesh of the Logos, *Instrumentum divinitatis*: Retrieving an Ancient Christological Doctrine." *International Journal of Systematic Theology* 23 (2021) 313–32.

Moses, Robert Ewusie. *Practices of Power: Revisiting the Principalities and Powers in the Pauline Letters.* Minneapolis: Fortress, 2014.

Moss, Candida R. *Divine Bodies: Resurrecting Perfection in the New Testament and Early Christianity.* New Haven: Yale University Press, 2019.

Moss, Charlene McAfee. *The Zechariah Tradition and the Gospel of Matthew.* New York: Walter de Gruyter, 2008.

Mournet, Terence C. *Oral Tradition and Literary Dependency: Variability and Stability in the Synoptic Tradition and Q.* Tübingen: Mohr Siebeck, 2005.

Moyaert, Marianne. "Redemptive Suffering after the Shoah: Going Back and Forth between Jewish and Christian Traditions." In *Atonement and Comparative Theology: The Cross in Dialogue with Other Religions*, edited by Catherine Cornille, 189–213. New York: Fordham University Press, 2021.

Moyise, Steve. *Was the Birth of Jesus according to Scripture?* Eugene, OR: Cascade, 2013.

Müller, Gerhard. *Was heißt: Geboren von der Jungfrau Maria? Eine theologische Deutung.* Basel: Herder, 1989.

Müller, Mogens. *The Expression 'Son of Man' and the Development of Christology: A History of Interpretation.* London: Equinox, 2008.

Murphy, Francesca Aran. *God is Not a Story: Realism Revisited.* Oxford: Oxford University Press, 2007.

Myers, Alicia D. *Blessed among Women? Mothers and Motherhood in the New Testament.* Oxford: Oxford University Press, 2017.

———. "Jesus the Son of God in John's Gospel: The Life-Making Logos." In *Portraits of Jesus in the Gospel of John*, edited by Craig R. Koester, 141–55. London: Bloomsbury, 2018.

Nellas, Panayiotis. *Deification in Christ: The Nature of the Human Person.* Translated by Norman Russell. Crestwood, NY: St Vladimir's Seminary Press, 1987.

Nelson, R. David. "Creation and the Problem of Evil after the Apocalyptic Turn." In *Evil and Creation: Historical and Constructive Essays in Christian Dogmatics*, edited by David J. Luy, Matthew Levering, and George Kalantzis, 134–59. Bellingham, WA: Lexham, 2020.

Nepil, John L. *A Bride Adorned: Mary-Church Perichoresis in Modern Catholic Theology.* Steubenville, OH: Emmaus Academic, 2023.

Neusner, Jacob. *A Rabbi Talks with Jesus: An Intermillennial, Interfaith Exchange.* New York: Doubleday, 1993.

Newman, Barbara. *From Virile Women to Woman Christ: Studies in Medieval Religion and Literature.* Philadelphia: University of Pennsylvania Press, 1995.

Newman, Carey C. "From (Wright's) Jesus to (the Church's) Christ? Can We Get There from Here?" In *Jesus and the Restoration of Israel: A Critical Assessment of N. T. Wright's Jesus and the Victory of God*, edited by Carey C. Newman, 281–87. Downers Grove, IL: InterVarsity, 1999.

———. "God and Glory and Paul, Again: Divine Identity and Community Formation in the Early Jesus Movement." In *Monotheism and Christology in Greco-Roman Antiquity*, edited by Matthew V. Novenson, 98–138. Leiden: Brill, 2020.

———. *Paul's Glory-Christology: Tradition and Rhetoric.* Leiden: Brill, 1992.

———. "Resurrection as Glory: Divine Presence and Christian Origins." In *The Resurrection: An Interdisciplinary Symposium on the Resurrection of Jesus*, edited by Gerald O'Collins et al., 59–89. Oxford: Oxford University Press, 1997.

Newman, Francis. *Phases of Faith, or, Passages from the History of My Creed.* 2nd ed. London: Watts & Co., 1907.
Nguyen, Theresa Marie Chau, OP. *The Splendor of the Church in Mary: Henri de Lubac, Vatican II, and Marian Ressourcement.* Washington, DC: Catholic University of America Press, 2023.
Nicolas, Jean-Hervé, OP. *On the Incarnation and Redemption.* Book 2 of *Catholic Dogmatic Theology: A Synthesis.* Translated by Matthew K. Minerd. Washington, DC: Catholic University of America Press, 2023.
Nicolas, Marie-Joseph, OP. "Essai de synthèse mariale." In *Maria: Études sur la sainte Vierge*, vol. 1, edited by Hubert du Manoir, 707–41. Paris: Beauchesne, 1948.
———. "Le corps humain et sa resurrection." *Revue Thomiste* 87 (1979) 533–45.
Nichols, Aidan, OP. *Chalice of God: A Systematic Theology in Outline.* Collegeville, MN: Liturgical, 2012.
———. *Deep Mysteries: God, Christ, and Ourselves.* Lanham, MD: Lexington, 2019.
———. *Romance and System: The Theological Synthesis of Matthias Joseph Scheeben.* Steubenville, OH: Emmaus Academic, 2021.
———. *The Theologian's Enterprise: A Very Short Introduction.* San Francisco: Ignatius, 2020.
———. *There Is No Rose: The Mariology of the Catholic Church.* Minneapolis: Fortress, 2015.
Nichols, Terence L. "Miracles in Science and Theology." *Zygon* 37 (2002) 703–15.
Niederbacher, Bruno, SJ. "The Same Body Again? Thomas Aquinas on the Numerical Identity of the Resurrected Body." In *Personal Identity and Resurrection: How Do We Survive Our Death?*, edited by Georg Gasser, 145–59. Aldershot: Ashgate, 2010.
Nimmo, Paul T., and Keith L. Johnson, eds. *Kenosis: The Self-Emptying of Christ in Scripture and Theology.* Grand Rapids: Eerdmans, 2022.
Nitzan, Bilha. "The Benedictions from Qumran for the Annual Covenantal Ceremony." In *Dead Sea Scrolls: Fifty Years after Their Discovery: Proceedings of the Jerusalem Conference, July 20–25, 1997*, edited by L. H. Schiffman et al., 263–71. Jerusalem: Israel Exploration Society, 2000.
Nolan, Philip, OP. "Christ's Human Nature and the Cry from the Cross: St. Thomas Aquinas on Psalm 22:2." *Nova et Vetera* 21 (2023) 1219–44.
Nolland, John. "No Son-of-God Christology in Matthew 1.18–25." *Journal for the Study of the New Testament* 62 (1996) 3–12.
North, J. Lionel. "Jesus and Worship, God and Sacrifice." In *Early Jewish and Christian Monotheism*, edited by Loren T. Stuckenbruck and Wendy E. S. North, 186–202. London: T. & T. Clark, 2004.
North, Wendy E. S. "Monotheism and the Gospel of John: Jesus, Moses, and the Law." In *Early Jewish and Christian Monotheism*, edited by Loren T. Stuckenbruck and Wendy E. S. North, 155–66. London: T. & T. Clark International, 2004.
Novakovic, Lidija. *Messiah, the Healer of the Sick: A Study of Jesus as the Son of David in the Gospel of Matthew.* Tübingen: Mohr Siebeck, 2003.
Novenson, Matthew V. *Christ among the Messiahs: Christ Language in Paul and Messiah Language in Ancient Judaism.* Oxford: Oxford University Press, 2012.
———. *The Grammar of Messianism: An Ancient Jewish Political Idiom and Its Users.* Oxford: Oxford University Press, 2017.

———. "Jesus the Messiah: Conservatism and Radicalism in Johannine Christology." In *Portraits of Jesus in the Gospel of John*, edited by Craig R. Koester, 109–23. London: Bloomsbury, 2018.

Nutt, Roger W. "*Christus Est Unum Simpliciter*: On Why the *Secundarium* of Thomas Aquinas's *De Unione Verbi Incarnati* Is Not a Numerically Second *Esse*." In *Thomas Aquinas and the Crisis of Christology*, edited by Michael A. Dauphinais et al., 70–88. Ave Maria, FL: Sapientia, 2021.

Oakes, Edward T., SJ. *Infinity Dwindled to Infancy: A Catholic and Evangelical Christology*. Grand Rapids: Eerdmans, 2011.

———. *A Theology of Grace in Six Controversies*. Grand Rapids: Eerdmans, 2016.

O'Callaghan, Paul. *Christ Our Hope: An Introduction to Eschatology*. Washington, DC: Catholic University of America Press, 2011.

———. "La formula 'Resurrección de la carne' y su significado para la moral Christian." *Scripta Theologica* 21 (1989) 777–803.

O'Collins, Gerald, SJ. "Augustine on the Resurrection." In *Saint Augustine the Bishop: A Book of Essays*, edited by Fannie LeMoine and Christopher Kleinhenz, 65–75. New York: Garland, 1994.

O'Connor, Michael. *Cajetan's Biblical Commentaries: Motive and Method*. Leiden: Brill, 2017.

O'Donnell, Douglas Sean. "Insisting on Easter: Matthew's Use of the Theologically Provocative Vocative (κύριε) in the Suppliant Narratives." In *The Earliest Perceptions of Jesus in Context: Essays in Honour of John Nolland on His 70th Birthday*, edited by Aaron W. White et al., 185–200. London: Bloomsbury, 2018.

Oegema, Gerbern S. *The Anointed and His People: Messianic Expectations from the Maccabees to Bar Kokhba*. Sheffield: Sheffield Academic, 1998.

O'Keefe, John J. "Impassible Suffering? Divine Passion and Fifth-century Christology." *Theological Studies* 58 (1997) 39–60.

O'Meara, John J. "Parting from Porphyry." In *Congresso Internazionale su S. Agostino nel XVI Centenario della Conversione, Roma, 15–20 settembre 1986*, Atti 2, 357–69. Rome: Institutum Patristicum Augustinianum, 1987.

O'Murchu, Diarmuid. *Incarnation: A New Evolutionary Threshold*. Maryknoll, NY: Orbis, 2017.

Olson, Roger. "The Self-Realization of God: Hegelian Elements in Pannenberg's Christology." *Perspectives in Religious Studies* 13 (1986) 207–33.

Origen. *Spirit and Fire: A Thematic Anthology of His Writings*. Edited by Hans Urs von Balthasar. Translated by Robert J. Daly, SJ. Washington, DC: Catholic University of America Press, 1984.

Orlov, Andrei A. *Demons of Change: Antagonism and Apotheosis in Jewish and Christian Apocalypticism*. Albany, NY: SUNY Press, 2020.

———. *Embodiment of Divine Knowledge in Early Judaism*. London: Routledge, 2022.

———. *The Glory of the Invisible God: Two Powers in Heaven Traditions and Early Christology*. London: T. & T. Clark, 2019.

———. *Yahoel and Metatron: Aural Apocalypticism and the Origins of Early Jewish Mysticism*. Tübingen: Mohr Siebeck, 2017.

Ormerod, Neil. "Sacred Heart, Beatific Mind: Exploring the Consciousness of Jesus." *Theological Studies* 79 (2018) 729–44.

Ounsworth, Richard OP. *Joshua Typology in the New Testament*. Tübingen: Mohr Siebeck, 2012.

Paddison, Angus. *Scripture: A Very Theological Proposal*. London: T. & T. Clark, 2009.

Pannenberg, Wolfhart. *Jesus: God and Man*. 2nd ed. Philadelphia: Westminster, 1977.
Palaver, Wolfgang. "Sacrificial Cults as 'the Mysterious Centre of Every Religion': A Girardian Assessment of Aby Warburg's Theory of Religion." In *Sacrifice and Modern Thought*, edited by Julia Meszaros and Johannes Zachhuber, 83–99. Oxford: Oxford University Press, 2013.
Parrinder, Geoffrey. *The Son of Joseph: The Parentage of Jesus*. Edinburgh: T. & T. Clark, 1992.
Pasnua, Robert. *Thomas Aquinas on Human Nature*. Cambridge: Cambridge University Press, 2002.
Peacocke, Arthur. *Theology for a Scientific Age: Being and Becoming—Natural, Divine, and Human*. London: SCM, 1993.
Pederson, Ann Milliken, et al. "Fully Human and Fully Divine: The Birth of Christ and the Role of Mary." *Religions* 6 (2015) 172–81.
Peeler, Amy L. B. *You Are My Son: The Family of God in the Epistle to the Hebrews*. London: Bloomsbury, 2014.
———. *Women and the Gender of God*. Grand Rapids: Eerdmans, 2022.
Pennington, Jonathan T. *Jesus the Great Philosopher: Rediscovering the Wisdom Needed for the Good Life*. Grand Rapids: Brazos, 2020.
———. *The Sermon on the Mount and Human Flourishing: A Theological Commentary*. Grand Rapids: Baker Academic, 2017.
Peppard, Michael. *The Son of God in the Roman World: Divine Sonship in Its Social and Political Context*. Oxford: Oxford University Press, 2011.
Perriman, Andrew. *The Coming Son of Man: New Testament Eschatology for an Emerging Church*. Milton Keynes: Paternoster, 2005.
Perrin, Nicholas. *Jesus the Priest*. Grand Rapids: Baker Academic, 2018.
———. *Jesus the Temple*. Grand Rapids: Baker Academic, 2010.
Pesch, Rudolf. *Der Besessene von Gerasa*. Stuttgart: Katholisches Bibelwerk, 1972.
———. "Zur Entstehung des Glaubens und die Auferstehung Jesu." *Theologische Quartalschrift* 153 (1973) 103–17.
Peters, Ted. "Resurrection: The Conceptual Challenge." In *Resurrection: Theological and Scientific Assessments*, edited by Ted Peters et al., 297–321. Grand Rapids: Eerdmans, 2002.
Philippe, Jacques. *The Eight Doors of the Kingdom: Meditation on the Beatitudes*. New York: Scepter, 2018.
Philo, *On Flight and Finding*. In *Philo: On Flight and Finding. On the Change of Names. On Dreams*, translated by F. H. Colson and G. H. Whitaker, 7–133. Loeb Classical Library, no. 275. Cambridge: Harvard University Press, 1934.
Pidel, Aaron, SJ. *The Inspiration and Truth of Scripture: Testing the Ratzinger Paradigm*. Washington, DC: Catholic University of America Press, 2023.
Pierce, Madison N. *Divine Discourse in the Epistle to the Hebrews: The Recontextualization of Spoken Questions of Scripture*. Cambridge: Cambridge University Press, 2020.

Pitre, Brant. "The Historical Jesus and the Apocalyptic 'Thunderbolt' (Matthew 11:25–27 // Luke 10:21–22)." In *The Figure of Jesus in History and Theology: Essays in Honor of John Meier*, edited by Vincent T. M. Skemp and Kelley Coblentz Bautch, 169–85. Washington, DC: Catholic Biblical Association of America, 2020.
———. *Jesus the Bridegroom: The Greatest Love Story Ever Told*. New York: Random House, 2014.
———. *Jesus and Divine Christology*. Grand Rapids: Eerdmans, 2024.

———. *Jesus and the Jewish Roots of Mary: Unveiling the Mother of the Messiah.* New York: Random House, 2018.

———. *Jesus and the Last Supper.* Grand Rapids: Eerdmans, 2015.

———. *Jesus, the Tribulation, and the End of the Exile: Restoration Eschatology and the Origin of the Atonement.* Grand Rapids: Baker Academic, 2005.

Pitre, Brant, Michael P. Barber, and John A. Kincaid. *Paul, a New Covenant Jew: Rethinking Pauline Theology.* Grand Rapids: Eerdmans, 2019.

Pius XII. Encyclical Letter *Ad Caeli Reginam.* https://www.vatican.va/content/pius-xii/en/encyclicals/documents/hf_p-xii_enc_11101954_ad-caeli-reginam.html.

———. Encyclical Letter *Mystici Corporis.* https://www.vatican.va/content/pius-xii/en/encyclicals/documents/hf_p-xii_enc_29061943_mystici-corporis-christi.html. Pitstick, Alyssa Lyra. *Light in Darkness: Hans Urs von Balthasar and the Catholic Doctrine of Christ's Descent into Hell.* Grand Rapids: Eerdmans, 2007.

Pius XI. Encyclical Letter *Ad Diem Illum.* https://www.vatican.va/content/pius-x/en/encyclicals/documents/hf_p-x_enc_02021904_ad-diem-illum-laetissimum.html.

Pohle, Joseph. *Mariology: A Dogmatic Treatise on the Blessed Virgin Mary, Mother of God.* Edited by Arthur Preuss. St. Louis: B. Herder, 1941.

Polkinghorne, John. "Eschatological Credibility: Emergent and Teleological Processes." In *Resurrection: Theological and Scientific Assessments*, edited by Ted Peters, et al., 43–55. Grand Rapids: Eerdmans, 2002.

———. *Science and Christian Belief.* London: SPCK, 1994.

Pomplun, Trent. "Matthias Joseph Scheeben and the Controversy over the *Debitum Peccati*." *Nova et Vetera* 11 (2013) 455–502.

Pontifical International Marian Academy. *The Mother of the Lord: Memory, Presence, Hope.* Translated by Thomas A. Thompson, S.M. Staten Island, NY: Alba, 2007.

Popkes, Enno Edzard. *Die Theologie der Liebe Gottes in den johanneischen Schriften: Zur Semantik der Liebe und zum Motivkreis des Dualismus.* Tübingen: Mohr Siebeck, 2005.

Porter, Stanley E. "Luke: Companion or Disciple of Paul?" In *Paul and the Gospels: Christologies, Conflicts and Convergences*, edited by Michael F. Bird and Joel Willitts, 146–68. London: T. & T. Clark, 2011.

Powell, Samuel M. *The Trinity in German Thought.* Cambridge: Cambridge University Press, 2001.

Prothro, James B. *The Apostle Paul and His Letters: An Introduction.* Washington, DC: Catholic University of America Press, 2021.

———. "Semper Virgo? A Biblical Review of a Debated Dogma." *Pro Ecclesia* 28 (2019) 78–97.

Pryor, John W. *John: Evangelist of the Covenant People: The Narrative and Themes of the Fourth Gospel.* Downers Grove, IL: InterVarsity, 1992.

Puech, Émile "Fragment d'une apocalypse en Araméen (4Q246=psDand) et le 'Royaume de Dieu.'" *Revue Biblique* 99 (1992) 98–131.

Pusey, Edward Bouverie. *First Letter to the Very Rev. J. H. Newman, D.D., In Explanation Chiefly in Regard to the Ever-Blessed Theotokos, and the Doctrine of Her Immaculate Conception.* London: James Parker & Co., 1869.

Queiruga, Andrés Torres. "Jesus: Genuinely Human." Translated by Paul Burns. In *Jesus as Christ: What Is at Stake in Christology?*, edited by Andrés Torres Queiruga et al., 33–43. *Concilium* 2008/3. London: SCM, 2008.

Quitterer, Josef. "Hylomorphism and the Constitution View." In *Personal Identity and Resurrection: How Do We Survive Our Death?*, edited by Georg Gasser, 177–90. Aldershot: Ashgate, 2010.

Rae, Murray A. *Resurrection and Renewal: Jesus and the Transformation of Creation.* Grand Rapids: Baker Academic, 2024.

Rahner, Johanna. *"Er aber sprach vom Tempel seines Leibes": Jesus von Nazaret als Ort der Offenbarung Gottes im vierten Evangelium.* Bodenheim: Philo, 1998.

Rahner, Karl, SJ. "Christology in the Setting of Modern Man's Understanding of Himself and of His World." In *Theological Investigations*, vol. 11, translated by David Bourke, 215–29. New York: Seabury, 1974.

———. "Current Problems in Christology." In *Theological Investigations*, vol. 1, translated by Cornelius Ernst, OP, 149–200. Baltimore: Helicon, 1961.

———. "Dogmatic Considerations on Knowledge and Consciousness in Christ." In *Dogmatic vs. Biblical Theology*, edited by Herbert Vorgrimler, 241–68. Baltimore: Helicon, 1964.

———. *Foundations of Christian Faith: An Introduction to the Idea of Christianity.* Translated by William V. Dych. New York: Seabury, 1978.

———. "Jesus Christ and Christology." In *A New Christology*, edited by Karl Rahner and Wilhelm Thüsing, translated by David Smith and Verdant Green, 3–41. New York: Seabury, 1980.

———. "The Position of Christology in the Church Between Exegesis and Dogmatics." In *Theological Investigations*, vol. 11, translated by David Bourke, 185–214. New York: Seabury, 1974.

———. "On the Theology of the Incarnation." In *Theological Investigations*, vol. 4, translated by Kevin Smyth, 105–20. New York: Seabury, 1974.

———. "Unity of Spirit and Matter in Christian Faith." In *Theological Investigations*, vol. 6, translated by Karl-H. Kruger and Boniface Kruger, 153–77. Baltimore: Helicon, 1969.

———. "*Virginitas in Partu*: A Contribution to the Problem of the Development of Dogma and of Tradition." In *Theological Investigations*, vol. 4, translated by Kevin Smyth, 134–62. New York: Seabury, 1974.

Räisänen, Heikki. "Begotten by the Holy Spirit." In *Sacred Marriages: The Divine-Human Sexual Metaphor from Sumer to Early Christianity*, edited by Martti Nissinen and Risto Uro, 321–44. Winona Lake, IN: Eisenbrauns, 2008.

———. "Resurrection for Punishment? The Fate of the Unrighteous in Early Christianity and in 'New Testament Theology.'" In *Resurrection of the Dead: Biblical Traditions in Dialogue*, edited by Geert Van Oyen and Tom Shepherd, 361–81. Leuven: Peeters, 2012.

Raith, Charles, II. "Aquinas, Allegory, and Paul's Use of the Old Testament in Galatians 4:21–24, Romans 9:6–9, and 1 Corinthians 1:19." In *Engaging Catholic Doctrine: Essays in Honor of Matthew Levering*, edited by Robert Barron, et al., 165–88. Steubenville, OH: Emmaus Academic, 2023.

———. "Thomas Aquinas's Pauline Theology of the Atonement." In *T&T Clark Companion to the Atonement*, edited by Adam J. Johnson, 195–211. London: Bloomsbury, 2017.

Ralston, Joshua. "Judgment on the Cross: Resurrection as Divine Vindication." In *Atonement and Comparative Theology: The Cross in Dialogue with Other Religions*, edited by Catherine Cornille, 214–38. New York: Fordham University Press, 2021.

———. "A Schleiermachian Rejoinder to Thomas Joseph White's *The Incarnate Lord*." *Nova et Vetera* 20 (2022) 613–28.
Ramage, Matthew J. "Unless You Believe, You Will Not Understand: Biblical Faith according to Thomas Aquinas and Benedict XVI." In *Thomas Aquinas, Biblical Theologian*, edited by Roger W. Nutt and Michael Dauphinais, 35–59. Steubenville, OH: Emmaus Academic, 2021.
Ranke-Heinemann, Uta. *Eunuchs for the Kingdom of Heaven*. London: Penguin, 1991.
Ratzinger, Joseph. *Daughter Zion: Meditations on the Church's Marian Belief*. Translated by John M. McDermott, SJ. San Francisco: Ignatius, 1983.
———. "The End of Time." In *The End of Time: The Provocation of Talking about God*, edited by Tiemo Rainer Peters and Claus Urban, translated by J. Matthew Ashley, 4–25. New York: Paulist, 2004.
———. *Eschatology: Death and Eternal Life*. Translated by Michael Waldstein, revised by Aidan Nichols, OP. Washington, DC: Catholic University of America Press, 1988.
———. *Introduction to Christianity*. Translated by J. R. Foster. San Francisco: Ignatius, 2004.
———. *Jesus of Nazareth*. Vol. 1, *From the Baptism in the Jordan to the Transfiguration*. Translated by Adrian J. Walker. New York: Doubleday, 2007.
———. *Jesus of Nazareth*. Vol. 2, *Holy Week: From the Entrance into Jerusalem to the Resurrection*. Translated by the Vatican Secretariat of State. San Francisco: Ignatius, 2011.
———. *Jesus of Nazareth*. Vol. 3, *The Infancy Narratives*. Translated by Philip J. Whitmore. New York: Random House, 2012.
———. "Nachwort zur 6. Auflage." In *Eschatologie—Tod und Ewiges Leben*, 6th ed., 186–206. Regensburg: Friedrich Pustet, 2007.
Ratzinger, Joseph, with Vittorio Messori. *The Ratzinger Report: An Exclusive Interview on the State of the Church*. Translated by Salvator Attanasio and Graham Harrison. San Francisco: Ignatius, 1985.
Reardon, Patrick Henry. *Reclaiming the Atonement: An Orthodox Theology of Redemption*. Vol. 1, *The Incarnation*. Chesterton, IN: Ancient Faith, 2015.
Reasoner, Mark. "*Dei Verbum* and the Twentieth-Century Drama of Scripture's Literal Sense." *Nova et Vetera* 15 (2017) 219–54.
Reichmann, James. "Aquinas, Scotus and the Christological Mystery: Why Christ Is Not a Human Person." *The Thomist* 71 (2004) 451–74.
Reisenauer, Augustine M., OP. *Augustine's Theology of the Resurrection*. Cambridge: Cambridge University Press, 2023.
Reiser, Marius. *Jesus and Judgment: The Eschatological Proclamation in Its Jewish Context*. Translated by Linda M. Maloney. Minneapolis: Fortress, 1997.
Reno, R. R. *The End of Interpretation: Reclaiming the Priority of Ecclesial Exegesis*. Grand Rapids: Baker Academic, 2022.
Resch, Dustin. *Barth's Interpretation of the Virgin Birth: A Sign of Mystery*. London: Routledge, 2012.
Resnick, Irven M., and Franklin T. Harkins. "Introduction." In *On Resurrection*, by Albert the Great, translated by Irven M. Resnick and Franklin T. Harkins, 3–21. Washington, DC: Catholic University of America Press, 2020.

Reynolds, Benjamin E. "Apocalyptic Revelation in the Gospel of John: Revealed Cosmology, the Vision of God, and Visionary Showing." In *The Jewish Apocalyptic Tradition and the Shaping of New Testament Thought*, edited by Benjamin E. Reynolds and Loren T. Stuckenbruck, 109–28. Minneapolis: Fortress, 2017.

———. *The Apocalyptic Son of Man in the Gospel of John*. Tübingen: Mohr Siebeck, 2008.

———. *John among the Apocalypses: Jewish Apocalyptic Tradition and the "Apocalyptic" Gospel*. Oxford: Oxford University Press, 2020.

Ricoeur, Paul. "Objectivity and Subjectivity in History." In *History and Truth*, translated by Charles A. Kelbley, 21–40. Evanston, IL: Northwestern University Press, 1965.

Riches, Aaron. *Ecce Homo: On the Divine Unity of Christ*. Grand Rapids: Eerdmans, 2016.

Rillera, Andrew Remington. *Lamb of the Free: Recovering the Varied Sacrificial Understanding of Jesus's Death*. Eugene, OR: Cascade, 2024.

Rissi, Mathias. *Die Theologie des Hebräerbriefs Ihre Verankerung in der Situation des Verfassers und seiner Leser*. Tübingen: Mohr Siebeck, 1987.

Rival, Laura. "The Aztec Sacrificial Complex." In *Sacrifice and Modern Thought*, edited by Julia Meszaros and Johannes Zachhuber, 163–79. Oxford: Oxford University Press, 2013.

Robbins, Vernon K. *Jesus the Teacher: A Socio-Rhetorical Interpretation of Mark*. Philadelphia: Fortress, 1984.

Roberts, Kyle. *A Complicated Pregnancy: Whether Mary Was a Virgin and Why It Matters*. Minneapolis: Fortress, 2017.

Rodriguez, Rafael. *Structuring Early Christian Memory: Jesus in Tradition, Performance and Text*. London: T. & T. Clark, 2010.

Rogers, Eugene F., Jr. *After the Spirit: A Constructive Pneumatology from Resources Outside the West*. Grand Rapids: Eerdmans, 2005.

———. *Blood Theology: Seeing Red in Body- and God-Talk*. Cambridge: Cambridge University Press, 2021.

Rohof, Jan. *La sainteté substantielle du Christ dans la théologie scolastique. Histoire du problème*. Fribourg: Suisse Éditions St-Paul, 1952.

Rohr, Richard. *The Universal Christ: How a Forgotten Reality Can Change Everything We See, Hope for, and Believe*. New York: Convergent, 2019.

Ronning, John. *The Jewish Targums and John's Logos Theology*. Grand Rapids: Baker Academic, 2010.

Roose, Hanna. "Umkehr und Ausgleich bei Lukas: Die Gleichnisse vom verlorenen Sohn (Lk 15.11–32) und vom reichen Mann und armen Lazarus (Lk 16.19–31) als Schwestergeschichten." *New Testament Studies* 56 (2009) 1–21.

Rosa, Guglielmo Forni. *The "Essence of Christianity": The Hermeneutical Question in the Protestant and Modernist Debate (1897–1904)*. Translated by Marisa Luciani and Jane Stevenson. Atlanta: Scholars, 1995.

Rosati, Connie. "Self-Interest and Self-Sacrifice." *Proceedings of the Aristotelian Society* 109 (2009) 311–25.

Rösel, Martin. "Die Jungfrauengeburt des endzeitlichen Immanuel. Jesaja 7 in der Übersetzung der Septuaginta." *Jahrbuch für Biblische Theologie* 6 (1991) 135–51.

Rosen, Robert. *Essays on Life Itself*. New York: Columbia University Press, 2000.

Rossé, Gérard. *The Cry of Jesus on the Cross: A Biblical and Theological Study*. New York: Paulist Press, 1987.

Rowe, C. Kavin. *Early Narrative Christology: The Lord in the Gospel of Luke*. Berlin: de Gruyter, 2006.

———. *World Upside Down: Reading Acts in the Graeco-Roman Age*. Oxford: Oxford University Press, 2009.

Rowland, Christopher, and Christopher R. A. Morray-Jones. *The Mystery of God: Early Jewish Mysticism and the New Testament*. Leiden: Brill, 2009.

Rowlands, Jonathan. *The Metaphysics of Historical Jesus Research: Prolegomenon to a Future Quest for the Historical Jesus*. London: Routledge, 2015.

Rutledge, Fleming. *The Crucifixion: Understanding the Death of Jesus*. Grand Rapids: Eerdmans, 2015.

Ryliškytė, Ligita. *Why the Cross? Divine Friendship and the Power of Justice*. Cambridge: Cambridge University Press, 2023.

Salmanticenses (Discalced Carmelites of Salamanca). *On the Motive of the Incarnation*. Translated by Dylan Schrader. Washington, DC: Catholic University of America Press, 2019.

Sanders, E. P. *Jesus and Judaism*. Minneapolis: Fortress, 1985.

———. *The Historical Figure of Jesus*. London: Penguin, 1995.

———. *Paul and Palestinian Judaism: A Comparison of Patterns of Religion*. Philadelphia: Fortress, 1977.

Sanders, Jack T. *Ethics and the New Testament: Change and Development*. London: SCM, 1985.

Sarisky, Darren. *Reading the Bible Theologically*. Cambridge: Cambridge University Press, 2019.

Satlow, Michael L. *How the Bible Became Holy*. New Haven: Yale University Press, 2014.

Saward, John. *Redeemer in the Womb: Jesus Living in Mary*. 2nd ed. Elk Grove Village, IL: Word on Fire, 2023.

Sawicki, Marianne. *Seeing the Lord: Resurrection and Early Christian Practices*. Minneapolis: Fortress, 1994.

Schaberg, Jane. *The Illegitimacy of Jesus: A Feminist Theological Interpretation of the Infancy Narratives*. San Francisco: Harper & Row, 1987.

Schäfer, Peter. *Two Gods in Heaven: Jewish Concepts of God in Antiquity*. Translated by Allison Brown. Princeton: Princeton University Press, 2020.

Schall, James V., SJ. *Liberation Theology in Latin America: With Selected Essays and Documents*. San Francisco: Ignatius, 1982.

Shauf, Scott. *Jesus the Sacrifice: A Historical and Theological Study*. Lanham, MD: Fortress Academic, 2022.

Scheeben, Matthias Joseph. *Handbook of Catholic Dogmatics*, Book Five: *Soteriology*, Part Two: *The Work of Christ the Redeemer and the Role of His Virgin Mother*. Translated by Michael J. Miller. Steubenville, OH: Emmaus Academic, 2021.

———. *The Mysteries of Christianity*. 2nd ed. Translated by Cyril Vollert, SJ. Steubenville, OH: Emmaus Academic, 2023.

Schenck, Kenneth L. "Keeping His Appointment: Creation and Enthronement in Hebrews." *Journal for the Study of the New Testament* 66 (1997) 91–117.

Schillebeeckx, Edward, OP. *Interim Report on the Books Jesus and Christ*. Translated by John Bowden. London: Bloomsbury, 2014.

———. *Jesus: An Experiment in Christology*. Translated by Hubert Hoskins. New York: Seabury, 1979.

Schleiermacher, Friedrich. *The Christian Faith*. Edited by H. R. Mackintosh and J. S. Stewart. Translated by D. M. Baillie, et al. Edinburgh: T. & T. Clark, 1989.

Schlesinger, Eugene R. *Salvation in Henri de Lubac: Divine Grace, Human Nature, and the Mystery of the Cross.* Notre Dame: University of Notre Dame Press, 2023.

Schloss, Jeffrey P. "From Evolution to Eschatology." In *Resurrection: Theological and Scientific Assessments,* edited by Ted Peters et al., 56–85. Grand Rapids: Eerdmans, 2002.

Schmemann, Alexander. "Mary: The Archetype of Mankind." In *Sermons,* vol. 3: *The Virgin Mary,* translated by John A. Jillions, 45–55. Crestwood, NY: St Vladimir's Seminary Press, 1995.

Schmidt, Bettina E. "Blood Sacrifice as a Symbol of the Paradigmatic Other: The Debate about Ebó Rituals in the Americas." In *Sacrifice and Modern Thought,* edited by Julia Meszaros and Johannes Zachhuber, 197–213. Oxford: Oxford University Press, 2013.

Schmisek, Brian. *Resurrection of the Flesh or Resurrection from the Dead: Implications for Theology.* Collegeville, MN: Liturgical, 2013.

Schnabel, Eckhard J. *Jesus in Jerusalem: The Last Days.* Grand Rapids: Eerdmans, 2018.

Schrader, Dylan. *A Thomistic Christocentrism: Recovering the Carmelites of Salamanca on the Logic of the Incarnation.* Washington, DC: Catholic University of America Press, 2021.

Schreiner, Patrick. *The Body of Jesus: A Spatial Analysis of the Kingdom in Matthew.* London: Bloomsbury, 2016.

Schröter, Jens. *From Jesus to the New Testament: Early Christian Theology and the Origin of the New Testament Canon.* Translated by Wayne Coppins. Waco, TX: Baylor University Press, 2013.

Schuchard, Bruce G. *The Word from the Beginning: The Person and Work of Jesus in the Gospel of John.* Bellingham, WA: Lexham, 2022.

Schweitzer, Albert. *Das Messianitäts- und Leidensgeheimnis. Eine Skizze des Lebens Jesu.* Tübingen: 1901.

———. *The Quest of the Historical Jesus.* Translated by William Montgomery et al. Minneapolis: Fortress, 2001.

Sebald, W. G. *The Rings of Saturn.* Translated by Michael Hulse. London: Harvill, 1998.

Segal, Alan F. "Heavenly Ascent in Hellenistic Judaism, Early Christianity and Their Environment." *Aufstieg und Niedergang der römischen Welt* 23 (1980) 1333–94.

———. "Paul's Thinking about Resurrection in Its Jewish Context." *New Testament Studies* 44 (1998) 400–419.

———. *Two Powers in Heaven: Early Rabbinic Reports about Christianity and Gnosticism.* Leiden: Brill, 1977.

Seidensticker, Philip. *Die Auferstehung Jesu in der Botschaft der Evangelisten.* Stuttgart: 1967.

Semmelroth, Otto. *Mary, Archetype of the Church.* Dublin: Gill, 1964.

Senior, Donald, CP. *The Passion of Jesus in the Gospel of John.* Collegeville, MN: Liturgical, 1991.

Setzer, Claudia. *Resurrection of the Body in Early Judaism and Early Christianity: Doctrine, Community, and Self-Definition.* Leiden: Brill, 2004.

Shively, Elizabeth E. *Apocalyptic Imagination in the Gospel of Mark: The Literary and Theological Role of Mark 3:22–30.* Berlin: Walter de Gruyter, 2012.

Shoemaker, Stephen J. *Ancient Traditions of the Virgin Mary's Dormition and Assumption.* Oxford: Oxford University Press, 2002.

Siegert, Folker. "Der Logos, 'älterer Sohn' des Schöpfers und 'zweiter Gott': Philons Logos und der Johannesprolog." In *Kontexte des Johannesevangeliums: Das vierte Evangelium in religions- und traditionsgeschichtlicher Perspektive*, edited by J. Frey and U. Schnelle, 277–94. Tübingen: Mohr Siebeck, 2004.

Simoens, Yves. *La gloire d'aimer. Structures stylistiques et interprétatives dans le Discours de la Cène (Jn 13–17)*. Rome: Biblical Institute, 1981.

Sirico, Robert. *The Economics of the Parables*. Washington, DC: Regnery Gateway, 2022.

Skinner, Christopher W. "Virtue in the New Testament: The Legacies of John and Paul in Comparative Perspective." In *Unity and Diversity in the Gospels and Paul: Essays in Honor of Frank J. Matera*, edited by Christopher W. Skinner and Kelly R. Iverson, 304–15. Atlanta: SBL, 2012.

Sklar, Jay. *Sin, Impurity, Sacrifice, Atonement: The Priestly Conceptions*. Sheffield: Sheffield Academic, 2015.

Smith, Barry D. *The Meaning of Jesus' Death: Reviewing the New Testament's Interpretations*. London: T. & T. Clark, 2017.

Smith, D. Moody. *The Theology of the Gospel of John*. Cambridge: Cambridge University Press, 1995.

Smith, Julien. *Christ the Ideal King: Cultural Context, Rhetorical Strategy, and the Power of Divine Monarchy in Ephesians*. Tübingen: Mohr-Siebeck, 2011.

Smith, Morton. *Jesus the Magician*. San Francisco: Harper & Row, 1978.

Smith, Stephen H. "Parapsychology, Hallucinations, Collective Delusions, and Jesus' Post-Resurrection Appearances: A Response to Glenn Siniscalchi." *Journal for the Study of the Historical Jesus* 21 (2023) 228–53.

Smith, Thomas Allan. "Introduction." In Sergius Bulgakov, *The Burning Bush: On the Orthodox Veneration of the Mother of God*, translated and edited by Thomas Allan Smith, xi–xxiv. Grand Rapids: Eerdmans, 2009.

Snodgrass, Klyne. "Baptized into Christ: Romans 6:3–4—the Text on Baptism and Participation." In *Cruciform Scripture: Cross, Participation, and Mission*, edited by Christopher W. Skinner et al., 106–22. Grand Rapids: Eerdmans, 2021.

Sobrino, Jon, SJ. *Christ the Liberator: A View from the Victims*. Translated by Paul Burns. Maryknoll, NY: Orbis, 2001.

———. *Christology at the Crossroads: A Latin American Approach*. Translated by John Drury. Maryknoll, NY: Orbis, 1978.

———. "The Coming Kingdom or God's Present Reign." In *Jesus as Christ: What Is at Stake in Christology?*, translated by Paul Burns and edited by Andrés Torres Queiruga et al., 44–54. Concilium 2008/3. London: SCM, 2008.

———. *Jesus the Liberator: A Historical-Theological Reading of Jesus of Nazareth*. Translated by Paul Burns and Francis McDonagh. Maryknoll, NY: Orbis, 1993.

Söding, Thomas. *Die Verkündigung Jesu—Ereignis und Erinnerung*. 2nd ed. Freiburg: Herder, 2011.

Somme, Luc-Thomas. *Fils adoptifs de Dieu par Jésus Christ*. Paris: J. Vrin, 1997.

Sommer, Benjamin D. *The Bodies of God and the World of Ancient Israel*. Cambridge: Cambridge University Press, 2009.

Sonderegger, Katherine. "Anselmian Atonement." In *T&T Clark Companion to the Atonement*, edited by Adam J. Johnson, 175–93. London: Bloomsbury, 2017.

———. "Christ." In *The New Cambridge Companion to Christian Doctrine*, edited by Michael Allen, 70–86. Cambridge: Cambridge University Press, 2022.

Spence, Alan. *The Promise of Peace: A Unified Theory of Atonement*. London: T. & T. Clark, 2006.

Spezzano, Daria. *The Glory of God's Grace: Deification According to St. Thomas Aquinas.* Ave Maria, FL: Sapientia, 2015.

———. "Is Jesus Judgmental? Aquinas on Christ as Eschatological Judge." In *Thomas Aquinas and the Crisis of Christology*, edited by Michael A. Dauphinais et al., 368–89. Ave Maria, FL: Sapientia, 2021.

Spohn, William C. *Go and Do Likewise: Jesus and Ethics.* New York: Continuum, 2007.

Sri, Edward. *Queen Mother: A Biblical Theology of Mary's Queenship.* Steubenville, OH: Emmaus Academic, 2005.

———. "Release from the Debt of Sin: Jesus' Jubilee Mission in the Gospel of Luke." *Nova et Vetera* 9 (2011) 183–94.

———. *Rethinking Mary in the New Testament.* San Francisco: Ignatius, 2018.

Staniloae, Dumitru. *The Person of Jesus Christ as God and Savior.* Vol. 3 of *The Experience of God: Orthodox Dogmatic Theology.* Translated and edited by Ioan Ionita. Brookline, MA: Holy Cross Orthodox, 2011.

Stanton, Graham. *The Gospels and Jesus.* 2nd ed. Oxford: Oxford University Press, 2002.

Stanton, Vincent Henry. *The Jewish and the Christian Messiah.* Edinburgh: T. & T. Clark, 1886.

Staples, Jason A. "'Lord, LORD': Jesus as YHWH in Matthew and Luke." *New Testament Studies* 64 (2018) 1–19.

Staudt, R. Jared. *The Primacy of God: The Virtue of Religion in Catholic Theology.* Steubenville, OH: Emmaus Academic, 2022.

———. "Substantial Union with God in Matthias Scheeben." *Nova et Vetera* 11 (2013) 515–36.

Stauffer, Ethelbert. "Jeschu ben Mirjam: Krontroversgeschichtliche Anmerkungen zu Mk 6.3." In *Neotestamentica et Semitica*, edited by Earl E. Ellis and M. Wilcox, 119–28. Edinburgh: T. & T. Clark, 1969.

Sterling, Gregory. *Historiography and Self-Definition: Josephos, Luke-Acts, and Apologetic Historiography.* Leiden: Brill, 1992.

Stern, David. *Parables in Midrash: Narrative and Exegesis in Rabbinic Literature.* Cambridge: Harvard University Press, 1991.

Stern, Frank. *A Rabbi Looks at Jesus' Parables.* Lanham, MD: Rowman & Littlefield, 2006.

Stevenson, Austin. *The Consciousness of the Historical Jesus: Historiography, Theology, and Metaphysics.* London: Bloomsbury, 2024.

Strauss, David Friedrich. *Das Leben Jesu für das deutsche Volk bearbeitet.* Leipzig: F. A. Brockhaus, 1864.

Strauss, David Friedrich. *The Life of Jesus, Critically Examined.* 2 vols. Translated by George Eliot. Cambridge: Cambridge University Press, 2010.

Strauss, Mark L. *Jesus Behaving Badly: The Puzzling Paradoxes of the Man from Galilee.* Downers Grove, IL: InterVarsity, 2015.

Stroumsa, Guy G. *The End of Sacrifice: Religious Transformation in Late Antiquity.* Translated by Susan Emanuel. Chicago: University of Chicago Press, 2009.

Stuckenbruck, Loren T. *Angel Veneration and Christology: A Study in Early Judaism and in the Christology of the Apocalypse of John.* Tübingen: J. C. B. Mohr, 1995.

———. "Messianic Ideas in the Apocalyptic and Related Literature of Early Judaism." In *The Messiah in the Old and New Testaments*, edited by Stanley E. Porter, 90–113. Grand Rapids: Eerdmans, 2007.

Stuckenbruck, Loren T., and Gabriele Boccaccini. "1 Enoch and the Synoptic Gospels: The Method and Benefits of a Conversation." In *Enoch and the Synoptic Gospels: Reminiscences, Allusions, Intertextuality*, edited by Loren T. Stuckenbruck and Gabriele Boccaccini, 1–17. Atlanta: Society of Biblical Literature, 2016.

Stump, Eleonore. *Atonement*. Oxford: Oxford University Press, 2018.

Tacitus, *Histories, Books 4–5. Annals, Books 1–3*, translated by Clifford H. Moore. Loeb Classical Library 249. Cambridge: Harvard University Press, 1931.

Talbert, Charles H. "Miraculous Conceptions and Births in Mediterranean Antiquity." In *The Development of Christology during the First Hundred Years and Other Essays on Early Christian Christology*, 161–70. Leiden: Brill, 2011.

Tan, Kim Huat. *The Zion Traditions and the Aims of Jesus*. Cambridge: Cambridge University Press, 1997.

Tanner, Kathryn. *Jesus, Humanity, and the Trinity: A Brief Systematic Theology*. Edinburgh: T. & T. Clark, 2001.

Tappenden, Frederick S. "Luke and Paul in Dialogue: Ritual Meals and Risen Bodies as Instances of Embodied Communion." In *Resurrection of the Dead: Biblical Traditions in Dialogue*, edited by Geert Van Oyen and Tom Shepherd, 203–28. Leuven: Peeters, 2012.

Teilhard de Chardin, Pierre. *Christianity and Evolution*. Translated by René Hague. New York: Harcourt Brace Jovanovich, 1971.

———. *The Heart of Matter*. Translated by René Hague. New York: Harcourt Brace Jovanovich, 1978.

Teubner, Jonathan D. "Jesus and the Ascent of *Wissenschaft*: A Reassessment of Adolf von Harnack's *wissenschaftliche Theologie*." In *Theology, History, and the Modern German University*, edited by Kevin M. Vander Schel and Michael P. DeJonge, 267–91. Tübingen: Mohr Siebeck, 2021.

Thalhofer, Valentin. *Das Opfer des Alten und Neuen Bundes*. Regensburg: Manz, 1870.

Thate, Michael J. *The Godman and the Sea: The Empty Tomb, the Trauma of the Jews, and the Gospel of Mark*. Philadelphia: University of Pennsylvania Press, 2019.

———. *Remembrance of Things Past? Albert Schweitzer, the Anxiety of Influence, and the Untidy Jesus of Markan Memory*. Tübingen: Mohr Siebeck, 2013.

Thate, Michael J., et al. *"In Christ" in Paul: Explorations in Paul's Theology of Union and Participation*. Grand Rapids: Eerdmans, 2018.

Theissen, Gerd. *Miracle Stories of the Early Christian Tradition*. Translated by Francis McDonagh. Edinburgh: T. & T. Clark, 1983.

———. "The Political Dimension of Jesus' Activities." In *The Social Setting of Jesus and the Gospels*, edited by Wolfgang Stegemann, et al., 225–50. Minneapolis: Fortress, 2002.

Theissen, Gerd, and Annette Merz. *The Historical Jesus: A Comprehensive Guide*. Translated by John Bowden. London: SCM, 1996.

Thiessen, Matthew. *Jesus and the Forces of Death: The Gospels' Portrayal of Ritual Impurity within First-Century Judaism*. Grand Rapids: Baker Academic, 2020.

———. *A Jewish Paul: The Messiah's Herald to the Gentiles*. Grand Rapids: Baker Academic, 2023.

———. "The Legislation of Leviticus 12 in Light of Ancient Embryology." *Vetus Testamentum* 68 (2018) 297–319.

Thomas, Joseph. "If Not Parthenogenesis Why Not 'In Vivo Embryogenesis' with Mary as a Birth Mother." *The Journal of Maternal-Fetal & Neonatal Medicine* 28.15 (2015) 1850.

Thompson, James W. *The Beginnings of Christian Philosophy: The Epistle to the Hebrews*. Washington, DC: Catholic Biblical Association of America, 1982.

Thorsteinsson, Runar M. *Jesus as Philosopher: The Moral Sage in the Synoptic Gospels*. Oxford: Oxford University Press, 2018.

Tilling, Chris. *Paul's Divine Christology*. Grand Rapids: Eerdmans, 2012.

Torrance, Alexis. *Human Perfection in Byzantine Theology: Attaining the Fullness of Christ*. Oxford: Oxford University Press, 2020.

Torrance, Thomas F. *Atonement: The Person and Work of Christ*. Edited by Robert T. Walker. Downers Grove, IL: InterVarsity, 2009.

———. *Space, Time and Resurrection*. Edinburgh: T. & T. Clark, 1998.

Torrell, Jean-Pierre, OP. *Encyclopédie Jésus le Christ chez saint Thomas d'Aquin*. Paris: Cerf, 2008.

———. "S. Thomas et la Vierge Marie." In *Jésus le Christ chez Thomas d'Aquin. Texte de la Tertia Pars (ST IIIa) traduit et commenté, accompagné de Données historiques et doctrinales et de cinquante Textes choisis*, 1093–1101. Paris: Cerf, 2008.

———. "Nature and Grace in Thomas Aquinas." In *Surnaturel: A Controversy at the Heart of Twentieth-Century Thomistic Thought*, edited by Serge-Thomas Bonino, OP, translated by Robert Williams, revised by Matthew Levering, 155–88. Ave Maria, FL: Sapientia, 2009.

Treat, Jeremy R. "Atonement and Covenant: Binding Together Aspects of Christ's Work." In *Locating Atonement: Explorations in Constructive Dogmatics*, edited by Oliver Crisp and Fred Sanders, 101–17. Grand Rapids: Zondervan, 2015.

———. "Covenant." In *T&T Clark Companion to the Atonement*, edited by Adam J. Johnson, 431–35. London: Bloomsbury, 2017.

———. *The Crucified King: Atonement and Kingdom in Biblical and Systematic Theology*. Grand Rapids: Zondervan, 2014.

Treier, Daniel J. "The New Covenant and New Creation: Western Soteriologies and the Fullness of the Gospel." In *So Great a Salvation: Soteriology in the Majority World*, edited by Gene L. Green, Stephen T. Pardue, and K. K. Yeo, 14–37. Grand Rapids: Eerdmans, 2017.

———. "Virgin Territory?" *Pro Ecclesia* 23 (2014) 373–79.

Troeltsch, Ernst. *The Absoluteness of Christianity and the History of Religions*. Translated by David Reid. Louisville: Westminster John Knox, 2005.

Tsutserov, Alexander. *Glory, Grace, and Truth: Ratification of the Sinaitic Covenant according to the Gospel of John*. Eugene, OR: Wipf & Stock, 2009.

Turek, Margaret M. *Atonement: Soundings in Biblical, Trinitarian, and Spiritual Theology*. San Francisco: Ignatius, 2022.

Turner, Denys. "The Human Person." In *The Cambridge Companion to the* Summa Theologiae, edited by Philip McCosker and Denys Turner, 168–80. Cambridge: Cambridge University Press, 2016.

———. *Thomas Aquinas: A Portrait*. New Haven: Yale University Press, 2013.

Turner, James T., Jr. *On the Resurrection of the Dead: A New Metaphysics of Afterlife for Christian Thought*. London: Routledge, 2020.

Twelftree, Graham. *Jesus the Exorcist: A Contribution to the Study of the Historical Jesus*. Tübingen: Mohr Siebeck, 1993.

Vall, Gregory. "Two Trajectories in the Reception of *Dei Verbum*." In *Ecclesial Exegesis: A Synthesis of Ancient and Modern Approaches to Scripture*, 73–120. Washington, DC: Catholic University of America Press, 2022.

———. "Psalms and the Christ Event in the Epistle to the Hebrews." In *Ecclesial Exegesis: A Synthesis of Ancient and Modern Approaches to Scripture*, 267–90. Washington, DC: Catholic University of America Press, 2022.

———. Review of *A Quest for the Historical Christ: Scientia Christi and the Modern Study of Jesus*, by Anthony Giambrone, OP. *The Thomist* 88 (2024) 129–35.

van der Kooi, Cornelis, and Gijsbert van den Brink. *Christian Dogmatics*. Translated by Reinder Bruinsma with James D. Bratt. Grand Rapids: Eerdmans, 2017.

Van Dyke, Christina. *A Hidden Wisdom: Medieval Contemplatives on Self-Knowledge, Reason, Love, Persons, and Immortality*. Oxford: Oxford University Press, 2022.

van Inwagen, Peter. "The Possibility of Resurrection." *International Journal for Philosophy of Religion* 9 (1978) 114–21.

Van Loon, Hans. *The Dyophysite Christology of Cyril of Alexandria*. Leiden: Brill, 2009.

van Tilborg, Sjef, and Patrick Chatelion Counet. *Jesus' Appearances and Disappearances in Luke 24*. Leiden: Brill, 2000.

Van Wart, T. Adam. "Aquinas's Eschatological Historiography: Job, Providence, and the Multiple Senses of the Historical Event." *Pro Ecclesia* 30 (2021) 32–50.

Vander Schel, Kevin M. *Embedded Grace: Christ, History, and the Reign of God in Schleiermacher's Dogmatics*. Minneapolis: Fortress, 2013.

Vatican Council II. *Dei Verbum*. In *Vatican Council II: Constitutions, Degrees, Declarations*, vol. 1: *The Conciliar and Postconciliar Documents*, rev. ed., edited by Austin Flannery, 750–65. Northport, NY: Costello, 1996.

———. *Lumen Gentium*. In *Vatican Council II: Constitutions, Degrees, Declaration*, vol. 1: *The Conciliar and Postconciliar Documents*, rev. ed., edited by Austin Flannery, 350–426. Northport, NY: Costello, 1996.

Vermes, Geza. *Jesus the Jew: A Historian's Reading of the Gospels*. London: Collins, 1973.

Vermigli, Peter Martyr. *Loci Communes*. London: John Kyngston, 1576.

Verseput, Donald J. *The Rejection of the Humble Messianic King: A Study of the Composition of Matthew 11–12*. New York: Peter Lang, 1986.

Vidu, Adonis. *Atonement, Law, and Justice: The Cross in Historical and Cultural Contexts*. Grand Rapids: Baker Academic, 2014.

von Harnack, Adolf. *What Is Christianity?* Translated by Thomas Bailey Saunders. Philadelphia: Fortress, 1986.

Vonier, Anscar, OSB. *The Spirit and the Bride*. Worcester, MA: Assumption, 2013.

von Rad, Gerhard. *Theologie des Alten Testaments*, vol. 2. Munich: Kaiser, 1960.

Walck, Leslie W. *The Son of Man in the Parables of Enoch and in Matthew*. London: T. & T. Clark, 2011.

Ward, Thomas M. *Ordered by Love: An Introduction to John Duns Scotus*. Brooklyn: Angelico, 2022.

Ware, James. "Paul's Understanding of the Resurrection in 1 Corinthians 15:36–54." *Journal of Biblical Literature* 133 (2014) 809–35.

Weaver, J. Denny. "Narrative *Christus Victor*: The Answer to Anselmian Atonement Violence." In *Atonement and Violence: A Theological Conversation*, edited by John Sanders, 1–29. Nashville: Abingdon, 2006.

Wedderburn, A. J. M. *Beyond Resurrection*. London: SCM, 1999.

Weil, Simone. *Intimations of Christianity among the Ancient Greeks*. London: Routledge, 2003.

Weill, Marie-David. *L'Humanisme eschatologique de Louis Bouyer. De Marie, trône de la Sagesse, à l'Eglise, épouse de l'Agneau*. Paris: Cerf, 2016.

Weinandy, Thomas G., OFM Cap. "The Annunciation and Nativity: Undoing the Sinful Act of Eve." *International Journal of Systematic Theology* 14 (2012) 217–32.

———. "Aquinas: God *IS* Man: The Marvel of the Incarnation." In *Aquinas on Doctrine: A Critical Introduction*, edited by Daniel A. Keating et al., 67–89. London: T. & T. Clark, 2004.

———. *Does God Change?* Still River, MA: St. Bede's, 1985.

———. *Does God Suffer?* Notre Dame: University of Notre Dame Press, 2000.

———. *Jesus Becoming Jesus*. Vol. 1, *A Theological Interpretation of the Synoptic Gospels*. Washington, DC: Catholic University of America Press, 2018.

———. *Jesus Becoming Jesus*. Vol. 3, *A Theological Interpretation of the Gospel of St. John: The Book of Glory and the Passion and Resurrection Narratives*. Washington, DC: Catholic University of America Press, 2022.

Welburn, Andrew. *Myth of the Nativity: The Virgin Birth Re-examined*. Edinburgh: Floris, 2006.

White, L. Michael. *From Jesus to Christianity: How Four Generations of Visionaries and Storytellers Created the New Testament and Christian Faith*. San Francisco: HarperSanFrancisco, 2004.

White, Thomas Joseph, OP. "Divine Perfection and the Kenosis of the Son." In *Kenosis: The Self-Emptying of Christ in Scripture and Theology*, edited by Paul T. Nimmo and Keith L. Johnson, 137–56. Grand Rapids: Eerdmans, 2022.

———. *The Incarnate Lord: A Thomistic Study in Christology*. Washington, DC: Catholic University of America Press, 2015.

———. "Mariology and the Sense of Mystery: The Virgin Mary and the Spiritual Practice of Catholic Theology." In *Thomas Aquinas as Spiritual Teacher*, edited by Michael A. Dauphinais et al., 211–44. Ave Maria, FL: Sapientia, 2023.

———. "On the Ecumenical Work of Reforming Christology: *Sacra Doctrina*, *Analogia Entis*, and Kenosis." *Nova et Vetera* 20 (2022) 649–72.

———. "One God in Two Testaments: On the Biblical Ontology of Trinitarian Monotheism." In *Engaging Catholic Doctrine: Essays in Honor of Matthew Levering*, edited by Robert Barron, et al., 191–207. Steubenville, OH: Emmaus Academic, 2023.

———. "The Precarity of Wisdom: Modern Dominican Theology, Perspectivalism, and the Tasks of Reconstruction." In *Ressourcement Thomism: Sacred Doctrine, the Sacraments, and the Moral Life*, edited by Reinhard Hütter and Matthew Levering, 92–123. Washington, DC: Catholic University of America Press, 2010.

———. "The Trinitarian Consciousness of Christ." In *Thomas Aquinas and the Crisis of Christology*, edited by Michael A. Dauphinais et al., 99–125. Ave Maria, FL: Sapientia, 2021.

———. *The Trinity: On the Nature and Mystery of the One God*. Washington, DC: Catholic University of America Press, 2022.

———. "The Two Natures of Christ in the Crucifixion: The Cross as a Revelation of Divine Love." *Angelicum* 97 (2021) 121–51.

White, Vernon. *Atonement and Incarnation: An Essay in Universalism and Particularity*. Cambridge: Cambridge University Press, 1991.

Wilkins, Jeremy D. *Before Truth: Lonergan, Aquinas, and the Problem of Wisdom*. Washington, DC: Catholic University of America Press, 2018.

———. "Love and Knowledge of God in the Human Life of Christ." *Pro Ecclesia* 21 (2012) 77–99.

Williamson, Paul R. *Sealed with an Oath: Covenant in God's Unfolding Purpose*. Downers Grove, IL: InterVarsity, 2007.
Wilson, Brittany. *The Embodied God: Seeing the Divine in Luke-Acts and the Early Church*. Oxford: Oxford University Press, 2021.
Wink, Walter. "Our Stories, Cosmic Stories, and the Biblical Story." In *Sacred Stories: A Celebration of the Power of Story to Transform and Heal*, edited by Chares Simpkinson and Anne Simpkinson, 209–22. San Francisco: HarperSanFrancisco, 1993.
Wise, Michael O., et al. *The Dead Sea Scrolls: A New Translation*. 2nd ed. New York: HarperCollins, 2005.
Witherington, Ben, III. *Grace in Galatia: A Commentary on Paul's Letter to the Galatians*. Grand Rapids: Eerdmans, 1998.
———. *Jesus the Sage: The Pilgrimage of Wisdom*. Minneapolis: Fortress, 1994.
———. *Jesus the Seer: The Progress of Prophecy*. Peabody, MA: Hendrickson, 1999.
———. *The Many Faces of the Christ: The Christologies of the New Testament and Beyond*. New York: Crossroad, 1998.
———. *The Problem with Evangelical Theology: Testing the Exegetical Foundations of Calvinism, Dispensationalism and Wesleyanism*. Waco, TX: Baylor University Press, 2005.
Wold, Benjamin. "Jesus among Wisdom's Representatives: 4QInstruction." In *Enoch and the Synoptic Gospels: Reminiscences, Allusions, Intertextuality*, edited by Loren T. Stuckenbruck and Gabriele Boccaccini, 317–35. Atlanta: SBL, 2016.
Wood, Jordan Daniel. *The Whole Mystery of Christ: Creation as Incarnation in Maximus Confessor*. Notre Dame: University of Notre Dame Press, 2022.
Wray, Judith Hoch. *Rest as a Theological Metaphor in the Epistle to the Hebrews and the Gospel of Truth: Early Christian Homiletics of Rest*. Atlanta: Scholars, 1998.
Wrede, William. *Das Messiasgeheimnis in den Evangelien. Zugleich ein Beitrag zum Verständnis des Markusevangeliums*. Göttingen: Vandenhoeck & Ruprecht, 1901.
Wright, N. T. *After You Believe: Why Christian Character Matters*. New York: HarperCollins, 2010.
———. *History and Eschatology: Jesus and the Promise of Natural Theology*. Waco, TX: Baylor University Press, 2018.
———. *How God Became King: The Forgotten Story of the Gospels*. New York: HarperOne, 2012.
———. *Jesus and the Victory of God*. Minneapolis: Fortress, 1996.
———. *Paul and the Faithfulness of God*, Book II: Parts III and IV. Minneapolis: Fortress, 2013.
———. *The Resurrection of the Son of God*. Minneapolis: Fortress, 2003.
Wright, William M., IV. "*Dei Verbum*." In *The Reception of Vatican II*, edited by Matthew L. Lamb and Matthew Levering, 81–112. Oxford: Oxford University Press, 2017.
———. *The Lord's Prayer: Matthew 6 and Luke 11 for the Life of the Church*. Grand Rapids: Baker Academic, 2023.
Wright, William M., IV, and Francis Martin. *Encountering the Living God in Scripture: Theological and Philosophical Principles for Interpretation*. Grand Rapids: Baker Academic, 2019.
Xeravits, Géza G. *King, Priest, Prophet: Positive Eschatological Protagonists of the Qumran Library*. Leiden: Brill, 2003.
Yai-Chow Wong, Teresia. "The Problem of Preexistence in Philippians 2:6–11." *Ephemerides Theologicae Lovanienses* 62 (1986) 267–82.

Yong, Amos. *Beyond the Impasse: Toward a Pneumatological Theology of Religions.* Grand Rapids: Baker, 2003.

———. *Theology and Down Syndrome: Reimagining Disability in Late Modernity.* Waco, TX: Baylor University Press, 2007.

Zaas, Peter. "Who Was Jesus? A Jewish Response." In *Who Was Jesus? A Jewish-Christian Dialogue,* edited by Paul Copan and Craig A. Evans, 15–20. Louisville: Westminster John Knox, 2001.

Zaas, Peter, and William Lane Craig. "Interactive Discussion." In *Who Was Jesus? A Jewish-Christian Dialogue,* edited by Paul Copan and Craig A. Evans, 29–35. Louisville: Westminster John Knox, 2001.

Zacharias, H. Daniel. *Matthew's Presentation of the Son of David: Davidic Tradition and Typology in the Gospel of Matthew.* London: T. & T. Clark, 2017.

Zachhuber, Johannes. "The Absoluteness of Christianity and the Relativity of All History: Two Strands in Ferdinand Christian Baur's Thought." In *Ferdinand Christian Baur and the History of Early Christianity,* edited by Martin Bauspiess et al., translated by Robert F. Brown and Peter C. Hodgson, 287–304. Oxford: Oxford University Press, 2017.

———. "Modern Discourse on Sacrifice and Its Theological Background." In *Sacrifice and Modern Thought,* edited by Julia Meszaros and Johannes Zachhuber, 12–28. Oxford: Oxford University Press, 2013.

Zetterholm, Magnus. "Introduction." In *The Messiah in Early Judaism and Christianity,* edited by Magnus Zetterholm, xxi–xxvii. Minneapolis: Fortress, 2007.

Zimmermann, Johannes. *Messianische Texte aus Qumran. Königliche, priesterliche und prophetische Messiasvorstellungen in den Schriftfunden von Qumran.* Tübingen: Mohr Siebeck, 1998.

Zimmermann, Ruben. *Puzzling the Parables of Jesus: Methods and Interpretation.* Minneapolis: Fortress, 2015.

Zizioulas, John D. *Being as Communion: Studies in Personhood and the Church.* Crestwood, NY: St Vladimir's Seminary Press, 1997.

Index

1 Enoch, 17n43, 117, 195n47, 199n61, 350n141, 370–72, 377n62, 381

Abigail (David's wife), 164
Adam, 9, 17n43, 28, 53, 57, 71, 79, 85, 130, 225n137, 232n159, 236n5, 245n30, 254n59, 257, 259, 284n165, 290, 309, 311n21, 320n50, 325, 345–48, 349n137, 358n164, 360–62, 366, 406–7, 417
adopted sonship, 80–81
adoption, 59n9, 80, 185, 258n74, 361n3, 386–87, 415
adoptionism, 59n9, 387
adoptive sonship, 71, 255
Albert the Great, 52, 88n108, 308, 316, 319–20, 331–38, 344, 356, 406
Allison, Dale, 8n13, 20n48–49, 44n119, 55n1, 99n1, 111, 115–16, 131n95, 151, 180n5, 206, 211, 312n23, 323n59, 354, 357, 358n164, 375n56
Alpetragius, 336
altar, 51, 123n76, 239n14, 241, 248–49, 251, 254, 262n89, 270–71, 276n136, 280–82, 284, 285n170, 288, 291, 295, 297n204–205, 412, 415
Ambrose, St. 316
anamnesis, 251–52
Anatolios, Khaled, 256n67, 277n142, 279n149–50, 280n152, 281n154, 281n156, 282n161, 283n162, 284n168, 285n171, 285n173, 286n174, 294–95, 299–300

Anderson, Gary, 3n4, 64n27, 125n80, 236, 248n41, 250n147, 257n170, 277n140
Andrew of Crete, 346, 348, 406
Annunciation, 55n1, 84n98, 86n103, 87–88, 95, 161, 229, 287, 291, 396
Anselm, 42n110, 89n112, 243n25, 245n30, 277n142, 283n162, 316–17, 360n1, 406
apocalyptic day, 110
apostles, 27n69, 35n90, 65n28, 106–7, 196, 204n69, 216, 304n1, 328, 347, 380, 398, 403, 409, 419
Apostles' Creed, 55n1, 67
Areopagus, 304
ark of the covenant, 66, 73, 165, 285n170, 292, 309, 345, 347
Aslan, Reza, 17–19
Assefa, Daniel, 174
Assumption, 13, 20, 52–53, 64n26, 84n98, 85n100, 93, 115, 183n14, 212, 272n122, 308–9, 310n17, 313n25, 332, 344–46, 354n156, 358, 400; Dormition, 346–48, 400
Athanasius, St., 105, 413n3
atonement, 37n99, 38n101, 43n114, 88n109, 202n68, 227n143, 232n159, 240n17, 242–43, 244n29, 245n30, 246, 247n36, 253, 276, 277n141, 283, 284n168, 292, 297n205, 298n207, 300n214, 302n219, 363, 383–85, 386n85, 409n168, 412

479

INDEX

atoning sacrifice, 24, 238n11, 239, 246n33, 275
Attridge, Harold, 3, 14n37, 239, 240n16, 255n 61, 311n21, 386n87, 389, 392n110
Augustine, St., 29n77, 42n110, 45, 52, 82n89, 83, 86–87, 156–57, 222, 235n2, 260n82, 280, 296n204, 307–8, 316, 318n41, 319–20, 325–30, 332, 337, 344, 353–54, 356, 358

baptism, 2, 59, 64n25, 114n53, 147, 172, 177n2, 241n18, 250n47, 254n39, 271, 296, 302–3, 348, 381n73, 392n110, 393n114, 409n168, 417
Barber, Michael, 18n43, 24, 116n58, 146n128, 149n139, 167n194, 195n47, 237, 239, 251n49, 252n50, 253, 254n58, 296n203, 377n60, 394, 396, 397n122
Barron, Robert, 157n161, 263, 361–62
Barth, Karl, 178n4
Barton, Stephen, 75
Bauckham, Richard, 17n43, 76n67, 205–6, 115n56, 255, 256n64, 265n96, 269n114, 270, 371n42, 382n74, 388n99
beatitudes, 101, 104, 108, 147, 149n140, 158–59, 160n175–76, 161, 394
Bede, St., 165, 222
Behr, John, 9n18, 10n18, 86n103, 144n127
Bernard of Clairvaux, St., 54, 85, 164–66, 316, 406
Bérulle, Pierre de, 11
Bethlehem, 65n29, 97, 98n132, 161, 396
Biblical exegesis, 14, 21n50, 22, 402n143
biblical literalism, 55n1, 179, 221, 411
Billot, Charles, 45
blasphemy, 75n66, 113, 114n52, 115–16, 144, 297n205, 370
bodiliness, 8, 51–52, 305–9, 311, 315, 317–20, 325, 327, 331, 337–38, 343–44, 348, 350–53, 354n156, 357–58, 412

body; human body, 74, 79, 305, 322, 324n62, 327, 328n71, 333, 335n93, 341, 355n158, 356n160, 357n161, 412; earthly body, 310–12, 316, 318n41, 326, 331, 335, 337–39, 341, 354n156, 355, 357, 358n162; glorified body, 7–8, 51–52, 305, 308, 310–12, 314–15, 317–18, 321, 323, 325–26, 328n71, 329, 333–38, 340, 342–43, 345, 351, 353–54, 356–58, 412; Mystical Body, 91, 106n23, 224, 226, 290n185, 293n199; resurrected body (bodies), 52, 310, 311n21, 312n23, 314, 316, 318n41, 319, 320n50, 322, 323n59, 324n62, 325, 327, 330–32, 339–40, 410; risen body (bodies), 304–5, 310n17, 311, 312n23, 313n25, 315, 320, 322, 325, 326n65, 327–28, 330, 336, 339, 341, 343–44, 352n150, 354n156, 355, 357n161; spiritual body, 312, 316, 318, 323n59, 329–30, 339, 357
Bolt, Peter, 187n25, 203, 204n70, 244n29
Bonaventure, 16n42, 23n55, 88n108, 164–65, 179, 186–91, 196–97, 200, 205, 211–12, 317, 406, 411
Bond, Helen, 363
Borg, Marcus, 111, 116n59
Bouyer, Louis, 5n9, 9, 13n31, 16n42, 44n188, 54, 71, 75, 88, 225n137, 361n2
Braine, David, 76n67, 81
Bread of Life Discourse, 147
Bride, 12, 53, 75, 81n87, 134, 163n182, 202n68, 231, 234, 261, 289n181, 292–93, 301–2, 346, 348, 358, 366, 399n128, 400–401; virginal Bride, 73, 91
Bridegroom, 71, 113, 162n181, 231, 234, 261, 328n70, 348, 400
Brown, Raymond, 3n4, 5n9, 59–61, 61n15, 63, 64n25, 75n66,

480

113n52, 258–59, 288, 293n197, 295, 302
Brown, Sherri, 51, 242, 254n59, 263, 266, 270–74
Brunner, Emil, 70
Bühner, Ruben, 21n52, 22n54, 24n58, 29–30, 53n142, 60n11, 115, 116n56, 177n61, 144n124, 145n127, 368n29, 370n37–38, 371n42, 373n48, 377n60, 377n62, 380n72, 388n97, 397n124, 414n5
Bulgakov, Sergius, 5n9, 38n101, 52, 84n98, 178n4, 225n137, 307, 317–18, 330
Bullard, Collin, 169
Burkett, Delbert, 118
Burkitt, F. C., 107
Bynum, Caroline Walker, 326n65, 331n78, 350

Caesar Augustus, 97
Caird, G. B., 391, 392n108
Cajetan, Thomas de Vio Cardinal, 16, 235n2
Cana, 6, 50, 53, 162, 163n182, 166, 180, 223, 228–29, 231, 234, 256n65, 259, 262, 263n90, 273, 288n180, 301, 417
Canaanites, 134
Cantilupe, Thomas, St., 222
Capernaum, 104, 176, 189
causality, 80n82, 183n14, 299n211, 305
Celsus, 63
centurion's slave, 186–88, 211
Chalcedon, 31n80, 34, 54n143, 67, 77–78, 93n124, 382n74
charity, 14n35, 42, 94, 102, 124n77, 146n129, 167, 227n143, 229, 235n2, 276n136, 397, 402, 413n3, 414–15
Chemnitz, Martin, 317
Chennattu, Rekha, 51, 242, 263, 266–69
Cho, Bernardo, 113–14n52
Choumnos, Nikephoros, 232
Christocentrism, 90, 32n81, 38n101
Christology; conciliar Christology, 36; Davidic Christology, 24; high Christology, 22n54, 29, 49, 144n124, 368n29, 390n105; Spirit Christology, 2
Clement of Rome, 315
Coakley, Sarah, 320
cognitional theory, 42
Collins, Raymond, 14n37, 41n108, 68n41, 114n52, 117n60, 349, 361n3, 369n30
Coloe, Mary, 241n19, 260, 261n83, 262n89, 268n106–7, 270n115, 395n119
Commandments, 111n40, 126n83, 156n157, 165, 248, 250n45, 264, 268–69, 383
communication of idioms, 178
communion of saints, 230, 404
concupiscence, 70
Congregation for Catholic Education, 11, 411
consciousness, 42, 45, 171n204, 172–73, 180, 309n15, 350n140; consciousness of Christ, 32n81, 35n89, 37n99, 41, 182, 184, 191n34; mission-consciousness, 37, 112n145; self-consciousness, 113, 311n22, 44n117, 45; supra-consciousness, 45
consummation, 14n35, 28n72, 54, 102n11, 103, 173–75, 193n38, 224, 282n161, 298, 340, 360, 396–97, 415
contemplation, 12, 15n38, 37n98, 49, 71, 73, 90, 154n154, 162, 308, 346n124
continuity, 22n54, 38n101, 73, 79n82, 189n28, 238n12, 267, 305n4, 307–8, 311–12, 313n25, 315–16, 322, 324–27, 339–41, 344, 351, 354–55n156, 357, 358n162, 412
contrition, 283n162, 285n171, 294n200, 299–300
conversion, 138–39, 142
Coredemptrix, 289, 290n185
Corporeality, 89, 311, 313n25, 318, 330, 412
Cortez, Félix, 52, 376, 381–86, 397
cosmic battle, 205, 208

481

cosmos, 233, 296n203, 338, 340–41, 352, 358, 361n2, 378, 399n128, 408, 412
Council of Ephesus, 67, 77–78, 83, 85, 93n124, 275
Council of Trent, 275, 279
Creator, 17n43, 47n131, 64n27, 68n41, 115, 145, 169, 185n21, 203, 205, 211, 221, 225, 231, 233, 237n7, 311, 323, 327, 361n2, 363, 388–91, 393, 400, 412
Creed of Toledo, 275
critical history, 40, 171n204
Crowe, Brandon, 232n159, 263, 276n136
Crucifixion, 18, 30n78, 77n70, 108, 115n56, 117n60, 144, 173n212, 236n5, 242, 245n30, 254, 262n89, 270, 274, 276n136, 281, 298, 303, 307n10, 379n64, 405
cultic discourse, 378
cultic victim, 257, 282
Cyril of Alexandria, 54n143, 58, 77–79, 89n115, 93n124, 97, 236, 237n8

Daley, Brian, 4n6, 22n53, 78n73, 89n115, 320n50, 346
Dalton, Andrew, 9n17, 395, 414n4
Damascene (John of Damascus), 39n102, 78, 89, 91, 346–48, 406
Daniélou, Jean, 55, 57, 63n23
Daughter of Sion, 71
Dauphinais, Michael, 4n7, 26n68, 102
Davidic King, 63, 91, 97–98, 245n29, 297n205, 382–83, 385–87, 396, 397n122, 398, 406
Davidic Messiah, 20n48, 116n58, 374n52, 378, 383, 388, 396
Day of Atonement, 240n17, 242n23, 244n29, 283, 383–85, 386n85
Day of Jubilee, 369
Day of Preparation, 270
de Aldama, Joseph, 224–27, 405–7
de Chardin, Pierre Teilhard, 4n7, 310n17, 351, 352n149
de Liguori, Alphonsus, 226n138, 231, 406

de Lubac, Henri, 11, 12n27, 13, 52n141, 310n17, 415
Dead Sea Scrolls, 17n43, 365n17, 368n30, 374
Decalogue, 125, 152n150, 265n97
Dei Verbum, 25n62, 103, 105–6, 118
deification, 10n18, 62, 287n177, 294, 316, 348, 405
demoniac(s), 6, 49–50, 179, 180n5, 198, 200, 201n64, 202–3, 205, 206n77, 207–9, 212, 216–21, 233
demons, 6, 19n46, 50n137, 134n100, 187, 191n34, 192n37, 193–94, 198, 199n61, 200–201, 203, 205–8, 215–21, 329, 367n23, 378n64, 393
denarius, 131, 141
deposit of faith, 6, 65n28
discipleship, 100, 150, 263, 266, 288n180, 293n197, 377n60, 411
divine communion, 257, 262, 301n216
divine life, 50, 92, 94, 150n145, 185n19, 263n91, 358n162
divine person, 10n18, 35n89, 41, 177
divine providence, 20
divine will, 39n102, 133n98, 170, 190n32, 300n215, 301n215
divinity, 2n3, 4n6, 13n31, 17n43, 18n46, 19, 20n49, 24n58, 30n78, 31n80, 44–45, 54n143, 60n12, 69n43, 71, 77, 81, 83, 94, 103, 112, 115, 145n127, 151n145, 169n200, 178n4, 185n21, 196n49, 197, 231, 276n136, 281, 362n7, 379, 382n74, 387, 389n99, 391n106, 411, 413n3
dogma, 3n3, 7n12, 13, 67–69, 77n71, 84n98, 107, 354n156
Dörnyei, Zoltán, 96, 97n129
Douglas, Mary, 252n50, 408
Dozeman, Thomas, 249
Dunn, James, 28, 100, 113, 115n54, 119n66, 184n17, 191n34, 244, 256n67, 373n50, 392n110, 393n112

INDEX

ecclesiology, 13, 58n6, 66n31, 417
Eden, 301, 322n59, 347
Ehrman, Bart, 110-11, 114n54
Elijah, 20n48, 185n21, 190, 194n42, 195, 197, 204n69, 214, 303n221, 345, 374n53, 375n56, 418; New Elijah, 28
Elisha, 197, 214
Elizabeth (Mary's cousin), 40n108, 90n117, 164, 224n134
Emmaus, 304n1, 313, 336-37
empty tomb, 32, 69, 209, 350n140
enthronement, 41n108, 52-53, 114n52, 360, 362, 365, 371n42, 376-80, 382, 385-88, 390, 395, 397, 398n126-27, 413
epistemology, 23n57, 43
Erickson, Millard, 66
eschatological battle, 6, 221, 367
eschatology, 5n8, 28n75, 33, 48n135, 58n6, 73, 99n1, 107-8, 121n70, 125n80, 131n95, 135n101, 149, 194n42, 310n17, 315, 342, 344, 350n141, 351, 353
eschaton, 48n135, 111n40, 173, 238n11, 312n23, 320, 352, 368n27, 394, 415
Eskola, Timo, 52, 365, 376-80, 381n73, 386-88, 392-93, 412n2
Essenes, 46, 368n30
eternal life, 93-94, 125, 127, 138, 168n195, 287n177, 302n219, 306, 316, 317n40, 322, 334n90, 341, 357n162, 358n162, 371, 409, 411
eternal procession, 74
Eubank, Nathan, 65n29, 168-69
Eucharist, 47, 136n104, 188, 235n2, 253, 254n59, 255, 256n64, 263n91, 267, 271, 275n134, 302-3, 317, 408-9
Eusebius of Caesarea, 76-77
Eve, 9, 12, 53, 73, 85, 225n137, 254n59, 255, 257-59, 263, 288n180, 290, 309, 320n50, 345-48, 358n164, 366, 401, 406-7, 417
Eve, Eric, 176n1, 193, 198

exile, 47n131, 135, 160, 162n181, 171n204, 226n139, 236, 240n17, 244n29, 301
exodus, 28, 60n11, 74n62, 162n181, 191n35, 214, 244n29, 251-53, 263-64, 268, 288, 303n221, 361, 386, 393n114, 418
exorcism, 6, 49, 50n137, 176, 179, 187, 191, 192n35, 193, 194n42, 198, 199n61, 200n62, 201n63, 202, 206, 208, 211-12, 218, 220-21

Fagerberg, David, 360, 361n2
Farewell Discourse, 255, 266, 269, 350
Farrow, Douglas, 408-9
Feast of Tabernacles, 395
feasting, 140
fellowship, 8n14, 31n80, 36, 100n5, 122, 167, 202n67, 203n68, 239n14, 262, 280, 297n204
fiat, 87n107, 88n109, 225-26, 247, 291-92, 403, 405n155
Fitzmyer, Joseph, 44n119, 46n130, 51, 248, 251, 252n50
Fletcher, Patrick, 17n43, 121n70, 326n65, 351, 352n150, 353
Footwashing, 153n153, 267
forgiveness, 5n8, 35, 42, 125, 139-40, 154n154, 156n158, 181n9, 185, 188, 192, 193n38, 202n67, 236, 243n25, 244n29, 245n30, 246n33, 250, 251n49, 257, 269n113, 270, 294, 298-99, 300n215, 362n7, 369, 385, 417
Fourth Lateran Council, 355
freedom, 35n90, 39n102, 54n143, 87, 88n109, 105n15, 107n26, 130n92, 141, 149n140, 171n206, 178n4, 209, 221n124, 243n23, 244n29, 287n177, 290n185, 317, 334, 351, 353n150
friendship, 42, 235, 299n209

Gabriel (angel), 63, 64n25-26, 161, 164, 166, 367n26, 369n37, 396, 401
Gaine, Simon, 14-17, 102n11, 172-73

483

INDEX

Galilee, 6, 18n45, 47n131, 97n131, 108, 114n54, 131, 141, 148n135, 149n138, 171n206, 184, 188, 198, 200, 207, 220, 229, 258n74, 273, 301, 367n23
Gathercole, Simon, 299n209, 388, 389n101, 390
Gentiles, 120, 123, 130, 133n98, 136, 138–39, 187, 199n61, 200n62, 201, 202n67, 296n203, 394
Gerhard, Johann, 52, 308, 316–17, 357
Gerhardsson, Birger, 143
Germanus of Constantinople, 406
Giambrone, Anthony, 16n40, 24–25, 28, 29n75–76, 46–47, 62, 123n77, 167, 172, 190n30, 253, 367, 374–75, 387n96, 389n99
Gibbon, Edward, 19, 106
Gilson, Caitlin Smith, 307, 308n13, 327n70, 328n71
Girard, René, 199n58, 237n7
glorification, 10n18, 51, 101n9, 128n87, 236n5, 253n57, 273–74, 277n142, 279, 280n150, 282n161, 283n162, 285, 286n173, 295, 300, 303, 308, 325, 338, 345, 349n137, 351, 354, 357–58, 361n2, 368, 369n30, 397, 412
Gnostics, 72, 306n5
God-bearer, 5, 77
Golden Calf, 264
Graebe, Brian, 81n87, 83n93, 84
Gregory of Nazianzus, 316, 320n50
Gregory of Nyssa, 52, 82n89, 308, 316, 318n41, 319–25, 339, 344, 354, 356n160
Gregory the Great, 222, 316
Grindheim, Sigurd, 49, 113, 117–18, 169n200, 172
Guardini, Romani, 53
guilt, 136–37, 140, 181n9, 237n7, 243, 245n30, 247n36, 251n49
Günther, Anton, 45

Harris, Steven, 52, 305–6, 314n28, 315, 317n40
harvest, 25, 109, 141

healing, 33n87, 74, 112n45, 142, 149n140, 178n3, 179n5, 187–88, 189n30, 193, 195, 197n54, 198, 200n62, 203, 205, 206n77, 207, 211–12, 215–17, 219, 223–24, 246, 259n75, 365, 396
heavenly Jerusalem, 385, 415
Hegesippus, 76
Heil, John Paul, 253, 258
Heim, Mark, 298
Helvidius, 86
Henderson, Suzanne Watts, 166, 167n191
Hengel, Martin, 101, 162n181, 174, 237n7, 374, 379n66, 388n97, 390n104, 392n110
Herod, 71, 128, 171n206
Herrmann, Wilhelm, 180–81, 184
historical-critical (biblical) scholarship, 1, 9–10, 14–15, 19, 21, 23n57, 26, 62n19, 84n98, 106, 109n38, 118n64, 180
historical reconstruction, 20, 21n50, 23–24, 61, 86n103, 90n117, 171n204
historical research, 23n56, 25, 59n8
historiography, 20, 207, 304
holiness, 9n17, 73, 75, 88n109, 150, 158, 160, 203n69, 269n114, 279, 294n200, 345, 354n156, 393n112, 397, 400
Horbury, William, 372
householder, 131
Huizenga, Leroy, 28, 250
human will, 39n102, 89
humanity, 7n12, 10n18, 13n31, 30n79, 34n87, 36, 43n114, 46n126, 52–53, 54n143, 58n8, 69n43, 70, 73, 77–78, 80n82, 81, 83, 87n107, 88, 90, 93n124, 94–95, 155n155, 157, 169, 173n212, 178n4, 182n9, 203n69, 265n96, 280, 281n155, 282–83, 287, 289, 290n185, 292–93, 294n200, 298, 300n214, 305, 318, 320n50, 323, 333, 348, 349n140, 353, 358n164, 361n3, 362n7, 371n42, 382n74, 386, 413n3

484

humility, 12n28, 42n110, 53n143, 54n143, 91, 95, 130n91, 162, 164–66, 188, 231, 298, 366n20, 377n60, 399, 402–3, 416
hypostasis, 89n115, 93, 277n142
hypostatic union, 3n3, 4n6, 6n12, 10n18, 32n81, 34–35, 39, 45, 58, 78, 93, 225n137, 282, 283n162, 288, 314n28

idolatry, 20n49, 137, 187, 199, 201n63, 205, 381
Ignatius of Antioch, 315
Ignatius of Loyola, 172
ignorance, 45, 173–74
Ildephonsus of Toledo, 406
illegitimacy, 18, 61, 114n52
illegitimate child, 63
illumination, 45, 306
Imbelli, Robert, 409
imminent kingdom, 24n59, 43, 105, 177n1, 195n48
immortality, 46n126, 317, 319, 323n59, 327, 328n71, 332, 349, 353, 357n161
impurity, 126n83, 194n42, 202–3
incorruptibility, 325, 345, 357n161
individuation, 45
indwelling, 35n89, 37, 236, 281–82, 395
infancy narratives, 55n1, 56n4, 58, 59n9, 61, 65, 66n29, 68, 86n103, 411
integrity, bodily integrity, 48, 74, 84–85, 86n101; integrity of faith, 74; physical integrity, 82; spiritual integrity, 74; virginal integrity, 5, 73–75, 81, 83, 85
intertestamental texts, 380, 391n106
Irenaeus, St., 57, 72, 82n89, 222, 262, 316
Isaac, 60n11, 124, 292, 295n201, 28; New Isaac, 28n72, 235, 250n47

Jefferson, Thomas, 106, 107n26
Jenkins, Philip, 222 n126
Jeremias, Joachim, 174
Jericho, 142, 213n99
Jerome, St., 82n89, 314, 315n29, 316n35

Jipp, Joshua, 143, 373n49, 398n126–27, 410
John Paul II, Pope St., 88, 168n195, 225n137, 228–29, 290n185, 314
John the Baptist, St., 2, 18n43, 20, 46, 116, 124n77, 154n154, 186, 196n50, 224n134, 241n19, 263, 270, 368n30, 375n56, 417–18
Johnson, Luke Timothy, 50, 179, 199n60, 205, 207–14, 220–22, 237n7, 242n23
Jonah, 214
Joseph, St., 3, 56, 59, 63n23, 64, 71, 76n67, 77n70, 81, 86, 90n117, 95, 97n131, 165, 230n152
Josephus, 18n45, 126, 195n47, 196n50, 198n55, 217, 220, 362n8
Journet, Charles, 12n27, 237
Judaism, 1, 17n43, 24n58, 26, 30, 31n80, 50n138, 60n11, 68, 105, 111n44, 114n52, 116n56, 123–24, 125n80, 131n95, 133n98, 136, 145n127, 167, 191n34, 202n67, 281n153, 297, 366, 370n38, 371n42, 372, 375n57, 376, 378n64, 381n73, 388n99, 390n104, 413, 414n5; anti-Judaism, 139, 158n166, 384n81; Pharisaic Judaism, 139; Rabbinic Judaism, 139, 387; Romanized Judaism, 18; see also "Second Temple"
Judea, 62, 97n131, 148n135, 184, 397
judgment, 43, 60n12, 62n19, 75, 100, 102n11, 111n40, 117n60, 124n77, 135, 155n157, 158n166, 168n197, 169, 174n214, 189n29, 195, 198, 199n61, 206, 213n99, 214n102, 236n5, 238, 240n17, 241n22, 244n29, 245, 283n162, 284n168, 298, 320, 332, 354n156, 368n30, 371, 378, 418; final judgment, 43, 111n40, 117n60, 168n197, 169, 320, 332, 354n156, 371
judicial discourse, 378

INDEX

justice, 31, 35n90, 37, 41–42, 53n141, 91, 95, 101n9, 120n68, 131n95, 133n98, 141, 151, 155, 159n169, 163, 168n197, 169, 246, 277n142, 279, 281n156, 287n177, 302n219, 342, 362, 394n115, 396, 413–16

Keener, Craig, 14n37, 44n119, 118n66, 222–24, 229, 257–58, 260n82, 313n24, 350n141
Keith, Chris, 145n128, 146, 148, 170n201–2, 180n5
kenosis, 53n143, 232n159, 328n71, 392n110
King David, 3, 28, 43, 55, 65, 90n117, 134, 161, 164, 236, 250n47, 278n144, 281, 309n16, 362, 367, 372n47, 375n56, 377, 379–80, 383, 385, 391n106, 392n110, 396–98; new David, 28, 309n16, 345
Klawans, Jonathan, 50n138, 205, 237n7, 367n26
Knohl, Israel, 113, 367n26, 368–69, 372n47
Kromholtz, Bryan, 331n78, 341n112, 353n153, 355, 356n159

Lamb of God, 241, 256, 262–63, 266, 268, 270, 414
Last Supper, 43, 47, 51, 100, 136n104, 202n67, 221n124, 236, 238, 239, 240n17, 245, 247–49, 251–52, 263, 267, 271, 276n136, 298–300, 396
lawyer, 125, 126n83, 156n157
Lee, Aquila, 15, 44n117, 113, 379n66
legion(s), 192n35, 194n42, 199n61, 201, 208–9, 218–19
Lehtipuu, Outi, 308n12, 312n23, 314n26, 315n32–33, 316, 322n57, 358n162
Leithart, Peter, 202n68, 204, 261n87–88, 262n89, 295–98, 300, 301n216, 394n115
Leo XIII, Pope, 225n137, 227, 229, 259n79

Levine, Amy-Jill, 49, 99, 103, 120–33, 136–42, 151n148, 156, 157n160, 167–68, 258n74, 261n85
liberal Protestantism (liberal Protestants), 36, 179, 217
liberation theology, 36n95, 46, 52n141
Lincoln, Andrew, 48, 56n3, 58–59, 69n43, 80n82
liturgical rites, 47
Lohfink, Gerhard, 16n42, 49, 103, 120, 134–43, 167–68, 342n112
Loisy, Alfred, 31n80, 107, 111
Lonergan, Bernard, 19n47, 39–43, 43n113, 236n7
lordship, 143, 162n179
Lourdes, 223
Lüdemann, Gerd, 61
Lumen Gentium, 12–13, 57n6, 85, 228–29
Luther, Martin, 16, 29n77
Lyonnet, Stanislas, 41

Magnificat, 94–95, 166
Mariology, 5n9, 9n17, 11–13, 58n6, 66n31, 67n35, 71n51, 72, 85n100, 97, 223, 228n145, 231n156, 241, 289n181, 290n185, 402, 405, 405n155
Maritain, Jacques, 45
marriage, 12, 53, 59, 64n26, 71, 77n70, 88, 100, 134n100, 153n152, 162, 228, 234, 242n23, 258n74, 286n175, 300–301, 310, 316n35, 323n59, 327, 346, 348, 400, 402, 409
Martin, Francis, 301 162n182
Martyrdom, 395, 413
Matera, Frank, 27n69, 49, 148–54, 157–58, 160, 160n176
Materiality, 310, 336n93, 351, 356n159
Maximus the Confessor, 39n102, 178, 231, 320n50
McDonough, Sean, 390
McFarland, Ian, 362–64, 408
McKnight, Scot, 26n66, 27n69–70, 29, 51, 143, 238, 239n13, 245n30, 284n168, 394n114

486

INDEX

meal(s), 25, 94n126, 47n131, 100n5, 236, 239n14, 248, 250–52, 263n91, 267, 280, 297
Mediator, 13, 34n88, 43, 191, 227, 229, 230n150, 283, 284n165, 288, 292, 362n8, 405, 416
Mediatrix, 226–28, 229n150, 230n153, 290n185
meditation, 74, 94, 197, 403
Meier, John, 16n42, 19–21, 116n58, 143, 154n153, 200n62, 204n69
Melchizedek, 47n131, 145n127, 280, 368n29, 369, 378, 385, 389
mercy, 14n35, 95, 100, 126n83, 129, 137–42, 149n140, 163, 167, 168n197, 169, 181n8, 187, 189, 197, 208, 242n23, 243, 249n43, 264, 279, 299, 301–2, 311n21, 377n60, 378, 380, 404–5, 416
merit, 5n8, 92n120, 125n80, 168n197, 169, 227n143, 244n29, 278, 280, 285, 370
Merkabah mysticism, 365, 376, 380, 387–88
Messianic age, 5, 133n98
messianic era, 272
messianic kingship, 398, 410
Messianic secret, 108
messianology, 366n23, 380
Meszaros, Julia, 298, 299n209
metaphysics, 3n3, 4n6, 6n11, 14, 23n57, 32n81, 38n101, 43
Methodical history, 40
Moloney, Francis, 51, 153n153, 254n59, 255–57, 259–60, 263, 265n96, 272n120, 304n1, 370n38
Moltmann, Jürgen, 8n14, 66, 306, 357n162, 358n162
Moraldi, Luigi, 41
Morales, L. Michael, 408
morality, 134, 169
Mosaic covenant, 241, 250, 251n49, 254–55, 265, 267, 272, 274–75, 293, 412
Moses, 17n43, 24n58, 28, 43, 51, 60n11, 111, 130, 148, 161n176, 185n21, 191, 197, 214, 239n14, 241, 248–49, 254, 262n89, 263n90, 264–65, 266n99, 271–72, 283, 288, 291–93, 302, 303n221, 380n68, 381n73; New Moses, 28, 101, 191, 214, 241, 254, 262n89, 265, 288, 292, 298, 303n221, 394n114
Moss, Candida, 250n45, 306n5, 311n22, 315n33, 319n46, 324n59, 351, 351n144
motherhood; human motherhood, 72; Mary's motherhood, 51, 72–73, 76n66, 79, 80n82, 83n95, 87n105, 92, 93n124, 94, 225n137, 229–30, 288, 289n181, 292n197, 293, 345, 400, 406; spiritual motherhood, 224, 228, 259, 293n199, 224; virginal motherhood, 57–58, 66, 70–74, 85n101, 89, 91, 94–96
Mount Tabor, 233, 253n57
Mount Zion, 171, 189n29, 190, 385, 415

Nain, 187, 189–91, 195, 216, 222
narrative history, 40
nature, divine nature, 39n102, 53, 78, 145n127, 178n4, 301n215, 325, 362n7, 382n74, 401; human nature, 4n6, 7n12, 32n81, 33n87, 39n102, 45, 46n126, 54n143, 59n8, 78–79, 80n82, 81, 87–89, 92–93, 97, 140, 177, 178n4, 225n137, 230n153, 284, 301n215, 319, 320n50, 323–25, 333, 346, 356n160, 362n7, 413n3; spiritual nature, 184
neo-scholastic, neo-scholastics, 16, 42, 309n15; neo-scholastic theologians, 54; neo-scholastic theology, 39, 309n15
Nepil, John, 13n31, 289n181, 293n199, 405n155, 417
Nestorianism (Nestorians), 34, 77, 79, 89, 411; anti-Nestorian (anti-Nestorianism), 48, 58, 79, 83, 89, 97
New Aaron, 28
New Abraham, 235
New Phineas, 28

new theology, 121, 217
Newman, Carey, 112, 264n94
Newman, John Henry, 40, 107, 226n138
Nguyen, Theresa Marie Chau, 13
Nichols, Aidan, 49, 85n99, 91n120, 92, 93n124, 223n132, 226n140, 230, 235, 271n118, 280n152, 284n165, 290n185, 308n15, 345n124
Nicodemus, 100
Nicolas, Jean-Hervé, 43–46, 287, 290n185, 354n156
Nicolas, Marie-Joseph, 230
Novenson, Matthew, 145n127, 366, 372–74

obedience, 12, 14n37, 32n81, 38n101, 53, 54n143, 72, 87, 90, 95–96, 104n15, 126n83, 150n144, 155n157, 162–63, 166, 178n4, 181n9, 204n69, 236n5, 241, 245n30, 250, 267–68, 273–74, 278, 285, 288, 290n185, 300n215, 330, 362n7, 382n74, 389–90, 392, 419
old theology, 217
Olshausen, Hermann, 217–18
Omnipotence, 182
ontological union, 34, 45
Origen, 10n18, 52, 63, 86n103, 200n62, 307, 315–18, 321, 330, 353, 354n156, 356n160
original sin, 70, 84n98, 230n153, 276n139, 283n162, 323, 365
orthodox Protestantism, 217
orthopraxis, 36
Ounsworth, Richard, 28, 386n87

Palamas, Gregory, 54, 231, 400–402
parable, Good Samaritan, 49, 103, 107n26, 124–26, 128–29, 132, 141, 143, 167, 233; Laborers in the Vineyard, 103, 129, 130n92, 131n95, 132, 140, 143, 168; The Lost Son, 121, 136; parable of the lost coin, 136; parable of the lost sheep, 136; Prodigal Son, 103, 120, 123n77, 127, 132, 136–40, 142, 171n204
Parousia, 9n17, 102n11, 108, 135, 151n149, 313n25
Paschal lamb, 240, 252n50, 260
Passion, 9n18, 38n101, 47n132, 53, 56, 62n19, 86n103, 232, 235n2, 236n5, 238n1, 243, 254n59, 261, 271n118, 278n144, 286, 291, 323, 325, 332, 334n90, 357n161, 365, 374n52, 383, 416
Passover, 24–25, 47, 94n126, 142, 236, 238n12, 240, 241n18, 244n29, 245, 246n33, 248, 251–53, 256, 263, 270, 418
patriarch(s), 136, 377n62, 380
Peacocke, Arthur, 339
Peeler, Amy, 12, 56n4, 60n11, 62–63, 64n26, 80n82, 87n105, 88n107, 92n123, 96, 166, 166n189, 291n190, 393n112, 411
penalty, 85n101, 95, 104n15, 123n76, 150n145, 153n151, 235, 243, 245n30, 246–47, 278–79, 285, 286n175, 294–95, 297n205, 415
Pennington, Jonathan, 101, 104n15, 105n16, 149n140, 150n145, 153n152, 157n162, 159n168, 160n175–76
Pentecost, 2, 166, 239n13, 273, 302n218, 398, 403
Perrin, Nicholas, 3n4, 47n131, 50, 74n62, 99, 100n2, 103, 113, 154n154, 155, 159n168, 160n176, 161, 167, 172n208, 179, 200–201, 202n66–67, 204–5, 204n69, 250n47, 253n54, 272n122, 281n153, 375n56
Persecution, 120n68, 160, 238n1, 374, 395, 417
Persians, 217
Peter, St., 2n3, 24, 27n69, 35, 133n98, 166, 215, 242n23, 267, 304n1, 367n23, 393, 398, 409, 416
Peters, Ted, 52, 339–40
Petrine office, 24, 43
Pharisaic Jews, 120

488

INDEX

Pharisees, 104n15, 122, 123n74, 124n77, 125–26, 130n92, 137–39, 145n128, 148n135, 163n185, 190n32, 193n38, 214–15, 394n115
Philippe, Jacques, 101
pillar of cloud, 264
Pitre, Brant, 21n50, 24–25, 44n119, 49, 51, 77n70, 86n101, 114, 116, 117n60, 118n65, 169n200, 172, 185n21, 238n12, 239, 244n29, 252–53, 296n203, 299–300, 309, 344–45, 361, 399, 408
Pius XI, Pope, 290n185, 406
Pius XII, Pope, 4n6, 225n137, 399n128, 406
Plato, 56n2, 104n15, 299n209, 329–30
Pohle, Joseph, 345
Polkinghorne, John, 52, 324n62, 339–41, 358
Pope Leo the Great, 81n87, 85, 177
Pope Leo's Tome, 81n87, 85
Porphyry, 329–30
prayer, 44, 49–50, 74n62, 154n154, 164, 166, 171n204, 176n1, 222–24, 228, 230–31, 255n62, 262n89, 267, 269, 272n122, 278, 291, 363, 416
preexistence, 3n3, 29, 41n108, 44, 117n60, 376, 388–90, 393
pregnancy, 64n25–26, 96
presentation in the Temple, 291
priesthood, 24, 47, 166n189, 229n150, 249, 253n54, 261, 276n136, 280, 364–65, 379, 385, 409n168, 416
priestly hierarchy, 47
procreation, 58, 318
prophet(s), 2, 20n48, 24n59, 32, 34, 48–49, 86, 98n132, 112n46, 122n74, 129, 134, 148n135, 161n177, 176n1, 190–92, 194n42, 195, 196n50, 197, 214, 264n94, 280n152, 364, 387, 391n106; apocalyptic prophet, 6, 17, 19, 99n1, 103, 107; eschatological prophet, 38, 105, 177n1, 179–80, 204n69
prostitute, 186
Prothro, James, 76, 77n71, 83n95, 240

Pseudo-Dionysius, 92
Purification, 21n52, 162, 203n69, 249, 280, 383–84
purity, 49n135, 61n13, 73, 84n98, 100n5, 111n40, 122n74, 124, 127, 146n128, 155n157, 180, 194n42, 201n66, 202, 203n69, 210n91, 287n177, 296

queen(s), 12, 346–47, 366, 399–408, 410, 417
queenship, 9, 13, 53, 399, 402–7, 408n164
Qumran, 47n131, 52, 111n42, 113, 117, 123n76, 145n127, 161n177, 194n42, 367–69, 373n50, 380, 418

Rabbi Akiba, 172n207, 372
Rahner, Karl, 32–34, 35n89–90, 45, 65n28, 86n101, 112n45, 178n4, 236n5, 284n168, 302n220, 310n17, 351, 352n149–50
ransom, 107, 236n5, 244, 290n185
rationalism, 35n90, 212–13, 217
Ratzinger, Joseph, 13, 16n42, 23n55, 25n62, 32n80, 36n91, 63–65, 66n29, 88–89, 96, 147–48, 315, 348, 351, 352n149, 352n150, 353, 354n156
Reardon, Patrick Henry, 44n117, 46n126, 88n109, 241, 360, 418
recapitulation, 80n82, 262, 409
reconciliation, 26n68, 37, 124, 126n81, 129, 132, 136, 142, 178n4, 227, 243n25, 245n30, 280, 348, 392n110, 394n115, 409n168
Redeemer, 2, 9n17, 13, 65n28, 70, 173, 184n18, 190–91, 205, 214, 229n150, 230n153, 289, 301–2, 379, 404, 414
Redemption, 4n6, 7, 13, 39, 41–42, 43n114, 46, 66n31, 87n107, 91, 137, 139, 173n212, 180–81, 183n16, 227n143, 229–30, 245n29, 247n36, 276n136, 277, 279, 287, 289–90, 301, 366n20, 369, 377n60, 400, 407, 414–15
Reformation, 8, 11, 16

489

INDEX

reincarnation, 320, 339, 354n156
religious liberalism, 16, 31n80, 36
Renaissance humanism, 16
Repentance, 5n8, 100, 124n77, 125, 137–40, 142, 150n145, 180, 243, 299, 378n64, 394n114, 417
Ressourcement, 16, 17n42
restitution, 139, 277n142
resurrection, bodily resurrection, 8n13, 210, 306n5, 311n22, 312n23, 314, 320–21, 323, 324n60, 325–26, 332, 337–39, 354, 357n162, 358, 417; general resurrection, 314, 321–22, 326–27, 329, 331–32, 339, 345–47, 349; resurrection of the dead, 210, 304, 314, 317, 332, 349, 351n144, 371, 376, 379, 388
retribution, 151, 155
revelation, 6, 15n39, 27n69, 67, 69–71, 86n101, 88, 91, 101, 105, 109, 132n96, 160n175, 182, 185n19, 210, 224, 226, 229, 241n22, 253n57, 259, 261n88, 263–64, 265n97, 273–74, 308n15, 318, 323n59, 342, 344–45, 347, 364, 367n26, 370n38, 375n56, 393n114, 397, 399, 405, 409, 414–15, 418–19
reverence(s), 24n58, 87n107, 182, 188
Riches, Aaron, 89–91, 97
righteousness, 9n17, 95, 100n5, 120, 149n140, 153n151, 157n162, 158–59, 236n5, 245n30, 268–69, 275, 278, 304, 362, 373n50, 384n81, 414, 419
ritual, 49n135, 124, 126, 127n83, 194n42, 199n61, 202n67, 203, 204n69, 241, 250, 267, 295n201, 383–84
Roger of Conway, 222
Roman military, 208
rosary, 403, 406
royal enthronement, 52, 360, 362, 365, 376, 385–86, 413
rulership, 393
Ryliškytė, Ligita, 42

Sabbath, 104, 113n47, 122n74, 127, 136, 145n127, 146n128, 148n137, 189, 204n69, 270, 374
sacrament(s), 74, 111n40, 210, 230n153, 254n59, 256n64, 302n219, 408, 416
sacrificial blood, 53, 241, 248–49, 251, 254, 262n89, 292–93
Sadducees, 113, 123n74, 314n26
salvation, 4, 9n16, 12, 18, 27, 34n88, 35, 36n95, 39, 43, 46, 47n131, 52, 73–74, 77, 83n95, 85n101, 87, 106, 112, 118, 120, 138, 149n140, 150n144, 159, 162, 164, 166, 175, 188, 190n32, 191, 192n35, 193, 202n68, 204, 224n134, 226n138, 227, 229, 230n153, 233n165, 236, 238n11, 243n23, 256n64, 259, 276, 279, 280n150, 282n159, 290, 298, 301n215, 302, 307, 308n13, 309n15, 360, 365, 367n26, 369, 380, 387–88, 395, 403, 411–12, 413n3, 415, 418n10, 419
Samaria, 127, 129, 397
Sanctuary, 250n47, 262n89, 268, 281, 289n181, 296n204, 363, 378, 383–86, 395
Sanders, E. P., 49n135, 107n26, 110, 145n128, 153n153, 155n157, 373n50
Satan, 50n137, 95, 122n74, 150n144, 192–94, 199n61, 203, 205, 207–9, 216, 217n108, 232, 247, 378n64, 393, 405, 409n168, 410
Satisfaction, 42, 51, 235, 243, 244n29, 245n30, 246, 276n138, 277–81, 285, 295, 297n205, 298n207, 299n209, 300, 412
Savior, 11n20, 12n29, 19, 29, 41, 55, 94, 161, 230n153, 287, 292n197, 377, 396, 406
Saward, John, 11, 172n210
scapegoat, 199n58, 199n61, 205, 226n139, 238n11, 384
Schaberg, Jane, 61, 63n22
Schäfer, Peter, 387

Schillebeeckx, Edward, 35–36, 52n141, 65n28, 181n9
Schleiermacher, Friedrich, 32n81, 37n99, 69–70, 180, 182–84, 217, 219
Schlesinger, Eugene, 415
Schloss, Jeffrey, 52, 339, 342–44, 358
scholasticism(s), 16, 245n30
Schreiner, Patrick, 309, 310n17
Schweitzer, Albert, 16n42, 19, 24n59, 44n119, 49, 103, 107–11
Science, 62n19, 182, 308, 319, 338–39, 344, 349n140
Sebald, W. G., 198–99, 204
Second Coming, 135, 346, 373
Second Temple, Second-Temple context, 19, 27, 43, 162n181, 197n54, 236; Second Temple Judaism, 1–2, 17n43, 23, 24n58, 26–31, 48, 50n138, 60n11, 63n20, 79n80, 115, 116n56, 117, 125n80, 144n124, 167, 170, 172n207, 176n1, 179, 186, 191n34, 194, 216, 219, 226n139, 281n153, 365–66, 368n29, 370n38, 371n42, 372, 374, 375n57, 376–77, 379n68, 381, 391n106, 388n99, 409, 412n2, 413; Second Temple Literature, 52, 276n136, 367n23, 376, 378n64, 379; Second Temple messianism, 60n11, 115, 116n56, 370n37
self-offering, 46, 227n143, 253–54, 263, 269n114, 292, 297, 300n215, 409
self-sacrificial love, 9, 232, 311n21, 350, 414
self-understanding, 29n75, 31n79, 34n88, 47n131, 103n14, 112, 114–15, 116n58, 119, 161, 166, 201, 203n69, 237, 368n30
senses of Scripture, allegorical sense, 187; literal sense, 10n18, 188, 294; spiritual sense(s), 186, 197, 205, 221; tropological or moral sense, 188
Septuagint, 44, 60n11, 238n12

Sermon on the Mount, 49, 101, 103–4, 107n26, 119, 133n98, 147–49, 150n144, 151n145, 158, 167
Sermon on the Plain, 104, 148, 186, 196
session, 363, 365, 409n168
Shauf, Scott, 240, 246n33
Shechem, 127
shekinah, 64
sign(s), 5, 30, 47n131, 48, 52, 55, 57, 61n13, 66n31, 69–70, 73–75, 79, 82n89, 83n95, 85n101, 94, 98, 105, 115n56, 141, 146n130, 154n153, 183, 186, 188, 190, 191n35, 192, 195n47, 211, 214–16, 229, 231–33, 251n49, 253, 258, 260n81, 265, 273–74, 291, 300, 309n15, 321, 332, 367n26, 401, 413–14, 417
Simeon, 94, 291
Simoens, Yves, 266
Simon bar Kokhba, 172n207, 372–73
Sinai, 101, 162, 163n182, 185n21, 239, 241, 248–52, 254–55, 263–66, 271–73, 300
sinner(s), 49n135, 101n9, 120n68, 121–22, 124n77, 126n81, 131n95, 132n96–97, 138–40, 142, 152, 157n162, 166, 168n197, 180, 181n9, 193, 197, 202n67, 237n7, 243, 260, 277n142, 279, 285–86, 294n200, 298n207, 299n209, 303n222, 378n64, 399, 404, 418
skepticism, 21n50, 50, 59, 112, 206, 210n89, 222, 224, 331, 412
slave, 12, 92n123, 186–88, 211, 394
slavery, 12n28, 187, 193, 209, 232, 251–52, 296n203, 317, 414
Sobrino, Jon, 32n81, 35n89, 36–37, 65n28
soteriology, 16n42, 294n200, 360
Soubirous, Bernadette, 223
sovereignty, 18n43, 70, 71n50, 75, 96, 229, 371n42
Spouse of the Holy Spirit, 225
Staniloae, Dumitru, 48, 51
Strauss, David Friedrich, 19, 50, 107, 179, 183, 212–22, 233, 412

INDEX

Stump, Eleonore, 50, 237n7, 243, 284n168
Suárez, Francisco, 34n87, 406
Suffering Servant, 44, 238n11, 245, 256n67, 278, 369
synagogue(s), 104, 123, 148n135, 149n138, 188–89

tabernacle, 3n4, 5n9, 64n25, 203n69, 262n89, 268, 270n115, 395, 402
Tacitus, 63n20
Taille, Maurice de la, 45, 276n136
Tanner, Kathryn, 52, 308, 317, 319, 332
Taylor, Katherine, 222
teleology, 23n56, 340
Temple cult, 235, 237, 412
Tent of Meeting, 264
Tertullian, 316, 324n59
theandric synergy, 89
Theissen, Gerd, 21n50, 171n206, 193
theophany (theophanies), 30 172, 185n21, 249, 381n73, 393n114
Theotokos, 5, 58, 77, 85, 88n107, 89, 97
Thiessen, Matthew, 8, 9n15, 50, 126n83, 179, 202–5
Third Council of Constantinople, 39n102, 89, 178
Thyatira, 409
tomb(s), 32, 69, 86n103, 202–3, 207–9, 214, 216, 233, 346, 348, 350n140
Torah, 14n37, 28, 100–101, 108, 125–28, 132, 139–43, 146n130, 148n137, 149, 151, 153n152, 155–56, 158, 170n201, 188n28, 195, 197, 203n68, 272, 296n204, 297–98, 301, 394n115
Torrell, Jean-Pierre, 34n87, 79, 81n87, 88n108
Transfiguration, 28, 64n25, 99, 116, 147, 165, 172n207, 185n21, 232, 253n57, 279, 317, 336, 360n1, 374, 381n73
transmigration of souls, 320, 354n156
transposition, 38n101, 42–43, 57n4, 277n142
Treier, Daniel, 9n16, 79n82, 83–84
tribe(s), 47n131, 109n37, 142, 236, 244n29, 248–49, 300, 362

Trinity, 7n12, 38n101, 53n143, 112n45, 172, 178n4, 225, 261, 294n199, 320, 334n90, 388n96, 393n114, 403, 413n3
Tsutserov, Alexander, 51, 242, 263, 265–66
Twelftree, Graham, 191–92, 194, 198
twelve-pillared altar, 254
type (typology / typologies), 21n50, 28–29, 57n4, 57n6, 71, 73–74, 95–96, 211n94, 258, 276n136, 345n121

unity, 3n3, 5, 20n49, 26, 32n81, 41, 53n143, 89n115, 112n45, 119n67, 145n127, 197, 221n124, 228n143, 236, 259, 280, 282n159, 352n149, 353n153, 358, 379

Vatican II (Second Vatican Council), 13n31, 25, 31n80, 33n87, 57n6, 66n31, 85, 103, 105, 226n140, 227n140, 228, 282n158
Vawter, Bruce, 41
vengeance, 369, 378n64, 151–52
Vermigli, Peter Martyr, 305
vices, 158
vineyard, 103, 129–32, 134, 140, 143, 168
violence, 7n12, 122n74, 126, 129, 151, 195n47, 247, 295, 297, 373n48, 394n115
virgin birth, 11n23, 12n29, 48, 55–59, 60n12, 61–62, 65–71, 73–75, 81, 83–85, 90–91, 96, 411
virgin God-bearer, 77
virginitas in partu, 58, 74, 79, 81n87, 83n93, 84, 86n101, 401
virginity, 5, 56, 67, 72n54, 73–75, 77n71, 79, 82–83, 85n101, 86, 345
virtue(s), 9n17, 32n81, 54n143, 80n82, 104n15, 149n140, 154n153, 159n169, 169, 177n3, 178n4, 279n149, 231, 294n200, 320n50, 354n156, 357n162, 377, 400, 402

vocation(s), 94, 143, 166, 170, 244n29, 289, 345, 360–63,
Voltaire, 275
von Balthasar, Hans Urs, 13n31, 17n42, 36n95, 37, 38n101, 48, 57, 66, 71, 112n45, 118, 147, 173n212, 178n4, 303n222, 403, 405n155
von Harnack, Adolf, 31n80, 36n91, 107, 111
Vonier, Anscar, 397–98

Ward, Thomas, 366
Weaver, Denny, 50, 247, 247n36
Weinandy, Thomas, 72n54, 73n60, 85n101, 256n65, 306, 413n3
Wesley, John, 29n77, 222
White, Michael, 105
White, Thomas Joseph, 2, 4n6, 6n12, 10, 21–22, 24, 32n81, 33n87, 34, 36, 38n100–101, 39n102, 54n143, 112n45, 170, 173, 174n214, 177–78, 225n137, 227n143, 300n215, 303n222, 305
widow's son, 186, 190, 194–95, 222
Williamson, Paul, 245
Wink, Walter, 223, 151n148
Wisdom, 3n4, 5n9, 6–7, 14n37, 17n43, 19, 22n52, 22n54, 24n58, 31n79, 41n108, 44, 48–49, 91, 100, 102n13, 103–4, 106n23, 111–12, 116n59, 124, 134, 146n129, 148, 149n140, 154n154, 160n175, 161, 163n185, 165–67, 169, 170n202, 174–75, 189, 211–12, 228, 238n11, 298, 333–34, 349, 370–71, 376n60, 379n68, 390–92, 396, 399, 411, 413n3, 414–15, 419
Wold, Benjamin, 169
worship, 7, 20n49, 24n58, 31n79, 46, 47n131, 115n54, 117n60, 119n67, 123, 127n85, 128n87, 169n200, 199n60, 202, 204n69, 208n82, 235, 239n14, 240–41, 247, 264, 271n118, 280, 284n165, 286n173, 361n2, 362, 370, 371n42, 379n68, 380n68, 381, 387–88, 414–15
Wrede, William, 107–8, 374
Wright, N. T., 8n13, 16n42, 21n50, 28n72, 49–50, 104n15, 110n38, 111n44, 112n45–46, 114n52, 135n104, 143, 169n198, 170–71, 172n207, 179, 186, 191–200, 204–5, 207, 209, 212, 221, 236, 244n29, 296n203, 310n20, 311n21
Wright, William, 50n137, 52, 73n62, 162n182, 174, 255n61, 273n123, 301, 302n219

Zachhuber, Johannes, 23n56, 275
Zechariah, 188, 197, 201n63, 244n29, 249, 250n48, 251n49, 252, 261, 270, 278n144, 302n220, 375, 382, 394, 400n131
Zion, 12, 66, 75, 81n87, 88, 90–91, 96, 100n2, 163n182, 171, 189n29, 190, 259, 385, 415
Zizioulas, John, 10